EAST ANGLIAN ARCHAEOLOGY

Contents

List of Plates

List of Figures

List of Tables

Contributors

Sue Anderson
CFA Archaeology (human bone, Early Anglo-Saxon pottery, CBM, fired clay, heat-altered flint)

Anthony Barton
Independent illustrator (Early Anglo-Saxon costume reconstruction)

Sarah Bates
formerly NAU Archaeology (worked flint)

Iain Bell
Illustrator with Essex County Council, Historic Environment Branch (Early Anglo-Saxon iron weaponry)

Stuart Boulter
Suffolk County Council Archaeological Service (Senior Project Officer)

Rose Broadley
Independent (vessel glass)

Birte Brugmann
Independent (Early Anglo-Saxon beads and Early Anglo-Saxon chronology)

John Crowther
University of Lampeter (soil phosphate analysis)

Julie Curl
formerly NAU Archaeology (animal bone)

Vanessa Fell
English Heritage (conservation)

Val Fryer
Independent palaeoenvironmental specialist

Rowena Gale
Independent wood anatomist

Richenda Goffin
Suffolk County Council Archaeological Service (Finds Manager)

Sue Holden
Independent (graphics co-ordinator, site and finds illustration)

Janet Lang
Independent (metallurgical analysis)

Kate Morton
Independent illustrator (Early Anglo-Saxon iron, non-weaponry)

Sarah Paynter
Independent (metal working waste)

Sarah Percival
Independent (prehistoric pottery)

Rob Read
Independent illustrator (Early Anglo-Saxon non-ferrous finds))

Ian Riddler
Independent (Early Anglo-Saxon weaponry and knives)

Clive Ruggles
University of Leicester (archaeoastronomy)

Stephanie Spain
Independent (Early Anglo-Saxon shield fittings)

Tom Srahan
Illustrator with The Anglo-Saxon Laboratory (distribution maps and diagrams)

Cathy Tester
Suffolk County Council Archaeological Service (Roman pottery)

Penelope Walton Rogers
The Anglo-Saxon Laboratory, York (Early Anglo-Saxon Team Leader)

Jacqui Watson
English Heritage (mineral-preserved wood)

Donna Wreathall
Illustrator with Suffolk County Council Archaeological Service (flint, glass and non-ferrous finds)

Acknowledgements

A project of this size and complexity can only be completed with the help of a large number of people whose input in a variety of ways have contributed to this publication.

The FLN 008 excavation in Hill Pit was principally undertaken by the Field Group of the Suffolk Institute of Archaeology and History (excavation team including Gilbert Burroughes, Pat Carter, Mike Hardy and Joanna Martin) under the direction of Edward Martin of Suffolk County Council's Archaeological Service. This excavation team was augmented by members of the Suffolk County Council's Archaeological Service Field Team (Alan Smith, Mark Sommers and Jonathan Van Jennians). Thanks must also be extended to Allen Newport Ltd. for allowing the excavation to proceed and their assistance during the fieldwork. The FLN 008 claw beaker was conserved and reconstructed by Mary Davis of Norwich Castle Museum.

The excavations at Flixton Park Quarry were all carried out under the direction of Stuart Boulter by staff from Suffolk County Council's Archaeological Service Field Team including: Gemma Adams, John Ames, John Blow, Tim Browne, James Bullingham, Phil Camps, Tristan Carter, John Craven, Roy Damant, Tony Fisher, Clare Good, John Fulcher, Steve Hickling, Tom Loader, Allan Smith, Kevin Sparkes, Leah Towlson, Jonathan Van Jennians and Zoe Woods. A good working relationship was maintained throughout with the quarry operatives (at that time RMC Aggregates) whose staff, particularly Quarry Manager Brian Beales and 360° excavator driver Maurice Lawn, provided much appreciated support.

Post-excavation processing and archiving work was undertaken by in-house Suffolk County Council Archaeological Service staff including: Sue Anderson, Elizabeth Macdonald-Gibson, Amy Jones, Anna West and Alexis Willett. Richenda Goffin (Suffolk County Council) undertook the complex task of managing the finds work and also had a major input into the editing phase of the project. The research of the Anglo-Saxon cemeteries was co-ordinated by Penelope Walton Rogers (The Anglo-Saxon Laboratory), who compiled and edited Part III.

In addition to the contributors named above, a number of people have been consulted regarding specific aspects of the project work including: Edward Martin, Colin Pendleton, Jude Plouviez, James Rolfe and Keith Wade (all Suffolk County Council), Alex Bayliss, Diana Briscoe (Archive of Anglo-Saxon Pottery Stamps Matthew Canti, Derek Hamilton, Simon Mays, David Earle Robinson and Peter Murphy (English Heritage), Barry Bishop (independent archaeologist), John Blair (Oxford University), Alice Cattermole (Norfolk Museums and Library Service), Hilary Cool (Barbican Research Associates), Helen Geake (Cambridge University), Allan Hall (University of York), Philip de Jersey (Guernsey Museum Service), Richard Macphail (Institute of Archaeology UCL), Sonja Marzinzik (British Museum), Lorraine Mepham (Wessex Archaeology), Jim Rose and Danielle Schreve (Royal Holloway, University of London), Alan Vince (Archaeological Consultant), John Peter Wild (University of Manchester) and freelance specialist Karen Høilund Nielsen. Sarah Percival would also like to thank the following for the invaluable information and editorial comments they provided: Trevor Ashwin, Frances Healy and Edward Martin. Radiocarbon determinations were undertaken by Scottish Universities Research and Reactor Centre, the Radiocarbon Dating Laboratory, University of Waikato, New Zealand and Oxford Radiocarbon Accelerator Unit. At the assessment stage of the project, metalwork was radiographed by Bob Entwhistle (Ipswich Museums and Galleries) and Vanessa Fell (while at the Institute of Archaeology, Oxford) while Glynis Edwards (English Heritage) examined preserved organics.

Site photographs used in the publication were taken by various Suffolk County Council excavation staff and Essex County Council, while the photographs of artefacts were taken by Ian Cartwright (Institute of Archaeology, Oxford), Faye Minter and Gemma Adams (Suffolk

County Council Archaeological Service), Vanessa Fell and Jacqui Watson (English Heritage), the former who also provided the Scanning Electron Micrographs assisted by Roger Wilkes. In addition to Sue Holden (graphics co-ordinator), finds illustration was undertaken by Iain Bell (Early Anglo-Saxon iron weaponry, Essex County Council, Historic Environment Branch) and Donna Wreathall (flint, glass and non-ferrous finds, Suffolk County Council Archaeological Service) and independent illustrators, Kate Morton (Early Anglo-Saxon iron, non-weaponry) and Rob Read (Early Anglo-Saxon non-ferrous finds). Other drawings were provided by Tom Srahan (distribution maps and diagrams, The Anglo-Saxon Laboratory) and independent illustrator Anthony Barton (Early Anglo-Saxon costume reconstruction). Help in the search for photographs was provided by Chrystel Brandenburgh (Leiden City Archaeologist) and Evert Kramer (Friesmuseum, Netherlands). Digitisation of site plans was carried out by John Duffy (Suffolk County Council Archaeological Service).

At various times during the last decade the following people have been involved in the management and administration of the project: John Newman and Edward Martin (Suffolk County Council Archaeological Service), Kath Buxton, Tom Cromwell and Philip Walker (English Heritage), Simon Collcutt and David Griffiths (Oxford Archaeological Associates Ltd) and Adrian Havercroft (The Guildhouse Consultancy). Funding for the project, both fieldwork and post-excavation, was provided by RMC Aggregates Ltd (now Cemex), English Heritage and the Aggregates Levy Sustainability Fund.

Summary

Flixton Park Quarry lies on the south side of the Waveney Valley in an area that has been subject to aggregate extraction for many decades. While historically there was virtually no archaeological recording, the areas opened up since 1995 have all been subject to formal archaeological excavation under the auspices of archaeological planning guidance PPG 16 (1990). This volume represents the first in a series that will cover the extensive and significant archaeological deposits recorded at the quarry. The multi-phase format that will be employed for the publication series is essentially a product of the chronologically extended phased nature of the project and the fact that Volume I is largely funded by an Aggregates Levy Sustainability Fund (ALSF) grant.

Volume I includes features/structures of prehistoric, Late Iron Age/Early Roman and Early Anglo-Saxon date.

The prehistoric archaeology in this volume is dominated by three monumental structures. The earliest, dating to the Late Neolithic, is described as a post-hole circle of approximately 18m in diameter, although actually exhibiting a somewhat eccentric, but still symmetrical shape with an entrance to the north-west. While an internal sub-rectangular post-hole structure was recorded, its function remains unclear. Various interpretations are explored that include its use for both specialised and more mundane functions along with the possibility that astronomical alignments were invested in the monument. The site of the Late Neolithic structure was subsequently overlain by an Early Bronze Age funerary monument in the form of a unurned cremation and its surrounding ring-ditch. A second ring-ditch excavated in the adjacent quarry to the north is also described, which subsequently became the focus for burial in the Early Anglo-Saxon period (Flixton I). Its central mound was re-used as the site of a windmill in the later medieval or early post-medieval periods.

The Iron Age/Roman archaeology in this volume, while peripheral to a wider area of activity of this date, included an enigmatic palisaded enclosure comprising a series of closely spaced posts set in a series of slots and individual post-holes and describing a near-perfect circle of 27m diameter. Direct dating evidence was sparse, but a series of pits adjacent to the post-hole circle included a pottery assemblage of a transitional type suggesting that the activity dated to about the time of the Conquest. Various functions for the use of the post-hole circle have been explored, including its being associated with an enigmatic rectangular post-hole structure of similar date that was recorded in a later phase of the quarry.

The Anglo-Saxon period is represented at Flixton by two burial grounds (designated Flixton I and II) and a settlement, although only the cemeteries will be considered in detail in this volume. Flixton I seems to have been a small plot associated with a prehistoric barrow: only one grave has been excavated, but metal-detected finds indicate some further burials. Flixton II was larger and at first contained within a rectangular plot close to another barrow. Fifty-one of an estimated 200 or more graves have been excavated there. In a later phase, burial at Flixton II shifted southwards onto the barrow itself, where eleven more graves were identified. The date range of the excavated graves in Flixton II is from the end of the 5th century to the middle of the 7th century and the plot at Flixton I is likely to have been contemporary with its earliest phase. The material evidence has been used as a base from which to discuss the social make-up of the community who buried their dead in the two burial grounds. The role of this community in the southern marches of the former Iceni territory has also been explored.

Later volumes will cover the subsequent excavations, during which the archaeology of a significant area of the landscape was recorded in detail, revealing its development during the Neolithic period with sporadic activity and some funerary monument construction, the latter including a long barrow, the first to be formally excavated in Suffolk. During the Early Bronze Age the number of funerary monuments in the landscape increased with the construction of a series of round-barrows. These monuments varied considerably in size, morphology and the character of the burials with which they were associated. The quarry has also provided significant evidence for Bronze Age, Iron Age, Roman and Early Anglo-Saxon occupation with a wealth of structural evidence and a large assemblage of finds. More recent features include those associated with Flixton Hall and its surrounding parklands and evidence for World War I training activity in the form of extensive trench systems.

Together, the archaeological remains at Flixton provide an insight into how a significant area of our present landscape has developed through time. The evidence suggests that the position of the earlier funerary monuments had a repeated influence on the location of later monument construction and land-use, the latter characterised by periods of abandonment, or at least a much reduced level of activity, interspersed with more protracted occupation.

Résumé

Flixton Park Quarry est situé sur le côté sud de la Waveney Valley dans une zone où l'on extrait des agrégats depuis des décennies. Alors que sur le plan historique, il n'existait pratiquement pas de données archéologiques, des fouilles ont été entreprises en bonne et due forme dans toutes les zones ouvertes depuis 1995 sous l'égide de la directive PPG16 (Planning Policy Guidance 16) qui date de 1990.

Ce volume est le premier d'une série qui portera sur les larges dépôts significatifs qui ont été recueillis dans la carrière de Flixton Park. Cette série se compose de plusieurs phases. Deux raisons essentielles à cela : le projet s'organise en fonction de grandes étapes chronologiques ; le volume I est largement financé par une subvention de l'ALSF (Aggregates Levy Sustainability Fund). Ce volume comprend des éléments et des structures datant de la préhistoire, de la fin de l'âge du fer et du début de la période romaine ainsi que de la première période anglo-saxonne.

Trois structures monumentales dominent l'archéologie préhistorique qui est présentée dans ce volume. La structure la plus récente date de la fin du néolithique. Elle correspond à un trou de poteau d'un diamètre d'environ 18 m. Ce cercle présente une forme quelque peu excentrique qui reste toutefois symétrique avec une entrée tournée vers le nord-ouest. Sa fonction n'est toujours pas éclaircie alors même que le trou de poteau présente une structure interne sub-rectangulaire. Il existe différentes interprétations qui attribuent à ce monument un usage à la fois banal et spécialisé, sans exclure la possibilité d'alignements astronomiques. Le site de la structure du néolithique tardif fut par la suite recouvert par un monument funéraire du début de l'âge du bronze qui prit la forme d'une crémation sans urne placée dans un fossé circulaire. Un second fossé circulaire fait également l'objet d'une description. Il a été mis à jour dans la carrière voisine située au nord et il est devenu le centre des inhumations dans la première période anglo-saxonne (Flixton I). Le monticule central a été réutilisé comme site d'un moulin à vent dans la période médiévale tardive ou dans la première période post-médiévale.

L'archéologie de l'âge du fer et de la période romaine présentée dans ce volume se situe à la périphérie d'une zone d'activités plus large qui s'est développée à cette époque. Elle comprend toutefois une énigmatique enceinte à palissades. Cette dernière se compose d'une série de poteaux rapprochés placés dans une succession de fentes et de trous de poteaux distincts qui décrivent un cercle quasi- parfait de 27 mètres de diamètre. Même si les preuves d'une datation directe sont limitées, une succession de fosses situées à côté du cercle dessiné par le trou de poteau contenait un ensemble de poteries de type transitoire, ce qui donne à penser que l'activité développée remontait grosso modo à l'époque de la conquête. Différentes hypothèses concernant l'utilisation du trou de poteau circulaire ont été formulées ; il a ainsi été associé à une énigmatique structure rectangulaire de trou de poteau, datant à peu près de la même époque, qui a été rattachée à une phase tardive de la carrière.

La période anglo-saxonne est représentée à Flixton par deux lieux d'inhumation (désignés par les termes Flixton I et II) et par une implantation. Toutefois, seuls les cimetières seront analysés en détail dans ce volume. Flixton I était vraisemblablement un petit espace associé à un tumulus préhistorique. Une seule tombe a fait l'objet de fouilles ; cependant des opérations de détection de métaux ont révélé la présence d'autres tombes. D'une superficie plus grande, Flixton II était d'abord contenu dans un espace rectangulaire situé à côté d'un autre tumulus. Le nombre total des tombes est estimé à 200 au minimum et 51 d'entre elles ont été fouillées. Dans une phase ultérieure, Flixton II a connu un déplacement des inhumations qui ont eu lieu sur le tumulus lui-même où onze autres tombes ont été identifiées. La datation des tombes fouillées à Flixton II est comprise entre la fin du 5ème et le milieu de 7ème siècle de notre ère. Quant à Flixton I, il est probablement contemporain de la toute première phase de Flixton II. Les chercheurs se sont appuyés sur la découverte de preuves matérielles pour examiner la structure sociale de la communauté qui enterrait ses morts dans les deux lieux d'inhumation. Le rôle de cette communauté située dans les marches sud de l'ancien territoire des Iceni a également été étudié.

Les prochains volumes traiteront des fouilles ultérieures qui ont permis de consigner avec précision l'archéologie d'une zone significative du paysage. Il est apparu qu'une activité sporadique s'y est développée au cours du néolithique. Des monuments funéraires ont également été construits dont un long tumulus qui fut le premier à être véritablement fouillé dans le Suffolk. Au début de l'âge du bronze, le nombre de monuments funéraires augmenta dans le paysage avec la construction d'un ensemble de tumulus circulaires. Ces monuments varièrent considérablement par leur taille, leur morphologie et par la nature des tombes qui leur étaient associées. D'abondantes preuves structurelles ainsi qu'un grand nombre d'objets ont été découverts dans la carrière, ce qui prouve amplement que le lieu était occupé à l'âge du bronze, du fer, à la période romaine et au début de la période anglo-saxonne. Des découvertes plus récentes concernent Flixton Hall et ses espaces verts environnants ainsi qu'un large système de tranchées lié à des activités d'entraîne- ment au cours de la première guerre mondiale.

L'ensemble des restes archéologiques de Flixton nous montre comment une partie importante de notre paysage s'est développée au fil du temps. Les preuves rassemblées suggèrent que la position des premiers monuments funéraires a exercé une influence persistante sur l'emplacement des monuments postérieurs et sur l'utilisation de la terre, qui se caractérise par une alternance de périodes d'abandon, ou du moins d'activité très réduite, avec des périodes d'occupation prolongée.

(Traduction: Didier Don)

Zusammenfassung

Der Flixton-Park-Steinbruch liegt südlich des Waveney-Tals in einer Gegend, in der seit Jahrzehnten Gestein abgebaut wird. Während in der Vergangenheit jedoch kaum eine archäologische Befundaufnahme stattfand, unterlagen die seit 1995 in offizieller Mission ausgegrabenen Areale den Leitlinien für die archäologische Planung (PPG 16) von 1990.

Der vorliegende Band ist der erste in einer Reihe, die der Aufzeichnung der umfangreichen und bedeutsamen Kulturschichten des Steinbruchs dient. Das mehrphasig gestaltete Format der Reihe ist im Wesentlichen der zeitlichen Ausdehnung des Projekts sowie der Tatsache geschuldet, dass Band I vornehmlich durch Mittel aus dem «Aggregates Levy Sustainability Fund» (ALSF) finanziert wird. Band I behandelt die prähistorischen, späteisenzeitlichen/frührömerzeitlichen sowie frühangelsächsischen Befunde und Baustrukturen.

Die prähistorische Archäologie des Bandes wird von drei Großbauwerken dominiert. Das älteste geht auf das Spätneolithikum zurück. Es ist als Pfostenkreis mit einem ungefähren Durchmesser von 18 Metern beschrieben, obwohl die tatsächliche Form nicht wirklich rund, aber dennoch symmetrisch ist und einen Eingang im Nordwesten aufweist. In seinem Inneren wurde eine nahezu rechteckige Pfostenkonstruktion ungeklärter Funktion ausgemacht, zu der verschiedene Interpretationen erörtert werden, etwa die Verwendung für spezielle wie auch alltägliche Aufgaben sowie eine mögliche astronomische Ausrichtung des Gebäudes. Das spätneolithische Bauwerk wurde in der Folgezeit durch ein frühbronzezeitliches Grabmonument überlagert, das aus einem Brandgrubengrab mit umliegendem Kreisgraben bestand. Darüber hinaus wird ein zweiter, im nördlich angrenzenden Steinbruch ausgegrabener Kreisgraben beschrieben, der sich zu Beginn der frühangelsächsischen Periode zum zentralen Bestattungsort entwickelte (Flixton I). Dessen mittlerer Erdhügel wurde entweder im Spätmittelalter oder in der frühen Neuzeit für den Bau einer Windmühle genutzt.

Zu den archäologischen Befunden aus der Eisen- bzw. Römerzeit am Rand einer größeren Aktivitätszone jener Periode zählt eine rätselhafte Palisadeneinhegung, bestehend aus einer Reihe eng zusammenstehender, in Vertiefungen eingelassener Pfosten, die einen nahezu kreisrunden Ring von 27 Metern Durchmesser bilden, sowie einzelnen Pfostenlöchern. Zwar gab es kaum direkte Datierungsmerkmale, doch fanden sich in mehreren Gruben unmittelbar neben dem Kreis Keramikgegenstände eines Übergangstyps, die darauf hindeuten, dass die Befunde aus der Zeit der römischen Eroberung stammen. Dem Pfostenkreis werden verschiedene mögliche Funktionen zugeordnet. Dabei wird unter anderem vermutet, dass er mit einer rätselhaften rechteckigen Pfostenanlage ähnlichen Datums in Zusammenhang stehen könnte, die bei späteren Steinbrucharbeiten aufgezeichnet wurde.

Die angelsächsische Zeit ist durch zwei Gräberfelder (Flixton I und II genannt) und eine Siedlung vertreten, wobei dieser Band nur die Gräberfelder im Detail betrachtet. Flixton I war offenbar ein kleines, mit einem prähistorischen Grabhügel in Verbindung stehendes Gelände. Es wurde lediglich eine Grabstätte ausgegraben, mittels Metalldetektoren ermittelte Befunde deuten jedoch auf weitere Gräber hin. Flixton II war größer und lag anfangs in einem rechteckigen Areal in der Nähe eines weiteren Grabhügels. Insgesamt wurden dort 51 der schätzungsweise mindestens 200 Grabstätten ausgegraben. In einer späteren Phase wurden die Bestattungen von Flixton II in Richtung Süden auf den Grabhügel hin verlagert, wo elf weitere Gräber ausgemacht wurden. Die untersuchten Grabstätten von Flixton II fallen in die Zeitspanne von späten 5. bis Mitte des 7. Jahrhunderts, während Flixton I vermutlich mit der Anfangsphase von Flixton II zusammenfiel. Anhand des Fundmaterials wird die soziale Zusammensetzung der Gemeinschaft erörtert, die die beiden Gräberfelder zur Beisetzung ihrer Toten nutzte. Zusätzlich wird die Rolle dieser Gemeinschaft im südlichen Grenzgebiet des früheren Icener-Territoriums untersucht.

In den Folgebänden werden die daran anschließenden Ausgrabungen beschrieben, die zur detaillierten Aufzeichnung der archäologischen Befunde eines bedeutsamen Landschaftsareals führten. Die Grabungen enthüllten sporadische Aktivitäten und den Bau vereinzelter Grabmonumente in der Jungsteinzeit, etwa des ersten Langhügelgrabs, das in Suffolk formal ausgegraben wurde. In der frühen Bronzezeit erhöhte sich die Zahl der Grabmonumente in der Landschaft durch den Bau mehrerer Rundhügelgräber, die ihrer Größe, Morphologie und der Art der zugehörigen Bestattungen nach große Unterschiede aufwiesen. Die zahlreichen Baustrukturen und umfangreichen Fundkomplexe innerhalb des Steinbruchs liefern zudem wichtige Hinweise auf die bronzezeitliche, eisenzeitliche, römerzeitliche und frühangelsächsische Siedlungstätigkeit. Neuere Befunde betreffen unter anderem Flixton Hall und die umliegende Parklandschaft sowie ausgedehnte Grabensysteme, die militärischen Übungen zur Zeit des Ersten Weltkriegs dienten.

Zusammen genommen zeigen die archäologischen Hinterlassenschaften von Flixton, wie sich ein nennenswertes Gebiet unserer heutigen Landschaft mit der Zeit verändert hat. Die Funde deuten darauf hin, dass sich die Lage der frühen Grabdenkmäler wiederholt auf den Bau der späteren Grabstätten und die Landnutzung auswirkte, wobei Letztere durch Perioden der Aufgabe oder stark verringerter Aktivitäten mit zwischenzeitlich ausgedehnteren Siedlungsphasen gekennzeichnet war.

(Übersetzung: Gerlinde Krug)

Part I

Introduction

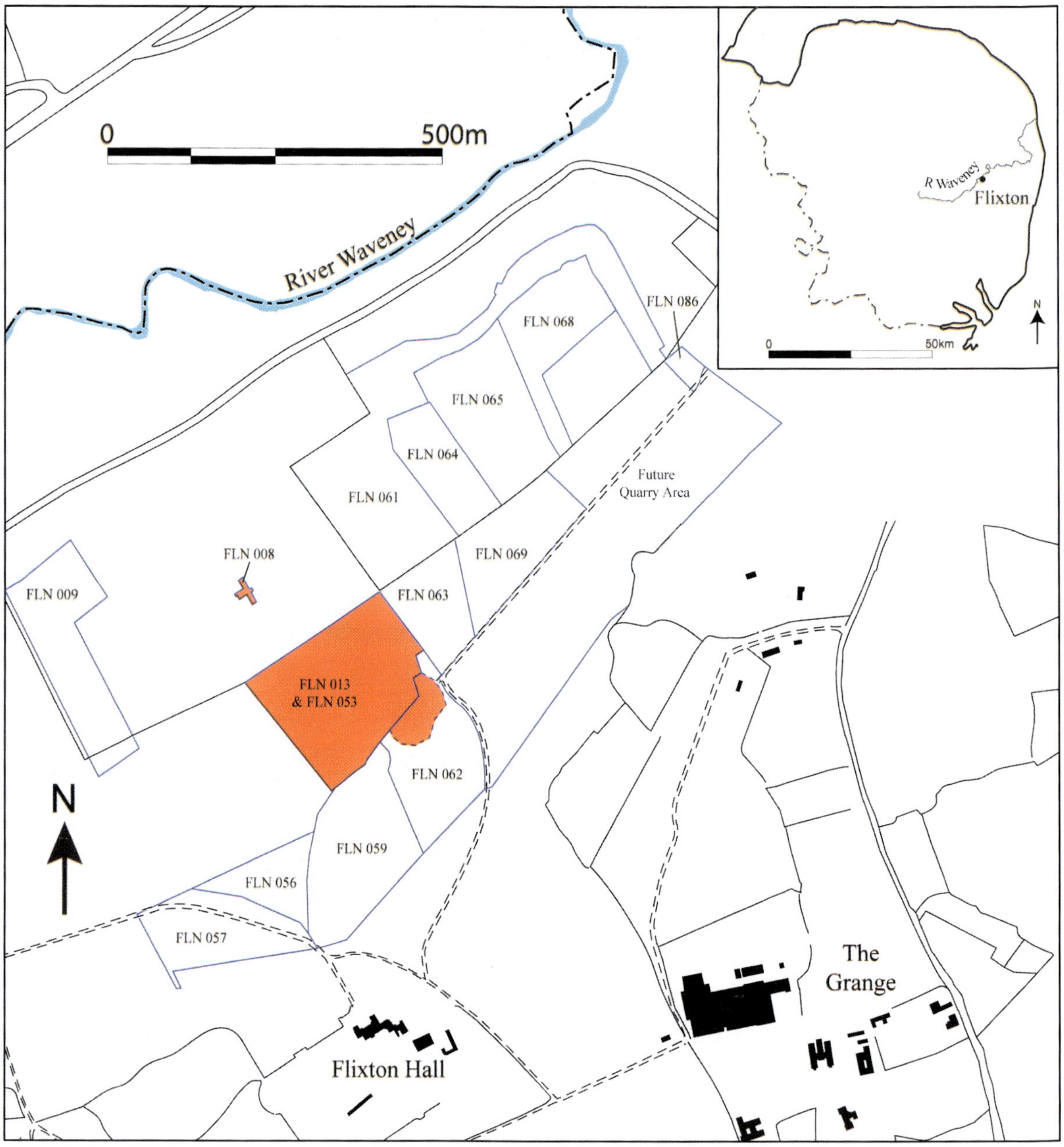

Figure 1.1 Site location. 1:10,000

Chapter 1. Introduction to the Excavations

by Stuart Boulter

I. Background

Fig. 1.1

There have been large scale quarrying operations in the vicinity of Flixton Park since the middle of the 20th century and while very little formal archaeological work was carried out, evidence from piecemeal recording and aerial photographs give testament to the rich and varied archaeological landscape that has been lost. The planning consent covering the extraction at Flixton was old, pre-dating archaeological planning guidance PPG 16 (1990). In 1995, the renewal of this earlier consent resulted in the addition of an archaeological condition stating that continued quarrying would be dependent on the applicant (then RMC Aggregates) providing for a programme of archaeological works. Since that time, the archaeology in all new quarry areas has been comprehensively recorded by continuous monitoring and, where necessary, open area excavation. All of this work has been carried out by Suffolk County Council's Archaeological Service Field Team (hereafter SCC) and funded by the quarry owners.

This volume deals with the archaeological remains excavated under the Historic Environment Record (HER) codes FLN 008, FLN 013, FLN 053 and the north-east corner of FLN 062 immediately south of its boundary with FLN 053 (Fig. 1.1). The other sites shown on Figure 1.1 will be reported on separately (see Section V below for details).

II. Topography and geology

Flixton Park Quarry and the adjacent Tarmac Quarry (previously Hill Pit) are located on the extensive north-east to south-west orientated river terrace gravels on the south side of the River Waveney (centred on TM 2990 8640) (Fig. 1.1). At this juncture, the river forms the boundary between Suffolk and Norfolk and lies approximately 500m to the north of the excavation areas.

Locally, the FLN 008, FLN 013, FLN 053 and FLN 062 sites lie at the head of a shallow south-west to north-east aligned depression/valley within the gravel terraces, which respects the orientation of the present river valley.

The depositional environment and date of the gravels are still a source of study and debate. In a recent post-graduate study undertaken at Flixton, the deposits recognised included Early Pleistocene marine sediments overlain by Anglian and post-Anglian deposits including tills, fluvial sediments and outwash deposits (Heirman 2006).

During topsoil stripping it was revealed that shallow localised variations in the topography were often reflected in the underlying geology with gravel and stone areas standing proud from those where sand was the principal component. The intervening troughs often contained a significant thickness (up to 1m) of fine silty sand deposits which, judging by the included artefactual evidence, must at least partially have accumulated after the Roman Period. Prior to the accumulation of this layer, the natural undulations of the site would have been far more pronounced.

Within the areas covered by this volume, the maximum elevation was *c.* 16.3m OD on the western edge of the FLN 013 site, reducing to just below 15m OD on the northern side of the FLN 053 area.

III. The sites

Fig 1.2

Figure 1.2 illustrates all of the FLN 013 and FLN 053 features and those of FLN 062 relevant to this publication, with the location of the limited FLN 008 trenches and projected extent of the ring-ditch also shown.

FLN 008

The HER code FLN 008 was one of those allocated during the 1970s to a series of ring-ditches identified on aerial photographs (centred on TM 3020 8653). As the quarry operations at Alan Newport's Hill Pit began to encroach on the ring-ditch in 1990, a local amateur archaeologist (Mike Hardy), who had previously fieldwalked the area, visited the site and realised the importance of what was being lost. As no funding was available at that time, members of the Suffolk Archaeological Field Group undertook the excavation fieldwork on a voluntary basis under the direction of a SCC archaeologist (Edward Martin). As resources were limited, total excavation was not an option. An area of approximately 460m^2 was opened up in the form of linear trenches cut through the surviving mound and surrounding ditch.

FLN 013

Another of the HER codes previously allocated specifically to a ring-ditch feature visible on aerial photographs, FLN 013 (centred on TM 3028 8631) was then used to cover all of the archaeological deposits recorded in what was known as Quarry Phase 4. Initial excavation of the ring-ditch was undertaken by SCC early in 1996 along with limited evaluation trenching with a combined area of 1,100 square metres. The identification of further archaeological remains immediately to the north of the ring-ditch, including a Late Neolithic post-hole structure, led to another phase of fieldwork by SCC late in 1996, when the archaeology in the remaining 8,900 square metres of Quarry Phase 4 was recorded. At this juncture, the Late Neolithic post-hole structure was allocated the HER code FLN 054, but was excavated and recorded entirely within the FLN 013 context sequence. As such, in order to prevent confusion, the HER code FLN 054 has not been used further in the text of this volume, with the exception of the overall phasing table in Chapter 2, and does not appear on any of the plans.

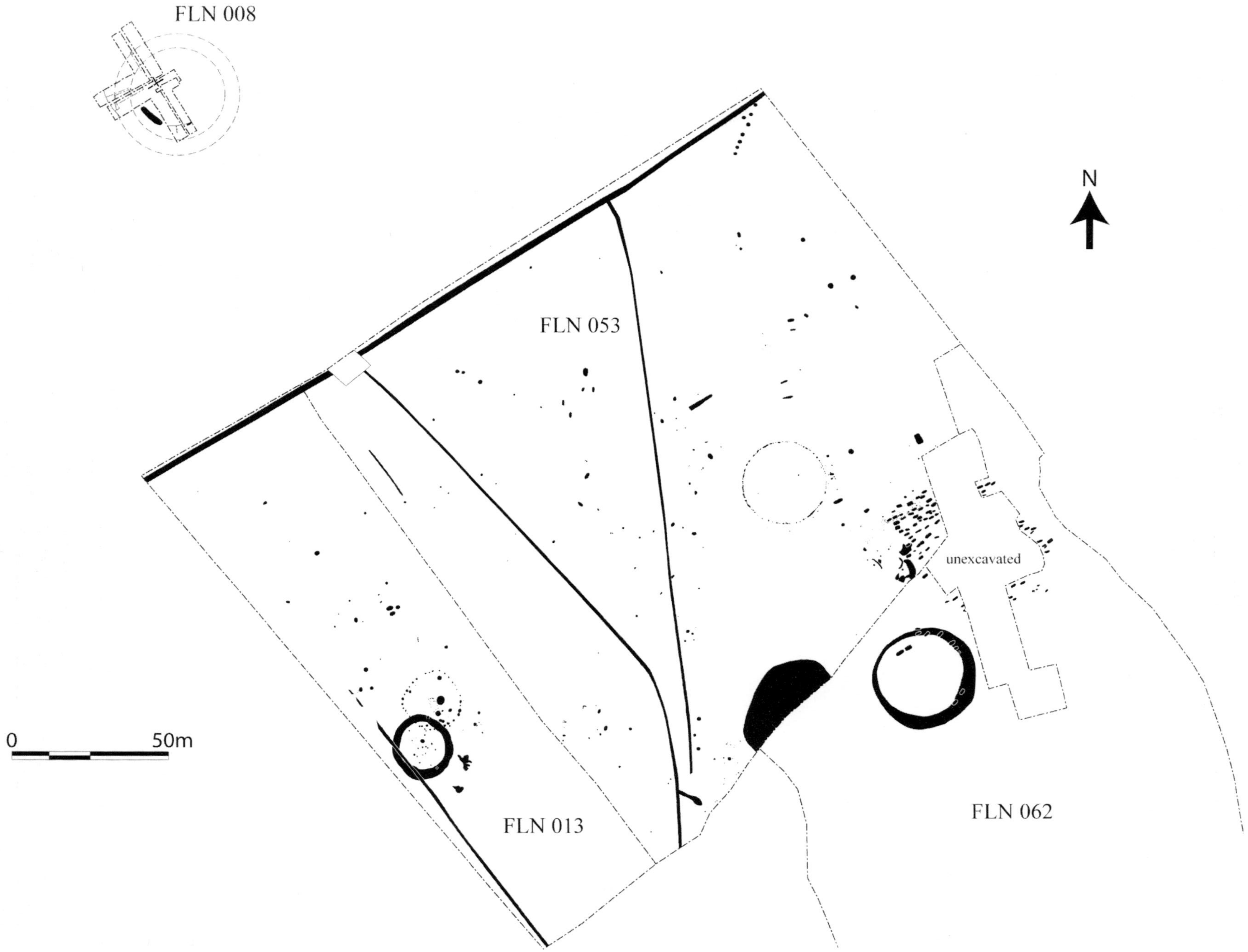

Figure 1.2 Overall feature plan

FLN 053

Quarry Phases 5 and 6, covering an area of approximately 25,000m^2 (centred on TM 3060 8640) and adjoining the eastern edge of FLN 013, were allocated the HER code FLN 053. Following the identification of significant, but scattered, archaeology in the adjacent FLN 013 area, the decision was made by the Mineral Planning Authority's Archaeological Advisor that continuous archaeological monitoring of all newly stripped areas would be undertaken. All subsequent archaeological monitoring and excavation work in this area was carried out by SCC archaeologists.

During the summer of 1997 approximately sixty percent of the FLN 053 area was stripped, leaving a triangular shaped plot forming the south-east corner of an existing rectangular field. The remainder of FLN 053, with the exception of a narrow strip underneath overhead power cables, was stripped in the summer of 1998.

It was during the monitoring of stripping in the final area that a metal detector survey revealed the presence of the Early Anglo-Saxon cemetery in the south-east corner of the field. The cemetery clearly continued out to the south, under the existing farm track, and to the east, under the overhead power cables. The capped budget put in place to deal with the archaeology in these quarry phases was not sufficient to deal with the unexpected costs that the exposed burials entailed, and fortunately English Heritage stepped in to provide the funding required in order to complete the excavation of the stripped area of the cemetery.

FLN 062

The area excavated by SCC as FLN 062 in 2001 equated to New Phase 7 of a revised quarry phasing and covered an area of 22,500m^2 to the south of and adjoining FLN 053 (centred on TM 3047 8628). There was no doubt that the Early Anglo-Saxon cemetery identified in FLN 053 continued into this area and another known ring-ditch (FLN 010) was also close to where the burials could be expected to occur at the northern end of the site. With a view to defining the extent of the cemetery, soil stripping was initiated at the southern end of the plot, working northwards towards the known burial area.

Significant archaeological deposits, predominantly of Late Iron Age and earlier Roman date, but also including a reasonable scatter of prehistoric features, were recorded throughout the area with a major concentration of the former towards the south, including two aisled buildings and two pottery kilns. The edges of the Early Anglo-Saxon cemetery were encountered, allowing clear definition of its overall area and revealing that the FLN 053 excavation had probably only accounted for about twenty-five percent of the graves. In addition, a further eleven Early Anglo-Saxon burials were identified in association with ring-ditch FLN 010. It was subsequently found necessary to excavate a total of seventeen of the exposed burials: eleven associated with the ring-ditch, a group of four small graves defining the south-east corner of the main cemetery, another isolated on the west side of the main cemetery and one on the west side, the latter due to grave goods being exposed at the surface. The FLN 010 ring-ditch was excavated and recorded within the FLN 062 context sequence (062:*0808*) and with the exception of the overall phasing table in Chapter 2 and the introduction to the feature in Chapter 3.II, the FLN 010 HER code is not referred to in the text and only appears on one plan (Fig. 3.1).

The financial resources that would have been required to excavate and publish what appeared to be in the region of 150 further burials was a daunting prospect. As the cemetery was located towards the edge of the designated quarry area, where its influence on the ground levels associated with the reinstatement landscaping would be relatively small, an agreement was reached with the Mineral Planning Authority's Archaeological Advisor whereby the remainder of the burials would be preserved *in situ*.

When assessing which aspects of the Flixton archaeology should be included in this volume, it was considered desirable from an archaeological point of view to include all of the Early Anglo-Saxon burials. While this complicated the funding of the project, the FLN 062 site was covered by PPG 16 and the responsibility of the quarry company, it was agreed that the Early Anglo-Saxon burials would be included, leaving the remainder of the FLN 062 archaeology for a later publication.

IV. Previous and subsequent investigations

Prior to the small rescue excavation in 1990 (FLN 008 included in this volume) there are no records of any formal archaeological work in either Hill Pit (subsequently worked by Tarmac and now Cemex) or Flixton Park Quarry (now owned by Cemex). In 1959, a small scale rescue excavation of a Roman pottery kiln was undertaken in the neighbouring Homersfield Quarry (TM 2882 8529; SEY 002) by Norman Smedley and Elizabeth Owles of the Ipswich Museum (Smedley and Owles 1959, 168–84).

There are also HER entries relating to a number of stray finds and finds scatters from the wider area of Flixton Park, predominantly prehistoric, Roman and medieval in date. Many of these were identified by amateur archaeologist Mike Hardy during fieldwalking exercises. Other HER codes have been allocated to monuments visible as cropmarks on aerial photographs, the majority of which are ring-ditches and also presumably of prehistoric date. One exception, FLN 009, visible on aerial photographs as a square enclosure with entrance on its western side, was excavated by SCC in 2003 and found to be post-medieval in date, enclosing a square footing of crushed brick and tile and interpreted as a folly associated with Flixton Hall (Boulter 2004).

Immediately prior to the FLN 013 excavation in 1996, a combined geophysical (topsoil magnetic susceptibility and magnetometry) and hand-augering survey was commissioned by Oxford Archaeological Associates Ltd. on behalf of the quarry company and undertaken by Oxford Archaeotechnics (Johnson 1996). The survey covered elements of what were known as Quarry Phases 4 to 6, effectively the areas that were to become FLN 013 and FLN 053. The targeted geophysical survey confirmed the presence of a ring-ditch feature (FLN 013) previously known only from aerial photographs. A second targeted geophysical survey (gradiometry and resistivity) and fieldwalking was undertaken by Archaeological Services WYAS in Quarry Phases 5 and 6 following the SCC excavation of FLN 013 late in 1996 (WYAS 1997). No concentrations of artefacts were recognised during the fieldwalking and anomalies in the geophysical results were not confirmed as features during the subsequent soil-strip.

It is, however, the subsequent archaeological work associated with the expanding quarry, undertaken seasonally by SCC since 1999, that has provided a vast body of archaeological evidence that is of relevance to the earlier excavations covered by this volume and will be discussed further in Chapter 16. The archaeology within an area covering approximately 31 hectares has now been formally recorded and significant deposits relating to a number of archaeological periods have been identified including the following:

Palaeolithic	Hand-axes and Levallois flake from the quarry gravels
Neolithic:	Earlier Neolithic long barrow and small ring-ditch. Later Neolithic structured pits
Early Bronze Age:	Early Bronze Age ring-ditches, burial and pit groups
Indeterminate Bronze Age or Iron Age:	Occupation including a series of four and six post structures
Late Iron Age/early Roman:	Occupation, enigmatic multi-post building/structure, ditches and multiple burial
Roman:	Occupation including two pottery kilns and two aisled buildings
Early Anglo-Saxon:	Occupation including both sunken featured buildings (SFBs) and 'halls' with a possible shrine within a ditched enclosure
Post-medieval:	Features relating to Flixton Hall and its surrounding parkland and a World War I training complex

V. Publication strategy

A vast body of multi-period archaeological evidence has been recovered from Flixton Park Quarry over thirteen years of seasonal excavations by SCC since 1996, with *c*.31 hectares opened during that time and a further *c*.12 hectares of the present permission remaining to be excavated by phase over the next few years. A project of this scale is actually dealing with the archaeology of a significant area of a landscape and its continuing development. The publishing of such a long-running site, with its great wealth of multi-period archaeology, is not without its problems from both a financial and logistical point of view. In order to avoid the impracticalities of waiting for the whole quarry permission area to be exhausted before producing a single integrated volume, or a series of volumes by period, it was decided that multi-period publication by quarry area would be the best way to proceed.

Although the bulk of the Flixton archaeology will be published with funding provided by the quarry company under the auspices of PPG 16, they had already fulfilled their financial obligations regarding the FLN 013 and FLN 053 areas. While not considered the ideal way in which to proceed, the availability of Aggregates Levy Sustainability Fund (hereafter ALSF) funding meant that in order to elicit publication of those areas of the site which qualified for this grant, it became necessary to tailor the project size to that which could be accommodated by the strict ALSF project time frame. The subsequent publication proposal included a site where there had been no funding for the original excavation or publication (FLN 008), two sites where the capped budget had been spent due to unforeseen circumstances (FLN 013 and FLN 053) and one, FLN 062, which was included on archaeological grounds and funded by the present quarry owners (Cemex) under PPG 16. At this stage it is envisaged that there will be at least two more Flixton publications, probably monographs in the EAA series, relating to the present Flixton permission area, the second of which would include an overview of the detailed landscape development of the entire site.

Figure 1.1 shows the phases of Flixton Park Quarry and the adjacent quarry (formerly Hill Pit) in which archaeological recording has taken place and differentiates clearly between the areas covered in this volume and those which will be dealt with in subsequent publications or, in the case of the FLN 010 site in Hill Pit, an Archive Report only. Also shown is the remaining area of the current permission for Flixton Park Quarry. A brief summary listing the dating and kinds of archaeological deposits encountered in the wider excavations is included above (Section IV), while the overall Flixton phasing is tabulated in Chapter 2 (Table 2.1). A more detailed summary describing the significant aspects of the archaeology from both Flixton Quarries that do not fall within the remit of this volume is presented in Chapter 16.

Chapter 2. General Excavation Details
by Stuart Boulter

I. Excavation methodologies

In general terms, the excavation methods and techniques remained fundamentally the same for the FLN 013, FLN 053 and FLN 062 components of the project and conformed to the Institute of Field Archaeologists' *Standards and Guidance for Archaeological Excavations*. There is very little information available for the FLN 008 site, but the surviving archive suggests that standard excavation methods were used throughout.

Soil-stripping in Flixton Park Quarry (sites FLN 013, FLN 053 and FLN 062) was carried out using a 360° mechanical excavator equipped with a toothless ditching bucket and no heavy plant being allowed to run over the newly exposed surface until the archaeology had been fully recorded. Both ploughsoil and any intervening subsoil were removed to reveal the underlying sands and gravels. Large areas of the site, those with only a low concentration of archaeological features, were recorded using minimal resources while the soil-stripping was in progress. More complex areas, the prehistoric ring-ditch and post-hole circle, the Late Iron Age/early Roman post-hole circle and the Early Anglo-Saxon cemetery, were treated as set-piece excavations with an SCC field team undertaking the work.

In the less complex areas of archaeology, surface cleaning was limited to the immediate area of visible features. In contrast, the set-piece excavation areas were manually cleaned in their entirety, in order to identify and define features that had often been filled with re-deposited natural sands and gravels. The whole site was subjected to a metal detector survey.

Site plans and sections were drawn at scales of 1:50, 1:20 and 1:10 depending on their complexity. Planning was initially undertaken by triangulation from a 10m grid, conforming to the national grid, that had been left in place following the geophysical survey over the known ring-ditch FLN 013 undertaken by Oxford Archaeotechnics earlier in 1996. Subsequent phases of the quarry were planned using a grid extrapolated from this original setting. Levels were related to Ordnance Datum from temporary benchmarks transferred to the site from the earlier survey work. A full photographic record was made including both monochrome prints and colour slides.

Features, their stratigraphic elements and small finds were given OP (observed phenomena) numbers within a 'unique continuous numbering system' under the appropriate HER code. For pit-like features, bulk sieving was carried out for fifty percent of the fill of those that were not obviously modern; the latter were hand sorted only. Where significant artefactual evidence was recovered, the percentage of the fill subjected to bulk sieving was increased to one hundred percent. One hundred percent of post-hole fills were sieved. The FLN 013 ring-ditch was divided into quadrants with fifty percent of each quadrant excavated (fifty percent of the whole feature) and fifty percent of each excavated section subjected to bulk sieving (twenty-five percent of the whole feature). All artefacts recovered were retained: there was no discard policy.

Following advice from Peter Murphy (English Heritage's then Regional Scientific Advisor) bulk samples were taken from feature fills that fulfilled two out of three of the following criteria:

- the sampled fill should appear to include a high concentration of burnt organic material;
- the features should not be stratigraphically isolated;
- the sampled fill should include significant artefactual evidence which could benefit from its direct association with any subsequent radiocarbon dates that might be obtained.

II. Post-excavation assessment and analysis

This volume presents the results of post-excavation analysis relating to a number of discrete phases of fieldwork and brings together specialist reports and stratigraphic analysis first undertaken in isolation.

Very little post-excavation specialist analysis had been carried out on the FLN 008 site archive prior to that associated with this publication. However, the FLN 013, FLN 053 and FLN 062 sites had been subjected to some previous examination. The FLN 013 area was covered by two assessment reports (Boulter 1996a and 1996b), an archive report (Boulter 1998), and was then included in a combined assessment report with FLN 053 (Boulter and Anderson 2000) and a revisited assessment report with FLN 008, FLN 053 and FLN 062 (Boulter 2006a). FLN 053 had also been the subject of a specific interim assessment report (Boulter 1997). FLN 062 was also covered in another assessment report (Boulter 2006b).

III. Understanding the site codes and context numbering used in this publication

The publication has firstly been divided by archaeological period. Beyond this, further subdivisions have been made depending on what was considered most appropriate: variously by site/area, artefact category/material, feature category and type of analysis conducted. In the case of the Early Anglo-Saxon phase, this has resulted in some chapters having multiple authorship and contributions by an author are sometimes divided between different chapters or sections.

The integrated presentation of context information within this publication posed problems due to the fact that data from four different sites, all with their own individual HER code and hierarchy of OP/context numbers, would often be included in the same section of text. In order to reduce confusion, where context numbers are included in the text they are always italicised, regardless of whether they relate to a feature cut, fill or artefact, and prefixed with their HER code number (*e.g.* 013:*0001*). However, it was not considered necessary to always prefix the site code number with the Flixton code letters FLN as all of the

Period	*Site phase*	*Date range*	*Identified in these areas (those in italics are covered in this volume)*
Prehistoric	I.a.	Palaeolithic, *c*.10,000+ BP	FLN 057, FLN 061, FLN 064
	I.b.	Mesolithic, *c*.8000–4000 BC	FLN 057
	I.c.	Early Neolithic, *c*.4000–3200 BC	FLN 056, FLN 057, FLN 059, FLN 061, FLN 062, FLN 069
	I.d.	Late Neolithic, *c*.3200–2400 BC	***FLN 013 (FLN 054), FLN 053,*** FLN 057, FLN 059, FLN 061, FLN 062
	I.e.	Early Bronze Age, *c*.2400–1500 BC	***FLN 008,*** FLN 009, ***FLN 013,*** FLN 057, FLN 059 (FLN 055), FLN 061, ***FLN 062 (FLN 010),*** FLN 063, FLN 064, FLN 069, FLN 086 (FLN 011)
	I.f.	Late Bronze Age, *c*.1000–650 BC	FLN 009, FLN 061
	I.g.	Late Bronze Age/Early Iron Age *c*.800–400 BC	FLN 056, FLN 057, FLN 059, FLN 062
	I.h.	Middle Iron Age, *c*.400 – 1st century BC	FLN 057
	I.i.	Indeterminate Bronze Age/Iron Age *c*.2400 BC – 43 AD	FLN 057, FLN 059, FLN 062
Roman	II.a.	Late Iron Age/Early Roman *c*.1st BC–E.2nd century AD	***FLN 053,*** FLN 056, FLN 057, FLN 059, FLN 062, FLN 063
	II.b.	Roman, *c*.E.2nd–L.3rd century AD	FLN 062
	II.c.	Roman, *c*.L.3rd–4th century AD	FLN 057, FLN 059, FLN 062
	II.0	Roman, Unspecified date	FLN 059, FLN 062, FLN 063, FLN 069?
Saxon	III	Early Anglo Saxon, *c*.410–E.7th century	***FLN 008, FLN 053,*** FLN 057, FLN 061, ***FLN 062***
Medieval	IV	*c*.1066–1480	***FLN 008, FLN 013,*** FLN 057, FLN 059, FLN 061
Post-medieval	V.a.	L.15th–17th centuries	***FLN 008,*** FLN 062
	V.b.	*c*.17th–19th centuries	FLN 009, ***FLN 013, FLN 053,*** FLN 057, FLN 059, FLN 061, FLN 062, FLN 063, FLN 064, FLN 065, FLN 068, FLN 069, FLN 086
	V.c.	*c*.1914–1918	FLN 009, FLN 061
	V.d.	*c*.20th century	FLN 009, ***FLN 013, FLN 053,*** FLN 059, FLN 061, FLN 065, FLN 068, FLN 069, FLN 086

Table 2.1 Flixton Park Quarry and Hill Pit, overall framework of phasing/dating

excavated areas were within that parish. In addition, where, for example, all of the information in a Table or Figure relates to one of the discrete sites that has been included in the title, or a group of OP/context numbers from the same site are presented in brackets, then the site number has been omitted from in front of the individual context numbers.

Also for clarity, the two spatially distinct Early Anglo-Saxon cemeteries are referred to in the text as Flixton I, for that associated with the ring-ditch in FLN 008, and Flixton II, for the burials in FLN 053 and FLN 062. Subsequently, as part of the analysis stage of the project, the sixty-two burials in Flixton II were issued another number (1–62) in order to place them within a single concordant series, while the one discrete burial in Flixton I was called Grave A. Artefacts numbers have been written in the formula 00/00, which represents the grave number followed by the find number as it appears in the inventory (Chapter 15) and on the grave plans. Each bead string has been numbered in this way, but individual beads have, in addition, their original (excavation) find context numbers in italics, 00/00*:0000*. Unstratified finds from FLN 008 and FLN 053 cemetery areas that were almost certainly derived from burials are referred to in the text by the cemetery number, either I or II, followed by NG, representing Non Grave, followed by the number allocated in the inventory (*e.g.* I/NG00). In references to other sites, 'G' has been used as an abbreviation for 'grave'.

IV. Chronology and phasing

Table 2.1

While it would have been possible to prepare a phasing based solely on the archaeology covered by this report, it was considered to be more sensible in the long term to utilise a phasing framework that incorporates all of the archaeological periods identified at Flixton. In this way, consistency will be maintained throughout the planned series of publications. A breakdown of the phasing framework appears as Table 2.1. The sites covered by this volume are shown in italics.

V. Finds and archive

Following their ordering into a stable, fully cross-referenced and indexed archive, the entire body of site records, including the bulk finds, small finds (the latter following conservation) and accompanying documentary material, has been deposited in the Suffolk HER and curated under the controlled conditions of the Suffolk County Council's Archaeological Service Store at Shire Hall, Bury St Edmunds (conforming to MGC standards, MGC 1992). A copy of the digital records has been deposited with the Archaeology Data Service (ADS). Guidance for compiling the overall archive was provided by *Management of Archaeological Projects* (English Heritage 1991), particularly Appendix 6.

Part II

Prehistoric and Roman

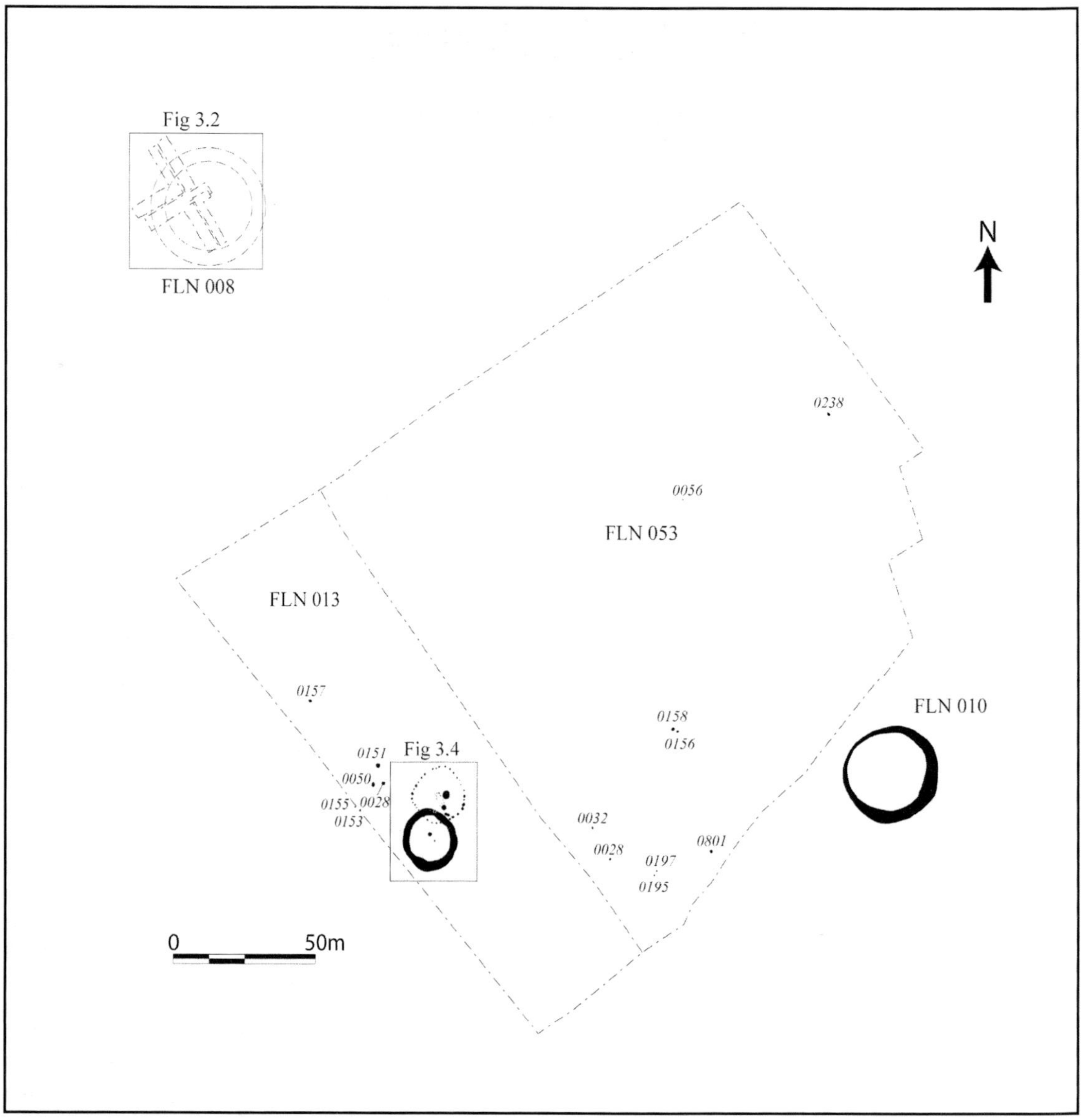

Figure 3.1 Period I.d. and I.e., Late Neolithic and Early Bronze Age features (Areas FLN 008, 013, 053 and 062)

Chapter 3. Prehistoric

by Stuart Boulter

I. Introduction

Fig. 3.1

Features attributed prehistoric dates were identified in all of the areas covered by this volume (Fig. 3.1). The earliest features were Late Neolithic in date and recorded in FLN 013 and FLN 053 comprising a sub-circular post-hole setting and a series of pits. In addition three Early Bronze Age ring-ditches, one each in FLN 008, FLN 013 and FLN 062, were also excavated.

II. The features

Site FLN 008

The 'rescue' excavation at this location was targeted on the known ring-ditch and when evidence for later, Period III (Early Anglo-Saxon) and Period IV/V (medieval/post-medieval), activity was encountered it was completely unexpected.

Ring-ditch (008:*0100*)
Figs 3.2–3.3

The previously known ring-ditch FLN 008 was located approximately 230m NNW of the FLN 013 ring-ditch and 60m south-west of another large ring feature (FLN 045) with a diameter of approximately 60m, which had previously been destroyed without record during quarrying operations.

Although clearly visible in the edge of the quarry, the ditch did not show up easily in the excavation trenches primarily because its upper fill graded imperceptibly into an intervening layer of subsoil that occurred between the ploughsoil and the underlying gravels. The excavators also identified a shallow, roughly circular mound surviving to a height of 0.65m and the trenches had been positioned accordingly. However, it became clear that the mound related more to the later, probably medieval or early post-medieval, reuse of the feature for the base of a post-mill type windmill, with its characteristic cross-shaped footing at its centre (008:*0103*). The centre of the ring-ditch was approximately 10m to the south-east and actually outside the excavation area.

An estimate for the diameter of the ring-ditch, measured from known points, gives a figure in the region of 40m (Fig. 3.2). One full, but rather oblique, north-east to south-west orientated section was excavated through the ditch on its western side (Fig. 3.3). The section revealed a markedly shouldered profile with an overall width of 4.7m and a depth of 1.69m, the latter measured from the base of the ploughsoil. Also in this position was an external lip, with a maximum depth of 0.25m, an irregular base and a vertical edge that did not follow the line of the main ditch. Within the confines of the limited excavation area it was not possible interpret this feature, although its orientation was more consistent with it being related to the later windmill phase than the original ring-ditch.

While a hint of stratification was recorded throughout, two main fill components were recognised. An upper fill comprised yellow/brown through to darker brown silty sand with moderately frequent stones (008:*0101*), the latter often defining the stratification. This upper fill overlay a stonier component (008:*0106* and *0107*) almost entirely confined within the 1m wide, v-shaped central deepening of the ditch. Fills 008:*0106* and 008:*0107* were clearly derived directly from the adjacent naturally occurring sand and gravel subsoil. Provided the ditch was not periodically cleaned out, this material represented a primary filling that would have started to accumulate immediately after the initial excavation of the feature. The upper fill (008:*0101*) would have accumulated over a far longer period of time, with its homogenous character suggesting continuous natural processes rather than deliberate episodes of backfilling. A large quantity of worked flint totalling 595 pieces was recovered from the fills in the excavated sections of the ring-ditch (Chapter 3.III).

Other features

One additional feature (008:*0114*) was tentatively attributed a prehistoric date and was considered to be broadly contemporary with the ring-ditch. Recorded during the subsequent bulldozing of the site, this trough-like feature, measuring approximately 9m long and 2m wide internal to and concentric with the ring-ditch at about 5m in from its western edge (Fig. 3.2). While not formally recorded, the feature was seen to be 0.3m deep with a fill that included a 0.05m thick layer of charcoal and heat-altered flint. The internal edge followed a similar alignment to an edge seen crossing the southern end of the south-west and south-east trenches. Here, it was initially interpreted as the internal edge of the ring-ditch, but later, following its excavation (008:*0112*), was found to represent a shallow depression inside the line of the ditch proper. The fill excavated as 008:*0112* also included heat-altered flint and charcoal and, given its similarities with 008:*0114*, it seems reasonable to assume that they are both part of a shallow, sometimes irregular, feature related to and respecting the internal edge of the ring-ditch.

Feature 008:*0113*, recorded as cutting the internal edge of the south side of the ring-ditch, was identified as an Early Anglo-Saxon grave and is described in Chapter 15.

Pottery spread

A dispersed surface scatter of pot sherds recorded in the southern end of the south-east trench (Fig. 3.2) was found in association with fragments of cremated bone. With the larger, more diagnostic fragments having since been identified as part of a collared urn, it was primarily these finds which were used as evidence to confirm the interpretation of the ring-ditch as the ploughed out remains of an Early Bronze Age round barrow, with at least one associated urned cremation burial.

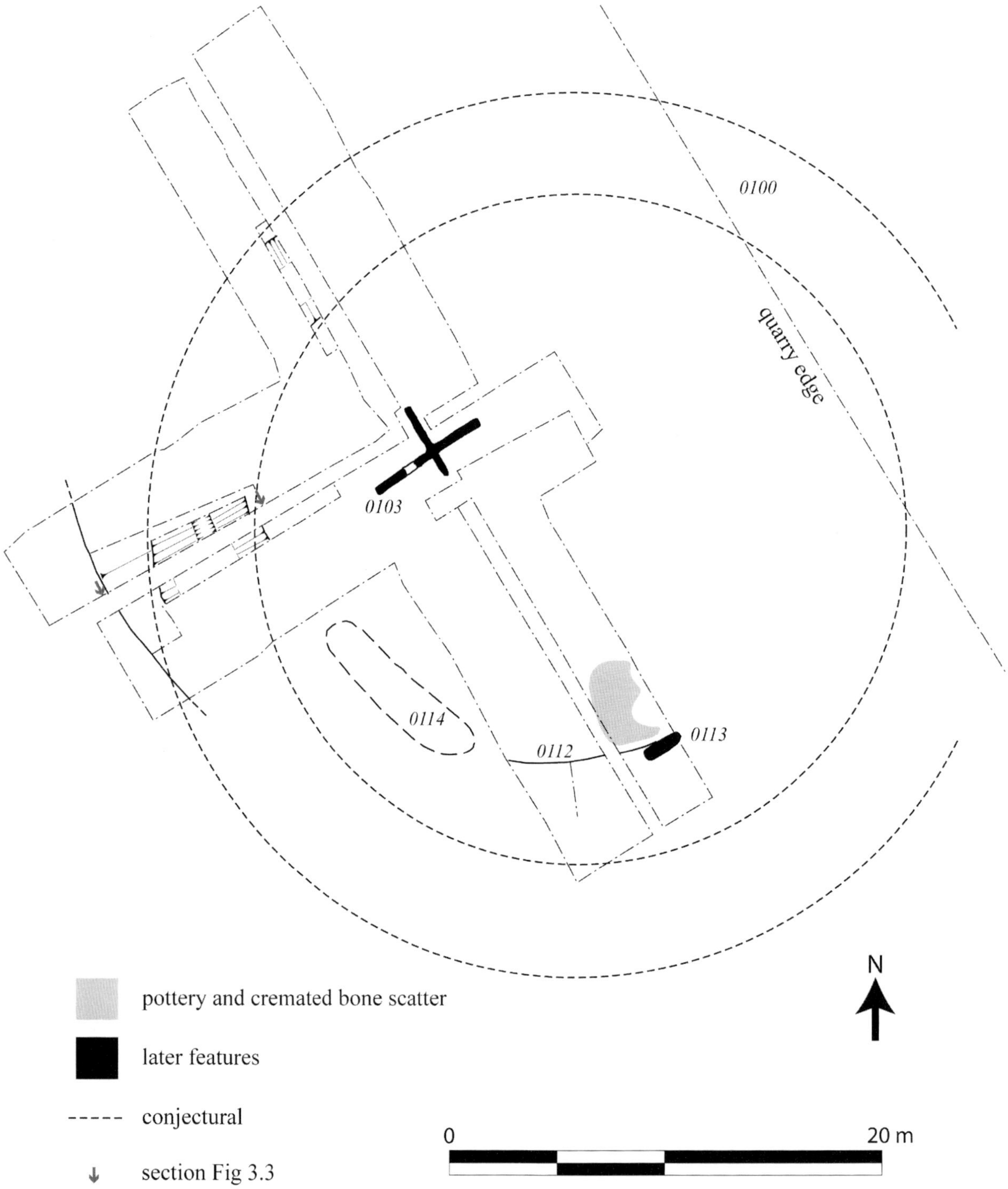

Figure 3.2 FLN 008: excavation plan

Sites FLN 013 and FLN 053

Datable prehistoric features were concentrated towards the southern end of the combined FLN 013 and FLN 053 area (Fig. 3.1), although some of the more widespread undated features, of which 199 were recorded, may have been contemporary. Artefactual evidence, backed up by a limited number of radiocarbon determinations, suggested that activity dated to the Late Neolithic (Period I.d.) and Early Bronze Age (Period I.e.) and was based around the construction of two very different monuments: a sub-circular post-hole circle and a ring-ditch. Other than the monuments themselves and their associated components, contemporary features were confined to a series of pits.

Sub-circular post-hole circle (013:*0147*) *and associated internal structure* (013:*0148*)

Figs 3.4–3.6; Pl. 3.1

During the manual cleaning undertaken prior to the excavation of the known ring-ditch, a series of post-holes was identified to the north and extending within the northern part of the monument. Within the confines of the initial excavation it was impossible to deduce the overall character of the structure, but it was clearly cut by what

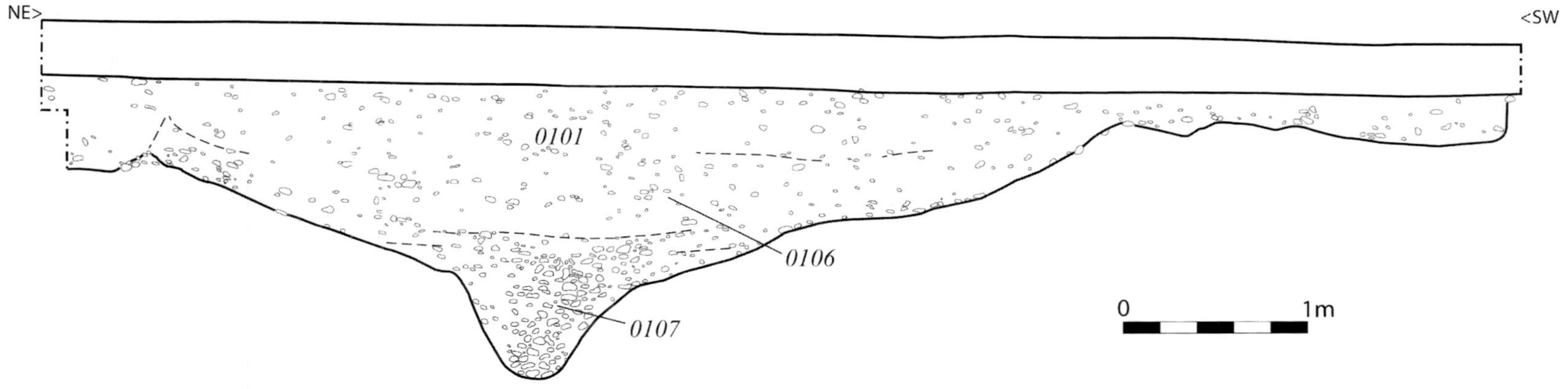

Figure 3.3 FLN 008: ring-ditch *0100*, section in NW quadrant

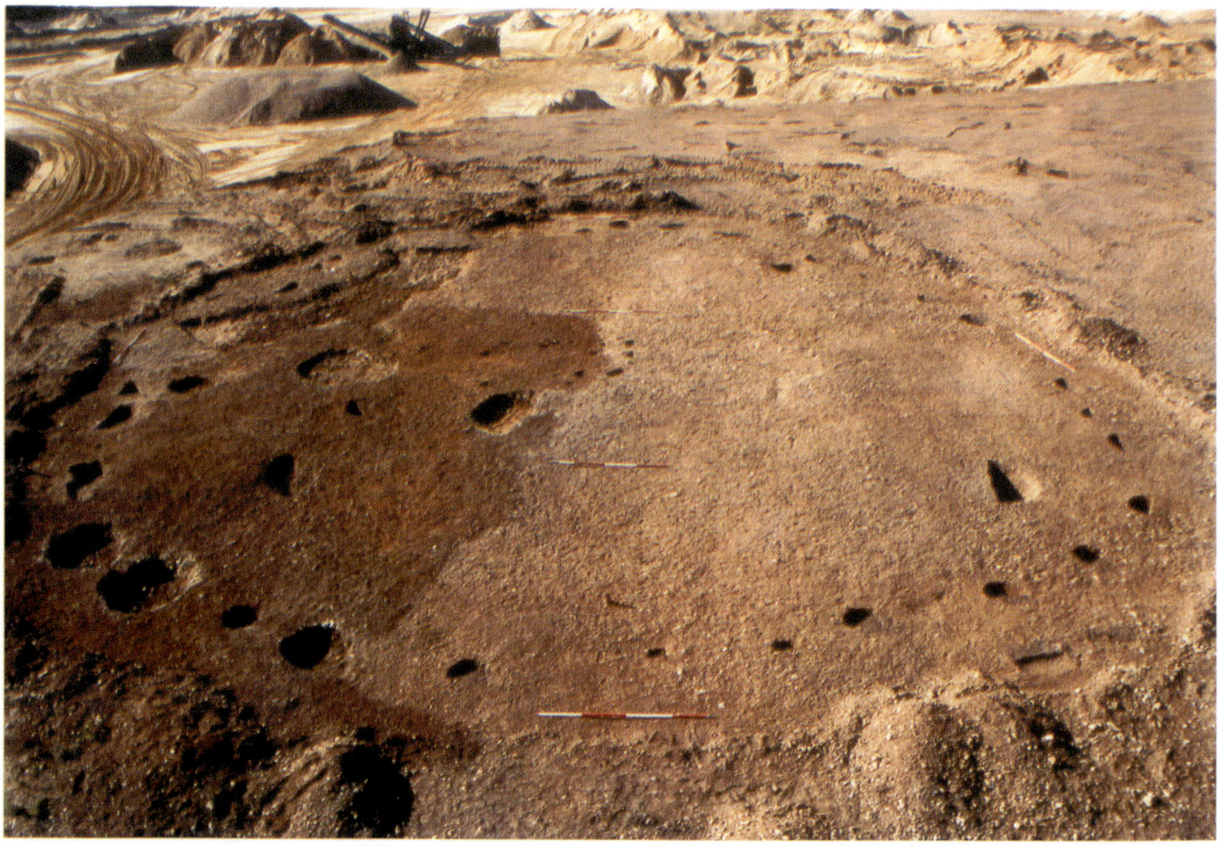

Plate 3.1 FLN 013: post-hole circle *0147* and internal structure *0148*

was presumed to be the prehistoric, probably Early Bronze Age, ring-ditch (Fig. 3.4; Pl. 3.1). The dating of the monument is discussed in Sections VI and VII below.

The structure itself (013:*0147*) comprised thirty three post-holes, detailed in Table 3.1, although based on the recorded intervals between the surviving features, it is calculated that thirty-six post-holes would have been present prior to its truncation by the later ring-ditch. Originally described as a post-hole circle, the actual shape was somewhat more complex. At first glance the geometry of the structure suggests that it may simply represent a poorly laid out circle with a diameter of approximately 18m. However, on closer inspection, a north-west to south-east line of symmetry can be identified. The south-east side of the structure would originally have comprised twelve post-holes arranged in a semicircular arc with a radius of 9m. Of these, ten (013:*0471*, *0467*, *0465*, *0410*, *0408*, *0406*, *0068*, *0064*, *0108* and *0112*) survived the partial truncation by the later ring-ditch. In contrast, the south-west side, comprising six surviving post-holes (013:*0120*, *0118*, *0116*, *0114*, *0443* and *0445*), with another lost to the truncation by the later ring-ditch, and the north-east side, comprising six post-holes (013:*0176*, *0159*, *0161*, *0174*, *0172* and *0166*), were essentially straight, approximately 8m in length and parallel with each other. The north-west side comprised eleven post-holes (013:*0416*, *0414*, *0412*, *0404*, *0188*, *0186*, *0169*, *0184*, *0182*, *0180* and *0178*) arranged in a 12m long arc with a radius of 14m, giving this end of the structure a rather flattened appearance when compared to the opposite, south-east end. A gap of 2.8m recorded between the six and seventh post-holes (013:*0169* and *0184* respectively) along the north-east side, counted from the western end, was interpreted as being the only entrance to the structure. While this gap did not conform to the apparent symmetry of the overall structure, with its long axis running equidistantly between post-holes 013:*0169* and 013:*0186* to the north-west and between 013:*0406* and 013:*0408* to the south-east, its significance was emphasised by the alignment of the internal post-hole structure (013:*0148*). The long axis of 013:*0148*, if projected to the north-west, passes directly through the proposed entrance. One other post-hole has been included as a numbered feature on Figure 3.4 (013:*0110*) as it continued the line of the north-east side of the circle. However, it was probably not an integral part of its formal structure.

Post-holes forming the main enclosure were all circular or sub-circular and although exhibiting a wide variation in their dimensions, the majority fell within a relatively narrow range. The diameters varied between 0.25m (013:*0172*) and 1.2m (013:*0064*), with depths from 0.2m (013:*0116*) through to 0.8m (013:*0068*). In addition, zones of dimensionally similar post-holes were identified around the circle. Those on the straight, south-west and north-east sides tended to be small while those on the north-west and south-east sides fell within a middle range. In contrast, a small group towards the south-east were large, in some part due to the presence of very unconsolidated and stony natural subsoil in this area which was prone to collapse.

Similarly, the spacing between individual post-holes was not uniform, although the majority again fell within a relatively narrow range. With the exception of the 2.8m gap between post-holes 013:*0169* and 013:*0184* marking the proposed entrance, the distance separating successive

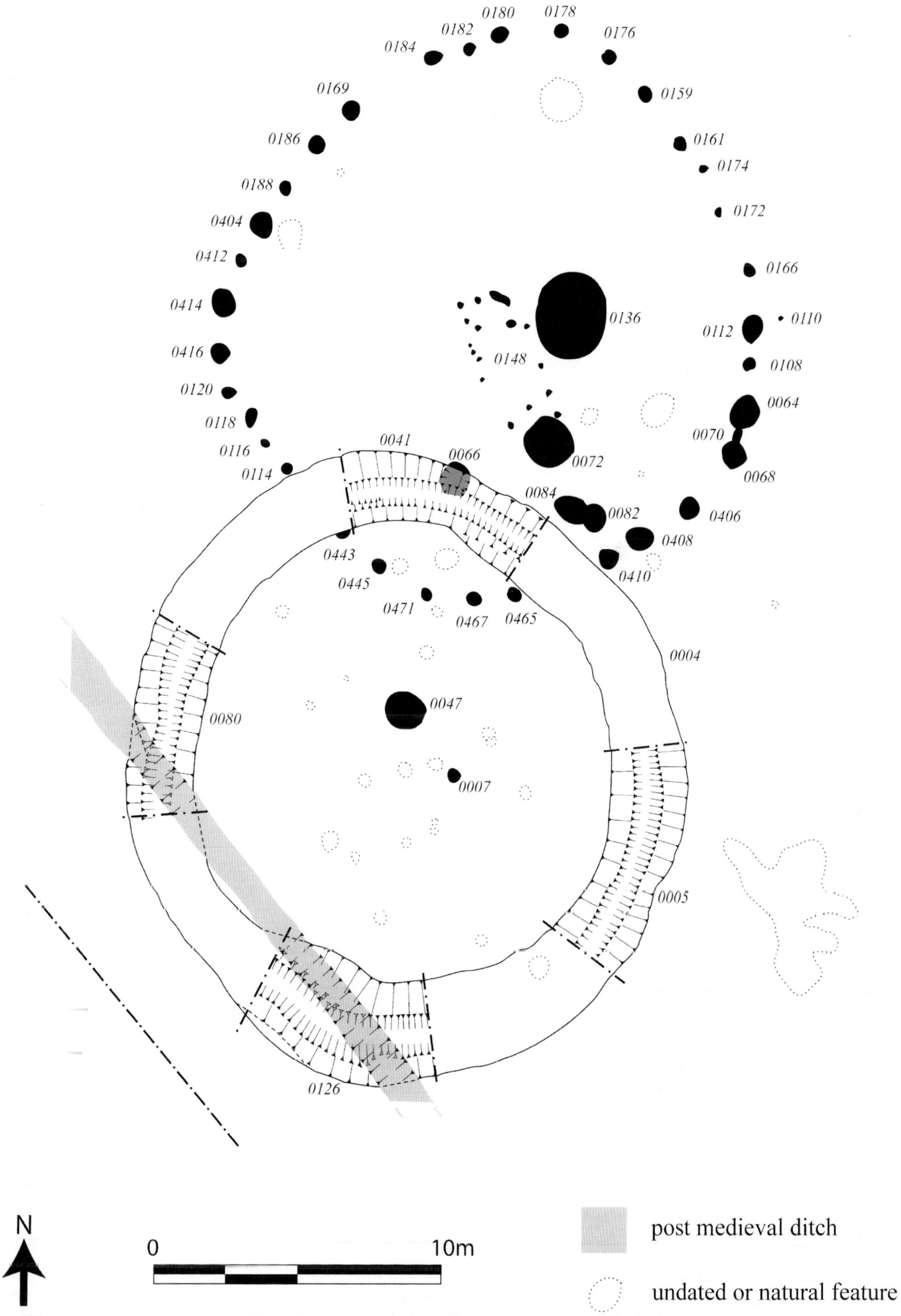

Figure 3.4 FLN 013: detail of post-hole circle and ring-ditch

Post-hole Context No.	*Diameter (m)*	*Depth (m)*	*Distance to next post-hole*	*Description*	*Pottery*	*Worked flint*	*Heat altered flint*	*Other*
0184	0.60	0.44	0.78	Vertical south-west side, slightly less steep to north-east, relatively flat-bottomed. The fill (*0185*) included a central component of homogenous brown silty sand, lighter towards edges (post-pipe?).	5 sherds of Grooved Ware (18g). Includes Fig. 3.9.1	5 pieces	5 pieces (58g)	
0182	0.40	0.34	0.60	Vertical sided, angled base. The fill (*0183*) comprised homogenous brown silty sand with occasional stones. Pottery (*0171*) possibly deliberately placed on top of feature as closure deposit.	15 sherds of Beaker (98g). Includes Fig. 3.9.23	3 pieces	4 pieces (220g)	
0180	0.60	0.48	1.60	Vertical south-west side, slightly less steep to north-east, relatively flat-bottomed. The fill (*0181*) comprised homogenous brown silty sand with occasional stones.			1 piece (25g)	
0178	0.50	0.44	1.40	Steep sided, rounded base. The fill (*0179*) comprised homogenous brown silty sand with occasional stones.				
0176	0.44	0.50	1.20	Vertical sided, angled base. The fill (*0177*) comprised homogenous brown silty sand with occasional stones.			1 piece (41g)	
0159	0.60	0.42	1.60	Steep sided, flattish base. The fill (*0160*) comprised homogenous brown silty sand with occasional stones.				
0161	0.48	0.30	0.70	Moderately sloping sides, rounded bottom. The fill (*0162*) comprised homogenous brown silty sand with occasional stones.		2 pieces	8 pieces (80g)	
0174	0.30	0.28	1.25	Steep sided, flat base. The fill (*0175*) comprised homogenous brown silty sand with occasional stones.				
0172	0.25	0.28	1.80	Vertical sides, rounded base. The fill (*0173*) comprised homogenous brown silty sand fill with occasional stones.				
0166	0.50	0.50	1.20	Steeply sloping, almost shouldered sides, rounded base. The fill (*0167*) comprised homogenous brown silty sand with occasional stones.			3 pieces (9g)	
0112	0.80	0.60	0.60	Steep sides, rounded base. The fill (*0113*) comprised homogenous grey/brown silty sand with occasional stones and charcoal.		1 piece	48 pieces (372g)	
0108	0.40	0.25	0.80	Steep sides, rounded base. The fill (*0109*) comprised homogenous grey/brown silty sand with occasional stones/gravel, concentrated at base, and charcoal.		1 piece, possible spurred scraper tool (Fig. 3.10.4)	103 pieces (1305g)	
0064	1.20	0.65	0.40	Moderately steep sides, greater to north, flattish base. Stratified fill (*0065*) comprised layers of light and dark brown silty sand with slumped stone/gravel around sides.		5 pieces	234 pieces (2092g)	
0068	1.00	0.80	1.50	Steep sides, rounded base. The fill (*0069*) comprised homogenous brown silty sand central fill with darker component towards base and slumped stone/gravel around sides.			26 pieces (184g)	
0406	0.70	0.30	1.20	Near vertical north-east side, slightly less steep to south-west, flat-bottomed. The fill (*0407*) comprised homogenous brown silty sand with frequent stone/gravel inclusions. Pottery sherd same fabric as decorated sherd in post-hole *0184* on the opposite side of the circle.	1 sherd (1g)			
0408	1.00	0.30	0.42	Steep north-east side, less so on south-west where it curves into the flattish base. The fill (*0409*) comprised homogenous brown silty sand with frequent stone/gravel inclusions.		2 pieces, includes possible blade core		
0410	0.70	0.65	Ring-ditch	Vertical north-east side, less steep to south-west, irregular base. The fill (*0411*) comprised homogenous brown silty sand with frequent stone/gravel inclusions.		2 pieces	2 pieces (280g)	

0465	0.60	0.40	0.86	Stepped south-east side, steeply sloping to north-west with a rounded base. The fill (*0466*) comprised homogenous brown silty sand with frequent stone/gravel inclusions.				
0467	0.50	0.38	1.20	Steep sides, rounded base. The fill (*0468*) comprised homogenous brown silty sand.				
0471	0.30	0.30	1.45	Steep sides, rounded base. The fill (*0472*) comprised homogenous brown silty sand.				
0445	0.50	0.50	1.18	Near vertical sides, angled base. The fill (*0446*) comprised homogenous brown silty sand with frequent stone/gravel inclusions.		3 pieces	6 pieces (487g)	
0443	-	0.40	Ring-ditch	Steep southern side, cut by ring-ditch to north. The fill (*0444*) comprised homogenous brown silty sand.				
0114	0.38	0.40	0.80	V-shaped profile. The fill (*0115*) predominantly homogenous brown silty sand with occasional stone/gravel inclusions.		3 pieces	3 pieces (48g)	
0116	0.30	0.20	0.50	Vertical sides, rounded, although slightly irregular base. The fill (*0117*) comprised homogenous brown silty sand with occasional stones.		1 piece	2 pieces (13g)	
0118	0.70	0.40	0.60	Steep, near vertical northern edge, more gently sloping and shouldered to the south. The fill (*0119*) comprised homogenous brown silty sand with charcoal flecks.				
0120	0.65	0.40	0.80	Relatively shallow sloping sides with a rounded base. The fill (*0121*) comprised homogenous brown silty sand with occasional stones.	2 sherds of Grooved Ware, 1 sherd of ind. Neo/LBA (4g)	6 pieces	5 pieces (68g)	
0416	0.80	0.44	0.90	Relatively shallow sloping sides with a restricted, but flat base. The fill (*0417*) comprised homogenous brown silty sand with frequent stone/gravel inclusions.		4 pieces	1 piece (17g)	
0414	1.00	0.44	0.90	Shallow sloping side to south, steep to the north, reducing to a gentle slope down to an open-v-shaped base. The fill (*0415*) comprised homogenous brown silty sand with occasional stones. Sand and gravel slump against northern edge.		2 pieces		
0412	0.44	0.40	0.80	Steep sides, rounded base. The fill (*0413*) comprised homogenous brown silty sand.	2 sherds of ind. Neo/LBA (1g)		3 pieces (128g)	
0404	0.85	0.40	0.80	Moderately sloping sides, rounded base. The fill (*0405*) comprised homogenous brown silty sand fill with frequent stone/gravel inclusions.			3 pieces (404g)	
0188	0.40	0.44	1.20	Moderately steep sides, rounded base. The fill (*0189*) comprised homogenous brown silty sand with occasional stones.	1 sherd of Grooved Ware (4g) (Fig. 3.9.8),	1 retouched flake	2 pieces (47g)	
0186	0.60	0.30	1.00	Near vertical sided, flat-bottomed. The fill (*0187*) has a central component, possibly a post-pipe comprised very dark brown silty sand with charcoal flecks and an outer fill of homogenous light brown silty sand.		2 pieces	188 pieces (1851g)	3 heat-altered stones (35g), 1 calcined bone (human wrist?)
0169	0.75	0.50	2.80	Moderately sloping sides, rounded base. The fill (*0170*) includes a central component, possibly a post-pipe comprised dark brown silty sand with charcoal flecks and an outer fill of brown silty sand with occasional stone/gravel inclusions		4 pieces	114 pieces (1366g)	1 heat-altered stone (19g)

Table 3.1 FLN 013: post-hole circle 0147, detail of post-holes

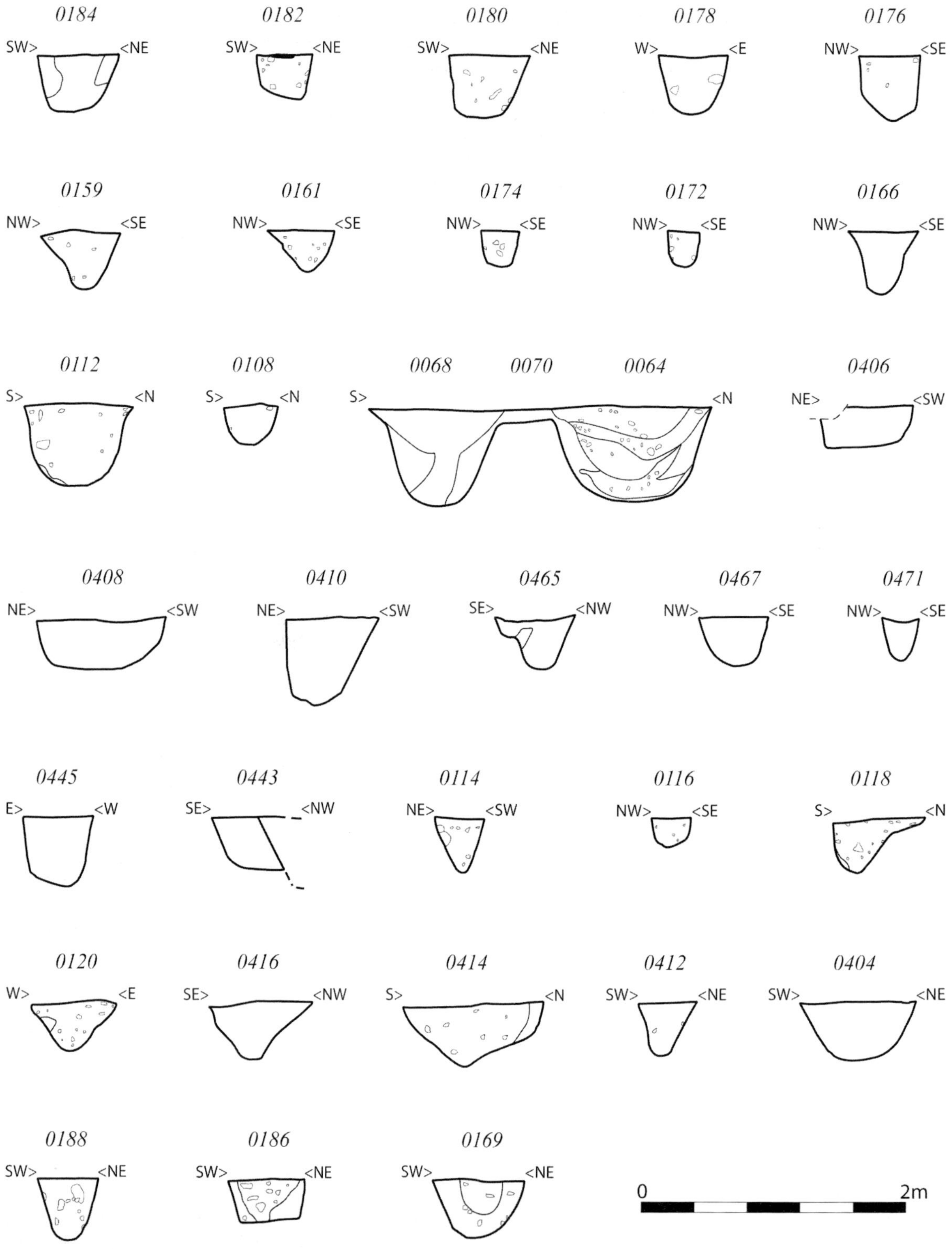

Figure 3.5 FLN 013: post-hole circle *0147* section drawings

features ranged from 0.5m (between 013:*0116* and *0118*) to 1.8m (between 013:*0172* and *0166*).

Post-hole profiles (Fig. 3.5) also showed some variation with the majority exhibiting a rounded bottom with steeply sloping sides (*e.g.* 013:*0404*). Variations included V-shaped (013:*0114*), flat-bottomed (013:*0186*), shallow sloping shouldered sides (013:*0414*) and asymmetrically sided (013:*0118*).

The fills were generally homogenous, comprising brown silty sand with charcoal flecks and varying proportions of gravel to pebble sized flint inclusions. Notable exceptions were 013:*0169* and 013:*0186*, immediately west of the entrance, either side of the line of symmetry through the structure, both of which had a central fill rich in charcoal and heat-altered sand. In addition, a group of post-holes towards the south-east of the structure (013:*0064*, *0068*, *0112* and *0108*) exhibited very dark coloured fill components and included heat-altered flints in relatively large quantities. There were multiple fills in 013:*0064* and 013:*0068*, with the former exhibiting a series of discrete layers and the latter a discrete central component. With the exception, possibly, of the central fill elements in features 013:*0068*, *0169* and *0186*, there was little evidence, post-pipes/ghosts *etc*., to prove that these features had actually functioned as post-holes, although this would still seem to be the most logical interpretation.

Artefactual evidence recovered from the post-hole fills comprised pottery, worked flint, heat-altered flints and a single human bone (Table 3.1). The relatively small quantity of ceramic finds included both Grooved Ware and Beaker, the latter dominated by fifteen sherds from a single vessel (013:*0171* in post-hole 013:*0182*) possibly representing a closure deposit at the top of a post-hole deliberately placed when the monument became redundant. The quantity of pottery was significant and its condition (relatively large unabraded sherds) suggested that, similarly to the pottery recovered from the broadly contemporary pits, it should be considered to be in its primary context of deposition. When the distribution of artefact type is examined a distinct pattern emerges. Of the six post-holes from which pottery were recovered (013:*0120*, *0182*, *0184*, *0188*, *0406* and *0412*), four (013:*0182*, *0184*, *0188* and *0412*) lay on the north-west side of the structure, two each side of the entrance. This includes 013:*0182*, which produced the fifteen sherds from a single Beaker. Furthermore, the only flint tool, a scraper, and a single burnt human bone (?wrist) were recovered from post-hole 013:*0186*, also on the north-west side of the structure. Heat-altered flints and undiagnostic worked flint (flakes) were more common throughout the structure, although the north-west side was again the most productive, with the concentration continuing around to the west and a further concentration from the large post-holes to the south-east. In addition, there appeared to be a positive relationship between worked flint and heat-altered flint, with only six post-holes producing one or other of these categories of find and sixteen which produced both.

Twenty-one features enclosed by the post-hole circle were positively attributed prehistoric dates, five pits and sixteen post-holes, the latter forming a rectangular post-setting (013:*0148*) central to the monument. Post-setting 013:*0148*, based on its spatial relationship with the surrounding post-hole circle, can be considered to be contemporary. However, the same cannot be said for the pits, as similar features were recorded outside the post-hole circle, although the artefactual dating suggests that they were broadly contemporary. These pits are described in greater detail in Chapter 3.II, Pits.

A further eight features were recorded within the area enclosed by the post-hole circle (shown dotted on Fig. 3.4). With the exception of one pit (013:*0451*) that was attributed a post-medieval (Period V.b.) date based on the presence of ceramic tile in its fill, these features remain undated. Three were described as post-holes (013:*0122*, *0447* and *0455*) and four (013:*0061*, *0449*, *0473* and *0475*) as pits. All exhibited fills comprised predominantly homogenous orange/brown moderately silty sand with varying concentrations of gravel/stones. Artefactual evidence from these features was limited to a few heat-altered flints and worked flint flakes and while this did not contradict a prehistoric date, their association with the surrounding monument was uncertain and they could not, therefore, positively be recognised as contemporary. Indeed, in some instances, it was unclear whether these were genuine archaeological features and it is unlikely that they would have been recognised without the repeated manual cleaning undertaken in this area. However, given their juxtaposition to the significant Late Neolithic structure it was considered prudent to record them in detail.

Rectangular post-hole setting 013:*0148* (Fig. 3.6) measured *c*.5m from north-west to south-east and *c*.2m from the south-west to north-east with its long axis lining up with the apparent entrance to the post-hole circle. While the arrangement of the post-holes was somewhat irregular, with variable intervals between the individual features, the overall footprint of the structure was clearly defined.

Details of the post-holes are listed in Table 3.2. All but one of the post-holes were circular or sub-circular, with one exception (013:*0457*) which was oval in shape, measuring 0.9m from north-west to south-east and 0.3m from south-west to north-east. While this odd shape could be a genuine reflection of the original feature, it may also have been the result of root or animal disturbance increasing its size or, alternatively, two separate post-holes could have been erroneously excavated as a single feature. Most of the post-holes were of relatively uniform size, although there was some variation with diameters between 0.08m (013:*0493*) and 0.38m (013:*0481*) and depths ranging from 0.1m (013:*0457*) through to 0.32m (013:*0461*).

The post-hole fills were generally homogenous, comprising silty sand with varying proportions of gravel and pebble-sized stone inclusions. One exception was 013:*0461*, which included a significant amount of charcoal in its fill. Artefactual evidence was limited to a worked flint scraper in 013:*0457* and undiagnostic worked flints from 013:*0457* and 013:*0459*, with heat-altered flints in 013:*0457*, 013:*0459*, 013:*0461* and 013:*0487*.

Ring-ditch (013:*0004*) *and associated cremation* (013:*0007*)
Fig. 3.7; Pl. 3.2

The known ring-ditch FLN 013 became the target of the initial 30m by 30m open area excavation in 1996. Although clearly visible following the mechanical removal of the topsoil, manual cleaning was undertaken further to enhance its definition. All artefacts identified during the cleaning were plotted, revealing that while the quantity of material, particularly worked flint, was relatively high, finds were evenly dispersed around the ditch.

The ditch described a slightly irregular circle with an internal diameter of approximately 15m and an external diameter of nearly 20m (Fig. 3.4; Pl. 3.2). Irregularities in shape were in some part the result of tree root and animal disturbance, which also explained the inclusion of intrusive material in fill context 013:*0019*.

Excavated sections were distributed regularly around the ditch revealing a relatively consistent profile and a fill composition that varied only in detail (Fig. 3.7). A distinct shouldered profile was recorded, with a depth varying between 0.8m in the north-west quadrant and 1m in the remaining three quadrants. Width measurements varied between 2m and 3.3m. The fill in all of the excavated sections comprised two overall basic components. However, there were distinct layers within each

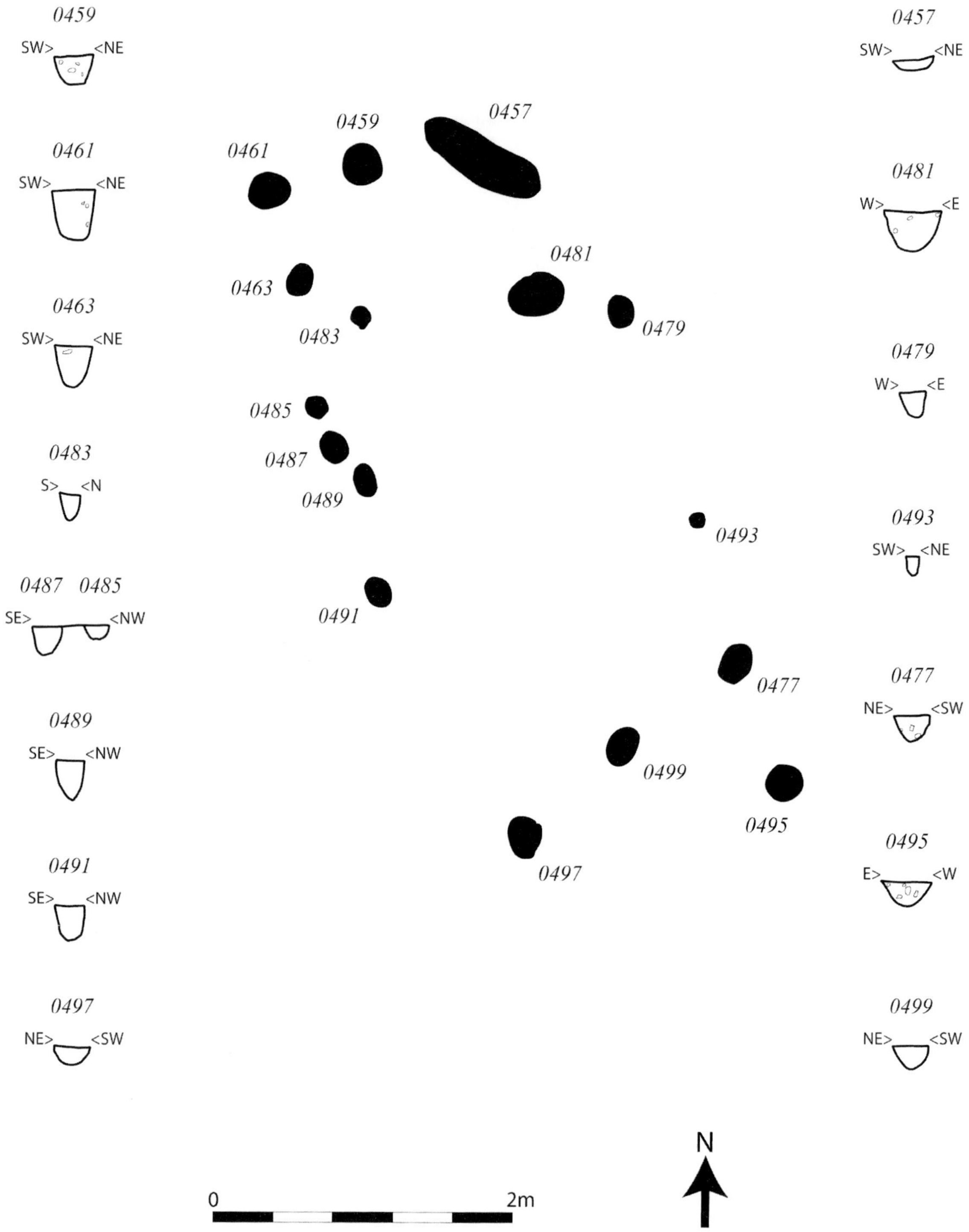

Figure 3.6 FLN 013: structure *0148*, detailed plan and section drawings

component and minor variations between each quadrant. Upper components generally comprised brown silty sand with varying concentrations of gravel to cobble sized flint inclusions. The lower component (primary fill, 013:*0168*) comprised yellow/orange sand with gravel and flints in varying proportions. The character of this layer appeared to depend directly on the composition of the juxtaposed naturally-occurring subsoil in the relevant section of the ditch. Where the sides of the feature comprised almost totally of gravel then the lower component of ditch fill also included a high proportion of that material. This suggests that the lower fill was generated directly by the slumping of the side of the ditch, provided the ditch was not periodically emptied, probably soon after its initial excavation, while the upper fill represented a more long term accumulation of material in the feature. The upper fills almost certainly include material derived from a central mound that would have been thrown up within the area enclosed by the ditch. However, this was not reflected by the attitude of the tip lines, which suggest there had been significant input from both external to and internal to the monument, possibly indicative of an external bank as well as an internal mound.

Post-hole Context No.	*Diameter (m)*	*Depth (m)*	*Location*	*Description*	*Worked flint*	*Heat altered flint*
0457	0.90 x 0.30	0.06	North-east corner of setting	Elongated feature, possibly two excavated as one or damaged by rooting/animal burrows. Homogenous grey/brown silty sand fill (*0458*).	5 pieces, includes a scraper	1 piece (60g)
0459	0.26	0.20	Central to north side of setting	Steep sided, flat bottomed. Homogenous dark grey/black silty sand fill with occasional gravel/stone inclusions, some charcoal (*0460*).	2 pieces	7 pieces (7g)
0461	0.28	0.32	North-west corner of setting	Steep sided, flat bottomed. Homogenous dark grey/black silty sand fill with charcoal (*0462*).		1 piece (59g)
0463	0.25	0.29	West side of setting	Steep sided, rounded base. Homogenous brown silty sand fill (*0464*).		
0477	0.24	0.18	South-east corner of setting	Steep sided, rounded base. Homogenous brown silty sand fill with gravel/stone inclusions (*0478*).		
0479	0.20	0.18	East side of setting	Steep sided, rounded base. Homogenous brown silty sand fill with gravel/stone inclusions (*0480*).		
0481	0.38	0.26	Stepped in from east side of setting	Moderately steep sided, rounded base. Homogenous brown silty sand fill with gravel/stone inclusions (*0482*).		
0483	0.16	0.16	Stepped in from west side of setting	Steep sided, rounded base. Homogenous brown silty sand fill with gravel/stone inclusions (*0484*).		
0485	0.16	0.10	West side of setting	Moderately steep sided, rounded base. Homogenous brown silty sand fill (*0486*).		
0487	0.20	0.18	West side of setting	Steep sided, rounded base. Homogenous brown silty sand fill (*0488*).		1 piece (70g)
0489	0.20	0.26	West side of setting	Steep sided, narrow angled base. Homogenous brown silty sand fill with gravel/stone inclusions (*0490*).		
0491	0.22	0.22	West side of setting	Steep sided, rounded base. Homogenous brown silty sand fill with gravel/stone inclusions (*0492*).		
0493	0.14	0.08	East side of setting	Near vertical sided, rounded base. Homogenous brown silty sand fill (*0494*).		
0495	0.32	0.16	South end of setting	Relatively gently sloping sides, round bottomed. Homogenous brown silty sand fill with gravel/stone inclusions (*0496*).		
0497	0.24	0.12	South-west corner of setting	Moderately steep sided, rounded base. Homogenous brown silty sand fill (*0498*).		
0499	0.24	0.16	Central and stepped in from south end of setting	Relatively gently sloping sides, round bottomed. Homogenous brown silty sand fill (*0149*).		

Table 3.2 FLN 013: structure *0148*, detail of post-holes

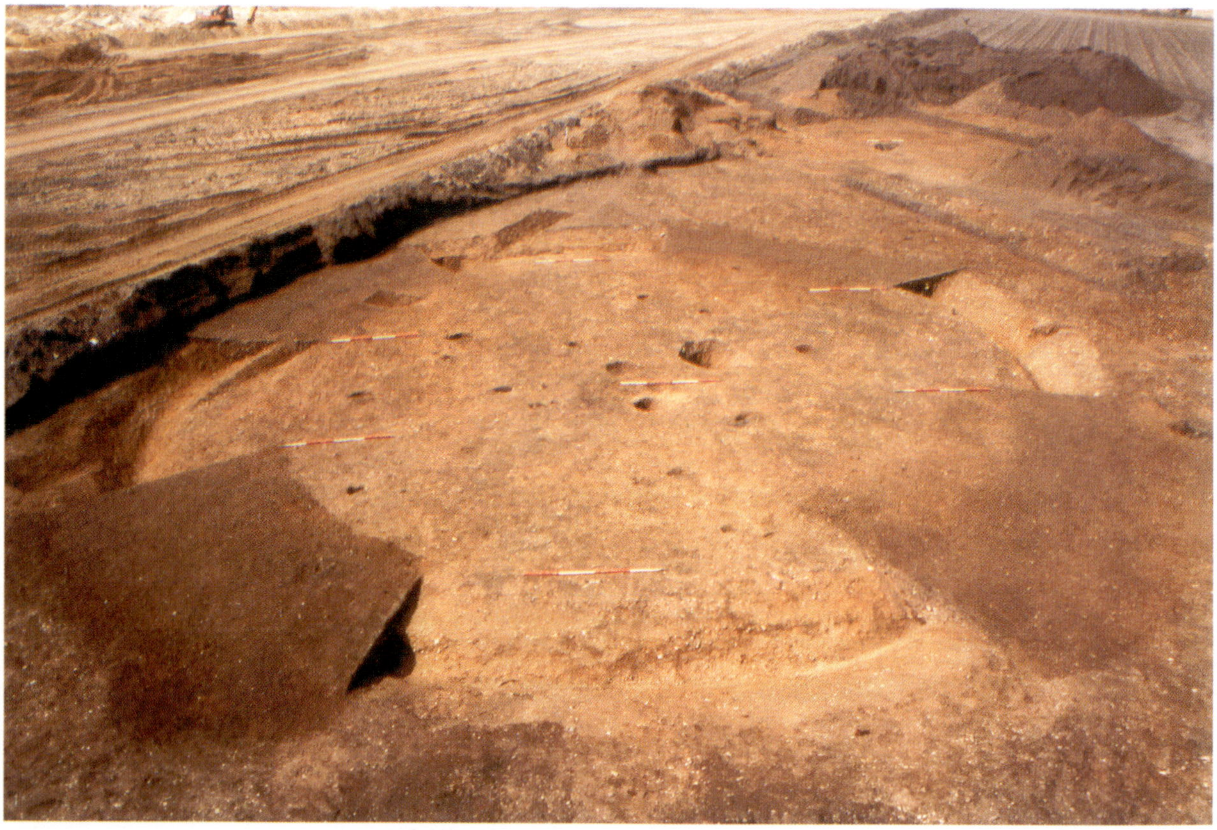

Plate 3.2 FLN 013: ring-ditch *0004*

Artefactual evidence, the majority of which was recovered from the upper fill component, included pottery sherds (predominantly abraded Grooved Ware, although indeterminate Later Neolithic/Early Bronze Age types were also represented). In addition, a considerable quantity of worked flint, including diagnostic tools of Late Neolithic date, was recovered from the ditch fill. As radiocarbon dating determined that the cremation associated with the ring-ditch was of Early Bronze Age date (Chapter 3.VI) and the ditch itself cut a pit proven by radiocarbon dating to be of Late Neolithic date (Chapter 3.VI), these finds must be considered residual and derived from earlier activity.

A single un-urned cremation (013:*0007*) was identified within the area confined by the ring-ditch located just to the east of centre (Fig. 3.4). The circular, 0.4m in diameter, 0.3m deep cremation pit was vertical sided with a shallower lip, a flat base and a fill, excavated in 0.05m spits (013:*0008–0013*), comprising dark grey/black charcoal-rich sand with many obvious bone fragments and heat-altered flints. The entire cremation pit fill was retained and details of the recovered human remains are included in this volume (Chapter 3.IV). Analysis of the charcoal found it to be composed almost entirely of Oak, although a small quantity of Ash (*Fraxinus* sp.) was also present, a sample of which was submitted for radiocarbon dating (Chapter 3.VI).

In addition to the contemporary cremation 013:*0007*, Period I.d pit 013:*0047* and an arc of five post-holes forming part of the Period I.d post-hole circle 013:*0147*, a further twenty features were recorded within the area enclosed by the ring-ditch (dotted on Fig. 3.4). The features were distributed in a random manner but, by excluding individual features, a number of sub-rectangular, square or circular configurations can be proposed as formal arrangements, although none can be substantiated. The features were all circular or sub-circular with diameters varying between 0.2m (013:*0014*) to 0.8m (013:*0449*), the latter one of those also within the confines of the earlier post-hole circle. Depths varied between only 0.08m (013:*0030*) and 0.4m (013:*0449*) with fills generally comprising homogenous orange/brown silty sand with varying concentrations of gravel/stones. One exception was 013:*0128* with a stratified fill, collectively 013:*0129*, comprising layers of silty and clean sand.

Like the majority of the features recorded within post-hole circle 013:*0147*, those within the ring-ditch only became apparent after protracted manual cleaning and would probably not have been recognised elsewhere on the site. Even if these were genuine features, there were no datable artefacts or other evidence to directly link them to any of the more securely dated phases, other than their juxtaposition to the Period I.e monument.

Pits

Fig. 3.8; Pl. 3.3

Nineteen pits were positively identified as prehistoric based almost entirely on their included artefactual evidence, eleven in the FLN 013 area and eight in FLN 053 (Figs 3.1 and 3.4). All were considered to belong in Period I.d. Late Neolithic. A number of the undated pits were also almost certainly prehistoric, particularly those containing undiagnostic worked flint and heat-altered flints. However, they could not be positively attributed to a Period or Phase due to the lack of secure dating evidence. Details of the prehistoric pits are listed in Table 3.3, with section drawings presented as Figure 3.8. With the

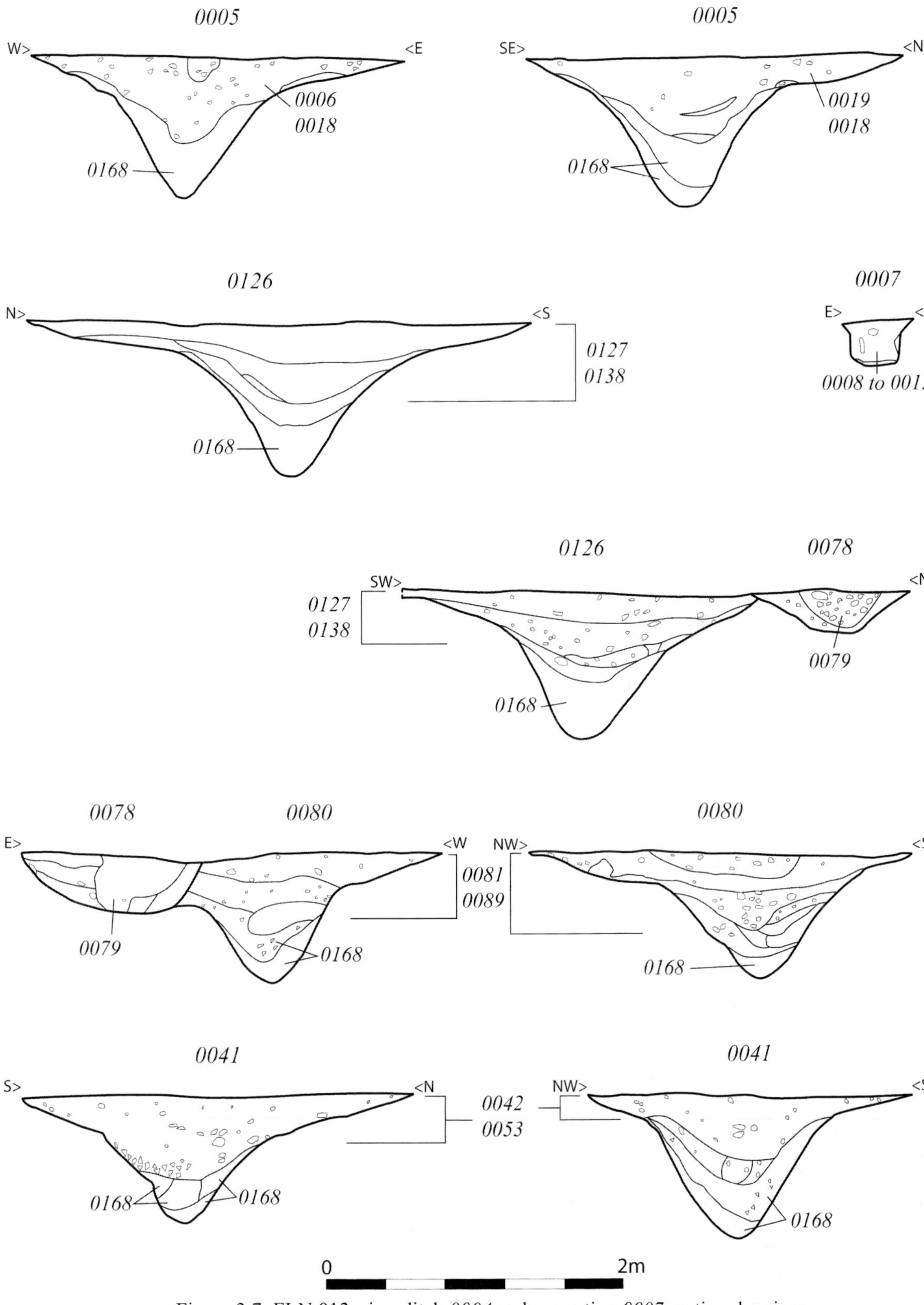

Figure 3.7 FLN 013: ring-ditch *0004* and cremation *0007* section drawings

exception of 053:*0238*, located towards the eastern edge of the overall excavated area, all of these features were recorded in the southernmost third of the site, the main concentration within the areas enclosed by the FLN 013 post-hole circle and ring-ditch, or immediately to the north-west and east of these monuments. However, it is difficult to say which, if any, of these features were directly contemporary with the use of the monuments, although they had undoubtedly, at some stage, become the localised focus for activity that was at least broadly contemporaneous. This was particularly the case for the earlier of the two monuments, the post-hole circle, as the majority of the dated adjacent pits contained later Neolithic Grooved Ware pottery.

Pit Context No.	*Dimensions (m)*	*Depth (m)*	*Description*	*Pottery*	*Worked flint*	*Heat-altered flint*
FLN 013						
0028	1.20	0.50	Circular. Semicircular profile. Stratified fill (013:*0029*, *0034*, *0035*, *0036*). The central, darker component (013:*0036*) included the majority of the artefactual evidence.	77 sherds of Grooved ware (653g). Includes Fig. 3.9.4-6, 15-19	193 pieces, includes 6 scrapers (4 illustrated Fig. 3.10.5-8), 3 cores, a notched flake, a possible piercer, 7 retouched flakes, 2 utilised flakes and 2 utilised blades (1 illustrated, Fig. 3.10.9)	198 pieces (2522g)
0047	1.30	0.92	Circular. Steeply sloping sides, shouldered towards top, flat bottomed. Stratified fill (013:*0048*, *0052*, *0077*), darker component (013:*0048*) at top, charcoal flecks throughout.	5 sherds of Grooved Ware (21g)	55 pieces, includes three cores, two retouched flakes and one scraper (Fig. 3.11.25)	30 pieces (971g)
0050	1.20 x 1.55	0.30	Oval. Gently rounded profile. Stratified fill (collectively 013:*0051*) with a darker upper component.	2 sherds of Grooved Ware (9g). Includes Fig. 3.9.11	4 pieces	-
0066	1.20	0.48	Sub-circular. Moderately steep sided, flat bottomed. Cut by FLN 013 ring-ditch. Stratified fill (0013:*0067*, *0075*, *0076*), includes darker middle component rich in charcoal (013:*0076*). The majority of the heat-altered flints were in fill 013:*0075*.	31 sherds of Grooved Ware (241g). Includes Fig. 3.9.7, 9	13 pieces, includes 1 retouched flake	48 pieces (285g)
0072	1.80	1.00	Circular. Steep sided, shouldered towards top, flat bottom curves up to meet sides. Stratified; darker upper fill (013:*0073*), charcoal-rich central band (013:*0074*) with a sandy basal fill (013:*0086*). The majority of the artefactual evidence was recovered from the upper fill.	33 sherds of Grooved Ware (278g). Includes Fig. 3.9.13, 20, 21	36 pieces, includes 1 scraper (Fig. 3.10.10), a possible serrated blade (Fig. 3.10.11), a piercer and a utilised flake	79 pieces (1628g)
0082	0.80	0.26	Circular. Cut pit 013:*0084*. Moderately steep sides, sloping base. Fill collectively 013:*0083* included central dark brown silty sand with charcoal flecks, outer component of lighter coloured sand and gravel.	1 sherd of Grooved Ware (1g)	14 pieces, includes a flake struck from a polished implement (Fig. 3.11.26), 2 scrapers (1 illustrated Fig. 3.11.27) and part of an edge ground knife (Fig. 3.11.28)	3 pieces (63g)
0084	1.20 x 0.90	0.14	Oval. Cut by 013:*0082*. Shallow dish-like profile. Homogenous brown silty sand fill (013:*0085*) with occasional gravel/stone inclusions.	1 sherd of GroovedWare (6g)	4 pieces, includes a possible broken scraper	28 pieces (446g)
0136	3.00 x 2.60	0.16	Oval. Shallow dish-like profile. Homogenous brown silty sand fill (013:*0137*) with occasional gravel/stone inclusions.	-	27 pieces, includes a scraper and a retouched blade	7 pieces (117g)
0151	1.50	0.64	Sub-circular. Moderately steep sides with a flat bottom. Stratified fill (013:*0152*), upper dark brown silty sand component (013:*0163*), lower components of cleaner sand and gravel (013:*0164* and *0165*). Finds concentrated in upper fill 013:*0163*.	29 sherds of Grooved Ware (167g). Includes Fig. 3.9.2, 10, 14	25 pieces, includes 3 scrapers (Fig. 3.10.12-14)	21 pieces (377g)
0153	0.40	0.20	Circular. Rounded profile. Paired with undated pit 013:*0155*. Grey silty sand fill (013:*0154*), includes charcoal.	2 sherds of Grooved Ware (2g)	-	1 piece (2g)
0157	1.26 x 0.80	0.24	Sub-rectangular with well-rounded corners. Moderately sloping sides, flat bottomed. Exhibited two fills, collectively 013:*0158*, a central brown silty sand with an outer stonier component. Charcoal flecks throughout.	87 sherds ind. Neo/LBA (346g)	33 pieces, includes 2 scrapers (1 illustrated, Fig. 3.11.29) and a utilised blade	4 pieces (110g)

FLN 053						
0028	0.74	0.24	Sub-circular. Rounded profile. Fill comprising an upper central layer of brown silty sand with an outer dark grey/black component (collectively 053:*0029*).	9 sherds of Grooved Ware (26g)	44 pieces, includes two scrapers (1 illustrated, Fig. 3.10.15), a retouched flake and a utilised hard hammer struck flake	85 pieces (1886g)
0032	0.80 x 0.60	0.16	Sub-oval. Moderately sloping sides with a concave base. Fill comprising dark grey/black sand and brown silty sand (collectively 053:*0033*).	9 sherds of Grooved Ware (34g)		28 pieces (851g)
0156	0.80	0.30	Circular. Steep sided, rounded base. Fill comprising dark grey/brown silty, stony sand, darker towards base 053:*0157*.		2 pieces, includes a fabricator (Fig. 3.11.30)	4 pieces (283g)
0158	1.08	0.12	Circular. Moderately steep sided, flat base. Dark grey silty, stony sand fill 053:*0159*		9 pieces, includes a knife (Fig. 3.11.31) and 2 scrapers (1 illustrated, Fig. 3.11.32)	3 pieces (77g)
0195	0.50	0.16	Sub-circular. Moderately sloping sides with a flat base. Fill (053:*0196*) comprising yellow clay with darker, greyish area at top with charcoal.	19 sherds of Grooved Ware (59g)	8 pieces, includes 3 scrapers (Fig. 3.10.17-19)	1 piece (34g)
0197	0.50	0.26	Sub-circular. Moderately sloping sides, angled base. Fill (053:*0198*) comprising grey/brown silty sand, darker towards top, with some charcoal.	4 sherds of Grooved Ware (22g)	12 pieces, includes a serrated blade (Fig. 3.10.20), 2 scrapers (Fig. 3.11.21 and 22)	7 pieces (104g)
0238	1.30 x 0.90	0.25	Oval. Shallow dish-like profile. Stratified fill comprising dark grey/brown silty sand with charcoal (053:*0239*) over brown silty sand (053:*0240*). Artefactual evidence all from the upper fill.	30 sherds Grooved Ware (869g). Includes Fig. 3.9.3, 22	44 pieces, includes 2 scrapers (Fig. 3.11.23 and 24), a tested piece and a core fragment	19 pieces (2720g)
0801	1.10	0.44	Circular. Rounded profile. Fill (053:*0802*) comprising homogenous dark brown silty with stones.		4 pieces, includes 1 scraper	3 pieces (25g)

Table 3.3 FLN 013 and 053: detail of prehistoric pits

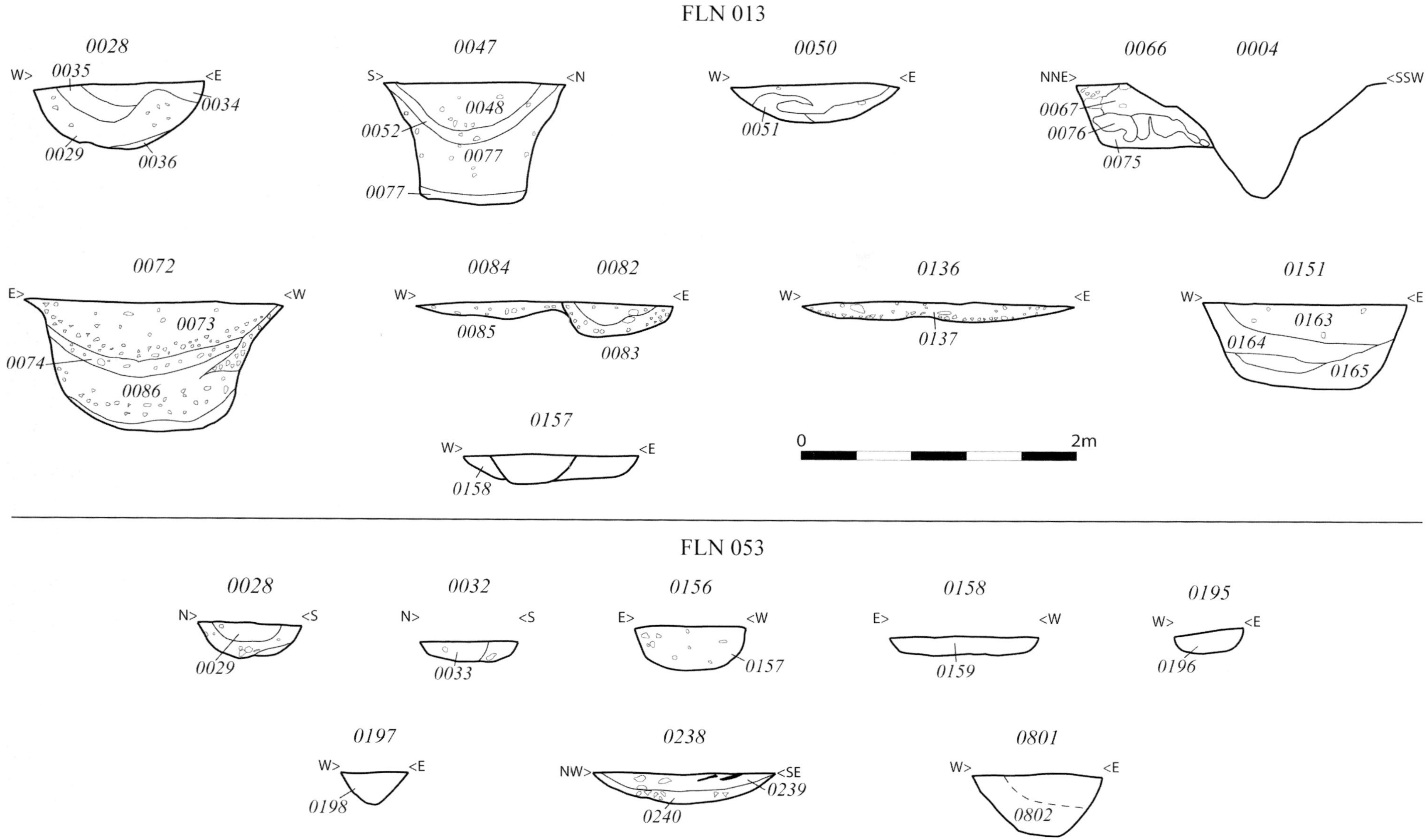

Figure 3.8 FLN 013 and FLN 053: prehistoric pits section drawings

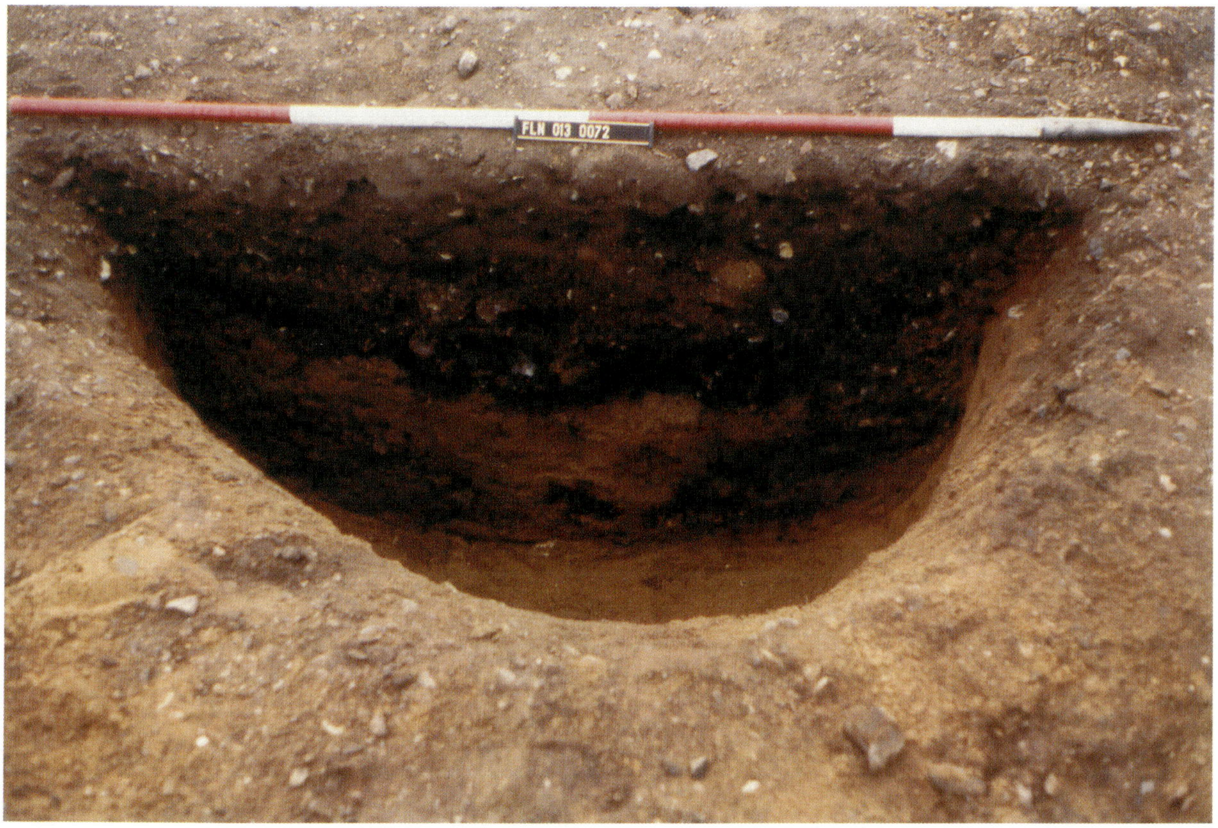

Plate 3.3 FLN 013: pit *0072*

The pits varied in both size and character. Some were small and originally described as post-holes in the site records. However, with no evidence to confirm their use as such, it was considered reasonable to change their description as the term post-hole actually invests a function to the feature that may not be entirely accurate.

The smallest of these features (013:*0153*), with a diameter of 0.4m, a depth of only 0.2m and a fill (013:*0154*) comprising grey silty sand with charcoal, was located 20m west of the two monuments and was paired with undated pit 013:*0155*.

The two largest pits (013:*0072* and *0136*) were both located within the confines of post-hole circle 013:*0147*, the former immediately to the south-east of the central post-setting (013:*0148*) and the latter immediately to the east of the same (Fig. 3.4). Both were dated as Late Neolithic (Period II.d.): 013:*0072* (Pl. 3.3) based on both ceramic and worked flint finds and 013:*0136* on worked flint only. While covering the largest area, an oval measuring 3.0m by 2.6m, 013:*0136* was also shallow, with a maximum depth of 0.16m, and could be interpreted as a naturally formed depression or hollow rather than a deliberately incised feature. In contrast, pit 013:*0072*, with its regular circular shape, 1.8m in diameter, steep sides continuing down to a depth of 1m and its stratified fill, was clearly different in character (Fig. 3.8; Pl. 3.3). In addition, its location central to the rear of the enclosure on the long axis of the internal post-setting is compelling evidence for its direct association with the surrounding monument.

Of particular note from an artefactual point of view were pits 013:*0028*, with seventy-seven sherds of Grooved Ware and 193 pieces of worked flint, including a number of tools and utilised flakes and blades, and pit 013:*0157* with eighty-seven sherds of indeterminate Late Neolithic or Early Bronze Age pottery and thirty-three pieces of worked flint, including two scrapers and a utilised blade. Pit 013:*0157* was located to the north of, and somewhat divorced from, the group of features clustered to the north-west of two monuments and was found to contain most of the indeterminate Late Neolithic or Early Bronze Age pottery recovered from the sites. Other pits which included a moderate quantity of finds in their fills were 013:*0066* (thirty-one Grooved Ware sherds and thirteen worked flints), 013:*0072* (thirty-three sherds of Grooved Ware and thirty-six worked flints), 013:*0151* (twenty-nine sherds of Grooved Ware and twenty-five worked flints) and 053:*0238* (thirty sherds of Grooved Ware and forty-four worked flints). It should also be noted that pits with a reasonable quantity of pottery or worked flint were also those which contained the majority of the heat-altered flints and could be taken as evidence that the three materials were introduced together within a mixed deposit derived from a pre-pit context, possibly a midden (Garrow 2006, 114).

While there was considerable variability in both the dimensions of the pits and the character of their fills, there were also certain similarities which suggest that some shared a commonality in the processes involved in their generation. In a number of the pits, for example 013:*0028*, the artefactual evidence, often including large unabraded pottery sherds and flint tools, was concentrated within a discrete fill, in this case 013:*0036*, that was far darker in colour than its neighbouring fill components. At the time of excavation these fills were often described as 'charcoal-rich' due to their almost black colour, but when sampled, were found to include only moderate quantities of that material. When fills of this type were seen *in situ* by soil scientist Richard Macphail, he interpreted them as representing degraded topsoil-like material that would have included a relatively high percentage of organic matter. Clearly, this component of fill and its incorporated finds had been introduced to the feature in a single event and must be considered, therefore, to represent a deliberate, controlled action. In other instances, the finds, usually in smaller quantities and in the case of the ceramics with more abraded surfaces, were dispersed throughout a relatively homogenous fill (*e.g.* 013:*0085* in pit 013:*0084*) and their inclusion more likely to be the result of a generalised introduction of artefact-rich fill material rather than deliberate acts of selection. With adjoining pottery sherds noted in at least two separate pits (053:*0195* and *0197*) it seems likely that the material was derived from a similar source, possibly a surface midden, before being transferred to the features. These 'pre-pit' contexts have been recognised on other East Anglian sites (Garrow 2006, 114).

Cremation

A small feature (053:*0056*) was recorded central to the FLN 053 area (Fig. 3.1). It included a small amount of calcined human bone, possibly juvenile, in the central, dark grey/black silty sand, component of its fill (053:*0057*). The feature was circular, 0.4m in diameter, had a depth of 0.16m with angled sides and a flat bottom. Even allowing for truncation of the upper levels, the amount of calcined bone was small and its identification as a full cremation burial is questionable. However, the presence of the calcined human bone does suggest that it was associated in some way with the cremation process. A number of similar features have been recorded in subsequent phases of the quarry where their stratigraphic and spatial association with other features suggests a prehistoric date and it is on that basis that a prehistoric date is proposed for the FLN 053 example.

Site FLN 062

For the purposes of this publication a brief description of ring-ditch FLN 010, excavated in the FLN 062 area, will be presented due to its perceived influence as the focus for eleven of the Early Anglo-Saxon graves.

Ring-ditch (062:*0808*)

While excavated under the overall context number 062:*0808*, the ring-ditch had already been allocated its own HER number (FLN 010; Fig. 3.1) after it was first recognised from aerial photographs during the 1970s. It was found to have a diameter of approximately 35m with a maximum ditch width of 5.6m to the south and east, reducing to 1m to north-west where it had been partially truncated by the existing farm track. The ditch profile varied considerably between the excavated sections, probably due to the variable character of the natural subsoil into which it had been cut, with less consolidated material slumping more and softening the profile in those areas. With a maximum depth of 1.4m, the profile varied from round-bottomed, open V-shaped with a slight shoulder and heavily shouldered. Where intact profiles survived without truncation, three fill components were noted: a basal, primary fill comprising clean sand and gravel derived entirely from the sides of the ditch soon after its initial excavation, a central fill of brown silty sand that would have accumulated over a longer period of time and an upper fill comprising very dark brown silty sand. Artefactual evidence recovered from the upper fill included a significant quantity dating to the Late Iron Age/Early Roman (Flixton chronology Period II.a.) indicating that the ditch was at least partially open at that time and may have been used for the disposal of domestic waste from the adjacent occupation area.

Manual cleaning within the area confined by the ring-ditch failed to identify any associated features.

III. The artefacts

Prehistoric pottery

by Sarah Percival

Introduction

This report covers the prehistoric pottery from all four of the Flixton sites discussed in this volume (FLN 008, FLN 013, FLN 053 and FLN 062). The ceramics are predominantly of later Neolithic to earlier Bronze Age date and include a significant assemblage of Grooved Ware, the largest so far excavated from the county of Suffolk. The assemblage is considered by individual site with the exception of FLN 013 and FLN 053 which are combined. There is an overall discussion at the end.

Methodology

The assemblage was analysed using the pottery recording system described in the Norfolk Archaeological Unit Pottery Recording Manual and in accordance with the Guidelines for analysis and publication laid down by the Prehistoric Ceramic Research Group (PCRG 2010). All the pottery was quantified and a full catalogue is available in the archive. The sherds were examined using a binocular microscope (x10 magnification) and divided into fabric groups defined on the basis of inclusion types. Fabric codes were prefixed by a letter code representing the main inclusion type present (F representing flint, G grog and Q quartz). Vessel form was recorded (R representing rim sherds, B base sherds, D decorated sherds and U undecorated body sherds) and the sherds were counted and weighed to the nearest whole gram. Decoration and abrasion were also noted. Details of the recognised fabrics and decoration form codes are listed below.

Grooved Ware and Late Neolithic/Early Bronze Age fabrics

G1: moderate, rounded **grog**; moderate, sub-angular **quartz sand**. Interior: smoothed, mid brown; core: dark brown inner, orange to buff outer; exterior: orange buff. Soft.

G2: moderate, rounded **grog**; moderate, sub-angular **quartz sand**, occasional, angular **calcined flint**. Interior: smoothed, mid brown; core: dark brown inner, orange to buff outer; exterior: orange buff. Vesicular surface and matrix. Soft.

G3: moderate, rounded **grog**; occasional, angular **calcined flint**. Interior: smoothed, mid orange brown; core: dark brown inner, orange to buff outer; exterior: orange buff. Vesicular surface and matrix Soft.

G4: moderate, rounded **grog**; moderate, sub-angular **quartz sand**. Interior: smoothed, mid brown; core: dark brown inner, orange to buff outer; exterior: orange buff. Soft.

Q1: abundant, rounded **quartz sand**; occasional, angular **calcined flint**. Dark to buff orange brown, core: dark grey to black, exterior: buff orange to brown. Slightly vesicular surface. Hard.

Q2: abundant, rounded **quartz sand**. Dark brown throughout. Hard.

Q3: abundant, rounded **quartz sand**; occasional, angular **calcined flint**. Dark to buff orange brown, core: dark grey to black, exterior: buff orange to brown. Slightly vesicular surface. Hard.

F2: moderate rounded **quartz sand**; occasional, angular **calcined flint**; moderate, sub-rounded quartz sand. Interior:

smoothed, dark brown, core: dark grey to black, exterior: buff orange to grey brown. Hard.

Iron Age and indeterminate fabrics

F1: abundant angular **calcined flint**; moderate, sub-rounded **quartz sand**. Interior: smoothed, dark to buff orange brown, core: dark grey to black, exterior: buff orange to brown. Laminated fracture. Hard.

Q4: abundant, rounded **quartz sand**.

Site FLN 008

A small and highly fragmentary assemblage was recovered, the majority from a scatter identified during surface cleaning in association with fragments of cremated bone. The bulk of the forty-eight sherds, which weigh 103g, are undatable scraps in grog-tempered fabrics (Table 3.4). A small quantity of undiagnostic flint tempered pottery was also found. Two larger sherds (individually numbered 008:*0024* and *0040*) in grog tempered fabric with distinctive wiped surfaces, are probably Earlier Bronze Age, perhaps derived from a small, collared urn. A further two small sherds in flint-tempered fabric may be of earlier Neolithic or Iron Age date. The remainder of the assemblage is entirely composed of undecorated body sherds which cannot be assigned to a pottery form.

Fabric code	*No.*	*% No.*	*Wt (g)*	*% of total wt*
F1	2	4.2	6	5.8
G	1	2.1	1	1.0
G1	27	56.3	54	52.4
G2	3	6.3	13	12.6
Q2	2	4.2	3	2.9
U	13	27.1	26	25.2
Total	**48**	**100.0**	**103**	**100.0**

Table 3.4 FLN 008: quantity and weight of prehistoric pottery by fabric

Sites FLN 013 and FLN 053

A total of 418 sherds weighing 3,027kg were collected, representing a minimum of eleven vessels. A significant proportion of the pottery is Grooved Ware of the Durrington Walls sub-style. Smaller quantities of indeterminate later Neolithic to Early Bronze Age (LNEBA) sherds were also found along with Iron Age and indeterminate prehistoric pottery (Table 3.5).

The sherds are in varied condition with some being moderately large and well preserved whilst most are small and many abraded. The majority of the Grooved Ware was recovered from pits, but sherds were also found in the fill of the ring-ditch (013:*0004*) and within the fills of post-holes including post-hole circle (013:*0147*). The pits and the post-hole circle (013:*0147*) produced moderately large and well-preserved sherds, in contrast to those from the ring-ditch which were smaller and more abraded. No complete profiles were found.

Grooved Ware

The Grooved Ware assemblage comprises 278 sherds weighing 2426g and includes rims from a minimum of ten vessels. Other diagnostic sherds represent a further thirteen vessels, giving a total of 23, each highly fragmentary and most represented by only a small number of sherds.

Eight LNEBA fabrics were identified (Table 3.5). The majority of the fabrics are found in both the Grooved Ware and indeterminate LNEBA assemblages. Two fabrics, G2 and G3, are unique to the Grooved Ware assemblage and two, G4 and Q3, are only found within the indeterminate LNEBA sherds.

Within the Grooved Ware assemblage fabrics which contain grog are most abundant, making up 69% of the total assemblage by weight. Within this group individual fabric types are characterised by grog in combination with quartz-sand and calcined flint (Table 3.5). The inclusions resemble those identified in Grooved Ware at Durrington Walls (Wainwright and Longworth 1971, 55) and are similar to fabrics found at Spong Hill, Norfolk (Healy 1988, fig. 78) and Great Bealings and Martlesham, Suffolk (Martin 1993, 44, 51). The Grooved Ware from Flixton does not contain shell, which is a characteristic component of the Durrington Walls assemblage (Wainwright and Longworth 1971, 55) and is found at some sites within the region including Redgate Hill, Hunstanton, Norfolk (Cleal 1993, table 29). Around one quarter of sherds contain vacuoles indicating that a component of the fabric has been lost (Fabric G3).

The Grooved Ware is mostly of the Durrington Walls sub-style though some elements of the Clacton sub-style are also present (Wainwright and Longworth 1971, 55–9). The pots have been constructed using smoothed coils of clay to build up the profile, evidenced by several examples of distinctive fractures along the line of a coil join (Fig. 3.9.1, 2 and 3). Most body sherds show some convex curvature and this, along with the flat concave bases, suggests that many vessels from Flixton have the barrel-shaped form characteristic of the Durrington Walls sub-style (Fig. 3.9.3, 4: Wainwright and Longworth 1971, 56). A similar range of rims to those identified at Durrington Walls is present, including pointed upright (Fig. 3.9.5), rounded upright (Fig. 3.9.6), everted rim with

Period	*Fabric*	*No.*	*% No.*	*Wt (g)*	*% Wt*
Early Bronze Age	F2	5	1.2	12	0.4
	G1	15	3.6	50	1.7
	G4	7	1.7	16	0.5
	Q1	3	0.7	2	0.1
	Q2	1	0.3	4	0.1
	Q3	15	3.6	98	3.2
Totals		*46*	*11.0*	*182*	*6.0*
Grooved Ware	F2	3	0.7	16	0.5
	G1	135	32.3	751	24.8
	G2	35	8.4	171	5.7
	G3	26	6.2	763	25.2
	Q1	54	12.8	584	19.3
	Q2	22	5.3	134	4.4
	U	3	0.7	7	0.2
Totals		*278*	*66.5*	*2426*	*80.1*
Iron Age	F3	6	1.4	12	0.4
	Q4	12	2.9	60	2.0
Totals		18	4.3	72	2.4
Indet. prehistoric	F1	74	17.7	346	11.4
	G2	2	0.5	1	0.1
Totals		*76*	*18.2*	*347*	*11.5*
Totals		**418**		**3027**	

Table 3.5 FLN 013 and 053: quantity and weight of prehistoric pottery by period and fabric

internal bevels (Fig. 3.9.7 and 8; Wainwright and Longworth 1971, 55–9) and in-turned (Fig. 3.9.9, 10; Durrington Walls type 8; Wainwright and Longworth 1971, fig. 20, P384, fig. 55). Both simple and concave base forms were found (Durrington Walls forms A and B; Fig. 3.9.11–13). Most bases are undecorated with the exception of one highly decorated example from pit 013:*0151* (Fig. 3.9.14) and one with possible remains of an incised herringbone motif.

Decorated sherds constitute 40% of the Grooved Ware assemblage, the remainder being plain, indicating that some vessels or parts of vessels were undecorated. The decorative motifs fall within the range described by Wainwright and Longworth (1971). Decorative techniques employed vary slightly across the site with finger-tip and fingernail rustication and twisted cord impressions being common (Fig. 3.9.9), along with incised grooved chevrons (Fig. 3.9.2, 3, and 15) and applied or pinched-out cordons (Fig. 3.9.4, 9, 16–18) impressed cord maggots (Fig. 3.9.19), or stab-and-drag impressions (Fig. 3.9.20 and 21). Two body sherds (Fig. 3.9.1 and 2) have internal incised decoration combined with external surface treatment and one rim (Fig. 3.9.8) has incised decoration to the internal bevel. Two other rims (Fig. 3.9.6 and 7) are decorated externally, the former with cord impressed bands and the latter with fingernail impressed bands.

Less common are vessels with applied or pinched-out cordons. The cordons are either plain or decorated with transverse strokes (Fig. 3.9.3 and 22). The cordons are present all over the body of the vessels, often defining horizontal and vertical panels with the area between the panels being plain or filled with impressed or incised decoration (Fig 3.9.3, 17 and 22). The presence of vertical cordons dividing the exterior of the vessel into panels and the use of cord impressions are defining characteristics of the Durrington Walls sub-style (Wainwright and Longworth 1971). A small number of sherds (for example those from pit 013:*0066* which is contained within timber circle 013:*0147*) have stabbed decoration characteristic of the Clacton style (Fig. 3.9.12, 20).

Most of the Grooved Ware sherds were recovered from Period I.d. pits, which produced 90.6% (2288g) of the total Grooved Ware assemblage. These sherds are quite large and well preserved with a mean sherd weight of 9.6g. Pits containing Grooved Ware are located in clusters, pairs or as individual isolated features (Percival 2004; Garrow 2006, 114). One possible loose cluster containing two pits producing Grooved Ware (013:*0066* and 013:*0072*), as well as other empty pits, lay within the area enclosed by the post-hole circle. Similar feature formations were seen at Over, Cambridgeshire (Garrow 2006, fig. 6.16), a broadly contemporary site which also had a rectangular post-hole structure similar to 013:*0148*.

To the north of the post-hole circle, one pit (013:*0028*), produced substantial quantities of highly decorated Grooved Ware and formed one of a possible pair with 'empty' pit 013:*0050*. Isolated pits included (013:*0151*) which lay some 10m to the north of post-hole circle (013:*0028*) plus a further five pits within FLN 053 which showed no grouping or clustering.

The taphonomy of the pits falls within three broad depositional 'types' ('general', 'selective' or 'arranged') as identified by Garrow (2006, 113). Pits displaying 'general deposition' are characterised by a mix of fragmentary pots and flint within a dark soil matrix. This type of fill appears to be composed of material 'scooped up from (an) artefact and charcoal rich 'pre-pit context'' and dumped within the newly excavated pit (Garrow 2006, 114). Pit 013:*0028* is a particularly striking example of this, having the majority of the pottery and flint (Bates below) concentrated within the lower fill of the pit (013:*0036*) with smaller quantities present in the upper fills (013:*0035*) and (013:*0034*). Other examples include isolated pits (053:*0028*) and (053:*0032*), which each produced small assemblages. In both pits the pottery was combined within a dark sandy fill, perhaps representing redeposited material from a 'pre-pit context'. In other examples sherds from the same vessel appear in more than one feature. Pits 053:*0195* contained nineteen small sherds (59g) from a maximum of six vessels including a distinctive vessel rim, all found within a dark sandy fill (053:*0196*). Pit 053:*0197* contained two small rim sherds from the same distinctive vessel, along with a further three undecorated body sherds. The presence of sherds from the same vessel within the two features suggests that the material within their fills was derived from the same source.

Other pits have deposits which include large distinctive sherds which may have been highly recognisable to the person burying them and may represent Garrow's 'selective' deposition. One example, pit 013:*0151*, had multiple fills with the majority of the Grooved Ware concentrated in the upper components, including a large decorated base which features incised vertical lines filled with incised chevrons (Fig. 3.9.5) and a distinctive end scraper (Bates below). This decorative style is not found elsewhere on the site and suggests that the highly recognisable base may have been selected for placement within a discrete fill or possibly a re-cut in the top of the feature (013:*0163*). A second pit, 053:*0238*, contained two fills with a black/grey upper fill and a yellow sandy weathered base. Thirty sherds (869g) from at least three vessels were recovered from the upper fill (053:*0239*) including large sherds from the base of an undecorated vessel, a base decorated with fine incised lines and a large rim sherd (Fig. 3.9.22).

Pits 013:*0066* and 013:*0072*, which lay within the post-hole circle, are difficult to characterise, particularly pit 013:*0066* which is cut through by ring-ditch 013:*0004* and is heavily disturbed. Pit 013:*0072* is strikingly similar in profile and number and type of fills to pit 013:*0151* and may also have had an earlier incarnation. Undecorated flint-tempered sherds and grog-tempered impressed sherds (Fig. 3.9.19 and 20), which may be of earlier Neolithic date, were found in the lower fills and the majority of the Grooved Ware in an artefact-rich upper fill within a possible re-cut.

Other features to produce Grooved Ware pottery include 'timber circle' (013:*0147*). Although only two sherds of identifiable Grooved Ware came from the feature, this is significant as it is the only monument of its kind to have produced Grooved Ware in Norfolk and Suffolk. The type site for the Durrington Walls style Grooved Ware is itself a timber circle and Gibson has recently stressed the close relationship between this class of monument and Grooved Ware pottery (Gibson 1999). Within the post-hole circle the Grooved Ware sherd with the most complex decoration was found in post-hole 013:*0184* which lay immediately to the east of the

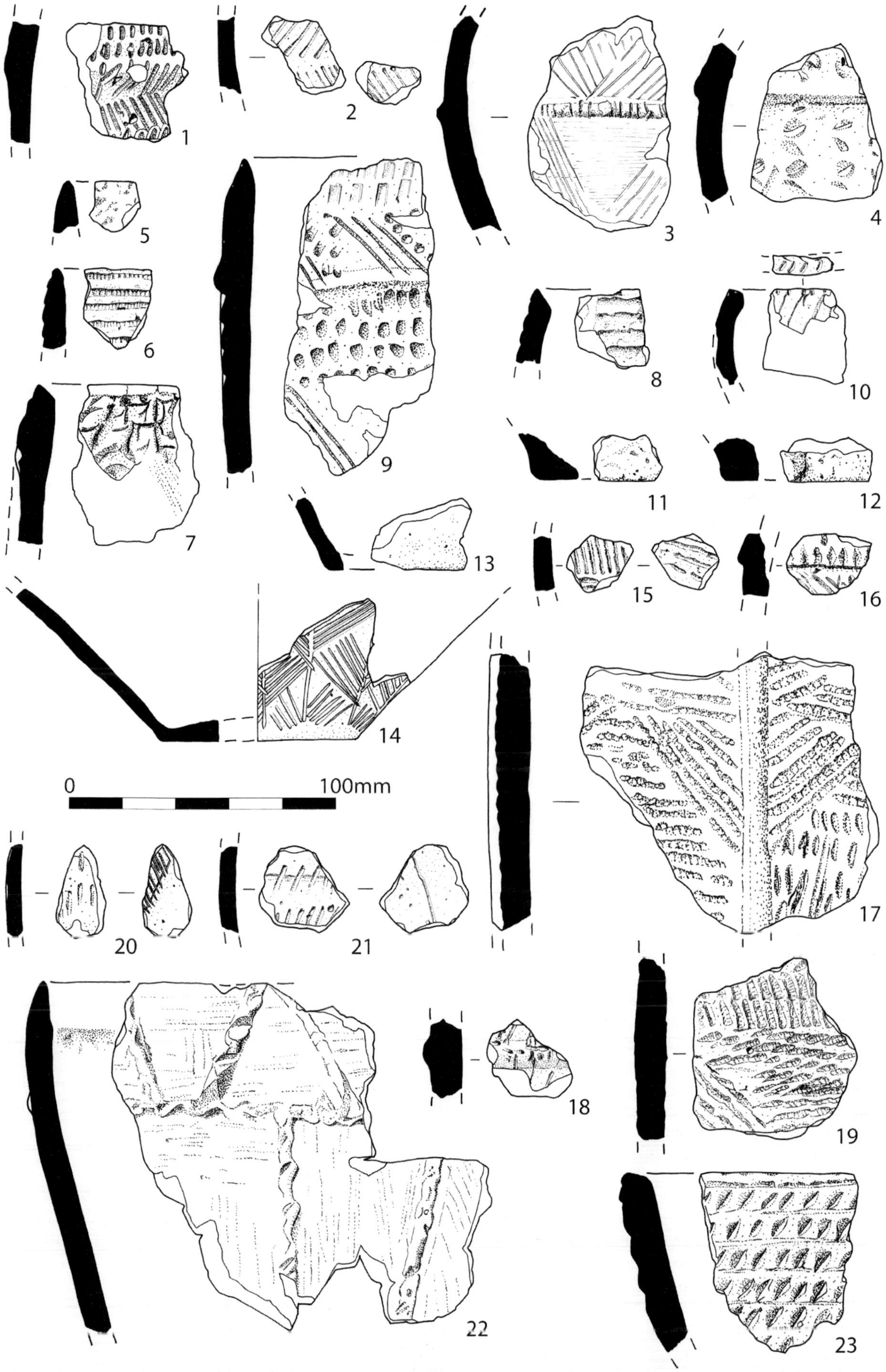

Figure 3.9 FLN 013 and FLN 053: prehistoric pottery (scale 1:2)

north-west facing entrance (Fig. 3.9.11). A decorated rim sherd (Fig. 3.9.4) came from post-hole 013:*0188*, which lay to the west of the entrance and would have been on the left of an observer standing within the circle. The emphasis of artefacts on the north-western sector of the monument is paralleled at Balfarg, Scotland (Richards 1993) and within the ditches of Mount Pleasant IV (Wainwright 1979). The small quantity of pottery found within the post-hole circle is paralleled at Maxey, Cambridgeshire, where the excavator interpreted the lack of finds as an indication that the monument had been kept clean (Pryor 1985). It is also possible that large quantities of pottery were not used at the circle or those monuments were not the proper location for the disposal of ceramic material (*cf.* Richards 1993, 192).

Late Neolithic/Early Bronze Age

A total of 31 further Late Neolithic/Early Bronze Age sherds weighing 84g were identified by distinctive surface treatment. The sherds were in six fabrics (Table 3.5). Five fabrics (F2, G1, Q1 Q2 and F2) are similar to Grooved Ware types) whilst two (G4 and Q3) were associated exclusively with sherds of Late Neolithic/Early Bronze Age type. Most of the sherds are undecorated, two are bases and only one, a large rim and body sherd may be tentatively identified as Beaker (Fig. 3.9.23).

The Beaker, comprising a large rim fragment and body sherds with single fingertip impressions, collectively numbered 013:*0171*, was recovered from post-hole 013:*0182* within post-hole circle 013:*0147* which also contained Grooved Ware. Two further post-holes containing plain undecorated sherds also lay within the north-western arc of the circle (013:*0120* and *0412*) whilst a third, which contained a fragment of pot weighing less than a single gram, was situated within the south-western quarter of the monument (013:*0406*). At Woodhenge, Grooved Ware and Beaker deposits within post-holes in separate rings of the multi-ring structure have been interpreted as representing different phases (Gibson 1999, 80). Gibson notes that the Beaker from the Woodhenge post-holes occurs high up in the post-hole fills. A similar pattern is present at Flixton, where the Grooved Ware sherds were recovered from within the fills of the post-holes, whilst the broken Beaker vessel was recorded lying flat near the top of fill 013:*0183* in post-hole 013:*0182*. Period I.d. pits 013:*0047,* 013:*0050* and 013:*0066* each contained small numbers of sherds of later Neolithic to earlier Bronze Age pottery, probably intrusive material accidentally incorporated. Ring-ditch 013:*0004* assigned to Period I.e., contained 38g of later Neolithic to earlier Bronze Age pottery, again redeposited within the backfill of the feature.

Other prehistoric pottery

Eighteen sherds of possible Iron Age pottery were found (in hearth 053:*0070* and pit 053:*0258*). The indeterminate prehistoric pottery which was too small and abraded to identify to type was found in ring-ditch 013:*0004* and pit 013: *0157*. This pottery is summarised in Table 3.5.

Catalogue of illustrated prehistoric pottery sherds (FLN 013 and FLN 053)

Fig. 3.9

1. Impressed and incised body sherd fabric Q1, context 013:*0185*, post-hole 013:*0184*.

2. Incised body sherds, fabric G2, context 013:*0165*, pit 013:*0151*.

3. Grooved Ware body sherd with narrow incised decoration and decorated cordon, fabric G1, context 053:*0239* pit 053:*0238*.

4. Finger-tip impressed body sherd with cordon, fabric Q1, context 013:*0036*, pit 013:*0028*.

5. Undecorated rim sherd, Durrington Walls rim form 1, fabric Q1, context 013:*0036*, pit 013:*0028*.

6. Rim sherd, decorated with cord impressed bands, Durrington Walls rim form 7, fabric Q1, context 013:*0036*, pit 013:*0028*.

7. Rim sherd, decorated with fingernail impressed bands on the body below the rim, Durrington Walls rim form 8/21, fabric Q1, context 013:*0063*, pit 013:*0066*.

8. Rim sherd, Durrington Walls rim form 8/21, fabric Q1, context 013:*0189*, post-hole 013:*0188*.

9. Rim sherd, Durrington Walls rim form 8/21, impressed and incised decoration, fabric G1, context 013:*0075*, pit 013:*0066*.

10. Rim sherd, decorated with fingernail impressions on body and herringbone motif on top of rim. Fabric G3, context 013:*0164*, pit 013:*0151*.

11. Base sherd, form B, fabric G1, context 013:*0051*, pit 013:*0050*.

12. Base sherd, form B, fabric G1, context 013:*0053*, ring-ditch 013:*0004*, section 013:*0041*.

13. Base sherd, form A, fabric G3, context 013:*0073*, pit 013:*0072*.

14. Highly decorated base sherd, form A, fabric G3, context 013:*0163*, pit 013:*0151*.

15. ?Comb-impressed body sherd, fabric G1, context 013:*0036*, pit 013:*0028*.

16. Cord-impressed and incised body sherd with cordon, fabric Q1, context 013:*0036*, pit 013:*0028*.

17. Impressed and incised body sherd with cordon, fabric Q1, context 013:*0036*, pit 013:*0028*.

18. Impressed and incised body sherd with cordon, fabric G2, context 013:*0036*, pit 013:*0028*.

19. Cord-impressed body sherd, fabric Q1, context 013:*0036*, pit 013:*0028*.

20. Body sherd spatula-impressed on interior and incised on exterior, fabric G1, context 013:*0086*, pit 013:*0072*.

21. Body sherd incised on exterior and on interior, fabric G1, context 013:*0086*, pit 013:*0072*.

22. Grooved Ware rim with cordons forming triangles above cordon and rectangular panels below, fabric G3, context 053:*0239* pit 053:*0238*.

23. Rim sherd, decorated with fingernail impressions and raised bands. Fabric Q3, context 013:*0171*, post-hole 013:*0182*. Post-hole circle 013:*0147*.

Site FLN 062

Only the prehistoric pottery recovered as residual finds from the Early Anglo-Saxon grave fills has been included here (9 sherds weighing 66g). Some of the pottery could be attributed to two ceramic phases, with other sherds being undiagnostic.

Earlier Neolithic

Two small undiagnostic sherds body sherds (29g) in quartz sand-rich fabric (Q3) were recovered from the fill of Grave 46. The sherds were tentatively identified as being earlier Neolithic, however the dating remains uncertain.

Later Neolithic to earlier Bronze Age

Two small grog-tempered sherds (9g) were found in the fills of Grave 57. The sherds are small, and both are abraded with the internal surfaces missing. The sherds are in a similar fabric to Beaker and other later Neolithic to earlier Bronze Age sherds found elsewhere on the site but cannot be identified to an exact pottery type.

Other prehistoric pottery
Three adjoining sherds (062:*1871*) (total weight 123g) were recorded as possible grave goods in Grave 51 due to their juxtaposition with other finds and the body stain. The vessel is undecorated with quartz and grog temper and dates to the earlier Iron Age. A further five sherds (28g) from Grave 55 are prehistoric but are too small and undiagnostic to be closely datable.

Discussion and regional parallels
The small assemblage from FLN 008 is largely undatable, although the grog-tempered sherds are almost certainly of a broad Bronze Age date. It is unclear if they are contemporary with the bulk of the pottery from the other sites discussed here which are predominantly of later Neolithic to earlier Bronze Age date. However, the presence of calcined human bone within the pottery scatter in the south-east trench quadrant suggests that an urned cremation had been present, probably directly associated with the ring-ditch, which was subsequently damaged and dispersed. The flint-tempered sherds may be of earlier Neolithic or perhaps Iron Age date.

The Grooved Ware from FLN 013 and FLN 053 has many similarities in fabric, form and decoration with the assemblages from the other Grooved Ware sites within Flixton Quarry. The vessels are predominantly tub /barrel-shaped in grog and sand tempered fabrics, with pinched-out cordons dividing the bodies of the pots into broad panels filled with incised decoration (Fig. 3.9.17). While this is characteristic of the Durrington Walls sub-style, stabbed decoration more typical of the Clacton style (Fig. 3.9.9) is also present. Durrington Walls style Grooved Ware (Longworth 1971) is found on the majority of the sites excavated within the quarry including FLN 057, FLN 061, FLN 062 and FLN 059. However sherds of possible Clacton style were also found at FLN 057 and Clacton style pottery forms the majority of the Grooved Ware assemblage at FLN 009.

The location of Flixton Park, on low lying ground with easy access to water, is typical of Grooved Ware sites in East Anglia (Garrow 2006, 81) and more widely within southern England (Cleal 1999, 5). Like the majority of Grooved Ware sites in the region the pottery is predominantly deposited in pits. Garrow in his recent review of Neolithic and earlier Bronze Age pottery styles deposited in pits in East Anglia noted that Grooved Ware sites with large numbers of pits, indicating recurring, sustained or high density occupation, such as Flixton, produce Durrington Walls style Grooved Ware mixed with Clacton style vessels, whilst sites with low numbers of pits mostly contain Clacton style pots (Garrow 2006, 80).

It remains unclear whether the ceramic styles identified by modern archaeologists held any meaning for the Grooved Ware users, however the presence of sherds from highly recognisable decorated vessels within certain selected deposits may be linked with the individual users of the pots, with the deposits representing 'statements' commemorating individual people, locations or events (Garrow 2006, 80). At FLN 053, the distribution of certain highly decorated sherds within a small number of features may indicate deliberate selection and deposition perhaps of a ritual nature.

While the similarities between different elements within the FLN 013 and FLN 053 assemblage indicate that they are roughly contemporary, it is also possible that some stylistic differences, for example between Woodlands and Durrington Walls style Grooved Ware and the absence of cord impressions from the FLN 053 pottery, are chronological (Garwood 1999, 157).

A radiocarbon determination undertaken on a charcoal sample from the fill of one of the pits (013:*0066*, fill *0075*) located internally to the FLN 013 post-hole circle produced a calibrated date of 2620–2344 BC (AA-22185; 3980±45 BP) (Boulter 1998). Garwood in his 1999 review of radiocarbon evidence suggests that Grooved Ware was current in southern Britain in the period between 3000–2000 BC (Garwood 1999, 152). This suggests that the Flixton assemblage was in use towards the middle of Grooved Ware currency, making the site broadly contemporary with other Grooved Ware sites in East Anglia such as Redgate Hill, Hunstanton and Storeys Bar Road, Fengate and just a little earlier than the Grooved Ware phase at Grimes Graves (Garwood 1999, table 15.3). The radiocarbon date for the Flixton Grooved Ware overlaps with the beginning of the widespread use of Beaker which began around 2600 BC continuing until approximately1800 BC (Kinnes *et al.* 1991). However the presence of mostly late Beaker styles at Flixton might suggest that the two pottery types were in use contiguously rather than contemporaneously.

The small pottery group recovered from the FLN 062 Early Anglo-Saxon graves is made up of residual sherds which will be included with the overall prehistoric assemblage from the site in a subsequent volume.

Worked flint
by Sarah Bates

Introduction
A total of 3072 pieces of struck or shattered flint was recovered from sites FLN 008 (675 pieces), FLN 013 (2066 pieces) and FLN 053 (331 pieces). This figure includes residual flint present in later features, the majority of which is likely to be prehistoric. About three quarters of the flints are complete (67% by number of pieces from FLN 008 and 75% from FLN 013 and 053), about half has cortex (51% and 56% respectively) and 20% and 18% of the flint is patinated. Possibly of note (see discussion) are differences in amounts of complete and cortical flint at FLN 053 compared to the other sites. A further twenty-eight pieces of flint, from the fills of the Early Anglo-Saxon graves excavated at site FLN 062 and presumed to be residual prehistoric material, have also been included in the report. The flint from each main site is considered separately, with a synthetic discussion at the end.

Site FLN 008
A total of 675 struck flints were recovered from FLN 008. The assemblage is summarised in Table 3.6.

Period I.e. Early Bronze Age: Flints from contexts associated with ring-ditch 008:*0100*
A total of 595 struck flints was recovered from fills of the ring-ditch. Five pieces are classified as cores or fragments from cores. There are two irregular flake cores, a flake used as a core and two core fragments.

There are 408 flakes, thirty-five blade-like flakes and ten blades. Most of these pieces are quite small and quite sharp – although a few are slightly edge-damaged. Squat flakes, many of them clearly struck by hard hammer, predominate and several flakes have cortical platforms where they have been struck haphazardly from their parent core. One flake, however, has neat scars on its dorsal surface and its platform is facetted; it is probably from a prepared, or more carefully used, core. In one context, 008:*0107*, several flakes have the same distinctive cortex and almost certainly came from the same core. Quite a few pieces, including some of the blade-like material is quite 'jagged' in nature. Twenty-three jagged shatter pieces and 105 spalls are also present.

A squat subcircular flake from context 008:*0110* has retouch around its distal edge and sides and a neat thin flake is retouched around its broader distal end (Fig. 3.10.1). Two piercers have slightly retouched distal points and another fragment has possible utilisation of a point. There are four miscellaneous retouched flakes.

A roughly triangular, quite thick, fragment of thermal origin has one edge retouched as a scraper and one corner broken, probably accidentally, to a broad notch.

Eleven flakes, a blade and a retouched flake came from 'cutting' 008:*0109* near the centre of the mound. The flakes are all quite small and are mostly squat in shape and quite sharp. The blade, which is slightly irregular, is patinated white and is from quite a large core.

Period III Early Anglo-Saxon

Thirteen flakes, two shatter pieces and a spall came from the fill of Grave A (008:*0113*). The flakes are generally small and squat and several have cortex on their platforms.

Unstratified

Thirty-four struck flints were recovered during the initial stripping of the site. As well as flakes, a few blade-like pieces, shatter pieces and spalls, there are six scrapers, three piercers, three miscellaneous retouched pieces and two utilised flakes. A small disc scraper (008:*0115*) has been formed on a subcircular primary piece with a bulbar ventral face (possibly due to thermal fracture). It has neat abrupt retouch of all but its proximal edge (Fig. 3.10.2). The others are all classified as end scrapers, one of which is illustrated (008:*0116*, Fig. 3.10.3). Three of them are neat rectangular/ovate flakes, one of them quite thin. All have their distal edges retouched. The other two are squatter in shape.

Sixteen other flints came from FLN 008, essentially recovered from the subsoil layer internal to the ring-ditch, possibly representing a pre-barrow soil or the vestiges of the barrow itself. They include a flake core with abraded and patinated cortex, a keeled core with an abraded and slightly patinated former surface, a tested piece and a core fragment. There are three flakes, two of them retouched. The flakes are generally thin and neat. There are also eight scrapers including two end scrapers, an end/side scraper and a variety of other types. A blade-like flake, classified as a knife, has its proximal end missing but its convex right edge has neat quite fine semi-abrupt retouch and slight 'wear' of its extreme edge.

Type	*No.*
Flake core	3
Keeled core	1
Core fragment	3
Core/tool	1
Tested piece	1
Shatter	27
Flake	445
Blade-like flake	38
Blade	11
Spall	109
Scraper	17
Piercer	6
Knife	1
Retouched blade	1
Retouched flake	9
Utilised flake	2

Table 3.6 FLN 008: summary of flint

Catalogue of illustrated worked flint

Fig. 3.10

1. End scraper, context 008:*0110*, ring-ditch 008:*0100*
2. Disc scraper 008:*0115*, unstratified context
3. End scraper 008:*0116*, unstratified context

Site FLN 013 and FLN 053

A total of 2397 pieces of flint were recovered from FLN 013 and FLN 053. The assemblage is summarised in Table 3.7. The flint is mostly mid to dark grey in colour; some of it is dull grey and some has a slightly mottled appearance. A small number of pieces have cherty inclusions. Cortex, where present, is mainly cream coloured and of thin to medium thickness.

Flint associated with Grooved Ware (Period I.d.)

Forty-eight flints came from post-holes which were part of circle 013:*0147*. The majority of these were small flakes, chips and spalls. A fragment from the platform edge of a possible blade core came from post-hole 013:*0408* and a small fragment, possibly from a core or possibly deliberately retouched as an irregular spurred scraper-type tool, came from post-hole 013:*0108* (Fig. 3.10.4). Only one other retouched piece, a thin slightly curving flake, was found, in post-hole 013:*0186*. The greatest concentration of flints occurred in a few post-holes in the north-western part of the circle and corresponded with the distribution of the sherds of Grooved Ware within the post-holes of the circle.

The rest of the flint found associated with Grooved Ware was from pits.

One hundred and eighty-eight flints came from fills of pit 013:*0028* which was located to the north-west of the ring-ditch. A well-used multi platform flake core with flakes struck from all around its surfaces and two fragments from probable blade cores, one of them possibly a deliberate trimming flake, came from the pit as well as three irregular struck fragments. One hundred and one flakes, eleven blade-like flakes and one blade were found in the pit. All of the material was sharp or quite sharp and the pieces were predominantly small. Fifty-seven percent of this material (by number of pieces) is uncorticated and it is notable that many of these tertiary pieces are thin. Ten jagged shatter pieces and thirty-nine spalls were also found in the pit.

Six scrapers came from pit 013:*0028*. Three of them are neatly retouched end scrapers (including 013:*0296*,

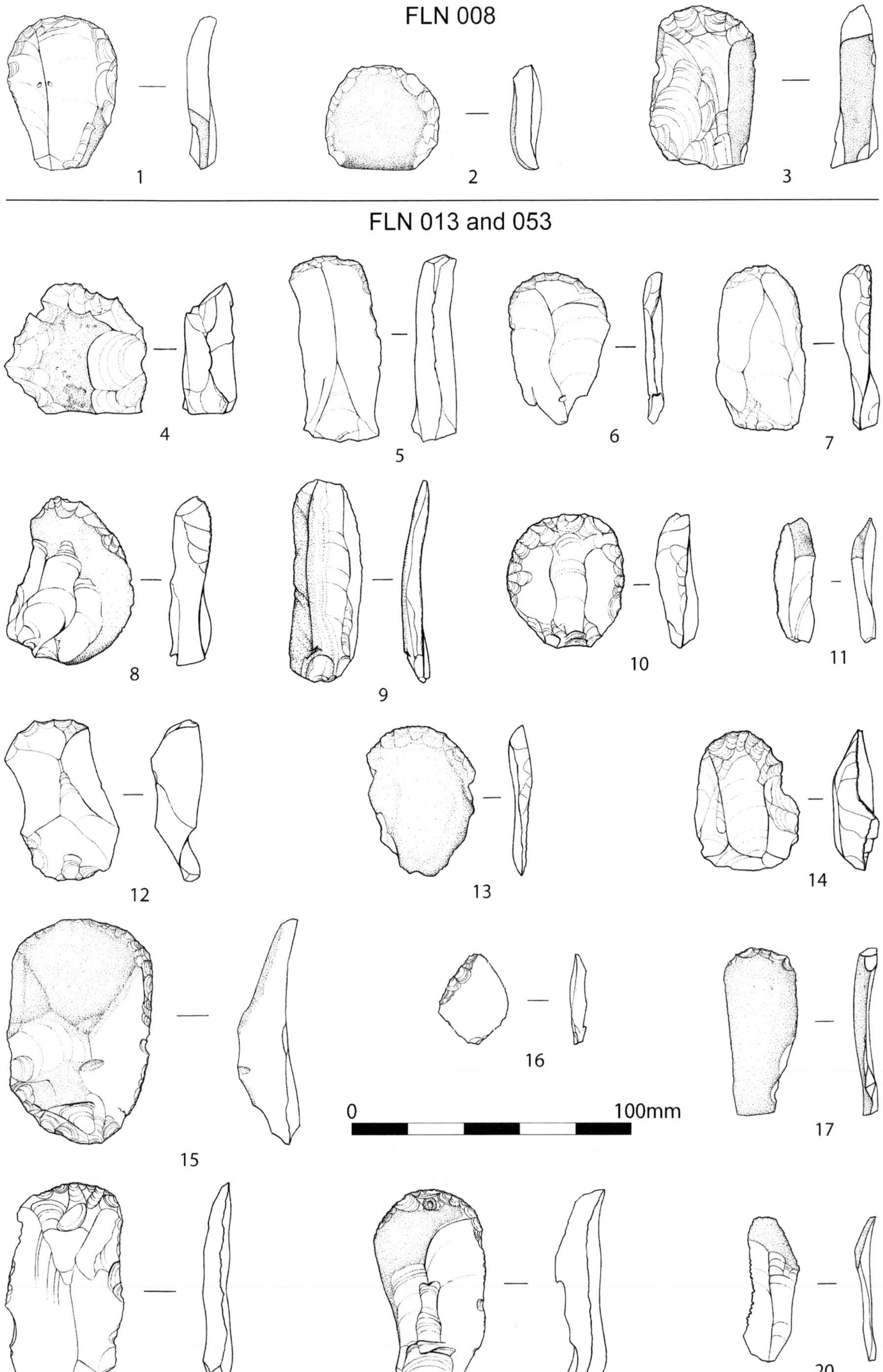

Figure 3.10 FLN 008, FLN 013 and FLN 053: worked flint (1–20) (scale 1:2)

Type	*No.*
Flake core	12
Blade core	1
Keeled core	3
Core fragment	9
Struck/tested piece	20
Core trimming fragment	1
Core/tool	2
Shatter	106
Flake	1572
Blade-like flake	77
Blade	51
Polished flake	2
Spall	354
Chip	18
Scraper	54
Piercer	10
Arrowhead	5
Polished axe	1
Fabricator/'strike-a-light'	1
Denticulate	4
Spurred piece	2
Serrated blade	3
Edge ground knife	1
Knife	1
Notched flake	3
Truncated blade	2
Retouched flake	40
Retouched fragment	3
Utilised blade	11
Utilised flake	28

Table 3.7 FLN 013 and FLN 053: summary of flint

Fig. 3.10.5 and *0348*, Fig. 3.10.6), one is an end/side scraper on a neat blade-like flake 013:*0349* (Fig. 3.10.7) and two are miscellaneous other types (including 013:*0366*, Fig. 3.10.8, which is burnt and a minimally retouched cortical piece in fill 013:*0036*).

A possible notched flake and a quite thick flake, a point of which may have been used as a piercer, were also found in the pit as well as seven miscellaneous retouched flakes, two utilised flakes and two utilised blades (including 013:*0350*, Fig. 3.10.9).

Of the flints from pit 013:*0028*, 159 pieces were from the dark coloured lower fill of the pit. These included all the retouched pieces apart from two miscellaneous retouched flakes.

Thirty-six flints were found in pit 013:*0072* which was located immediately north of the ring-ditch, within the post-hole circle and immediately south-east of its internal post-setting (013:*0148*) close to some other pits of earlier Neolithic date. There are twenty-two flakes with some quite thick, and a few thin, pieces. There are also two blades, a shatter piece and seven spalls. The debitage is all quite sharp. A very neat subcircular scraper has retouch around its distal edge and both sides 013:*0353* (Fig. 3.10.10). Upper fill component 013:*0073* also included a small thin blade with possible serrations (Fig. 3.10.11) on one edge, and a small thin flake with a protruding point utilised as a piercer. Part of a possibly quite large flake with a facetted platform has a utilised edge. Most of the flint from the pit was from the upper fill of brown sand but a few pieces, including the scraper, were recovered from the underlying dark coloured fill component 013:0074.

Nine flakes, four of them blade-like, three spalls and a retouched flake came from pit 013:*0066* which was just to the south-west of pit 013:*0072* and cut by the ring-ditch. The flakes are mostly quite small and the cortical nature of most of them suggests that they were struck from small gravel pebbles.

Twenty-five flints were found in pit 013:*0151* which was located within a cluster of features to the NNW of the ring-ditch. They include eighteen flakes, a blade and three spalls. The debitage is generally quite irregular and, mostly, quite sharp. Three scrapers came from the pit. There is an end scraper on a thick blade-like flake with a cortical platform from fill 013:*0164* (Fig. 3.10.12), a thin primary flake with neat semi-abrupt retouch of its distal part and an irregular thick piece with neatly retouched distal edge both from context 013:*0152* (Fig. 3.10.13 and 14). Some of the flint may have come from a 'central' dark/black sandy fill.

Two flakes, a spall and a neat utilised blade came from pit 013:*0050*.

Forty-four flints came from pit 053:*0028*. They include thirty-one flakes, one of them blade-like and most of them moderately sharp. Most of the pieces are quite small and irregular, although there are a few neater thin flakes. Ten spalls are also present. There is a sub-rectangular double end scraper 053:*0100* (Fig. 3.10.15), a neatly retouched flake and a utilised hard hammer struck flake.

One hundred and sixteen flints were found in pit 053:*0032*. These are almost all small flakes and spalls – many of which were recovered from samples. The flakes are predominantly thin and sharp tertiary pieces – very few have any cortex. There are four blade-like flakes. There is also an irregular flake core and a possible arrowhead. This latter piece is a small 'leaf-shaped' flake which has been bifacially retouched along the distal part of its right edge (Fig. 3.10.16). It may be an unfinished leaf-shaped arrowhead of earlier Neolithic date and residual in this pit.

Five flakes and three end scrapers came from pit 053:*0195*. Most of the flint from this pit is patinated a pale bluish-grey in colour. The three scrapers (Fig. 3.10.17, 18 and 19), all from context 053:*0196*, are all blade-like in nature with retouched distal ends, one of them (17) is a primary flake, and one (18) is quite thin and has a facetted platform.

Twelve flints came from the fill (053:*0198*) of pit 053:*0197*. There are seven flakes, one of which is a smooth curving piece with a facetted platform, and a shatter piece with abraded white patinated cortex. There is also a small serrated blade with an abraded platform (Fig. 3.10.20), and two scrapers, one of them a quite neat subcircular piece with a worn distal edge (Fig. 3.11.21). The other scraper is of similar size and shape but much thinner with more slight retouch (Fig. 3.11.22).

Forty-four flints, mostly flakes and irregular shatter pieces, came from the upper/central fill of pit 053:*0238*. Some of the material has abraded cortical surfaces and all is sharp or quite sharp. There is also a tested piece, a core fragment, a struck fragment and a small blade. Two broad subcircular scrapers 053:*0104* and 053:*0105* (Fig. 3.11.23 and 24 respectively) have relatively shallow retouch of their edges; the former is incomplete.

FLN 013 and 053

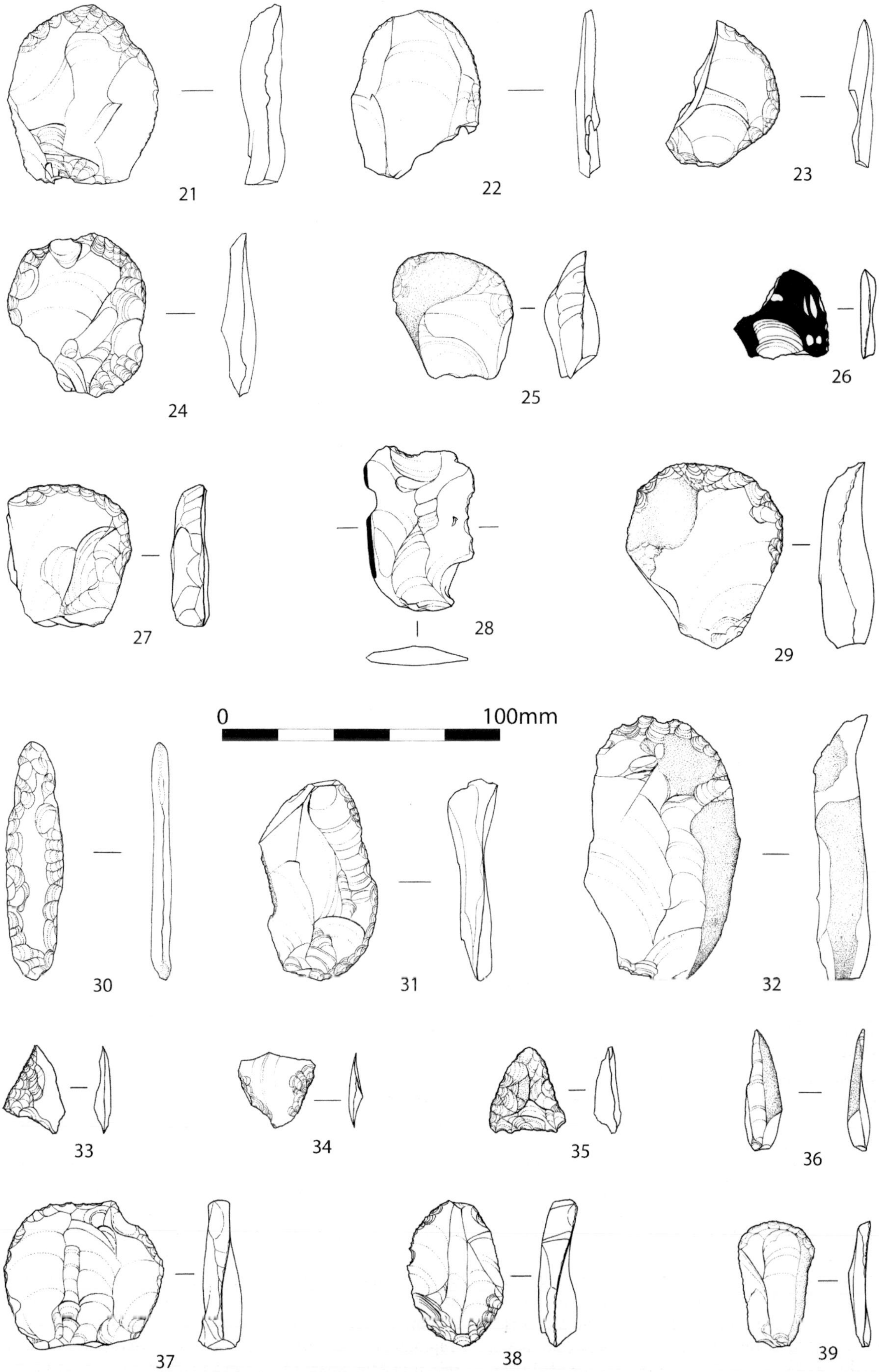

Figure 3.11 FLN 013 and FLN 053: worked flint (21–39) (scale 1:2)

Flint from other later Neolithic contexts (Period I.d.)

Fifty-four flints were found in pit 013:*0047* which was situated near the centre of ring-ditch 013:*0004* but which contained a few sherds of pottery of probable later Neolithic date. The flints include three flake cores – one of them quite neat and with some blade-like flakes having been struck from it. There are also thirty flakes, four blade-like flakes, four shatter pieces and ten spalls. The flakes are all quite sharp and are mainly quite small. They include both irregular and neat pieces. One scraper came from the pit. It is on a thick hard hammer struck flake which is retouched around its, cortical, distal edge 013:*0297* (Fig. 3.11.25). Two miscellaneous retouched flakes were also found. The flints were collected, in roughly equal numbers, from the 'central' and 'outer' fills of the pit with the single scraper and two retouched flakes the only tools recovered from the feature.

Fourteen flints were found in pit 013:*0082* which appeared to form part of the group of pits just north of the ring-ditch. A sherd of pottery of probable late Neolithic date was also found in the pit. There are eight flakes, a blade-like flake and a blade. Most of the pieces are quite small and two have abraded platforms. One flake has a polished surface and has been struck from a polished implement (Fig. 3.11.26). There are also two neatly retouched scrapers both quite broad with retouched distal edges. One, 013:*0354* (Fig. 3.11.27), has retouch extending around part of the right edge, whilst the other is an end/side scraper. Also present is part of an edge-ground knife of later Neolithic date 013:*0352* (Fig. 3.11.28), with its left edge polished on both faces. There are two notches, one on either side and on opposing faces. Their patina is slightly different to that of the rest of the piece and they may have been caused, probably accidentally, during or subsequent to use.

Thirty-three flints were found, along with pottery of probable Neolithic date in pit 013:*0157* which was located about 50m to the north-west of the post-hole circle. There are nineteen flakes, four blade-like flakes, six blades and a spall. They are mostly small and quite sharp and the pieces, especially the blades, are notable for their neat thin nature. Two blades have abraded platforms. There are two quite neatly retouched scrapers; one is the distal part of a probable end scraper, the other is a larger broader piece which may be broken on one side of its proximal end (Fig. 3.11.29), and a utilised blade.

Four flints came from pit 013:*0084* which was cut by pit 013:*0082*. There are two flakes, a retouched flake and a long narrow fragment with steep retouch of its distal edge. This latter is probably part of a longitudinally broken end scraper.

Twenty-seven pieces of flint came from pit 013:*0136* which was located within the area enclosed by the post-hole circle. They include a small struck fragment, twenty flakes, two blades (one with an abraded platform) and two shatter pieces. A small blade with white patinated cortex is possibly truncated by retouch at its distal edge and an irregular flake is retouched as a scraper.

Four squat or broad flakes and a neat 'horseshoe'-shaped end scraper came from short linear feature 013:*0457* and two spalls were found in post-hole 013:*0459*. Both of these features were part of post-hole structure 013:*0148*.

Two flakes came from pit 013:*0451* – one of them is from a blade core and has a facetted platform. The other is a small primary flake. The presence of the blade-like piece, and the fact that the pit was located within the post-hole circle, suggests that the feature was of Neolithic date.

A long narrow parallel-sided piece – probably a blade, has been bifacially worked along both its edges and around each end to form a very neat implement and was found in pit 053:*0155* (Fig. 3.11.30). It could be broadly classified as a fabricator although these rod-like tools are generally much thicker and far less elaborate (Saville 1981, 65). Its edges at each end are heavily worn and suggest that it was used as a 'strike-a-light'. Such a carefully made piece was probably well-used and curated (Butler 2005, 56).

Six small flakes, a knife and two scrapers were found in the single fill of pit 053:*0158*. The knife is on an irregular ovate flake with some cortex on its left side and neat abrupt retouch along the entirety of its right edge which curves to the platform at its proximal end (Fig. 3.11.31). There are two or three chips from the retouched edge – probably caused during use. One scraper is on a fairly large thick ovate flake which had some preparation of its platform and was probably soft hammer struck (Fig. 3.11.32). The distal end is quite neatly retouched but some slight notches give the edge a 'spurred' appearance. These may have occurred during use or have been deliberately formed. The patina and regularity suggest the former. The other scraper is on a smaller squatter flake with slight retouch of its edges. The fairly neat nature of the retouch, and of the flakes themselves, suggests a Neolithic date is likely for the material although no pottery was found in the pit. Most of it is quite sharp.

Two irregular flakes and a small blade-like flake were found along side pottery of probable prehistoric date in pit 053:*0192*.

Flints from contexts associated with ring-ditch 013:*0004* (Period I.e.)

A total of 1553 flints came from contexts associated with ring-ditch 013:*0004*.

Twenty pieces are broadly classified as cores. These are mostly flake cores and are generally quite small and irregular. There is one small exhausted blade core and two are classified as 'keeled' – although they are both quite irregular. There are also some core fragments and tested pieces. One fragment is probably from another blade core. Ten other pieces are classified as miscellaneous struck fragments. One piece may have been used as a core and/or as a crude denticular tool.

A total of 1111 unmodified flakes was recovered. The flakes are predominantly small or moderately small and often quite squat in shape. Many are irregular with some thick pieces, although a few neater thinner flakes were found in a small number of contexts. A range of raw material is represented: there is creamy orange quite coarse cortex from gravel lumps and nodules, as well as thinner abraded cortex from weathered pebbles and glossy white patinated former surfaces. The flakes are mostly quite sharp or sharp although a few contexts contain edge damaged pieces. One flake has slight traces of possible polish on its surface and might be from a polished implement. Twenty-nine flakes are classified as blade-like, most of them are sharp or quite sharp. Sixty-nine irregular shatter pieces, 191 spalls and nine small chips are also present in the deposits associated with the ring-ditch.

Twenty-three blades came from fills of the ring-ditch. Most of these are small and only a few are very neat or have abraded platforms indicative of careful production.

Three probable arrowheads came from the ring-ditch fills. All are of probable later Neolithic date. A small oblique arrowhead has neat bifacial retouch of one edge and slight retouch of its base 013:*0246* (Fig. 3.11.33). A small triangular fragment in context 013:*0006* (Fig. 3.11.34) has bifacial flaking of one edge, and more minimally on the opposite edge, the third, and 'cutting' edge is unworked and has part of one side slightly broken – perhaps during use. It is probably a chisel arrowhead (Clark's type C1, Clark 1934). There is also a quite thick triangular piece with retouch over most of its dorsal face and a small area of cortex surviving, also in context 013:*0006* (Fig. 3.11.35). There is also some slight retouch of its ventral edges – especially at the proximal edge where the bulb has been removed – but it seems likely to be an unfinished piece.

Nine pieces from the ring-ditch are broadly classified as piercers. Mostly, these are quite small flakes with their distal points either slightly retouched or utilised. A small pointed blade 013:*0240* (Fig. 3.11.36) has a slight retouch of the cortical left side at its distal tip. Another neat blade, found in context 013:*0127*, has a utilised point at one side of its obliquely broken proximal end. Two piercer-type tools are more closely categorised as spurred pieces, one in context 013:*0081*, and the other a spot-find 013:*0298* in context 013:*0053* (Fig. 3.11.37).

Two denticulates are present. One is an irregular flake and the other fairly neat; each has crude retouch on one edge. Another small quite thick blade has slight retouch forming a serrated edge.

Thirteen scrapers were found in deposits associated with the ring-ditch. A thick ovate flake has retouch of its distal and proximal ends (013:*0364*, Fig. 3.11.38) and another proximal fragment is steeply retouched and might be another double end scraper. Four end scrapers (including 013:*0357*, Fig. 3.11.39), some of them quite broad ovate pieces, and one smaller quite thin blade-like piece have retouched distal ends. Other pieces are more irregularly or minimally retouched.

A quite thick ovate flake has slight retouch around much of its circumference and is classified as a disc scraper 013:*0360* (Fig. 3.12.40) and a much smaller subcircular scraper with some bifacial retouch of both sides has been classified as a 'thumbnail' type in context 013:*0053* (Fig. 3.12.41). Five other pieces are miscellaneous/other scrapers. They vary from broad through to blade-like in shape and have retouched distal and, sometimes, other edges.

Sixteen miscellaneous retouched flakes, three retouched fragments, four utilised blades and nine utilised flakes were also found in the deposits associated with the ring-ditch. One of the flakes (Fig. 3.12.42) from context 013:*0042* has traces of polish on its dorsal face and is probably from a part-polished axe.

Features within ring-ditch 013:*0004*

A very small flake and a spall came from pit 013:*0037*. A fairly thick cortical flake from an abraded pebble, with slight retouch on its distal edge, was found in pit 013:*0090*. A very small blade and a spall came from pit 013:*0043*.

Flint from later features

A small number of flints were found residually in features of probable Romano-British date (Period II.a.). There is an unusual notched flake in fill 053:*0256*, from pit 053:*0255*. It is triangular in shape with small, unifacially worked, notches on either side just below its proximal apex (Fig. 3.12.43). These may have been used for hafting the piece. Its straight steep distal edge has some chips from its – possibly due to use. An irregular blade from the same pit is probably utilised.

A blade-like flake and an unusual flint tool came from the fill (053:*0276*) of pit 053:*0275* (Fig. 3.12.44). The latter is on a thermally fractured fragment from a nodule and has a knob-like protrusion on its upper cortical face. One edge appears to have been retouched to a steep crudely denticular edge. It seems likely that the piece was utilised due to the 'handle'-like knob.

Other material from Romano-British features include flakes, shatter pieces, spalls and a chip. Two scrapers including a small piece in the fill (053:*0798*) of pit 053:*0797* (with two star-shaped fossils within it), a possible notched flake and a utilised flake are also present.

A flake and a possible denticulate (the latter heavily abraded) came from Period III post-hole 053:*0346*.

Nine flakes, a blade and an utilised flake came from a Period V ditch 013:*0078*. Several of the flakes had cortical platforms suggesting that they were quite randomly struck and probably of quite late date. They are residual in the modern ditch but they may well date to the period of activity associated with the ring-ditch

Period 0 Undated features

One small hard hammer struck flake was found in pit 013:*0087* and a small neat blade slight utilisation/wear of its right edge was found in pit 013:*0427*. A small quite neat subcircular scraper, only slightly retouched on a cortical naturally scraper-like flake, came from post-hole 013:*0100* and single small flakes came from pit 013:*0429* and post-hole 013:*0455*. A total of twenty-four flints came from ten undated features at FLN 053. They are mostly small irregular flakes. An end/side scraper and a utilised flake are also present.

Unstratified

Eighty-five flints, many slightly edge damaged, came from unstratified contexts (some with individual 'spot find' context numbers) They include a neat keeled core, part of a blade core, twenty-eight flakes (mostly small and several quite irregular), five blade-like flakes and four blades. There are also eight scrapers. These include a side scraper, a possible end/side scraper and six miscellaneous types, one of which is a bifacially retouched thin fragment with shallow flaking from one end and its other face steeply retouched to an irregular scraper-like edge (in sub-context 013:*0150*) (Fig. 3.12.45).

A small triangular chisel arrowhead is present (Clarke's Type C2, Clark 1934). Its broadest edge is an unworked primary flake edge. The other two edges are retouched with slight edge retouch on their opposite faces (Fig. 3.12.46). An obliquely truncated truncated blade with additional retouch of its left edge to a point and a possible denticulate were also found.

One other unstratified piece has slight possible utilisation of its distal point and may have been used as a

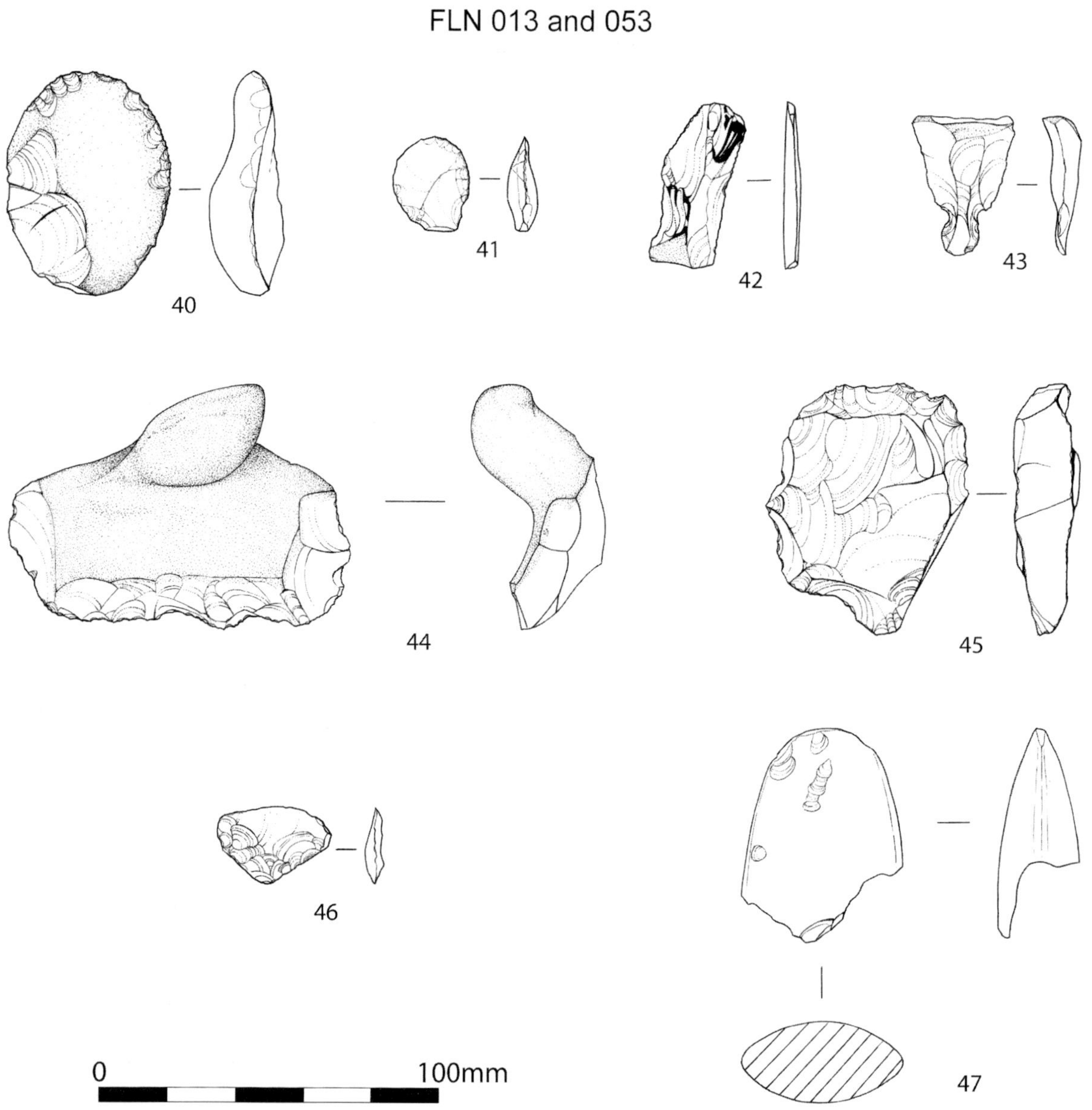

Figure 3.12 FLN 013 and FLN 053: worked flint (40–47) (scale 1:2)

piercer. There are also eight miscellaneous retouched flakes, an utilised blade and ten utilised flakes.

The rounded end fragment of a polished flint axe was found 053:*0001* (Fig. 3.12.47); polish extends over both faces and the edge and there are one or two flakes from each face and slight edge damage to the end of the axe. As such a small part of the axe survives it is difficult to describe it further or assign it to a particular type.

Catalogue of illustrated worked flint (FLN 013 and 053) Figs 3.10–3.12

FLN 013 and FLN 053

4. Core/tool, context 013:*0109*, post-hole 013:*0108* in post-hole circle 013:*0147*

5. End scraper 013:*0296*, context 013:*0036*, pit 013:*0028*

6. End scraper 013:*0348*, context 013:*0036*, pit 013:*0028*

7. End/side scraper 013:*0349*, context 013:*0036*, pit 013:*0028*

8. Scraper 013:*0366*, context 013:*0036*, pit 013:*0028*

9. Utilised blade 013:*0350*, context 013:*0036*, pit 013:*0028*

10. Scraper 013:*0353*, context 013:*0074*, pit 013:*0072*

11. Serrated blade, context 013:*0073*, pit 013:*0072*

12. End scraper, context 013:*0164*, pit 013:*0151*

13. Scraper, context 013:*0152*, pit 013:*0151*

14. Scraper, context 013:*0152*, pit 013:*0151*

15. End scraper 053:*0100*, context 053:*0029*, pit 053:*0028*

16. Arrowhead, context 053:*0033*, pit 053:*0032*

17. End scraper, context 053:*0196*, pit 053:*0195*

18. End scraper, context 053:*0196*, pit 053:*0195*

19. End scraper, context 053:*0196*, pit 053:*0195*

20. Serrated blade, context 053:*0198*, pit 053:*0197*

21. Scraper, context 053:*0198*, pit 053:*0197*

22. Scraper, context 053:*0198*, pit 053:*0197*

23. Scraper, context 053:*0239*, pit 053:*0238*

24. Scraper, context 053:*0239*, pit 053:*0238*

25. Scraper 013:*0297*, context 013:*0052*, pit 013:*0047*

26. Polished flake, context 013:*0083*, pit 013:*0082*

27. End/side scraper 013:*0354*, context 013:*0083*, pit 013:*0082*

28. Edge ground knife 013:*0352*, context 013:*0083*, pit 013:*0082*

29. Scraper, context 013:*0158*, pit 013:*0157*

30. Fabricator, context 053:*0156*, pit 053:*0155*

31. Knife, context 053:*0159*, pit 053:*0158*

32. End scraper, context 053:*0159*, pit 053:*0158*

33. Oblique arrowhead 013:*0246*, ring-ditch 013:*0004*

34. ?Chisel arrowhead, context 013:*0006*, ring-ditch 013:*0004*

35. ?Unfinished triangular arrowhead, context 013:*0006*, ring-ditch 013:*0004*

36. Piercer 013:*0240*, ring-ditch 013:*0004*

37. Spurred piece 013:*0298*, context 013:*0053*, ring-ditch 013:*0004*

38. Double end scraper 013:*0364*, context 013:*0127*, ring-ditch 013:*0004*

39. End scraper 013:*0357*, context 013:*0042*, ring-ditch 013:*0004*

40. Disc scraper 013:*0360*, context 013:*0081*, ring-ditch 013:*0004*

41. Thumbnail scraper, context 013:*0053*, ring-ditch 013:*0004*

42. Polished flake, context 013:*0042*, ring-ditch 013:*0004*

43. Notched flake, context 053:*0256*, fill 053:*0255*

44. Retouched fragment/tool, context 053:*0276*, pit 053:*0275*

45. Scraper, unstratified context 013:*0150*

46. Chisel arrowhead, unstratified context 013:*0001*

47. Polished axe fragment, unstratified context 053:*0001*

Site FLN 062

A total of twenty-seven flints was recovered from the fills of two graves of Anglo-Saxon date which cut the fills of another ring-ditch excavated to the south of FLN 053 at FLN 062. They were almost all small flakes, some are quite sharp, others slightly edge-damaged. There are three blade-like pieces, one blade and two small utilised flakes. The vast bulk of the FLN 062 assemblage, including that from the ring-ditch, has not been considered for this report.

Overall discussion

The flint from the Flixton sites covered in this volume is wide-ranging in appearance, and includes both irregular and moderately thick flakes and thinner neater pieces.

The latter are often tertiary flakes, suggesting that cores were methodically used and not just randomly struck a few times before being discarded. This is also suggested by the presence of one or two neat and/or carefully used cores and fragments from probable blade cores – including possible trimming pieces. These factors all indicate that much of the material is contemporary with the Neolithic activity at the site. Although FLN 013 and FLN 053 are adjacent and part of the same site, it is notable that larger amounts of both complete and cortical flint came from FLN 013 (79% and 60% respectively) than from FLN 053 (50% and 34% respectively). This probably reflects the fact that most of the flint from FLN 053 was from Neolithic pits while at FLN 013 (and FLN 008 where similarly larger percentages were seen) flint also came from Bronze Age ring ditches. The thinner tertiary flakes more characteristic of the earlier period would be more susceptible to breakage, perhaps especially so if they were deliberately redeposited in the pits (see below). It is possible that some of the blade-like pieces may be of Mesolithic or earlier Neolithic date and an arrowhead may be of earlier Neolithic date but, in contrast to the sites to the south and north-west (Bates 2004), there are no flints from the present sites that date unequivocally to these periods or earlier. Notably, some cores which are recorded as being more irregular in nature came, generally, from deposits associated with the ring-ditches at FLN 013 and FLN 008 and a preponderance of small squat flakes came from the ring-ditch at FLN 008. These flints probably represent knapping dating to this later, Bronze Age, phase of activity.

As already pointed out by Martin with regard to FLN 013 (in Boulter 1996a and b), most, if not all, of the diagnostic tools from the site are of Neolithic date and those which can be more closely dated can be assigned to the later Neolithic period. These include four arrowheads, three of them recovered from the ring-ditch and the other unstratified, and the edge ground knife from pit 0013:*0082*. Two of the arrowheads are chisel types and one is an oblique type; these types have both been associated primarily with Grooved Ware (Healy 1988, 46) although it has been shown that chisel types have tended to be associated with the Woodlands sub-style of Grooved Ware (not seen at the present site) while oblique types have more commonly been found with the Clacton and Durrington sub-styles identified at Flixton (Green 1984). One chisel arrowhead is very similar to that recovered from a Grooved Ware pit at Markshall, Caistor St Edmund (Robins 2000, 198 fig.159, F40). The fourth piece may be an unfinished triangular arrowhead and is also likely to date to the later Neolithic. From FLN 053, Neolithic types include a serrated blade, a fabricator and part of a polished axe.

By far the most common type of tool found at Flixton is the scraper; a total of fifty-four pieces have been classified as such at FLN 013/FLN 053 and seventeen scrapers came from FLN 008. The scrapers from the FLN 013 area vary, with blade-like end scrapers, neatly retouched ovate and subcircular examples and more irregular or minimally retouched pieces all seen. The presence of a considerable number of quite neatly retouched pieces, including the end scrapers, suggests a predominantly Neolithic date for the material. Some more irregular pieces found in the ring-ditch fills are probably of later date; it seems likely that some neater flints from these contexts are residual Neolithic pieces. From FLN 053, the scrapers recovered from pits are, with one or two exceptions, larger than those from FLN 013 and although those from feature 053:*0195* are all long end scrapers, the pieces from the other pits are on broader ovate flakes, some of them quite thick. They are characteristically 'Neolithic' in type.

There has been much discussion about the possible deliberate or 'structured' deposition of material into pits and the selection of specific artefact types for placement in certain features during the Neolithic period. This practice has been considered with particular reference to later Neolithic Grooved Ware (Cleal 1984; Thomas 1991).

Comparison of the worked flint from different features at the Flixton sites suggests that it may be possible to define broad differences between the lithic material deposited with, or without, Grooved Ware. However the small number of features and the relatively similar nature of some of the flint from them does not provide sufficient evidence for a conclusive argument. Also it does not seem possible to show an inverse relationship between the significance of flint and pottery in pits from 'pairs' – as is suggested may be the case with the material from such pits at some sites (Percival 2004). Of the four pits with significant quantities of Grooved Ware in the FLN 013 area, three include at least one neatly retouched scraper on neat ovate or blade-like flakes. One pit also includes a serrated blade and a small piercer, and another has a blade with a distinctive striped appearance due to its cortex and inner rind. The fourth Grooved Ware pit has only a few flints, mostly small cortical flakes. The retouched pieces from the excavated pits that contain non-Grooved Ware pottery are slightly more irregular in type; two pits contain one and two scrapers – all irregular in some way. The third has one neatly and one minimally retouched, scraper, an edge ground knife and a flake from another polished implement. It is notable that the knife is quite smooth on its flaked surface; it may have been well-used, perhaps curated, before being deposited in the pit but it has two notches which appear to be accidental damage and so it may have been discarded as being no longer useful. In the FLN 053 area, there is less scope for the comparison of the flint from pits since Grooved Ware came from most of them. The majority of the neatly retouched scrapers do, however, come from the Grooved Ware pits.

The relatively high ratio of retouched flint to waste flakes in association with Grooved Ware has been documented by Thomas (1991, 73–4) and Garrow (2006, 90–91) where scrapers are noted as being as the most common tool type (the possible reasons for this are discussed by Garrow). This phenomenon might be perceptible at Flixton although the number of features in the study group is quite small. Retouched pieces, with scrapers being by far the most common formal tool type, comprise 10–12% (by number) of the lithic material from all four of the FLN 013 Grooved Ware pits while in the other pits the amounts are more inconsistent, ranging from 5% to 25%. In the FLN 053 area, the amounts are also inconsistent with the percentage of retouched flint (again, mostly scrapers) ranging from less than 1% to 37% in the pits containing Grooved Ware and being 33% in a pit that has no pottery at all.

At FLN 013 and FLN 053, concentrations of struck flint, including retouched pieces, came from the distinctive dark-coloured fills components of six pits, five of which contained Grooved Ware and the other – pottery of probable later Neolithic date with a few flakes also being found in a similar fill in an undated pit. Although lithic material was also found in pits with dissimilar fills, it does seem, as noted by Percival (in relation to pottery, Percival 2004), that there was some correlation between the dark-coloured fills and the greater concentrations of artefacts. The origin of this material is unknown; it may have come from existing middens but it is possible that some of the flint was deliberately selected for deposition. The relative frequency of the scrapers suggests that some selection did occur. It is noted also, that one scraper from pit 053:*0028* was heavily worn on its retouched edge. This is comparable with one of the group of scrapers recovered along with Grooved Ware from the dark-coloured fill of a pit excavated at Markshall, Caistor St Edmund (Ashwin and Bates 2000, 194). That fill contained a small amount of charcoal along with charred cereal and hazelnut shell. There is no clear evidence for the 'arranged' deposition of flint as suggested elsewhere (Garrow 2006, 113–5).

Although the analysis did not include any serious attempt at refitting, none of the material from any of the pits was noted as clearly having been struck from the same core. The only instance of such a possibility is at FLN 008 where several flakes are recorded as such from the ring-ditch fill 008:*0107*.

The flint found to the south of FLN 053 at Site FLN 062 was residual in the fills of the graves and is likely to relate to activity associated with the ring-ditch or with the earlier, Neolithic, activity in the vicinity.

Fired clay
by Sue Anderson

Introduction
Two fragments of fired clay from FLN 008 and FLN 013, one from each site, have been included in the prehistoric section of the finds reports based on their context, although neither was in any way diagnostic or closely datable.

Site FLN 008
One fragment (4g) of fired clay (008:*0031*) was collected from the south-east trench quadrant. It is a heavily abraded, chalk-tempered piece which is undiagnostic in terms of function. Fragments of similar colour and fabric have been identified as triangular loomweights (probably of Iron Age date) elsewhere at Flixton, but the fragment could equally be part of a broken-up oven dome.

Site FLN 013
One small, abraded fragment (24g) of medium sandy fired clay was collected from Period I.e. ring-ditch fill component 013:*0053*.

Heat-altered flint and stone
by Sue Anderson

Introduction
The vast majority of the heat-altered flint and sandstone was considered to be prehistoric in date and therefore the main section dealing with this material is incorporated here.

All heat-altered flint and sandstone was counted, weighed and a sample retained. The data was used to study spatial distribution of this material across the site, providing further evidence for the spread of prehistoric activity. From many contexts, particularly at FLN 013 and FLN 053, heat-altered flint and stone was the only artefact type recovered. It probably represents waste from cooking and may have been discarded along with animal bone and other organic remains which have not survived in the acidic soil.

Site FLN 008
Twenty-three fragments of heat-altered flint were recovered (29g) from four contexts.

Sites FLN 013 and 053
One hundred and thirty-four contexts contained 2363 fragments (55.740kg) of heat-altered flint and/or sandstone, generally associated with worked flint and/or pottery of Neolithic date. Seven features contained over 100 fragments of heat-altered flint/stone each. Overall, Period I.d. contained the most (1340 pieces), with 285 fragments from Period I.e., 51 were from eleven Period II.a. features, six from one Period III feature, five pieces from Period V and the remainder unphased. It is likely that most of the unphased features which contained this material were of prehistoric date. The largest groups in this category, all containing over thirty fragments and weighing more than 1kg, were from pits 053:*0036*, *0184* and *0190*.

The majority of heat-altered flint came from the area of the Period I.d. post-hole circle, Period I.e. ring-ditch and associated features. In total, the ring-ditch 013:*0004* contained 283 fragments (4621g). Period I.d. pit 013:*0047* contained thirty fragments (971g) and Period I.e. pit 013:*0037* one piece (20g), whilst three unphased pits (013:*0020*, *0025* and *0090*) produced four pieces (78g). The post-hole circle 013:*0147* contained 762 pieces (8635g). Within it, the Period I.d. post-hole structure 013:*0148* contained ten fragments (0196g), whilst seven pits (Period I.d. 013:*0066*, *0072*, *0082*, *0084* and *0136*; Phase V 013:*0451*; Unphased 013:*0449*) produced a total of 169 fragments (2645g).

To the west of the structures, three Period I.d. pits (013:*0028*, *0151* and *0153*) contained a total of 220 pieces (2901g), although most of this was from 013:*0028*. To the east, four features (Unphased 013:*0087*, *0102*, *0104* and *0110*) contained 147 fragments (1651g) between them, most of which came from pit 013:*0087*. To the north, unphased pit 013:*0196* contained seven fragments (269g).

Scattered features to the north-west (013:*0157*, *0420*, *0422*, *0427* and *0437*) contained 183 fragments (2832g) of which 166 pieces came from pit 013:*0427*. With the exception of Period I.d. 013:*0157*, all of these features were unphased.

In the FLN 053 area for Period I.d., three pits (053:*0195*, *0197* and *0801*) contained small amounts of heat-altered flint, but the largest groups were from pits 053:*0028*, *0032* and *0238*, producing 851g, 1886g and 2720g respectively. Unlike FLN 013, there is no particular concentration of features containing this material, although a group of pits close to the palisaded post-hole circle 053:*0346* did contain some of the larger quantities collected from the site. Pits 053:*0028*, *0036* and *0042* in this area all produced over a kilogram each. The palisaded post-hole circle 053:*0346* did not produce any heat-altered flint, although both post-holes (053:*0620* and *0632*) inside it contained small quantities. Perhaps surprisingly, given its wide dispersal, none of this material was recovered as residual finds within this part of the cemetery.

Site FLN 062

Seven fragments of heat altered flint or other stone were found in the grave fills (39g) at this site and were probably derived from the upper fill of the ring-ditch into which they had been cut.

Discussion

Isolated pits containing both small and large quantities of fire-cracked and heat-altered flint were dispersed over most of the excavated area. It is assumed that these represent domestic activity, most likely belonging to the early prehistoric phases of site use.

The largest concentration of heat-altered flint was associated with the post-hole circle at FLN 013. Almost every post-hole contained at least one fragment, ranging in weight from 7g in 013:*0416* to 2092g in 013:*0064*. Whilst this material may have been useful as packing for the support of posts, the diversity of quantities within even neighbouring post-holes might indicate a more structured inclusion of the objects, particularly given their association with worked flint and pottery. Alternatively, if the site were a focus for feasting, this might generate a large quantity of pot-boilers which were eventually incorporated into the fills of the post-holes.

IV. Biological evidence

Cremated bone

by Sue Anderson

Site FLN 008

Seventy-eight fragments of cremated human bone were collected from seventeen contexts during the excavation of the ring ditch, of which sixteen were in the south-east quadrant and one was in the south-west. Table 3.8 shows the quantification of cremated bone for the four main areas of the skeleton.

The contexts represent spot finds within the southern half of the ring ditch and it seems likely that the bone is the scattered remains of a single cremation burial, possibly in an urn, as a number of fragments were recovered from the same general area of the site. No duplication was noted in any of the groups, and all identifiable pieces were adult. There were no indicators of age or sex beyond the size of individual elements.

Identifiable bones included the left mandibular condyle, the superior part of the right zygoma, pieces of rib and vertebra, and fragments of humerus, radius, femur, tibia and fibula. The maximum dimensions recorded for fragments were 27mm for the skull and 58mm for the long bones.

As this was a heavily disturbed burial, little can be said about the cremation rites or methods. Clearly the total of 64g is well below the average weight for a typical adult cremated body, but this is certainly due to disturbance and not to poor collection of bone following cremation. The surviving bone was generally of a uniform creamy colour, fully oxidised, which indicates a firing temperature in excess of *c*.600°C (McKinley 2004, 11). However, less well-fired bone may have been lost in the acidic soils.

The cremated bone appears to represent a single scattered burial of possible Early Bronze Age date. Fragments of pottery found in association with it suggest that it may originally have been urned. The burial was that of an adult, but age and sex could not be determined.

Site FLN 013

A single cremation burial was excavated near the centre of ring ditch 013:*0004*. The pit containing burnt bone (013:*0007*) was excavated in 5cm spits from 013:*0008* at the top to 013:*0013* at the bottom. Preliminary analysis involved the separation of bone from each spit into specific areas of the skeleton (skull, axial, upper limb, lower limb) where possible. There was a total of 694 fragments weighing 2499g. By weight, 89.1% was identifiable. The quantities from each area by spit are recorded in Table 3.9.

There was no clear sorting of bones, although cranial fragments occurred more commonly in the top layers, particularly 013:*0009* which contained the largest pieces. Very little lower limb was present. Maximum long bone fragment size was 55mm (in spit 013:*0008*) and maximum skull fragment size was 50mm (in 013:*0009*). Identifiable fragments included pieces of femur, ?ulna, cervical vertebrae, ribs, finger phalanges, proximal right humerus, and scapula. Some fragments of cranium appeared unburnt, but most of the bone was fully oxidised.

	Skull		Axial		Upper limb		Lower limb		Unidentified		Total	
Context	No.	Wt (g)	No.	Wt (g)	No.	Wt (g)	No.	Wt (g)	No.	Wt (g)	No.	Wt (g)
0013									1	0.6	1	0.6
0021									8	2.9	8	2.9
0022							1	15.2	5	3.6	6	18.8
0023	6	2.9	2	0.1			4	4.0	11	2.4	23	9.4
0024	2	3.1							2	0.7	4	3.8
0025	1	0.7					1	1.5	4	1.2	6	3.4
0026			2	0.8			1	2.6	5	3.0	8	6.4
0027							1	1.9			1	1.9
0028	3	1.9									3	1.9
0029							1	2.3			1	2.3
0030			1	1.0					4	0.6	5	1.6
0034									1	0.3	1	0.3
0036									2	0.6	2	0.6
0037			4	0.8	1	0.6	1	2.4			6	3.8
0040							1	3.3			1	3.3
0042									1	0.8	1	0.8
0055					1	2.2					1	2.2
Total	**12**	**8.6**	**9**	**2.7**	**2**	**2.8**	**11**	**33.2**	**44**	**16.7**	**78**	**64.0**

Table 3.8 FLN 008: cremated bone quantities

The amount of bone present represents less than a quarter of the expected weight for an adult female, and considerably less for an adult male. Either collection following cremation was not very thorough or, more likely, the burial had been truncated. The relative proportion of cranial fragments by weight was 51.9%, the torso represented 11.4%, the upper limb 26.6% and the lower limb 10.0%. The skull should represent 18.2%, the torso 20.6%, the upper limb 23.1% and the lower limb 38.1% (McKinley 1994, 6). Perhaps the lower limb was deposited in the upper part of the burial and had been lost to truncation by ploughing.

The individual was an adult, probably relatively young as no signs of degeneration were noted on the remaining joint fragments and all cranial sutures were unfused. Epiphyseal fusion was complete, suggesting an age of around 25–35 years. No teeth were found, but fragments of alveolus were present and not closed. Sexing was not possible due to a lack of specific indicators. The burial probably represents a single individual and no animal bone was identified.

A few fragments of charcoal and heat-altered flint were included with the cremation, and were presumably collected from the area of the pyre when the bones were gathered.

Site FLN 053

The cremation burial 053:*0057*, deposited in a small pit 053:*0056*, was wet sieved and produced only ten small fragments of bone. With the exception of two fragments of skull and a possible rib, none of this is identifiable. The thickness of the cranial fragments indicates a possible juvenile. Small fragments of burnt bone were also collected during wet sieving of four other samples: 053:*0046*, 053:*0276*, 053:*0278* and 053:*0847*. Apart from a large fragment of ?human clavicle or large mammal rib in 053:*0046*, none of this material is identifiable to species.

Overall discussion

All three cremation burials were incomplete, and that from FLN 008 was scattered due to later disturbance. The largest assemblage of cremated bone, from FLN 013, was well below the expected weight for an average adult and is also likely to have been truncated. They probably represented two adults and a child.

	Skull		Axial		Upper limb		Lower limb		Unidentified		Total	
Context	No.	Wt (g)	No.	Wt (g)	No.	Wt (g)	No.	Wt (g)	No.	Wt (g)	No.	Wt (g)
0008	39	18.1	43	11.0	17	10.4	17	17.3	76	10.8	192	67.6
0009	107	74.9	13	5.6	43	23.7	-	-	72	6.2	235	110.4
0010	20	12.2	9	4.9	22	9.3	4	3.4	72	5.7	127	35.5
0011	23	9.4	6	1.6	35	12.1	-	-	38	2.4	102	25.5
0012	3	0.8	4	1.5	9	3.8	1	1.6	15	1.4	32	9.1
0013	1	0.3	1	0.8	-	-	-	-	4	0.7	6	1.8
Total	**193**	**115.7**	**76**	**25.4**	**126**	**59.3**	**22**	**22.3**	**277**	**27.2**	**694**	**249.9**

Table 3.9 FLN 013: cremated bone from pit 013:*0007*

V. Palaeoenvironmental analysis

Bulk soil samples
by Val Fryer

Introduction

Bulk soil-samples were submitted from the prehistoric features in the FLN 013 and FLN 053 excavation areas.

Methodology

The samples were processed by manual water flotation/washover, collecting the flots in a 500 micron mesh sieve. The cremation samples were initially passed through a 5mm sieve to extract the cremated bone for further examination. Residues were collected in a 1mm mesh sieve and sorted when dried. The dried flots were scanned under a binocular microscope at low power (up to x 40) and the macrobotanical and other remains noted. Plant macrofossils were preserved by charring. Modern contaminants including fibrous roots, seeds/fruits, small mammal/amphibian bones, invertebrates and molluscs were also present in some samples along with rare small coal fragments which were also considered to be intrusive.

Sites FLN 013 and FLN 053

Twenty-eight samples from prehistoric features were submitted for assessment and analysis (twenty-six from FLN 013, two from FLN 053); twenty-two were from contexts attributed a Period II.d., Late Neolithic date; nine were from pit fills (seven from FLN 013, two from FLN 053), eleven from post-holes forming part of circle 013:*0147* and two from post-holes forming part of its internal structure 013:*0148*. The remaining six constituted the entire fill of the un-urned cremation 013:*0007* located central to ring-ditch 013:*0004* and attributed a Period II.e., Early Bronze Age date.

With the exception of charcoal/charred wood fragments, plant macrofossils were extremely rare within the assemblages, comprising a single wheat (*Triticum* sp.) grain, a few indeterminate cereal grains, occasional seeds of grassland herbs and hazel (*Corylus avellana*) nutshell fragments. Although the pit fills possibly contained low density deposits of burnt food refuse, no other interpretable material was recovered. The small quantity of material incorporated within the post-holes was probably derived from scattered refuse that accidentally became incorporated within their fills.

Charcoal
by Rowena Gale

Introduction

Charcoal recovered from soil bulk samples from prehistoric features from sites FLN 013 and FLN 053 was submitted for identification and isolation of material suited to radiocarbon dating. In addition, a sample was submitted from a possible prehistoric feature from FLN 008.

Methodology

A total of twenty-four samples was examined, one from FLN 008, twenty-one from FLN 013 and two from FLN 053. Charcoal fragments measuring >2mm in radial cross-section were considered for species identification. The samples were prepared using standard methods (Gale and Cutler 2000). The anatomical structures were examined using incident light on a Nikon Labophot-2 compound microscope at magnifications up to x400 and matched to prepared reference slides of modern wood. When possible, the maturity of the wood was assessed (i.e. heartwood/sapwood).

Classification follows that of *Flora Europaea* (Tutin *et al.* 1964–80). Group names are given when anatomical differences between related genera are too slight to allow secure identification to genus level. These include members of the Pomoideae (*Crataegus*, *Malus*, *Pyrus* and *Sorbus*), Leguminosae (*Ulex* and *Cytisus*) and Salicaceae (*Salix* and *Populus*). When a genus is represented by a single species in the British flora, it is named as the most likely origin of the wood given the provenance and period, but it should be noted that it is rarely possible to name individual species from wood features and exotic species of trees and shrubs were introduced to Britain from an early period (Godwin 1956; Mitchell 1974). The anatomical structure of the charcoal was consistent with the following taxa or groups of taxa:

Betulaceae. *Alnus glutinosa* (L.) Gaertner, European alder
Corylaceae. *Corylus avellana* L., hazel
Fagaceae. *Quercus* sp., oak
Oleaceae. *Fraxinus excelsior* L., ash
Leguminosae. *Cytisus scoparius* (L.) Link, broom or *Ulex* sp., gorse
Malvaceae. *Tilia* sp., lime
Rosaceae. Subfamilies:

Pomoideae, which includes *Crataegus* sp., hawthorn; *Malus* sp., apple; *Pyrus* sp., pear; *Sorbus* spp., rowan, service tree and whitebeam. These taxa are anatomically similar; one or more taxa may be represented in the charcoal.

Prunoideae, which includes *Prunus avium*, wild cherry, *Prunus padus*, bird cherry; *Prunus spinosa* L., blackthorn. The anatomical features of these genera are overlapping and it is sometimes difficult or impossible to differentiate between the species

Salicaceae. *Salix* sp., willow, and *Populus* sp., poplar. In most respects these taxa are anatomically similar.

Site FLN 008

A sample of charcoal was recovered from an irregular curving feature (008:*0114*) located internal to and essentially concentric with the FLN 008 ring-ditch. The charcoal consisted mainly of chunks of alder (*Alnus glutinosa*) roundwood (exceeding 30mm in radius) from moderately fast-grown trees. Oak (*Quercus* sp.) heartwood and gorse/broom (*Ulex* sp./*Cytisus scoparius*) roundwood were also present. Since clearly not structural in origin, the charcoal probably represents fuel debris that was either dumped or accumulated in the feature.

Sites FLN 013 and FLN 053

Pits

Charcoal from eight pits (six FLN 013, two FLN 053) were examined. The taxa identified comprised hazel (*Corylus* sp.), oak (*Quercus* sp.), ash (*Fraxinus* sp.), lime (*Tilia* sp.), Rosaceae, Pomoideae, and *Prunus* spp.,

Post-hole circle 013:*0147* and structure 013:*0148*

Charcoal from seven post-holes in the circle 013:*0147*, and two from its internal structure 013:*0148* were studied. The taxa identified were hazel (*Corylus* sp.), Pomoideae, *Prunus* spp. and oak (*Quercus* sp.). Samples 013:*0170* and 013:*0417* included charcoal in which the structure was too poorly preserved to distinguish between alder and hazel.

The charcoal fragments were mainly too small to assess the maturity of the wood. Oak charcoal included heartwood and sapwood and, although the sapwood has been isolated, it was considered safer to use material from other species for radiocarbon dating. Short-lived species include hazel, members of the Pomoideae and *Prunus*.

Cremation burial 013:*0007*

The samples from cremation burial 013:*0007* were predominantly composed of *Quercus* (oak). *Fraxinus* (ash) was present in two samples (013:*0008* and 013:*0009*), but only in very small quantities. It was not possible to assess whether the ash included heartwood, but generally it is shorter lived than oak. The oak consisted of sapwood and heartwood. The charcoal fragments were fragmented but none appeared to originate from very roundwood (*i.e.* <10mm in diameter).

Overall discussion

With the exception of the charcoal in cremation 013:*0007*, which was clearly derived from the fuel from the cremation pyre (predominantly oak), the precise origin of the charcoal is inconclusive, although almost certainly representing debris from local hearths. There is little evidence to indicate the activities or events from which it might have resulted.

However, the evidence from the charcoal does suggest that the local environment during the later Neolithic and Early Bronze Age supported a diverse range of woodland trees and shrubs. It is probable that deciduous woodland flourished on the sheltered sides of the valley, probably with oak (*Quercus* sp.) as the major component, growing in association with ash (*Fraxinus excelsior*), hazel (*Corylus avellana*) and lime (*Tilia.* sp.). Willow (*Salix* sp.), poplar (*Populus* sp.) and alder (*Alnus glutinosa*) prefer seasonally rich damp/wet soils that would have been found on the valley floodplain to the north of the site. A number of shrubby or scrubby species were also named: hawthorn/ *Sorbus* group (Pomoideae), blackthorn (*Prunus spinosa*) and gorse/broom (*Ulex* sp./*Cytisus scoparius*), which, more typically, colonise open woodland or scrubland, and perhaps grew on the sandy soils of the river terraces or in clearings.

VI. Scientific analysis

Introduction

The presence of the cremation central to the FLN 013 ring-ditch confirmed its function as a funerary monument. However, interpreting the function of the earlier structure, post-hole circle 013:*0147* and its internal post-setting 013:*0148*, was not as straightforward. With a view to providing some insight regarding the original use of the monument, two surveys were carried out. The first, a soil-phosphate survey, was completed during the excavation phase of the project, with the second, a detailed examination of potential astronomical alignments preserved in the geometry of the post-hole circle, undertaken by Clive Ruggles as part of the analysis stage of the project, the latter summarised here with the full report available in the site archive.

In addition, four radiocarbon dating determinations were undertaken on samples of charcoal; one from a pit cut by ring-ditch the FLN 013 ring-ditch (013:*0004*), two from post-holes, one each from the post-hole circle (013:*0147*) and its internal structure (013:*0148*), and one from the cremation confined by the FLN 013 ring-ditch.

Soil-phosphate survey

by Stuart Boulter

Introduction

Although phosphates are present in all soils, the background level can be increased markedly by a number of anthropogenically derived means. Phosphates occur in a variety of organic materials (excreta, bone, meat, vegetable matter *etc.*) which are commonly associated with human activity.

The simplest form of phosphate analysis (spot-tests) was carried out on samples associated with post-hole circle 013:*0147* and structure 013:*0148*, as these tests could easily be carried out by in-house staff. The results would not define precisely what activity (if any) was carried out within the monument, but would pick up localised concentrations of phosphate and also identify more generally enhanced areas. While not definitive in their own right, it was hoped that the results would at least contribute towards the overall interpretation.

Methodology

Forty samples were taken at the intersections (where possible) of a 3m square grid (conforming to the national grid) covering the area enclosed by the post-hole circle. Seven control samples were taken at intervals across the wider site to ascertain the background phosphate level.

Results

Fig. 3.13

Phosphate levels of both the control samples and those from the post-hole circle exhibited considerable variation with thirteen assigned to the 'trace' category, twenty six as 'weak' and eight as 'positive' (Fig. 3.13). Of the eight positive samples, six were associated with the post-hole circle. The positive samples did not appear to represent a discrete area of higher phosphate level, although all were located within 1m of features making up the post-hole circle, particularly on its eastern side. There was certainly no apparent variation associated with the central post-setting. The most obvious inference to be made from these results is that the interior of the post-hole circle was not the location for any concentrated activity that would have resulted in a general area of phosphate enhancement. This appears to rule out its use as a livestock enclosure or as a repeatedly used funerary enclosure where human remains were laid out for any length of time. However, the analytical method applied does have its drawbacks and was only used in an attempt to identify major trends rather than more minor, localised variations representing more ephemeral activity.

Astronomical potential of the post-hole circle

by Clive Ruggles

General background

An amateur astronomer (Patrick Taylor) saw a plan of the FLN 013 post-hole circle soon after its excavation had been completed and was immediately struck by its geometry. In a subsequent paper (Taylor 1997) he suggested that the monument may have functioned as a 'lunar observatory', echoing a similar claim made for a number of British stone circles (in most cases more correctly termed 'rings') by the engineer Alexander Thom in the 1970s (Thom 1971). In order to test this specific theory and to examine the astronomical potential of the monument a detailed survey was undertaken.

Following advances in interpretative archaeology over the last two decades, any assessment of the function and use of a monument such as this needs to take account of the perceived relationships and associations that might have helped to endow it with cosmological meaning and significance (*e.g.* Bradley 1998). Relevant evidence might include, for example, architectural features reflecting in microcosm the features of the surrounding landscape such as prominent peaks, water sources, or caves (Bradley 2000a); alignments upon celestial objects such as the sun and moon (Ruggles 1999); or spatial patterning in formal deposition (*e.g.* Pollard and Ruggles 2001). It follows that

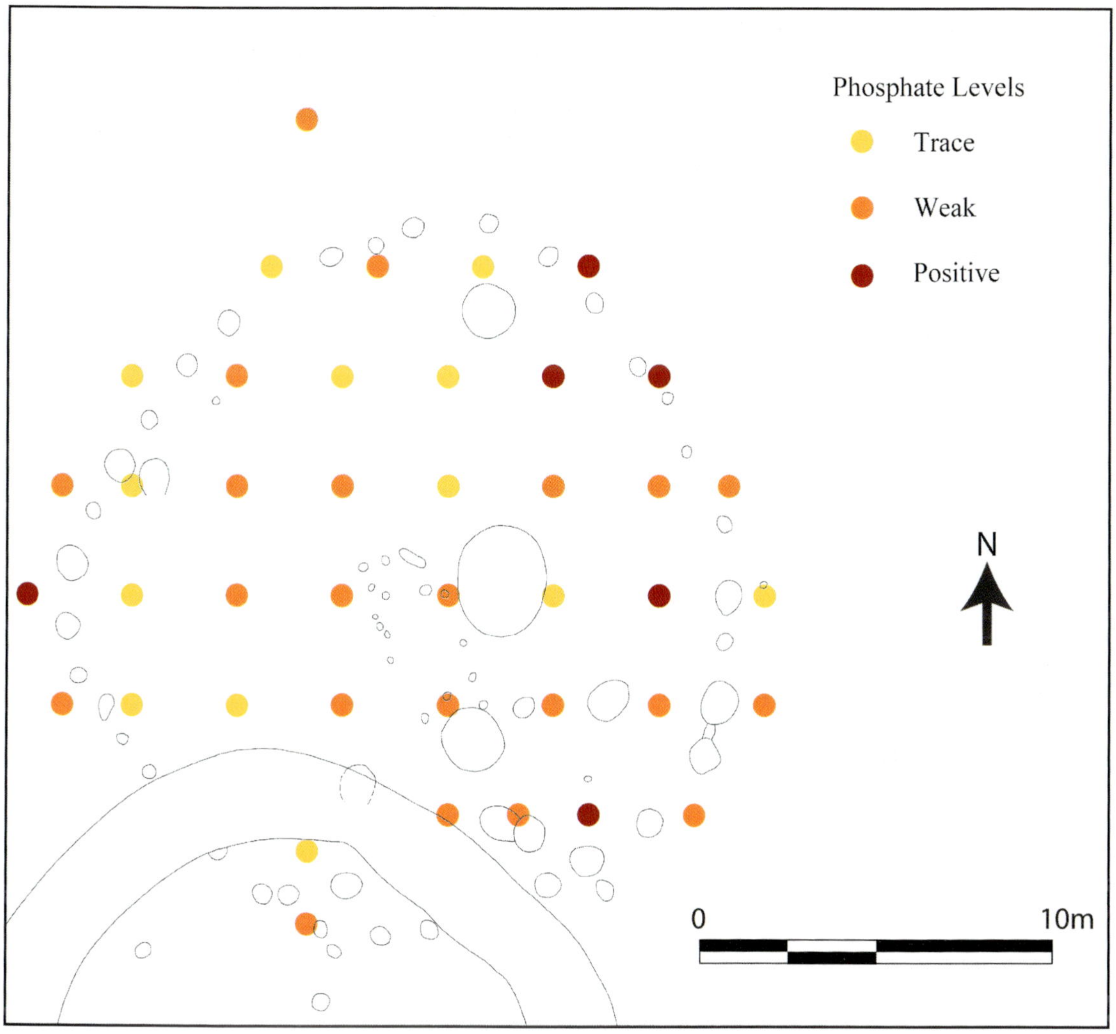

Figure 3.13 FLN 013: soil phosphate survey

the interpretation of Neolithic ritual monuments should include at least some consideration of how they relate to the sky and to the movements of the principal astronomical bodies.

Systematic studies of large groups of similar monuments can reveal consistent patterns of orientation related to the sun or moon (Ruggles 1999, chs. 5 and 6). Interpretations of single monuments remain problematic, because of the possibility of fortuitous astronomical alignments, and generally only succeed where there is a strong contextual argument. An example is the passage tomb at Balnuaran of Clava, where Bradley (2000b) has convincingly argued that structural integrity was compromised in order to make an astronomical alignment (upon the setting midwinter sun) effective. In Wessex, we have a halfway situation where four closely related and broadly contemporary Late Neolithic monuments were all aligned on the rising or setting position of the sun at the solstices, although not in a consistent manner. The significance of this last example to the current study is that two of the four monuments in question were built in timber rather than stone: the timber rings at Woodhenge and Durrington Walls Southern Circle (Parker Pearson *et al.* 2007; Ruggles 2007).

Patrick Taylor's claims that the Flixton site constitutes a lunar 'observatory' are based upon two observations (Taylor 1997):

(i) there is a clear axis of symmetry, and this axis of symmetry is aligned in the north-westerly direction upon the most northerly setting position of the moon;

(ii) there is a horizon 'notch' in this direction that could have provided a distant foresight.

Such ideas clearly reflect the influence of Thom, and the term 'observatory' is perhaps unfortunate given the symbolic/cosmological interpretation that would now be applied to astronomical alignments of Neolithic monuments where they exist. Nonetheless, as is clear from the background just set out, it is far from absurd to suggest that the Flixton timber circle might have been deliberately aligned upon a significant rising or setting position of the sun or moon.

In order to determine the astronomical potential of the site in general, and to assess Patrick Taylor's theory in particular, it was necessary to check both the basic data concerning potential astronomical alignments and the likelihood that any astronomical alignments identified were actually intended by the builders (since such alignments can arise fortuitously, through factors quite unrelated to astronomy).

The main stages in this process were as follows:

(i) identify the principal orientation and any other directions of potential significance from the Flixton ring using the excavation plans and determine their azimuths;

(ii) determine the azimuth, altitude and declination of potential horizon points in and around each of these directions;

(iii) generate a profile of the horizon in and around each direction of potential significance and identify any prominent horizon features;

(iv) assess the potential significance of the astronomical possibilities in each direction.

Summary of results

The existence of what appears to be a primary axis (axis of symmetry) running NW–SE provides two directions of possible significance, and the 'secondary axis' perpendicular to this provides another two. The astronomical data regarding these four directions can be summarised as follows:

There are no prominent features in the natural topography that could have acted as potential horizon foresights in any of the four directions. While the possibility can never be discounted that there once existed artificial, or more transient natural, foresights, there is no actual evidence of any permanent point of reference on any of the horizons that could have provided a visual point of reference enabling the rising or setting point of the sun or moon to be determined to within, say, one or two solar or lunar diameters (0.5–1°). In other words, there are no demonstrable astronomical associations of high precision.

The ring was oriented along an axis of symmetry running on an azimuth of approximately 140.5°/320.5° and in the north-westerly direction appears to have faced the most northerly setting position of the moon. The alignment in the opposite direction appears not to have had any astronomical significance, falling roughly midway between the rising points of the midwinter sun and the most southerly moon.

The secondary axis, perpendicular to the primary one, is oriented to the north-east about 2° to the right of the position of sunrise at midsummer, and to the south-west about 3° to the right of the position of sunset at midwinter.

The direction of orientation of the central post-hole structure, assuming it to have been broadly rectangular in form, and the direction of the putative entrance from the centre of the ring, yield an azimuth of approximately 161°. Neither this nor the opposite direction (azimuth 341°) has any significance in relation to the sun or moon.

If the Flixton timber circle were one of a known local group of similar monuments, then it would be possible to compare the orientations of each monument in the group and undertake a statistical analysis in order to assess the likely intentionality and significance of the astronomical alignments found. This not being possible, we are left with the following interpretative possibilities.

Weighing together all these factors, the four main interpretative possibilities can be summarised as follows:

(i) The lunar alignment of the principal axis was deliberate and significant.

(ii) The solstitial alignment (in both directions) of the secondary axis was deliberate and significant.

(iii) Both the lunar alignment of the principal axis and the approximate solstitial alignment of the secondary axis were deliberate and significant.

(iv) None of the observed solar and lunar alignments at Flixton was deliberate and significant.

In view of the unique nature of this site there are no firm grounds, at least on the basis of the evidence currently available, for strongly favouring any one of these options to the complete exclusion of the others.

Conclusion

Earlier claims that the Flixton timber ring might have functioned as a 'lunar observatory' cannot be substantiated. However, the fact that the ring was not a true circle does mean that there existed a clear axis of symmetry. The direction of this axis suggests that the monument may well have been deliberately oriented, in common with a number of British stone rings, with respect to the moon. If so, then the event in question might well have been the setting of the midwinter full moon, which would have occurred this far north along the horizon only in approximately every nineteenth year.

There is also a possibility that the monument had a broader association with the solar solstices expressed through its approximate orientation with regard to the four solar solstitial rising and setting positions, and particularly those to the north-east and south-west, in directions approximately perpendicular to the principal axis.

These astronomical associations make sense when interpreted as one aspect of the symbolism that helped to endow this monument with cosmological meaning and significance.

Radiocarbon dating determinations

by Stuart Boulter

Bulk soil-samples were taken from a range of contexts, primarily for the recovery of material for palaeo-environmental analysis. However, the presence of moderate quantities of charcoal within the majority of the samples lead to their examination by Rowena Gale with a view to isolating material suitable for radiocarbon dating, essentially short-lived species.

Samples were selected with the aim of dating both of the FLN 013 monuments and one of the pits, the latter with Grooved Ware in its fill and clearly cut by the later ring-ditch. Four samples were selected as being suitable for dating. Two of these, both from discrete concentrations of charcoal; the first from cremation 013:*0007* and the second from pit 013:*0066*, were sent to the Scottish Universities Research and Reactor Centre. The remaining two samples, sent to the Radiocarbon Dating Laboratory at the University of Waikato, were fragments of more dispersed material from contexts relating to post-hole circle 013:*0147* (the fills of post-holes 013:*0161* and *0186* respectively). It was recognised that submitting the dispersed fragmentary charcoal from the two post-holes was risky as this material may not have been in its primary context of deposition. However, there were no discrete concentrations of charcoal in any of the post-holes that would have represented a better proposition. During the analysis and publication phase of this project, the detailed information regarding the available samples was revisited with the aim of identifying others which could reliably, on taphonomic grounds, be subjected to radiocarbon dating. However, Derek Hamilton (the Assistant Scientific Dating Co-ordinator at English Heritage) was very concerned about the presence of modern contaminants identified by the project Palaeoenvironmentalist (Val

Laboratory	Lab. No.	Context	Sample type	Genus/Species	Date BP	Date cal BC (95%)
University of Waikato	5428	Post-hole 013:*0161*, fill 013:*0162*	Charcoal	Pomoideae	4477±81	3365–2922
University of Waikato	5427	Post-hole 013:*0186*, fill 013:*0187*	Charcoal	*Corylus* sp.	2455±68	767–406
SUERC	AA-22184	Cremation 013:*0007*, spit 013:*0008*	Charcoal	*Fraxinus* sp.	3410±55	1890–1530
SUERC	AA-22185	Pit fill 013:*0066*, fill 013:*0075*	Charcoal	Pomoideae	3980±45	2620–2340

Table 3.10 FLN 013: Radiocarbon determinations (calibrated using OxCal v3.10)

Fryer) and concluded that none of the retained samples were suitable.

The following results were calculated using the calibration curve of Reimer *et al.* (2004) and the computer program OxCal (v3.10) (Bronk Ramsey 1995; 1998; 2001). The calibrated date ranges (at 95% confidence) were calculated using the maximum intercept method (Stuiver and Reimer 1986).

The results from the samples sent to Waikato confirmed that at least one of the samples had included charcoal that did not relate directly to the feature from which it was recovered, contradicting both the stratigraphic and artefactual evidence. The dates obtained are shown in Table 3.10.

Given that the features forming the post-hole circle were contemporary, clearly forming part of the same structure, then the dates obtained should be consistent. While it could be argued that only one of the dates may have been obtained from intrusive or residual material, other evidence suggests that both are suspect. The sample from post-hole 013:*0186* gave a date in the Iron Age which, based on the fact that post-hole circle was cut by the Early Bronze Age ring-ditch, cannot be a fair reflection on the date of the feature. The date from post-hole 013:*0161* is more difficult to dismiss, with the calibrated date range placing it towards the end of the earlier Neolithic or early in the later Neolithic. If correct, this date extends the currency of the Flixton monument and its associated activity by a few hundred years. However, while it has been suggested that the finds evidence recorded in the post-holes relates to the redundancy of the monument, rather than its period of use, there is a lack of diagnostic material that would indicate a significantly earlier date for its construction and confirm the 013:*0161* radiocarbon determination. In addition, for this early date to be correct, the monument would have been constructed somewhat prior to the dates presently given for currency of timber circles which almost all fall between 2800 BC and 1000 BC (Gibson 1998, 47). While this does not preclude the possibility that there are earlier examples, on balance, it seems more likely that the currency of the Flixton monument was firmly in the later Neolithic and broadly contemporaneous with the adjacent pits.

Dating determinations (Table 3.10) obtained from the other two samples, both carried out by Scottish Universities Research and Reactor Centre, were found to be more consistent with the overall body of evidence.

These results confirmed that the cremation (013:*0007*), and by association its surrounding ring-ditch 013:*0004*, belonged to Period I.e. and was Early Bronze Age in date, while Grooved Ware pit 013:*0066* was approximately seven or eight hundred years earlier, attributable to Period I.d., and of Late Neolithic date.

Unfortunately, while pit 013:*0066* was located within post-hole circle 013:*0147* its chronological relationship with the surrounding monument was not directly ascertained, primarily due to the perceived failure of the radiocarbon dating on the two samples from the post-holes. However, the presence of similar Grooved Ware pottery in the fills of post-holes from the circle and both being cut by the later ring-ditch suggests that they were at least broadly contemporary.

VII. Overview of the prehistoric archaeology

The Period I (prehistoric) phases of archaeology were represented by two major monumental structures within the FLN 013 area, a post-hole circle and ring-ditch, with a second ring-ditch within FLN 008, only subjected to limited investigation, and another in FLN 062, the details of which will appear in a subsequent publication. Other features were limited to a few pits, the majority in FLN 013, with more isolated examples in FLN 053. It remains unclear, however, how many of the undated features actually belong in Period I.

For most of the features, the dating evidence was limited to the broad period framework provided by the ceramic finds and, to a lesser extent, the worked flint. However, two of the four radiocarbon dating determinations undertaken did provide at least some definition to the chronological range covered by the prehistoric activity on the site.

While limited to a low concentration of charred plant macrofossils and wood charcoal, the palaeoenvironmental evidence was able to show that the site lay within close proximity to a number of different habitats. Deciduous woodland appears to have dominated, probably on the well-drained terrace gravels and heavier clay soils to the south. However, recent micromorphological analysis of the palaeosol preserved beneath a Early Neolithic long barrow, excavated by SCC in 2006 in the FLN 069 quarry area 500m to the north-east, suggests that at least localised deforestation of the terrace gravels had occurred prior to its construction (French 2008). Also present were species suited to seasonally wet conditions, that would have occurred on the flood plain of the River Waveney to the north, and others indicative of open scrubby woodland.

The younger of the two FLN 013 monuments, the ring-ditch and its central unurned cremation deposit, was dated by a radiocarbon determination to the first half of the second millennium BC, which places it firmly in the Early Bronze Age (Flixton chronology Period I.e.). The evidence suggests that the ring-ditch feature formed part of a funerary monument. Originally, the ditch is likely to have enclosed a circular mound covering the single cremation burial and would have been constructed, at least partially, from the upcast spoil from the ditch. This monument forms part of a dispersed group of similar features occupying the river terrace gravels on both sides of the Waveney Valley. A number of examples have been excavated at Flixton, including the limited trenching at FLN 008 to the north and that in FLN 062, both detailed in this publication.

While the function of the FLN 013 ring-ditch is not in doubt, it is its spatial, stratigraphic and chronological relationships with the earlier post-hole circle that may have some significance. Both monuments lie on a low east-facing ridge overlooking a shallow south-west to north-east orientated depression/valley running parallel with the main Waveney Valley to the north (Chapter 16). It is entirely possible that this prominent position was the defining influence for the location of both monuments. It is also possible that one, or both, were originally positioned in relation to the Early Neolithic Long Barrow located some 500m to the north-east (FLN 069). This feature lay in the bottom of, and was aligned with, the shallow valley/depression and, when projected, its long-axis passes directly through the post-hole circle (Chapter 16). If this were the case, the presence of the earlier post-hole circle may have been unknown to the excavators of the ring-ditch and their juxtaposition no more than a coincidence resulting from other associations within the overall landscape. However, other factors may also have been involved. The ring-ditch clearly encroaches onto the groundplan of the earlier monument and vestiges of this feature could have survived in the landscape, or at least a memory of it remaining with the ancestors of those who built the original structure, prompting a re-use of the site. What is clear is that, unlike some other sites, for example, the barrow at Deeping St Nicholas (French 1991) and the Late Neolithic and Early Bronze Age palisaded ritual monument at Street House Farm, Loftus, Cleveland (Vyner 1988), there was no chronologically extended development of the initial structure by the addition of further phases that alter, but also respect and maintain the continuity of the original geometry of the monument. A discussion regarding the wider context of these features is included in Chapter 16.

The dating and interpretation of the earlier post-hole monument and pits was somewhat more problematic. While some of the pits were relatively isolated within the site, most were recorded close to or actually within the confines of the post-hole circle. A radiocarbon determination obtained from a charcoal sample from a pit that was internal to, but had no direct stratigraphic relationship with the post-hole circle itself, provided a date in the middle of the third millennium BC, firmly in Period I.d. (Late Neolithic) of the Flixton chronology. It cannot be stated with certainty that the pitting occurred contemporaneously with the activity associated with the post-hole circle, but it does seem reasonable to suggest that at least some were excavated while the monument was in use. The Flixton radiocarbon date falls well within the accepted currency of other timber circles (*c.*2800–1000 BC) provided by more directly associated radiocarbon dates (Gibson 1998, 47). This scenario is also consistent with the artefactual evidence although the chronological framework provided by the ceramic and worked flint finds lacks definition.

The post-hole circle exhibited certain characteristics shared with other field monuments of similar date, no two of which were ever absolutely identical. The general monument tradition includes stone circles, henges and post-settings, many of which were composite and include elements of all three. Using timber uprights may in part be the result of the lack of suitably sized stones available in the local area, although monuments such as the Durrington 68 timber circle in Wiltshire contradict this as a general assumption (Pollard 1995). Unfortunately, as the acidic well-drained soils of Flixton are not conducive to the preservation organic materials, including animal and human bone, with timber being used as the principal construction material, the surviving evidence was limited to the more durable finds and a groundplan. The original monument may have been far more complex than the surviving groundplan suggests (Gibson 1998, 77). While taking this into account, the Flixton monument is smaller and simpler in its design than many contemporary structures. While the character of the above-ground structure can only be a matter of conjecture, even to the point where, although remaining the most likely scenario, there is actually little evidence proving that the post-holes were once occupied by posts. Evidence from broadly contemporary structures suggest that in some instances the intervening gaps between individual posts were blocked with panels of wood or wattle and daub, with the intention of restricting access and views of the interior (Gibson 1998, 87–8). Given that some of the post-holes in the Flixton circle were relatively small, it seems reasonable to assume that they would have formed part of an integrated structure, helping to support panelling or other above ground elements, rather than simply a socket for a post which, in itself, would not have represented a particularly imposing feature. At the very least, one can envisage the presence of lintel-like components between the adjacent uprights similar to the outer circle of Stonehenge, a scenario also proposed in a reconstruction for the timber circle at Sarn-y-bryn-caled (Gibson 1998, figs 83, 94 and 95). Whether the diameter and depth of the post-holes directly relates to the size of the timber it once held is also open to conjecture, as is the effect of the variable intervals between the post-holes. Even if we assume some truncation of the original depth of the features, they are not large by monumental standards and an above ground height of more than 2m for the posts is unlikely for even those set in the larger post-holes. If the size/height of the post-hole were related directly to that of its associated post, then the monument may have exhibited an irregular profile, with a zone of larger/taller posts to the south-east, smaller/shorter posts on the north-east and south-west sides, and the remainder relatively uniform.

The diverse character of field monuments means that there is no absolute parallel for the Flixton structure. However, a mention should be made here of the later (Early Bronze Age) timber structure excavated at Holme-next-the-Sea on the north Norfolk coast, some 84km to the north-west of Flixton (Brennand and Taylor 2003). While not contemporary and very different in structural detail, 'Sea Henge', as it became known, does share certain similarities to the Flixton monument and may represent a later form within a varied, but related tradition. Firstly, neither structure is actually circular, both exhibiting a long axis of symmetry on an approximately north-west to south-east alignment. In each case, the presence of a long axis, with a secondary alignment at approximately 90 degrees, has been viewed as evidence that the monuments had been invested with meaningful celestial orientations. For 'Sea Henge' it was suggested that the principal alignment reflected the position of the midsummer rising sun, to the north-east, and midwinter setting sun, to the south-west (Chamberlain 2003, 66). At Flixton, a link to the four solar solstitial rising and setting positions was explored along with its relationship with the moon. It was also suggested that 'Sea Henge' had been constructed in four sections relating to the two axial alignments; these would have been marked and their posts the first to be inserted (Brennand and Taylor 2003, 65). The quadripartite partitioning of space within monuments (Darvill 1997) has also been explored in relation to the Flixton circle (Ruggles above). Given the geometrical uniformity of the structure, it is likely that, similarly to 'Sea Henge', it was constructed around the long axis and the possible secondary alignment, regardless of whether they were related to celestial phenomena, and it is these that would have been established as the first stage during the initial laying out process.

Due primarily to the limitations of the surviving evidence, the function of the circle and its associated structure remains uncertain, even after detailed study. Results of the soil phosphate analysis appear to rule out a simple domestic function as a stock enclosure, as there were no generally enhanced phosphate levels that would have been present throughout the interior if it had been used in that way. However, the results do not rule out activities that would leave only more locally enhanced areas such as excarnation, with the central structure representing a platform on which bodies were laid out. With very little evidence with which to make an interpretation, other than its possible use as an excarnation platform, the function of the internal post-hole structure also remains somewhat of an enigma. While it was clearly aligned on the probable entrance, it was dismissed by Ruggles as part of a sighting mechanism as it does not fit any of the potential astronomical alignments and the soil phosphate results suggest that it was not likely to have been associated with animal husbandry.

The apparent preferential deposition of artefacts within post-holes on the north-west side of the circle, flanking the entrance, may also be significant and similar occurrences have been recorded with other monumental structures (Gibson 1998, 81–3). Anderson has suggested that the apparent concentration of heat-altered flints found in the post-holes of the monument and in features in its immediate vicinity may be the result of associated cooking and feasting activities. In addition, at least one of the post-holes contained a large sherd of pottery placed towards the top of the fill that could not have been present with a post *in situ*. Percival has suggested that as this was potentially one of the later date sherds recovered from the structure, it may represent a closure deposit placed in the post-hole when the monument had become redundant or was being dismantled.

Considerable resources were invested in analysing the astronomical potential of the circle with regard to deliberate alignments that had been invested in its structure either as part of its function or purely for symbolic purposes. The results of Clive Ruggles' work assessed the earlier assertions made by amateur astronomer Patrick Taylor that the circle functioned as a lunar observatory (Taylor 1997). While not conclusive, analysis did identify a definite axis of symmetry within the monument which may have been aligned with regard to the moon. In addition, he recognises the possibility that a secondary alignment perpendicular to the axis of symmetry may reflect broader associations with the four solar solstitial rising and setting positions. While accepting that the evidence is limited, the astronomical alignment of the circle does remain an attractive interpretation and similar functions and symbolism have been proven beyond reasonable doubt for other similar and broadly contemporary field monuments. However, as Alex Gibson states '...proving sites could have been used in this way does not prove that they were' (Gibson 1998, 77). Another possibility is that the astronomical alignments were deliberate, but only symbolic, and have no bearing on the actual function of the monument. In reality the monument may have been the focus for a number of activities at different times, possibly on a seasonal basis. Some of these could have been ritualistic/sacred and associated with the astronomical alignments that seem to have been invested in the structure, while others more mundane, possibly simply as a recognised meeting point in the landscape, although access to its interior may still have been restricted to a selected elite. The position of the structure within its wider landscape context is discussed more fully in Chapter 16.

The Period I.d. (Late Neolithic) pits were not associated with any surviving structures or deposits positively indicative of domestic activity, although the artefacts recovered from their fills could have derived from domestic contexts. Given the currency of Grooved Ware, the number of features was small and could have been generated within a relatively short period of time during a concentrated period of activity or, alternatively, they could equally represent more extended ephemeral activity or episodic site visits, possibly on a seasonal basis. It should also be stated, however, that adjacent areas of the quarry, particularly those to the south of FLN 013 and FLN 053, have also included Period I.d. (Late Neolithic) pits with both isolated features and some loose concentrations/ clusters, although again no contemporary associated structures were recognised. The morphology of the pits, their artefactual content and spatial associations (isolated, clustered and paired) were consistent with features described by Garrow from a number of sites in East Anglia, indeed he included preliminary information from Flixton in his publication (Garrow 2006). The pits at Flixton included examples falling into all of the categories identified by Garrow in his Chapter 6 and those spatially closely associated with the post-hole circle were not obviously different in any way. Garrow's interpretation relies heavily on what he calls 'pre-pit' contexts, possibly midden deposits, which became the source of the bulk of the material subsequently placed in the pit. This was classed as 'general deposition' and is differentiated from 'selective deposition', where artefacts were deliberately selected for inclusion, but not placed in any particular way and 'arranged deposition' where artefacts were formally arranged or stacked in the feature. Examples of 'general deposition' and 'selective deposition' have been recognised at Flixton while the presence of 'arranged deposition' is open to discussion, but the writer argues that the juxtaposition of some of the finds within discrete fills does fulfil the criteria stated by Garrow (2006, 113–5). Regardless of any deliberate selective element involved in the process of deposition, or the possible association with a monument that may have performed a 'specialised' function, the material within the Flixton pit fills was domestic in character, or at least indistinguishable from material generated solely by domestic activity.

In summary, much weight is now given to the identification of 'specialised deposits' generated by 'non-domestic' or 'ritual' activity in prehistoric contexts, although the latter term could be considered to be overused, often simply to define enigmatic features that did not have a more obvious function. However, for the later Neolithic phase at Flixton, the separation of activities as being either 'sacred' or 'profane' is not straightforward. The distinction between the two, as we know them, would, to the later Neolithic community, not only have been blurred, but sometimes non-existent and artificially imposing these differences can actually detract from a meaningful interpretation. While the astronomic properties of the timber circle may be real, the structure almost certainly functioned in conjunction with more mundane everyday activities, probably associated with a low level of seasonal occupation in the vicinity of the site. The activity appeared to include the deliberate deposition of midden material and selected artefacts in pits which could be interpreted as part of the ritualistic closing of the site after each period of occupation, however brief that may have been. They may also have seen the burial of this material as taking it out of its normal everyday existence and turning it over to the unseen 'other world', that occupied by their ancestors or the other spiritual entities thought to be governing the ordered progression of the seasons and various natural phenomena which affected the everyday life of the community.

Chapter 4. Late Iron Age/Early Roman

by Stuart Boulter

I. Introduction

Fig. 4.1

Features attributed to Period II.a. were all located within the FLN 053 site, although significant deposits of this date have also been identified elsewhere in the quarry, particularly in the wider area of FLN 062 to the south, but are not covered in this publication. Generally, the features were concentrated towards the south-eastern corner of the FLN 053 area, although a small group lay to the south (Fig. 4.1). While a total of 116 discrete features were recorded, eighty-eight of these formed part of a composite structure, post-hole circle 053:*0346*. Of the remaining features, twenty-six were pits, one was a ditch and one was a curving slot.

II. The features

Palisaded circle 053:*0346*

Figs 4.2–4.4; Pl. 4.1

The overall structure comprised a total of eighty-eight discrete slots and post-holes, although this by no means represented the number of posts in the circle, as the morphology of many of the slots indicated that they represented multiple post-settings (Figs 4.2–4.4 and Pl. 4.1).

The term 'palisaded circle' has been used to describe the monument due to the limited separation between the posts that would have made up the structure, as indicated by the relatively close proximity of the individual post-settings. The structure described a perfect circle with a diameter of *c.*27m and evidence suggesting that a minimum of 113 post-settings had been present. There were five interruptions to the circuit which could have

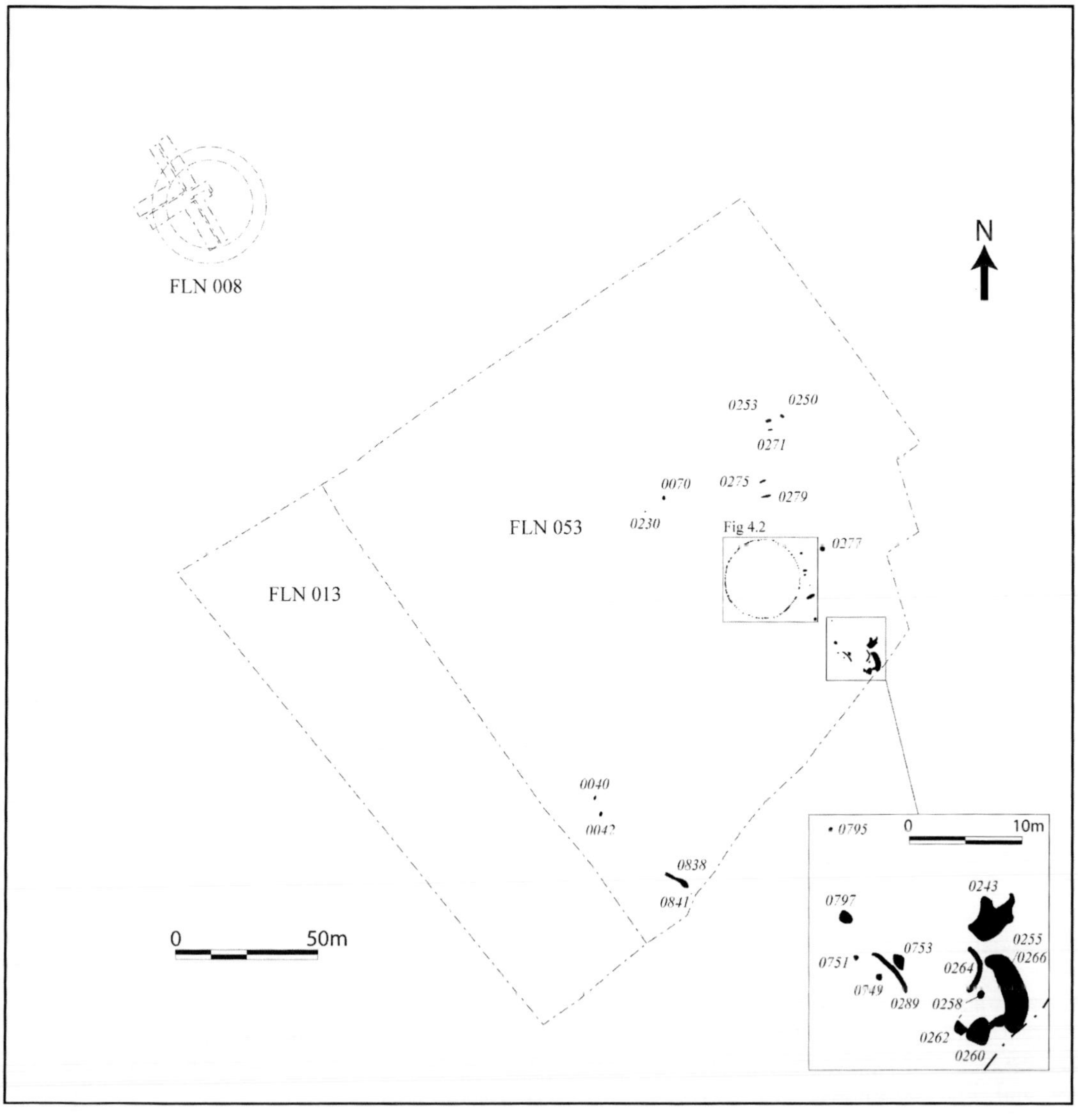

Figure 4.1 Period II.a., Late Iron Age/Early Roman features (Areas FLN 008, 013, 053 and 062)

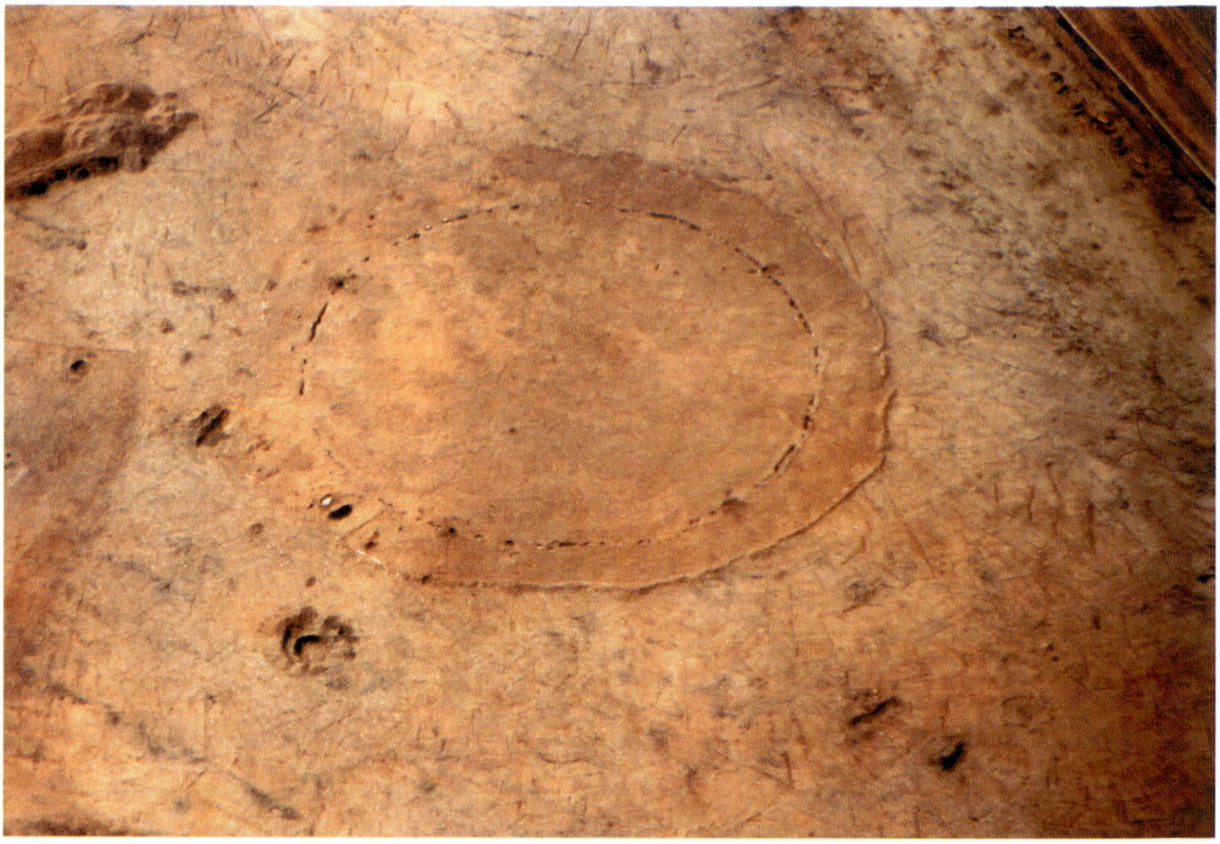

Plate 4.1 FLN 053: palisaded circle. North is at the bottom of the photograph

afforded access to the interior; one to the SSW (defined by post-holes 053:*0429*, *0443* and *0445*), one to the south (between post-holes 053:*0471* and *0473*), one to the ESE (between slot 053:*0491* and post-hole 053:*0493*), one to the east (between post-holes 053:*0515* and *0517*) and one to the north (between post-holes 053:*0563* and *0565*) (Fig. 4.2). Of the five possible entrances, that to the ESE was the widest, measuring 2.7m, while that to the SSW was defined by three adjacent post-holes with intervals of 1.8m and 2m between the adjacent features. The entrance to the east was formed by two post-holes (053:*0515* and *0517*) set slightly at odds with the otherwise uniform features forming the circle and was flanked externally by pits 053:*0281* and 053:*0593*, the former including significant artefactual evidence, principally ceramics, in its fill.

Details of the post-holes and slots are presented in Table 4.1 with sections as Figures 4.3 and part of 4.4. Diameters of the individual post-holes varied between 0.2m and 0.5m with a similar variation in the widths of the slots. Depths varied between only 0.04m and 0.33m. However, these cannot be seen as a genuine reflection of the original excavated depth of these features due to truncation of their upper levels, initially by ploughing and subsequently during the unsupervised, pre-excavation soil-strip. Fills comprised homogenous light-mid brown silty sand throughout with no post-ghosts visible.

Ceramic dating evidence was limited to twenty-one small, generally abraded sherds of pottery recovered from seven different features; slots 053:*0330* and 053:*0334* on the north-west side of the structure, slot 053:*0481* to the south-east and four post-holes, 053:*0541*, 053:*0545*, 053:*0547* and 053:*0563* to the north-east (Table 4.1). Other artefactual evidence was limited to three pieces of fired clay, two in post-hole 053:*0379* and one in slot 053:*0342* and single struck flints in post-holes 053:*0379*, 053:*0555* and 053:*0561* and another in slot 053:*0491* (Table 4.1).

Manual cleaning within the area enclosed by the post-hole circle revealed three small, undated features (Fig. 4.2) all described as post-holes based on their size rather than any direct evidence of their function. Post-hole 053:*0525* was close to the north-eastern edge of the circle, 053:*0620* was more central, but still in the north-eastern quarter, while 053:*0632* was within the south-east quarter of the circle. There was no evidence that positively associated these features with the surrounding circle and their juxtaposition may have been coincidental.

Pits

Fig. 4.5

A total of twenty-seven pits were attributed to Period II.a. with a wide range of sizes and morphologies. These are detailed in Table 4.2 with sections as part of Figure 4.4 and all of 4.5. Isolated examples were recorded, although the majority of these features formed a loose linear concentration arcing from a point approximately 45m to the north of the 'palisaded circle' through to a small cluster immediately east of the monument and then continuing to the southern edge of the site some 40m to the south (Fig. 4.1).

While the function of the pits was unclear, a number of them merit more detailed description primarily due to a combination of unusual characteristics in their morphologies and their included artefacts. Generally, the overall ceramic assemblage from the pits included a significant

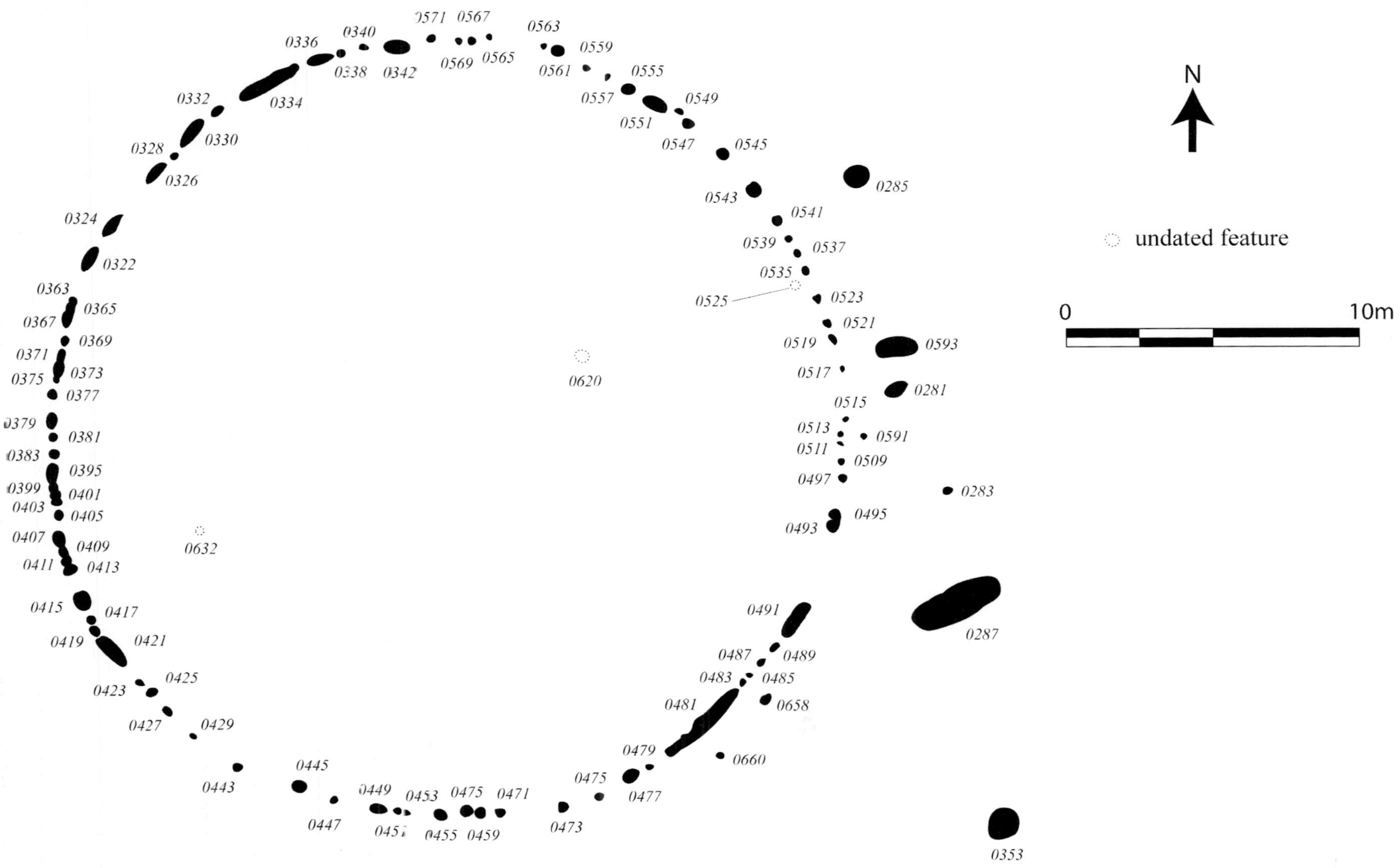

Figure 4.2 FLN 053: detail of palisaded circle *0346*

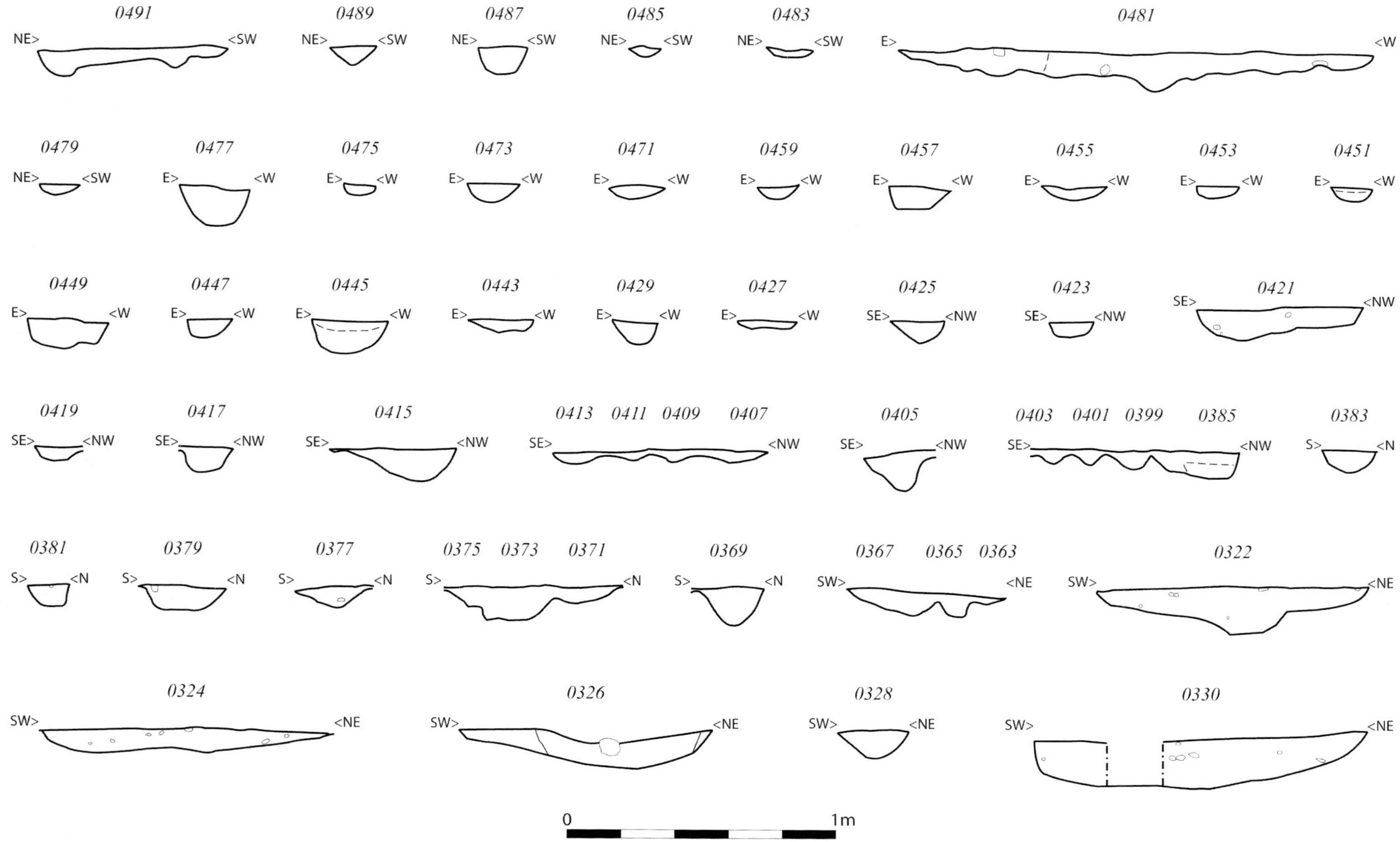

Figure 4.3 FLN 053: palisaded circle *0346*, section drawings

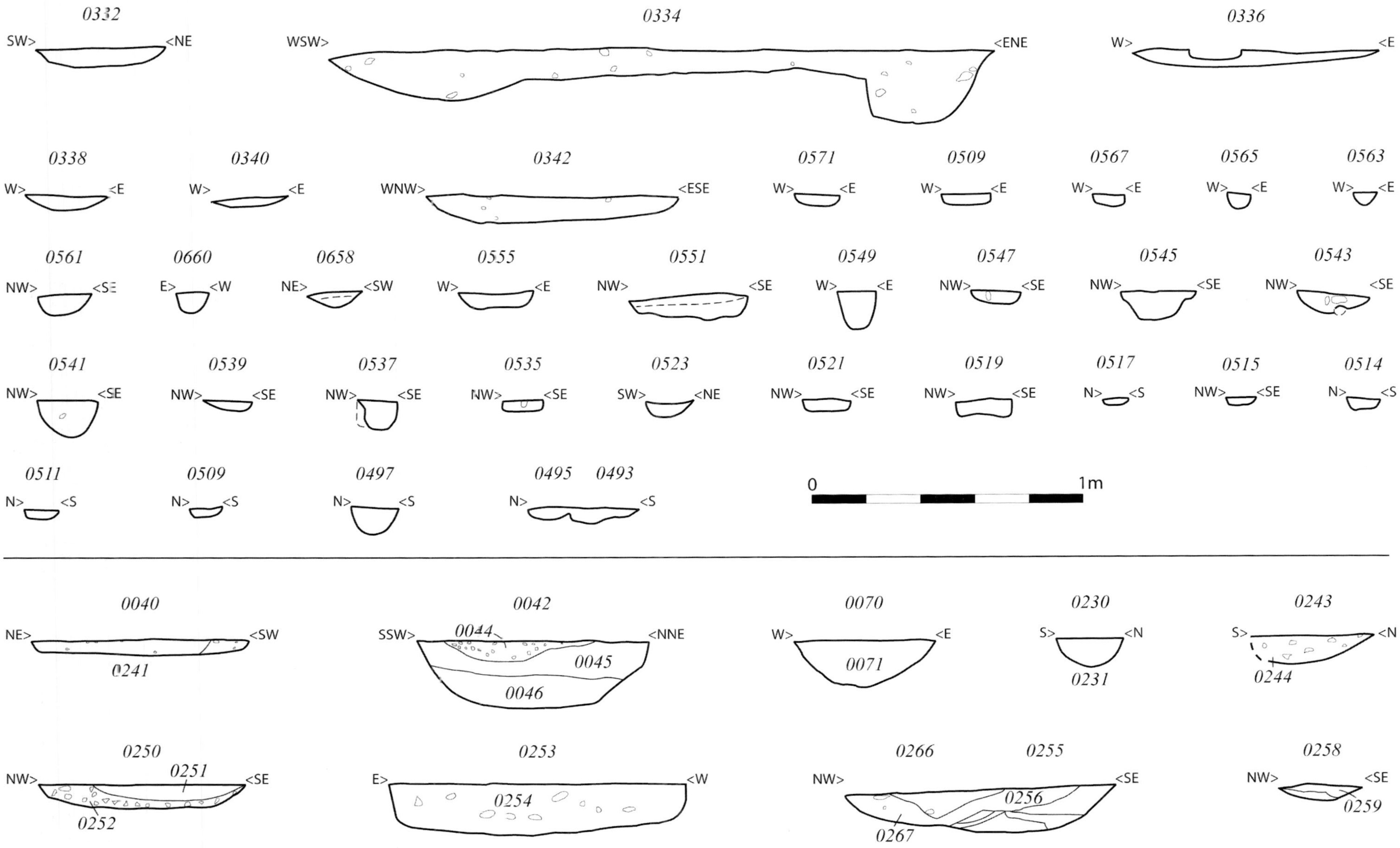

Figure 4.4 FLN 053: palisaced circle *0346* and other Late Iron Age/Early Roman features, section drawings

Context	*Dimensions (m)*	*Max depth (m)*	*Description*	*Pottery*	*Other finds*
0322	1.00 x 0.38	0.18	Slot. One central post-setting, shallower either side. Base slopes up from post-setting to moderately inclined edges. Fill 053:*0323* comprised homogenous brown silty sand with occasional stone/gravel inclusions.		
0324	1.06 x 0.36	0.10	Slot. No obvious post-settings. Flattish base, moderately sloping edge at SW end, shallow slope to NE. Fill 053:*0325* comprised homogenous brown silty sand with occasional stone/gravel inclusions.		
0326	0.90 x 0.35	0.12	Slot. No obvious post-settings. Dished base along long axis, moderately sloping edges. Fill 053:*0327* comprised homogenous brown silty sand with lighter outer component. Includes occasional stone/gravel inclusions.		
0328	0.26	0.10	Post-hole. Circular, moderately sloping sides with rounded base. Fill 053:*0329* comprised homogenous brown silty sand with occasional stone/gravel inclusions.		
0330	1.22 x 0.37	0.20	Slot. No obvious post-settings. Slightly dished base along long axis with steeply sloping edge at SW end, gentler slope at NE end grading into base. Fill 053:*0331* comprised homogenous brown silty sand with occasional stone/gravel inclusions.	2 abraded sherds (7g)	
0332	0.46 x 0.3	0.08	Post-hole. Oval shaped, flat base, moderately sloping sides. Fill 053:*0333* comprised homogenous brown silty sand with occasional stone/gravel inclusions.		
0334	2.44 x 0.46	0.28	Slot. Post-setting at each end, flat-bottom between settings with depth of 0.1 metres. Gently sloping edge at SW end grading into round-bottomed post-setting, steep sided at NE end with flat-bottomed post-setting. Fill 053:*0335* comprised homogenous brown silty sand with occasional stone/gravel inclusions.	7 abraded sherds (25g)	
0336	0.90 x 0.35	0.06	Slot. No obvious post-settings. Gently dished base along long axis continuing as shallow sloping sides. Fill 053:*0337* comprised homogenous brown silty sand with occasional stone/gravel inclusions.		
0338	0.30	0.05	Post-hole. Circular with rounded base. Fill 053:*0339* comprised homogenous brown silty sand with occasional stone/gravel inclusions.		
0340	0.28	0.04	Post-hole. Circular with rounded base. Fill 053:*0341* comprised homogenous brown silty sand with occasional stone/gravel inclusions.		
0342	0.92 x 0.45	0.10	Slot. Kidney shaped, no obvious post-settings. Moderately sloping ends and flat base. Fill 053:*0343* comprised homogenous brown silty sand with occasional stone/gravel inclusions.		1 frag fired clay (2g)
0363 *0365* *0367*	0.32 0.33 0.61 x 0.34	0.10 0.20 0.20	Slot. Three-lobed, each numbered separately. 053:*0363* and 053:*0367* had rounded bases continuing as gently sloping sides while 053:*0365* had steep sides and a flattish base. Fills 053:*0364*, 053:*0366* and 053:*0368* were indistinguishable, forming one continuous component comprising homogenous brown silty sand with occasional stone/gravel inclusions.		
0369	0.32 x 0.48	0.30	Post-hole. Oval-shaped, rounded base with moderately steep sides. Fill 053:*0370* comprised homogenous brown silty sand with occasional stone/gravel inclusions.		
0371 *0373* *0375*	0.45 x 0.30 0.50 x 0.38 0.20	0.10 0.25 0.18	Slot. Three-lobed, each numbered separately. 053:*0371* to N has a moderately sloping side continuing as a rounded base, 053:*0373* has steep sides and a flat base, while 053:*0375* has a flat base and moderately sloping S end. Fills 053:*0372*, 053:*0374* and 053:*0376* were indistinguishable, forming one continuous component comprising homogenous brown silty sand with occasional stone/gravel inclusions.		
0377	0.50	0.18	Post-hole. Circular with gently sloping sides and rounded base.		
0379	0.64 x 0.40	0.20	Post-hole. Oval-shaped. Moderately sloping edge at N end, steeper to south with a flat bottom. Fill 053:*0380* comprising homogenous brown silty sand with occasional stone/gravel inclusions.		2 abr. frags fired clay (2g); 1 flint flake
0381	0.30	0.18	Post-hole. Circular, steepish sides with angled base. Fill 053:*0382* comprised homogenous brown silty sand with occasional stone/gravel inclusions.		
0383	0.40	0.18	Post-hole. Circular, rounded profile. Fill 053:*0384* comprised homogenous brown silty sand with occasional stone/gravel inclusions.		

0385 *0399* *0401* *0403*	0.6 x 0.47 0.30 0.25 0.25	0.20 0.10 0.10 0.10	Slot. Four-lobed, each numbered separately. 053:*0385* to N had moderately steep sides and a flattish base, 053:*0399*, 053:*0401*, 053:*0403* all had rounded profiles. Fills 053:*0386*, 053:*0400*, 053:*0402* and 053:*0404* were essentially indistinguishable, forming one continuous component comprising homogenous brown silty sand with occasional stone/gravel inclusions. One small area of very dark brown silty sand was recorded in the base of the 053:*0385* setting.
0405	0.45	0.30	Post-hole. Circular, section shows feature adjoining 053:*0403* to N, but isolated on plan. Steep northern edge, moderately steep to the south with a rounded bottom. Fill 053:*0406* comprised homogenous brown silty sand with occasional stone/gravel inclusions.
0407 *0409* *0411* *0413*	0.62 x 0.50 0.36 0.33 0.42	0.10 0.10 0.10 0.10	Slot. Four-lobed, each numbered separately. All had gently sloping edges continuing into rounded bottoms. Fills 053:*0408*, 053:*0410*, 053:*0412* and 053:*0414* were essentially indistinguishable, forming one continuous component comprising homogenous brown silty sand with occasional stone/gravel inclusions.
0415	0.80	0.24	Post-hole. Sub-circular, rounded profile. Fill 053:*0416* comprised homogenous brown silty sand with occasional stone/gravel inclusions.
0417	0.36	0.18	Post-hole. Circular, section shows feature adjoining 053:*0419* to S, but isolated on plan. Fill 053:*0418* comprised homogenous brown silty sand with occasional stone/gravel inclusions.
0419	0.30	0.10	Post-hole. Circular, section shows feature adjoining 053:*0417* to N, but isolated on plan. Fill 053:*0420* comprised homogenous brown silty sand with occasional stone/gravel inclusions.
0421	1.20 x 0.51	0.24	Slot. Two (possibly three) post-settings. Moderately steep edges at ends, flat base at NW end, undulates and deepens to SE. Fill 053:*0422* comprised homogenous brown silty sand with occasional stone/gravel inclusions.
0423	0.30	0.10	Post-hole. Circular, steep sided with a flat bottom. Fill 053:*0424* comprised homogenous brown silty sand with occasional stone/gravel inclusions.
0425	0.40	0.15	Post-hole. Sub-circular, moderately steep sided with a rounded bottom. Fill 053:*0426* comprised homogenous brown silty sand with occasional stone/gravel inclusions.
0427	0.45	0.06	Post-hole. Oval, gently sloping sides with a flat bottom. Fill 053:*0428* comprised homogenous brown silty sand with occasional stone/gravel inclusions.
0429	0.34	0.15	Post-hole. Oval, moderately steep sided with a flat bottom. Fill 053:*0430* comprised homogenous brown silty sand with occasional stone/gravel inclusions.
0443	0.50	0.10	Post-hole. Sub-circular, gently sloping sides, flattish base. Fill 053:*0444* comprised homogenous brown silty sand with occasional stone/gravel inclusions.
0445	0.58	0.26	Post-hole. Sub-circular, with a rounded profile. Fill 053:*0446* comprised grey and brown silty, grvelly sand.
0447	0.34	0.14	Post-hole. Sub-circular, rounded profile. Fill 053:*0448* comprised homogenous brown silty sand with occasional stone/gravel inclusions.
0449	0.40 x 0.60	0.24	Post-hole. Oval, relatively steeply sided with undulating bottom (possibly two post-settings). Fill 053:*0450* comprised homogenous brown silty sand with occasional stone/gravel inclusions.
0451	0.30	0.12	Post-hole. Sub-circular, rounded profile. Fill 053:*0452* comprised homogenous brown silty sand with occasional stone/gravel inclusions.
0453	0.30	0.10	Post-hole. Sub-circular, rounded profile. Fill 053:*0454* comprised homogenous brown silty sand with occasional stone/gravel inclusions.
0455	0.50	0.10	Post-hole. Sub-circular, rounded profile.
0457	0.45	0.16	Post-hole. Sub-circular, angled profile with a flat base, steep-sided to the E, moderately sloping edge to the W. Fill 053:*0458* comprised homogenous brown silty sand with occasional stone/gravel inclusions.
0459	0.30	0.10	Post-hole. Sub-circular, rounded profile. Fill 053:*0460* comprised homogenous brown silty sand with occasional stone/gravel inclusions.
0471	0.40	0.10	Post-hole. Sub-circular, rounded profile. Fill 053:*0472* comprised homogenous brown silty sand with occasional stone/gravel inclusions.
0473	0.40	0.12	Post-hole. Sub-circular, rounded profile. Fill 053:*0474* comprised homogenous brown silty sand with occasional stone/gravel inclusions.

0475	0.22	0.08	Post-hole. Sub-circular, steep sides, flattish bottom. Fill 053:*0476* comprised homogenous brown silty sand with occasional stone/gravel inclusions.		
0477	0.52 x 0.44	0.30	Post-hole. Oval-shaped, steep sides, flat bottom. Fill 053:*0478* comprised homogenous brown silty sand with occasional stone/gravel inclusions.		
0479	0.30	0.08	Post-hole. Sub-circular, rounded profile. Fill 053:*0480* comprised homogenous brown silty sand with occasional stone/gravel inclusions.		
0481	3.50 x 0.60	0.30	Slot. Irregular-shaped, central deeper post-setting with undulating base either side. Fill 053:*0482* comprised homogenous brown silty sand with occasional stone/gravel inclusions.	2 abraded sherds (6g)	
0483	0.30	0.08	Post-hole. Sub-circular, gently sloping sides, flat bottom. Fill 053:*0484* comprised homogenous brown silty sand with occasional stone/gravel inclusions.		
0485	0.32	0.10	Post-hole. Circular, rounded profile. Fill 053:*0486* comprised homogenous brown silty sand with occasional stone/gravel inclusions.		
0487	0.38	0.20	Post-hole. Sub-circular, steep-sided, gently rounded base. Fill 053:*0487* comprised homogenous brown silty sand with occasional stone/gravel inclusions.		
0489	0.32	0.15	Post-hole. Sub-circular, moderately sloping sides, angled base. Fill 053:*0490* comprised homogenous brown silty sand with occasional stone/gravel inclusions.		
0491	1.40 x 0.47	0.20	Slot. Two post-settings; one at NE end of trench, the other near the SW end, gently sloping bottom between settings. Fill 053:*0492* comprised homogenous brown silty sand with occasional stone/gravel inclusions.		1 flint flake
0493 *0495*	0.50 0.40	0.10 0.08	Post-holes. Double, two lobed post-setting, both sub-circular. 053:*0493* had an undulating base while 053:*0495* exhibited a rounded profile. Fills 053:*0494* and 053:*0496* were indistinguishable, comprising homogenous brown silty sand with occasional stone/gravel inclusions.		
0497	0.34	0.20	Post-hole. Sub-circular, rounded profile. Fill 053:*0498* comprised homogenous brown silty sand with occasional stone/gravel inclusions.		
0509	0.24	0.08	Post-hole. Circular, moderately steep sides with a flat bottom. Fill 053:*0510* comprised homogenous brown silty sand with occasional stone/gravel inclusions.		
0511	0.25	0.08	Post-hole. Sub-circular, moderately steep sides with a flat bottom. Fill 053:*0512* comprised homogenous brown silty sand with occasional stone/gravel inclusions.		
0513	0.24	0.08	Post-hole. Sub-circular, moderately steep sides with a flat bottom. Fill 053:*0514* comprised homogenous brown silty sand with occasional stone/gravel inclusions.		
0515	0.22	0.06	Post-hole. Sub-circular, moderately steep sides with a flat bottom. Fill 053:*0516* comprised homogenous brown silty sand with occasional stone/gravel inclusions.		
0517	0.20	0.06	Post-hole. Sub-circular, rounded profile. Fill 053:*0518* comprised homogenous brown silty sand with occasional stone/gravel inclusions.		
0519	0.40 x 0.27	0.10	Post-hole. Oval-shaped, steep-sided with undulating base. Fill 053:*0520* comprised homogenous brown silty sand with occasional stone/gravel inclusions.		
0521	0.36	0.10	Post-hole. Sub-circular, steep-sided with a flat base. Fill 053:*0522* comprised homogenous brown silty sand with occasional stone/gravel inclusions.		
0523	0.34	0.12	Post-hole. Sub-circular, rounded base. Fill 053:*0524* comprised homogenous brown silty sand with occasional stone/gravel inclusions.		
0535	0.32	0.10	Post-hole. Circular, Steep-sided with a flat bottom. Fill 053:*0536* comprised homogenous brown silty sand with occasional stone/gravel inclusions.		
0537	0.30	0.20	Post-hole. Circular, rounded profile. Fill 053:*0538* comprised homogenous dark brown silty sand with occasional stone/gravel inclusions.		
0539	0.36	0.08	Post-hole. Sub-circular, rounded profile. Fill 053:*0540* comprised homogenous light brown silty sand with occasional stone/gravel inclusions.		
0541	0.44	0.33	Post-hole. Sub-circular, rounded profile. Fill 053:*0542* comprised homogenous dark brown silty sand with occasional stone/gravel inclusions.	3 abraded sherds (10g)	

0543	0.54	0.16	Post-hole. Sub-circular, rounded profile. Fill 053:*0544* comprised homogenous brown silty sand with occasional stone/gravel inclusions.		
0545	0.52	0.20	Post-hole. Sub-circular, rounded base, with a step/lip around upper edge. Fill 053:*0546* comprised homogenous dark brown silty sand with occasional stone/gravel inclusions.	3 abraded sherds (24g)	
0547	0.38	0.10	Post-hole. Sub-circular, rounded profile. Fill 053:*0548* comprised homogenous dark brown silty sand with occasional stone/gravel inclusions.	3 abraded sherds (20g)	
0549	0.38 x 0.25	0.30	Post-hole. Oval-shaped, steep-sided, rounded base. Fill 053:*0552* comprised homogenous dark brown silty sand with occasional stone/gravel inclusions.		
0551	0.90 x 0.48	0.20	Post-hole. Two-lobed, oval-shaped, moderately steep edges, undulating base. Fill 053:*0552* comprised homogenous dark brown silty sand with occasional stone/gravel inclusions.		
0555	0.54 x 0.38	0.12	Post-hole. Oval-shaped, moderately sloping sides, flat base. Fill 053:*0556* comprised homogenous dark brown silty sand with occasional stone/gravel inclusions.		1 flint flake
0557	0.34	0.16	Post-hole. Sub-circular, steep-sided to SE, gently sloping to NW with a rounded base. Post-hole. Oval-shaped, steep-sided, rounded base. Fill 053:*0558* comprised homogenous dark brown silty sand with occasional stone/gravel inclusions.		
0559	0.24	0.06	Post-hole. Sub-circular, rounded profile. Fill 053:*0560* comprised homogenous dark brown silty sand with occasional stone/gravel inclusions.		
0561	0.40	0.16	Post-hole. Sub-circular, moderately steep sides, rounded base. Fill 053:*0562* comprised homogenous dark brown silty sand with occasional stone/gravel inclusions.		1 flint blade
0563	0.18	0.10	Post-hole. Sub-circular, rounded profile. Fill 053:*0564* comprised homogenous dark brown silty sand with occasional stone/gravel inclusions.	1 abraded sherd (1g)	
0565	0.16	0.11	Post-hole. Sub-circular, steep-sided with a flattish base. Fill 053:*0566* comprised homogenous dark brown silty sand with occasional stone/gravel inclusions.		
0567	0.24	0.08	Post-hole. Sub-circular, steep-sided with a flattish base. Fill 053:*0568* comprised homogenous dark brown silty sand with occasional stone/gravel inclusions.		
0569	0.38	0.08	Post-hole. Sub-circular, steep-sided with a flat base. Fill 053:*0570* comprised homogenous dark brown silty sand with occasional stone/gravel inclusions.		
0571	0.34	0.08	Post-hole. Sub-circular, moderately steep-sided with a flattish base. Fill 053:*0572* comprised homogenous dark brown silty sand with occasional stone/gravel inclusions.		

Table 4.1 FLN 053: palisaded circle *0346*, details of post-holes and slots

quantity of near-complete vessels along with material which could be described as domestic-type waste.

The juxtaposition between some of the features with the larger and more unusual artefact assemblages and the palisaded circle may also be of significance. Three pits, 053:*0277*, 053:*0353* and 053:*0593*, located 10m north-east, 10m to the south-east and 2m to the east of the 'palisaded circle' respectively, included complete artefacts in their fill which may be indicative of deliberate deposition rather than general disposal of rubbish. Pit 053:*0277* included a complete fired clay triangular loomweight (053:*0117*) and a clay sling-shot (053:*0118*) within an assemblage which otherwise resembled domestic rubbish, while pit 053:*0353* included an iron tool (053:*1187*). Pit 053:*0593* again included a range of material that could be interpreted as domestic waste, but also a complete miniature ceramic vessel (053:*0610*) and the broken sherds from another substantially complete vessel. In addition, large, lightly heat-altered, flint cobbles within the fill of the pit, although not unusual in the local geology, were certainly not apparent in the immediately adjacent sediments and their inclusion must be considered to be deliberate rather than coincidental.

Five of the pits could be described as trough-like. Four of these (053:*0253*, *0271*, *0275* and *0279*) appeared to be arranged in parallel pairs, all aligned approximately east to west, and separated by distances of 2.4m (053:*0253* and *0271*) and 4.5m (053:*0275* and *0279*). While it was unclear whether this juxtaposition of similar features was significant, comparable evidence was subsequently recorded in FLN 062 approximately 300m to the south (Boulter 2006b). Also, perhaps significantly, the two main contexts containing metalworking slag were pits 053:*0253* and 053:*0279*.

Another group of features (053:*0243*, *0255*, *0260*, *0262* and *0266*), which from their similar characteristics and spatial association were probably related, formed the southern end of the linear concentration. These were generally irregular in shape with ill-defined edges and indiscernible relationships with adjacent features. The function of these pits was unclear, but Period II.a. slot 053:*0289* lies immediately to the west and the undated slot 053:*0264* both of which may be structural, could be considered to be associated with this group of features. While the fills predominantly appeared as mid to dark brown silty sands, they almost certainly represented the

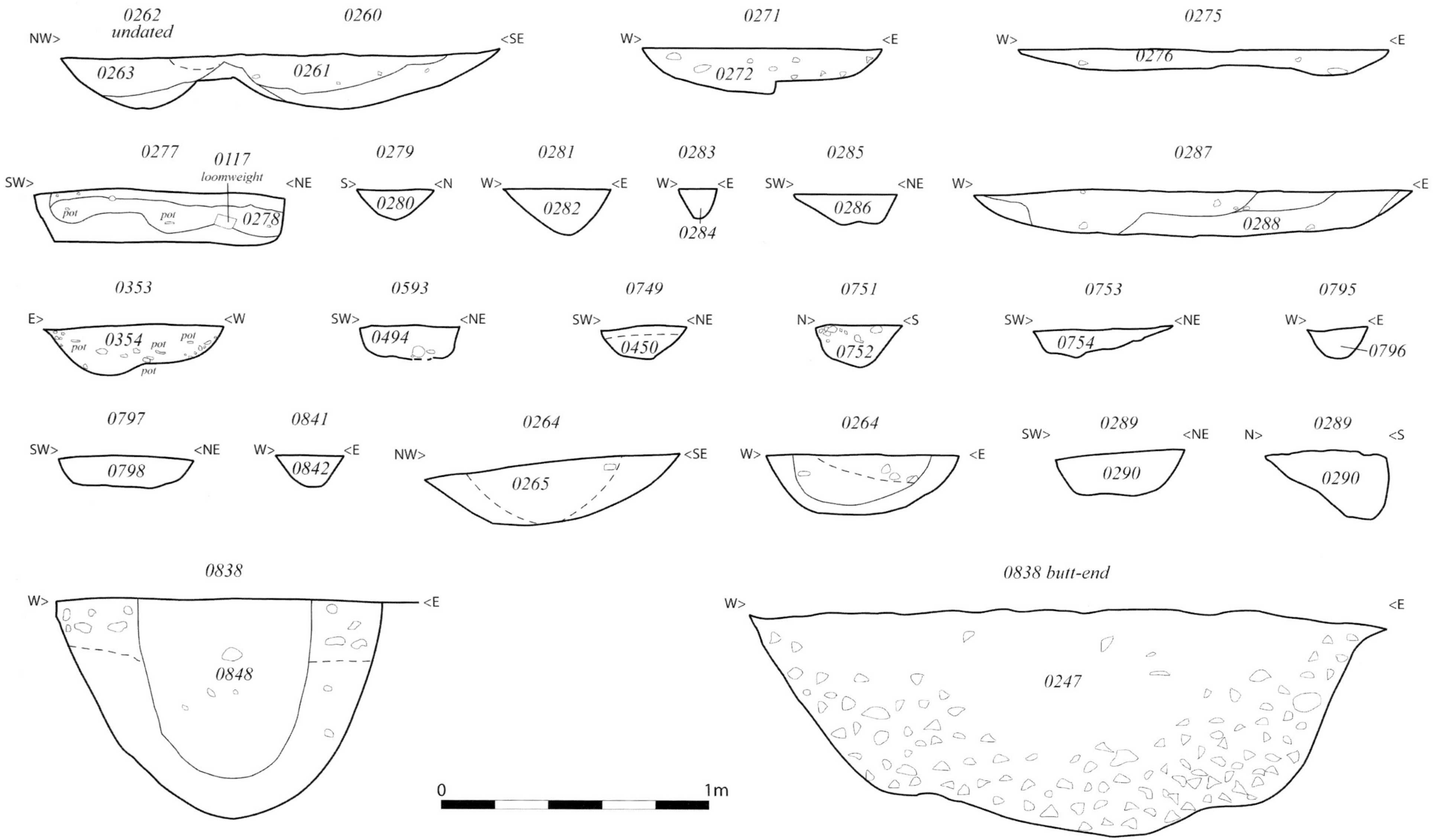

Figure 4.5 FLN 053: Late Iron Age/Early Roman features, section drawings

Context	*Dimensions (m)*	*Depth (m)*	*Description*	*Pottery*	*Fired clay*	*CBM*	*Small finds*	*Metalworking waste*	*Animal bone*	*Worked flint*	*Heat-altered flint*
0040	1.6 x 0.8	0.12	Shallow oval shaped, steep-sided with a flat bottom. Fill 053:*0041* comprised dark brown sand with occasional stones, lighter towards southern end.	7 sherds (49g)	2 pieces (17g), possible loomweight		053:*0103* fragment of Hertfordshire Puddingstone quern (1200g)				3 pieces (40g)
0042	1.7 x 1.13	0.5	Oval shaped, moderately sloping sides with a flat bottom. Stratified fill comprising upper component of sand/gravel (053:*0044*) over mid brown silty sand (053:*0045*) over dark brown silty sand (053:*0046*). Excavated together as 053:*0043* on south-east side.	205 sherds (2695g)	125 pieces (784g), possible loomweight		053:*0102*, iron nail		4 pieces (4g)		20 pieces (1273g)
0070	1.4 x 1.04	0.34	Oval shaped with a rounded profile. Fill 053:*0071* comprised homogenous brown silty sand with occasional stones.	2 sherds (22g)	7 pieces (22g)					1 piece	2 pieces (112g)
0230	0.5	0.2	Circular, rounded profile. Fill 053:*0231* comprising homogenous brown silty sand with charcoal flecks.		2 pieces (139g), possible loomweight or bar			1 piece (1g)			2 pieces (10g)
0243	3.2 x 5.0	0.2	Irregular shaped, gently sloping sides, flattish base. Fill 053:*0244* comprised homogenous brown silty, stony sand.	3 sherds (23g)	1 pieces (3g)					2 pieces	
0250	1.5 x 1.12	0.2	Sub-rectangular with rounded corners. Moderately sloping sides with a flat base. Upper fill (053:*0251*) comprising homogenous dark brown silty sand with charcoal with an outer fill (053:*0252*) of orange/brown sand and gravel.	11 sherds (85g)	3 pieces (14g), possible loomweight				3 pieces (4g)	1 piece	2 pieces (92g)
0253	2.2 x 1.06	0.4	Sub-rectangular 'trough-like' with well-rounded corners. Steep-sided with a flattish base. Relatively homogenous fill (053:*0254*) comprising dark brown silty, sand with inclusions of stones/gravel and charcoal flecks. Darker towards top.	52 sherds (628g)	13 pieces (91g), includes possible loomweight and daub		053:*0116*, part of a iron strap, 053:*0121*, part of a loop-headed spike, 053:*0254b*, part of a blade tool and 053:*0254*, 2 iron nails	30 pieces (959g), includes smithing hearth bottom	18 pieces (19g)	1 piece	3 pieces (121g)
0255	7.0 x 1.6	0.36	Irregular shaped, somewhat ill-defined with a rounded profile. Stratified fill (053:*0256* and *0257*) comprised light to mid brown silty sand with varying concentrations of stones/gravel inclusions. Disturbed by animal burrows etc.	31 sherds (295g)			053:*0123*, iron nail			2 pieces, includes sf 053:*0113*, a notched flake	
0258	0.6	0.12	Circular, originally described as a hearth due to presence of heat altered flints in fill, but lack of *in-situ* heat alteration of underlying sediments contradicts this interpretation. Fill 053:*0259* comprised an upper component of brown stony sand and a lower component of orange/brown gravel/sand.	10 sherds (38g)							9 pieces (90g)

0260	2.26 x 2.0	0.4	Irregular, possibly associated with 053:*0266*. Rounded profile. Fill 053:*0261* comprising mid-dark brown homogenous silty sand with occasional stones.	1 sherd (2g)	2 pieces (44g)					
0266	0.6 x ?	0.26	Irregular, possibly associated with 053:*0255*. Rounded profile. Fill 053:*0267* comprising homogenous brown silty sand.		7 pieces (38g), includes sf 053:*0110* and *0111*, the latter with needle-point dots					
0271	1.8 x 0.6	0.36	Sub-rectangular 'trough-like' with rounded corners. Gently sloping sides with a stepped base. Fill 053:*0272* comprised homogenous brown silty sand.	30 sherds (387g)	1 piece (44g), possibly a prop				1 piece	
0275	2.8 x 0.63	0.2	Trough-like with rounded ends. Gently sloping sides and an undulating base. Fill 053:*0276* comprised homogenous brown silty sand with occasional stones.	19 sherds (154g)	6 pieces (175g)				2 pieces, includes an unusual knobbed scraper tool	
0277	1.84	0.4	Circular. Steep, near vertical sides with a flat bottom. Stratified fill (collectively 053:*0278*) comprising a dark central layer between upper and lower components of homogenous brown silty sand.	36 sherds (66kg)	169 pieces (4301g), includes sf 053:*0117*, a near-complete loomweight , Fig. 4.7.1, 053:*0118*, a sling bullet, Fig.4.7.3 and a kiln bar fragment, Fig 4.7.5			95 pieces (252g)		2 pieces (63g)
0279	3.7 x 0.85	0.22	Trough-like, tapering towards the west. Moderately sloping sides and rounded base. Fill 053:*0280* comprised homogenous grey/brown silty sand.	4 sherds (103g)	6 pieces (108g), includes loomweight and vitrified hearth lining		1 piece (288g), smithing hearth bottom		1 piece	
0281	0.80 x 0.55	0.36	Oval shaped, moderately steeply sloping sides with a rounded base. Fill 053:*0282* comprised homogenous brown silty sand.	13 sherds (206g)	6 pieces (174g), includes square section bar, possible kiln furniture, Fig. 4.7.4	1 piece (10g)				
0283	0.3	0.22	Circular. Steeply sloping sides with a rounded bottom. Fill 053:*0284* comprised homogenous brown silty sand with charcoal flecks.	1 sherd (7g)						
0285	0.76	0.24	Circular. Variable sloping sides, uneven base. Fill 053:*0286* comprised homogenous light brown silty sand.	5 sherds (23g)	1 piece (60g)					
0287	3.2 x 1.2	0.34	Sub-rectangular 'trough-like' with well-rounded corners. Gently sloping sides grade into a flat bottom. Patchy fill (collectively 053:*0288*) comprising light orange/brown sand through to dark brown sand with occasional stone/gravel inclusions.	80 sherds (1616g)	3 pieces (10g)				2 pieces	2 pieces (94g)

0353	1.3	0.4	Circular. Moderately steeply sloping sides, stepped rounded base. Fill 053:*0354* comprised relatively homogenous brown silty sand with charcoal, darker at base.	154 sherds (1616g)	1 piece (83g), possibly kiln bar or weight, Fig. 4.7.6		053:*1187*, an iron tool, Fig. 4.8 and 053:*1425*, a piece of vessel glass	3 pieces (1g)	2 pieces	1 piece (13g)
0593	1.5 x 0.72	0.54	Sub-rectangular with well-rounded ends. Steep sides rounding to a flat base. Fill 053:*0594* comprise very dark brown/grey silty sand with some charcoal and large flint cobbles.	202 sherds (5150g). Includes intact vessel 053:*0610*	46 pieces (358g), includes possible crude vessel and a rim to an opening	1 piece (15g)		6 pieces (8g)	3 pieces	11 pieces (12235g)
0749	0.7 x 0.55		Oval. Rounded profile. Fill 053:*0750* comprises homogenous brown silty sand with occasional stones and charcoal flecks	2 sherds (5g)						
0751	0.48		Circular. Rounded profile. Fill 053:*0752* comprises homogenous dark brown silty sand with occasional stones.	1 sherd (7g)					1 piece	
0753	1.65 x 1.0		Irregular shape. Variable sloping sides, irregular base. Rounded profile. Fill 053:*0754* comprises homogenous dark brown silty sand with common stone/gravel inclusions.	5 sherds (5g)					1 piece	
0795	0.37	0.22	Sub-circular. Rounded profile. Fill 053:*0795* comprises homogenous orange/brown silty sand.	2 sherds (10g)						
0797	1.25 x 1.00	0.24	Irregular shape. Moderately sloping sides with a flat bottom. Fill 053:*0798* comprised homogenous dark grey/brown silty sand.	3 sherds (25g)					3 pieces, includes a scraper	
0841	0.55 x 0.41	0.24	Oval. Moderately sloping sides, rounded bottom. Fill 053:*0842* comprised homogenous orange/brown silty sand	3 sherds (6g)	3 pieces (4g)		Unidentified iron lump (5g)		3 pieces	

Table 4.2 FLN 053: details of the Period II.a., Late Iron Age/Early Roman pits

Fabric	*Code*	*No.*	*% No.*	*Wt (g)*	*% Wt*	*Eve*	*% Eve*
Hand-made sand tempered wares	HMS	103	9.3	1595	10.4	0.49	2.9
Hand-made sand/organic tempered wares	HMSO	84	7.6	1055	6.9	0.83	4.8
Total Later Iron Age hand-made coarsewares		*188*	*17.0*	*2661*	*17.3*	*1.32*	*7.7*
North Gaulish white fine ware	NGWF	6	0.5	23	0.1		
East Gaulish samian	SAEG	1	0.1	3	0.0		
South Gaulish samian	SASG	1	0.1	3	0.0		
Terra Nigra	TN	6	0.5	73	0.5	0.05	0.3
Terra Rubra	TR	1	0.1	27	0.2	0.19	1.1
Total imported finewares		*15*	*1.4*	*129*	*0.8*	*0.24*	*1.4*
Unspecified colour-coated wares	UCC	5	0.5	16	0.1	0.13	0.8
West Stow fine reduced wares	WSF	1	0.1	6	0.0		
Total local or regional finewares		*6*	*0.5*	*22*	*0.1*	*0.13*	*0.8*
Black-surfaced wares	BSW	446	40.3	6504	42.4	7.45	45.0
Miscellaneous buff wares	BUF	12	1.1	236	1.5		
Grey micaceous wares (black-surfaced)	GMB	180	16.2	1874	12.2	3.62	21.1
Grey micaceous wares (grey-surfaced)	GMG	1	0.1	22	0.1		
Grey micaceous wares (buff-oxidised)	GMO	5	0.5	54	0.4		
Grog-tempered wares (Belgic)	GROG	29	2.6	416	2.7	0.25	1.5
Miscellaneous sandy grey wares	GX	193	17.4	2801	18.2	4.04	23.6
Miscellaneous red fineware	RF	3	0.3	9	0.1		
Miscellaneous red coarse wares	RX	16	1.4	70	0.5		
Storage jar fabrics	STOR	14	1.3	553	3.6	0.10	0.6
Total local or regional coarsewares		*899*	*81.1*	*12539*	*81.7*	*15.46*	*90.1*
Total		**1108**	**100.0**	**15351**	**100.0**	**17.15**	**100.0**

Table 4.3 FLN 053: Late Iron Age and Roman pottery fabrics

original burial of topsoil-like material with a reasonable organic content (R. Macphail, pers. comm.).

Miscellaneous features

Fig. 4.5

Two other features were attributed to Period II.a.; a slot (053:*0289*) and a ditch (053:*0838*).

Slot 053:*0289* was located approximately 7m west of the irregular pit complex and undated slot 053:*0264* which was similar in character. The 4.7m long feature was 0.5m wide with a maximum depth of 0.2m and a round-sided flattish-bottomed profile. Orientated north-west to south-east, it described a very gentle curve with its concave side facing to the south-west. The included fill (053:*0290*) comprised homogenous brown silty sand. Similarly to the pit complex to the east, the ceramic finds were generally relatively abraded compared to those from the more northerly pits. While located within a cluster of small pit-like features, no formal arrangement was recognised and function of the slot is unclear, although a structural use cannot be ruled out.

Ditch 053:*0838* was orientated from south-east to north-west with a bulbous south-east facing butt-end, continuing for a distance of 10m to the north-west before becoming indistinct. Extensive manual cleaning in this area failed to locate it further to the west and no defined terminal was found. The bulbous butt-end had a maximum width of 2.4m while the rest of the feature was only 1.25m wide. A maximum depth of 0.9m was recorded with a fill (053:*0847* and *0848*) comprising predominantly dark brown silty sand with some stones/gravel inclusions and charcoal flecks. While the ceramic evidence suggested a similar date to the other Period II.a. features, the assemblage was distinctive and included all of the sites Gallo-Belgic platters, beakers and most of the flagons. The limited extent of this feature and its apparent isolation do not help in its interpretation and its function remains unclear. In addition, its orientation did not conform with elements of the broadly contemporary field ditch system recorded in adjacent areas of the quarry.

III. The artefacts

Late Iron Age and Roman pottery

by Cathy Tester

Introduction

All Late Iron Age and Roman pottery was recovered from FLN 053. A total of 1,108 sherds of pottery weighing 15.351kg, with an estimated vessel equivalent (eve) of 17.15 based on 84 measurable rims was collected from 42 contexts in 31 features or feature groups. The assemblage is dominated by local or regional coarsewares, mainly of Late Iron Age and early Roman date but a small amount is later. The quantities by fabric category are shown in Table 4.3 and a full catalogue by context forms part of the site archive.

Methodology

Late Iron Age (LIA) and Roman pottery was quantified using sherd count, weight and estimated vessel equivalent (eve). Each sherd family was given a separate entry in the database table and an individual spotdate when possible. Wheel-made (Late Iron Age) and Roman wares were classified using the type series devised for recording Roman pottery at Pakenham (unpublished) which is standard for recording Roman pottery in Suffolk but is supplemented by Hawkes and Hull's (1947) *Camulodunum* typology, Thompson's form series for Late Iron Age pottery (Thompson 1982) and the Chelmsford typology (Going 1987). Hand-made pottery was classified by major visible fabric inclusions. Fabrics were identified using a x10 binocular microscope.

The wares

Nineteen fabrics or fabric groups were identified. Two were hand-made and seventeen were wheel-made or wheel-finished. The hand-made wares were found in association with wheel-made and appeared to be contemporary in use and deposition.

Hand-made wares

A total of 188 hand-made sherds weighing 2661g, and with 1.32 eves based on nine measurable rims, were collected from twenty features. They are probably locally made and account for 17% of the total assemblage count and weight and nearly 8% of the eves. They were assigned to two broad fabric groups, both containing abundant quartz sand. General fabric descriptions are as follows:

HMS medium-coarse quartz sand; occasional larger sub angular quartz inclusions

HMSO medium-coarse quartz sand; occasional larger sub angular quartz inclusions and occasional organic

The two fabrics are very similar and the divisions are almost arbitrary, based only on the presence of visible organic material. Surface colours range from orange-brown to brown to dark brown and black and are sometimes 'patchy', but brown and dark brown–black are most common. The exterior surfaces are burnished or smoothed and decoration is rare. Only two pieces are decorated, one is scratched or scored and the other has incised lines.

Forms identified are simple curved jars with upright, slightly everted, rounded and pointed rims (Fig. 4.6.1 and 6) which were most common, as well as bowl/jars (Fig. 4.6.4 and 5, the latter of which is a Belgic form), a colander, a deep dish (Fig. 4.6.2) and a platter. Stylistically, the jars range in date between the mid to late Iron Age but there is no reason to assume that they are earlier than the early to mid 1st century AD wheel-made vessels with which they were associated.

Wheel-made wares

Seventeen wheel-made or hand-made and wheel-finished fabrics or fabric groups were identified which include imported finewares and local or regional wares.

Imported wares are rare. Of the fifteen sherds found, thirteen were from two Period II.a. features; ditch 053:*0838* and pit 053:*0040*. The remaining two sherds were residual in the Period V post-medieval quarry pit 053:*0805*.

The earliest imports are Gallo-Belgic finewares which belong to the first half of the 1st century AD. North Gaulish white fineware is represented by three vessels, a butt beaker (pit 053:*0040*) and two platters (ditch 053:*0838*). Terra Rubra is represented by a girth beaker *Cam* 84a (ditch 053:*0838*). Terra Nigra is represented by two vessels, both platters, (ditch 053:*0838*) a *Cam* 8 and an uncertain platter base with a partial central stamp reading '[...]^ O' or 'O V[...]' bordered, with two double incised circles, on its interior.

Two small sherds of samian, a South Gaulish Dr.15/17 platter, which is Nero-Flavian, and a non-diagnostic sherd of East Gaulish samian which is late 2nd to mid 3rd century were redeposited in the Period V, post-medieval quarry pit 053:*0805* (fill 053:*0806*).

Wheel-made local and regional wares, which make up the bulk of the pottery assemblage, are dominated by several broad coarseware groups from a variety of unknown but presumed local sources.

Black-surfaced wares (BSW) are the largest fabric group, consisting of all the non-micaceous black-surfaced wares and accounting for 40% of the sherds, 42% of the weight and almost half (45%) of the total eves. Early BSW is regarded as a transitional 'romanising' fabric and has its origins in the hand-made potting traditions of the Late Iron Age. It probably belongs to the early or mid 1st century if not earlier. Many of the vessels appear to be hand-made but wheel-finished, a feature which is most apparent on rim, shoulder and base sherds. A high proportion of the sherds contained fine black grog or burnt organic material which is a characteristic of early assemblages. The most common forms identified are jars including high-shouldered jars *Cam* 266 (Fig. 4.6.16), 'Braughing' jars *Cam* 260 (Fig. 4.6.11) and large storage jars *Cam* 270b (Fig. 4.6.15), cordoned and carinated jars *Cam* 218 (Fig. 4.6.7), a carinated bowl/jar (Fig. 4.6.3) and biconical jar type 5.1.2. Small bowls or cups were also identified including a Thompson type E1-4 carinated bowl (Fig. 4.6.9), concave-sided *Cam* 212 and other *Cam* 211–214 types. A copy of a *Cam* 14 platter and other uncertain platter forms were identified, as well as a *Cam* 252/253 type lid (Fig. 4.6.10).

Grey micaceous wares (GM) are another significant component of the coarseware assemblage and here they occur almost entirely in the black-surfaced variant (GMB) which accounts for 16% of the sherds, 12.5% of the weight and 21% of the assemblage Eves. GM wares have a fine-textured sandy fabric with abundant mica and few other inclusions and are very common in the northern part of Suffolk from the 1st century onwards. This fabric group emerges later than BSW and all of the material is wheel-made, dating from perhaps the second quarter of the 1st century and the Conquest but probably pre-Flavian. Kilns producing these fabrics are known at Flixton (FLN 062) and nearby Homersfield (SEY 002) and the range of forms identified here includes jars, bowls, beakers, cups and platters. There is a significant fineware element present that includes copies of Gallo-Belgic forms. Jars are high-shouldered 'Braughing' jars *Cam* 260, cordoned jars *Cam* 218 and other cordoned and carinated jars which could not be certainly identified. Globular beaker *Cam* 108, carinated beaker *Cam* 120, carinated bowls *Cam* 216, a larger sized *Cam* 214 type bowl (Fig. 4.6.8) and copies of Gallo-Belgic concave-sided cups or bowls *Cam* 211–214 types were also found, as well as a *Cam* 26a copy of Gallo-Belgic platter form *Cam* 12.

Other GM fabrics present were a single sherd of the grey-surfaced variant (GMG) and five sherds of GMO, a distinctive oxidised variant which is light brown to buff coloured. A single butt beaker sherd was identified amongst them.

A small amount (29 sherds, 416g, 0.25 eves) of Belgic grog-tempered wares belonging to the first half of the 1st

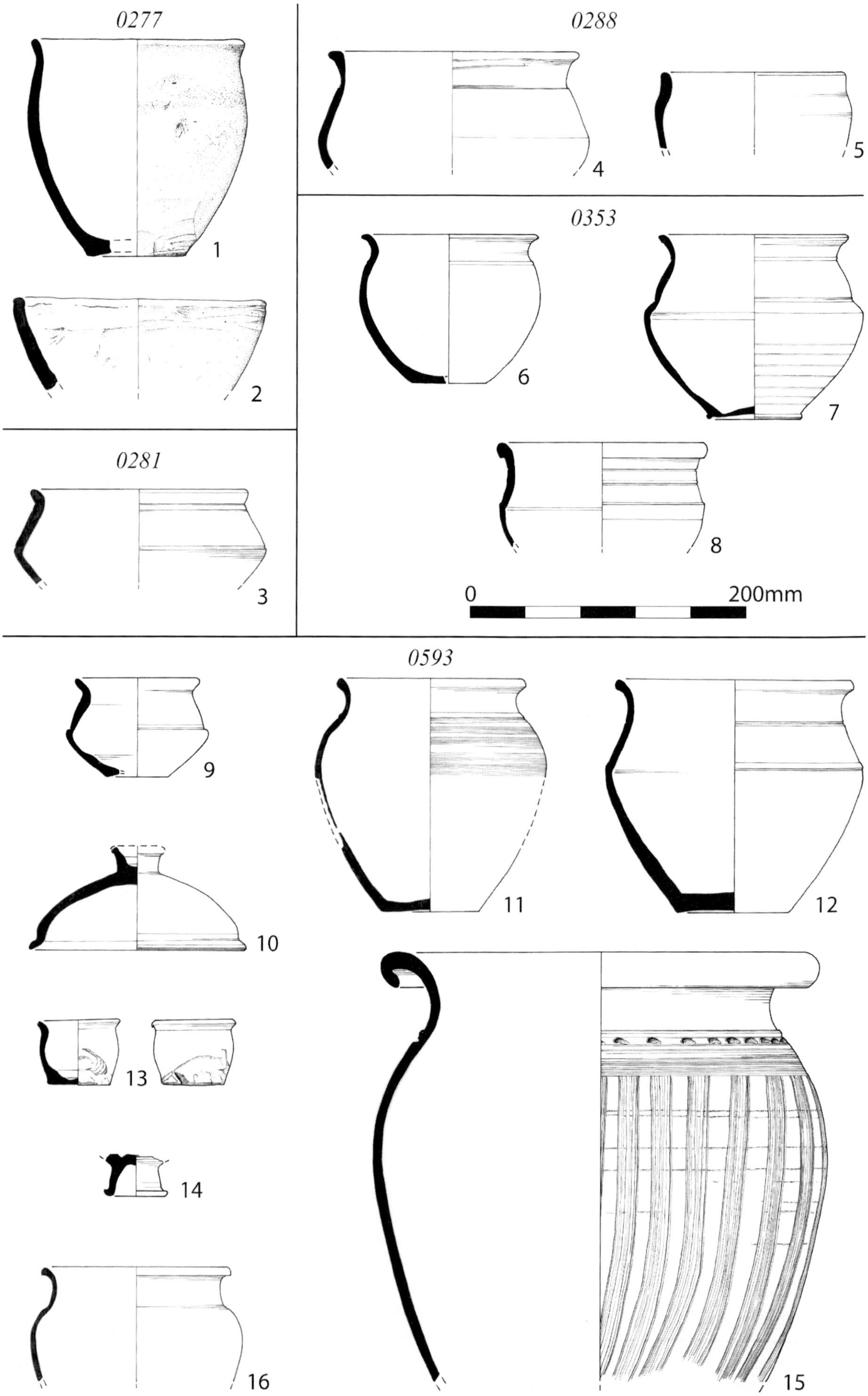

Figure 4.6 FLN 053: Period II.a., Late Iron Age/Early Roman pottery (1–15) (scale 1:4)

Period/Phase	No. of features	No.	% No.	Wt (g)	% Wt	Eve	% Eve	Ave wt (g)
II.a. Late Iron Age/early Roman	24	1010	91.2	14699	95.8	16.42	95.7	14.5
III. Early Anglo Saxon	2	16	1.4	69	0.4	0	0.0	4.3
V. Post-medieval	1	57	5.1	376	2.4	0.31	1.8	6.6
Unstratified		25	2.3	207	1.3	0.42	2.4	8.3
Total		**1108**	**100.0**	**15351**	**100.0**	**17.15**	**100.0**	-

Table 4.4 FLN 053: Late Iron Age and Roman pottery by phase

century AD was found in seven pits, six attributed to Period II.a. and one to Period III. Five sherds are from large storage jars and the rest are from standard-sized vessels. Forms identified are high-shouldered jars and *Cam* 218 cordoned jars. In the southern half of the county this fabric would be amongst the most common at this date, but at Flixton, it is more unusual as the area is well outside the Trinovantes tribal boundary. It is not known whether these sherds are locally-made or imported from further south.

Sandy greywares are the second most common coarseware fabric group identified and make up 17.4% of the count, 18.2% of the weight and 23.6% of the eves. Amongst these wares are some 'romanising' fabrics which contain a little grog and some of these sherds appear to have been hand-made and wheel-finished. The range of forms identified include a narrow-mouthed jar or flask, high-shouldered jars, a carinated jar (Fig. 4.6.12), cordoned carinated jars *Cam* 218 and a girth beaker. Most notable is a complete miniature vessel (Fig. 4.6.13) with 'string marks' not only on its basal exterior but up the side of its lower wall as if it was rather carelessly removed from the wheel. A hollow pedestal base from a *Cam* 204 urn (Fig. 4.6.14), a form that can be very early (1st century AD or earlier) was also found.

Fourteen miscellaneous storage jar sherds (553g, 0.10 eves) were found in three contexts.

The remaining fabrics are oxidised and are a minor components of the assemblage. Twelve miscellaneous buff ware sherds were collected. These are mostly undiagnostic, but two pieces may possibly come from flagons. Buff wares, which are usually represented by romanised tableware forms, are not common in this collection due to the predominantly 'native' character of the assemblage. It is interesting to note that half of these sherds, including the two possible flagons, came from ditch 053:*0838* which was notable for having a less 'native' and/or possibly higher status assemblage.

The redwares include three sherds from a single red fineware butt beaker. The vessel has red-orange surfaces and a black core and represents a 'native' attempt to copy continental finewares such as Terra Rubra. Red coarsewares consist of small undiagnostic sherds which occur singly and dispersed. One sherd is rouletted and is possibly from a butt beaker. Several pieces are abraded and may possibly be BSW with the surface worn off.

Catalogue of illustrated Late Iron Age/Roman pottery sherds

Fig. 4.6

1. Jar, HMS; Pit 053:*0277*; Fill 053:*0278*

2. Bowl/dish HMSO; Pit 053:*0277*; Fill 053:*0278*

3. Carinated bowl/jar BSW; Pit 053:*0281*; Fill 053:*0282*

4. Biconical bowl/jar HMSO; Pit 053:*0288*; Fill 053;*0289*

5. Bowl/jar HMSO; Pit 053:*0288*; Fill 053;*0289*

6. Jar, HMSO; Pit 053:*0353*; Fill 053:*0354*

7. *Cam* 218, BSW/GMB; Pit 053:*0353*; Fill 053:*0354*

8. Carinated bowl GMB; Pit 053:*0353*; Fill 053:*0354*

9. Thompson E1-4 carinated cup/bowl BSW; Pit 053:*0593*; Fill 053:*0594*

10. Lid, *Cam* 252/253 type BSW; Pit 053:*0593*; Fill 053:*0594*

11. 'Braughing jar' BSW; Pit 053:*0593*; Fill 053:*0594*

12. Jar, GX pit; Pit 053:*0593*; Fill 053:*0594*

13. Miniature GX; Pit 053:*0593*; Fill 053:*0594*

14. Pedestal base (*Cam* 204) GX; Pit 053:*0593*; Fill 053:*0594*

15. Storage jar, Thompson C6 STOR/BSW; Pit 053:*0593*; Fill 053:*0594*

16. Jar *Cam* 266 BSW; Pit 053:*0593*; Fill 053:*0594*

The Late Iron Age and Roman pottery by phase

The pottery quantities by phase are shown in Table 4.4. The vast majority of the pottery was found in Period II.a. features with only a small amount coming from later-dated or unstratified contexts. It is interesting to note that the average sherd weight in Period III (4.3g) and Period V (6.6g) is less than half the weight in Period II.a. (14.6g).

Distribution

Pottery was recovered from 29 features which included 25 pits, a ditch, a grave and structural features (post-holes and slots) associated with palisade circle 053:*0346*. A small amount was unstratified. Quantities by feature type are shown in Table 4.5.

Feature type	No	% No	Wt (g)	% Wt	Eve	% Eve	Ave wt (g)
Ditch	101	9.1	1056	6.9	0.75	4.4	10.5
Grave	1	0.1	2	0.0	0.00	0.0	2.0
Pits	942	85.0	13921	90.7	15.82	92.1	14.8
Post-holes	10	0.9	55	0.4	0.06	0.4	5.5
Slots	29	2.6	110	0.7	0.10	0.6	3.8
Unstratified	25	2.3	207	1.3	0.42	2.5	8.3
Total	**1108**	**100.0**	**15351**	**100.0**	**17.15**	**100.0**	-

Table 4.5 FLN 053: Late Iron Age and Roman pottery by feature type

Pits

The majority of the Late Iron Age and Roman pottery assemblage came from 25 pits and 23 of them were assigned to Period II.a. (78.5% count, 87.8% wt, 90.4% eves). The two other pits were Early Anglo-Saxon and post-medieval.

All of the Period II.a. pits seem to be broadly contemporary, with similar assemblage compositions, and fourteen of them included hand-made and wheel-made pottery fabrics which appear to be contemporary in use and deposition. Over 70% by weight of the total Late Iron Age and Roman pottery assemblage came from six Period II.a. pits (053:*0042*, *0253*, *0277*, *0287*, *0353* and *0593*) and they included some substantially complete vessels. The six most productive pits are described in more detail below.

Pit 053:*0042*

Three fills (053:*0043*, *0044* and *0045*) produced 205 sherds (2695g, 2.37 eves). About a quarter of the pottery (24%) was hand-made (HMS) and the forms identified are jars, one of which has 'scratched' decoration. BSW (36%) and GX (25%) account for most of the wheel-made wares and some of these sherds were 'romanising'. Micaceous fabrics GMB and GMO (8%), GROG (5%) and a few sherds of oxidised wares BUF and RX are also present. Forms identified are mainly cordoned jars *Cam* 218 and other jars which could not be certainly identified. Globular beaker *Cam* 108, copies of Gallo-Belgic cups and a butt beaker are also present.

Pit 053:*0253*

Pit fill 053:*0254* produced 52 sherds (628g, 0.72 eves). Hand-made fabrics (HMS and HMSO) account for 45% of the group and the form identified was a simple curved jar. Wheel-made fabric BSW comprised 43.3% and forms identified are *Cam* 218 cordoned jars and carinated beaker type 6.9.2.

Pit 053:*0277*

Pit fill 053:*0278* produced 36 sherds (665g, 0.42 eves). Hand-made pottery (HMS and HMSO) accounts for 83% of this group and forms identified are a simple curved jar (Fig. 4.6.1), other uncertain jars, a colander or strainer and a shallow bowl or dish (Fig. 4.6.2). Wheel-made fabrics include BSW (14%) and single sherds of GMB and BUF. Wheel-made forms are uncertain jars including carinated jars and a *Cam* 212 carinated bowl.

Pit 053:*0287*

Pit fill 053:*0288* produced 80 sherds (1616g, 1.30 eves). About a fifth (18%) of the pottery is hand-made (HMSO) and forms identified are a biconical jar (Fig. 4.6.4), a bowl (Fig. 4.6.5) and other uncertain jar or bowl sherds. Wheel-made fabrics GX (20%), GMB (18%), BSW (11%) and a single abraded BUF sherd are also present. Wheel-made forms identified are a narrow-mouthed jar or flask, uncertain jar forms, and a cordoned carinated bowl *Cam* 216.

Pit 053:*0353*

Pit fill 053:*0354* produced 154 sherds (1336g, 2.56 eves). Hand-made pottery (HMS, HMSO) accounts for 10.5 % and a simple curved jar (Fig. 4.6.6) was the only form identified. The largest wheel-made fabric group is GMB (51%) followed by BSW (23%) and GX (10%). Wheel-made forms identified are a *Cam* 218 cordoned jar (Fig. 4.6.7), uncertain jars and a carinated bowl (Fig. 4.6.8). A girth beaker, *Cam* 211–214 type concave-sided cups or bowls and a *Cam* 26a copy of *Cam* 12 Gallo-Belgic platter were also found.

Pit 053:*0593*

Pit fill 053:*0594* produced the largest group (202 sherds, 5150g, 602 eves) accounting for more than a third of the total assemblage weight and eves. Just two sherds of hand-made pottery (HMS, HMSO) were collected from this feature. The most common wheel-made fabric is BSW (76%) which includes many 'romanising' sherds and pieces that are hand-made but wheel-finished. GX accounts for 23% and a single sherd of GMB and oxidised fabrics RF and RX were also present.

BSW forms identified are jars including high shouldered jars, *Cam* 260 Braughing jars (Fig. 4.6.11), a *Cam* 266 (Fig. 4.6.16) and a *Cam* 270b storage jar (Fig. 4.6.15). Cordoned jars *Cam* 218, carinated jars or bowls (Fig. 4.6.7), a carinated cup or bowl Thompson type E1-4 (Fig. 4.6.9) and a *Cam* 252/253 lid (Fig. 4.6.10) were also found. GX forms include most notably a complete miniature vessel (SF 053:*0610*, Fig. 4.6.13) with string marks not only on its basal exterior, but up the side of its lower wall as it was rather carelessly removed from the wheel. A hollow pedestal base from a *Cam* 204 urn was also found (Fig. 4.6.14).

Ditch

The two fills of ditch 053:*0838* (053:*0847* and *0848*) produced 101 sherds weighing 1056g (average weight 10.4g) and 0.75 eves, which accounted for 9.1% of the sherds, 6.9% of the weight and 4.4% of the total eves. This assemblage composition is very different from that of the pits. Apart from one sherd from pit 053:*0040*, this is the only feature which contained Gallo-Belgic finewares TR, TN and NGWF (13%). Fineware forms identified were platters, including a *Cam* 8, girth beaker *Cam* 84a and globular beaker *Cam* 105a.

One hand-made (HMSO) sherd was found in this feature. The most common coarsewares of local manufacture are wheel-made GMB (30%), STOR (24%), BSW (12%), BUF (15%). Forms identified are flagons, jars, (including a large *Cam* 260 'Braughing' jar), and other uncertain cordoned and carinated jars, concave-sided *Cam* 211–214 type cups and a platter.

Palisaded circle 053:*0346*

Three slots (053:*0331*, *0335* and *0482*) and four of the post-holes (053:*0542*, *0546*, *0548* and *0564*) in this structure produced a small amount of pottery (21 sherds, 92g, 0.06 eves). The sherds are non-diagnostic, abraded and fragmentary (average weight 4.2g), some are small enough to be intrusive and of limited use for dating or interpreting the features. The fabrics identified are similar to fabrics which are found elsewhere on the site where they belong to the Late Iron Age and Roman period, none of which has to be later than 1st century.

The most diagnostic pieces found were a HMS rim and base from post-hole 053:*0546* which are similar to the hand-made pottery found in the pits.

Overall discussion

The majority of the pottery was recovered from a group of broadly contemporary Late Iron Age–early Roman pits which appear to line up loosely from north to south on the eastern side of the site. The pits containing the best groups of pottery were quite close to the south-east side of the palisade structure 053:*0346*. While the juxtaposition of the pits with the palisaded circle and the fact that they were broadly contemporaneous suggests that they are somehow related, this cannot be proven.

The most notable feature of this assemblage is the presence of hand-made sandy wares alongside wheel-made or at least hand-made and wheel-finished wares. There is no reason to assume that both types of pottery are not contemporary and although some of the hand-made forms began earlier than the wheel-made ones, they do continue to exist alongside the wheel-made fabrics, thus indicating the survival of the hand-made tradition well into the first half of the 1st century AD. The fourteen features which contained both types of pottery demonstrate the 'transitional' nature of the assemblage and this material represents the merging traditions of Mid to Late Iron Age technology and more sophisticated 'romanising' techniques such as kiln production and the use of the wheel.

Other sites in the region where hand-made forms continued in use alongside wheel-made wares include Burgh (Martin 1988a) and Elveden Center Parcs (Craven forthcoming) in Suffolk, and Fison Way, Thetford (Gregory 1992) and Saham Toney (Lyons 2000) in Norfolk.

On the whole, this is a 'native' assemblage consisting of products of indigenous pottery industries. It consists almost entirely of hand-made and wheel-made local and regional coarsewares used side by side during the first half of the 1st century AD and the activities which produced this assemblage were 'native' and not Roman in origin.

Fabric	*Code*	*No.*	*Wt (g)*
Medium sandy with coarse chalk	msc	166	4101
Medium sandy with moderate to large voids (?chalk)	msv	221	5616
Fine sandy with moderate voids (?chalk)	fsv	5	43
Medium sandy with few other inclusions	ms	84	333
Medium sandy with flint	msf	11	524
Fine sandy with few other inclusions	fs	3	63
Fine matrix with organic (?grass) tempering	org	18	142
Total		**508**	**10822**

Table 4.6 FLN 053: quantities of fired clay by fabric

The pottery has none of the elements of a 'fortress assemblage', a phrase used by Tyers (1996) to describe groups of pottery associated with a military presence, featuring ceramics such as Italian samian, Roman tablewares, and Gallo-Belgic finewares. There are no amphora, no flagons and no mortaria and the few continental imports are restricted to two features.

These transitional Late Iron Age forms, particularly the hand-made wares and more 'romanising' BSW fabrics, represent a local adaptation of the Belgic tradition. Although FLN 053 lies outside the Trinovantes (Belgic) boundary and within what is presumably Iceni territory, it is still within the Belgic 'sphere of influence'. Forms present here are illustrated in Thompson's (1982) type series for Belgic pottery and the assemblage also shows close links to material from *Camulodunum*.

The majority of the pottery falls within a very narrow chronological limit of early to mid 1st century AD and it is possibly all pre-Flavian. Some of the less diagnostic pieces could have a wider date range, but the most identifiable ones are pre-Flavian if not earlier. This suggests that activity did not continue for long after the Conquest on this site although it is known elsewhere in the near vicinity (most notably in FLN 062 immediately to the south). There is only one feature that has any later Roman pottery (late 2nd to mid 3rd-century); this material was redeposited in a Period V quarry pit and had been through long cycle of deposition.

Fired clay

by Sue Anderson

Introduction

Fired clay attributable to Period II.a. was primarily recovered from the FLN 053 site, although eight fragments (42g) were residual material from the FLN 062 Period III Early Anglo-Saxon graves and were also considered to be of this date (information in archive). The following report is a summary of a fuller version which is available in the archive.

Type	*No.*	*Wt (g)*
Daub	1	30
Kiln furniture	2	222
Triangular loomweight	153	5033
Sling-shot	4	20
Uncertain	350	5541

Table 4.7 FLN 053: quantities of fired clay by type

Site FLN 053

A total of 508 fragments of fired clay (10.822kg) from 39 contexts was studied. The assemblage includes both the bulk finds and fired clay objects collected as small finds. The fired clay was quantified by context, fabric and type, using fragment count and weights. The presence and form of surface fragments and impressions were recorded, and wattle dimensions measured where possible. Data were recorded in an MS Access database which is available in the site archive.

Seven very broad fabric types were identified; brief descriptions and quantities are shown in Table 4.6. The assemblage was dominated by chalk-tempered fabrics, though much of the chalk had been lost in the acidic soils. All other fabrics made up a much smaller proportion of the assemblage.

Approximately a third of the assemblage was abraded, the softer fabrics being the most affected as would be expected. Eighteen contexts contained fired clay with an average fragment weight of 5g or less.

Typology

Functional types were recorded where possible, but over half of this assemblage by fragment count falls into the 'uncertain' category. Table 4.7 shows the quantities of fragments identifiable to type.

The majority of identifiable fragments consisted of pieces of triangular loomweight. These include a near-complete example (SF 053:*0117* from pit fill 053:*0278*) weighing 3870g (Fig. 4.7.1). There are diagonal holes across two corners, one of which had been broken in use. The weight is made in a chalk-tempered fabric which has smoothed, reduced surfaces. Similar pieces were collected from twelve other contexts.

Four fragments of three sling-shots were collected. Two (SF 053:*0106* and *0118*) are substantially complete (Fig. 4.7.2 and 3). The first of these was collected from an unstratified spot-find, whilst the other almost complete example (SF 053:*0118)* came from pit fill 053:*0278*. The sling-shots are pointed oval types and measure 35–39mm long and 22–24mm in diameter. The other fragment (slot fill 053:*0343*) is small and its identification is uncertain.

Two pieces of possible kiln bars were identified. One fragment from pit fill 053:*0282* has a roughly square section (45 x 49mm) and tapers slightly along its length (Fig. 4.7.4). The other fragment (pit fill 053:*0278*) is incomplete in section but also tapers in length, measuring 41–44mm in width (Fig. 4.7.5). Both were reduced to dark grey in colour.

A possible kiln prop or weight was identified in pit fill 053:*0354* (Fig. 4.7.6). It consists of the ?base of a sub-rectangular section piece measuring 71 x 83mm at its widest point, but appearing slightly waisted close to the break, where it was 59mm wide. The base showed signs of wear.

One fragment of possible daub from pit fill 053:*0282* was roughly smoothed on the external surface and had a triangular impression on the inner side which may have been made by a cut timber.

Amongst the 'uncertain' fragments, some individual groups can be described. Several thin fragments (pit fills 053:*0280* and 053:*0807*) with a roughly smoothed surface and a flat underside may have been pieces of render or lining for a wooden box. Similar examples have been found at Carlton Colville (Anderson 2009, 247) and

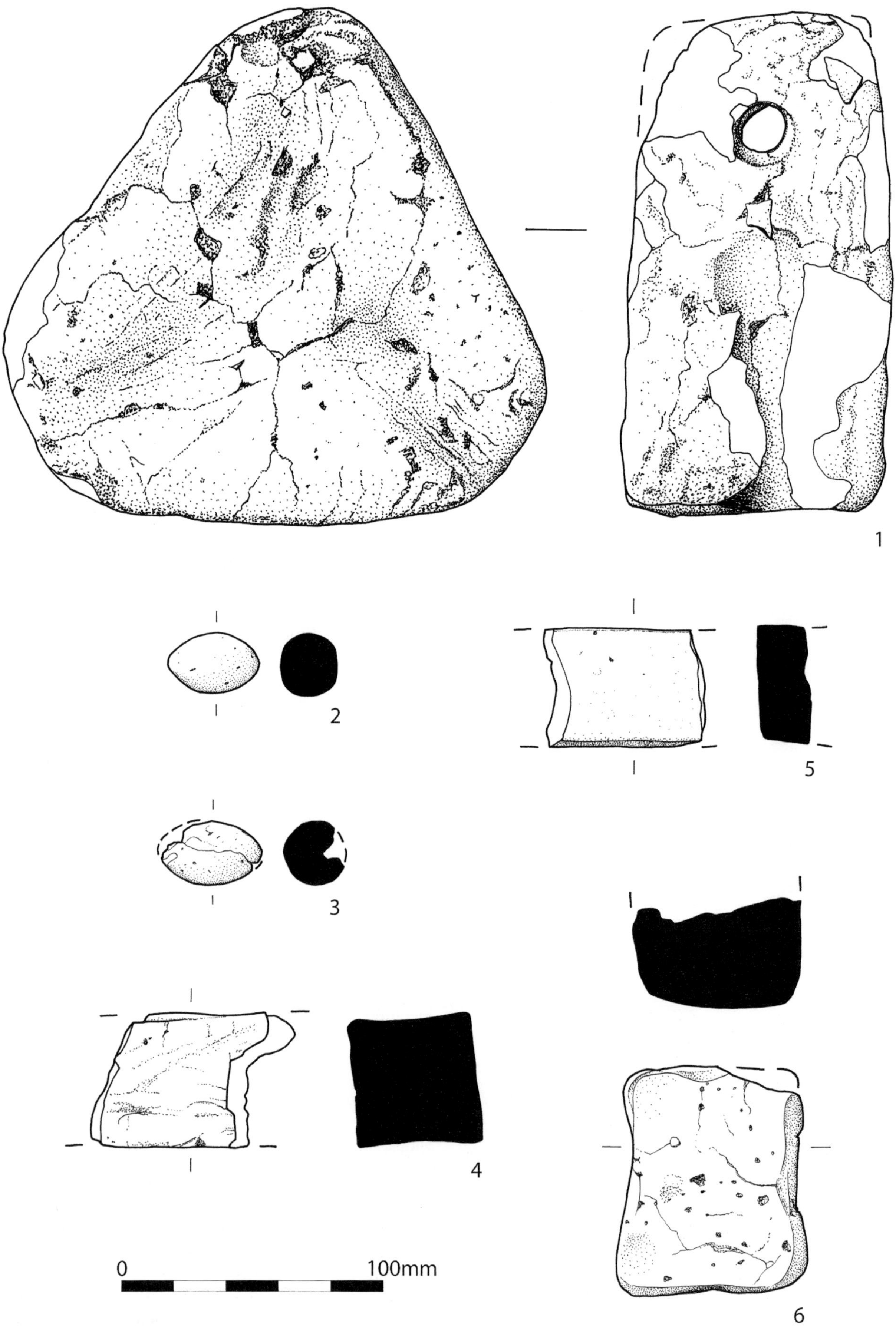

Figure 4.7 FLN 053: Period II.a., Late Iron Age/Early Roman fired clay objects (scale 1:2)

Brandon (Anderson forthcoming a). Two thin fragments (pit fill 053:*0594*) with smoothed surfaces in organic tempered fabrics may have been crude vessels. Some of this material is very similar to briquetage, although this would not normally be expected to occur on inland sites.

Distribution

Most of the fired clay was recovered from features assigned to Period II.a. (454 fragments, 10718g). A small quantity (37 fragments, 88g) is likely to be residual in contexts of Phase V, and the remainder was unphased. The majority of fired clay was collected from pits. A small group of features to the west of the site (053:*0034*, *0040* and *0042*) produced several fragments of possible loomweight, and further fragments were found in pits to the north of the palisaded circle (053:*0250*, *0253* and *0279*).

The largest group from a single feature came from pit 053:*0277*, a total of 171 fragments including one sling-shot and the intact loomweight. The pit was isolated to the north-east of the palisaded circle and contained the largest group of animal bone from the site, together with a relatively large assemblage of early Roman pottery. It would appear to be domestic rubbish, but given its isolation and proximity to the circle, a structured or special deposit is a possibility. The possible kiln bars came from this pit and nearby 053:*0281*, whilst the prop-like object came from another large pit (053:*0353*) to the south-east of the ring. Another relatively large group of fired clay was collected from pit 053:*0593*, east of the ring, and included the possible crude vessels and flat fragments.

Catalogue of illustrated fired clay objects (FLN 053)
Fig. 4.7.1–6

1. Triangular loomweight. Dimensions: 175 x 195 x 93mm. SF 053:*0117*, context 053:*0278*, pit 053:*0277*
2. Sling-shot 053:*0106*, unstratified spot find
3. Sling-shot 053:*0118*, context 053:*0278*, pit 053:*0277*
4. Kiln bar fragment, context 053:*0282*, pit 053:*0281*
5. Kiln bar fragment, context 053:*0278*, pit 053:*0277*
6. Kiln prop or weight, context 053:*0354*, pit 053:*0353*

Overall discussion

The majority of fired clay was collected from pits within FLN 053. The assemblage includes some large triangular loomweights which were in use with the warp-weighted looms of the Iron Age and early Roman period (Wild 1970, 61–3, 156). There are also three sling-shots of similar date. Less certain objects include fragments of kiln bar and a possible kiln prop, perhaps related to the kilns identified to the south at FLN 062, or alternatively debris from an oven. Fragments of flat clay may have been lining for box hearths. Only two fragments of possible daub were identified, suggesting that wattle-and-daub structures were not common on the site, or at least that none were burnt down. There are no certain examples of oven dome. It appears that fired clay in the later Iron Age and early Roman periods at this site was more likely to have been employed for small domestic objects than for any major structural purpose.

Ceramic building material

by Sue Anderson

Only a very small quantity of Roman ceramic building material (CBM) was recovered from all the sites with single pieces from SE quadrant 008:*0029* (8g) and pit fill 013:*0024* (31g), two pieces from pit fill 053:*0806* (239g) and six pieces (114g) from two Early Anglo-Saxon grave fills in FLN 062. Five were pieces of *imbrex*, and four were tiles of unknown type. Most of the fragments of Roman CBM from the sites covered in this volume are residual. The tiles are similar to those from larger assemblages of this period found during excavations at Flixton Quarry (Anderson in archive) and elsewhere in Suffolk. A large proportion of Roman tile found in the county is made in fine, soft orange fabrics, generally with few inclusions. The harder, well-fired tiles found elsewhere in the region appear to be less common here.

Feature	*SHB*	*Undiagnostic*	*Other slag*
LIA/Roman pit *0279* (fill *0280*)	288		
LIA/Roman pit *0253* (fill *0254*)	674	199	
Undated post-hole *0620* (fill *0621*)			4 (carbonaceous)
LIA pit *0230* (fill *0231*)			1 (fuel ash slag)
Totals	**962**	**199**	**5**

Table 4.8 FLN 053: weights of slag (g) by context

Heat-altered flint and stone

The vast majority of the heat-altered flint and sandstone is considered to be prehistoric in date (Chapter 3.III). Although the majority of the heat-altered stone from non-prehistoric phases is assumed to be residual, two features from FLN 053 contained material which may be Late Iron Age or Roman. Eleven stones weighing over 12kg were collected from mid 1st-century pit 053:*0593*. These large stones could have been cracked due to proximity to a fire and are unlikely to be prehistoric pot-boilers. The only other large group from a Roman feature was from pit 053:*0042* which produced twenty fragments weighing 1273g.

Metalworking waste

by Sarah Paynter

A small (1090g) assemblage of metalworking waste was recovered from only one of the Flixton sites covered in this volume, FLN 053. The different types of waste were identified on the basis of their appearance, according to the categories listed below (Bayley *et al.* 2001), and quantified by context (Table 4.8).

SHB (smithing hearth bottom) slag: a by-product of iron smithing, these lumps of slag form in the fuel bed of the smithing hearth and are typically plano-convex in shape.

Undiagnostic slag: slag lacking sufficient diagnostic features for identification.

The diagnostic slag is characteristic of iron smithing, and includes two complete smithing hearth bottom (SHB) slags (weighing 173g and 288g) and a number of fragmented examples. It is highly likely that the undiagnostic slag from the site is also smithing waste. This slag had been dumped in two nearby pits, contexts 053:*0279* and 053:*0253*, both attributed a Period II.a., Late Iron Age/early Roman date. No features relating to the smithing activity itself survives.

The remaining material in the assemblage comprises a small fragment of black, carbonaceous material and a piece of fuel ash slag. This type of slag is formed at high

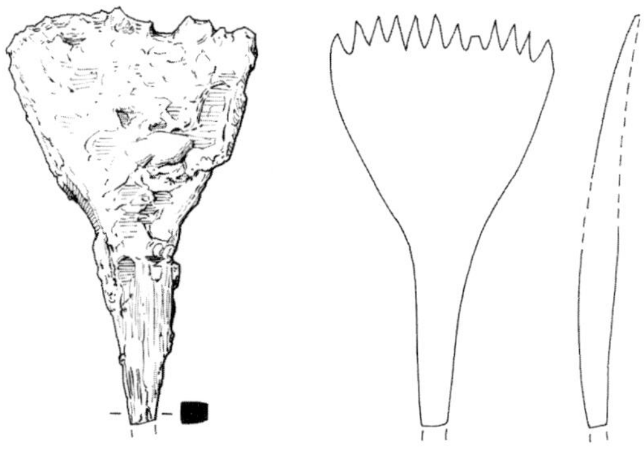

Figure 4.8 FLN 053: toothed implement *1187* (scale 1:2)

temperatures by the reaction of siliceous material, such as clay, with plant ashes, for example from charcoal or wood fuel. However, neither the carbonaceous material nor the fuel ash slag is necessarily associated with metalworking.

The assemblage indicates that iron smithing took place somewhere in the vicinity of the FLN 053 site during the Late Iron Age/early Roman period. The material comprises entirely waste fragments that have been dumped in pits and it is not possible to locate the activity more precisely.

Small finds

Introduction
by Richenda Goffin
Very few small finds were recovered from FLN 013 and FLN 053 which could be assigned to Period II.a. The small quantity of identifiable metal objects of this date from FLN 053 have been catalogued below, but the remains of nails and miscellaneous fragments which cannot be dated to a particular period have not been included. The ceramic small finds have been discussed in the fired clay report (Anderson above), but the vessel glass (053:*1425*) and the fragment of Hertfordshire puddingstone (053:*0103*) are described below. The small finds from the non-Saxon grave features from FLN 062 will be described in a separate publication.

Metalwork
by Ian Riddler
Fig. 4.8
An iron implement (053:*1187*) was recovered from pit 053:*0353*. It has a blunt, rectangular tang that widens to a broad, D-shaped blade with a series of short teeth along its edge (Fig. 4.8). Traces of mineralised organic material are present on the tang. The shape of the blade and the presence of a row of short teeth recall several distinct object types of Roman date associated with craft working. Roes published a number of iron and copper alloy objects with toothed blades, all of which are socketed, however, rather than tanged; most have only a small number of well-spaced teeth (Roes 1958). Some of these implements had previously been interpreted as tools used to dress plaster but she suggested that their short teeth could equally well provide a series of indentations of even space and depth, particularly when marking the location of stitch holes in leather working (Roes 1958, 245). In discussing an assemblage of thirty similar implements from Conimbriga, Wild felt that they might have been used instead as spacers in textile manufacture (Alarcaõ and da Ponte 1982; Wild 1985). The Flixton implement differs both from this series of objects and from the flat, toothed blades of Roman date (Frere 1957) for its closely-spaced teeth. Contemporary combs of iron are also known, largely from central European contexts, but these have longer teeth and their forms recall those of composite antler combs. Werner regarded them as woolcombs but it is more likely that they were used in combing human hair (Werner 1988; 1991).

A socketed iron implement with a D-shaped blade and seven teeth from Niederbieber is similar in form to the Flixton implement but the closest parallels are provided by an unpublished iron implement from a Roman context at Dolland's Moor in Kent and a similar implement from Dunadd (Riddler 2001; Bulleid and Gray 1911, 267–8 and fig. 56; Lane and Campbell 2000, 240). The closely-spaced sequence of short teeth distinguishes these three implements from those identified by Anna Roes. They are closer in form to modern pricking irons, which are used to stamp marks on leather to indicate the position of stitch holes, and that may have been their function. Gray felt that the Dunadd implement was a weaving comb but this is unlikely. The closely spaced teeth of all three objects are more likely to have been used to stamp organic material, but they could equally well have been drawn across a surface, scoring leather or ceramics.

In addition to two iron nails (053:*0254*), three iron small finds were recovered from the fill of pit 053:*0253*. The curved end of an iron implement (053:*0121*; dimensions: L.68mm, W.7mm), alongside its square section and tapering shaft, allow it to be identified as part of a loop-headed spike, a form of Roman structural ironwork (Manning 1985, 130). It fits into the longer of the two size groups of loop-headed spikes identified at Caister-on-Sea (Mould 1993, 103).

A fragment of an iron blade (SF 053:*0254b*; dimensions: L.60mm, W.23mm) stems from the lower part of a reaping hook and can be assigned to Manning's type 2 (Manning 1985, 57). Implements of this type are commonly found in Roman rural contexts and are well represented at Monkton, for example (MacDonald *et al.* 2008, 219 and fig. 2.65).

Part of a broad iron strap was recovered (SF 053:*0116*; dimensions: L.56mm, W.42mm) which widens towards one end, where it includes a central rivet hole. It has fractured across the opposite end and probably stems from a structural fitting.

In addition, single iron nails were recovered from pits 053:*0042* (053:*0102*), and 053:*0255* (053:*0123*), while an unidentified iron lump was found in pit 053:*0841*. All of these features contained significant quantities of Roman pottery.

Stone querns
by Richenda Goffin
A fragmentary piece of Hertfordshire Puddingstone (053:*0103*) was recovered from the fill of a shallow pit 053:*0040*. It is plano-convex in shape and is probably part of a bun-shaped rotary quern. The conglomerate is made of a cream matrix with frequent medium to large orange pebbles up to 43mm in length. It is Late Iron Age to early Roman in date. Pit 053:*0040* also contained seven sherds of pottery dated overall to the second half of the 1st century, so the stone may be residual or re-used.

Vessel glass
by Hilary Cool

Deep blue glass fragment 053:*1425* may be dated to the first century on the basis of its colour. Deep blue blown vessels were popular amongst the glass in use in the Roman world in AD 43, and started to be imported into Britain after the Conquest. Strongly coloured glass such as this was going out of fashion in the second half of the 1st century as a taste for paler, lighter tinted vessels developed. The most likely period of use for the vessel that this fragment came from would thus be from AD 43 to sometime in the 80s, but of course there is no way of telling how long it might have been curated on a rural site where it would have been an exotic novelty.

The fragment retains few clues as to the vessel it came from. From the general size a small beaker or drinking cup can be ruled out. The hint of a possible carination with a very shallow reverse S curve could suggest that it came from a tubular-rimmed bowl (Price and Cottam 1998, 78–80), a type of vessel that appears to have been adopted on rural sites in the first century. A deep blue example which retained a complete profile was found in a ditch with Neronian samian at Long Melford, Suffolk (Avent and Howlett 1980, 246, fig. 41). It must be stressed though, that there can be no certainty as to that identification for this fragment.

IV. Biological evidence

Animal bone
by Julie Curl

Methodology
The assemblage was examined primarily to determine range of species and elements present and the amount of material that could produce measurable, ageable bone, and whether bone, horn or antler working evidence was present in the assemblage. Butchering and any indications of skinning, hornworking and other modifications were recorded. When possible a record was made of ages and any other relevant information, such as pathologies. Counts and weights were noted for each context. All information was recorded on the faunal remains recording sheets. The assessment was carried out following a modified version of guidelines by English Heritage (Davis 1992).

Site FLN 053
A total of 213 animal bone fragments (310g) was hand-collected from ten contexts, of which 129 fragments (288g; 93% of the assemblage by weight) were recovered from seven contexts associated with six Period II.a. pits. The bone is generally in good condition although very fragmentary. Some bone had been burnt at high temperatures, resulting in some distortion. A summary of the overall FLN 053 animal bone quantification is provided in Table 4.9.

Taxon	*No.*	*% No.*	*Wt (g)*	*% Wt*
cattle (*Bos taurus*)	3	1.4	13	4.2
?cattle (*Bos taurus*)	80	37.5	7	2.3
sheep/goat (Ovicaprid)	15	7.0	55	17.7
pig (*Sus scrofa*)	7	3.3	102	32.9
large mammal	6	2.8	18	5.8
medium mammal	37	17.3	83	26.8
wigeon (*Anas penelope*)	1	0.5	1	0.3
Unidentifiable	64	30.0	31	10.0
Total	**213**	**100.0**	**310**	**100.0**

Table 4.9 FLN 053: summary quantification of animal bone by taxa

Four taxon groups and three broad categories were identified in this assemblage; sixty-three fragments were deemed unidentifiable. The broad categories can be defined as: large mammal – an animal approximately the size of a cow/horse/large deer; medium mammal – an animal approximately the size of a sheep/goat/pig/small deer.

The eighty fragments of ?cattle are not representative as these are very small fragments of one tooth. Therefore the medium-sized mammals dominate this assemblage, in terms of both number and weight. Only a very small number of fragments of each taxa is present and caution should be applied when considering the significance of these figures.

Most of the faunal remains were retrieved from pit 053:*0277*, which produced 44.6% of the total number of fragments and 81.3% of the total weight (74% of the total number of Period II.a. fragments, 87.5% by weight).

Many of the fragments have been exposed to heat and have turned white, hard and slightly distorted as a result, perhaps pointing to these animals being used as a food source. Nine fragments have this appearance and are from separate contexts (pit fills 053:*0043* and *0354*). Only two fragments were noted as being immature at the time of death. Few butchering marks are evident, but the tarsometatarsus from the Wigeon in pit fill 053:*0278* shows a fine cut mark, which suggests a use for food. The sheep/goat scapula has tooth puncture marks in it which were probably made by a dog or wolf and a few other fragments also show evidence of gnawing, all of which suggest some level of canid activity at this site. There is no obvious pathology on the animal bone fragments from this site.

The bones in this assemblage may represent a small amount of food waste although the very limited size of the sample and its fragmentary nature hinders any definite conclusions from being made. The presence of the butchered Wigeon, one of the smaller species of duck, is indicative of hunting of wild species for food use.

Site FLN 062
A small quantity of animal bone (24 fragments, 14g) was recovered from the Early Anglo-Saxon graves cutting ring-ditch 062:*0808*. The bones from Graves 46 and 60 should be considered as residual deposits originating in the upper fill of the ring-ditch which was then incorporated into the grave during its backfilling. The justification for including this material here is that the upper fill of the ring-ditch is interpreted as a midden/dump deposit of Period II.a. Late Iron Age/early Roman date.

Two taxon groups were identified with one fragment not identifiable to taxa.

The bone recovered from grave fills 062:*0894* (Grave 46) and 062:*1863* (Grave 60), the former comprising fourteen pieces of adult cattle teeth and the latter a single adult small mammal rib, is fragmentary and was recovered in small quantities. Nine small bones, identified as a juvenile rabbit, were recovered from the grave fill 062:*1856* (Grave 58). No butchery marks were observed on any of these bones and it is likely to be a rabbit which had burrowed into the grave or the remains of a more modern rabbit kill buried by a fox.

V. Palaeoenvironmental analysis

Bulk soil samples

by Val Fryer

Introduction

Bulk soil-samples relating to seventeen Period II.a., Late Iron Age/early Roman contexts, all from the FLN 053 site, were submitted for assessment and analysis; eleven were pit fills, four were slots or post-holes forming part of palisaded circle 053:*0346*, one was ditch fill and one was the fill of a complete pot.

Methodology

The samples were processed by manual water flotation/washover, collecting the flots in a 500 micron mesh sieve. Residues were collected in a 1mm mesh sieve and sorted when dried. The dried flots were scanned under a binocular microscope at low power (up to x40) and the macrobotanical and other remains noted. Plant macrofossils were preserved by charring. Modern contaminants including fibrous roots, seeds/fruits, small mammal/amphibian bones, invertebrates and molluscs were also present in some samples.

Results

Charred plant macrofossils

Charred cereals and/or seeds of common weed species were noted at a very low density in most samples. Preservation was poor to moderate. Cereal grains were frequently puffed, probably as a result of combustion at very high temperatures, and some subsequent fragmentation and abrasion had also occurred. Oat (*Avena* sp.) and wheat (*Triticum* sp.) grains were present. Spelt wheat (*T. spelta*) glume bases were noted in three samples (053:*0045*, *0278* and *0354*). Weed seeds were rare throughout but included brome (*Bromus* sp.), dock (*Rumex* sp.) and vetch/vetchling (*Vicia/Lathyrus* sp.). Hazel (*Corylus avellana*) nut shell fragments were recorded in six samples (053:*0282*, *0254*, *0276*, *0343*, *0354* and *0847*). A single spike-rush (*Eleocharis* sp.) fruit was recovered from sample 053:*0594*.

Other plant macrofossils

Charcoal fragments were present at varying densities in all samples (see below). Fragments of charred root, rhizome or stem were also noted along with heather (Ericaceae indet.) stem fragments and indeterminate seeds.

Other material

The fragments of black porous 'cokey' material and black tarry material which occurred in six samples are probably the residues of the combustion of organic materials, including cereal grains, at very high temperatures. Other materials included bone fragments, burnt or fired clay and burnt stone fragments and small pot sherds. Ferrous globules and hammer scale were included in sample 053:*0254*, the fill of pit 053:*0253*.

Overall discussion

The Period II.a. assemblages are probably derived from refuse from diverse origins. The presence of cereals, chaff and segetal weed seeds may indicate that some cereal processing debris is present, but at such low densities that it is unlikely to be indicative of processing in the near vicinity. It is considered more probable that it is derived from wind blown detritus from adjacent areas. Industrial residues including ferrous globules, hammerscale and vitrified material were present in one sample (053:*0254* from pit 053:*0253*) which also contained a quantity of metalworking waste/slag.

In conclusion, the very low density of material recovered precludes the identification of any specific on-site activities dating to the Late Iron Age/early Roman period. The recorded material was almost certainly generated by the disposal of refuse derived from domestic, agricultural and industrial sources in the surrounding area.

Charcoal

by Rowena Gale

Introduction

Charcoal from seventeen Period II.a., Late Iron Age/early Roman contexts, all from the FLN 053 site, was submitted for examination; eleven were pit fills, four were slots or post-holes forming part of palisaded circle 053:*0346*, one was ditch fill and one was the fill of a complete pot.

Methodology

See Chapter 3.V for method statement. In addition to species listed there, the following taxa or groups of taxa were encountered:

Aceraceae. *Acer campestre* L., field maple
Caprifoliaceae. *Sambucus nigra* L., elder
Cornaceae. *Cornus sanguinea* L., dogwood
Ulmaceae. *Ulmus* sp., elm

Results

Pits

Charcoal was present in a number of the pits and almost certainly represents fuel debris but, in the absence of conclusive evidence, it is not possible to attribute this to a specific activity (*e.g.* domestic, industrial or ritual hearths), although in view of the frequency of the pits, domestic waste seems the most likely. Eleven samples of charcoal were examined from the fills of ten pits (053:*0042*, *0253*, *0271*, *0275*, *0277*, *0279*, *0281*, *0287*, *0353* and *0593*). The charcoal was usually sparse and consisted of small fragments. Each pit included multiple species. Ash (*Fraxinus excelsior*), oak (*Quercus* sp.), the hawthorn/*Sorbus* group (Pomoideae) and blackthorn (*Prunus spinosa*) were more or less common to each pit, whereas field maple (*Acer campestre*), dogwood (*Cornus sanguinea*), hazel (*Corylus avellana*), willow/poplar (*Salix* sp./*Populus* sp.), elm (*Ulmus* sp.), gorse/broom (*Ulex* sp./*Cytisus scoparius*) and possibly birch (*Betula* sp.) were more sporadic. In most instances the charcoal was too comminuted to assess the original dimensions of the fuel. A fairly high proportion of the oak heartwood appeared to be from widish roundwood (*e.g.* poles/branches) rather than mature timber. The fill (053:*0851*) of whole pot (053:*0610*) from pit 053:*0593* was also examined and found to contain a few fragments of ash (*Fraxinus excelsior*) and oak (*Quercus* sp.) charcoal.

Palisaded circle 053:*0346*

Charcoal was examined from contexts associated with the ring structure 053:*0346*: post-holes 053:*0383*, 053:*0477* and 053:*0541* and slot 053:*0342*. The origin of this charcoal is obscure, although its similarity to that from the pits suggests a common or similar source. The charcoal included oak (*Quercus* sp.), ash (*Fraxinus excelsior*), field maple (*Acer campestre*), hazel (*Corylus avellana*), the hawthorn/*Sorbus* group (Pomoideae), blackthorn (*Prunus*

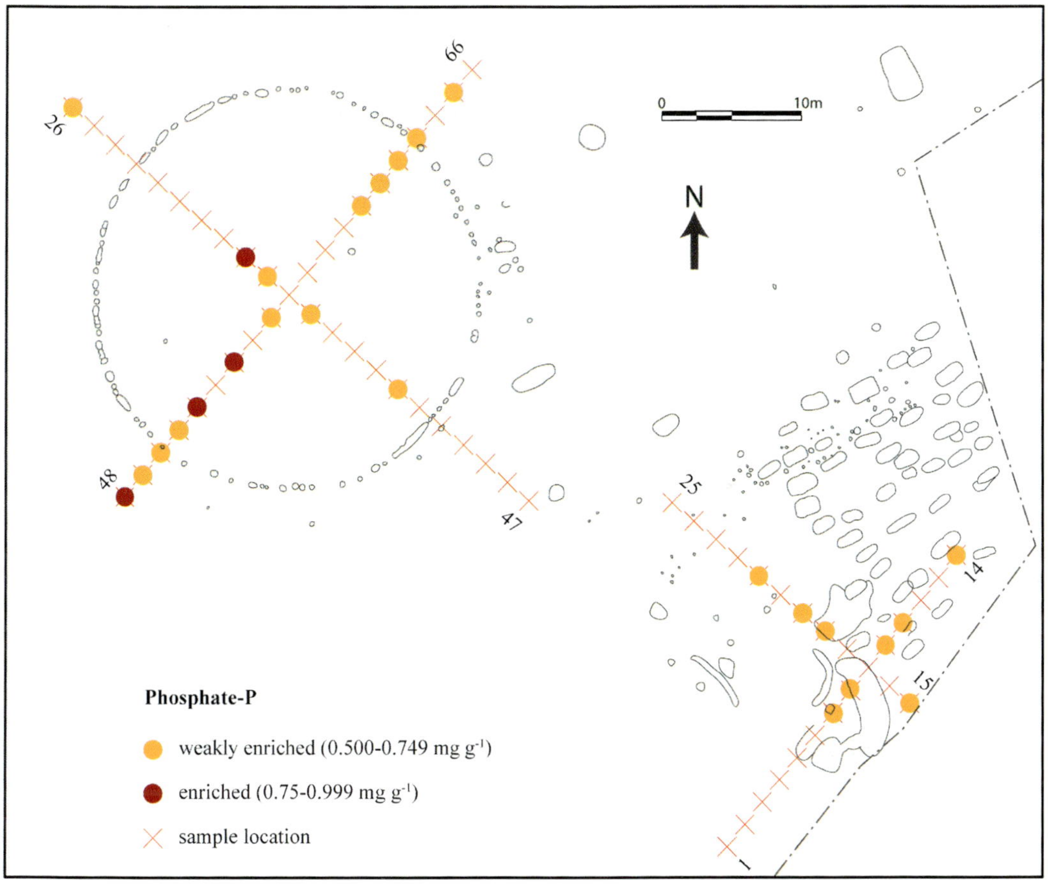

Figure 4.9 FLN 053: phosphate-P survey results

spinosa), willow/poplar (*Salix* sp./*Populus* sp.) and elder (*Sambucus* sp.).

Ditch

A deposit from ditch context 053:*0838* included ash (*Fraxinus excelsior*), oak (*Quercus* sp.), field maple (*Acer campestre*), hazel (*Corylus avellana*) and the hawthorn/*Sorbus* group (Pomoideae).

Overall discussion

Although almost certainly representing debris from local hearths, the precise origin of the charcoal is inconclusive. There was little evidence to indicate the activities or events which from which it might have resulted and on-site industrial activity was not recorded, although redeposited smithing waste was present.

Despite the absence of structural evidence within the site area at FLN 053, with the exception of the palisaded circle 053:*0346*, the frequency of pits dating to the Late Iron Age/early Roman period indicates settlement activity in the vicinity and subsequent excavations, particularly FLN 059 and FLN 062 to the south, have included evidence for significant levels of contemporary activity. It is likely then, that fuel debris dumped in the pits was generated by relatively local domestic and industrial activity.

The function of the Roman ring-structure (053:*0346*) is uncertain. Charcoal deposits from three post-holes and a slot were examined along with a sample from a broadly contemporary ditch (053:*0838*). The similarity of the deposits from these features indicates that a fairly uniform range of firewood was used across the site. The taxa identified included predominantly oak, ash, the hawthorn group and blackthorn and also, although less frequently, hazel, field maple, willow/poplar, elm, gorse/broom, dogwood, elder, and possibly birch. The charcoal was too fragmented to assess the use of coppiced stems or managed woodland.

Evidence from the charcoal suggests that the local environment had continued to support a diverse range of woodland trees and shrubs with broadly similar species present to those during the Late Neolithic and Early Bronze Age (Chapter 3).

Interestingly, however, although alder was present in the Early Bronze Age deposit at FLN 008, there was no evidence of its use in the Late Iron Age/Roman period. Although alder makes poor quality firewood, this is probably not the reason for its absence in the Late Iron Age/Roman deposits, since elm and willow/poplar, which are also considered as low grade firewood (Edlin 1949; Porter 1990), were exploited. A possible explanation could relate to environmental or climatic variations, perhaps a lowering of the water table or improved ground drainage for agricultural purposes. Alternatively, alder may have had more important uses in the local economy, *e.g.* hurdle-making and basketry.

Firewood was clearly collected from a range of habitats around the valley and although there appears to have been some preference for oak (*Quercus* sp.), ash (*Fraxinus excelsior*), blackthorn (*Prunus spinosa*) and the hawthorn/*Sorbus* group (Pomoideae), this selection could reflect distribution or availability.

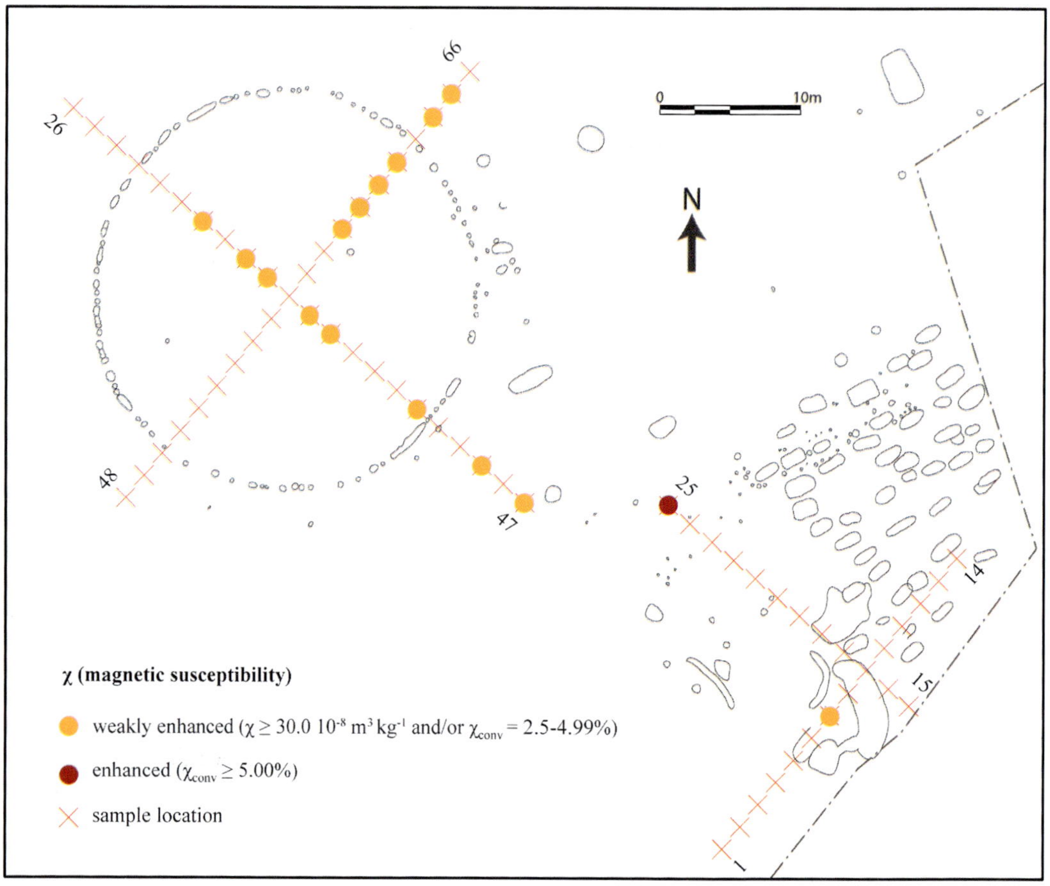

Figure 4.10 FLN 053: χ (magnetic susceptibility) survey

VI. Scientific analysis

Soil phosphate and magnetic susceptibility survey
by John Crowther

Introduction

Sixty-six soil samples were taken from a series of transect lines running through palisaded circle 053:*0346* and on into the Early Anglo Saxon cemetery Flixton II (Figs 4.9 and 4.10). The samples were analysed at the University of Wales Lampeter for both total phosphate (P) and magnetic susceptibility (χ).

Phosphates: phosphates occur naturally in all organic material (topsoil, plant tissue, excreta, bone, *etc*.). As they are released by organic decomposition processes, they tend to form insoluble compounds and thus become 'fixed' within the mineral fraction of soils and sediments. Many forms of human activity lead to phosphate enrichment and, under favourable conditions, this may remain detectable for 10^2–10^3 years (see reviews by Bethel and Máté 1989; Crowther 1997; Heron 2001).

Magnetic susceptibility: χ (low frequency mass-specific magnetic susceptibility) in soils and sediments largely reflects the presence of magnetic forms of iron oxide (*e.g.* maghaemite) – this being dependent upon the presence of iron (Fe) and occurrence of alternating reduction-oxidation conditions that favour the formation of magnetic minerals. Enhancement is particularly associated with burning, but is also caused by microbial activity in topsoils (see reviews by Clark 1996; Scollar *et al*. 1990).

Only the conclusions are presented here, with the full version of the report available in archive.

Conclusions

The analytical results demonstrate the potential of phosphate and magnetic susceptibility surveys on sites of this type, with both surveys revealing quite marked spatial variability which seem likely to be related to human activity in the past. While the phosphate data show definite areas of enrichment (Fig. 4.9), the results of the χ survey are less convincing, with only one sample showing clear signs of enhancement (4.10). Unfortunately, neither phosphate-P enrichment nor χ enhancement in subsoils can be linked to a particular phase of site occupation (*cf.* sealed contexts of known phase or date). In this case, the patterns that emerge from the survey results do not appear to correspond closely with the known archaeological features, other than the elevated phosphate-P concentrations in the area of the Period II.a. Late Iron Age/Early Roman pit group and extending into the Period III. Early Anglo-Saxon cemetery Flixton II, which seem likely to be associated with ground disturbance (rather than bone).

VII. Overview of the Late Iron Age/Early Roman archaeology
by Stuart Boulter

In addition to difficulties interpreting the character of the activity represented by the Late Iron Age/early Roman deposits in FLN 053, firm dating was also problematic, particularly with regard to defining pre and post-Conquest deposits. However, the overriding impression given by the ceramic evidence is of a later Iron Age native tradition continuing through the first half of the 1st century, beyond the Conquest, with only limited romanisation.

Within the confines of the areas covered by this publication, the features were limited to the palisaded circle, a series of pits, a slot and a short length of ditch. However, the features in the FLN 053 site only represented the northern limits of a more extensive area of Late Iron Age and Roman archaeology (see Chapter 16) concentrated in the quarry phases excavated as FLN 059 and FLN 062 (Fig. 1.1), with evidence of activity continuing into the middle of the 4th century. One component of the Late Iron Age/early Roman phase was a rectilinear system of field boundary ditches with its northern limit represented by a south-west to north-east ditch running through the above sites and continuing on to the south-west through the quarry areas excavated as FLN 056 and FLN 057 (Fig. 1.1). The FLN 053 features, which were at least broadly contemporary with the field system, were located beyond its northern limit in what was probably, at that time, open unenclosed ground, although boundaries defined solely by hedges cannot be completely ruled out.

Although domestic-type refuse and some industrial waste in the form of smithing slag was present within the pit fills, there were also elements of the assemblage that were suggestive of more deliberate deposition. Pits with a possible deliberate depositional element to their finds formed a cluster to the east of the broadly contemporary palisaded circle. A large proportion of the ceramic assemblage was recovered from only a small number of the pits and was considered, from its condition, to have been in its primary context of deposition. While the recovered material could still be described as domestic in character, the inclusion of one whole pot, a number of broken but comparatively complete vessels and objects such as loomweights and sling-shot does suggest that the pits may have performed a dual role.

The pits, which varied considerably in character, formed a loose linear concentration arcing from the southern edge of the FLN 053 area away to the north and passing close to the eastern side of the palisaded circle. These included a group of irregular features to the south, with more regular, circular, oval, sub-rectangular and trough-like pits to the north. An enhancement in the soil phosphate levels towards the southern edge of the site corresponds with the area of irregular pits and is consistent with the inclusion of organic material in their fill. The ceramic finds recovered from the fills of the irregular features tended to be more abraded than those to the north. It is unclear whether the overall semi-formal configuration of features was due to their respecting some element of the contemporary landscape that did not survive archaeologically, or that the apparent formality was fortuitous. The two, possibly associated, pairs of similarly orientated trough-like features may also be significant. If the material included in the pits was from domestic activity then the lack of accompanying structural evidence, other than the palisaded circle, suggests that it was generated elsewhere and subsequently moved to its final context of deposition. However, it is possible that some ephemeral evidence was lost to post-depositional processes such as ploughing or during the unsupervised site strip. In addition, an unknown number of the undated features may actually belong in this phase.

The palisaded circle was an unusual feature. No close parallels have been identified on other excavated sites and its function remains unclear. Artefactual evidence from the post-holes and slots was extremely limited and the ceramic finds were relatively undiagnostic and exhibited moderate to high levels of abrasion suggesting that they may not have been in their original context of deposition. If that were the case, then this also has implications regarding the dating of the structure, with the finds only providing a *terminus post quem.* While it is still considered that the artefactual evidence places the palisaded circle in Period II.a., it unfortunately remains unclear whether it was constructed prior to the Conquest or later in the 1st century AD. On balance however, given that the adjacent possibly associated pits strongly suggest a native tradition, it seems likely that, regardless of date, its influences were native rather than Roman.

The close spacing of the shallow post-settings, some within slots, gives the impression that the structure was formed using a large number of posts which individually may not have been substantial in character. Whether the gaps between the posts were left open or closed in some way, to make viewing of the interior difficult from the outside, is impossible to say. It also remains unclear as to how many entrances were present as the severe, unsupervised, machining of the site may have removed some of the shallower lain features. Two of the five gaps suggested as possible entrances are considered more likely to have been genuine for a number of reasons. The first, to the ESE, represented the widest break between successive features in the circuit (2.7m). The second was that to the east, due to the close proximity of pits external to the circle which included in their fills artefactual material that could be considered to be a deliberately structured deposit. In addition, the remarkably regular character of the circle was slightly interrupted at that point with the two post-holes flanking the 1.6m wide gap very slightly offset towards the exterior of the circle, particularly that to the south. Further considerations, when proposing that the gaps to the east and south-east represent genuine entrances, were made with reference to the extensive studies undertaken by Mike Parker Pearson (Parker Pearson 1996) and Rachael Pope (Pope 2007). Both of these publications involve the critical examination of orientations and the allocation of space within the layout of Iron Age structures and settlements, and the identification and interpretation of both chronological and regional trends. It is universally accepted that from the Middle Bronze Age through to the Roman occupation the native house form in Britain was round, but the assertion that entrances overwhelmingly tended to be on the eastern side (Parker Pearson 1996, 119), a trend repeated in Iron Age shrines, has not always been as well received (Pope 2007, 211). However, it is conceded that in the later and Roman Iron Age, the period attributed to the Flixton structure, a fairly standardised eastern orientation is evident in house design (Pope 2007, 224). While the function of the Flixton structure remains unclear, it does seem to conform to the trend described by Parker Pearson, providing that is, that the principal entrance(s) have been correctly identified. In the past, the eastern orientation of entrances has variously been interpreted as practical, to avoid the prevailing winds and to optimise the ingress of light, and symbolic, facing the rising sun (Parker Pearson 1996). In reality, this tradition probably developed as a combination of these and other similarly practical and more esoteric considerations, although it has also been suggested that exaggeration of the statistical data has made the practice seem more widespread than it actually is

(Pope 2007, 212). Given that the Flixton structure is large, and there is no evidence that it was ever roofed, it seems unlikely that the practical considerations of shelter and light were ever a major influence on the position of the entrances. However, other practical considerations, relating to purely local factors such as position in the landscape and its relation to contemporary activities, may have come to bear, although it seems logical to suggest that established tradition and the need to invest symbolic meaning may also have been influencing factors.

Soil phosphate and magnetic susceptibility surveys within the circle did not identify a discernible pattern relating to the structure and there was a lack of associated features internal to the circle, although the exclusion of activity may actually have been the whole point of the structure. Its location away from the focus of occupation may also be significant, along with its position in the shallow valley almost directly on the long axis of the Early Neolithic long barrow to the north-east, which also runs through the Late Neolithic timber circle some 140m to the south-west. The long barrow and circular barrows of the Early Bronze Age monuments would certainly have still been prominent features in the landscape and may have had some influence on the location of the later monument. It is entirely possible that the structure performed a perfectly normal function associated with the adjacent occupation. However, it may not be a coincidence that another, broadly contemporary, enigmatic structure, a rectangular post-hole building with three lines of internal post-holes, also lies north of the ditched field system approximately 140m to the SSW of the circle (Boulter 2006b). So far, no exact parallels have been found for this structure. Possible interpretations include its use as a large-scale granary raised on a platform supported by the rows of posts (the most likely), or as a temple or shrine, an interpretation for which there is less evidence. However two gold coins (both 'Irstead' type quarter staters) and two silver coins, all attributable to the Iceni (P. de Jersey pers. comm.) recovered from the immediate vicinity hint at an enhanced status for the structure (see Chapter 16). Identifying the function of this structure could have a major bearing on the interpretation of the palisaded circle. If it were found to be associated with a purely domestic activity, then this would more likely be the case for the circle as well. However, if the rectangular structure had performed a more specialised function such as a shrine or temple, it would strengthen the case for a similar scenario for the circle as part of a more extensive complex.

While not providing a close parallel for the palisaded circle, the excavations at Fison Way, Thetford do bear some comparison (Gregory 1992). The three major phases of activity represented at that site involved the successive construction and alteration of a series of enclosures and associated structures. Domestic occupation did not appear to be the prime reason for the construction of the site, although some industrial processes such as metalworking were clearly undertaken. The site has been interpreted as a major religious and ceremonial centre for the local Iron Age tribe, the Iceni, and it is structures dated to the final phase there, in the middle of the 1st century AD, that affinities with Flixton are tentatively recognised. Based on the tribal boundary between the Iceni to the north and the Trinovantes to the south, proposed by Edward Martin (Martin 1988b), the Flixton site was located within the territory of the Iceni, a fact that would seem to add weight to the comparisons made between the two sites. The Phase III site at Fison Way comprised a large rectangular double-ditched enclosure with three circular buildings and two other circular arrangements of posts, and it is the latter that merit comparison with the Flixton structure. The two post-hole circles recorded at Thetford were far smaller than that at Flixton, 10m rather than 27m, but were similarly interpreted as enclosures rather than roofed buildings, possibly acting as ceremonial fore-buildings to the adjacent roundhouses. Comprising shallow gullies with opposed entrances flanked by post-holes with two internal post-settings, the similarities with Flixton, where the palisaded circle represented the whole of the monument with no associated buildings or enclosing ditches, are not obviously apparent. However, in broad terms, it is the presence of circular structures on sites where their function does not seem to be entirely domestic in character that may be significant.

In summary, it is difficult to offer a meaningful interpretation for the Period II.a., Late Iron Age/early Roman deposits within FLN 053 as they were clearly peripheral to a wider area of contemporary activity. While the attribution of dates to individual features was not possible with any degree of precision, the currency of the deposits spanned the decades either side of the Conquest with no major evidence for disruption of what appears to have been only a moderately romanised native tradition (see also Chapter 16).

Part III

The Anglo-Saxon Cemeteries

Chapters 7–9 and 15 were written in 2007 and the rest of Part III in 2009

Chapter 5. Introduction to the Anglo-Saxon Cemeteries

I. Introduction
by Penelope Walton Rogers

The Early Anglo-Saxon period is represented at Flixton by two burial grounds, Flixton I and II, and a settlement. The main focus of this report is the substantial cemetery, Flixton II, excavated in two campaigns, in 1998–9 (FLN 053) and 2001 (FLN 062) (Fig. 5.1). A single grave discovered at Flixton I in 1990 (FLN 008) will also be included, along with some metal-detected finds that suggest at least one other burial in the same area (see Chapter 15). The settlement (FLN 061), however, is presented here in outline only (see Chapter 16.IV), for reasons described in Chapter 1.

Flixton II was at first contained in a rectangular plot, but later expanded towards the south, where there was a cluster of burials focused on a Bronze Age barrow. Most of the external boundary of the cemetery has been located and it is estimated that there were originally over 200 graves, of which sixty-two have been excavated. A single fragment of a 5th-century brooch was found in the general area of Flixton I, but no inhumations earlier than the late 5th or early 6th century have been recorded at either cemetery, no cremations have been detected, and only two sherds of 5th-century pottery have been identified from the settlement. While it is possible that early graves exist in the unexcavated portion of the site, on the evidence available at present, Flixton II appears to have been in use from the end of the 5th century to the middle of the 7th century and the settlement was mostly occupied in the 6th century, with some continuation into the 7th. Flixton I was probably contemporary with the earliest phase of Flixton II.

Flixton lies to the west of a small string of Waveney Valley sites that includes Bungay on the Suffolk side of the river and Broome, Earsham, Stockton and Kirby Cane on the Norfolk side (for details, see Chapter 14). They are to the south of the much larger group of cemeteries on the river systems of east-central Norfolk, which include Caistor St Edmund (Caistor-by-Norwich), Bergh Apton, Spong Hill and Morning Thorpe. Caistor St Edmund is the site of the capital of the *civitas* of the Iceni, Venta Icenorum, and it is thought to have retained some regional authority and administrative importance after the collapse of Roman government (Myres and Green 1973, 8–14; Scull 1992, 12, 14). Although Flixton is now separated from these sites by the county boundary, it originally lay inside the old Iceni territory (Dymond and Martin 1999, 41), and there would have been access to Venta Icenorum and the rest of the Norfolk group via the Roman road that crossed the river at Bungay (Plunkett 2005, 22).

Upriver from Flixton, to the west, there is a cluster of sites with 5th-century material, in the valleys of the upper Waveney and its tributary the Dove (see Chapter 14). Beyond these, on the opposite side of a shallow watershed, is the great arc of 5th- and 6th-century sites on the rivers flowing into the fens, such as the settlement at West Stow and the Cambridgeshire cemeteries. In the opposite direction, downriver, there may have been early post-Roman activity at Burgh Castle, close to the coast (Scull 1992, 14–15), but on the whole 5th-century evidence from the lower Waveney Valley is sparse and the settlement at Bloodmoor Hill, Carlton Colville, does not appear to have been founded until the 6th century (Lucy *et al.* 2009, 329, 427). Further away to the south, on the other side of the claylands, lies the Sandlings province, where barrow burials at Snape (Filmer-Sankey and Pestell 2001) and Sutton Hoo (Bruce-Mitford 1978, 1983; Carver 2005) mark the rise of a new elite in the later 6th and 7th centuries. This process runs parallel to the documented rise of the Wuffings, whose dynasty eventually established control over East Anglia (Plunkett 2005, 61–2).

Flixton therefore occupied a borderland position at the southern edge of the Norfolk group, and faced towards the rising power base in south-east Suffolk. It lay on a west–east route with access to the fen-edge sites, close to its intersection with a north–south Roman road and a river crossing. All of this would have put Flixton and its neighbouring sites in a significant position in the shifting politics of East Anglia.

II. The structure and aims of the report
by Penelope Walton Rogers

The first duty of any team working on an excavated cemetery is to reconstruct the lives of the people buried there and to explore the character of the community from which they came. To this end, the report has been structured so that it reviews the cemetery layout and burial practice, artefact assemblages and human remains, before moving on to more interpretative studies, which consider the individuals in the graves and how their gender roles and social background can be understood through the burial evidence. Between these two sections lies a pivotal chapter on chronology. The manner in which social roles were expressed through burial practice changed during the period in question, and recent advances in the chronology of East Anglian cemeteries (Penn and Brugmann 2007, 42–71) have allowed their pattern to be plotted with more precision than formerly.

Establishing the composite character of the community which buried its dead at Flixton has been hampered by the fact that both burial grounds have been only partially excavated. It has been difficult to plot family groups, for example, or to produce complete statistics on mortality rates. Time and budget did not permit isotope analysis of the teeth, which might have indicated the place of origin of some of the dead. Nevertheless, comparison with other sites and the use of established models of the social structure portrayed in more complete cemeteries

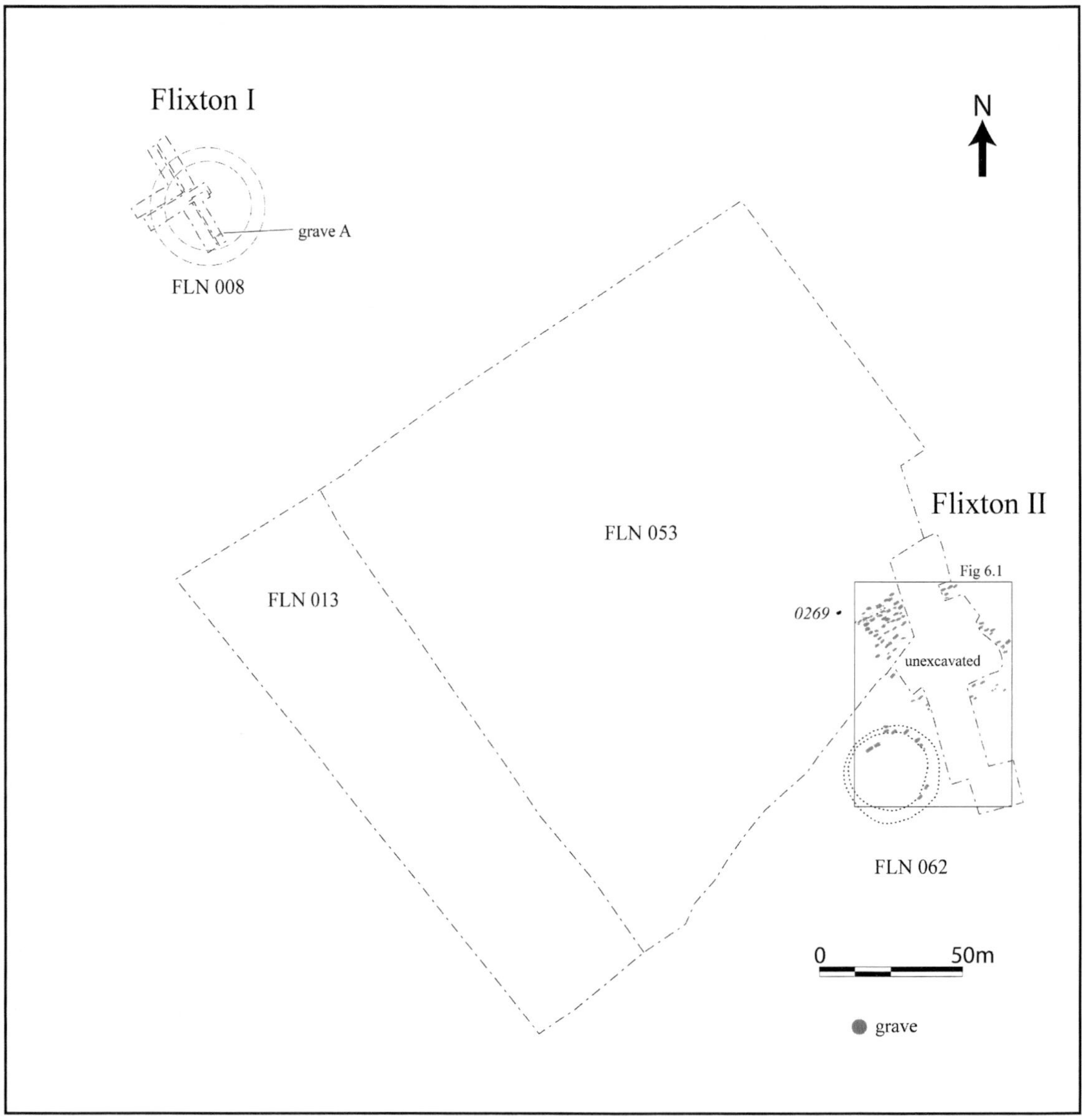

Figure 5.1 Period III, Early Anglo-Saxon features (Areas FLN 008, 013, 053 and 062). The settlement lies off the plan to the north-east

(Scull 1993; 1995; Härke 1997; Ravn 2003) has allowed some conclusions to be drawn concerning the likely make-up of the missing portion of the population, and artefact studies have produced evidence for their origins and affiliation. The significance of the separate burial ground, Flixton I, in relation to the large enclosed cemetery, Flixton II, has also been explored.

The second responsibility of the investigative team is to examine the contribution that the site can make to current research themes and debates. Population movement, interaction between ethnic groups and territories, gender roles, exogamy, spiritual beliefs and the impact of a changing ideology are all matters that can find expression in clothed and furnished burials, and Flixton has material to contribute on each of these subjects. These strands have been threaded through the main narrative and addressed in greater detail in the final section, where a hypothesis will be presented as to who the people at Flixton were, and what their relationship may have been with the rest of East Anglia. This is only the first part of the story, however. The cemeteries have provided a chronology and social structure for the community at Flixton, but attention will now turn to the settlement, its putative pagan shrine, and to the written sources. A study of Flixton as part of a 7th-century royal estate, given in endowment to one of the earliest Christian bishops, belongs more naturally in the next stage of investigation.

III. The excavation of the Anglo-Saxon cemeteries

by Stuart Boulter
Fig. 5.1; Pl. 5.1

Early Anglo-Saxon burials at Flixton were first identified during a limited rescue excavation in 1990 (FLN 008) targeted on a ring-ditch feature in the then Alan Newport Quarry known as Hill Pit (now Cemex). For the purposes of this publication this cemetery has been called Flixton I (Fig. 5.1). While only one grave was recorded cut into the southern side of the ring-ditch, the area of excavation was small. The presence of other graves was considered likely, as contemporary artefactual evidence was recovered from the north side of the excavated area during a metal-detecting survey.

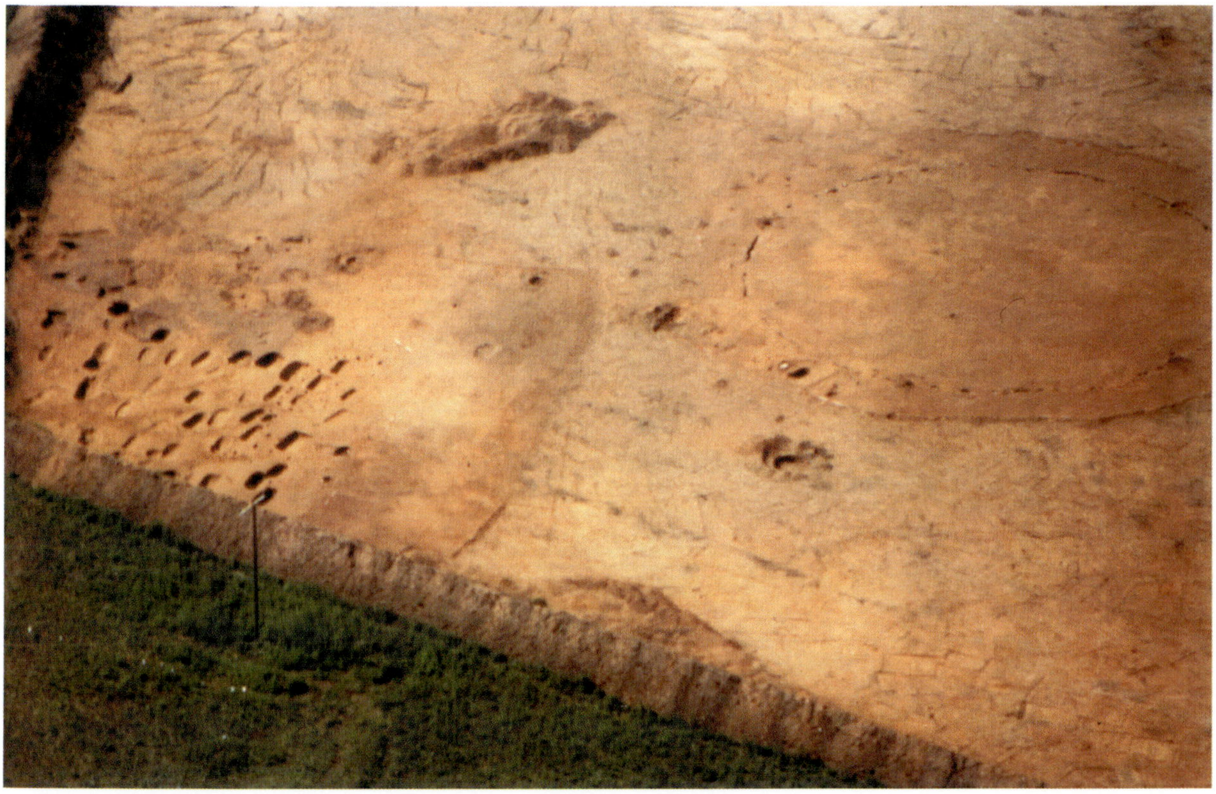

Plate 5.1 Overview of the northern part of the Flixton II cemetery (Area FLN 053). North is to the right of the photograph

Part of a more extensive cemetery, which is here termed Flixton II (Fig. 5.1), was uncovered in 1998 (FLN 053), comprising forty-five inhumations (Pl. 5.1). Its limits were defined and a further seventeen inhumations excavated in 2001 (FLN 062), the latter including eleven associated with a previously known ring-ditch feature (FLN 010). The ring-ditch would almost certainly have been accompanied by an internal barrow mound and it is this which would have formed the focus for the burials. Excavation evidence suggests that by this time, the ditch itself had been filled by a combination of natural accretion and then rubbish disposal during the Roman period. The main group of burials forming Flixton II occupied a tightly defined rectangular plot measuring approximately 40m from south-west to north-east, and 50m from north-west to south-east. There was no surviving evidence for a physical boundary around the main area of the cemetery, but the presence of some form of demarcation can be conjectured due to its regular shape.

While it is clear that the presence of earlier landscape features, Early Bronze Age round barrows and their associated ring-ditches, influenced the location of both Flixton I and Flixton II, in the case of Flixton II the existing topography may also have been a factor (see Chapter 16). A 1m interval topographic survey undertaken by the quarry company shows the main cemetery area lying immediately above the 16m contour within a small north-facing promontory overlooking the western end of a shallow eastern-facing depression immediately to the north (Chapter 16). There is no similar topographic information for Flixton I, but experience suggests that Early Bronze Age round barrows were often situated in locally prominent positions. In this instance, its subsequent reuse as the site for a windmill can be considered as further evidence that this was the case for the FLN 008 monument. It is also debatable whether subsoil geology influenced the position of the main group of burials forming Flixton II, as its western edge coincided with the change from a very stony subsoil to a relatively stone-free sand with gravel within the body of the cemetery. However, the character of the naturally occurring subsoil at Flixton changes laterally on a regular basis, both on a micro and macro scale, and the marked difference recorded on the edge of the cemetery may have been entirely coincidental.

IV. Post-deposition damage and quality of preservation

by Stuart Boulter

Information for Flixton I is limited to that retrievable from the archive, but photographs taken of the grave during excavation include a profile through the surrounding overburden. Ploughsoil can be seen overlying a slightly thinner layer of brown silty sand subsoil with a combined thickness estimated to be in the region of 0.5m. It is unclear whether the subsoil layer resulted from the degradation of the adjacent Early Bronze Age barrow/windmill mound, as opposed to representing a more laterally persistent naturally derived deposit. However, it would certainly have provided a degree of protection to the underlying grave from recent agricultural processes such as ploughing. This being said, the grave was only 0.15m deep and earlier post-depositional damage must be considered a possibility.

In the case of the FLN 053 component of Flixton II, graves towards the south-east of the excavated area lay immediately below the existing topsoil and had potentially been damaged by both ploughing and during the unsupervised soil-strip. Towards the north and west an increasing thickness of orange/brown sand subsoil had protected the graves from plough damage, but some disruption to the upper levels may have occurred during machining. It is likely then that the generally shallower depth of graves recorded towards the south-east in the FLN 053 area of Flixton II was the result of post-deposition damage rather than the influence of any other factor.

In the FLN 062 component of Flixton II the graves were encountered immediately below the ploughsoil. While this was similar to those recorded towards the south-east in FLN 053, in this instance the soil-strip was closely supervised and any post-depositional damage limited to that caused by earlier agricultural activities.

Chapter 6. Cemetery Location, Layout and Burial Practice

I. Location

The settlement stood on a low ridge that looked northwards across water meadows to the River Waveney and south towards the prehistoric monuments and the two Anglo-Saxon cemeteries (see Chapter 16). The large Flixton II cemetery was situated on a spur of land 500–600m directly to the south of the settlement, on the opposite side of a shallow depression, and Flixton I lay at a similar distance to the south-west. The space between the settlement and cemeteries is rather more than, for example, the 200–300m between the settlement and cemetery at West Stow (West 1985), but Flixton II would still be visible from the settlement, as would the mound with which Flixton I was associated. Since no other occupation has been located in the area, it has been assumed that both burial grounds served the same settlement.

The prehistoric earthworks seem to have been deliberately incorporated into the Anglo-Saxon use of the site. A double ring-ditch which must represent a relatively large barrow lay at the western end of the settlement, where it would have provided a suitable place for assembly; Flixton II was positioned directly in front of a smaller barrow to the south; and the recorded Flixton I burial lay inside the ring-ditch of a third. When viewed from the settlement, therefore, both cemeteries would have had an Early Bronze Age barrow for a backdrop.

The standing monuments were probably part of what drew the settlers to this site. Between a third and a half of Anglo-Saxon cemeteries in one survey proved to be associated with early monuments and most commonly these were prehistoric round barrows (Williams 1997, 4–6). Some burials were dug into the barrow itself (Williams 1997, 22), but most cemeteries were simply located in the vicinity of the monuments. Howard Williams argues that this was an attempt to relate the settlers to the area's ancestral and spiritual past, and to legitimise their claims to control land and local resources (Williams 1997, 25–6).

II. Cemetery layout and development

Fig. 6.1

As described in Chapter 5, Flixton II was contained within a rectangle, 40m x 50m, represented by two corners and the remains of at least three straight edges (Figs 5.1 and 6.1). The 51 graves (Graves 1–51) within this plot were often quite close, especially in the northern area where there were several instances of graves inter-cutting, and new burials inserted into old grave pits. Although there was no boundary ditch or post-hole alignment to mark the edges of the plot, it seems likely that there was some form of barrier, such as a hedge, to separate the cemetery from the land around it. Given that the excavation of this main plot accounted for close to 25% of the overall cemetery area, it is estimated that, with the same concentration of burials throughout, the cemetery will have accommodated approximately 200 individuals.

The rectangular shape of the plot is extremely unusual for the early part of the Early Anglo-Saxon period. Unbounded cemeteries are regarded as characteristic of the period up to the later 6th century and concomitant with settlements that are loosely structured and unfenced (Reynolds 2003, 103, 130). If, on occasion, they have a well-defined edge, it is usually because they have been constrained by the terrain or by earlier man-made structures. A 5th- and 6th-century cemetery at Wasperton, Warwickshire, for example, took its shape from a Romano-British enclosure, *c*.50m x 30m internally (Carver *et al*. 2009, 116–9). At Flixton there was no such earlier structure. The rectangular plot lay outside the northern limit of the ditched fields and enclosures of the Late Iron Age and early Roman periods, and the recognisable features in the underlying archaeology were curvilinear (see Chapter 4). It is possible to draw parallels with a smaller rectangular plot at Dover Buckland, Kent, for which a theory was advanced that it was a burial ground for settlers from outside the area, who had been granted a limited amount of space by the local population (Evison 1987, 143). Whether this can be applied to Flixton will be considered in a later chapter (Chapter 14).

To the south of the main plot there was a separate group of eleven graves, Graves 52–62, on and around the barrow. These have proved to be late burials and predominantly male (Chapters 9 and 11), a pattern that can be seen elsewhere and one which coincides with the raising of new barrows over princely burials, as at Snape and Sutton Hoo (discussed further in Chapter 11). It can be argued that it represents an attempt to claim the prestige of a barrow burial without the expense of raising a mound.

The single burial at Flixton I (Grave A) and the associated metal-detected finds, I/NG1–6, although also on a barrow, are earlier in date and are roughly contemporary with the earliest burials at Flixton II (see Chapter 9). The reasons why, at an early stage in the settlement's history, this group chose to bury its dead separately from the rest will be considered in Chapters 10 and 14.

III. Orientation of graves and bodies

Fig. 6.2

The rectangular plot and the graves within it were laid out on a WSW–ENE to SW–NE alignment (Fig. 6.2a), which almost certainly represents the west–east alignment of most East Anglian cemeteries (Fig. 6.2b), modified by the topography of the site. This stretch of the Waveney Valley runs south-west to north-east and the graves follow both the contours of the land and the alignment of the

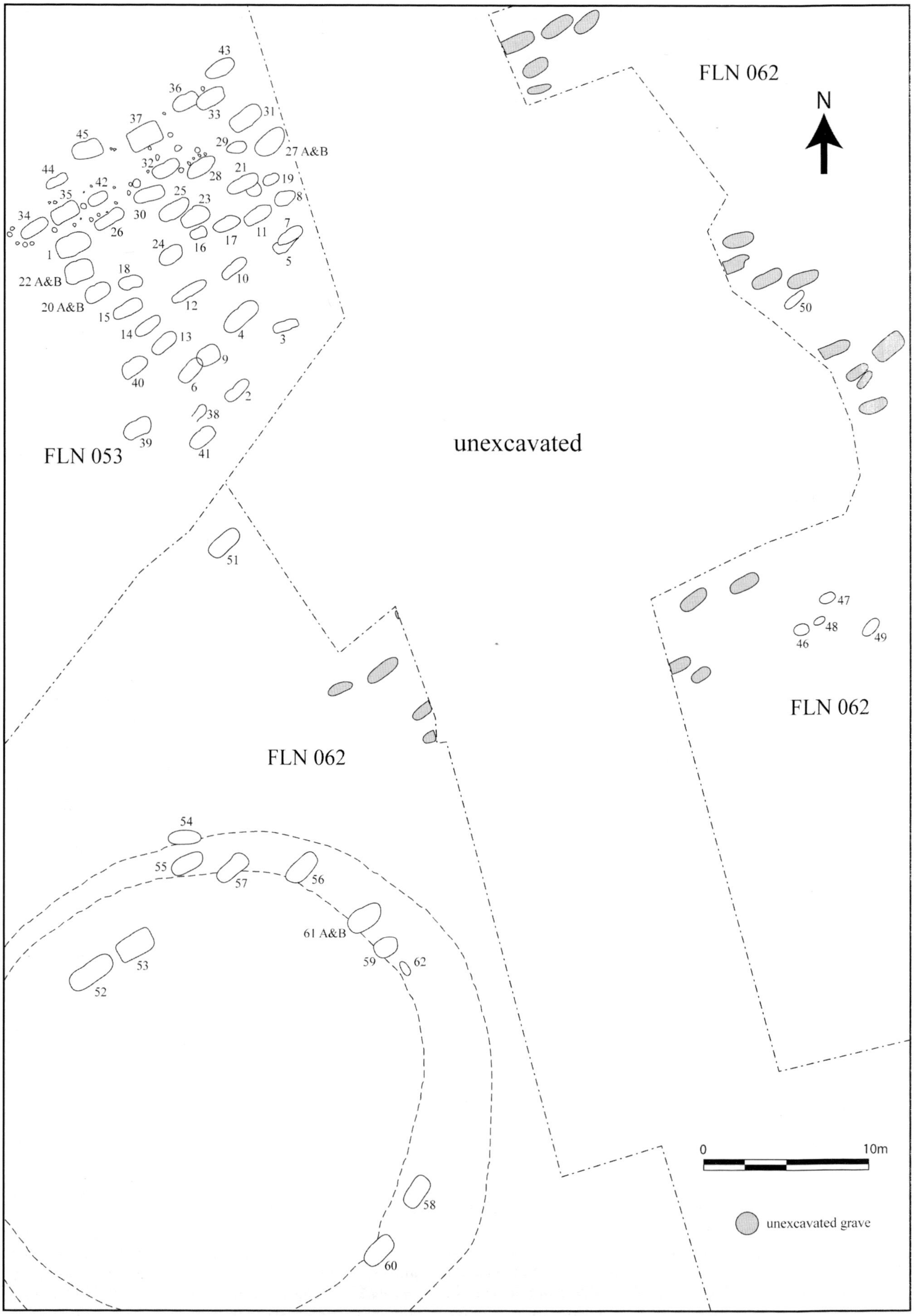

Figure 6.1 The numbering of the excavated graves at Flixton II (Areas FLN 053 and 062)

Romano-British field system to the south. Most variation occurs amongst the southerly cluster of graves, where the round barrow and its surrounding ring-ditch have influenced the orientation of the burial.

Where there was evidence for the orientation of the bodies in the graves, they were found to be almost exclusively head to the west (Table 6.1; Fig. 6.2a). Consequently, for the purposes of consistency in the inventory, the others have been presented in this way, as a measurement in degrees from grid north. In Grave 17, however, the arrangement of garment accessories combined with clothing details indicated that the body had been placed with head to the east. To add to the curious nature of this burial, a man's skull lay on the floor of the grave, at the woman's side.

There are other examples of women, and bodies with female accessories, laid out with the head to the east at Morning Thorpe G153, G207 and possibly G238 (Green *et al.* 1987, 6, 10, 100), Spong Hill G19 and G44 (Fig. 6.2 b) (Hills *et al.* 1984, 4), and Bergh Apton G5, G6 and G21 (Green and Rogerson 1978, 4: note that the E–W orientation of G7 in the cemetery plan is W–E in the catalogue). There are no examples from Snape (Filmer-Sankey and Pestell 2001, 13–14), Bury St Edmunds Westgarth Gardens (West 1988, 7), or Ipswich Boss Hall and Buttermarket/St Stephen's Lane (Scull 2009b), which suggests that this was primarily a Norfolk practice (further west, in Cambridgeshire and the Midlands, grave orientation is much more variable). The body may have been hidden from view in a coffin in one instance (Bergh Apton G6), but in the other examples the burial party must have been conscious of the body's orientation. This reverse burial appears to be a practice only applied to women. Where skeletons have survived, the men in the same cemeteries have been laid out with head to the west, and where they are absent, weapons follow the conventional layout, with spears pointing to the west and swords to the east. It has to be assumed that women were interred this way because of something in their lives that made them appear 'contrary' to the community who buried them.

IV. Grave construction

Graves were cut in a range of shapes, from oval, through parallel-sided with a rounded end, to rectangular (Table 6.1), but there was no detectable pattern in relation to date, gender or age. Grave size, however, had more significance, and there were obvious differences between the smaller graves in the early northern part of the main plot and those to the south. Even allowing for the fact that the area containing early graves had been machined before excavation, the later graves appear to have been dug to a greater depth than the others. The southern graves were also longer and wider, often over 2m long, even though there was no clear evidence for coffins or biers, and no grave goods large enough to require the extra space (unless they were of perishable materials). Once the site's chronology and the parameters for distinguishing male from female have been discussed, it will be shown that grave size was related to both gender and date (Chapters 9–11). The smallest graves, less than 1.5m in length, which often have no surviving bones or artefacts, have been classified as the burials of children.

In the tight layout of the northern part of the cemetery, some graves overlapped: Grave 6 cut into the end of Grave 9, Grave 7 was almost wholly inside Grave 5 and Grave 33 impinged on a corner of Grave 36. In at least one case a grave would appear to have been deliberately opened and re-used. In Grave 27, the burial of an adult (B) with male accessories, cut through another (A) with female accessories, a process which left some of the female-gender artefacts at the side of the grave and others in the grave fill. There may be a second example of this practice in Grave 17, where a male skull was found beside a body with female accessories, although this was the unusual case of reversed burial described above, and there may have been some other process at work. In Grave 4 the presence of two fills, one inside the other, and artefacts unusually positioned in the grave, is likely to represent a third case. These consecutive, 'stacked' burials are a recognised phenomenon. They often involve a man and a woman (35% of the sample: Stoodley 2002, 114) and they have sometimes been interpreted as burial in the grave of a pre-deceased spouse. The frequent disturbance of the earlier body led Stoodley to question this idea (Stoodley 2002, 114), but other evidence, especially from the Continent, has endorsed the view that consecutive burial, even when the first body was disturbed in the process, was an expression of a close relationship between the two people in the grave (Penn and Brugmann 2007, 77, 82, 87).

There were three examples of two bodies buried in the same grave, seemingly at the same time. In Grave 20 there were two bodies, A and B, both possibly adults and both with female accessories. In Grave 22 an adult of uncertain sex and without accessories, A, was buried with a child of 11–12 years, B. In Grave 61 a middle-aged female, A, was buried with a young man of 16–18 years old, B. In each case, the bodies had been laid out side-by-side with heads pointing in the same direction, and in Grave 22 they faced each other. This practice is found in all parts of Early Anglo-Saxon England, and several different combinations have been noted, the most common being a woman with a child, closely followed by a man with a woman (Stoodley 2002, 106, 113). A family relationship is often assumed in double burials that include a child, although no DNA analysis or matching features in the skeletons have as yet proved the point.

V. Chambers, coffins, biers and other furnishings

Preservation of skeletal remains and other organic materials, including containers in which the bodies had been placed, was poor throughout the site. Soil stains were generally concentrated in the base of the grave and when not interpreted as relating directly to a body, have been described in the catalogue as 'possible bier', due primarily to the absence of evidence for sides and lids that would indicate a coffin or chamber. An animal hide or heavy wool rug might leave a similar trace. In Grave 35, however, a rectangular grave cut and dark linear stains indicated either a coffin, or a timber grave-lining. Grave 37 also had a large straight-sided cut that suggested a small chamber, although no evidence for timber survived; and dark lines in the soil in Graves 3, 19 and 31 were thought to represent either coffins or rectangular biers.

These graves were all in the northern half of the main plot, but further evidence was found on artefacts from two

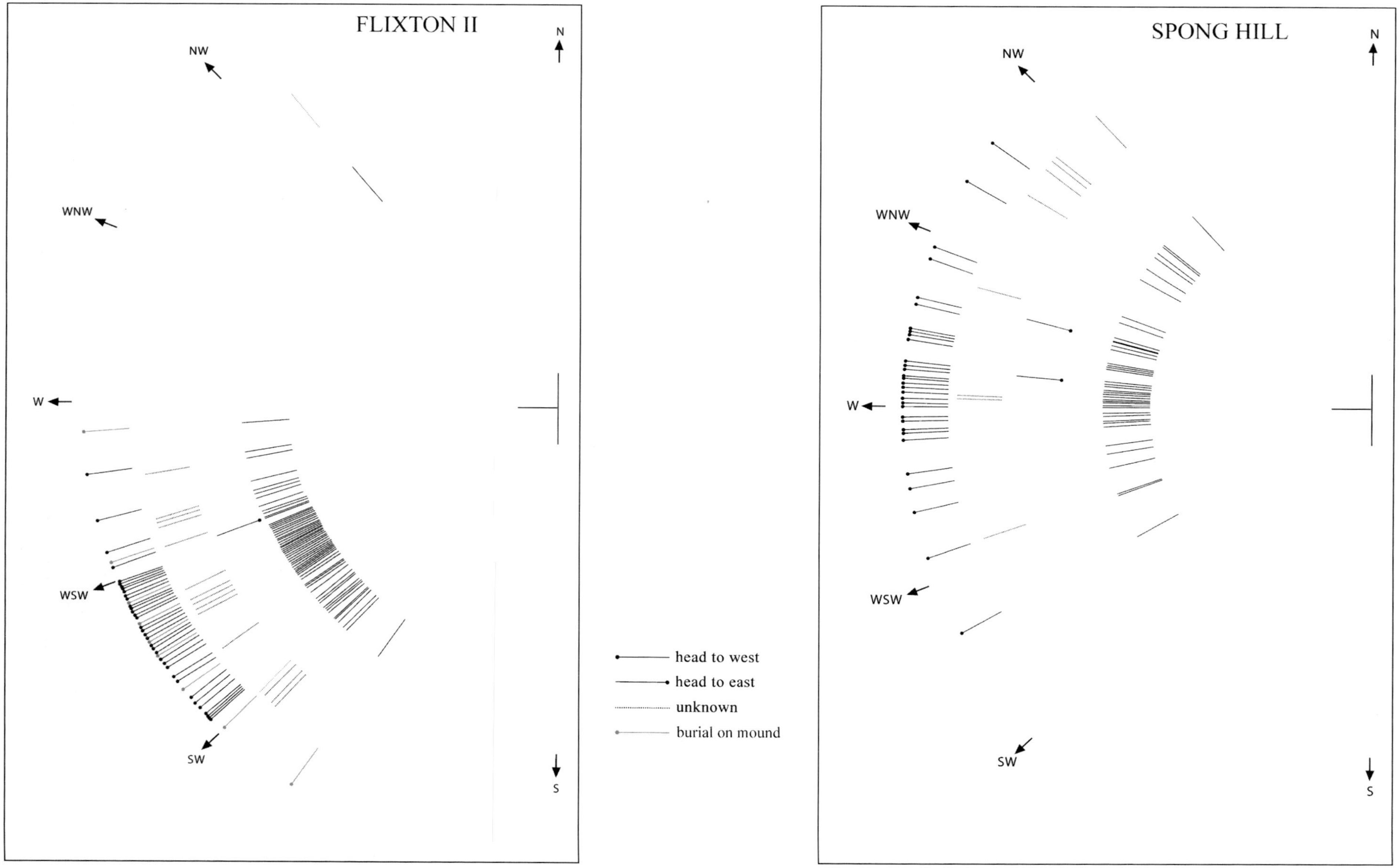

Figure 6.2 Orientation of graves (a) Flixton II and (b) Spong Hill (after Hills *et al.* 1984, Figure 2). The innermost arc includes all graves. The Anglo-Saxon Laboratory

Grave	Orientation	Grave shape	Grave size L x W x D (m)	Posture	Other features
Flixton I					
A	239°H	sub-rectangular	1.90 x 0.70 x 0.15	supine ext	-
Flixton II					
Rectangular plot					
1	244°H	irregular oval	2.10 x 1.30 x 0.56	-	plant cover
2	229°H	sub-rectangular	1.70 x 0.60 x 0.22	on R side legs flexed	plant cover
3	252°H	rectangular	1.57 x 0.55 x 0.22	supine ext	coffin (or bier)
4	228°H	apsidal/sub-rect	2.60 x 0.98 x 0.40	disturbed	one cut inside another; ?container for body
5	227°H	sub-rectangular	2.10 x 1.80 x 0.25	-	bier (or hide or rug); cut by 7
6	223°	sub-rectangular	1.70 x 0.80 x 0.22	-	bier (or hide/rug); cuts end of 9
7	242°H	sub-rectangular	1.52 x 0.60 x 0.44	supine ext	bier (or hide/rug); cuts into 5
8	239°H	sub-rectangular	1.35 x 0.60 x 0.18	-	-
9	239°H	apsidal/sub-rect	1.30 x 0.90 x 0.55	-	end truncated by 6; ?bier
10	227°H	apsidal	1.78 x 0.58 x 0.14–18	ext	-
11	240°H	apsidal	1.94 x 0.60 x 0.18	supine ext	-
12	239°H	apsidal	2.40 x 0.48 x 0.10	ext	-
13	227°H	apsidal	1.70 x 0.80 x 0.14	-	?bier
14	233°H	apsidal	1.70 x 0.65 x 0.20	supine ext	bier (or hide or rug)
15	242°H	sub-rectangular	1.90 x 0.70 x 0.20	supine ext	-
16	253°	oval	1.05 x 0.50 x 0.10	-	-
17	69°	apsidal	1.70 x 0.76 x 0.10	reversed; male skull at side	plant cover; bier (or hide or rug)
18	262°H	apsidal/oval	1.48 x 0.50 x 0.10	on L side, legs flexed	-
19	246°	sub-rectangular	1.02 x 0.55 x 0.14	-	coffin or bier
20	242°H	apsidal	1.68 x 0.86 x 0.32	A unknown; B supine legs ?flexed	-
21	244°H	apsidal	1.87 x 0.80 x 0.16–24	supine	-
22	250°H	sub-rectangular	1.80 x 1.20 x 0.46	A on L side; B on R side	- -
23	239°	sub-rect/apsidal	1.83 x 0.88 x 0.34	prob supine ext	bier (or hide or rug)
24	234°	apsidal	1.62 x 0.90 x 0.26	-	-
25	239°	sub-rectangular	2.20 x 0.75 x 0.15	-	-
26	237°H	sub-rectangular	1.95 x 0.60 x 0.26	supine ext	plant cover; ?bier
27	230°H	oval	2.20 x 1.10 x 0.46	A disturbed; B supine	B - plant cover; bier/hide/rug
28	236°H	apsidal	1.80 x 0.75 x 0.24	supine	bier (or hide/rug); post-holes
29	260°	oval	1.25 x 0.70 x 0.10	-	-
30	256°H	apsidal	primary cut 1.97 x 0.70 x 0.12; secondary cut 1.80 x 0.50 x 0.40	supine	?bier; post-holes
31	236°H	apsidal	2.26 x 0.90 x 0.30	ext	coffin or bier
32	244°H	rect/irregular	1.75 x 0.70 x 0.26	?supine ext	bier (or hide or rug)
33	240°H	apsidal	1.93 x 0.85 x 0.44	supine ext	cuts 36
34	238°H	apsidal	1.85 x 0.65 x 0.30	supine	post-holes
35	240°?H	rectangular	1.70 x 0.83 x 0.22	-	chamber (or coffin) ?post-holes
36	242°H	apsidal	1.75 x 0.80 x 0.38	prone ext	post-holes, cut by 33
37	244°H	rectangular	2.10 x 1.25 x 0.32	?supine ext	chamber; post-holes
38	223°	oval	0.80 x 0.50 x 0.24	-	-
39	244°H	oval	1.70 x 0.95 x 0.64	-	?bier (or hide or rug)
40	239°H	apsidal/oval	1.70 x 0.86 x 0.54	-	-
41	233°H	irregular oval	1.75 x 0.90 x 0.65	supine ext	-
42	246°H	apsidal	1.30 x 0.60 x 0.20	-	post-holes; ?bier
43	242°H	sub-rectangular	1.97 x 0.85 x 0.52	on L side, legs flexed	?bier
44	244°H	apsidal	1.40 x 0.50 x 0.20	-	?bier (or hide or rug)
45	253°	sub-rectangular	1.80 x 0.96 x 0.14	-	-
46	253°	oval	0.95 x 0.60 x 0.34	-	-

47	250°	apsidal/oval	1.00 x 0.54 x 0.34	-	-
48	243°	apsidal	0.70 x 0.38 x 0.16	-	-
49	224°	apsidal	1.30 x 0.56 x 0.45	-	-
50	239°	apsidal	1.50 x 0.56 x 0.16	-	-
51	227°	apsidal	2.30 x 1.10 x 0.50	on L side, flexed, almost crouched	-
Associated with ring-ditch/mound					
52	237°H	sub-rectangular	2.92 x 1.05 x 0.60	-	plant cover; planks over
53	241°H	rectangular	2.30 x 1.35 x 0.47	supine ext, ankles crossed	planks over
54	267°H	apsidal	1.92 x 0.82 x 0.30	-	-
55	244°H	apsidal	2.05 x 0.85 x 0.45	supine ext	plant cover
56	225°H	sub-rectangular	2.20 x 0.80 x 0.48	supine ext	-
57	232°H	apsidal	2.15 x 1.00 x 0.48	supine ext	-
58	215°H	apsidal	2.02 x 0.97 x 0.57	supine ext, legs crossed	-
59	251°H	apsidal/oval	1.62 x 1.08 x 0.48	supine ext	plant cover
60	225°	sub-rectangular	2.00 x 1.00 x 0.45	-	-
61	238°H	apsidal	2.27 x 1.22 x 0.65	A supine; B supine	-
62	320°	apsidal	1.00 x 0.47 x 0.14	-	-

Abbreviations
ext = extended; H = evidence for head to west, as indicated by bones, teeth or artefacts; apsidal = parallel-sided cut with a rounded end; depth indicates the depth dug into natural (depth of topsoil not known)

Table 6.1 Construction of the grave and other features of the burial rite

graves on the southern barrow, as described by Jacqui Watson: 'Wood has been preserved on the outer cone of some of the shield bosses, and this is likely to have come from a coffin or wooden planks laid over the burial. The shield boss from Grave 52 has the remains of ash with a tangential surface and the shield boss from Grave 53 has the remains of oak with a radial surface. The surfaces presented by these two sets of wooden planks indicate how the timber was reduced, the oak being radially split and the ash tree sawn or tangentially split – the standard method used to produce long planks from these trees (Morris 2000, 2102)' (Fell and Watson 2007).

Other organic wrappings of textile, leather or vegetable matter, which have largely been destroyed by post-depositional processes, have also been identified in mineralisation products on grave goods. They include a patterned coverlet in Grave 52 and a possible piled rug in Grave 32. Indeed, elements of the basal stains were almost certainly composite, in that the juxtaposition of the corpse and grave goods had preferentially preserved parts of a container and other organic materials, but only in the general area of the body or artefacts.

Chamber graves are usually associated with adult males of high status, as, for example, at Spong Hill G31 and G40 (Hills *et al.* 1984, 6, 80–2, 91–4). The number of artefacts in Grave 37 accords with this, but the absence of any finds in Grave 35 suggests that status did not always require metal artefacts for its expression. Coffins must also represent extra expenditure of time, effort and materials and in Graves 3 and 31 they were associated with comparatively well-dressed women, although the small example in Grave 19 was probably the burial of a child and, as is often the case with children, it lacked any artefacts. For many people of this period, however, burial was directly into the ground, with a hide or rug between the body and the bare earth.

VI. Posture

Most bodies were supine, with legs extended, which is the most common arrangement in East Anglia (72% of males and 71% of females: Stoodley 1999a, 58). In Grave 22, however, the young adult and child had been positioned on their sides, facing each other, and in three instances single bodies had been placed on their sides, on their left in Graves 18 and 51 and on the right in Grave 2. One of these was female (Grave 51), one was male (Grave 2), the third was unknown, and a male with legs flexed to one side (Grave 43) can be added to the list. Males over the age of 15 were most commonly supine (Härke 1997, 128) but it is possible that the male in Grave 2, classified as 'young adult', was regarded as youthful enough to be laid on his side.

In Grave 36, the brooches were face down and the knife on the right, instead of the more usual left, which suggests that the body was prone. There are certain examples of women buried face down who may have met a violent end, perhaps because of wrong-doing (Hirst 1985, 36–7), but in many cases a prone body is probably just another variant of the burial positions in which women and children are found (Lucy 2000, 78–80). Two males buried on or next to the southern mound had legs crossed, at the ankles in Grave 53 and above the knee in Grave 58. Such postures appear at first casual, but they may have had some significance not yet recognised.

VII. Covering the body

Pl. 6.1

Mineral-preserved plant remains were recorded in nine graves (Pl. 6.1). A sample taken from the layer on top of the sleeve clasps from Grave 17 (17/2) was examined by Dr Allan R. Hall, University of York, who comments as follows: 'The material was clearly a monocotyledonous stem with a ring of vascular bundles. A tiny patch of surviving epidermal cells visible on a fragment examined under a transmission microscope revealed narrowly rectangular cells with the strongly sinuous walls characteristic of grasses and sedges' (full report in site archive). Further samples on spearheads from Grave 2 (2/2) and Grave 55 (55/1) were examined by Dr David Earle Robinson, English Heritage Centre for Archaeology, and reported as 'monocotyledonous material, most probably grass or sedge'. Less well preserved, straw-like material was recorded on another spearhead, Grave 52 (52/1), on shield bosses from Graves 1 (1/3 i) and 27 (27B/7) and on knives from Graves 26 (26/7), 33 (33/1) and 59 (59/2). In each case, the plant matter was on one face only, and in Graves 1, 17 and 27 this could be shown to be the upper surface.

Placing a layer of plants over the dead was probably a relatively common practice, although the evidence is limited to those burials where there have been suitable conditions for the preservation of organic materials. A wide range of plants has been recorded. They include grass or flower stems at Sewerby G19, East Yorkshire; straw or grass at Mildenhall, Suffolk, Woodingdean G5, Sussex, and Monkton, Kent; bracken at Barnham, Suffolk, Snape G7, Suffolk, Swaffham G18, Norfolk, and Mucking, Essex; rushes at Berinsfield G102, Oxfordshire, and reeds or rushes at Lechlade G92, Gloucestershire; greenweed (*Genista tinctoria* L., dyers' broom or woadwaxen) at Finglesham G204, Kent; and, as well as the plant stalks found in several graves at Ipswich, seeds of yellow flag iris (*Iris pseudacorus* L.) and bogbean (*Menyanthes trifoliata* L.) were tentatively identified in Boss Hall G313 (Hirst 1985, 31; Hills and Wade-Martins 1976, 9, pl. VIII; Boyle *et al.* 1995, 51; West 1998, 273; Lucy 2000, 97; Filmer-Sankey and Pestell 2001, 242; Chadwick Hawkes and Grainger 2006, 149; Scull 2009b, 66).

Greenweed, yellow flag iris and bogbean are sources of dye (Grierson 1986, 83, 104, 122), and it is possible that the purple alkanet-like colorant that stained six burials at Snape also came from plants placed in the grave (Walton Rogers 2001a, 214). That being the case, a mineral pigment, ochre, found in G6573 at Springfield Lyons, Essex (Tyler and Major 2005, 6), probably forms part of the same pattern. Dyestuffs often had ritual significance in early societies (Forbes 1964, 99–104), and dyeplants frequently appear in later herbals and leech-books (Cockayne 1864–6). As Susan Hirst has commented, plants in graves may have been 'not just to protect the body from contact with the earth, but possibly for magic protection by virtue of a particular plant which was perhaps thought to have magical properties beyond death' (Hirst 1985, 31).

VIII. Grave markers

Features adjudged to be contemporary, due primarily to their juxtaposition to, and apparent formal association with, individual graves, were concentrated within the northern third of the main plot of Flixton II. In this area, a series of post-holes was recorded close to the edges of the graves and while positive attribution to an individual burial was not always possible, it was clear that their location was significant. The number of instances where graves encroached upon an earlier burial was small and

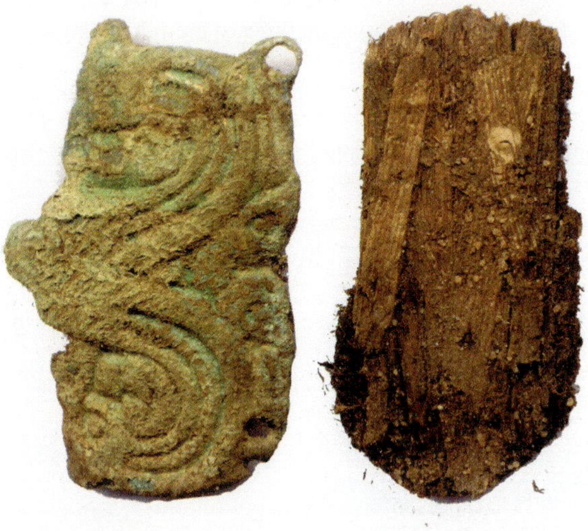

Plate 6.1 Grass or sedge from Grave 17. The organic layer has been lifted, face up, from the top of sleeve clasp 17/3 i, hook piece. Dimensions of clasp, 35 x 24mm. The reverse of the organic layer is shown in Plate 10.2. Image: The Anglo-Saxon Laboratory

their overall arrangement indicated a deliberate semi-formal layout, with graves lined up in south-west to north-east orientated end-to-end rows and also positioned side by side. On that basis it is reasonable to assume that a grave marker or above-ground structure was employed in order to facilitate the recognition of earlier burials and deter encroachment. The post-holes provide the only surviving physical evidence for such features.

A few of the post-holes, such as the two interpreted as being associated with Grave 36 (Fig. 6.1), were positioned on the long axis of graves and these have been interpreted as grave markers, primarily due to the absence of other post-holes along the grave sides. Where multiple post-holes were recorded in association with a grave, for example the ten around Grave 42 (Fig. 6.1), an alternative interpretation has been sought. One possibility involves their holding a series of posts forming part of a revetment structure or curbing around a small mound centred on the grave itself. Generally small, the circular post-holes ranged in diameter from 0.2m to 0.4m with depths also not exceeding 0.4m and fills comprising dirty brown silty sand with occasional gravel and pebble inclusions.

Post-built structures in association with cremations are well-known from the Thames Valley southwards, but they occur less frequently with inhumations (Down and Welch 1990, 29–33; Boyle *et al.* 1995, 123–4). There are examples with inhumations from Kent, at Finglesham and St Peters, Broadstairs (Hogarth 1973), and Castledyke, North Lincolnshire, where they were also concentrated in the northern part of the cemetery (Drinkall and Foreman 1998, 27, 213, 335). An example with four substantial posts around a double inhumation at Morning Thorpe, G148 (Green *et al.* 1987, I, 76–7), stakes supporting an organic cover in Snape G2 (Filmer-Sankey 1992, 48; Filmer-Sankey and Pestell 2001, 19–21, 241), and a central narrow trench thought to indicate a grave marker in three graves at Springfield Lyons, Essex (Tyler and Major 2005, 6) seem to be the only other representatives of the practice in the main part of East Anglia. In Cambridgeshire, however, at Edix Hill, there were ten graves with one or two post-holes, usually at the foot or head end of the grave, or sometimes at the side (Malim and Hines 1998, 44–79: Graves 5, 8, 10, 33, 59, 60, 73, 76, 84 and 88). At least four come from Phase 1, the Migration period (Malim and Hines 1998, 279–91), which is comparable with the dates of the Flixton graves with post-holes (see Chapter 9).

IX. Organisation of the cemetery

Although it is difficult to see an overall pattern when the cemetery has been only partially excavated, there is evidence for a change in the grouping of graves over time. In the northern part of the main cemetery, the graves of men, women and children from different phases were mingled together. This is typical of those cemeteries that are likely to represent individual households burying their dead in the same plot over successive generations (Penn and Brugmann 2007, 86–7). The graves with associated post-holes, ranged end-to-end close to the northern boundary, are most likely to represent the core of one particular family group. To the south, and on the mound, however, there is evidence for some form of segregation. There is a small group on the ring-ditch that includes a child, Grave 62, and possibly an adult woman, Grave 59, but most of the burials on and next to the mound are male. A cluster of four children's graves tucked away in the south-east corner of the main plot, Graves 46–49, also suggests some special grouping. The theory that these are all late graves and reflect changes in social structure in the late 6th and 7th centuries will be considered in Chapters 11 and 12.

X. Feasting the dead

Fig. 6.3

One feature (053:*0269*), located 7m north-west of the north-west corner of Flixton II, as defined by Grave 34, was tentatively associated with the cemetery at the time of excavation (Fig. 5.1). This interpretation was based entirely on morphological grounds and its similarity with a series of features closely associated with the Early Anglo-Saxon cemetery at Snape (Filmer-Sankey and Pestell 2001). The attribution of an Early Anglo-Saxon date contradicted the finds evidence – fifteen sherds of Late Iron Age/Early Roman pottery were recovered from fill 053:*0270* – but was subsequently justified by radiocarbon dating.

Hearth/pit 053:*0269* was sub-rectangular in shape, measuring 2m from south-west to north-east, 1.2m from north-west to south east and surviving to a depth of 0.25m with a flat bottom and moderately sloping sides (Fig. 6.3). The fill (053:*0270* and *0718*) comprised two components; the bottom and sides were covered in charcoal with individual branches locally defined with an overlying fill of gravel to cobble-sized heat-altered flints with small chippings and charcoal filling the gaps between the larger stones. Only a small representative sample of the heat-altered flints was retained. In addition, there was evidence for *in situ* burning, as the underlying naturally occurring sand subsoil was heat-reddened.

It had been realised prior to the initial assessment that radiocarbon dating could be crucial with regard to the interpretation of this feature and associating it with the adjacent cemetery. On that basis, wood anatomist Rowena Gale undertook a full identification of the charcoal from fill contexts 053:*0270* and 053:*0718* at this early stage of the project, rather than a more limited assessment. The species identified included *Corylus* sp., hazel, *Fraxinus* sp., ash, *Quercus* sp., oak (both sapwood and heartwood), *Prunus spinosa*, blackthorn, *Salix* sp./*Populus* sp., willow/poplar and members of the subfamily Pomoideae (Rosaceae) which includes hawthorn, apple, pear, whitebeam, rowan and wild service. All of these species were considered suitable for radiocarbon dating, although the oak heartwood was to be avoided. Subsequently, samples were submitted to Oxford Radiocarbon Accelerator Unit (ORAU) for dating. Two samples of different species (Pomoideae and *Prunus* sp.) were selected to test the integrity of the deposit. In addition, the Pomoideae sample was internally replicated by the laboratory as part of their internal quality assurance procedure. As the results were statistically consistent for the two sub-samples they were combined to give the calibrated date. The results were calculated using the calibration curve of Reimer *et al.* (2004) and the computer program OxCal (v3.10) (Bronk Ramsey 1995; 1998; 2001). The calibrated date ranges (at 95% confidence) were calculated using the maximum intercept method (Stuiver and Reimer 1986).

The combined results from the Pomoideae sub-samples dated to cal AD 430–555 (OxA-16710 and Oxa-16711; 1553±18 BP) while that from the *Prunus* sp. sample dated to cal AD 420–545 (OxA-16712; 1574±25 BP). All three results from the two samples were statistically consistent and suggest they were the same actual age, dating between the early–mid 5th century and the mid 6th century. The results almost certainly confirm that the use of pit 053:*0269* was contemporary with and in some way related to the adjacent cemetery.

A number of possible interpretations were explored for the similar features at Snape (Filmer Sankey and Pestell 2001, 259–61) with the most favourably looked upon involving their use in rituals associated with the cemetery, probably cooking and feasting. As there were no cremation burials associated with the Flixton cemetery, its use as a pyre seems unlikely. However, its marked similarity to a pit recorded adjacent to one of the 'hall' buildings in the contemporary settlement at Flixton (Area FLN 061 feature 061:*0604*) suggests that its function was one that was also required in a more domestic setting and on that basis, its use for cooking represents a reasonable interpretation of the evidence. Similar, but undated, features have been recorded in the Early Anglo-Saxon settlement of West Stow (West 1990, 27–30).

A feast close to the graveside seems to have formed part of the funeral ritual in Britain and on the Continent (Lee 2007, 87–103). The feast in itself would cement relationships between the surviving members of the kin group and food might also be shared symbolically with the dead. Food offerings were sometimes placed in the grave with the body, and evidence of a feast can be found in the grave fill (Lee 2007, 88–90). At Flixton, probable remains of graveside feasting include substantial pieces of ceramic vessels in the fills of Graves 1, 6, 13, 15 and 25 (single abraded sherds have not been included), charcoal in the fill of post-holes close to Grave 30 and charcoal flecks in the fill of Grave 52, although no animal bones, representing joints of meat, have survived.

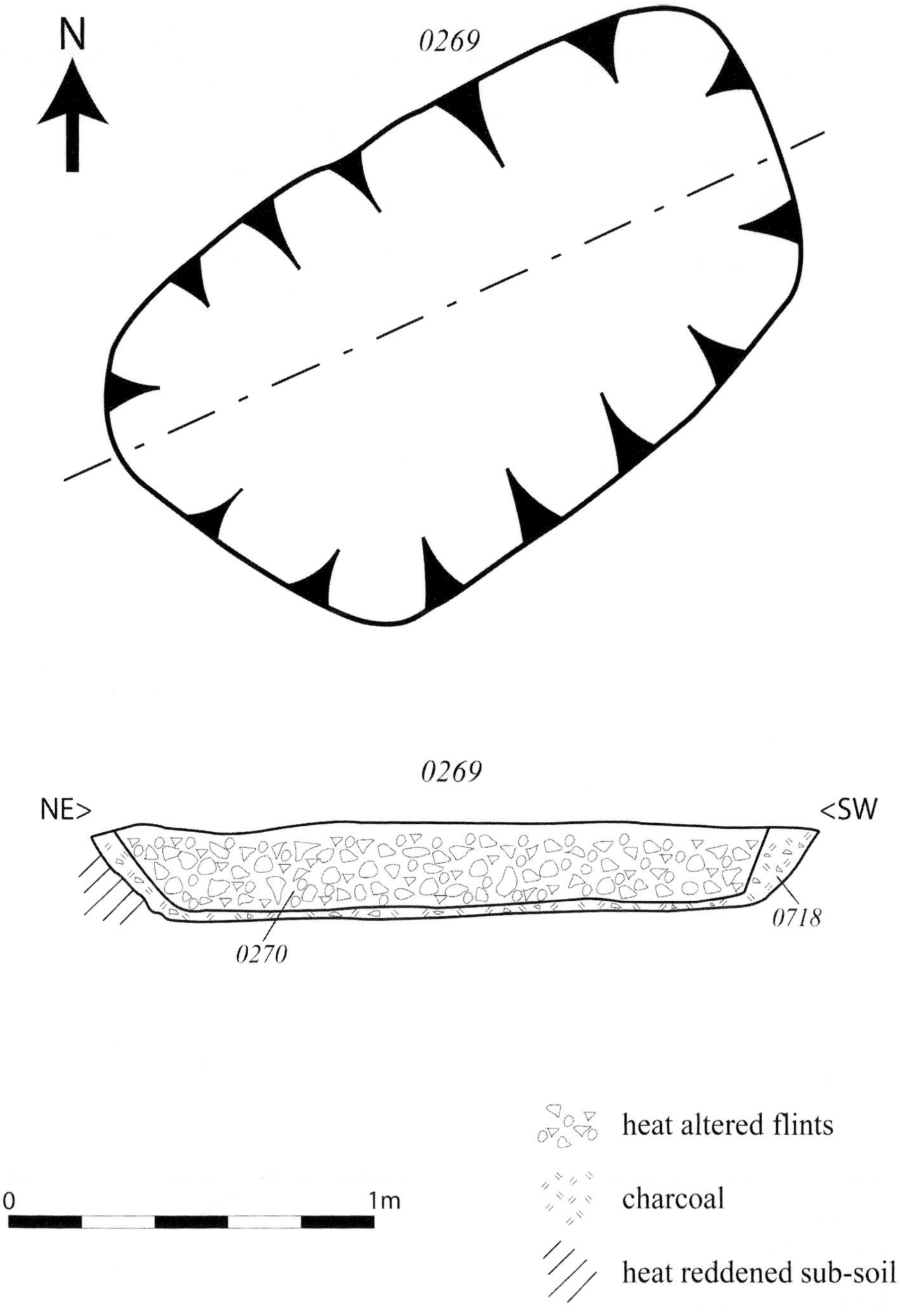

Figure 6.3 Hearth/pit 053:*0269*

Chapter 7. The Artefacts from the Graves

I. Introduction

by Penelope Walton Rogers

Despite the poor preservation of the skeletons, it is clear from the surviving artefacts and their disposition in the grave that the dead were placed in the grave fully clothed, and weaponry and personal equipment arranged on and around the body. The artefacts can be grouped according to function, as garment fasteners (brooches, clasps, pins and buckles), decorative accessories (necklaces and a finger ring), girdle groups (bag fittings, rings and keys), knives and tools, weapons (shield fittings, spearheads and ferrules) and domestic utensils (glassware and ceramics). To the burial party, however, much more would have been visible than has survived to greet the archaeologist. Clothing, blankets and coverlets, a wooden cup, wooden shield boards and spear shafts, leather belts and sheaths, and horn knife handles are all represented in the burial, although their appearance has to be reconstructed from the sparse mineral-preserved remains adhering to the metalwork.

The status of the people buried in the excavated sections of the two cemeteries is revealed through these accessories. There is little that is unusual or exotic, apart from the claw beaker from Flixton I Grave A, the battered sleeve clasps from Flixton II Grave 17, and the patterned coverlet from Flixton II Grave 52, and there are no men buried with swords, or women with extensive collections of jewellery. Most of the finds are simple, plain artefacts, which are often worn, damaged and repaired. Repairs to metalwork are not unusual in Anglo-Saxon cemeteries, but the re-use of broken artefacts is particularly common at Flixton.

In cultural terms, the finds are typical of the region and there are many comparisons to be made with the cemeteries across the county border in Norfolk, at Bergh Apton, Spong Hill and Morning Thorpe. Although the metalwork is typically Anglo-Saxon, Flixton shares with these sites textiles which indicate some survival of Romano-British skills. More surprisingly, among the women's garment accessories, there is a small group of finds with features of design and technology that have parallels, not in the local sites, but at Empingham II, Rutland, and its neighbouring cemeteries. Whether this is coincidental, or evidence for some introduction from the area around the Welland Valley will be considered later (Chapter 10).

Ascribing dates to the artefacts has presented difficulties, because the chronology of the Early Anglo-Saxon period is currently in the process of revision. The recently completed 'Four Cemeteries' project (Penn and Brugmann 2007) devised new type definitions for certain artefact groups, so that the material could be analysed by correspondence analysis, and this has led to a new phasing system for East Anglian cemeteries (see Chapter 9). The new phasing has pushed back many of the accepted dates for the artefacts used in the analysis, a process foreshadowed by John Hines' review of the '6th-century transition' in women's graves in Cambridgeshire (Hines 1999), in which he suggested that the archaeologically visible change in women's costume, regarded as marking the end of the Migration Period in Britain, should be moved from 570/80 to the 560s (and will therefore be presented in this volume as 560/80). The effect of the revised chronology on artefact groups not included in these studies and on sites outside East Anglia has yet to be established, although it is likely that similar adjustments will need to be made. Within this chapter, therefore, the traditional type definitions for artefacts have been retained, but where they have equivalents in the new phasing system, they have been added in italics with the prefix EAC (East Anglian Chronology). The usefulness of the EAC system will become clear when the development of the cemeteries is considered in later sections (Chapters 9–14).

The numbering system used for graves and artefacts has been described in Chapter 2.

II. Garment fasteners

by Penelope Walton Rogers

Cruciform brooches

Pl. 7.1

Only one cruciform brooch was recovered from a grave, 4/2), but a second, II/NG1, from an unstratified context, appears to be its pair (Fig. 15.7). In addition, two detached knobs, II/NG2 and II/NG3, also from an unstratified context, almost certainly derive from one or other of the two brooches. A fragment of a third cruciform brooch from Flixton I, I/NG3 (Fig. 15.3), is also not from a grave, but it is a significant find because it is the earliest Anglo-Saxon object recovered so far from the Flixton complex of sites.

The two near-matching brooches, 4/2 and II/NG1, can be classified as Mortimer Type B2, which has heart-shaped nostrils on the animal-head foot, simple half-round knobs and no side-lappets (Mortimer 1990, I, 61–5). Their lengths of 103–4mm, the separately cast side knobs and the stamped decoration are common features of this type group, although the square eyes on the animal head on both brooches seem to be unique. The only manufacturing detail which differentiates the two brooches is the stamped ring-and-dot ornament, which appears on the head, bow and foot in 4/2, but only on the bow in II/NG1. Both brooches have seen considerable wear and on 4/2 there is a running repair, where cords have been used to tie in place the transverse iron strut on the brooch back, which, in this type of brooch, holds both the pin spring and side knobs in place (Mortimer 1990, II, fig. 3.19). Brooch II/NG1 also has a large gash in the wing and head-plate. Vanessa Fell has shown that the damage is ancient and that the remains of a tin-based metal coating on the wing and head-plate, identified by X-ray fluorescence (XRF), may indicate that there was once a repair plate attached by solder to the front of the brooch (Pl. 7.1).

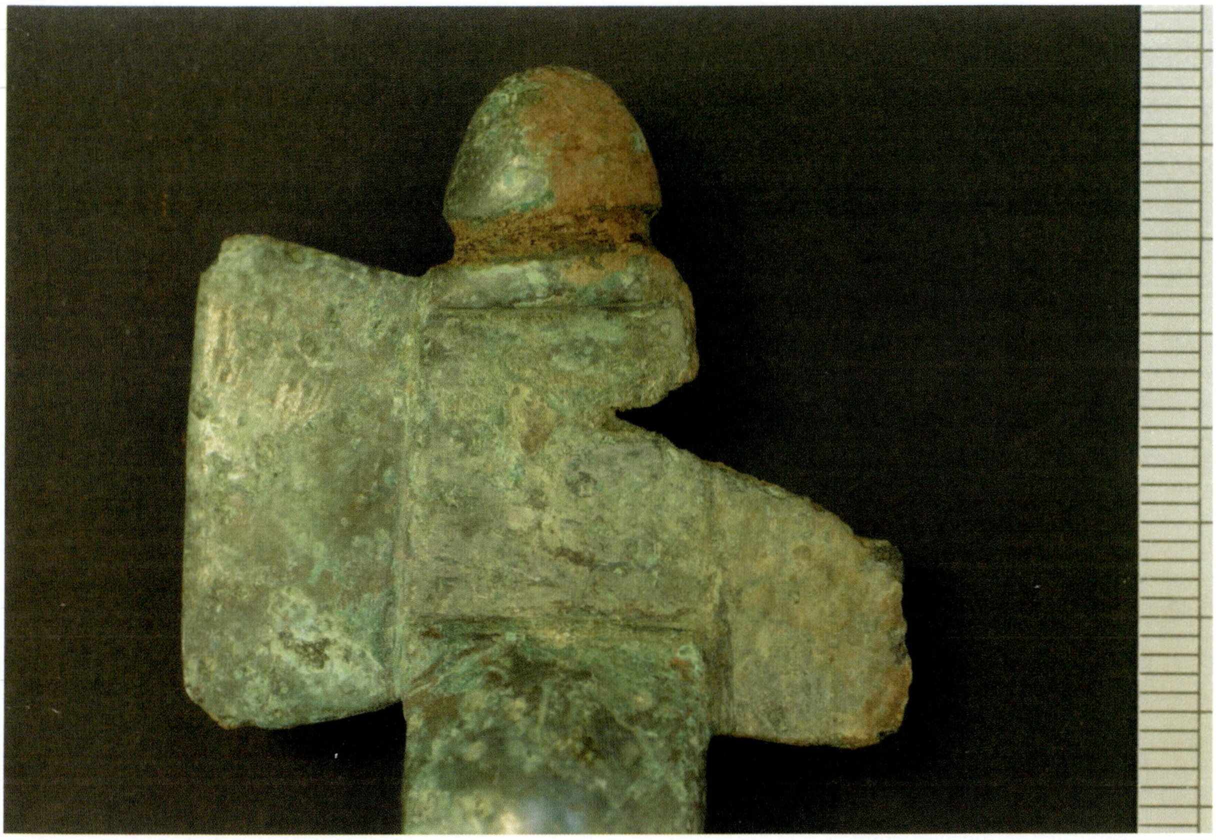

Plate 7.1 Cruciform brooch 053:*1157*, showing the gash on the head-plate. Scale in mm. Photo Vanessa Fell, English Heritage

Cruciform brooches of Type B2 have been found in almost fifty graves in Lincolnshire, the Midlands, East Anglia and Kent (Mortimer 1990, I, 61–5). In at least twelve they were worn as matching pairs, which supports the view that II/NG1 was originally from the same grave as brooch 4/2. In 1990, B2 brooches were attributed to the late 5th to mid 6th century, based on dating evidence available at the time (Mortimer 1990, 177), but within the EAC analysis they were subsumed in the large category *Xform1*, which proved to be most common in Phase FA1, up to AD *c*.480, with some examples in FA2a, *c*.480–510 (Penn and Brugmann 2007, 24, 70, fig. 5.21). A review of the graves with B2 brooches outside East Anglia (as listed by Mortimer) confirms the EAC dating. The brooches are often associated with Phase FA1 artefacts, namely A1 beads, B12 sleeve clasps, trefoil-headed small-long brooches and equal-armed brooches; and less frequently with FA2a objects, such as A2 beads, sleeve clasps of Type B13a/b (EAC *wcBar*) and B18d, and Class D cruciform brooches.

The fragment of brooch I/NG3 has a narrow head, a full-round top knob and wings which are angled back from the head-plate. The full-round knob and small head-plate place it in Type A1, or perhaps A2 amongst those closest to A1, since reflexed wings have previously been recorded in A2 but not A1 brooches (Mortimer 1990, I, 47–50, 266–8, II table 3.6, fig. 3.25). In East Anglia, such brooches have been found with cremations at Spong Hill C1216, C1468, C1469 (Hills 1977, 47, 57, 194), C2197 (Hills and Penn 1981, 60, 223) and C2656 (Hills *et al.*. 1987, 66, 172) and as stray finds in West Norfolk, Suffolk and Cambridgeshire (Penn 1998, 13–14; Malim and Hines 1998, 200–1; Mortimer 1990, 47, 48; West 1998, 294, 304), rather than in inhumations. They are undoubtedly a 5th-century type and Mortimer places A1 in the early part of the century and A2 somewhat later (Mortimer 1990, II, 177). Because they are rare in inhumations, they were not included in the EAC analysis, although they would naturally fall in the broad *Xform1* category. This brooch fragment forms part of a thin scatter of 5th-century material along the middle and lower stretches of the Waveney Valley, which appears to pre-date full-scale settlement.

Small-long brooches

An almost matching pair of small-long brooches, A/1 and A/2 (Fig. 15.3), was found at Flixton I, and a second non-matching pair came from a disturbed burial in Flixton II, 27A/2 and 27A/3 (Fig. 15.24). The first two have a trefoil head and A/2 has a sub-triangular foot (the foot terminal of A/1 is missing), but they are differentiated by faceting on the foot stem of A/1 and stamped decoration in the form of hollow triangles on A/2. The second pair includes a brooch which is also trefoil-headed, 27A/2, although it is larger than the previous pair. Brooch 27A/3 is quite different, with a cruciform head, knobs cast in one with the brooch and hooked lappets immediately below the bow (the foot is incomplete).

The three trefoil-headed brooches represent a common type, distributed across the Midlands, from the upper Avon Valley, through the upper Nene, to the middle reaches of the Ouse (Cambridgeshire) and its tributaries (Leeds 1945, fig. 6). To Leeds' original distribution plot may be added several more, including some outside the core territory, at West Heslerton, North Yorkshire, G12 and G97 (Haughton and Powlesland 1999, II, 18–19,

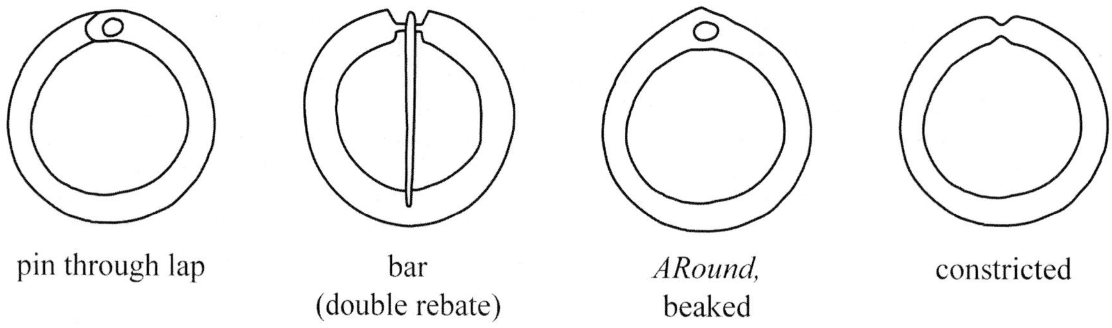

Figure 7.1 The main types of flat-banded annular brooch at Flixton. The Anglo-Saxon Laboratory

157–8), Castledyke, North Lincolnshire, G163 (Drinkall and Foreman 1998, 81–2, 189, 191), Norton-on-Tees, Cleveland, G21 (Sherlock and Welch 1992, 131–2), Empingham, Rutland, G67A (Timby 1996, 113, 200), Morning Thorpe G231 (Green *et al.*. 1987, 274) and Bury St Edmunds Westgarth Gardens G16 (West 1988, 24, 46), although the focus remains in the Midlands. Within the EAC system, trefoil-headed small-long brooches have been classified as *sm2*, and ascribed to Phase FA1, the 5th century up to *c*.480, with some continuation into Phase FA2a, *c*.480–510 (Penn and Brugmann 2007, 25, 58, fig. 5.9, 70, 5.21).

Brooch 27A/3 is a less common type. Cruciform-headed small-long brooches with a sub-triangular or spatulate foot are regarded by Hines as a form of cruciform brooch, Type Bb (Malim and Hines 1998, 200), and within the EAC analysis they have been classified as *Xform1* and given the same date-span as the *sm2* brooches just described (Penn and Brugmann 2007, 24). However, side lappets, in both small-long and cruciform brooches, are mostly a later feature (Mortimer 1990, 177; Malim and Hines 1998, 201) and this brooch has therefore been placed with other small-long brooches with lappets, as *sm3*, which has a stronger presence in Phase FA2a (Penn and Brugmann 2007, 58, fig. 5.9, 72, fig. 5.22). Hooked downward-pointing lappets on full-size cruciform brooches and on small-long brooches are characteristic of the Cambridgeshire region (Leeds 1945, figs 5e, 10f, 20f, 22h; Mortimer 1990, I, 83, II, fig. 2.41).

Annular brooches

Annular brooches were recovered from thirteen graves, as matching pairs in Graves 17, 20B, 21, 31, 34, and 36, non-matching pairs in Graves 11, 26, 30 and 51, and as singletons in Graves 8, 9 and 13. They are mostly of the common narrow-banded, flat-ring variety, but a small number of other types will be treated separately.

Flat narrow-banded copper-alloy brooches
Figs 7.1–7.2

The sixteen annular brooches of the flat narrow-banded form, are mostly circular, although some tend towards oval (20/7, 20/10, 36/1 and 36/2). They are 39–55mm in diameter, with bands 5–10mm wide, they have been cut from sheet metal 1.0–2.0mm thick, and they can be divided into three groups, based on technical features (Fig. 7.1). In three examples, the band is penannular and the open ends have been overlapped and perforated, so that the iron pin threaded through the circular perforation also holds the band ends together (34/1–2 and 51/1). The rest of the brooches have been made as an intact ring and in eight the band narrows into a thin, centrally placed bar (sometimes termed a 'double rebate emplacement'), which acts as a pivot on which the pin can rotate: (9/5, 11/5, 13/1, 17/4 (x 2), 36/1–2 and 51/2). The remaining five have a circular perforation for the pin attachment and four of these have a distinctive 'beak' or swelling in the rim beside the perforation (without beak 26/2; with beak 11/9, 20/7, 20/10 and 26/1).

It is obvious that these brooches were primarily functional with little decorative purpose. Several are very poorly crafted and 34/2, for example, has a miss-hit perforation. Most are plain, or ornamented with simple groups of transverse incised lines. There is stamped decoration on only two, a row of solid circles around the inner and outer edges of 17/4 (Fig. 15.16) and a row of rings in the same position on 26/1 (Fig. 15.21).

Narrow-banded annular brooches represent the single most common 6th-century brooch type in Anglian cemeteries from Durham to Suffolk. They do not form part

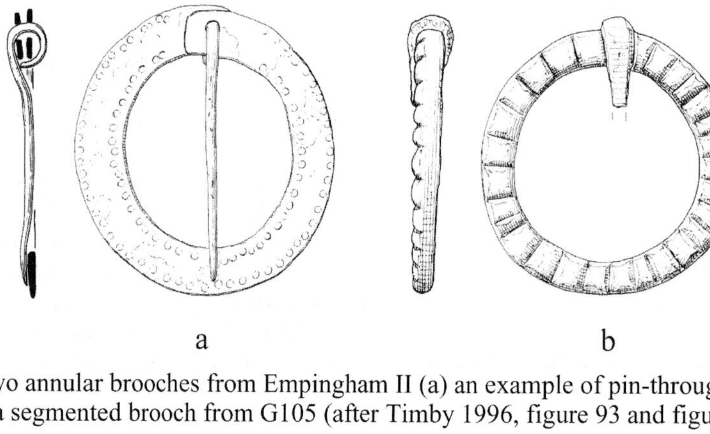

Figure 7.2 Two annular brooches from Empingham II (a) an example of pin-through-lap from G4A; (b) a segmented brooch from G105 (after Timby 1996, figure 93 and figure 152)

of the first tranche of Anglo-Saxon cultural goods (Høilund Nielsen 1997, 91), and the EAC analysis suggests that they appeared in East Anglia in the last two decades of the 5th century (Penn and Brugmann 2007, 25, fig. 5.9, 71). Those with a circular perforation for the pin (EAC *ARound*), of which there are eight at Flixton, emerged later still, possibly around AD 510 (*ibid.*). Their numbers were reduced in the period around AD 560/80 when there was a significant change in costume (see Chapter 10) although some variants continued in use into the 7th century.

No satisfactory type series has as yet been constructed for annular brooches (Leeds 1945, 46–9; Hines 1984; Hirst 1985, 55–6), almost certainly because they are the products of numerous locally-based metalworkers, all using a similar repertoire of techniques. Thus, features of the Flixton collection appear in brooches as far away as North Yorkshire, but exact matches are few and where they occur it may sometimes be by coincidence. In these circumstances it is difficult to establish a broad national framework. A better approach may be to begin locally and to identify zones and periods of use for idiosyncratic features or distinctive brooch types, before linking regional studies at a national level. With this in mind, two points can be made in relation to the Flixton collection.

First, the brooches with a 'beaked' outline find parallels at nearby sites in Norfolk, at Morning Thorpe G384 (Green *et al.* 1987, II, 342) and Bergh Apton G29 (Green and Rogerson 1978, 24–5, 66), and seem to be a local variant. Their circular perforation and associated grave goods place them in the period 510–60/80 (Chapter 9) and they were recorded with beads of Brugmann Group A2 at Bergh Apton, and silver bell and Group B glass beads at Morning Thorpe (Brugmann 2004, table 4).

Secondly, it can be argued that brooches with the pin through the lap-joint have their origins in Midlands technology. Annular brooches made with a lap-joint are found throughout the Anglian region, but they divide into two separate groups (Tables 7.1 and 7.2). In the first the lap is held together by the pin, as at Flixton, and in the second it is fixed by a rivet or solder and the pin emplacement is made separately (a rare third form made from two pieces riveted together will not be discussed here). The pin-through-lap type has been found in association with sleeve clasps of Type B7 (EAC *wcB7b*), A2 beads and cruciform brooches of EAC *Xform1* and *Xform2*, which suggest a period of use in Phase FA1–FA2 (the Group B beads in Morning Thorpe G371 probably come from a secondary burial). Matching pairs are likely

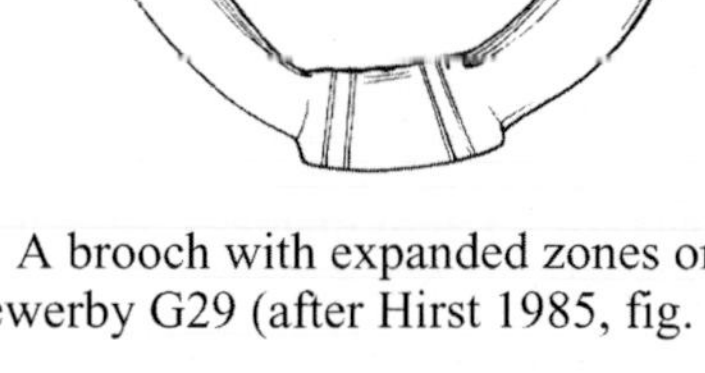

Figure 7.3 A brooch with expanded zones on band from Sewerby G29 (after Hirst 1985, fig. 43)

to indicate the core area of production and they predominantly come from Empingham, Rutland (Fig. 7.2a). They are almost always teamed with a third brooch or pin, there are on average forty-five beads per grave, and extra accessories are relatively common. The type with a separate pin emplacement, on the other hand, has been found with relatively few datable accessories, although the A1 and A2 beads and the Class D cruciform brooch (EAC *Xform3*) also suggest Phases FA1–FA2. The matching pairs are mostly found in East Anglia, beads average nineteen per grave and sleeve clasps and other accessories are few. There is an exception in Empingham II G85B, which is a well-furnished grave, but the brooches there have copper-alloy pins and a slot-like pin emplacement, which separates them from the rest of the group.

The pin-through-lap annular brooch is therefore associated with women well-provided with accessories, with the main focus on Empingham, and the brooch with separate pin emplacement occurs in poorer burials and is better represented in East Anglia. Although the Flixton graves in which the lap-jointed annular brooches occur are not well furnished, in terms of technology they belong with the Empingham group.

Segmented narrow-banded copper-alloy brooches from Grave 21

The two matching brooches from Grave 21 (21/2–3) (Fig. 15.20), are 41–2mm diameter and have bands 3mm thick, cut by deep transverse grooves which divide the brooch into twelve raised segments. The iron pin is attached by looping the end over a constriction in the band (Fig. 7.1). There are further examples of segmented brooches of the same size and with a similar form of pin attachment in the Empingham II cemetery, a singleton in G91 and a matching pair in G105, although the Empingham brooches have twenty-two and twenty-eight raised segments respectively (Fig. 7.2b) (Timby 1996, 120, 124, 219, 230). The Flixton grave offers little evidence for date, but Empingham G91, which Timby dates to the first half of the 6th century (Timby 1996, 93), includes a scutiform pendant, in the EAC analysis attributed to Phases FA2b–FB, *c.*AD 510 and later (Penn and Brugmann 2007, 26, 58 fig. 5.9).

Copper-alloy annular brooch from Grave 8

Fig. 7.3

The single annular brooch from Grave 8 (8/1) (Fig. 15.9), has a narrow band with widened areas which carry transverse grooves, and a bar pin emplacement. This seems to be an inexpertly made variant of the type of brooch in which four expanded areas jut out from the brooch (Fig. 7.3), of which there are examples from West Heslerton G39, North Yorkshire (Haughton and Powlesland 1999, II, 60–1), Sewerby G29, East Yorkshire (Hirst 1985, 57, 130) Morning Thorpe, G140 (Green *et al.*. 1987, I, 74; II, 247), Snape G16 (Filmer-Sankey and Pestell 2001, 52, 133) and Holywell Row G58, Suffolk (Lethbridge 1931, 30–32). Dating evidence for these burials is poor, although there are indications of Phase FA2 in a 6th-century florid cruciform brooch (Leeds and Pocock 1971, Type Vai) (*Xform2*) in the grave at Snape, and A2 beads and a D5 cruciform brooch (*Xform3*) at Holywell Row. At Flixton the brooch was associated with A2 beads.

Site	*Grave*	*Annular brooches*	*Third fastener*	*Sleeve clasps*	*Beads and pendants*	*Other artefacts excluding ceramics*
Empingham II, Rutland	G4A	matching pair	small-long brooch	*B7b*	17 beads	strap fittings
	G6	matching pair	cu/a pin	*B7b*	*c.*75 beads (A2)	finger ring, iron ring, buckle x 2, knife
	G16A	matching pair		*B7b*	6 beads	iron ring
	G83	matching pair	3rd annular brooch	*B7b*	76 beads (A2), amulet	girdle-hanger, keys, buckle, pouch fittings
	G100	matching pair	cruciform brooch, Z3 (florid), *Xform2*	B13 (*wcBar*)	*c.*43 beads	silver fragment, tweezers, iron ring, buckle, knife x 2
Sewerby, E.Yorkshire	G35	matching pair	cruciform brooch, C2, *Xform1*	*B7b*	53 beads (A2b), scutiform pendant	girdle-hanger, buckle, knife
Morning Thorpe, Norfolk	G371 probably two burials	single, paired with different annular	cruciform brooch, C1, *Xform1*; great square-headed	wrist area disturbed	18 beads (B1 and B2)	iron rings, buckle
	G407	single, paired with penannular	iron pin	B13c (*wcBar*)	74 beads (A2)	latch-lifter, cast ring, strap end

Compiled from data in Timby 1996; Hirst 1985, 131; Green *et al.* 1987, I, 144–5, 157–8; II, 334–5, 356–7; Brugmann 2004, table 11.

Table 7.1 Pin-through-lap annular brooches and their associated artefacts

Site	*Grave*	*Annular brooches*	*Third fastener*	*Sleeve clasps*	*Beads and pendants*	*Other artefacts excluding ceramics*
Empingham II, Rutland	G80	single, paired with bar annular	penannular brooch		*c.*75 beads	spindle whorl, cu/a fragments, knife
	G85B (child)	matching pair *ASlot*	pin, Ross VIII	?fragment	34 beads (A2)	lunula, girdle-hanger, latch-lifter, ivory ring, fittings, knife, buckle
	G126 (child)	single, at waist			6 beads	pin at neck
West Heslerton N.Yorkshire	G56	two non-matching				
Morning Thorpe, Norfolk	G91	single, paired with ?bar annular	cruciform 'associated D5b'		11 beads (A1)	?wooden bowl, knife
	G326	single, paired with annular			14 beads	
	G373 (?child)	single				
Bergh Apton, Norfolk	G11	matching pair	iron pin		26 beads (A2)	iron ring, buckle, knife
	G35	two non-matching		?B7	46 beads (A2)	
Spong Hill, Norfolk	G44	matching pair			7 beads (A2)	iron rings, knife
Great Chesterford, Essex	G124	?matching pair		B7	1 bead	buckle, knife
Eriswell 008, Suffolk	G22	matching pair	cruciform class D *Xform3*		10 beads	

Compiled from data in Haughton and Powlesland 1999, 87; Timby 1996; Green *et al.* 1987; Green and Rogerson 1978; Hills *et al.* 1984, 97–8, 146; Evison 1984, 168, 108–9; West 1998, 30, 49; Mortimer 1990.

Table 7.2 Annular brooches with lap-joint and separate pin emplacement, and their associated artefacts

Small bead-and-reel copper-alloy brooches from Grave 30
The small, non-matching pair of cast brooches from Grave 30 both have bead-and-reel moulding on the front and plain backs (Fig. 15.25). The pin, which is copper-alloy in 30/3 and iron in 30/4, has been looped over the ring without any special fixing. Ring-like brooches with moulded ornament occur over a wide date range, but those with a diameter of less than 30mm are most common in late burials (Geake 1997, 53–4). The association of the Flixton brooches with *B7b* clasps and their use as a pair on the shoulders suggests a pre-560/80 date, but their relatively small size, 32mm diameter, may indicate that they were made close to this horizon.

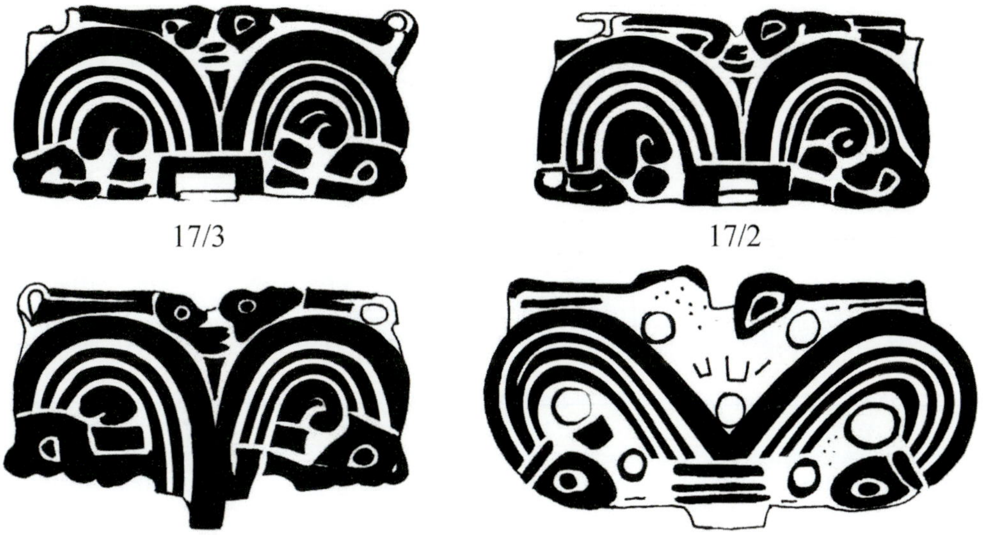

Figure 7.4 The design of the sleeve clasps from Grave 17. The Anglo-Saxon Laboratory

Ring-shaped iron brooches from Grave 31
The two brooches from Grave 31 have thin circular-section rings over which the pin has been looped (Fig. 15.29). The pin of 31/1 is incomplete, but on 31/2 it projected 10mm beyond the edge of the brooch when first recorded. Iron annular brooches are often regarded as a substitute for the copper-alloy ones, but they occur outside the core Anglian region – as, for example, at Portway G9, Andover, Hants (Cooke and Dacre 1985, 25, 67) – and the long pin on the brooches at Flixton and Norton G7, Cleveland (Sherlock and Welch 1992, 124–5), suggests a connection with native British or Welsh penannular brooches (Fowler 1960, 155; Dickinson 1982, 61–5). The grave goods associated with iron annular brooches indicate a broad period of use in the 5th and 6th centuries.

Sleeve clasps
Figs 7.4–7.6; Pls 7.2–7.3
Sleeve clasps, or 'wrist clasps', were recovered from five graves. In four graves, Graves 3, 11, 16 and 30, they were Class B clasps made from thin copper-alloy sheet, although they were fragmentary and sometimes difficult to attribute to a type-group. They can be summarised (after Hines 1993) as a pair of Hines Form B7 with two rows of small repoussé dots, 30/1–2; a catch piece from a plain variant of Form B7, 16/1; a pair of Form B13a with an attached bar, 11/4 i–ii; and a pair of Form B13b with an attached tube, 3/8–9. Sleeve clasps were usually worn as two pairs, one at either wrist, and remains of a second pair of undetermined type were recorded in Grave 11 (11/1 i–iii), and Grave 3 (3/7), but not in Graves 16 and 30. Fragments of another pair of Class B sleeve clasps, II/NG8, were recovered from the northern part of Flixton II, but not from a grave.

Metal clasps, used to fasten the cuff opening on the sleeve, were introduced from Scandinavia and became a standard feature of Anglian women's dress from the final quarter of the 5th century to the end of the Migration Period (Hines 1984, 35–109). Within the EAC system, Forms B13a and B13b were subsumed in the category *wcBar* and attributed to Phase FA2, *c.*480–530/50, while those examples of Form B7 which have small repoussé dots have been categorised as *wcB7b* and also placed in Phase FA2, but predominantly FA2b, *c.*510–530/50 (Penn and Brugmann 2007, 28–9, 58, fig. 5.9, 73, fig. 5.24). The plain variant of Form B7 has not been formally dated, but there is a cluster of examples at Morning Thorpe, in G20, G108, G148, G249 and G299 (Hines 1993, 116), in each case associated with *ARound* annular brooches, which suggests that they have a similar date-span to the *wcB7b* variants.

The clasps in the fifth burial, Grave 17, were cast in copper alloy and represent the worn and repaired remains of two different sets of Class C clasps. There is a hook piece (17/3 i) and two catch pieces (17/2 ii and 17/3 ii) from set A, and a single hook piece (17/2 i) from set B (Fig. 7.4, 15.16 and Pl.7.2). Both sets belong to Form C1, that is, cast clasps with an epsilon design and animal heads at the end of the epsilon arms, and all four pieces also have a pair of animals facing each other along the rear edge. Hook piece 17/2 i (set B), however, is larger than the others, differs in details of the design and it lacks the gilding of the other three (established by XRF analysis). It also lacks attachment lugs and it is likely that the circular

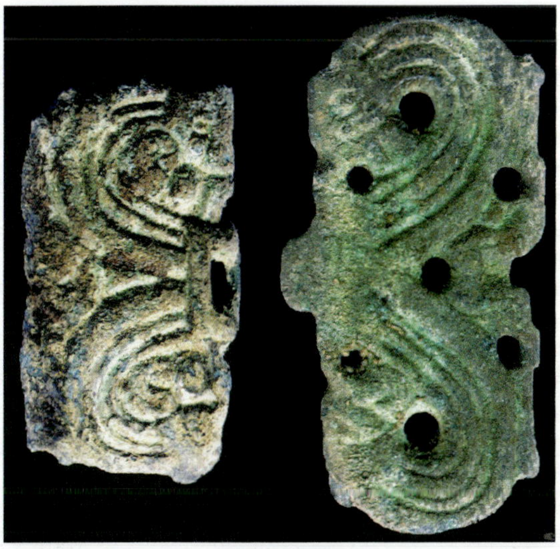

Plate 7.2 Sleeve clasps from Grave 17, 17/2, (i) catch piece, (ii) hook piece. Dimensions (i) 34 x 20mm, (ii) 45 x 24mm. Image: The Anglo-Saxon Laboratory

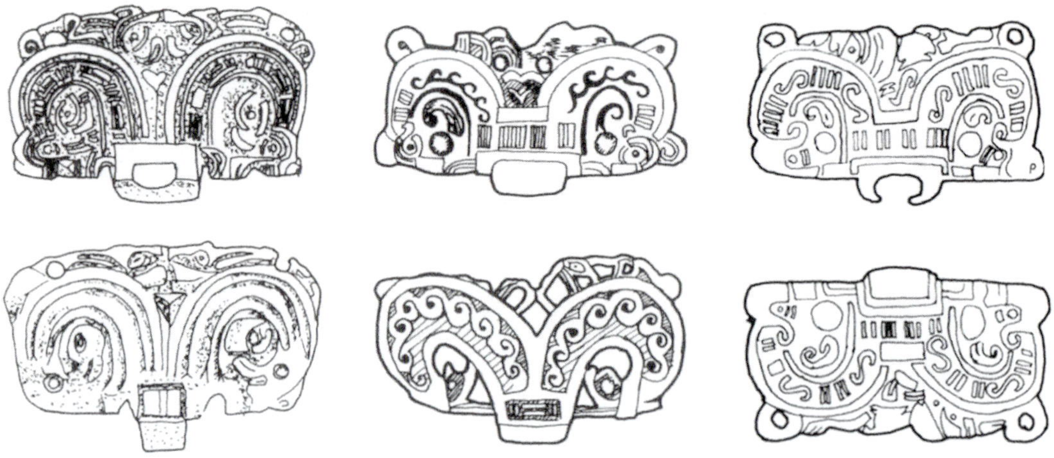

Figure 7.5 Comparable sleeve clasps of Hines Type C1iii–v (after Hines 1993, figs 131–3). C1iii top: Great Chesterford G54, bottom Londesborough G6/7; C1iv top: Saxonbury G13, bottom Haslingfield; C1v top and bottom: Thorpe Malsor, Northants. Courtesy of John Hines

holes enclosed by the epsilon arms originally held large rivets, although some smaller perforations added later were probably made so that the clasp could be stitched to the cuff. All four plates are extremely worn and both hook pieces have a replacement hook soldered to the plate (also examined by XRF).

There are three sub-categories of Form C1 which have animals facing each other along the rear edge, C1/iii, the Great Chesterford Type, C1/iv, the Saxonbury-Bidford Type, and C1/v, the Central Midlands Type (Fig. 7.5) (Hines 1993, 67–9, 125). The Flixton examples are not C1/v because they lack animal paws reaching into the V of the epsilon, but they have features of both C1/iii and C1/iv, which are only marginally differentiated and are perhaps variants of a single type (Hines 1993, 69). There are examples of the C1/iii from Great Chesterford G54, Essex (Evison 1994a, 99, 151, 229), Spong Hill Cremation 1323 (Hills 1977, 52, 209), Londesborough G6 and G7, North Yorkshire (Pl. 7.3; Swanton 1964, 270–5, pl. 1), and Bifrons, Kent (Conyngham Collection, Chadwick Hawkes 2000, 66, 71); and of C1/iv at Bidford-on-Avon G200, Warwickshire (Hines 1993, 69), Saxonbury G13, East Sussex (Craddock 1979, 91–2, pl. 7), and Haslingfield, Cambridgeshire (MacGregor and Bolick 1993, 181–2: Ashmolean 1909.245). The animal head on the ends of the epsilon in Flixton set A, with its eye at the outer corner and its segmented snout curled into the centre of the coil, finds parallels in both groups; the plain ridges forming the epsilon in set A and set B occur in the Spong Hill example and both the Londesborough pairs; and the unusually wide V of set B (17/2 i), and the perforations instead of attachment lugs, appear in the Haslingfield example. The two Londesborough pairs probably offer the closest comparison with Flixton set A (Pl. 7.3). Londesborough G6 includes a great square-headed brooch of Hines Phase 2 Group XIV (Hines 1997, 106–11) and a pair of *wcB7b* clasps, which together correspond with a dating in EAC Phase FA2b.

Class C clasps are prestige objects: they have cast zoomorphic ornament, are sometimes made of silver and several are gilded. As a class, they were in use during the last quarter of the 5th century and the first half of the 6th (Hines 1993, 67–73). They are dominated by the C1 form, which has a wide distribution, although the core area seems to be Cambridgeshire and the East Midlands (Fig. 7.6). Clearly, they are not local to Flixton.

Pins

Fig. 7.7

Pins were found in four of the Flixton II graves (Graves 3, 11, 12 and 20), although only one was complete. This was a copper-alloy pin, 3/5, which is 175mm long and has faceted decoration beneath a perforated head, and two triangular spangles originally attached by means of a wire ring passed through the perforation (Fig. 15.5). The iron pins, 11/11 and 20B/9, are both broken at the head end, but are still relatively long, 127mm and 92mm respectively, and 11/11 must have been used in its broken state, since it clearly pierces folds of textile. Another copper-alloy pin, 12/1, is a fragment only 49mm long and broken at both ends, but its position on the chest suggests that it, too, was a functioning garment fastener.

Pins with spangles are found throughout the North, Midlands and East Anglia, but 3/5 belongs to a small sub-group, Ross Type VIII variant iii, which has faceted or moulded decoration, and spangles attached by a ring

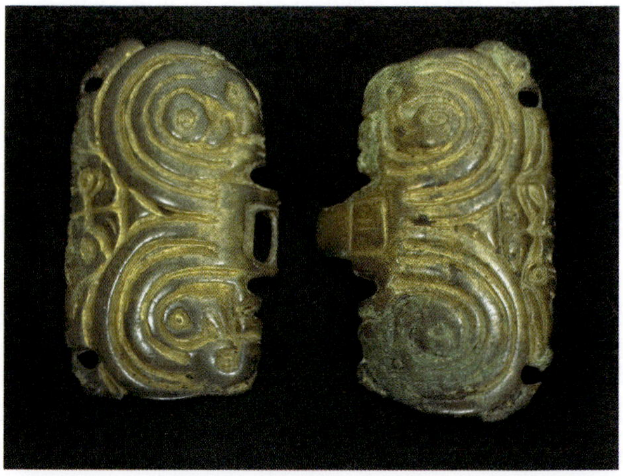

Plate 7.3 Sleeve clasps from Londesborough, North Yorkshire, G6/7. Courtesy of York Museums Trust (Yorkshire Museum). YORYM:1947.293.1 and YORYM:1947.293.2

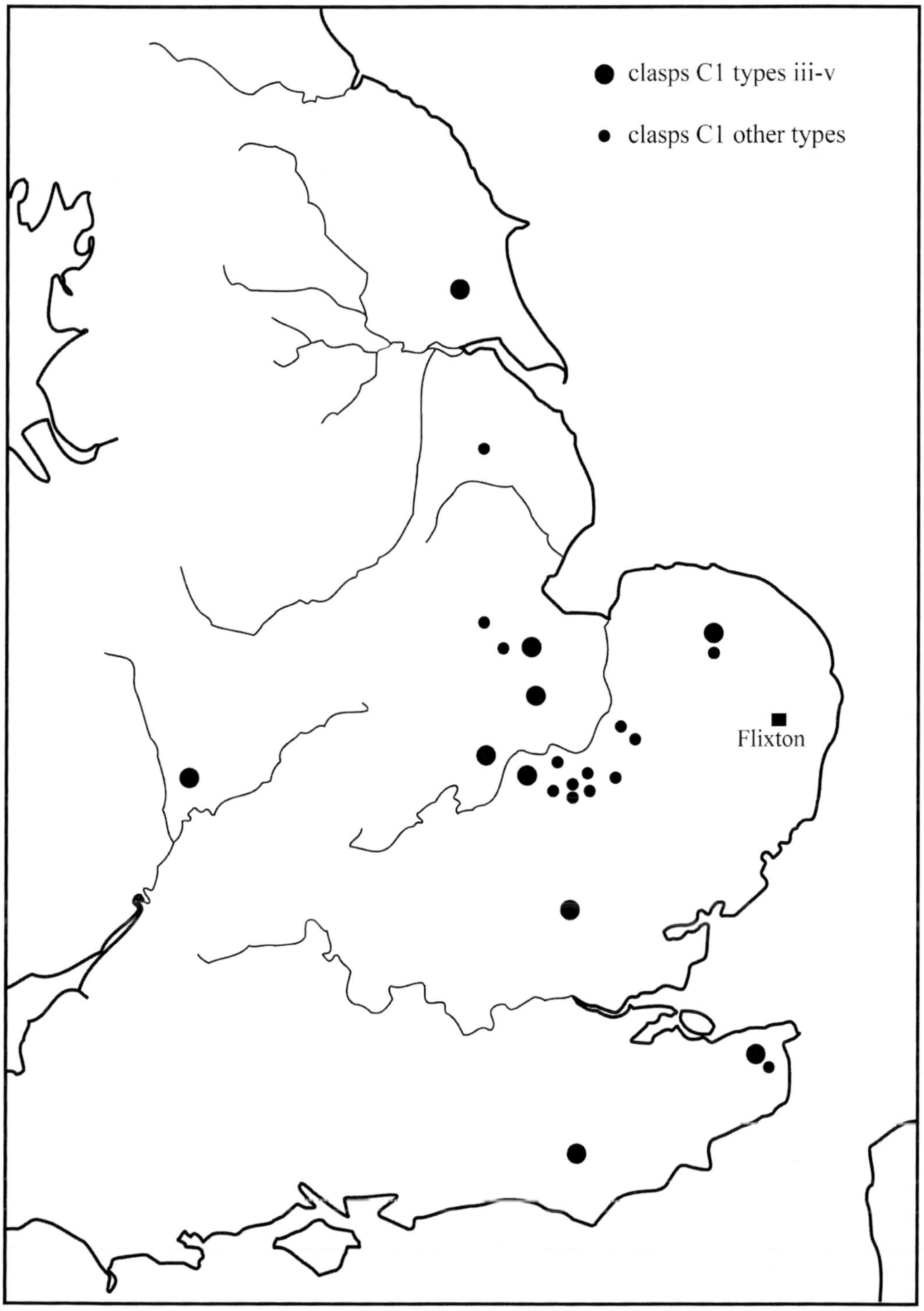

Figure 7.6 The distribution of C1 sleeve clasps in Early Anglo-Saxon England. The Anglo-Saxon Laboratory

without a distributor plate. There are four examples, from Haslingfield and Barrington in Cambridgeshire, Saxby, Leicestershire, and Wakerley, Northamptonshire (Ross 1991, 171–2, fig. 5.7). The example from Wakerley G82 is most like the Flixton pin, although it is shorter, at 126mm long (Fig. 7.7).

Pins were not numerous enough to be included in the EAC analysis, but Ross places all Type VIII pins with spangles in the period between the mid 5th century and 560/80, and a similar date range is indicated by the Wakerley example, associated with annular brooches with bar pin emplacement and A2 beads (Adams and Jackson 1989, 136–7, 149; Brugmann 2004, 55). The incomplete pins cannot be attributed to a particular type, but the lengths of 11/11 and 20/9 are consistent with a pre-560/80 date, since most pins after this date were shorter than 80mm (Walton Rogers 2007, 126).

Buckles

Fig. 7.8

Buckles were recorded in twenty-four graves of Flixton II, two in Grave 51, two in Grave 61, where there were two bodies, and one in each of the remainder. They were in positions that indicated they had been used on belts, and as

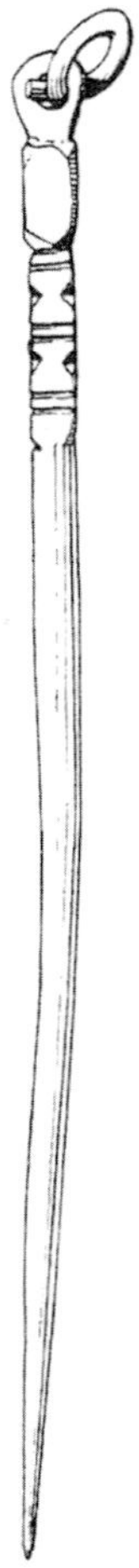

Figure 7.7 Pin from Wakerley G82, Northants, L.126mm (after Adams and Jackson 1989)

fasteners for pouches and shield straps. Most have simple iron loops of Marzinzik's Class I, in which the strap would be folded round the axis of the loop and stitched or riveted to itself (Fig. 7.8). They include three D-shaped buckles, Type I.10a-i (27/B/9, 36/4, 59/1), two D-shaped with an enlarged tongue rest, Type I.10b-i (32/2 and 56/3), three oval-to-D-shaped, Type I.10d-i (7/1, 37/8 and 43/2), six oval, Type I.11a-i (4/7, 11/12, 15/2, 23/3, 54/2, 57/1), two oval with an enlarged tongue rest, Type I.11b (55/3 and 61/3) and one circular buckle, Type 12a-i (51/3). Oval buckles predominate and even the D-shaped examples are essentially an oval with a short straightened area, so that there is a broad similarity in appearance amongst all the Class I examples.

Buckles of this kind are found throughout the Anglo-Saxon cemeteries and the I.10–I.12 type groups are little differentiated by region or date (Marzinzik 2003, 30–35). However, each type group contains many variations, reflecting different thickness of loop, width–length ratio, length of pin-axis, shape of cross-section and so on, and when the Flixton buckles are compared visually with others in the same groups, they sit most naturally with those in East Anglian cemeteries, particularly those in Norfolk. The Flixton D-shaped form with a short axis curving into the oval of the loop, for example, finds close parallels among Type I.10a-i and Type I.10b-i buckles at Morning Thorpe G27, G142, G225, G303, G174, G288 and Swaffham G16; and the Type I.11 buckles are most like those from Morning Thorpe G53, G211, G235, G239, G242, G274, G322, G409 and Spong Hill G46 (Marzinzik 2003, pls 27–34, 42–3, 52–3). Manufacture within the region therefore seems likely for the Flixton Class I buckles.

Class II buckles, in which a metal plate is folded over the axis of the buckle loop and the strap riveted between the two layers of the plate, are represented by ten examples, of which one, a fragment, 51/9, cannot be identified to type. Two, 20/5 and 61/1, have plain rectangular iron plates and belong to the most common and widespread of the Class II type groups, Type II.19a. One of these, 61/1, has the strip-like plate and enlarged tongue rest which defines the '*buckle1*' type, attributed to Phase FB in the EAC study (Penn and Brugmann 2007, 32, 58, fig. 5.9, 73, fig. 5.25). Two more are particularly small buckles, 31/7 and 9/4. Buckle 31/7 has a long tapering iron plate which places it in Type II.16, a 6th-century form which is not common in East Anglia, although there is an almost identical example from Bergh Apton G29 (Marzinzik 2003, 44–5, pls 88–91; Green and Rogerson 1978, 25, 66). The less well preserved buckle, 9/4, is probably an example of II.22a, which has a broad distribution, although those closest in shape to the Flixton buckle have been recorded at Thornham, near Hunstanton, Norfolk, G6 and G19, Ipswich Buttermarket G1356, and Wakerley G40, Northants (Marzinzik 2003, 48). They are thought to be pouch fasteners and are dated to the 6th or 7th century. The loops in all these Class II buckles resemble those of the Type I.10 and I.11 examples described above and may have been made by the same metalworkers.

Buckle 26/4 (Fig. 15.24) is the only example with a copper-alloy plate and has been categorised as Type II.19b. The plate is rectangular on the front, but it has trimmed-away corners on the back, and its single rivet is dome-headed on front and back. Type II.19b is a broad group, but the shaping of the back plate so that it is smaller than the front is a feature seen mostly in Midlands buckles of Types II.19b and II.21b. At Empingham, the feature occurs in five women's graves, where the buckles are associated with A2 beads (G22), Hines B13a sleeve clasps (G7, G69, G73), B13c sleeve clasps (G50) and a Mortimer D4 cruciform brooch (G69). The smaller back plate does not appear in the Norfolk cemeteries, unless an example in iron at Morning Thorpe G333 should be included (Green *et al.* 1987, I, 129; II, 308), but it has been recorded in Type II.19b buckles at Wakerley G82, accompanied by a pair of annular brooches with a bar pin emplacement and a pin of Ross Type VIII (Adams and Jackson 1989, fig. 72–3), and at Beckford B G68, Hereford and Worcester, where the buckle was part of a girdle group, and associated with a pair of disc brooches and an amber bead (Evison and Hill 1996, 87, fig. 31). This gives a pre-560/80 date for the feature, and in the Flixton grave, Grave 26, the buckle was found with a pair of annular brooches of the *ARound* type, which suggests *c.*510 to 560/80.

Four of the Class II buckles have iron plates fixed with decorative rivets. Buckle 14/2 has two rivets with large silver disc-shaped heads, which place it in the 6th-century type group, II.20 (Marzinzik 2003, 47). Buckle 3/2 is too fragmentary to allow its type to be identified, although the copper-alloy rivet head with encircling grooves on its upper face suggests Type II.20 or II.21. Buckles 53/7 and 58/1 have a row of rivets along the rear edge of the plate, four white-metal rivets on 53/7 and three copper-alloy

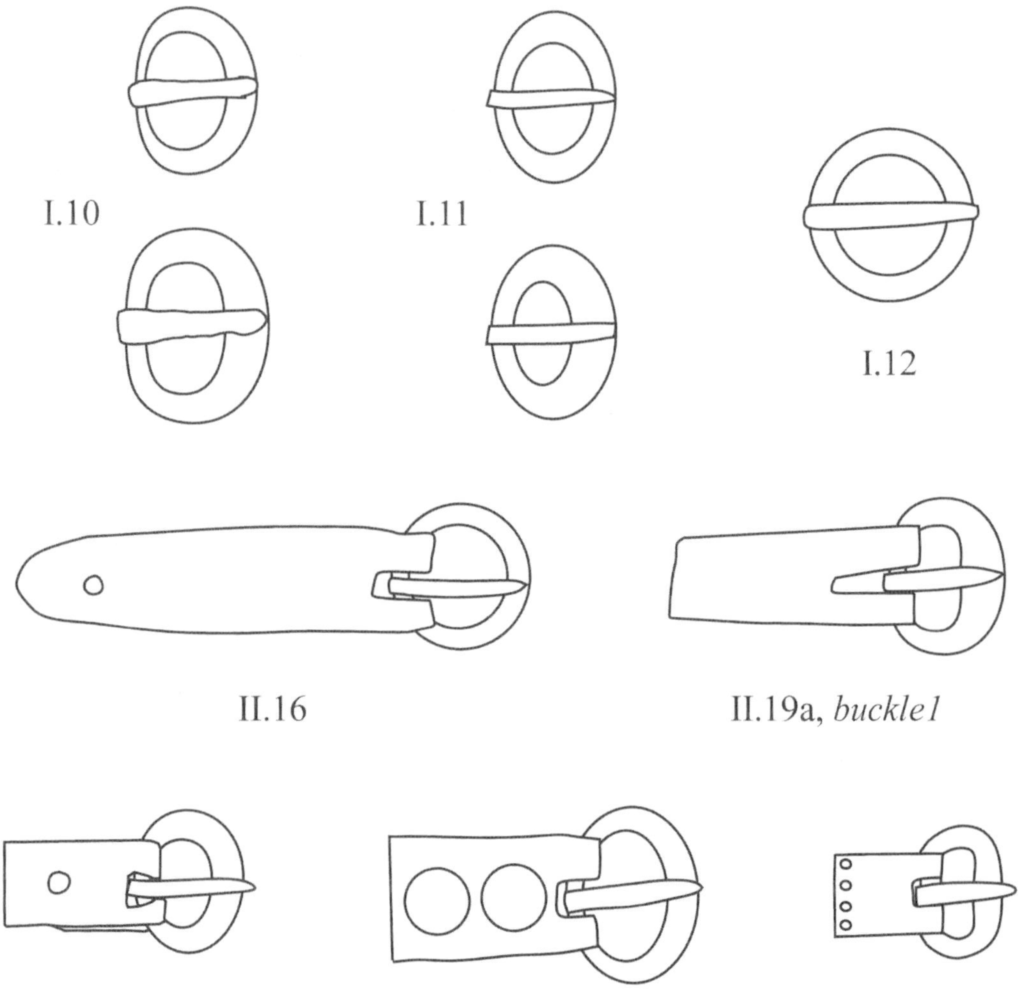

Figure 7.8 The main buckle types from Flixton, defined by their Marzinzik type codes. The Anglo-Saxon Laboratory

rivets with ornamented bosses on 58/1. They belong in Type II.24a, which is regarded as a 'type fossil' for the late 6th and 7th centuries (Marzinzik 2003, 51). These four buckles are broadly distributed types and cannot be attributed to any particular region.

Finally, four buckles were recovered within the area of the cemeteries but not from graves (Figs 15.3 and 15.48). Two include remains of a strap pierced by the buckle tongue and one has mineral-preserved textiles on front and back, which suggests that they come from disturbed burials. They are 053:NG/6, Type I.12a-I (Fig. 15.47), 053:NG/8, Type II.19a (Fig. 15.47), and a fragment, 008:NG/2, probably Type I.11a (Fig. 15.47). The fourth buckle, 008:NG/4 (Fig. 15.47), is represented by only a copper-alloy loop, which has an inset axis, a depression in the tongue rest and a cross-section which is flat on the inner face and concave on the back. There are two major groups which include these features, Types I.2–I.4 and Types II.11–II.14. These mostly have a distribution focused on the south-east, but Types I.2 (fiddle-shaped tongue) and I.4 (club shaped tongue) are also found in more northerly cemeteries. Both are essentially 6th-century types.

Straps

Remains of the strap fastened by the buckle were preserved on 11/12, 14/2, 20/5, 37/8, 53/7, 58/1 and 61/1. In every case the strap could be identified as an animal skin product, rather than textile, although in several instances only the thin epidermal layer had survived. In the buckle with silver rivet heads, 14/2, however, a well preserved piece, 3–4mm thick, with a surviving grain pattern, could be identified as leather made from cattle hide. In no case was it possible to measure the width of the strap, although the range of buckle loop sizes suggests that different widths were in use. Narrow straps were found with metal strap-ends, but since they were associated with girdle groups, they will be considered with pouch fittings, below.

III. Decorative accessories

by Penelope Walton Rogers

Introduction

Decorative accessories include beads and pendants, finger rings and a child's lunulate neck-ring. A toilet accessory has been included in the group even though it may have been functional, because it was probably worn suspended from the neck. From Grave 51 there was also an ornamented metal ring of a size appropriate to a small bangle, but it was found on the lower thigh with keys and pouch fittings and it will therefore be considered with the girdle groups.

Pierced Roman coins

Fragments of two Roman coins, I/NG5 and I/NG6 (Fig. 15.3), identified by Jude Plouviez as 4th-century bronze *nummi,* were found in an unstratified context in the FLN 008 area of the site (Flixton I). Their circular perforations indicate that they almost certainly originated in graves. Pierced Roman coins were hung around the neck, attached at the waist or incorporated into necklaces in the 5th and 6th centuries (Green *et al.* 1987, I, 54–7, II, 220; Evison 1987, 49; Timby 1996, 56–7; Archibald 1997 *et al*, 215). The coins are rarely of issues that were current at the end of Roman rule and it is likely that they were collected by the Anglo-Saxons as chance finds or by grave-robbing. Pierced Roman coins were worn by early Germanic women all over Europe and it is possible that they had an amuletic as well as decorative purpose (Meaney 1981, 220).

Bucket pendants

There were seven bucket pendants found in a group with beads, to one side of the disturbed burial in Grave 27 (27A/4), and three in a cluster at the neck in Grave 20 (20/8). They are of the standard form, with a disc-shaped base, a body made from a flat strip of copper-alloy curled into a cylinder and a handle formed from a second curved strip of metal. Raw flax fibre had been stuffed inside all three pendants from Grave 20.

Most copper-alloy bucket pendants come from the Anglian region (Hines 1984, 13, 342; Haughton and Powlesland 1999, I, 115), although there are twelve from grave HB2 at Bidford-on-Avon, Warwickshire (Dickinson 1993). Flixton G27A has been ascribed to EAC Phase FA1/FA2a, G20 to Phase FA2, and examples from Morning Thorpe G397, Bergh Apton G34 and Bury St Edmunds Westgarth Gardens G13 have also been placed in Phase FA2 (Penn and Brugmann 2007, 26). Burial in the first half of the 6th century, and perhaps as early as the late 5th century, has therefore been established, although this does not represent the full period of their use. Bucket pendants had a long history on the Continent before they came to Britain (Hines 1984, 13, 342; Dickinson 1993, 51) and single examples with wire handles from Harford Farm G28, Norfolk (in silver) (Penn 2000, 29, 51, 118), and Eastry Updown G15, Kent (Dickinson 1993, 51), demonstrate their continuation into the 7th century. The symbolic nature of bucket pendants will be considered in a later section (Chapter 10).

Other metal necklace fittings

Two small tubes of rolled copper-alloy sheet, one with a perforated disc soldered to one end, 42/1, and the other with sides crushed inwards, 42/2, were found in association with a single melon bead in a child's burial, Grave 42. The position of these objects with a bead in the region of the neck suggests that they had been used as part of a necklace. Three similar tubes, each with a transverse perforation, were found in a bead-string at Edix Hill G19B (Malim and Hines 1998, 110), although four rolled tubes, clenched around the remains of leather thongs, at the neck of a woman at Bidford-on-Avon grave HB2, were thought to be lace tags from a pouch (Dickinson 1993, 47, 50).

Glass and amber beads

by Birte Brugmann

Pls 7.4a–b

No beads were recovered from Flixton I, but Flixton II produced 201 beads found in sixteen inhumation graves, fifteen of these in the main plot (Graves 3, 5, 8, 9, 20, 21, 26, 27, 30, 31, 33, 39, 40, 42 and 51). The eleven graves around the prehistoric barrow included only a single grave with beads (Grave 59). Almost half the beads (ninety-nine) from Flixton are made of glass, the remaining 102 beads are made of amber.

Glass beads

Fifteen of the sixteen graves with beads at Flixton produced glass beads, numbers in a single grave ranging from one bead in Grave 42 to sixteen beads in Grave 3. *Circa* 35% of these beads are bi- or polychrome, the remaining monochrome and made of translucent or opaque glass. About two thirds of the ninety-nine glass beads are covered by a typology developed for a chronological framework of glass beads from Anglo-Saxon inhumation graves (Brugmann 2004). The national sample on which this study was based included the beads from Flixton FLN 053 (Brugmann 2004, 10), but at the time the analysis had to be restricted to a survey of datable glass bead types. A detailed catalogue of the Flixton beads was therefore only produced for the site publication.

The purpose of the study of a national sample of glass beads, which included the East Anglian cemeteries at Spong Hill (Hills *et al.* 1984), Morning Thorpe (Green *et al.* 1987), Bergh Apton (Green and Rogerson 1978) and Westgarth Gardens (West 1988), was to develop a selective typology based on attributes indicating related manufacture, and to use these types for a chronological framework for glass beads from Anglo-Saxon graves. If possible, types were defined to match existing type definitions of glass beads dated by contexts from Continental graves, as these types can link Anglo-Saxon and Continental chronological frameworks. This approach led to a patchwork of type definitions based on manufacturing techniques and further defined by shape, size, colour or decorative pattern, largely depending on existing typologies from various sources. A systematic typology covering all glass beads in the sample would have been beyond the scope of the project. In the course of further research on the East Anglian cemeteries at Spong Hill, Morning Thorpe, Bergh Apton and Bury St Edmunds Westgarth Gardens, however, it was possible to extend the typology for glass beads probably made in Norfolk (Brugmann 2004, 36 *et seq*; Penn and Brugmann 2007).

Table 7.3 provides a type series for the Flixton beads which follows the selection and definition of attributes as they were developed for the typology in Brugmann (2004), updated in Penn and Brugmann (2007) and used in the analysis of the beads from the Anglo-Saxon cemetery at Tittleshall, Norfolk (Brugmann forthcoming a). All glass bead type combinations from Flixton fall into one of the bead phases defined in Brugmann (2004, 44 *et seq.*). For a re-assessment of the absolute dates assigned to these phases, see Bayliss *et al.* (forthcoming).

Bead Phase A (A1 and A2)

The earliest bead type combination found at Flixton is probably the group of sixteen glass beads from Grave 3. The beads were found in two groups, a group of eleven mostly annular *Blue* beads (Type 1; Pl. 7.4a, 3/11:*1154*, *1165* and *1166*) and a second group of two larger *Blue* beads (Pl. 7.4a, 3/12:*1174* and 3/12:*1175*) combined with a *Traffic Light* bead (Type 15; Pl. 7.4a, 3/12:*1177*), two polychrome beads, *Polychrome1* (Types 20; Pl. 7.4a, 3/12:*1182*) and *Polychrome5* (Types 24) not covered in Brugmann (2004), and four amber beads. *Blue* and *Traffic Light* beads are the most common types of monochrome and polychrome beads in Bead Phase A1 (Brugmann 2004, 44). While *Blue* beads were common across Anglo-Saxon England, *Traffic Light* beads have been mainly found in East Anglia and were probably produced in this region (Brugmann 2004, 34 *et seq*, figs 37, 49). Large beads with wide crossing waves and dots (larger than type *Koch 20*, see below), such as bead *Polychrome1* from Grave 3, are common in bead strings of Bead Phase 1, but as the wide variety of colour combinations and shapes makes it difficult to identify workshops, such beads were not included in the typology in Brugmann (2004). The fragmented bead listed as *Polychrome5* was probably also such a bead. All in all, the combination of beads in Grave 3 is typical of Bead Phase A1.

The glass bead string from Grave 27 falls in Bead Phase A but cannot be assigned to Phases A1 or A2 specifically because *Constricted Segmented* beads (Type 5; Pl. 7.4b, 27/5:*1312*) were used throughout Phase A. Relatively large white beads with a red circumferential trail on a blue-green wavy trail (*Polychrome3*, Type 22; Pl. 7.4b, 27/5:*1307*) are known from Phase A but are not common enough to have been included in Brugmann (2004).

The glass bead strings from Graves 8 and 20 can be dated to Bead Phase A2 on the basis of the blue *Constricted Cylindrical* beads (Type 4; Pl. 7.4a, 8/4:*1173* and 20B/12:*1266*) associated with other glass bead types and amber beads (see Brugmann 2004, 44 *et seq*.). The bead from Grave 8 is associated with a blue bead that looks very similar but is not drawn but a wound imitation (Type 4a; Pl. 7.4a, 8/4:*1172*). The *blue-green globular* bead (Type 15; Pl. 7.4a, 8/4:*1171*) associated with these beads cannot be closely dated.

The *Constricted Cylindrical* bead in Grave 20 was associated with two *Cloak* beads (Pl. 7.4a, 20B/12:*1265* and *1267*) and a *BlueGreen Spiral* bead (Pl. 7.4a, 20B/12: *1273*) which fall in Bead Phase A (Brugmann 2004, 79 *et seq*). The small white bead with blue-green crossing trails and red dots (Type 14; Pl. 7.4a, 20A/11:*1264*) does not have the typical concave perforated side of type *Norfolk Short* defined in Penn and Brugmann (2007) but the size and decoration of the bead suggest that it is of related manufacture. The white globular bead (Type 16; Pl. 7.4a, 20A/11:*1261*) also found in Grave 20 is not closely datable.

In Grave 30, six yellow glass beads were found. Two of them have four ribs and represent type *Norfolk Melon* (Type 13; Pl. 7.4b, 30/7:*1361* and *1374*) defined in Penn and Brugmann (2007). These small beads were probably part of the same workshop or workshops that produced bead types mostly distributed in Norfolk and are dated to Bead Phase A2. The four yellow globular beads associated with them (Pl. 7.4a, 30/7:*1362, 1363, 1365* and one not illustrated) cannot be closely dated. The single *Norfolk Melon* bead from Grave 42 (Pl. 7.4b, 42/3:*1405*) dates the grave to Bead Phase A2 (or later).

The bead strings from Grave 26 and 31 include two small white globular beads with irregular blue trails (Type 12; Pl. 7.4a, 26/9:*1300* and Pl/ 7.4b, 31/8:*1330* respectively) which do not quite match the type description of *Norfolk BlueWhite* beads (Brugmann 2004, 79) because of their relatively carefully shaped perforated sides and their dark rather than light blue irregular trails, but they may well be related in manufacture. In both graves, these beads were associated with glass beads which cannot be closely dated (*white globular, yellow* and *Polychrome7*, Types 16, 17, 26; Pl. 7.4a, 26/9:*1296*, *1305* and *1306*; Pl. 7.4b, 31/8:*1337* and *1338*). The bead strings therefore cannot be assigned to Phase A2 with certainty.

Although a few *Norfolk* bead types (see Brugmann 2004, 36 *et seq*.), named after their main area of distribution, were found at Flixton, the numbers are low, and only one, or possibly two types are represented. Flixton produced too few beads to invite an analysis of regional characteristics.

Bead Phase A2b

Grave 51 produced two *Melon* beads (Type 11; Pl. 7.4b, 51/10:*1321* and *1362*), which in combination with *Reticella* beads define the rare but distinctive Bead Phase A2b (Brugmann 2004, 52), which runs roughly parallel with Bead Phases A2 and B1. *Melon* and *Reticella* beads were probably imported from the Continent (Brugmann 2004, 37). The two *Melon* beads from Grave 51 were associated with five monochrome beads (*yellow* and *red globular*, Types 17, 18; Pl. 7.4b, 51/10:*1355*, *1357* and *1358*) and an impressive collection of amber beads, which is typical for bead associations of Bead Phase A2b (see below).

Bead Phase B (B1 and B2)

The bead string from Grave 9 combines a *Traffic Light* bead (Type 15; Pl. 7.4a, 9/7:*1201*) of Phase A1 with a *Melon* bead (Type 11; Pl. 7.4a, 9/7:*1198*) of Phase A2b, a *Cylindrical Pentagonal* bead (Type 6; Pl. 7.4a, 9/7:*1219*) and a *Dot34* bead (Type 8; Pl. 7.4a, 9/7:*1210*), types which were introduced to Anglo-Saxon bead fashion only in Phase B (Brugmann 2004, 81). Other than on the Merovingian continent, 'quality heirlooms' are remarkably rare in Anglo-Saxon bead fashion before Bead Phase C, and it is therefore likely that this rare combination of a *Traffic Light* bead and a *Melon* bead with beads which were introduced in the early part of Phase B, date the grave to Phase B1 rather than B2. Grave 9 also included two highly fragmented beads which were probably *Blue* beads (most common in Phase A1, see above; Type 1a) and pairs of *red globular* beads (Type 18; Pl. 7.4a, 9/7:*1203*) and yellow beads with red crossing waves (*Polychrome6*, Type 25; Pl. 7.4a, 9/7:*1199* and *1205*), neither of which is closely datable.

The *Cylindrical Round* beads in Grave 5 (Type 7; Pl. 7.4b, 5/2:*0147a–d*) were not associated with any other types of glass beads and do not date the grave more closely than to Phase B. The *Cylindrical Round* bead in Grave 33 (Pl. 7.4b, 33/2:*1349*) was found with a bead of type *Koch20* (Type 9, Pl. 7.4b, 33/2:*1350*) introduced in Phase B1 (Brugmann 2004, 58 *et seq*). It seems, however, possible that the pair of small yellow beads (Type 17, Pl. 7.4b, 33/2:*1345* and *1347*) also found in the grave are related to the type *Segmented Globular*, which was introduced only in Phase B2 (Brugmann 2004, 39, 75).

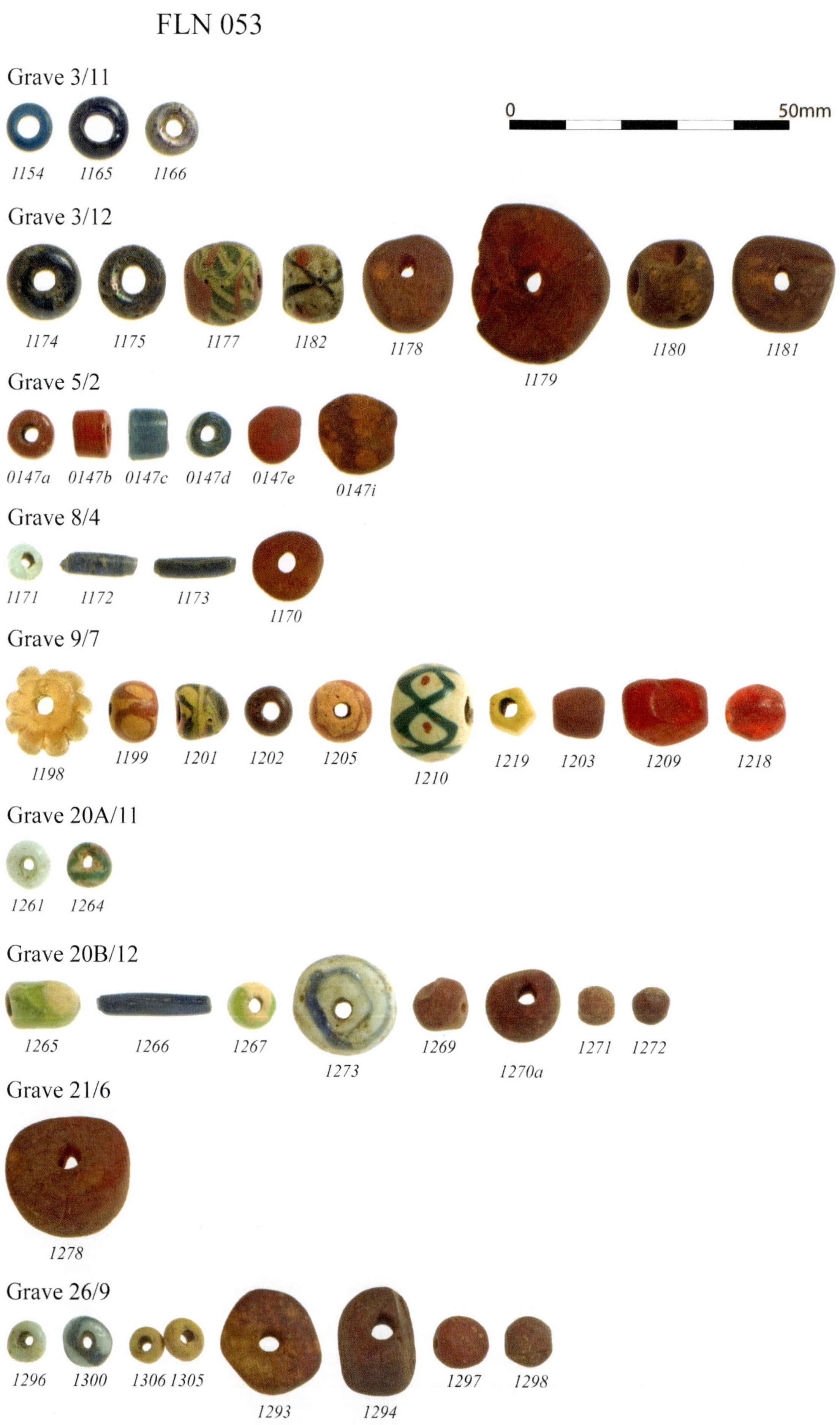

Plate 7.4a Selected beads (1:1)

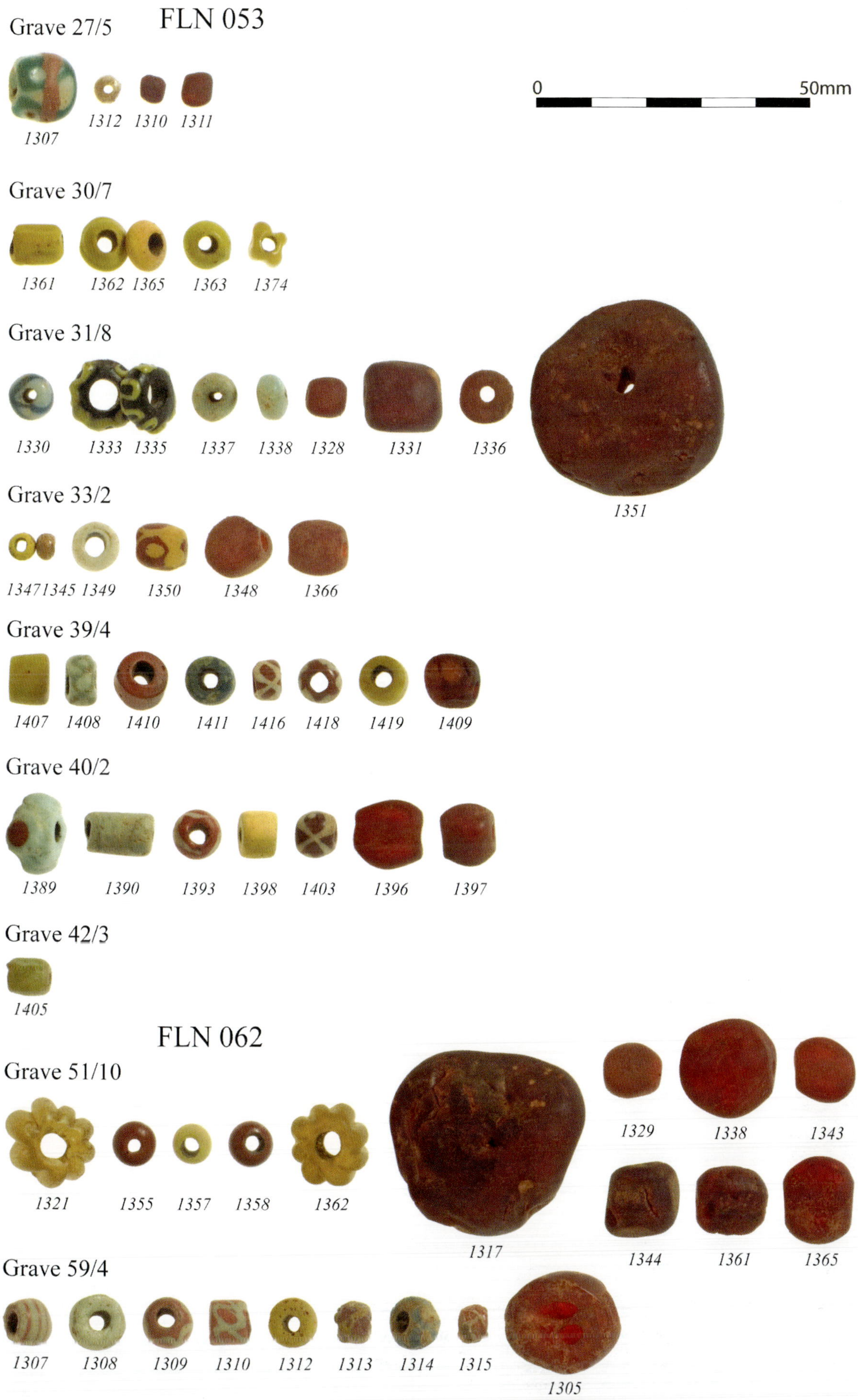

Plate 7.4b Selected beads (1:1)

type no	*type name*	*no. of beads*	*no. of segments*	*diameter of perforation*	*diameter of body*	*Length of body*	*proportion*	*bead making technology used for body*	*shape*	*translucency*	*body colour*	*technique used for decoration*	*motif*
bead types defined in Brugmann (2004) and Penn and Brugmann (2007), and related types													
1	**Blue**	**13**	**1**	**3.0–5.0**	**8–12**	**3–8**	**very short to short**	**wound**	**annular or globular**	**translucent**	**blue**	**none**	**none**
1a	**Blue?**	**2**	**1**					**highly fragmented**		**translucent**	**blue**		
2	**BlueGreen Spiral**	**1**	**1**	**3.5–4.0**	**17**	**4**	**very short**	**wound**	**globular**	**opaque**	**white**	**applied**	**translucent blue spiral**
3	**Cloak**	**2**	**1**	**2.0–3.5**	**8**	**9–12**	**medium to long**	**wound**	**cylindrical/ globular**	**opaque**	**yellow**	**applied**	**translucent yellow-green layer**
4	**Constricted Cylindrical**	**4**	**1**		**3–4**	**13–19**	**very long**	**drawn, perforated sides constricted**	**cylindrical**		**blue**	**none**	**none**
4a	Constricted Cylindrical, related	1	1		4	13	very long	wound, perforated sides constricted	cylindrical		blue	none	none
5	**Constricted Segmented**	**3**	**1**		**3–5**	**4**		**drawn layers, perforated sides constricted**	**globular**		**light**	**none**	**none**
6	**Cylindrical Pentagonal**	**1**	**1**	**3.0–3.5**	**7**	**9**	**medium**	**wound, perforated sides marvered flat**	**cylindrical, pentagonal cross section**	**opaque**	**yellow**	**none**	**none**
6a	Cylindrical Pentagonal, related	1	1	2.0–3.5	7	12	medium	wound, one peforated side marvered flat	cylindrical, slightly pentagonal cross section	opaque	white	none	none
7	**Cylindrical Round**	**10**	**1**	**2.0–4.0**	**7–9**	**5–7**	**short to medium**	**wound, perforated sides marvered flat**	**cylindrical, round cross section**	**opaque**	**greyish blue, red, yellow, white**	**none**	**none**
7a	Cylindrical Round, related	1	1	4.0-5.0	8	7	medium	wound, perforated sides around large oval perforation not marvered flat	cylindrical, round cross section	opaque	greyish blue	none	none

8	**Dot 34**	**1**	**1**	**5.0–7.0**	**16**	**12**	**medium**	**wound**	**globular**	**opaque**	**white**	**applied**	**greyish blue narrow crossing waves and red dots**
9	**Koch 20**	**2**	**1**	**2.0–3.0**	**8**	**7–9**	**Medium**	**Wound**	**globular**	**opaque**	**red**	**applied**	**white or yellow wide crossing waves and three dots**
10	**Koch 34**	**13**	**1**	**2.5–5.0**	**6–9**	**4–7**	**short to medium**	**Wound**	**globular or cylindrical**	**opaque**	**white or red**	**applied**	**narrow crossing trails (opaque white on red or translucent blue on white)**
10a	Koch 34 related	1	1	3.0–3.5	7	6	medium	Wound	globular (irregular)	opaque	red	applied	yellow irregular trail
10b	Koch 34 variant	1	1	3.0–3.5	8	6	medium	Wound	globular	opaque	red	applied	white spiral
11	**Melon**	**3**	**1**	**4.0–5.5**	**13–15**	**11–12**	**short to medium**	**Wound**	**globular, 8-9 ribbed cross section**	**translucent**	**yellow**	**none**	**none**
12	**Norfolk BlueWhite related***	**2**	**1**	**1.5–3.0**	**8–9**	**5–6**	**short to medium**	**wound, no concave perforated side, both reworked**	**globular**	**opaque**	**white**	**applied**	**translucent dark blue irregular trail**
13	**Nolfolk Melon**	**3**	**1**	**2.0–4.0**	**7–8**	**7–9**	**medium to long**	**Wound**	**globular or cylindrical, 4 ribbed cross-section**	**opaque**	**yellow or yellow-green**	**none**	**none**
14	**Norfolk Short?**	**1**	**1**	**2.0–3.5**	**7**	**4**	**short**	**wound, irregular; perforation square at smaller end**	**short, globular**	**opaque**	**white**	**applied**	**translucent blue-green wide crossing waves and three red dots**
15	**Traffic Light**	**2**	**1**	**3.0–4.0**	**9–13**	**8–12**	**medium**	**Wound**	**globular**	**opaque**	**red**	**applied**	**translucent green and yellow twisted trail**
Other bead types													
16	*blue-green globular*	*1*	*1*	*1.5–2.0*	*5*	*6*	*medium*	*Wound*	*globular*	*translucent*	*blue-green*	*none*	*none*
17	*white globular*	*4*	*1*	*1.0–3.0*	*7–8*	*4–5*	*short*	*wound (with one possible exception)*	*globular*	*opaque*	*white*	*none*	*none*

18	*yellow*	*11*	*1*	*1.5–4.5*	*4–9*	*3–6*	*short to medium*	*Wound*	*globular or cylindrical (perforated sides not marvered flat)*	*opaque*	*yellow*	*none*	*none*
19	*red globular*	*6*	*1*	*2.0–3.0*	*7–8*	*4–5*	*short*	*Wound*	*globular*	*opaque*	*red*	*none*	*none*
polychrome													
20	*Polychrome1*	*1*	*1*	*3.0–4.0*	*13*	*10*	*medium*	*wound*	*globular*	*opaque*	*white*	*applied*	*translucent green wide crossing waves and three red dots*
21	*Polychrome2*	*1*	*1*	*2.5–3.5*	*13*	*8*	*short*	*wound*	*globular*	*opaque*	*white*	*applied*	*lost wide crossing waves and three red dots*
22	*Polychrome3*	*1*	*1*	*2.0–4.0*	*11*	*11*	*medium*	*wound*	*globular*	*opaque*	*white*	*applied*	*red circumferential trail on blue-green wave*
23	*Polychrome4*	*1*	*1*	*1.5–2.0*	*7*	*6*	*medium*	*wound*	*cylindrical*	*opaque*	*white*	*applied*	*translucent green wide crossing waves*
24	*Polychrome5*	*1*	*1*			*8*		*wound, fragment*	*globular*	*opaque*	*white?*	*applied*	*probably translucent blue decoration*
25	Polychrome6	2	1	2.0–3.0	10	8	medium	wound, sharp edges to perforation	globular	opaque	yellow	applied	opaque narrow crossing waves
26	Polychrome7	2	1	5.0–5.5	12	5	short	wound	globular		dark	applied, not marvered in	opaque yellow wave

Bold script marks glass bead types defined in Brugmann (2004) and Penn and Brugmann (2007). Italic script marks type definitions summarising beads with particular attributes but not necessarily of related manufacture

Table 7.3 Typology covering the glass beads from Flixton II

Unfortunately such small globular beads can only be distinguished from earlier productions of small yellow globular beads if they were produced as segmented beads. The bead string from Grave 33 therefore cannot be dated more closely than to Phase B.

The bead combination from Grave 40 also includes a bead of type *Koch20* (Type 9; Pl. 7.4b, 40/2:*1403*), introduced in Phase B1, and a larger bead originally with wide crossing trails and three red dots (*Polychrome2*, Type 21, Pl. 7.4a, 40/2:*1389*) which was probably made in Bead Phase A. The monochrome white bead in this grave (Type 6a; Pl. 7.4a, 40/2:*1390*) is probably a carelessly made *Cylindrical Pentagonal* bead. The *Koch34* bead (Type 10; Pl. 7.4a, 40/2:*1393*) is decorated with white narrow crossing trails on a red body and was carefully made as an individual bead rather than having been produced as part of two or more segments (Brugmann 2004, 38, table 7), as were many of the white beads with blue trails of the *Koch34* series increasingly common in Bead Phase B2. The combination of this typologically early example of a type *Koch34* bead with beads introduced in the early part of Phase B or before suggests that the bead string from Grave 40 dates to the transition from Bead Phase B1 to B2 rather than later.

The bead strings of Graves 39 and 59 include two variants of type *Koch34* beads: red beads with white narrow crossing waves (Type 10; Pl. 7.4b, 39/4:*1416* and *1418*; 59/4:*1309*, *1310* and *1315*) and white beads with blue narrow crossing waves (Pl. 7.4b, 39/4:*1408*; 59/4:*1314*). The five *Koch34* beads from Grave 39 are associated with four *Cylindrical Round* beads (Type 7; Pl. 7.4b, 39/4:*1407*, *1410*, *1411* and *1419*) and firmly place the bead string from this grave in Phase B2. The seven *Koch34* beads in Grave 59 were associated with a *Cylindrical Round* bead (Pl. 7.4b, 59/4:*1308*) and a not closely datable monochrome yellow bead (Type 17; Pl. 7.4b, 59/4:*1312*). The manufacture of a red bead with an irregular yellow trail (Type 10a; Pl. 7.4b, 59/4:*1313*) and a red bead with a white spiral trail (Type 10b; Pl. 7.4b, 59/4:*1307*) from this grave are probably related to that of type *Koch 34* (*cf.* Brugmann forthcoming b). Grave 59 does not seem to include any glass bead 'heirlooms' and can also be firmly placed in Bead Phase B2. It includes typologically late versions of type *Koch34* (segments snapped off other segments, including a cylindrical bead) and may well represent the latest bead collection buried with an individual in the excavated graves at Flixton.

Amber beads

The 102 amber beads from Flixton II add up to *c.*94g (Fell and Watson 2007, Appendix 1). The thirty-three amber beads from Grave 51 account for about half of this weight (*c.*50g), and the remaining beads are shared by thirteen graves with between one and thirteen amber beads, with a total weights of between 0.3g (Graves 8 and 39) and 13.1g (nine beads in Grave 31). Most beads show signs of wear at the perforated sides.

Due to their small size, the seven amber beads from Grave 27 together weigh less (0.4g) than the single amber beads in Graves 21 (2.6g) and 59 (2.1g). The amber beads from Flixton vary in diameter from 3mm to 33mm. For cataloguing and analysis, they were put into three main size categories according to the maximum diameter of their cross section: 3–5mm (seven beads), 6–10mm (37 beads), 11–15mm (43 beads), and 16–21mm (12 beads). Three beads are considerably larger, with maximum diameters between 26mm and 33mm.

The shapes of the Flixton amber beads fall into three main types, 'rounded' beads mostly medium in proportion with a rounded show side but an irregular cross-section, 'faceted' beads medium (or rarely long) in proportion and without any regular section, and short or very short 'irregular' beads without any regular section; the longitudinal section is quite often 'wedge-shaped', *i.e.* asymmetrical in a way that leads to wear on the perforation in a particular spot, with time creating a drop-shaped cross section. The only bead from Flixton not falling into any of these types is the amber bead from Grave 59, which is a functional fragment of a carefully shaped bead with two perforations (Pl. 7.4b, 59/4:*1305*). It seems likely that this is an 'heirloom' considered to be valuable despite the damage because of its regular shape and relatively large size (17mm diameter).

A detailed analysis of the amber beads from the 1994 excavations at Dover Buckland, Kent, suggests that amber bead fashion changed along with the glass bead types defining Bead Groups A2 and B (Brugmann forthcoming b). It was possible to demonstrate a tendency for the small drawn glass beads of Group A2 to be associated with small rounded amber beads and the more substantial glass beads of Group B with larger faceted amber beads. As single beads, short irregular amber beads were worn throughout the Early Anglo-Saxon period, possibly as amulets, but a detailed analysis would probably show that as part of bead strings they were most common in Bead Phase A1 (Brugmann 2010).

At Flixton, relatively low numbers of beads were found, and the pattern is therefore somewhat patchy. The glass beads from Grave 3 dated to Phase A1 (see above) are associated with three short irregular amber beads out of four and thus seem to fit the pattern well enough. The single, short irregular amber bead from Grave 21 is likely to fall into the 'amulet' category. In the four graves with glass bead associations dated to Phase A2, only seven amber beads were found, a single short irregular one in Grave 8, and six in Grave 20 with an average weight of *c.*0.2g. The most substantial collection of amber beads from Flixton, the thirty-three beads from Grave 51, were associated with beads of Bead Phase A2b, characterised by relatively large glass beads, and the mostly large faceted amber beads from this grave are typical for such strings (average weight *c.*1.3g). The six graves dated to Bead Phase B (Graves 5, 9, 33, 40, 39 and 59) produced thirty-one beads with an average weight of *c.*0.5g, 27 of them faceted.

Summary

Although the number of beads found at Flixton is low compared with Spong Hill, Morning Thorpe, Westgarth Gardens and Bergh Apton (Penn and Brugmann 2007), fifteen of the sixteen bead strings or single beads can be dated according to the framework in Brugmann (2004):

Group A1	(AD *c.*450–530)	Grave 3
Group A	(AD *c.*450–570)	Graves 26, 27, 31
Group A2	(AD *c.*480–570)	Graves 8, 20, 30, 42
Group A2b	(AD *c.*530–580)	Grave 51
Group B1	(AD *c.*550–600)	Grave 9
Group B	(AD *c.*550–650)	Graves 5, 33
Group B2	(AD *c.*580–650)	Graves 39, 40, 59

Lunulate iron neck-ring or 'lunula'
by Penelope Walton Rogers
Figs 7.9–7.10; Pl. 7.5

Fragments of an iron object resembling a flattened torc, 22/1, were found with a child of 11–12 years in Grave 22 (Fig. 15.20). The skeleton was poorly preserved but the object appeared to be in the region of the neck. It is approximately 120mm in diameter and is in the form of a crescent moon: the tips of the crescent are extended into arms which are fastened by means of a hook on one end and a perforation in the other. The term 'lunula' (Latin: crescent moon) is sometimes used for these objects (Clarke *et al.* 1985, 90–1, 182–6, 260–3; Walton Rogers 2007, 132–3).

Eight examples of similar neck-rings have been recorded in Anglo-Saxon burials and there is a fragment of a ninth from an occupation site (Table 7.4). They are made of silver or copper alloy, and they are often ornamented, mostly with stamped decoration, but sometimes with studs and other attachments. In the five instances where the skeleton has been preserved, the bodies are those of children, ranging from three years old at Empingham II G118, to 13–15 years at Empingham II G85B (Fig. 7.9), and they have been found with both male-gender (three examples) and female-gender (four examples) accessories. The diameters of all of those from burials, 100mm to 125mm, are appropriate to children, and contrasts with the adult sizes of the Continental examples, which are mostly over 140mm.

The same hook-and-perforation fastening was sometimes used for late Romano-British and Merovingian bracelets or arm rings (Clarke 1979, fig. 85; Hartmann 1981, 36–7; Swift 2000, 61–4), and the male arm ring and neck-ring could be made as a matching set (Wiexzorek *et al.* 1997, I, 88–9, pl. 66; II, 824). A lunulate ring with a twisted wire fastening, from Caistor-by-Norwich G13, was found in a disturbed grave with an adult, probably male, jaw bone, and at 88mm diameter it is almost certainly an arm ring (Myres and Green 1973, 223, fig. 61). There is another, with a button-and-perforation fastening, of similar size from the cemetery at West Stow (West 1985, I, 144; II, fig. 266).

Most lunulate neck-rings come from the east Midlands, where there are five from three sites within 20km of each other, Wakerley, Empingham II and Market Overton II (Fig. 7.10). The example from Flixton represents only the third from East Anglia and it is possible that it represents yet another introduction from the Empingham area. On the other hand, the cemetery at Empingham II has a particularly large number of well-furnished female graves, and burials with lunulate neck-rings are often accompanied by more artefacts than is usual for children (Table 7.4). The concentration of neck-rings in the east Midlands may, then, be influenced by the wealth of the sites as much as geography.

The associated artefacts provide some indication of date. In West Heslerton G100 there was a pair of annular brooches with a bar pin emplacement and a pin of Ross Type VIII, and at Emscote a pair of saucer brooches, both of which indicate a pre-560/80 date. In Empingham II G85B the child wore a pair of *ASlot* annular brooches and A2 beads, but an adult woman buried in the same grave, seemingly at the same time, had a variety of accessories including a florid cruciform brooch of Mortimer Type Z1 (EAC *Xform2*), so that the burial can be regarded as in the equivalent to EAC Phase FA2, *c.*480–530/50. Bergh Apton G50 has been attributed to EAC Phase MA2, *c.*510–560/70 (Penn and Brugmann 2007, 31) and in Wakerley G40 there was a Swanton E1 spearhead (see below) and a 6th- or 7th-century buckle of Type II.22a (Marzinzik 2003, 48, 216). The fragment from Handford Road in Ipswich comes from a 5th/6th-century sunken-featured building (Boulter 2005). The exact date range of Anglo-Saxon lunulate neck-rings is therefore uncertain, although it seems to centre on the first half of the 6th century.

The Anglo-Saxon form almost certainly has its origins in Continental neck-rings, which are in turn related to the gold torcs given to foreign soldiers by the Roman army (Stout 2001, 82–4; D'Amato and Sumner 2005, 3, 40, 45). Gold neck-rings have been found in hoards on the Continent dated to the end of the 4th and the first quarter of the 5th century (Martin 1997, 51–4, pls 12, 14; Alkemade 1997, 185–6, pls 50–1), and in simple silver and copper-alloy forms they appear in both men's and women's graves (Böhme 1974, 118–20). They were made in a variety of styles, but those most like the Anglo-Saxon type are found in The Netherlands. There are elaborate examples from Rhenen-Achterberg and Olst (Alkemade 1997, pls 50–1), and simpler ones from the Frisian *terpen*, including an example, 162mm diameter, from the Cornjum, near Leeuwarden, Friesland, dated to the 5th century (Pl. 7.5; Boeles 1951, 320–3). Another, 145mm diameter, comes from further away, at Altenerding G421 in southern Germany, where it was found in a burial with a mix of artefacts that suggested a woman with connections outside the region (Sage 1984, I, 421; II, 120–1).

Some of the Continental neck-rings are made from plain wire, and further examples from Anglo-Saxon burials indicate that these also transferred from adult to child when they came to Britain. There is a simple copper-alloy wire neck-ring in the burial of a 2–6 year old at West Heslerton, G172 (Haughton and Powlesland 1999, II, 300), an incomplete example made from iron wire around the neck of a 1–2 year old at Lechlade Butler's Field G48, Gloucestershire (Boyle *et al.* 1998, 75, 162, 209), iron

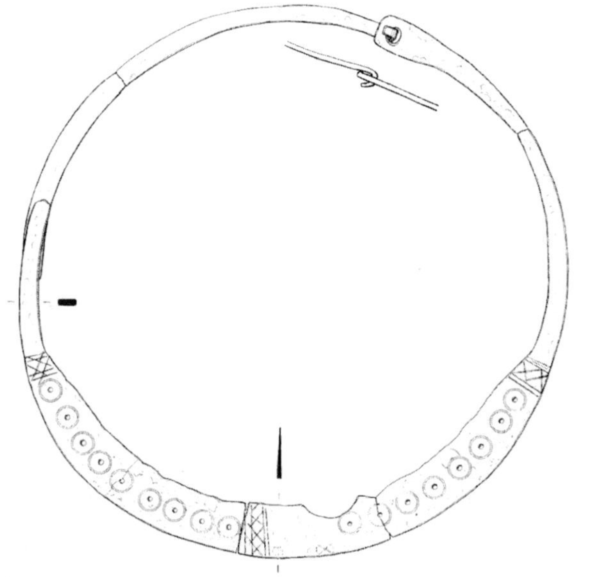

Figure 7.9 A copper-alloy lunulate neck-ring from Empingham II G85B (after Timby 1996, fig. 136)

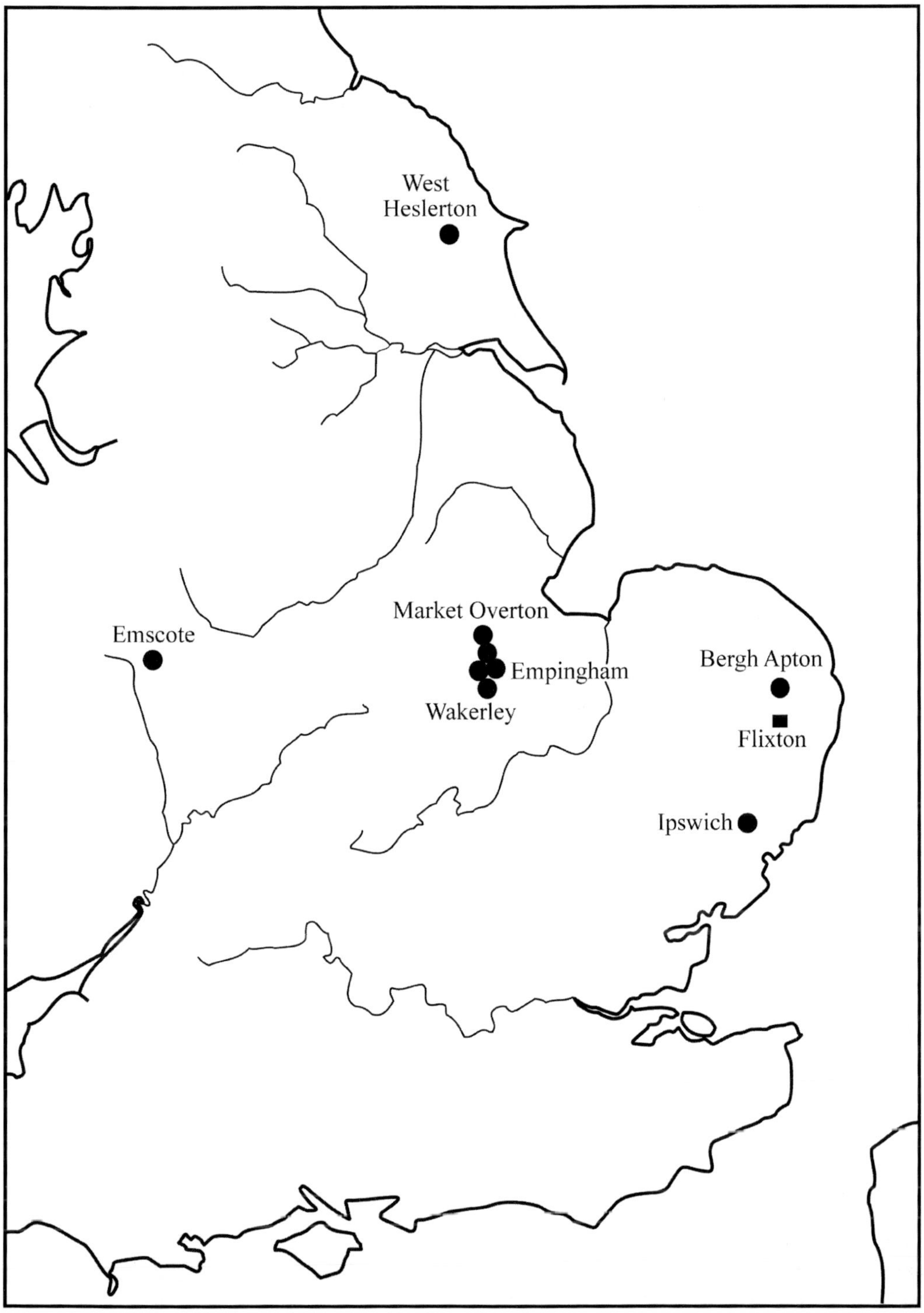

Figure 7.10 The distribution of lunulate neck-rings in Early Anglo-Saxon England. The Anglo-Saxon Laboratory

examples with four children aged from about 18 months to three years at Blacknall Field, Pewsey, Wiltshire, G33, G52, G53 and G96 (Annable and Eagles 2010), and another of iron with a juvenile at Bainesse Farm, Catterick, North Yorkshire (Wilson *et al.* 1996, 36–7). The Lechlade burial can be dated by a late 5th- or early 6th-century buckle (Marzinzik 2003, 37–8), the West Heslerton one by bucket pendants (see above), while one of the Blacknall Field burials, G53, includes beads of the late 5th or early 6th century (Annable and Eagles 2010). The Catterick burial has been dated to the 7th century on the basis of the small size of the circular iron buckle at the hip (Wilson *et al.* 1996, 3), although such buckles are not exclusively late (Marzinzik 2003, 34). An adult-size variant of the wire neck-ring was recovered from Ipswich Hadleigh Road (West 1998, 52–3, 176), but this was threaded with a bead and almost certainly forms part of a separate, 7th-century, adult female fashion, which included bracelets and other wire rings with attached beads (*e.g.* Harford Farm G11, G18, G20 and G33: Penn 2000, 109, 112, 115, 120).

Site, Grave	*Age (bones and teeth)*	*Gender (artefacts)*	*Material*	*Diameter*	*Fastening*	*Ornament*	*Position*	*Associated with*
West Heslerton G 100, N.Yorks	Child 2–5 yrs	Female	Cu/a (brass)	*c*.110 mm	Hook and perforation	Stamped circles.Tinned spangles	Around neck	Pair annular brooches, pin, 2 amber beads, pot, knife, cu/a staple
Bergh Apton G50, Norfolk		Male	Cu/a	*c*.125 mm	Two hook-and-perforation fastenings	Three perforations on front plate	No skeleton, but probably region of neck	Small spearhead, buckle, knife, wooden object
Wakerley G40 Northants	Juvenile	Male	Silver	100 mm	Hook and perforation	Stamped ring-and-dot and Vs	To right of shoulder	Small spearhead, buckle, knife, ceramic bowl
Empingham II G85B, Rutland	Sub-adult 13–15 yrs, female	Female	Cu/a	116–119 mm	Hook and perforation	Stamped large ring-and-dot and transverse zones of Xs between parallel lines	By neck	Pair annular brooches, pin, 3 glass and 29 amber beads, ?clasps, girdle-hangers, ivory ring, pouch fittings, knife. Also adult female with pair annular brooches, cruciform brooch, sleeve clasps, 52 beads, keys, cu/a needle, glass fragments
Empingham II G96C, Rutland	Child 5 yrs	Male	Cu/a	100 mm	Hook and perforation	Stamped triangles	Around neck	Spear, buckle, anklet. Part of triple burial with two other juveniles: 8-year-old ?female with spear, arrowhead, buckle, knife, pot; 15–16 year-old ?male with knife, buckle potsherds.
Empingham II G118, Rutland	Child 3 yrs	Female	Cu/a	110 mm	Not preserved	Repousse dots and transverse zones of incised Xs	Around neck	Amber bead(s)
Market Overton II, Rutland			Silver	*c*.115 mm	Hook and wire loop	Stamped triangles and ring-and-dot		No grave association
Emscote, Warks		Female	Silver	115–120 mm	Hook and perforation	Stamped Us and Vs, edged with tooled lines	Thought to have been at neck originally	Two gilt saucer brooches
Handford Road, Ipswich	Occupation site		Cu/a	Fragment	absent	Stamped ring-and-dot between rows of triangles		Sunken-featured building
Flixton G22, Suffolk	Child 11–12 yrs		Iron	120 mm	Hook and perforation	None visible	Region of neck	Knife, ceramic vessel, knife fragment, glass fragments. Also in grave a young adult without accessories.

Cu/a = copper-alloy. Compiled from data in Haughton and Powlesland 1999, I, 116, II, 161; Adams and Jackson 1989, 106, 156–7; Timby 1996, 59, 118, 122, 126–7, 136, 214, 224, 235; Baldwin Brown 1915, IV, 424, pl. 101; Chatwin 1925, 269–70, pl. 30; Green and Rogerson 1978, 35,76; Boulter 2005.

Table 7.4 Metal lunulate neck-rings from Early Anglo-Saxon sites

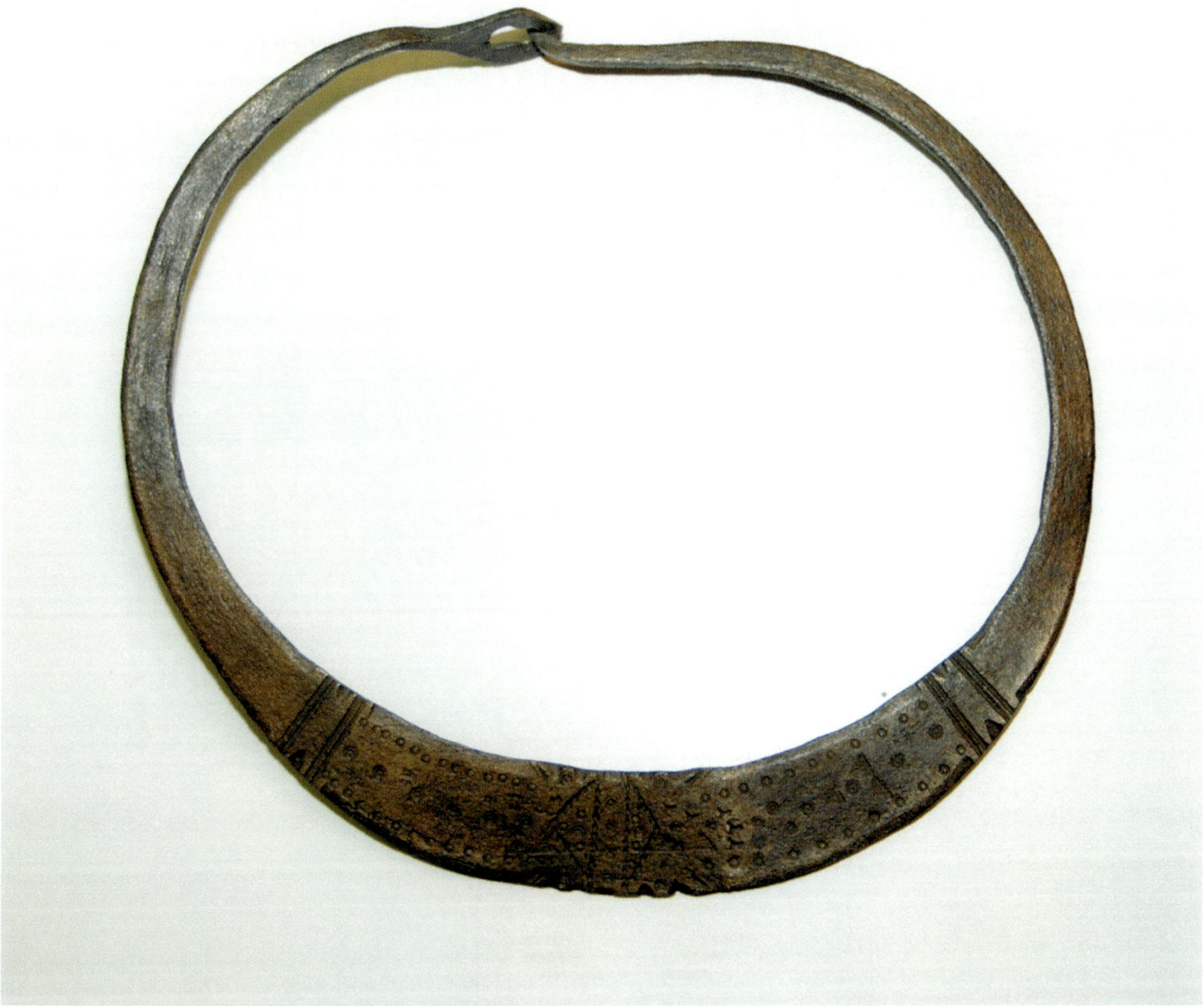

Plate 7.5 A lunulate neck-ring from Cornjum terp, now in the Friesmuseum, Leeuwarden, The Netherlands. Diam. 162mm. Courtesy of the Friesmuseum

Ear scoop

Toilet sets, consisting of an ear scoop and two pin-like objects of different sizes, are found on the chest in graves in southern England, from Oxfordshire to Hampshire. Outside this area, complete sets sometimes occur (Sherlock and Welch 1992, 53; Malim and Hines 1998, 218), but mostly the items are found separately. At Flixton, a single ear scoop, 3/6, was found in a burial with female accessories, Grave 3 (Fig. 15.5). It is of a standard type, with twisted stem, flat round terminal at one end and suspension loop at the other. Examples from the Upper Thames Valley have been dated to the later 5th or earlier 6th century (Dickinson 1976, I, 223–4) and at Flixton the scoop was associated with A1 beads, AD *c*.450–530 (see above).

Finger rings

There was a copper-alloy finger ring, 11/6, still with remains of human tissue adhering to the inner face, in a female-gender burial, Grave 11. It was in the region of the chest, where the hand must have lain across the body, although no hand or arm bones survived. It is plain, cast, 25mm diameter and has a D-shaped section. Another ring of lead (the metal identified by XRF by Vanessa Fell) with a similar diameter and a circular section, 4/5, was found in a similar position in another burial without surviving bones, Grave 4, although this grave may have been disturbed and the ring was not certainly from a finger. Lead seems an unusual metal for something worn on the hand. It may have been regarded as a cheap substitute for silver, although in the classical world it was associated with the underworld (Aldhouse-Green and Aldhouse-Green 2005, 163).

Early Anglo-Saxon finger rings are more commonly made in expanding spiral or coiled forms, but a small number of the plain cast type seen here have been found in 6th- and 7th-century graves and their main period of use is regarded as the mid 6th century (Boyle *et al.*, 1995, 88). At Flixton, Grave 4 has been placed in Phase FA1/FA2a and Grave 11 in Phase FA2, on the basis of the accompanying grave goods.

IV. Textiles

by Penelope Walton Rogers

Introduction

Remains of clothing, textile covers and cords were found adhering to metalwork in twenty-nine graves. Over seventy different items were registered, but due to their variable preservation full technical details of weave, spin and thread-count could be recorded in only forty-five

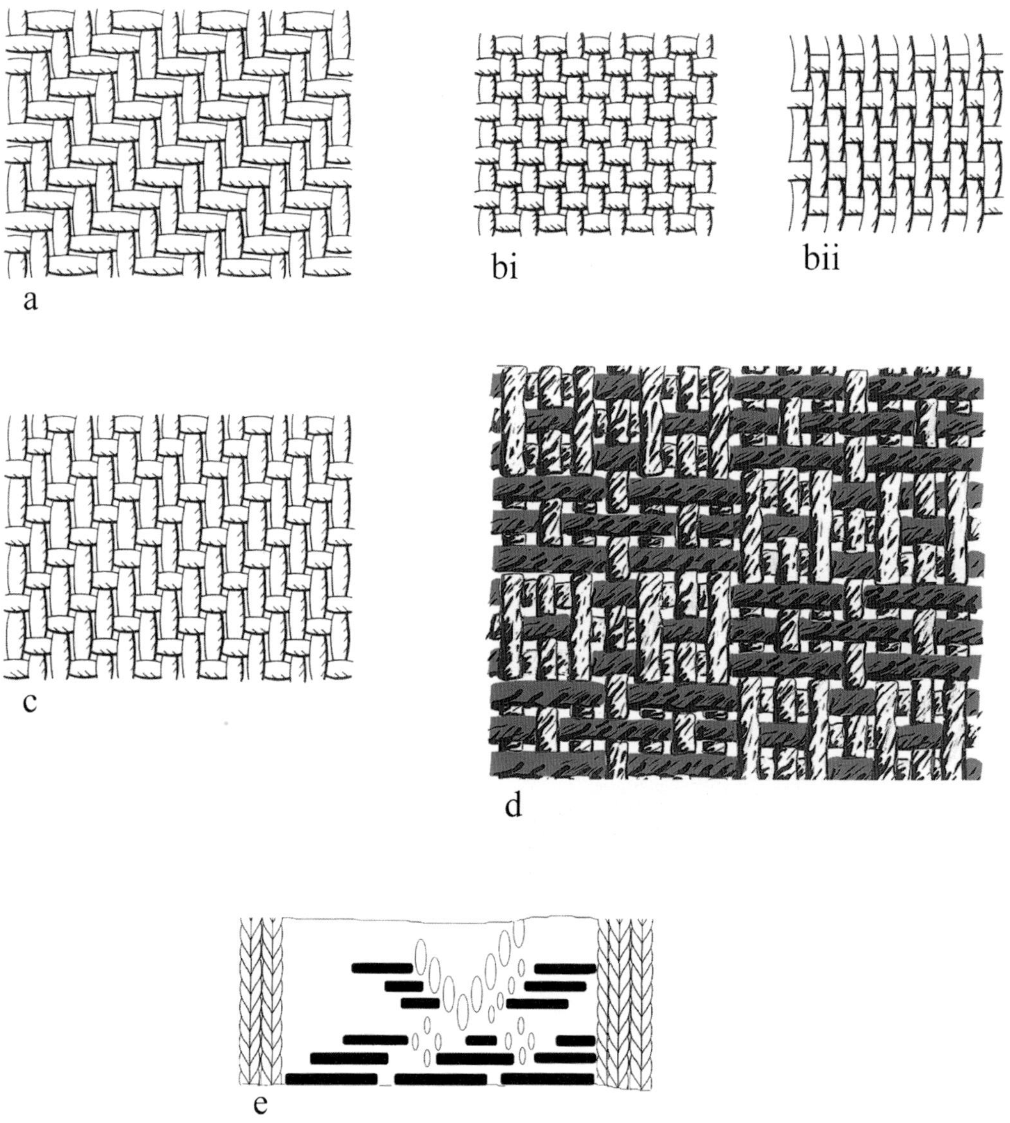

Figure 7.11 The weaves of the Flixton textiles: (a) 2/2 twill (b) tabby, (i) plain, (ii) repp (c) 2/1 twill (d) 3/1 coverlet weave (e) patterned tablet weave from Grave 17. The Anglo-Saxon Laboratory

(Table 7.5). The raw materials of the textiles were successfully identified in twenty-eight cases, using a combination of transmitted-light (optical) microscopy carried out by the author and scanning-electron micrographs (SEM) prepared by Vanessa Fell. A single example of wool twill from sleeve clasp 17/2 i–ii (Pl. 10.2) was well enough preserved to allow identification of the dye by absorption spectrophotometry and thin-layer chromatography (Walton and Taylor 1991). Details of the individual textiles have been placed in archive and a summary appears in Table 10.5.

The main cloth types

Figs 7.11–7.12

The weaves of the different Flixton textiles are illustrated in Figure 7.11. The Flixton collection is dominated by textiles woven in plain 2/2 twill, with yarn spun Z in warp and weft (ZZ 2/2 twill), of which at least half are wool and only a small proportion linen (Table 7.5). They represent 54% of all the textiles from the site and 70% of the total for the three main Anglo-Saxon loom-woven cloth types, which are ZZ 2/2 twill, ZS 2/2 twill and ZZ tabby. The ZZ twills occur in coarse and medium qualities, with counts of 7 x 6 to 15 x 15 threads per cm, and there is one fine example in wool, 16 x 16 per cm, on a pair of brooches 21/2–3, and another in flax or hemp (linen), 20–24 x 12–14 per cm, on another pair of brooches 51/1–2. One medium-weight ZZ twill pinned by annular brooch 8/1 may have been made from goat hair, since it had numerous fine fibres of 15–16 microns diameter combined with coarser ones over 60 microns, although it did not include

Textile type	*Wool*	*Linen*	*Fibre not id.*	*Total*
ZZ tabby	0	3	2	5
ZZ tabby repp	0	2	1	3
ZZ 2/2 twill	13	4	7	24
ZS 2/2 twill	1	0	2	3
ZZ 2/1 twill	0	1	0	1
other weaves	1	0	1	2
tablet weaves	2*	2	3	7
Total	**17**	**12**	**16**	**45**

* One wool tablet band has some linen yarn

Table 7.5 Textiles from 29 graves at Flixton II. Only confident identifications have been included

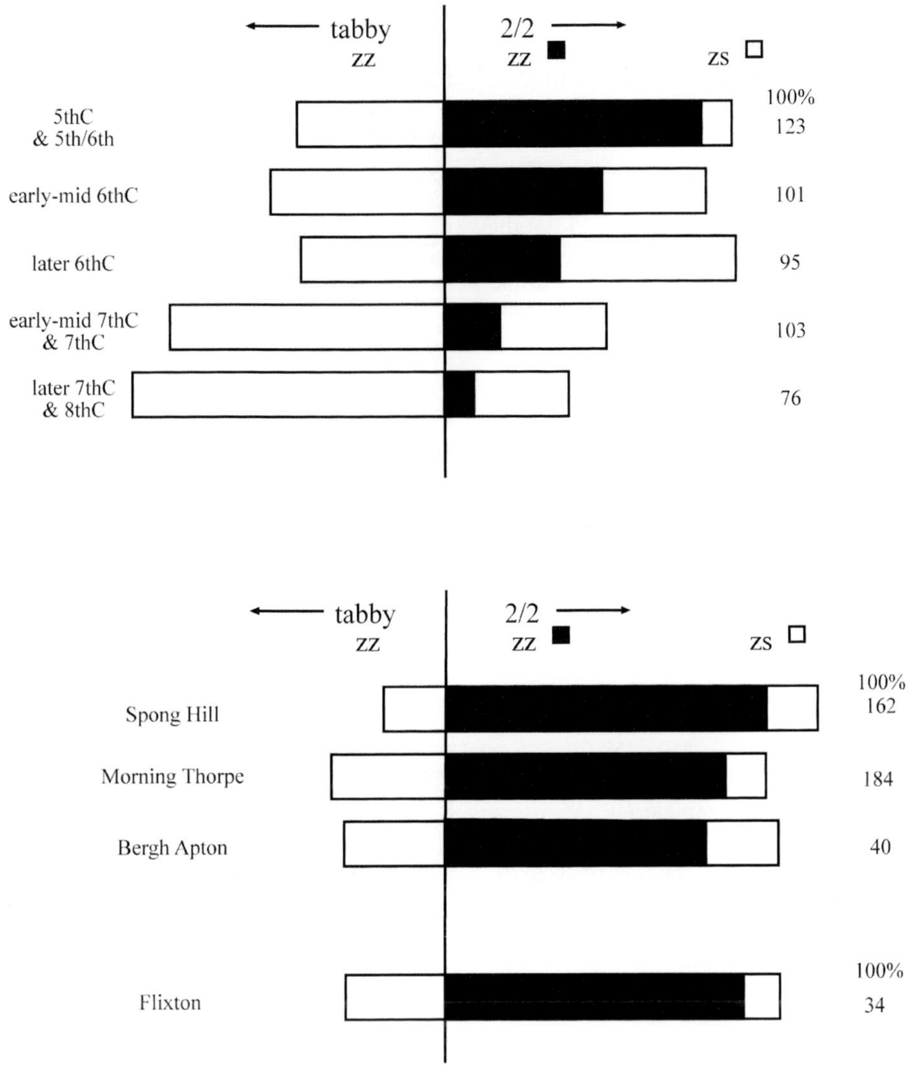

Figure 7.12 Above: the three main textile-types of Early Anglo-Saxon England, arranged by date. Below: The three main textile-types in the Norfolk cemeteries, compared with Flixton

the full range of fibres diagnostic of goat (Appleyard 1978, 10–11, 62–4; Textile Institute 1975, 60–1, 163–4). Individual details of interest in this group include a ribbed border over 10mm wide, probably a selvedge, running across the brooch pins on both 21/2 and 21/3; and the combination of woad and a tannin-based dye on white wool, for a blue-black colour in the twill on 17/2.

Textiles from Anglo-Saxon cemeteries form a remarkably consistent pattern, despite the variation in soil conditions. According to a recent survey of a national sample, ZZ 2/2 twill was the main clothing fabric of the 5th and early 6th centuries, but its use in burial textiles declined during the course of the 6th century (Fig. 7.12 upper plot; Walton Rogers 2007, 104–7). The Norfolk cemeteries of Morning Thorpe, Bergh Apton and Spong Hill were not included in the original bar chart (Fig. 7.12 upper plot), because their dates were not available at the time of its compilation, but now that it is known that Spong Hill has proportionately more early graves, Bergh Apton more late graves and that Morning Thorpe covers the full date span of the other two (Penn and Brugmann 2007, 69, fig. 5.20), the same decline in ZZ 2/2 twill can be demonstrated for these sites (Fig. 7.12 lower plot). On the other hand, the three sites maintain a higher proportion of ZZ 2/2 twill (60–74%) than the national average of 49% (as a percentage of the three main cloth types). The same is true of cemeteries of the 'Saxon' region, from the upper Thames Valley southwards (Walton Rogers 2007, 109), which suggests that certain core areas of Anglo-Saxon England were slow to adapt to the 6th-century changes. Flixton, with 70% ZZ 2/2 twill, therefore fits the local Norfolk pattern better than the national sample.

There are only three examples of ZS 2/2 twill, which is a textile type that arrived at the end of the 5th century, and it seems to have been a particularly late arrival in the Flixton cemetery: one grave has been dated (see Chapter 9) to EAC Phase FB1, Grave 9, the second to Phase MB, Grave 52, and the third, Grave 57, is undated, although situated in a cluster of late graves.

ZZ tabby, mostly made from flax or hemp, was found eight times, and in one instance, 8/1, it could be confidently identified as flax, from the plant *Linum usitatissimum* L., by the presence of nodes, fine lumen, well-spaced cross-markings and a clockwise rotation in the 'drying-twist test' (Textile Institute 1975, 16, 78, 168–9; Catling and Grayson 1982, 12–17). The raw flax in the bucket pendants from Grave 20 (see above) was identified by the same means. The ZZ tabby textiles have thread-counts ranging from medium, 10 x 10 per cm, to fine, 18 x 14 per cm and one, on annular brooch, 9/5, has a ribbed or repp-effect border running across the line of the brooch pin. On another example, representing a head veil in Grave 20A, there are two fine tablet-woven borders marking the front edges of the veil. Two of the eight tabbies are repp weaves, where the dominant system of threads lies straight and the crossways system weaves round it. They were found on objects in the region of the waist, a ring and latch-lifter, 31/5, and a knife, 52/4: the latter is probably hemp, to judge from the variable size of the lumen and the close, dense cross-markings (Catling and Grayson 1982, 22–3). Repp has only recently been separated from the other tabby weaves. At present it seems to be most common in the south-east, especially Kent (Walton Rogers forthcoming a), but there are comparable examples in Suffolk at Holywell Row G37 and Sutton Hoo Mounds 1, 5 and 7 (Bender Jørgensen 1992, 206; Walton Rogers 2005).

Romano-British textile techniques
Pl. 7.6
In the national survey, it was shown that certain techniques which are likely to be Romano-British in origin cluster at certain sites (Walton Rogers 2007, 230–2). The techniques are 2/1 twill, the tubular selvedge and the process of 'soft-finishing', by which is meant the raising of a nap on the surface of the fabric. They often occur at sites with Roman antecedents and one of the largest clusters occurs in the Norfolk cemeteries, Morning Thorpe and Bergh Apton, east of the Roman *civitas* capital of Venta Icenorum, and Spong Hill. Flixton once more proves its relationship with these sites, with one or possibly two examples of 2/1 twill, and two of soft-finishing, although no tubular selvedges were noted. The 2/1 twill weave is difficult to identify when corroded to metalwork, but a folded linen example on strap-end 9/3 conveniently shows the front and back face of the weave (Pl. 7.6) and a fragment on annular brooch 17/4 is probably the same. Soft-finished textiles were also noted on annular brooch 9/5 and annular brooch 20A/10. This evidence does not indicate that the occupants of Graves 9, 17 and 20 necessarily came from Romano-British stock, but rather that there was within Norfolk and northern Suffolk a zone in which Romano-British textile skills had been preserved. This is supported by the late example of an Iron Age/Romano-British style of spindle whorl in Grave 40.

Specialist textiles
Pl. 7.7
On one face of the socket of spearhead 52/1, there is a thick patterned wool textile which has been woven in a simplified variant of the weave known as 'summer-and-winter' (Pl. 7.7; for the weave diagram, see Fig. 7.11d). Three examples of true summer-and-winter have been recorded so far, one on a spearhead in G931 at Mucking II, Essex (Crowfoot 2009, 431), one on some metalwork of uncertain identity in G23 at Market Lavington, Wiltshire (Walton Rogers 2006, 112–3) and the third on a shield boss in G85 at Wakerley Northants (Crowfoot 1989). Summer-and-winter has pattern rows of 3/1 and 1/3 construction alternating with rows of tabby, but in the simplified version the tabby rows are omitted. Another example of the simple variant was found in G37 at Snape, Suffolk, where it was a grave lining, and this is identical with the Flixton piece in terms of thread-count and spin

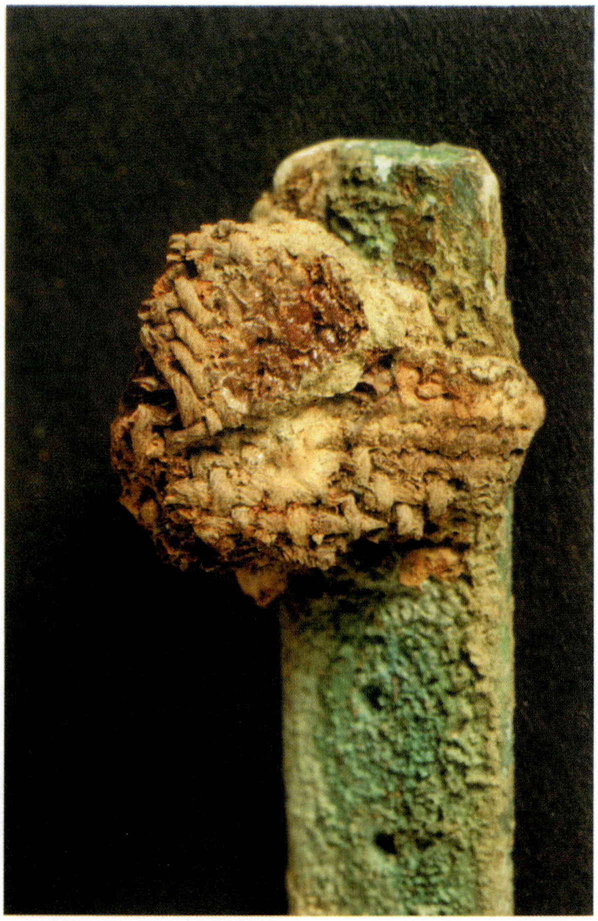

Plate 7.6 A fold of 2/1 twill on a strap end, 9/3, showing front and back of the weave. Photo Vanessa Fell, English Heritage

(Crowfoot 2001, 208–10, reviewed in Walton Rogers 2007, 80–2). Summer-and-winter is almost certainly a Sasanian or Byzantine import and was probably woven on the *zilu* pattern loom (Walton Rogers 2007, 82, 236, *contra* Walton Rogers writing in 1992, published 2006, 113). No such loom would have existed in Anglo-Saxon England, but it is possible that the simpler variant of the weave could be woven on simpler apparatus. If that is correct, then it might be argued that the Snape and Flixton textiles were an Anglo-Saxon copy of the imported coverlets, although experimental work would be needed to confirm this point.

On the back of a buckle, 32/2, at the side of the body in Grave 32 there is another heavy twill made of wool or goat hair, from which emerges a single large tuft of unspun raw fibre. It is impossible to be certain of an identification based on such a small piece, but in its raw material, ground weave and general appearance, this textile shows all the characteristics of a pile weave. Some of the earliest piled textiles come from women's graves, but in the 7th century they were exclusive to male-gender graves, where they have been identified as cloaks and rugs (Walton Rogers 2007, 85–6). Where they were made in the Early Anglo-Saxon period is unclear, although they may have been imported (*ibid.*) and they are usually found in well furnished graves.

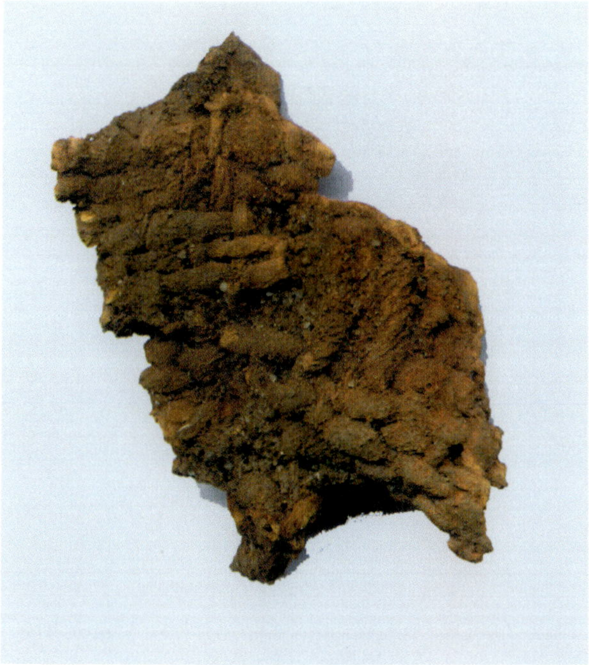

Plate 7.7 The coverlet weave on the socket of spearhead 52/1. The Anglo-Saxon Laboratory

Tablet weaves

Narrow bands woven with tablets were identified in six different graves, all burials with female accessories. There were two different bands in Graves 3 and 20 and one each in Graves 11, 17, 30 and 31. In its simplest form, tablet weaving consists of parallel cords held together by a weft, and there are examples of this type, worked on four-hole tablets (so that the cords are four-ply) on sleeve clasp 3/8, annular brooches 11/5, 20/6 and 20/10. The cords mostly twist in opposite directions, ZSZSZS, indicating that the tablets have been threaded alternately left and right, but in the example on the sleeve clasp from Grave 3 they are SSS, which is most probably a border on a different form of tablet weaving. There are further poorly preserved tablet weaves of uncertain construction on annular brooches 30/2 and 31/2.

The remaining bands are all patterned, although it is difficult to establish the exact technique because of their mineralised state. The wide band binding the iron ring 3/4, for example, has areas of twill-effect and repp-effect weave combined with plain areas where the cords are twisted ZSZSZS. The narrow bands on the two annular brooches and the buckle in Grave 20 have been worked with two-hole tablets, a technique which gives a thin, lightweight band suitable for the linen veil that they border, and irregularities in the weave suggest some form of decorative effect. Finally, the better preserved tablet-woven bands on the sleeve clasps from 17/2 and 17/3 display intricate patterning in wool and linen. These represent sleeve cuffs 28mm wide and the best-preserved cuff on 17/2 has simple corded borders, SZSZ[?SS] on one side and SSZSZS on the other, flanking a patterned zone (Fig. 7.11e). The patterning is made up of twill-effect tablet-weaving which gives a prominent central V, on either side of which are brocaded areas. At the tip of the V, the pattern begins to reverse and there is a four-spot pattern in white linen on dark wool. The wool yarns are all made from non-pigmented (white) fleece and their dark colour is almost certainly due to dye.

Most of these examples are standard Anglo-Saxon tablet weaves, and the twill-effect structure is particularly common in the Anglian region (Walton Rogers 2007, 91–2). The combination of techniques seen in the cuff bands from Grave 17, however, is highly unusual. No exact matches have been found, although some related techniques have been recorded in the wealthy Viking Age cemetery at Birka, Sweden, where the bands were worked in linen and silk with silver brocade, instead of the linen and wool with wool brocade seen at Flixton (Geijer 1938, 76–87; Hansen 1990, 57, 68–9, 107–9). Several of the Anglian tablet weaves have their ancestry in Scandinavia and the Flixton cuffs probably represent one further example. The virtuosity of their construction fits the prestigious nature of the sleeve clasps with which they were found, although there was nothing else in this grave to suggest any degree of affluence or status.

Needlework and cords

Fine plied yarns had been used for stitching on the tablet-woven bands associated with the iron ring, 3/4, and annular brooch, 11/5. The sewing thread on 11/5 was linen, but wool had been used to stitch the tablet bands to the clasps from Grave 17. These yarns are all plied Z2S (that is, two Z-spun yarns twisted together in the S-direction) and thicker cords, made by twisting several linen Z2S yarns together in the Z-direction, were used for the repair on cruciform brooch 4/2. On this brooch the broken pin support has been tied back in place and to judge from the best preserved area on the brooch arm, where there is a neat criss-cross of yarns square to the brooch, the cord binding must have covered most of the brooch head. Cord repairs are not unusual in cruciform brooches, but they are generally worked as a diagonal criss-cross, with a bracing thread round the bow, and this careful binding, square to the brooch, seems to be unique.

V. Girdle groups

by Penelope Walton Rogers

Introduction

Clusters of objects were found in the region of the left waist, hip or thigh, in Graves 3, 9, 11, 20, 21, 26, 31 and 51, in each case a burial with female-gender accessories. They would almost certainly be suspended from the belt, or relate to a bag suspended from the belt, and they have therefore been classified as 'girdle groups'. Two metal rings higher up the body in Graves 34 and 39 have been included for comparison.

Metal rings

Pl. 7.8

The small sliding-knot ring made from copper-alloy wire, 26/5, from a girdle group in Grave 26, and another, 39/2, from the region of the chest in Grave 39, are typical of the rings used to suspend lightweight items such as tweezers and toilet sets (Boyle *et al.* 1995, 89). They were not, however, attached to metalwork in the Flixton graves and the example from Grave 39 may have formed part of a necklace.

Sturdy, cast rings of 22–25mm diameter, in iron, 21/1, and copper alloy, 34/3, may also have been used for suspension and can be compared with the iron ring, 21mm diameter, linked through the looped end of a key or latch-lifter, 31/5. The function of the cast iron rings, 35–52mm diameter, 3/4, 11/2 ii, 20/2 and 21/4, is less clear. The well-preserved organic remains around 3/4 suggested that the ring had been tied to a transverse object, possibly the sheath or shank of the mysterious finial-like object, 3/3.

There are also two large cast copper-alloy rings, 49mm and 55mm diameter. The first, 26/3, has been ornamented with groups of transverse grooves and a particularly clear wear pattern indicates that it, too, has been used for suspension. The larger of the two, 51/7, has a triangular section and is ornamented with transverse lines and rows of punched dots (Pl. 7.8). This ring was found with a riveted clip and leather, as was a copper-alloy ring with moulded ornament from West Heslerton G140 (Haughton and Powlesland 1999, II, 238–9), which suggests the presence of a pouch. Some cast rings may be Roman in origin (Boyle *et al.* 1995, 90) and some may have been amulets or curing stones (Meaney 1981, 12–13, 170–8), although others appear to have had a practical purpose, as suspension hoops and as frames for the mouths of purses (Evison 1987, 119).

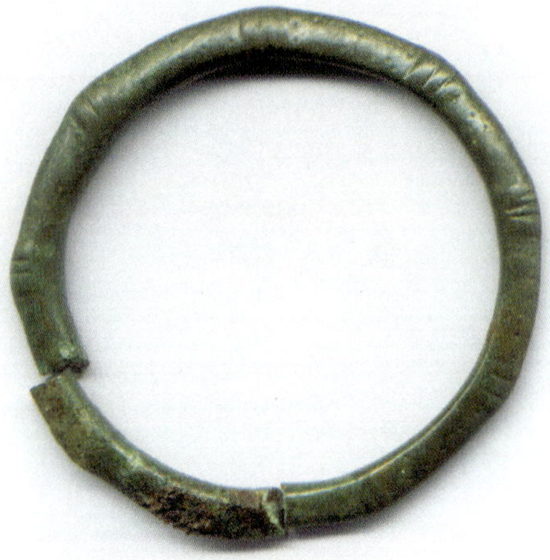

Plate 7.8 Cast copper-alloy ring, 51/7. D. 55mm. The Anglo-Saxon Laboratory

Leather/skin fittings

Riveted clips associated with animal skin – either leather or oil-dressed skin – in two girdle groups, 9/6 and 51/8ii, are likely to represent a pouch of some sort carried at the hip. Further riveted clips, one of which had remains of an iron pivot or loop passing through the fold of the clip, were found in the region of the upper body in Grave 20B/4. These last were associated with strap-ends, as were the others, and it is possible that this complex represents a pouch placed on the woman's chest (see Chapter 10).

Keys and latch-lifters

Fig. 7.13

Iron keys and latch-lifters, 145mm to 235mm long, with a suspension loop at one end, were recovered from five graves, one each from Graves 11, 20, 26 and 31 and two from Grave 51 (Fig. 7.13). Only one, 20/1, is a latch-lifter of the standard 'crooked finger' form. Three, 11/2i, 31/5–6, 51/6, have a working end formed from three inwards bends, and an incomplete example, 26/6, probably represents another the same. The final piece, 51/4, is a variant of the T-shaped key, with a forked end and terminals turned backwards like an anchor. In the two items from Grave 51, the suspension loop has been curled to one side, whereas the loops on the others are all curled on the same axis as the crooked end. A small iron ring is linked through the end of 31/5. All five graves incorporated pairs of annular brooches and all except Grave 31 had at least one of the *ARound* type, which suggests they belong to the *c.*510–560/80 period.

Angular crooked-finger latch-lifters are found in the North, Midlands, East Anglia and Kent. At Edix Hill they were most commonly buried in the pre-560/80 period (Meaney 1998, 272) and a brief review of twelve other sites suggests a similar pattern, although the type still appears intermittently in later graves. The T- or anchor-shaped key, in contrast, appears in some pre-560/80 graves, such as Morning Thorpe G108 and G249, Norfolk (Green *et al.* 1987, I, 65–6, 103–4, II, 237, 280) and Norton G21 and G29, Cleveland (Sherlock and Welch 1992, 131–2, 138–140), but is most common in later graves, at sites such as Harford Farm, Norfolk (Penn 2000, 54–5), Dover Buckland, Kent (Evison 1987, 116–7) and Finglesham, Kent (Chadwick Hawkes and Grainger 2006). The anchor-shaped key combined with three crooked-finger latch-lifters in Edix Hill G83 was originally placed in Edix Hill Phase I, pre-560/80 (Malim and Hines 1998, 283), but this can now be moved to AD *c.*580–650 on the basis of the glass beads of Group B2 (Brugmann 2004, 60). The keys usually have the suspension loop curled on a different axis from the working end and the same feature is adopted in several of the later latch-lifters, such as those at Castledyke G138 and G155, North Lincolnshire (Drinkall and Foreman 1998, 75–6,79, 184, 186), Edix Hill G54 (Malim and Hines 1998, 66, 119) and Dover Buckland G53 and G58 (Evison 1987, 231–2, 299).

The type with three inward bends is less common and it is not clear whether it should be regarded as a latch-lifter or a pot hook. There is a relatively small, rounded version from Morning Thorpe G221 (Green *et al.* 1987, I, 94, II, 272), EAC Phase FA2 (*c.*480–530/50), but the rest are large and angular, and come from burials of different dates. One, 227mm long, from West Heslerton G119 was associated with annular brooches and B19 clasps (Haughton and Powlesland 1999, 197–200); a second from West Heslerton G143, over 165mm long (incomplete), was associated with *B7b* clasps, and a Class D cruciform brooch (*ibid.*, 244–8); a third, *c.*230mm long, was with a short pin and chatelaine at Beakesbourne G29, Kent (Faussett 1856, 151, pl. 15); and a possible fourth, over 215mm, from a late grave at Edix Hill, G54 (Malim and Hines 1998, 66, 119), was with a buckle of Type II.24bii (Marzinzik 2003, 118); a final example, *c.*200mm long, came from an undated grave, Wakerley G69, Northamptonshire (Adams and Jackson 1989, 126). The suspension loop was preserved on the Morning Thorpe example, where it was curled on the same axis as the working end, and on the undated Wakerley and the later Edix Hill pieces, where it was turned to the side. Since both anchor-shaped keys and latch-lifters with the

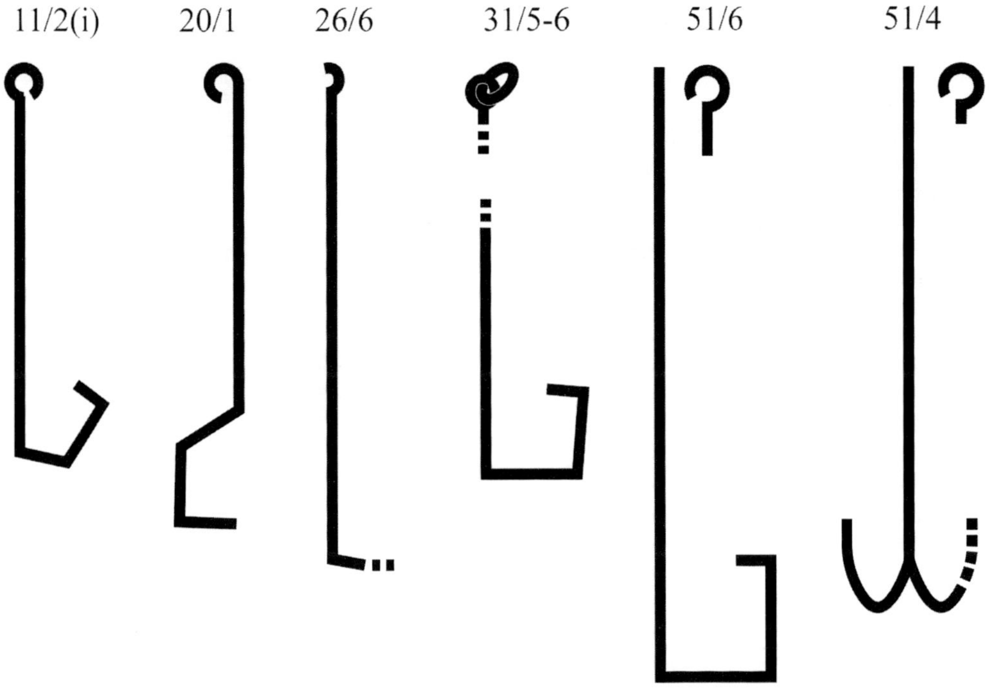

Figure 7.13 Latch-lifters and keys from Flixton graves. Drawn to scale. L.51/6 235mm. The Anglo-Saxon Laboratory

suspension loop turned to the side are more common in late graves, it is possible that Grave 51, which incorporates a pair of annular brooches and beads of Brugmann Group A2b, is from a transitional phase.

Strap-ends

Strap-ends were recovered from three graves with female accessories, as a trio in Grave 9, a trio with a separate singleton in Grave 20, and as a pair in Grave 51. The trios were probably from straps for pouches, since they were associated with a girdle group in Grave 20, probably body B, and Grave 51, and skin/leather and a pouch fitting in Grave 9. It is probable that the single strap-end, 20B/6, associated with a buckle and other metal fittings, 20/4–5, in the region of the chest of body B in Grave 20, also came from a pouch (see Chapter 10). Each strap-end has been made from a pair of copper-alloy plates held together by a single rivet. The set of three from Grave 9 (9/3), are long and tapering (39mm x 8mm) with a row of punched dots on both faces. The strap-ends of the second trio, 20/3, are fragmentary (over 30mm x 6.5mm), but probably a plain variant of the same type. The pair from Grave 51 (51/8i), are relatively short (16mm x 9mm), with a squarer end and incised cross decoration on one face, and the single strap-end on the chest in Grave 20 (20B/6), is similar (25mm x 9mm), but plain.

The narrow, tapering, two-plate strap-end is found throughout the North, Midlands and East Anglia and there are matching sets of three associated with girdle groups in twelve graves (Table 10.4). Decoration varies, but Empingham II once more provides the closest parallels with a single line of punched dots on the trios from both graves. Incised crosses are more usual in East Anglia, although there are punched dots around the edges of some single strap-ends from Holywell Row G52 (Lethbridge 1931, 28, 38) and Edix Hill G13B (Malim and Hines 1998, 48–50), and double and single rows of stamped marks down the centre of the trios from Bergh Apton G29 and G34. In eleven of the twelve graves with trios (Table 10.4), the strap-ends are associated with latch-lifters and/or girdle-hangers, and each burial also has a pair of annular, or openwork brooches. Third garment-fasteners are limited to a cruciform brooch of Class D in Morning Thorpe G253 and a pin of Ross Type VIII in West Heslerton G167, but sleeve clasps of different types were recorded in six graves, and A2 beads in seven (Table 10.4). This places most tapered strap-end trios in EAC Phase FA2, *c*.480 to 530/50. Flixton 20, fits the pattern, since the burial includes A2 beads, but the trio in Grave 9 is associated with only one annular brooch and a B1 bead, which places it in Phase FB1 (see Chapter 9).

Square ended strap ends are not a common type, and have been found as singletons, at Empingham G50, Holywell Row G7 and G68 and Morning Thorpe G249 (Timby 1996, 111, 195; Lethbridge 1931, 3–4, 33, 44, Green *et al.* 1987, II, 280), and as a trio with a fourth larger strap-end at Edix Hill G19B, where they were associated with a pair of Midlands-style openwork brooches (Malim and Hines 1998, 110–11). They appear with male and female accessories and their date range is as yet unclear, but the Flixton examples have been allocated to Phase FA2 (Grave 20) and FB1 (Grave 51) on the basis of associated artefacts.

Straps in strap-ends

Remains of a narrow leather or skin strap were preserved in several of the strap-ends, the best preserved being in 9/3, where, in each case, the last 13mm of a neatly cut, square-ended strap had been riveted between the two parts of the strap-end. A small buckle, 9/4, is associated with this complex. Relatively thin straps were recorded in 20/3 and 51/8ii, and another small buckle, 51/9i, was recorded near the straps in Grave 51.

Unidentified object, 3/3

Fig. 7.14; Pl. 7.9

The cast copper-alloy hoop with a thick shank, 3/3, from Grave 3, cannot be identified with confidence (Pl. 7.9). It has the remains of an iron rod embedded in the shank, and it seems likely that the hoop was a terminal or suspension loop for a utensil. The way in which mineral-preserved textiles curve around a cavity next to the shank end of the object suggests that the iron rod was originally encased in some organic material which has since decayed. Because the combination of cast copper-alloy on an iron rod is rare in the Early Anglo-Saxon period, the object was at first thought to be a Roman artefact. However, Dr Hilary Cool, a specialist in Roman artefacts, could not find any obvious parallels, although she noted that a copper-alloy terminal on an iron shank was the kind of combination seen on Roman keys and furniture fittings (H. Cool, pers. comm.).

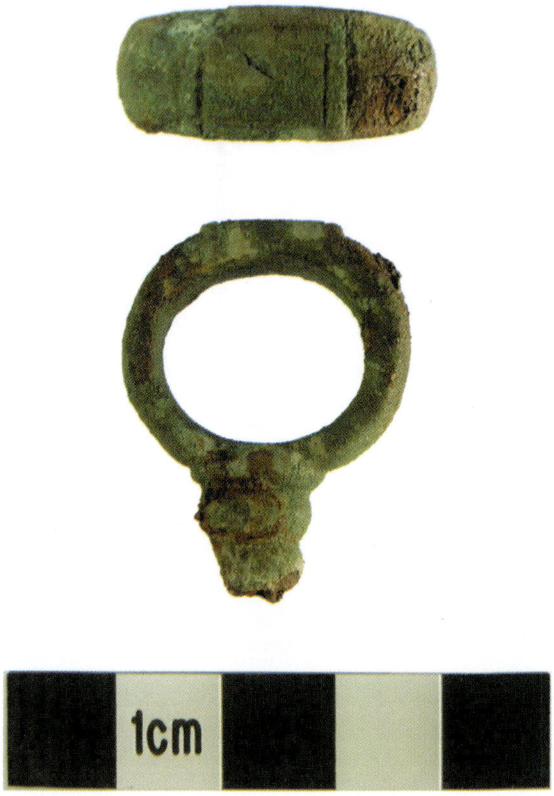

Plate 7.9 Unidentified object, 3/3. Ring D.25mm

There is a smaller artefact from a late 7th-century grave, Dover Buckland G161 (Buckland Phase 6), which shares some features with this item. It was classified as a pin, although its description suggests, rather, a small stiletto in a sheath (Fig. 7.14a; Evison 1987, 84–5). Its cast copper-alloy terminal represents the head of a man wearing a horned helmet, and the shape of the horns forms a loop similar to that on 3/3. Its iron shaft is inlaid with a contrasting metal, and it is encased in a wooden sheath. A range of similar items from Sweden, one possibly Vendel and the others early Viking Age, have been found in women's burials, where they were associated with accessories such as tweezers, shears, knives and keys (*ibid.*). The Buckland and Flixton objects both lay in the region of the woman's left waist, alongside a knife. In the Flixton grave there was also an iron ring which had originally been tied to a crossways object, possibly the shaft of 3/3. The Buckland artefact was described as a 'probable cult object', but the grave was considerably later in date than the Flixton burial, which has been placed in Phase FA2a (see Chapter 9). An iron rod with a tubular copper-alloy handle, with moulded decoration and gilding, was found with a girdle group in Bergh Apton G42 and is conceivably a variant of the same artefact type (Fig. 7.14b; Green and Rogerson 1978, 31–2, 74).

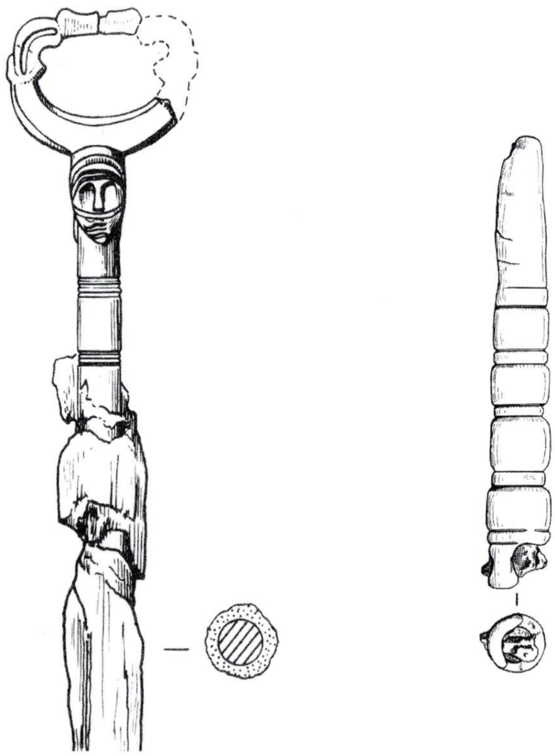

Buckland I G161 Bergh Apton G42

Figure 7.14 (a) object from Buckland I G161, copper-alloy with iron blade/shank encased in wood (after Evison 1987, fig. 63, copyright English Heritage); and (b) object from Bergh Apton G42, copper-alloy with iron core (after Green and Rogerson 1978, fig. 89). Drawn to scale. L. of object on right 78mm

VI. Knives and hand tools

Knives

by Ian Riddler

Figs 7.15–7.16

Thirty-six knives were recovered from thirty-two graves. Most of the knives are complete or near complete, but seven are fragments, having lost all or a part of the tang, and one (41/3) lacks both the tip of the blade and the end of the tang. The knives have been catalogued and assigned to type using Drinkall's system (Drinkall and Foreman 1998, 279–84), which is a revision of that devised by Vera Evison for the Buckland cemetery (Evison 1987, 113–5), where the diagnostic attribute is the shape of the blade, rather than the size of the knife (Fig. 7.15). Ascriptions to type are based on an examination of the knives themselves, as well as their radiographs. Size groups (as Härke 1989) have not been used, but the dimensions of the knives are considered below. Almost all of the knives can be assigned to type, with the exception of one fragment. In a few cases, described below, they do not fit precisely into a single type.

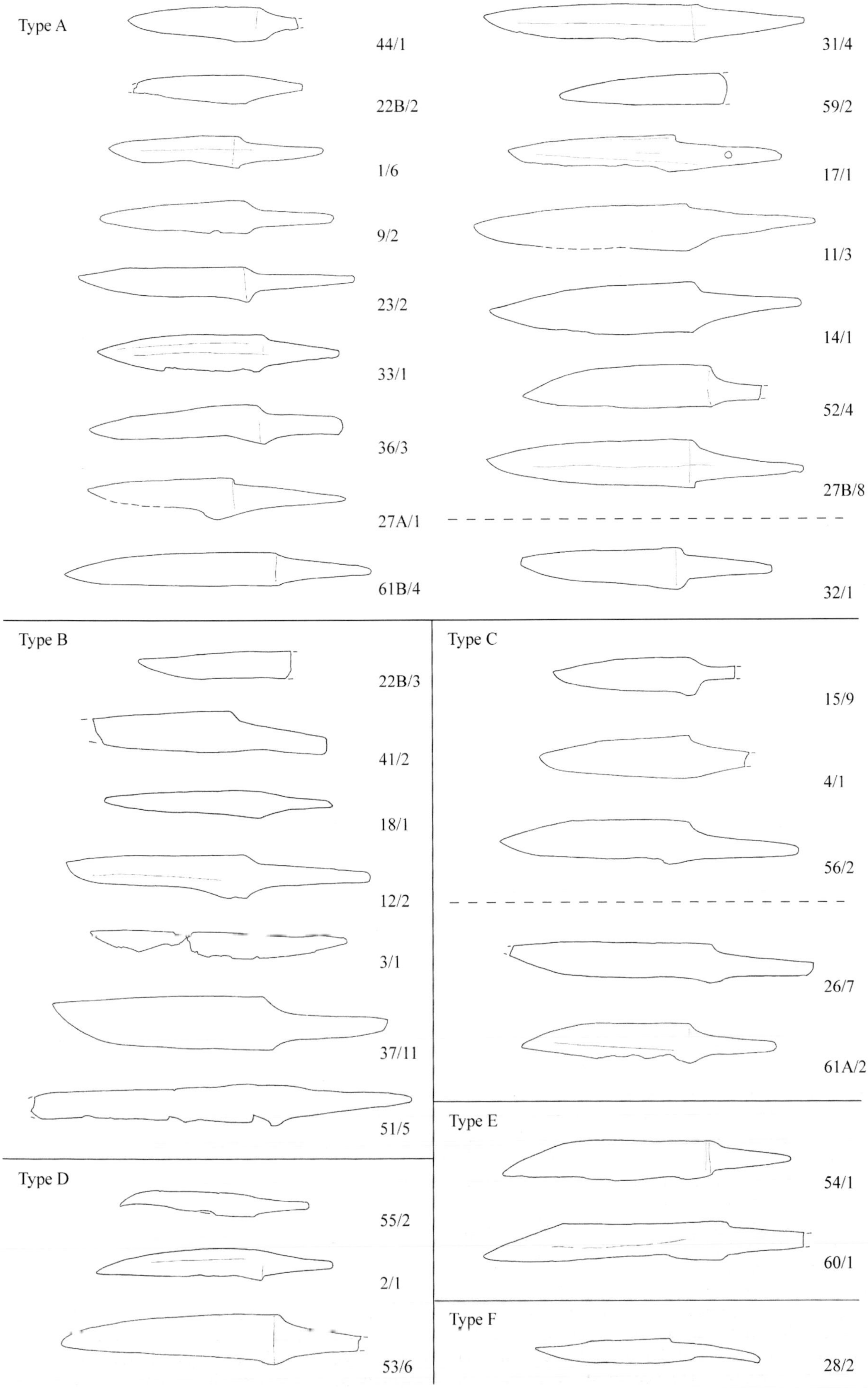

Figure 7.15 The knife types at Flixton II. Ian Riddler

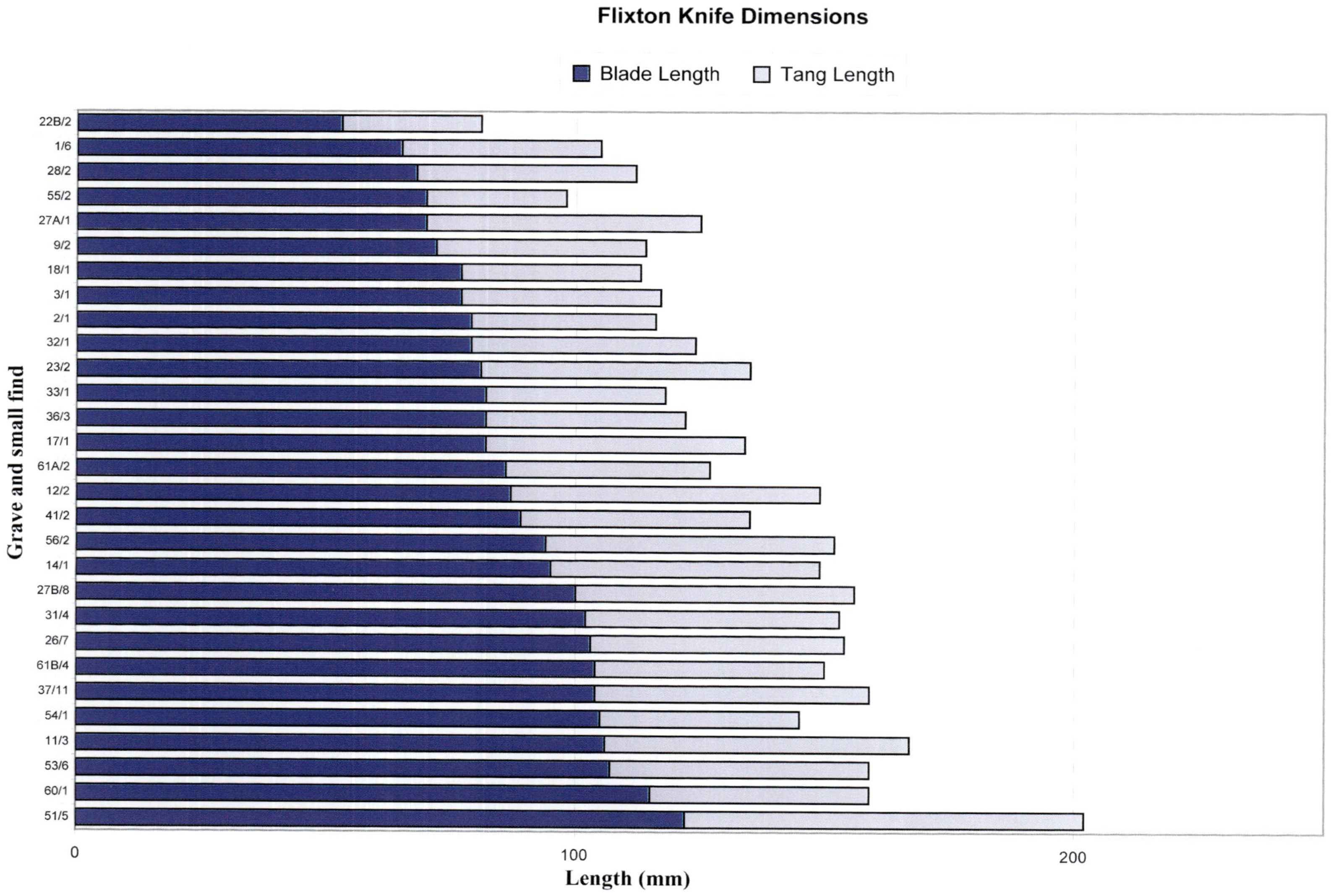

Figure 7.16 The lengths of the knives from Flixton II. Ian Riddler

Seventeen knives belong to Type A, the most common knife form of the Early Anglo-Saxon period. With this type the back of the blade and the cutting edge are broadly parallel before converging at the tip. One knife (32/1) is almost a hybrid between Types A and C, the lack of an angled front section to the blade placing it closer to the former type than the latter. Type A occurs throughout the entire Anglo-Saxon period and cannot be closely dated. Seven knives have been placed in Type B. It is essentially a 6th-century knife form, possibly extending into the early part of the 7th century (Evison 1987, 115; Böhner 1958, 214–5) and is defined by a straight back to the blade (often dipping slightly at the tip), with a rising cutting edge. There are two slender versions of this form (3/1 and 51/5), as well as a comparatively large knife for this assemblage (37/11) and one (18/1) for which the cutting edge is straight and slopes towards the back before curving at the front edge. Five knives have been placed in Type C, although two of these are slight variants. Type C is similar to Type A, but has an angled front portion to the back of the blade. It can also be confused quite easily with Type E, although with Type E the cutting edge does not rise to the tip. One of the variants (61A/2) is close to a Type A whilst the other (26/7) has only a slight incline to the front of the blade. Type C is of mid 6th- to 7th-century date and it may have served as a precursor to the related Type E, although it is possible that both forms originated at roughly the same time (Evison 1987, 115). Three knives belong to Type D, a type defined by its curved back and straight cutting edge, which usually does not rise to the tip. Type D is found in both 6th- and 7th-century contexts. Two examples (2/1 and 55/2) are slender and narrow, whilst a third knife (53/6) is both broader and larger. Type E occurs initially in the late 6th century and gains in popularity across the 7th century. One of the pair of knives of this type (60/1) has a slightly rising cutting edge, but is better viewed as a Type E than a Type C. Both knives have long parallel blades with the angle confined to a small section at the front. One (54/1) has a groove just below the back, behind the angled descent. A single, slender example of a Type F knife (28/2) has a concave curve to the front section of the blade and a rising cutting edge. It is the rarest form of early Anglo-Saxon knife, occurring in both 6th and 7th century contexts.

The knives vary in overall length between 81mm and 202mm, with their blades extending from 53mm to 122mm (Fig. 7.16). Two-thirds of the blades are less than 100mm in length. There are no large knives (as defined by Härke 1992a, 91) or *seaxes* in the assemblage and no obvious divisions into size groups are apparent. Härke (1989, 144–5; 1992a, 91 and table 5) preferred to separate knives into three size groups on the basis of their blade lengths. Whilst a distinction could be made for the Finglesham cemetery between blade lengths of 60–99mm (Type 1) and those of 100–129mm (Type 2), no such grouping is apparent either at Flixton or within a sample of knives from several east Kent cemeteries (Riddler and Trevarthen forthcoming). Figure 7.16 shows a continuum of blade sizes with no clear separation of size groups. Almost all of the knives would fall within Härke's Group 1, with just a few belonging to Group 2.

A Type A knife (17/1) from Grave 17 has a circular perforation through the tang. This is an unusual feature for a knife of this period, but it is not unknown. Similar tang perforations have been observed on knives from Carlton Colville, Spong Hill, Cuxton, Berinsfield, Dover Buckland, Saltwood and Winnall (Härke 1995, 75; Meaney and Hawkes 1970, fig. 13.8; Scull 2009a, 409; Riddler and Trevarthen forthcoming). In most cases there is just one perforation, set close to the blade, which can enclose a rivet. On a knife from Saltwood, the rivet secured a handle of bone or antler, whilst in other cases the handle is thought to have been horn. In most cases they may have been used to secure the handle to its tang. Two perforations are visible on a knife from Spong Hill and three on a knife from Carlton Colville (Hills *et al.* 1984, fig 71.7b; Scull 2009a, 403 and fig 7.23). These knives can be regarded as perforated whittle tangs, rather than proper scale tangs. Knives with scale tangs are commonly thought to have been unknown in England before the 13th century (Scull 2009a, 409) but a growing number have been found in earlier contexts, including examples from Thetford and Winchester that go back to the 10th to 12th centuries (Riddler and Walton Rogers 2006, 271).

Knife handles and sheaths

by Vanessa Fell

Pls 7.10–7.11

Mineralised horn survives on the tangs of twenty-seven of the thirty-six knives from the graves (Pl. 7.10); five others show evidence of having had a handle at the time of burial although the material cannot be identified and the remainder either do not have tangs or no evidence of a handle has survived. One knife (37/11) may have a repaired handle, because the horn ridges are orientated diagonally on one side of the tang. Evidence for horn handles is commonly found on Anglo-Saxon knives (*e.g.* Watson 1984; 2001; 2002), although their ridged structure has often been confused with wood grain (Watson and Edwards 1990, 103).

There are twenty-seven knives, and possibly two others, that retain evidence of mineralised animal product. These may include containers and grave wrappings, although some were certainly sheaths. The material can be identified as leather or untanned skin where collagen fibres are visible. The grain pattern survives particularly well on one blade (37/11) and can be identified as bovine, probably calf (Pl. 7.11), and another knife (14/1) has a very faint grain pattern, again bovine. One sheath was seamed at the cutting edge (41/3) whereas another was seamed along the spine (23/2).

Fire-steels

by Ian Riddler

An iron fire-steel (61/5) lay to the left of the knife associated with one of the burials in Grave 61 (Fig. 15.45). The lower edge is straight and rises to form curled birds head terminals at either end, with a lightly rounded upper edge. There is no buckle or other form of attachment evident on the fire-steel and it was aligned vertically in the grave, suggesting that it was suspended from one of its curled ends. It belongs to the group of fire-steels succinctly described by Evison as 'sub-triangular in shape with a straight back, convex curve on the opposite side and curled ends' (Evison 1987, 111). They are widespread in contexts of the late 6th century onwards (Hawkes 1973, 195; Geake 1997, 79–80). The tight curls of this example and its low convex upper edge suggest that it belongs to the late 6th to early 7th century. Later 7th century examples occur in at least two forms. One group, seen at Burwell and

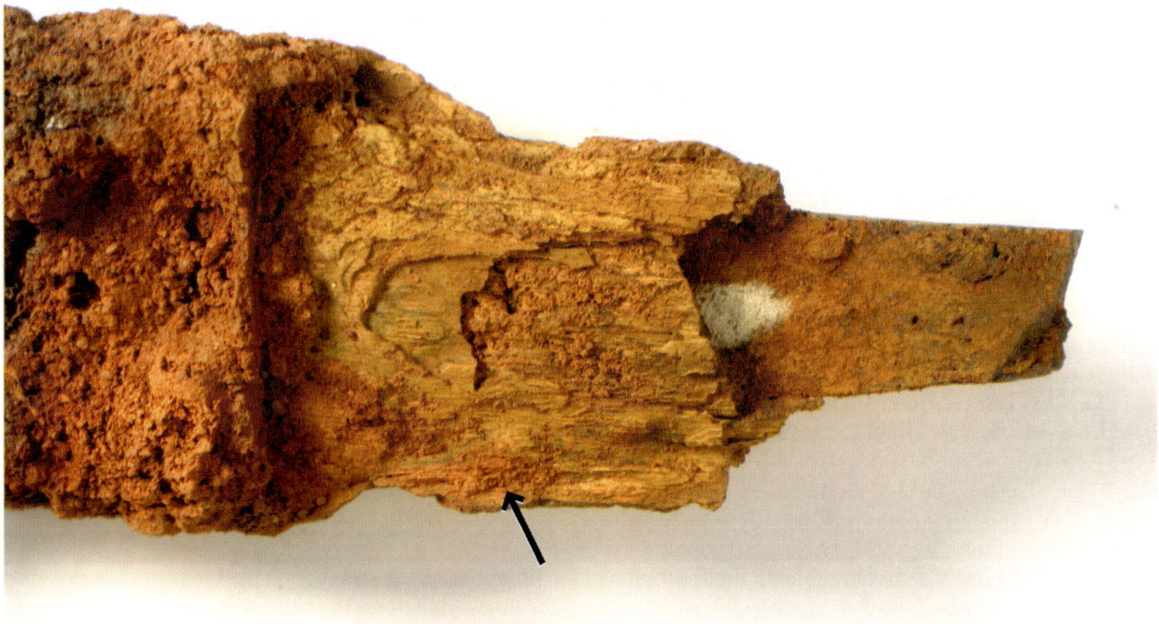

Plate 7.10 Knife 53/6 showing well-preserved horn (arrowed) on the tang. The edge of the original handle is revealed by the vertical line to the left. Photo Vanessa Fell, English Heritage

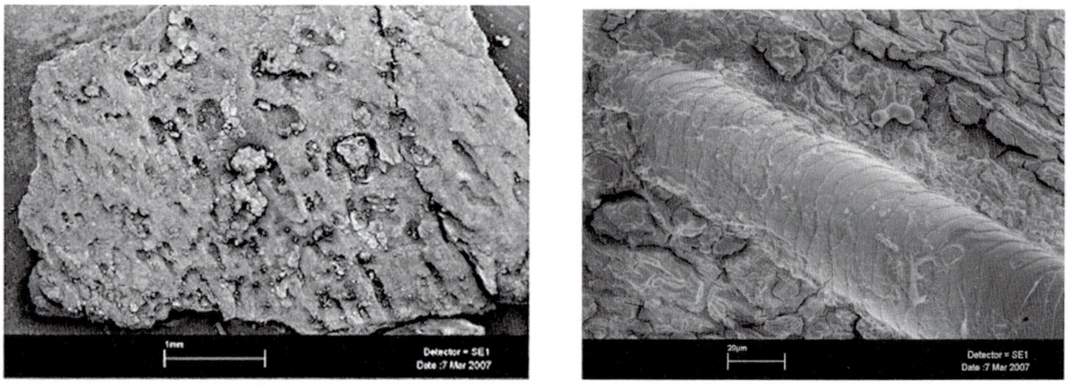

(a) (b)

Plate 7.11 The remains of a sheath on knife 37/11: (a) Scanning Electron Micrograph of the grain pattern and (b) SEM of fibre with scale pattern of cattle, probably calf. Images Vanessa Fell, English Heritage

Caistor St Edmund, is more triangular in shape, with long curved arms (Penn 2000, 58 and fig 69). A second form, occurring at Westgarth Gardens, Burwell and Shudy Camps, has a flat lower edge and tightly bound curls, again with a triangular upper edge.

A fragment of a second fire-steel (18/2) was found with a knife in Grave 18, possibly the burial of a child (Fig. 15.15). It has a hooked end with a rounded terminal and a straight main body that is scarcely wider than the hook. It has fractured about its midpoint and at the terminal but it could still have been used, even in this incomplete form. The shape of the fire-steel recalls an example from G41 at Dover Buckland, as well as several from the Mill Hill cemetery (Evison 1987, 110, fig. 24.7; Parfitt and Brugmann 1997, 76, figs 40.70b, 40.74d and 44k). Evison noted the similarity of this type to several examples found at Lavoye (Joffroy 1974, 39–40, fig 20) and Kazanski has recently listed comparable examples from Merovingian contexts, where the emphasis is firmly on a 6th century dating (Kazanski 2002, 47). The same can be said for Alamannic fire-steels of this type, which have been considered by Koch (2001, 305) and placed in SD Phase 3–4, of *c.*AD 480–530. The majority of fire-steels of this type occur in Frankish or Alamannic graves, as well as graves in east Kent, and they are not common in East Anglia.

Spatulate iron tool

by Penelope Walton Rogers

An iron tool, 60/2, 135mm long, was found with the knife in Grave 60 (Fig. 15.45). It has a flat section and tapers from a rounded end to a blunt point. It bears a resemblance to the single-ended pin beaters used with the two-beam vertical loom, but these were usually made of bone or antler rather than metal (Walton Rogers 1997, 1755–7; 2001b, 158–61). It seems more likely that, although it lacks a clearly defined tang, it is an example of the spatulate tools sometimes found with the knife in graves of the later 6th, 7th and early 8th century (Hirst 1985, 89; Evison 1987, 110; Drinkall and Foreman 1998, 283–4). It was found with a late form of knife, 60/1, amongst the late graves at the foot of the southern barrow.

Spindle whorl

by Penelope Walton Rogers

The lead spindle whorl, 40/1, still has remains of the wooden spindle on which it would have been mounted inside the spindle hole (Fig. 15.34). It is of the simple disc-shaped form, B1, which was relatively common in the Iron Age and Roman period, especially in lead, but continued in decreasing numbers into the Early and Middle Anglo-Saxon periods (Walton Rogers 1997, 1743; 2007, 23–6). It has been shown that the size of the spindle hole increases with time (*ibid.*) and the relatively late date suggested by the 8mm diameter of the 40/1 spindle hole is confirmed by the B2 beads in the same grave. During the 6th century, plano-convex spindle whorls (Forms A1 and A2) were introduced, along with ZS twills, and both eventually became standard in the eastern half of England. The late survival of an Iron Age/Romano-British style of spindle whorl in Grave 40 corresponds with the continued use of ZZ twill for wool textiles and the persistence of Romano-British textile technology, both here at Flixton and in the Norfolk sites.

VII. Weaponry

Spears

by Ian Riddler

Fig. 7.17

Fifteen spearheads were recovered from fourteen separate graves at Flixton II, whilst a further example was unstratified. Most of the spearheads are complete but in two cases (Graves 2 and 6) only the sockets remain, whilst the unstratified spearhead is fragmentary and most of the blade is missing. The majority of the graves contained a single spearhead but there were two in Graves 1 and 37. In Grave 37, one was on the left and the other was with the shield on the right, whilst the two spearheads in Grave 1 lay side by side at the head of the grave.

The spearheads have been assigned to type using both the Swanton typology and that devised by Karen Høilund Nielsen for the EAC project (Swanton 1973; 1974; Penn and Brugmann 2007). The types are summarised in Table 7.6 and they are discussed here in a broad chronological sequence. Whilst some of the spearheads fit neatly into established typologies, others do not, as is often the case (Härke 1992a, 86).

For convenience, the Swanton typological scheme is described here first, in discussing the form and the broad dating of the various spearhead types. Under Swanton's scheme the earliest spearheads would be those of Types

Object no..	*Swanton Type*	*EAC Outline Group*	*EAC Size Group*	*EAC Phase*
Graves in rectangular plot				
1/1	C2	Angular	Medium 1	MA2
1/2	C2	Angular	Medium 2b	MA2
23/1	E2	Concave	Long 1b	MA1
27B/6	E2	Angular	Medium 1	MA2/B
28/1	H1	Concave	Medium 1b	MA1
37/1	H3	Concave	Long 1a	MA2
37/6	H2	Angular	Medium 2b	MA2
41/1	E2	Parallel	Long 1	MB
43/1	E1 variant	Angular	Medium 1	MA2/B
Graves associated with ring-ditch/mound				
52/1	E3	Angular	Long 1	MA2/B
53/1	E2	Angular	Long 1	MA2/B
55/1	D3	Lanceolate	Long 1	MA2/B
56/1	E3	Parallel	Long 2	MC

Table 7.6 The spearheads from Flixton II

H1 and H2. They were considered to be relatively early in date by Swanton and were current in the Upper Thames and Sussex regions from the late 5th to the mid 6th century (Swanton 1973, 105; Welch 1983, 132–3; Dickinson and Härke 1993, 11) and they do not appear in Geake's study of the artefacts from 7th-century and later graves (Geake 1997, 68–70). The same dating applies also to the H3 series (Dickinson and Härke 1993, 17). Spearheads of Type E2 are the most common to be found at Flixton and Morning Thorpe and they were also present at Bergh Apton and Brooke. Type E2 spearheads are not found in 5th-century contexts (Härke 1992a, 86 note 98, contra Swanton 1973, 79) but are found in the 6th and early 7th centuries, extending perhaps to the middle of that century, as are spearheads of Type E3 (Down and Welch 1990, 94). D3 spearheads belong essentially to the 6th century, with an emphasis on the second half of that century (Riddler and Trevarthen forthcoming). The single example of an E1 spearhead has curved blade edges, in the manner of leaf-shaped blades, and represents a variant of that series, although it shares elements of both angular and leaf-shaped blades. The dating of Type E1 spearheads is fairly broad (Geake 1997, 69). Swanton believed that the same broad dating applied to C2 spearheads but the majority come from contexts of the late 6th to 7th century (Swanton 1973, 53; Dickinson and Härke 1993, 12; Geake 1997, 68).

The spearheads have also been allocated outline types and size groups from the East Anglian Chronology analysis (Penn and Brugmann 2007, 17–22). The correlation of the two schemes is not quite exact but this merely highlights the small but often significant variations in blade forms and spear sizes, which makes it difficult to assign them unequivocally to precise single types. The E1 variant spearhead from Grave 43 tends to defy precise classification under either scheme. Some of the spearheads fall into unexpected outline types but in general the dating evidence is similar from either system, the EAC analysis generally providing a more precise chronology. Two spearheads belong to phase MA1 (Table 7.6), the concave outline of their blades forming a decisive

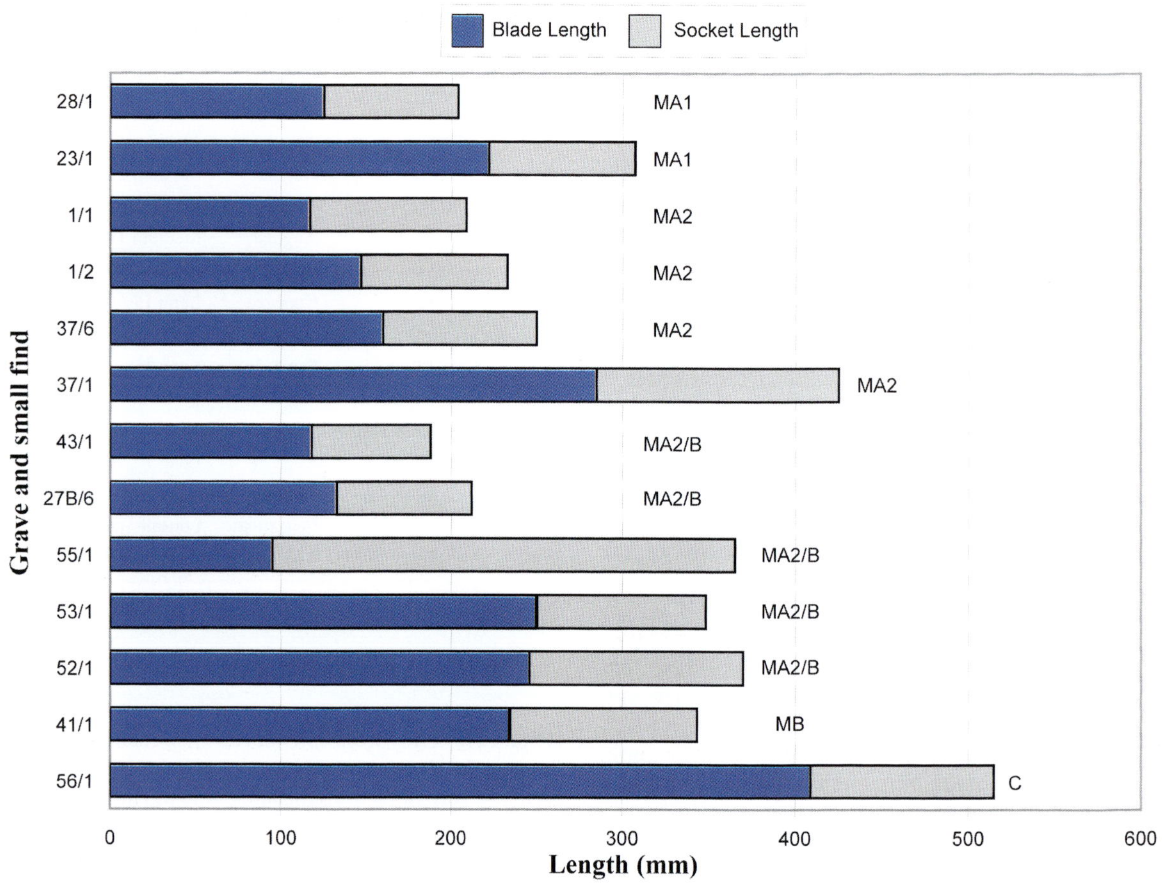

Figure 7.17 The lengths of spearheads from Flixton II, arranged by phase (for phasing see Chapter 9). Ian Riddler

chronological indicator. Four spearheads can be placed in phase MA2 and a further five belong to phase MA2/B.

The group as a whole encompasses the standard East Anglian blade forms, except for Swanton's Type C2, and includes D3 which is essentially a Kent type. The spearheads of phase MA2 are confined to the northern part of the cemetery, but three of the five graves of phase MA2/B are on the ring barrow to the south. The Type D3 spearhead from Grave 55 is included in the latter group. The two latest spearheads include one example (41/1) from Grave 41 and one (56/1) from Grave 56, which is one of the latest items from the entire cemetery. The key element of both of these spearheads is the parallel sides of their blades. The latest spearhead is also the longest from the cemetery and a gradual increase in lengths can in fact be seen across the phases (Fig. 7.17).

Just one of the spears, from Grave 37, was equipped with an iron ferrule, whilst a second ferrule occurred without a spearhead in a burial with female-gender accessories, Grave 9 (see Chapter 10). Both of the ferrules are conical in shape and taper to a rounded point, which is the standard type of the period (Härke 1992a, 87). Eight of the spearheads were fastened to their shafts with the aid of lateral nails, set between 8 and 35mm above the base of the spear socket. In seven cases the nails were parallel with the plates and passed across the cleft of the socket. In the eighth case, with the spearhead from Grave 43, the nail passes from the back of the socket into the cleft space in an unusual and inefficient method of securing the shaft. An iron ring lay midway along the socket of one of the spearheads (37/6) from Grave 37 and was also intended to secure the spearhead to its shaft.

Jacqui Watson was able to identify the wood types used on all of the spear shafts, as well as the two ferrules, and twelve out of sixteen examples are ash (this includes the spearhead and ferrule from Grave 37 which both contain ash) (Fell and Watson 2007). In a sense this is the expected result, given that one of the terms used to describe a spear in Old English is *æsc*, meaning ash wood, and this is the only spear term to refer directly to a specific wood type (Pollington 2001, 138, table 11). Ash also dominates the spear shafts from Worthy Park in Hampshire (Watson 2003, 196), but this contrasts with the situation seen elsewhere, and particularly outside of East Anglia, where hazel is often the dominant wood (Table 7.7). The Flixton sample is too small to identify reliably any trends over time and the earliest and the latest spears both included shafts of ash, but other woods are present from phase MA2 onwards.

Cross-sections of the wood could be seen in twelve cases and with all of these shafts the preference was for mature wood, rather than saplings or coppiced poles. Jacqui Watson (Fell and Watson 2007, citing Urbon 1991) has noted that mature timber increases the accuracy of flight of the projectile, suggesting that the spears were meant to be thrown. The size and shape of their blades accords well with this idea. They are relatively small and narrow blades and there are few examples of later, sword-like forms that may have been retained in the hand and used as weapons in combat.

	Flixton	Snape	Worthy Park	Edix Hill	Castledyke South	Empingham	West Heslerton
Ash	11	7	11	2			4
Possibly Ash	1			1	1		
Hazel	2	1		5	4	13	9
Alder	1						3
Hazel or Alder			1		1		
Willow or Poplar	1	1	1		1	9	5
Beech		1					
Beech or Holly		1					
Birch						1	

Table 7.7 Wood species identified for spear shafts from selected cemeteries

The metallurgy of the spearheads
by Janet Lang

The fifteen spearheads from graves were radiographed by Vanessa Fell at the English Heritage laboratories in Portsmouth and did not show any particularly distinctive features. Six were selected for further examination after an inspection of the radiographs and a consideration of their contexts and styles. These were 1/1–2, 23/1, 37/6, 41/1 and 55/1. Unfortunately one of the samples, 55/1, proved to be completely corroded, and did not provide any useful information. Details of the metallographic examination of sections removed from the selected spearheads and mounted in resin and the micrographs can be found in the site archive. A table of hardness values, or HV (diamond pyramid microhardness, 100g wt), is given in Table 7.8.

The quality of the metal varies, as indicated by the number and size of the inclusions in the blades. The inclusions in 23/1 and 37/6 are quite large (especially 23/1) and numerous. Their distribution is also inhomogeneous: the metal of 41/1 contains a concentration of inclusions in one small area, but has very few elsewhere, either in the ferrite or pearlite bands: this may be the result of the breaking up of a larger inclusion. A concentration of inclusions also occurs in 1/1, in an area of small-grained ferrite. Unusually, this is accompanied by a small amount of pearlite, perhaps demonstrating that it was made from an inhomogeneous bloom fragment.

Several blades appear to have been constructed with layered structures. In 1/2, 37/6 and 41/1 the central layers are slightly richer in carbon which might have been expected to result in an increase of hardness at the cutting edge but this has only occurred in 1/2, although it is possible that the harder edges of other blades were lost to corrosion.

There is little sign of heat treatment, although the blades are perhaps harder than might be expected from the appearance of their microstructures. In the low-carbon metal, some carbon was evidently retained in solution by rapid cooling and has precipitated within the grains in an aging process. This can increase the hardness up to a maximum, after which it declines (for example by aging at 50°C over five days, the hardness of very low carbon iron can be increase from *c.*100 HV to a maximum of *c.*200 HV after which it declines to 150 HV after seven days: this is discussed by Samuels 1980, 107). Whether this could have come about as a result of holding for a while at an elevated temperature as a final process or by a long-term aging process is not known. It has been suggested by Blakelock and McDonnell (2007, 53–4) that these effects can result from cremation rites, although at Flixton the spears had been placed in inhumations. The spearheads are harder than the microstructure might indicate. Phosphorus in solution in the iron increases hardness: in some of the sections its presence was indicated by characteristic 'ghost' structures (a difference in response to etching which gives a relief appearance in the microsection).

	1/1	1/2	23/1	37/6	41/1
Cutting edge	148	211	128	125	181
Middle	127	164	164	219	191

Table 7.8 Table of hardness values, average of three readings (HV_{100})

A comparison of the two blades found in Grave 1 shows that they have one common characteristic: the cutting edges of the blades are harder than the cores, but otherwise there is little similarity between them. Unfortunately, spearhead 55/1, the D3 type more commonly found in Kent, was completely corroded, so that it could not be compared with the East Anglian types. Of the C-type spearheads found in Grave 1, 1/2 appears to have a layered structure, with the middle layer richer in carbon, a construction which is also observed in 37/6 and 41/1, which are East Anglian types.

In terms of chronology, the earliest spearhead is probably 37/6: this blade contains variable slag and has a soft cutting edge and a hard core. The comparable later blade is 41/1. This is also layered with a carbon-richer middle layer, from core to cutting edge, but it has far fewer inclusions. Although the cutting edges of both blades are softer than the cores, the edge of 41/1 is little different to its core and is harder than 37/6.

Considering the differences in blade and socket shapes, the blade of 23/1 is long and wide. It is made of ferrite with many inclusions: the metal itself would bend easily but the inclusions would increase the likelihood of snapping. Spearhead 41/1 is long and narrow: with a small-grained pearlite and ferrite central layer, it would have been tough and reasonably shock-resistant.

With such small numbers of samples it is impossible to come to any conclusions which have any general applications. Metal quality varied. It is clear that layered structures were used and they probably included a central steel layer by choice. The use of a harder central layer in blade making may date to the 7th century BC (Panseri *et al.* 1957). It has the advantage that even after a number of sharpening operations, the edge can still be sharpened, whereas with a harder layer either welded to the surface or introduced by means of carburisation, it can be worn away by frequent grinding. It is difficult to know if this was as important for spearheads as it was for swords.

Apart from the outer layers of the ferrite grains in 41/1, which show some elongation parallel to the surfaces, there are few signs of cold working, although these may have been lost to corrosion. In contrast, the structure of a spearhead from Dover Buckland G264a showed marked distortion from cold working (Lang forthcoming).

In general, it may be said that the spearheads are similar to those from Edix Hill (Barrington A), in that the quality of construction was not particularly good (Malim and Hines 1998). Between half and a quarter of the Edix Hill blades were constructed so that the cutting edge was harder than the rest of the spearhead. The results of the hardness tests on the Flixton blades gave a similar ratio (Table 7.8).

Shields

by Stephanie Spain

Shield remains were recovered from six graves at Flixton II (Graves 1, 15, 27, 37, 52 and 53) and there was an unstratified find from area FLN 053. The unstratified shield boss is the earliest on the site, dating to the late 5th or early 6th century (Dickinson and Härke 1993, 11–12). The remainder of the shield bosses are later types, traditionally thought to span the 6th and early 7th centuries. Shield grips were found in all the graves except Grave 27 and four shields also had board mounts. These are all of common types but the long grip from Grave 15 is unusual for the region, though widespread elsewhere. This shield also had a small lozenge-shaped mount which was very probably some kind of repair.

The shield fittings

The unstratified boss, II/NG6, belongs to Dickinson's Group 1, a common type in the area, dating to the later 5th century or first half of the 6th century. The Flixton boss is a little smaller than most other Group 1 bosses in the area, suggesting that it may date later rather than earlier within this range. As the boss has a straight rather than concave cone, it should strictly be classified as Group 1.1. Its large apex disc is typical locally, and bosses of the same shape include Morning Thorpe G259, which has similar dimensions.

Three bosses fall within Dickinson's Group 3, dating from the 6th to early 7th century, and all are very interesting (Dickinson and Härke 1993, 14–17). Two belong to Group 3 subtypes, identified in a study of shield bosses from Kent, where the Group 3 type is most prevalent (Spain 2000). The Grave 1 boss (1/3 i) fits subtype 3a, the earliest form of Group 3 which combines the low, broad and heavily carinated shape of earlier Group 1 with the convex Group 3 cone. It therefore dates on the early side for Group 3, before or around the mid-6th century. The Flixton example is similar to one from Westgarth Gardens G62 in both size and shape.

The Grave 37 boss (37/2), fits subtype 3b(ii), which has a broad flange relative to diameter and an unusually high wall combined with shallow convex cone, giving a distinctive profile (Spain 2000). A boss of the same type from Wheatley G15 was included by Dickinson in her miscellaneous Group 8 (Dickinson and Härke 1993, 21–2) and in Kent bosses of this type have been found in several high status graves dating to the second half of the 6th century (Saltwood G1048, Broadstairs I G66 and G74 and Dover Buckland G265B). Though there are East Anglian bosses with similarly tall walls, I have so far been unable to find any local examples with this profile. The third Group 3 boss, from Grave 15 (15/1 i), has a fairly tall wall, but its flange width, carination and height are typical of standard Group 3. The boss had silver-plated copper-alloy flange rivets.

The remaining three bosses all belong to Dickinson's Group 6, which developed from the Group 3 form and dates from the late 6th into the first half of the 7th century (Dickinson and Härke 1993, 20). The Grave 27 boss (27B/7), is slightly larger than the other two and is similar in size and shape to Holywell Row G56. The two smaller group 6 bosses, from adjacent Graves 52 (52/2), and 53 (53/2), are more similar to each other than to other examples in the region, both having a fairly tall wall. Dickinson based her Group 6 on Evison's 'low curved' and 'low straight' subtypes and 53/2 is a perfect example of the latter, which has slightly larger dimensions than the former (Dickinson and Härke 1993, 20).

It has not been possible to correlate the Flixton bosses exactly with the EAC typology, but the Group 1 and Group 3a bosses are broadly equivalent to the SOC types, the Group 3 bosses to the COV/COS types and the Group 6 bosses to the CAS/SOS types.

Four shields had strap grips of Härke's Type Ia(1), essentially flat strips of iron which flare slightly towards the terminals with a rivet at either end for fastening to the shield board (Dickinson and Härke 1993, 24–7). The Group 3 bosses were fitted with broader versions, while the Group 6 bosses had much narrow examples, as is usual with the later boss type.

The shields in Graves 1 (1/4–5), and 37 (37/3–5, 9), had sets of four large disc mounts, arranged in pairs either side of the boss. Belonging to Härke's Group 'a', these are a reasonably common find with 6th-century bosses (Dickinson and Härke 1993, 27–30). The Grave 52 and 53 shields both had a 'double-rivet' style mount, formed of conjoined disc-headed rivets (Dickinson and Härke 1993, 27). These seem always to occur with Group 6 bosses and narrow strap grips and are thus characteristic of the early 7th century. They are not found very frequently, however, and do not occur with any of the five examples of this boss and grip combination at nearby Morning Thorpe (G218, G255, G333, G374 and G367; Green *et al.* 1987).

The long grip from Grave 15 is Härke's Type IIb, which has a flanged central section flanked by separate rivet plates before continuing as long, narrow extensions ending in small terminals (Dickinson and Härke 1993, 24–7). In this case the narrow extensions end in one lozenge-shaped and one discoid terminal, and the inner pair of rivets are copper alloy to match the boss flange rivets. Though the long grip is closely associated with Group 3 bosses and is fairly common in Kent, it is not usually found in East Anglia (Dickinson and Härke 1993, 27). This shield had copper alloy disc-headed rivets positioned on the board around the end of the discoid grip terminal. These may be associated with a small buckle found close to the shield, indicating fittings for a possible carrying strap. It also had a lozenge-shaped mount with a tiny knob-headed rivet in each corner, probably used to repair the wooden shield board.

Grave	*Shield Group*	*Board details*	*Grip*	*Diameter*	*Thickness at boss*	*Thickness at fitting*
Unstratified	1	Thin layer of leather preserved on flange; also leather/skin/pelt on outside of cone.	-	-	-	-
1	3	Shield board made from ash (TLS), with leather on the front c.2.2mm thick, and back 3.6-4mm thick. Plant stems on the front of large studs (1/5).	Cut out	>0.4m	14.0mm	14.0mm
15	3	Shield board made from willow or poplar (RLS), grip same. Thin layer of leather over the front, and thicker layer of leather on back. Evidence for a carrying strap pulled through the grip.	Rebated	>0.45m	10.0mm	10.0mm
27B	6	Wood (TLS). Rebated grip visible with wooden portion 18-21mm wide. Thin layer of leather between flange and wood. Chopped plant stems on front of shield boss.	Rebated	-	> 10.0mm	-
37	3	Shield board possibly made from ash (TLS), with leather on the front c.2mm thick, and on the back 3.5-4mm thick, wood 6mm thick. The grip also has leather on the outer side, c.4mm thick, and underneath layers of textile. The shield was probably placed against the side of grave cut and on top of spearhead (37/6).	-	>0.26m	-	12.0mm
52	6	Wood (TLS). Leather preserved on front c.1mm thick, and back 2.4mm, wood 7mm. Very degraded textile on the outside of grip. Wood preserved on front of boss and studs ash (TLS), probably represents a grave cover.	?rebated	>0.445m	c.10.4mm	-
53	6	Wood (both TLS and RLS) - possibly indicates the use of several sawn planks. Leather covered on both sides, front c.1mm thick, back c.3.6mm. Wooden board recessed to take boss flange, and counter sunk on the reverse to take the stud rivets. Wood preserved on front of shield mount, oak (RLS), possible evidence for a grave cover,	-	>0.36m, or c.0.46m from soil stain	-	8.4mm

Shield Group typology follows Dickinson and Härke 1993; TLS = tangential longitudinal section and RLS = radial longitudinal section

Table 7.9 Details of the organic materials preserved on the shield fittings from Flixton II

The technology of the shields
by Jacqui Watson
Pls 7.12–7.16

The wood used on the shield board of the Group 1 shield, II/NG6, could not be identified but two of the Group 3 shields utilised ash and one used willow or poplar (Fell and Watson 2007). Two of the Group 6 shields included boards of lime or maple and one was alder. The choice of woods is unusual in that willow or poplar is under-represented, although the sample size is small. Willow/poplar normally accounts for around 50% of the shields, followed by lime (25%), and six other species including ash and alder the remainder (Watson 1995, 37).

At least two of the shields (from Graves 15 and 27B) and possibly a third (Grave 52) had rebated grips (Table 7.9), where a separate piece of wood had been inserted into the front of the shield board (Dickinson and Härke 1993, 36). This can be clearly seen on the rivet used to attach the iron grip, 15/1 ii, on the shield from Grave 15 (Pl. 7.12), as well as on the flange of boss 27B/7 (Pl. 7.13). On the shield boss from Grave 53 (53/2), a fragment of the wooden shield board extends beyond the flange and it is possible to see that it has been cut and rebated to fit the boss flange (Pl. 7.14). The thin leather covering on the front of the shield folds around the edge of the flange. Presumably this was to make the upper side of the boss flange level with shield board. On the same shield, the outer pair of decorative mounts also have extensive organic remains and it can be seen that on the reverse of the shield the rivets were countersunk into the wooden surface with the leather compressed into the recessed area (Pl. 7.15). The metal washers are not preserved, just an impression in the surface of the leather, but they may have been made from copper alloy as there are low levels of tin and calcium around the iron rivet shank that may have been re-deposited there from the corroding washers.

All the wooden shield boards were covered in leather, and there seems to be a consistent choice of thin leather over the front, with a thicker type on the back, as for example, on the shield stud from 15/1 ii. Three hypotheses can be put forward. First, the front may have been decorated with relief carving in the wooden surface, which would be taken up by the thin leather when applied wet and left to dry on the wood: designs could also be made using coils of coarse thread between the wood and leather, as used on book bindings and sword scabbards (Cameron 2000). Second, perhaps the thin leather would take up dyes, or be easier to paint; or, third, thick leather, especially if shrunk to fit, would be very hard and effective at holding the shield together.

There is evidence for a carrying strap on the shield from Grave 15. The leather strap has been pulled around the grip 15/1 ii (Pl. 7.16) and there is a small buckle positioned near the shield rim, which may have been used to attach the strap like the examples from G96, Boss Hall, Ipswich (Watson 2001) and G46, Edix Hill, Barrington (Watson 2002). A reconstruction of how this shield may have looked when placed in the grave appears in Chapter 11.

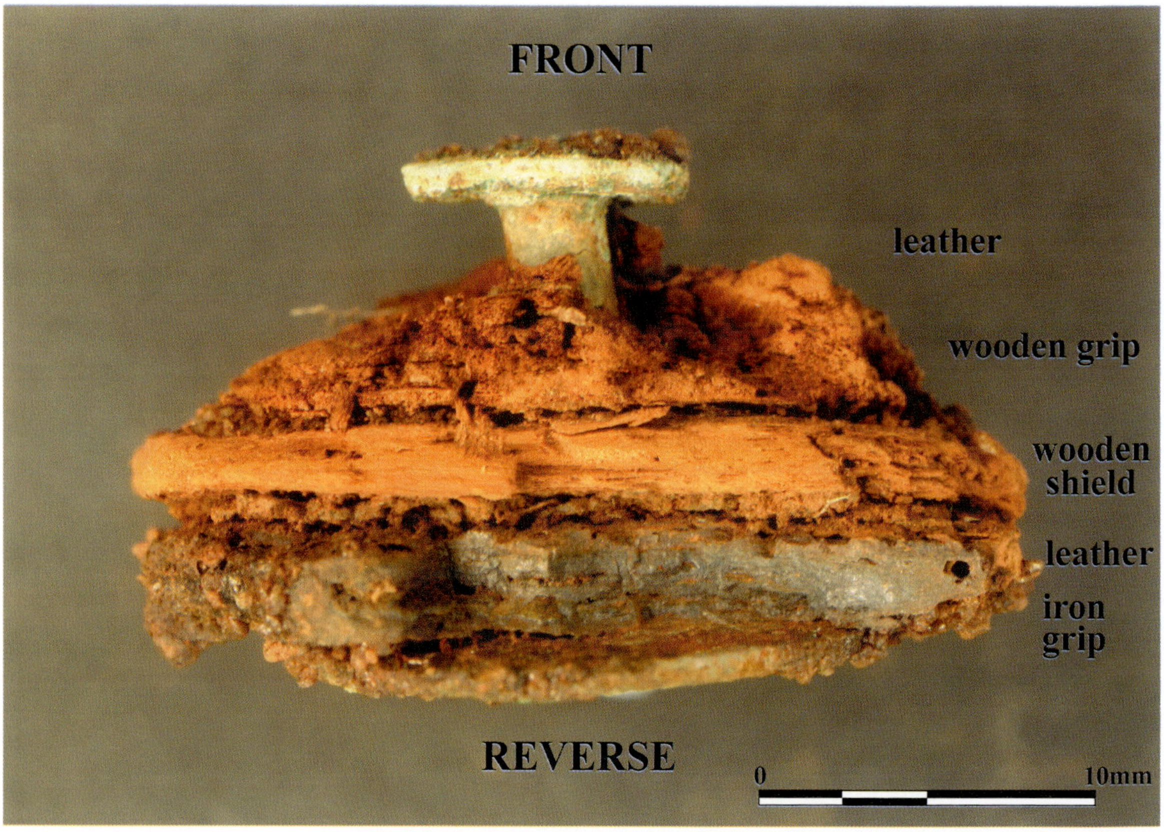

Plate 7.12 Layers of organic material preserved on the copper-alloy stud, 15/1b, used to attach the iron grip to the shield board. Photo Vanessa Fell, English Heritage

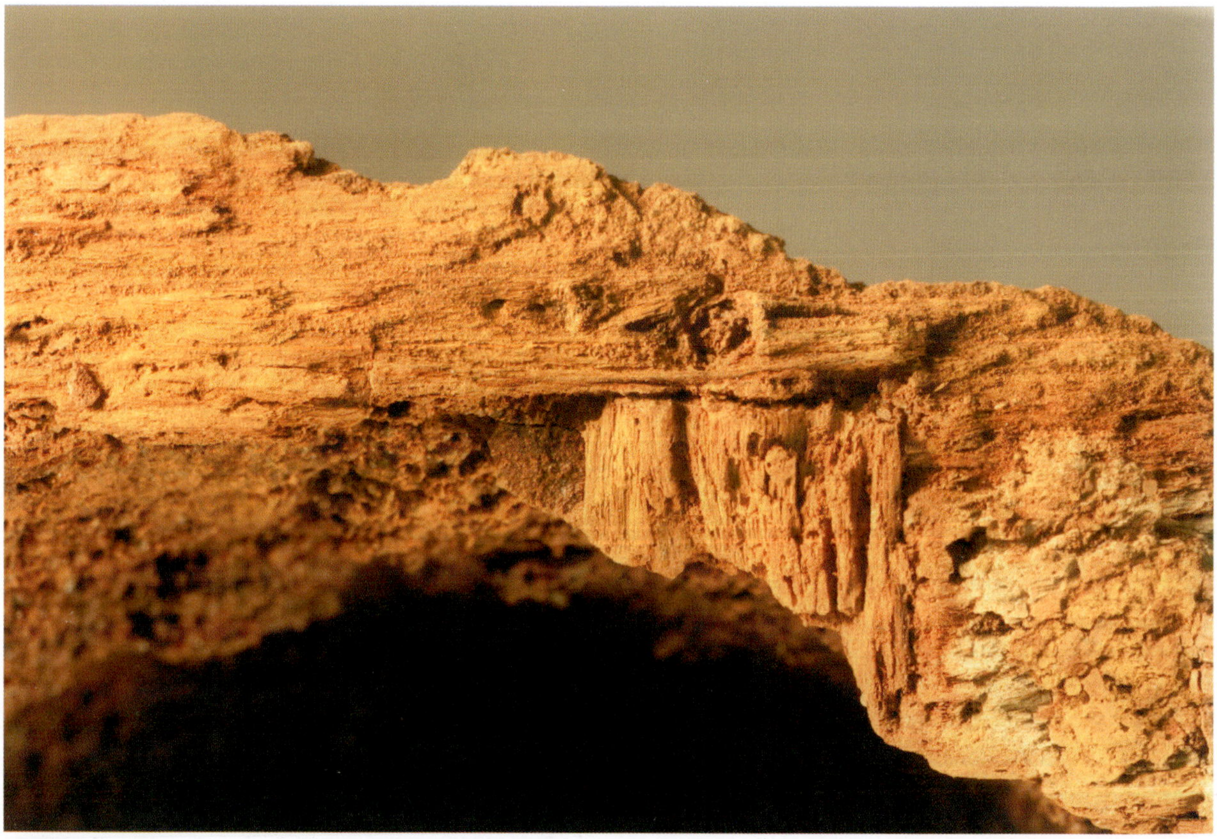

Plate 7.13 Separate wooden grip rebated into the front of the wooden shield board on boss 27B/7. Photo Vanessa Fell, English Heritage

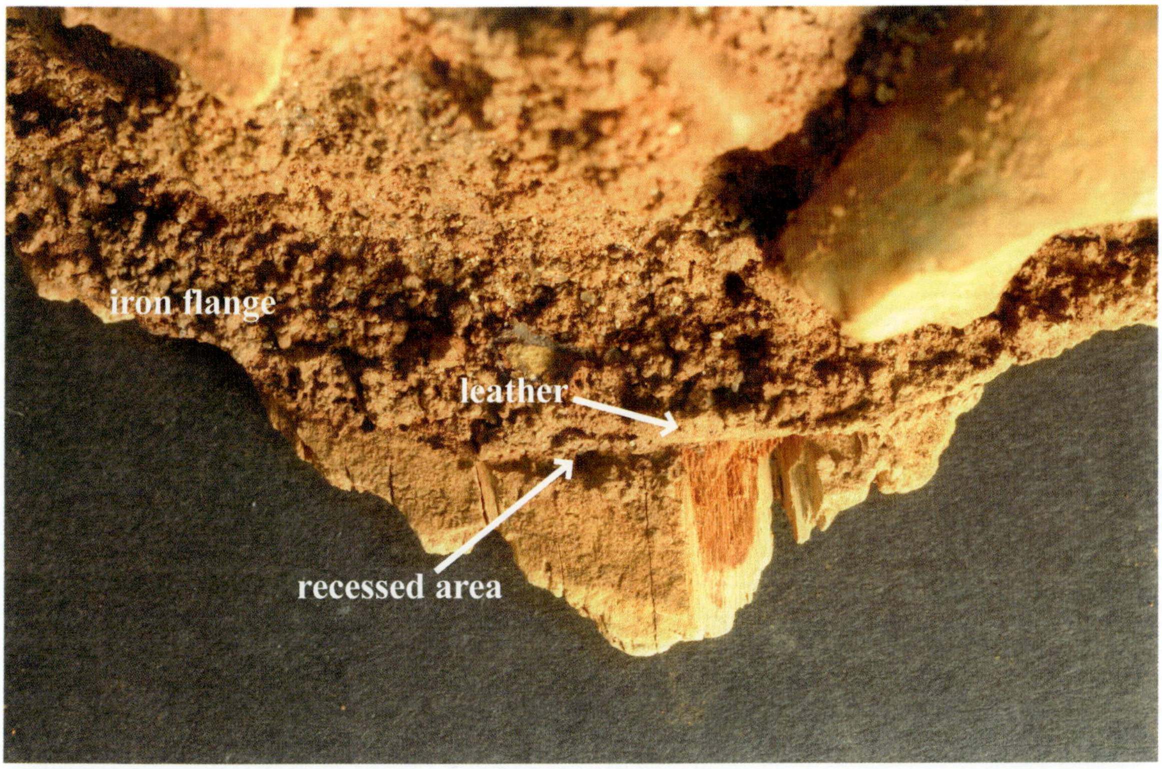

Plate 7.14 Wooden shield board rebated to take the boss flange, 53/2. Photo Vanessa Fell, English Heritage

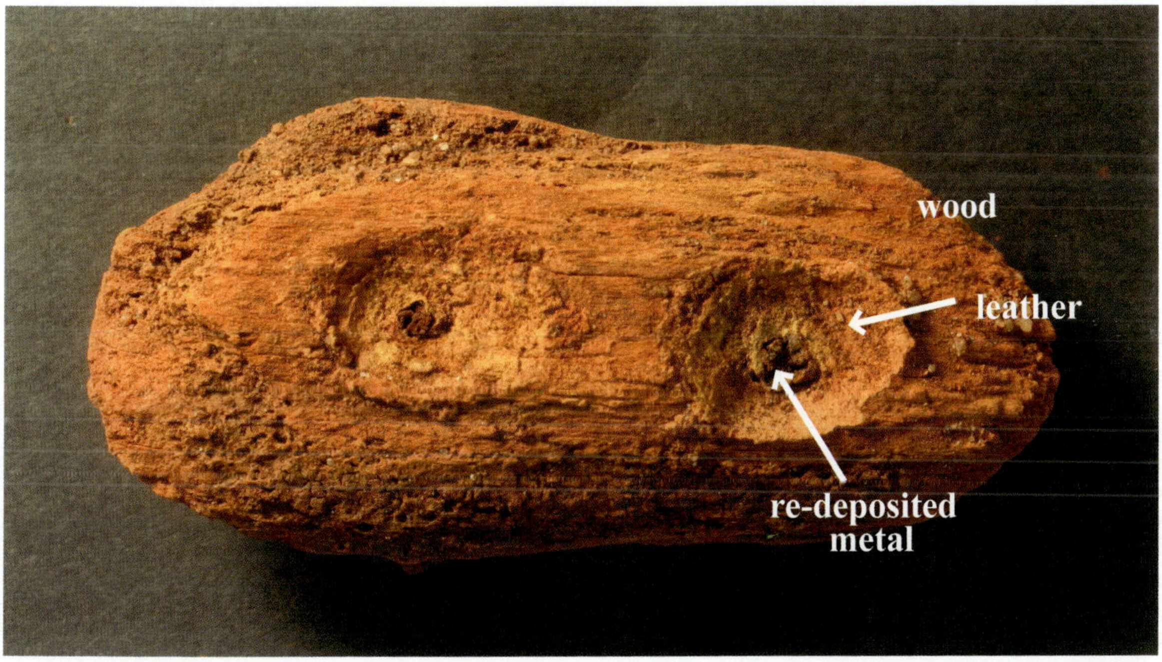

Plate 7.15 Decorative mounts, 53/4, with counter-sunk areas in the wood. Photo Vanessa Fell, English Heritage

VIII. Vessels

Glass beaker

by Rose Broadley
Pls 7.17–7.18

The vessel from Flixton I is substantially complete and has been carefully conserved A/3 (Pls 7.17 and 7.18). It is 167mm tall and *c*.98mm in diameter at the rim. The rim has a rounded profile, which is typical of Early Anglo-Saxon glass vessels. The vessel has a distinct and concave foot, measuring 37mm in diameter, which was finished in the same way as the rim. The metal of the body of the vessel is a pale translucent green, marbled with very dark red glass. The vessel is 3mm thick at the base, 2mm thick at the rim and paper-thin in the middle in the zone where the claws are attached – the latter attesting to the skill of the glassmaker. The claws themselves are arranged in two rows of four claws, which are slightly offset from each other so that they form a zigzag of eight claws. The claws are made from very dark, almost opaque red glass,

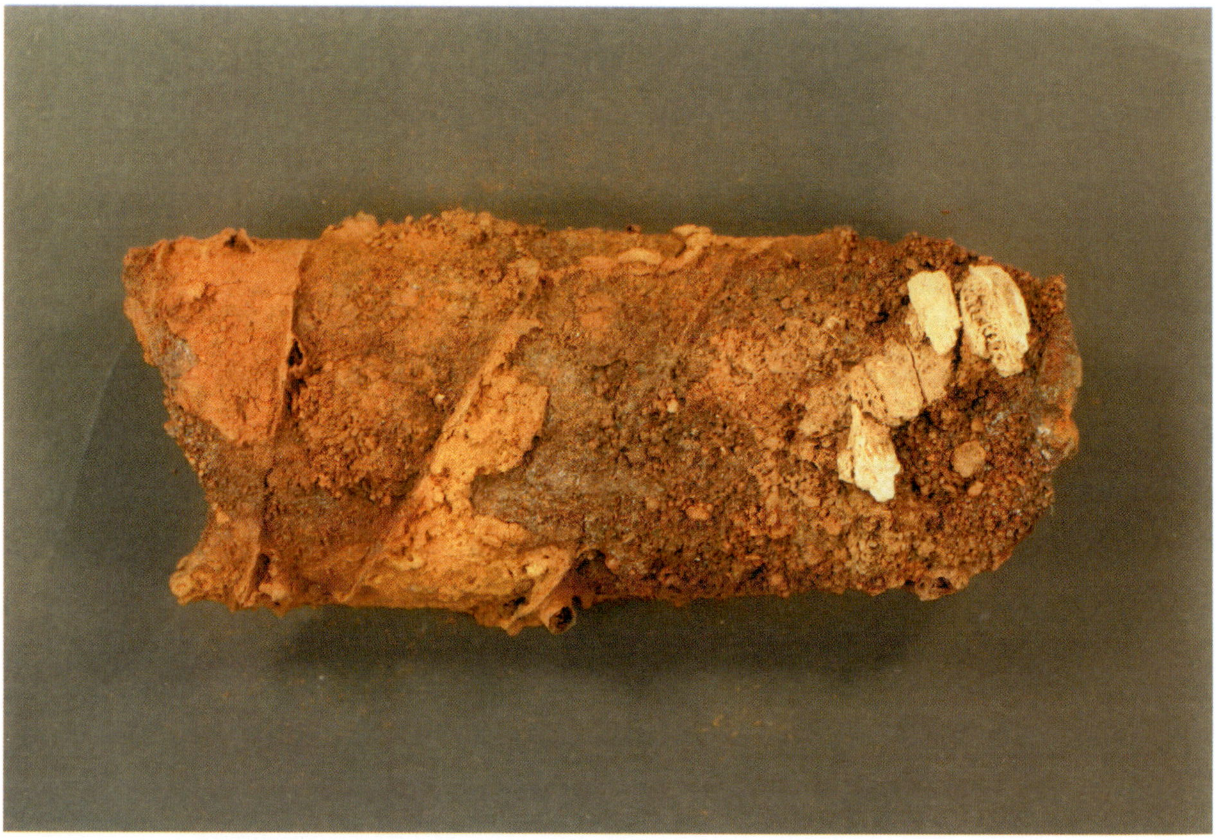

Plate 7.16 Iron shield grip, 15/1 ii, with remains of leather carrying strap pulled over grip. Photo Vanessa Fell, English Heritage

meaning that in reflected light they appear black. They feature the thick indented vertical trails characteristic of this type of claw beaker. Both above and below the claws the vessel is decorated with very fine trailing in the same very dark red used in the claws and the marbling.

The main body of the glass was free-blown, meaning that a ball of hot glass was attached to the end of a long glass-blowing tube, known as a pontil rod, and was then blown into the basic shape required without the aid of a mould. As with all glass made in this way, there is a clear pontil mark on the base, made by the long tube used to blow the glass. The red marbling of the pale green glass that was used to make the body of the vessel would have been added during this initial blowing phase, and may have been achieved by controlling the temperature of the furnace very carefully to allow the two colours to swirl and blend, but not merge completely. The presence of this effect indicates that this vessel was made by an expert craftsman.

The claws were made by applying a hot blob of glass to the wall of a pre-blown vessel, which was then blown itself and hooked downward to form a claw. This technique was developed in the late Roman period and appears to have originated in Germany. The trails were applied skilfully by stretching molten glass into a long skein and trailing it rapidly around the body of the vessel – in this case the trails are particularly fine and tightly-wound, adding to the overall impression of a very well-made glass vessel.

This glass vessel is a clear example of the Evison Type 3c claw beaker, dating to the first half of the 6th century. The arrangement and number of the claws, the indented trails on the claws and the fine trailing on the upper and lower thirds of the vessel are all absolutely typical of the type. The vessel height and rim diameter also match the average dimensions of this type almost exactly (although the diameter of the foot is smaller than usual, making this particular vessel rather unstable).

Such a rare and high status artefact is a significant find. In 2000, Vera Evison was able to list only thirty-one known examples of the Type 3c claw beaker, nearly half of which were fragmentary. She listed two found in Suffolk, one from Snape and one (fragmentary) from Hut 50 at West Stow. Almost half of Evison's thirty-one known examples were found in East Anglia. Eight were discovered in cremations at Spong Hill, Norfolk, two at Mucking, Essex (one in G92 and one in Hut 166), one from G122 at Great Chesterford, Essex, and one found in Cambridgeshire in 1875, which is now in the British Museum. The most 'productive' site outside East Anglia is Loveden Hill, Lincolnshire, where five were found in cremation burials. In contrast, only four in total have been found in Kent, which is the county that has yielded the most Early Anglo-Saxon glass vessels, particularly from inhumations. Evison suggests, based on the distribution of find-spots, that the Type 3c beaker was manufactured in England, perhaps north of the Thames. She makes a convincing case that these and the 'Kempston' type of cone beaker were manufactured in England, and suggests that production of glass vessels in Britain may have continued unbroken from the Roman period (Evison 1982, 53–9; Evison 2000, 72).

The red marbling in the metal of the main body of the beaker is undoubtedly the most unusual aspect of this vessel, coupled with the fact that the claws and the trails were all created using the same dark red glass – most examples of this type are monochrome pale green or

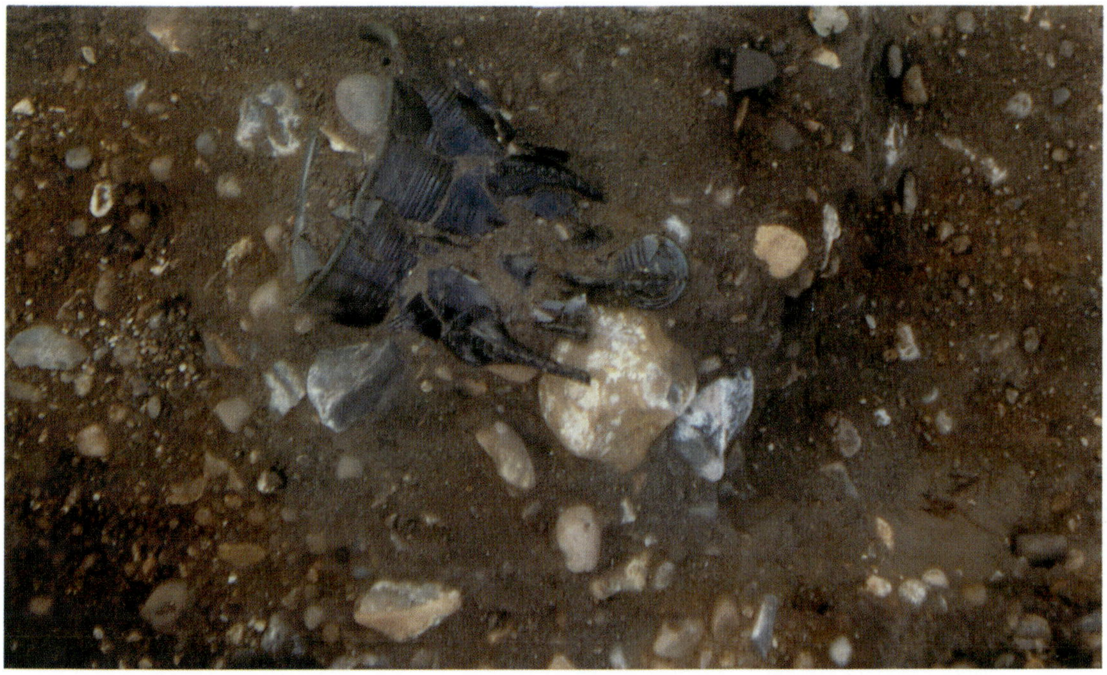

Plate 7.17 Claw beaker A/3 taken during the excavation of Flixton I, Grave A

brown vessels. No exact parallels are currently known by the author for the decoration of this vessel from England – the only other bichrome examples of Type 3c claw beakers are a claw fragment from a cremation at Spong Hill, Norfolk (Evison 1988, fig. 3; Evison 1994b, 29–30), which is a blue claw with a light green trail, and the unique claw beaker from Castle Eden (Evison 1982, pl. VIIa), which has blue indented trails on a light blue-green beaker. The red marbling in the metal of the body has parallels in blue globular beakers from a well at Chew Stoke and from mound 2 at Sutton Hoo (Evison 2000, 71), both of which are likely to date from between AD 550 and 650. There may also be an interesting connection with two Swedish claw beakers where the light blue-green glass is streaked with red, and some of the applied trails are streaked green and red (Evison 2000, 71; Arwidsson 1932, 252). Evison indicates that some distinctive Anglo-Saxon vessels were exported during the period AD 550–700, including claw beakers of two different types to Sweden (2000, 90–91). Given that the only other red-marbled claw beakers currently known were found in high-status graves in Sweden, it is tempting to suggest that the Flixton beaker was a late example of its type, perhaps made in East Anglia around AD 550, and that the Swedish exemplars were exported there from England at around the same time.

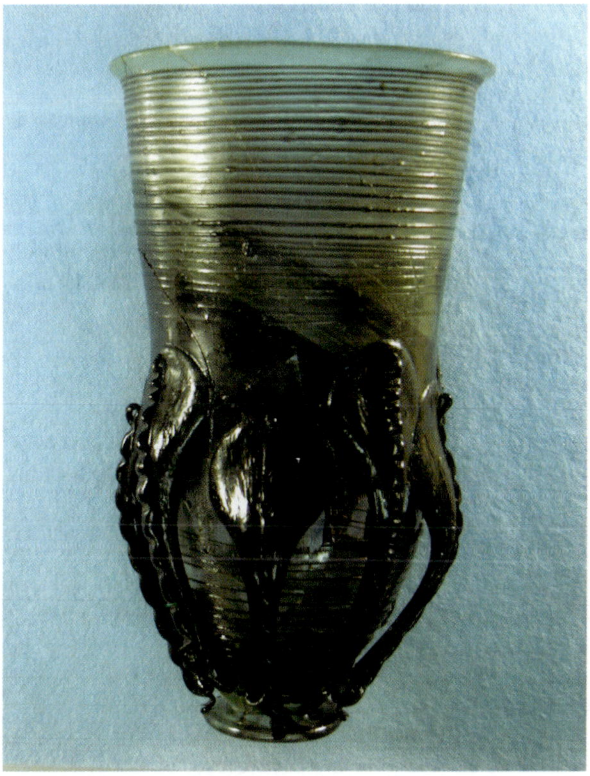

Plate 7.18 Claw beaker A/3 after reconstruction. Ht of object 167mm

Wooden vessel

by Jacqui Watson

Fig. 7.18

Three pieces of copper alloy from Grave 11 are probably a vessel rim mount (with a tubular rivet) and two repair staples, which were attached to a small wooden bowl or bottle made from maple (*Acer* sp.). The position of the rim mount (11/10) and the staple (11/8) on the grave plan indicate that the vessel had a diameter in the region of 85mm, with sides 3–5mm thick. As only one fragment of wood remains it is possible to produce two variations of body shape for this vessel (Fig. 7.18).

The grain orientation of the wooden fragment suggests that it is from a face-turned vessel with external surfaces of transverse and radial sections (Morris 2000, 2122). All the copper alloy pieces were attached to a transverse section, the wood surface that is prone to splitting, so it is quite likely that the staples (11/7–8) were holding together a crack on this side of the vessel. The fragment of wood attached to the rim mount does not appear to be broken, and the wood surface appears to be covered in little knots

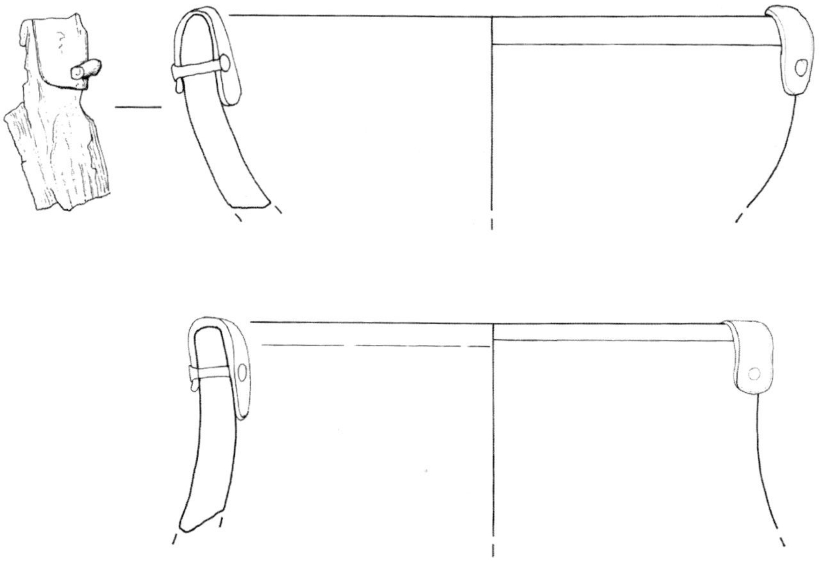

Figure 7.18 Alternative profiles for the wooden vessel associated with mounts 11/7 and 11/8 in Grave 11 (scale 1:1). Jacqui Watson, English Heritage

of wood that would have given the vessel an attractive appearance.

This may have been similar in form to two of the wooden cups from Sutton Hoo, Suffolk (Cups 2 and 7: Bruce-Mitford 1983, 368, 372), but these are much smaller, with rim diameters of around 35mm (although the body is wider than the rim). Maple was used for vessels at both Sutton Hoo and Taplow, Buckinghamshire, as well as being the traditional material for 'mazers' (wooden cups) where again a type of burr wood was chosen for its decorative appearance.

Pottery

by Sue Anderson

Introduction

One vessel was recovered from Grave A within the ring-ditch at Flixton I, while the other sherds from this site were unstratified spot-finds from a single vessel, probably displaced from this or another burial. The main part of the assemblage was from the cemetery at Flixton II.

Methodology

Quantification was carried out using sherd count, weight and estimated vessel equivalent (eve). Where possible, sherd families were recorded, and a minimum number of vessels (MNV) was estimated for each context. A full quantification by fabric, context and feature is available in the archive. All fabric codes were assigned from the Suffolk post-Roman fabric series, which includes Norfolk, Essex, Cambridgeshire and Midlands fabrics, as well as imported wares. A ×20 microscope was used for fabric identification and characterisation. Form terminology follows Myres (1977) and Hamerow (1993). Recording uses a system of letters for fabric codes together with number codes for ease of sorting in database format. The pottery was recorded directly onto an Access database.

Flixton I

Fragments of two Early Anglo-Saxon vessels were recovered in the south-east quadrant of the ring-ditch excavation, I/NG1 from immediately north of Grave A and A/4 partially within the grave itself. Find I/NG1 consisted of three sherds of a globular or sub-biconical vessel decorated with square cross stamps and incised vertical lines in a medium sandy fabric (Fig. 7.19.1). Find A/4 was a near-complete hemispherical bowl with a flat base (twenty-five sherds), undecorated and in a granitic fabric (Fig.7.19.2). The outer surface of the bowl had been smoothed, but the inner surface was heavily worn leaving the coarse grits exposed. It is likely that both vessels came from graves of 6th-century date. Both were sooted and had probably been used in a domestic context before their final burial.

Illustrated vessels

Fig. 7.19; see also illustrated grave groups

1. Body sherds of ?sub-biconical or globular vessel, medium sandy with occasional coarse quartz inclusions, light brown externally and blackened internally. Decorated with square cross stamps: Briscoe Type C3ai. (I/NG1 in grave inventory)
2. Near-complete hemispherical bowl with flat base and plain rim, coarse granitic inclusions, patchy brown/black. Inner surface worn to expose grits, external surface smoothed and sooted. Rim D.*c*.60mm, 25% complete. (A/4 in grave inventory)

Flixton II

A total of 389 sherds (4.822kg) of Early Anglo-Saxon pottery was collected from twenty-three graves in the cemetery. Six basic fabric groups were distinguished on the basis of major inclusions. However, it should be noted that, as with all handmade pottery, fabrics were extremely variable even within single vessels and categorisation was often difficult. Background scatters of chalk, flint, grog, white mica and other less common inclusions, such as felspar and ferrous pieces, were present in many of the vessels. All were handmade, and colours varied throughout from black through grey, buff and brown to red, often within single vessels. Many sites in East Anglia have produced similar fabric groups, although they occur in different proportions. General fabric descriptions are listed below.

ESO1 Heavily grass tempered with few other inclusions

ESO2 Grass tempered but containing a much greater proportion of sand than ESO1

ESMS Medium sand tempering with few other inclusions, sand grains generally well-sorted

ESFS Fine sand tempering with few other inclusions

ESCF 'Charnwood Forest' type, sparse to moderate felspar and occasional gold mica

ESOM Granitic inclusions with grass temper

Table 7.10 shows the quantities of pottery by fabric group from the cemetery. In addition, there was one unstratified body sherd of ESO2 (5g) and one small rim sherd (1g) of ESMS from a post-hole within the palisaded ring. If the latter is not intrusive, it may be of Iron Age date. These sherds will not be considered further.

In this group, organic and granitic-tempered vessels were more common than sandy types. Organic-tempering is thought to increase markedly in the 6th and particularly the 7th centuries in Essex (Hamerow 1993, 31) and Suffolk (K. Wade, pers. comm.). Forms in this ware at other sites in Suffolk have generally tended to confirm this view.

It has been suggested that granite tempered pottery may have been brought from Charnwood Forest in Leicestershire (Williams and Vince 1997), although there is also a possibility that granite erratics could be obtained from the local boulder clays (A. Vince, pers. comm.). A small piece of granite was collected during excavations at Flixton, so it seems likely that the material was available for inclusion in pottery made in the area. The similarity of the organic tempered vessels to those tempered with both grass and granitic inclusions suggests that they were likely to have been made in the same area. This is mirrored by similar findings from a site at Foulsham, Norfolk (Anderson forthcoming b), where several vessels both with and without granitic inclusions contained the same type of red grog. Thin section analysis would be required to confirm these findings, but it seems that granite may sometimes have been specifically chosen as a temper in areas where it was not widely available.

No calcareous wares, which are common to the south and west, were present in this group. A decrease in calcareous wares was noted at Mucking after the 6th century. At Handford Road in Ipswich, calcareous wares made up 71% of the assemblage and organic-tempered wares only 1%. However, the lack of shelly wares in this area may be more related to the local geology than to date.

The estimated vessel equivalent for this group was 3.18; no rims were too small for measurement in the cemetery group. Measurements of handmade vessels are always approximate unless a large proportion of the rim is present. For this reason, the minimum number of vessels (MNV), based on sherd families, was estimated for each context, producing a total MNV of twenty-nine vessels. Given the nature of the site, this MNV is likely to be very close to the true number of vessels represented in the assemblage.

Very few vessels were complete and all but one were heavily fragmented, presumably the result of later disturbance and truncation of many of the graves. It was possible to reconstruct the profile of most of the more complete examples, and the types present are shown in Table 7.11.

Rim and base types were classified following Hamerow (1993, fig. 26). There were eight vessels with vertical rims, three with everted rims and one with an incurving rim. One vessel had an upright beaded rim.

Description	*Fabric*	*No.*	*Wt (g)*	*Eve*	*MNV*
Grass-tempered	ESO1	110	1,511	0.41	10
Grass and sand tempered	ESO2	19	313	0.45	1
Fine sandy	ESFS	16	757	0.85	4
Granitic-tempered	ESCF	25	923	0.98	3
Grass and granitic tempered	ESOM	144	847	0.06	6
Medium sandy	ESMS	75	471	0.43	3
Totals		**389**	**4,822**	**3.18**	**29**

Table 7.10 Early Anglo-Saxon pottery quantities by fabric from Flixton II

Three vessels had flat-rounded bases, six had rounded bases and four were flat-angled. No foot-ring types were present in this assemblage. Rim diameters varied from 90mm to 190mm, though most were between 110mm to 160mm.

Surface treatment – in the form of smoothing, grass-wiping, or occasionally burnishing – was very common in this group, most sherds showing some signs of one type, even if worn away in places. Only two vessels were decorated and both were incomplete so the schemes were uncertain. A sub-biconical jar from Grave 2, of which only a small proportion of the upper half survived, had two multiple ring stamps (Type A2) above the carination (Fig. 7.19.3). A globular jar from Grave 5 had segmented-S stamps (Type H2) around the neck and possibly in panels on the body (Fig. 7.19.5).

The pot dates are based on form and fabric evidence from Mucking (Hamerow 1993) and Carlton Colville (Tipper 2009) and compare favourably with the phasing of the graves based on other artefacts, as presented in Chapter 9. This would tend to substantiate the theory that organic tempering was more common in the 6th and 7th centuries. It also adds weight to Tipper's suggestion that granitic pottery was more likely to occur in the 6th century at Carlton Colville. Study of granite-tempered vessel types at other Suffolk sites during assessment by the author has also resulted in the impression of a 6th-century date for this fabric type, but further work is required on most of these assemblages.

Discussion

The majority of vessels in this assemblage were in grass-tempered or granitic fabrics. This is an unusual

Type	*Form*	*MNV*
With corner point	biconical jar?	1
	round-bellied bowl	1
Without corner point	globular jar	1
	globular vessel?	1
	offset-shouldered bowl	2
	curved bowl	1
	sub-biconical jar	1
Simple	baggy jar (straight-sided ovoid)	4
	straight-sided bowl	1
	inturned-rim bowl	1

Note: 'type' follows Hamerow (1993, fig. 24); form includes Myres' terminology

Table 7.11 Early Anglo-Saxon pottery forms at Flixton II

distribution in comparison with other sites in the region, although study of seventeen settlement and cemetery sites in Essex, Cambridgeshire, Norfolk and Suffolk by the author has shown that in general Early Anglo-Saxon assemblages are extremely variable in their make-up. Even the three adjacent cemetery sites and settlement at Eriswell have produced four very different assemblages (Anderson 2003). The assemblage from the broadly contemporary Flixton settlement (FLN 061) has been recorded for assessment (Anderson 2006a), and has a wide variety of fabrics. Very little organic-tempered pottery was present in comparison with the cemetery, with sandy fabrics predominating. Some shell-tempered wares were present and there was a relatively high proportion which contained red grog, including some vessels which had both grog and granitic inclusions. In total, eleven basic fabric groups were recorded in the settlement, compared with only six in the cemetery.

Geographically, the closest pottery assemblage to have been analysed recently is the settlement group at Bloodmoor Hill, Carlton Colville. That assemblage was dominated by quartz-tempered vessels (41%), followed by organic (26%), with granite making up only *c.*10% of the total weight (Tipper 2009, 202). Calcareous, sandstone and grog fabrics were also identified there. At Morning Thorpe, near Long Stratton, the greatest proportion of pottery was quartz-tempered, but some organic, granitic, bone, grog and oolitic tempered vessels were also present (Friedenson and Friedenson 1987). The most comparable cemetery site in terms of fabrics is probably Tittleshall in Norfolk (Anderson forthcoming b) which had a high proportion of organic pottery, though fine sandy wares were more common than granite-tempered vessels there. Sutton Hoo Visitor Centre site at Bromeswell (Anderson 2000) also produced a high proportion of organic and granitic pottery, but there the dominant type was shelly.

As a rule, settlement sites tend to have a wider range of fabrics than cemeteries (Morning Thorpe being an exception), so Flixton is consistent with this pattern at least. Tipper noted a greater diversity of fabric types in the outlying areas of settlement at Bloodmoor Hill, with a more uniform fabric distribution in the central area where organic and sandy fabrics were more frequent. He has suggested that this distribution may have a temporal link, with greater diversity occurring in the earlier phase at that site. This would fit with the theory that there was an increase in the use of organic wares in the later 6th/7th centuries in southern East Anglia. No analysis of the distribution of fabric types within the Flixton settlement was carried out during the assessment, but this will be studied during future work. Possibly the greater number of fabrics at the settlement could indicate that it started earlier than the excavated part of the cemetery.

Fourteen vessels in this group were identifiable to form. Six were 'simple' types – baggy jars and bowls. There were six globular or sub-biconical types and a round-bellied bowl. Only one 'early' form was present, a possible biconical jar. The majority of forms would fit best in the 6th–7th centuries. Baggy, globular and sub-biconical types were also the most common forms in the settlement.

Very little decoration was present in this assemblage, only three vessels having stamps. Four vessels consisted of the base only, however, so it is possible that their upper bodies were decorated. This lack of decoration is more typical of inhumation cemeteries, which do not generally produce the highly decorated forms seen in the earlier cremation cemeteries such as Spong Hill. This may be because the vessels used were not specifically made for the funerary ritual. The Flixton settlement produced a wider variety of decoration, which included some 5th-century types such as *Schlickung*, but incised decoration and a few examples of stamped schemes were the most common types.

Two types of stamps from Flixton have been identified as a C 3ai (I/NG1) and an H 2ai (5/1) by Diana Briscoe (Figs 7.19.1 and 7.19.5). The former is a common type in the Midlands and North, but has only three local parallels, at Caistor St Edmund and Bergh Apton in Norfolk. The H 2ai stamp is relatively rare in the Archive of Anglo-Saxon Pottery Stamps but is distributed widely from Hampshire to Lincolnshire. Local examples have been found at Caistor St Edmund and West Stow. None of the parallels were made with the same dies as those from Flixton. Briscoe suggests that the types of stamps present suggest connections to both the north and the south of the region, but the evidence is slight due to the small size of the sample (summarised from Briscoe in archive). The third stamp identified in this group is a type A2 ring stamp (2/3, not seen by Briscoe) (Fig. 7.19.3).

Illustrated pottery (FLN 053 and FLN 062)
Fig. 7.19; see also illustrated grave groups

3. Four sherds of a grass-tempered (ESO1) sub-biconical jar with flat-angled base, decorated with type A2 ring stamps above the slight carination, smoothed but outer surface spalled, sooted. Grey surfaces, red-brown core. (2/3 in grave inventory)

4. Small straight-sided medium sandy bowl (ESMS with occasional burnt-out organics) with vertical rim and flat-rounded base, slight spalling and cracking, worn and sooted internally, smoothed externally. Brown with blackened areas inside. Rim D.150mm, 15% complete. (3/10 in grave inventory)

5. Rim and body of a fine sandy globular jar (ESFS with occasional quartz conglomerates) with everted rim, burnt food residue inside, smoothed/burnished externally with Briscoe's type H2ai segmented-S stamps. Red-brown to black externally, black internally. Rim D.160mm, 15% complete. (5/1 in grave inventory)

6. Baggy/globular grass-tempered (ESO1) jar with short vertical/in-turned rim and rounded base, burnt food residue inside, sooted, slight burnishing. Grey/brown externally, black internally. Rim D.160mm, 10% complete. (6/2 in grave inventory)

7. Small globular offset-shouldered grass-tempered (ESO1) bowl with vertical rim and flat-rounded base, sooted. Oxidised orange-brown externally, dark grey internally. Rim D.150mm, 11%. (8/3 in grave inventory)

8. ?Biconical grass-tempered (ESO1) jar with short vertical rim, smoothed. Grey. Rim D.120mm, 8% complete. Possibly redeposited. (11/13 i in grave inventory)

9. Inturned-rim globular grass-tempered bowl (ESO2, large voids probably from seeds) with thick rounded base, sooted, smoothed externally. Dark grey/brown. Rim D.120mm, 45% complete (base 100%). (11/14 in grave inventory)

10. Very fragmented grass-tempered (ESO1 with occasional chalk) baggy jar with vertical rim and rounded base, smoothed. Orange-brown externally, grey internally. Rim D.110mm, 6% complete. (16/2 in grave inventory)

11. Baggy jar, grass/granitic-tempered (ESOM but organics sparse), very small vertical rim with signs of wear or deliberate rubbing, sooted, burnt food residue internally. Buff-brown externally, black internally. Rim D.120mm, 6% complete. (21/5 in grave inventory)

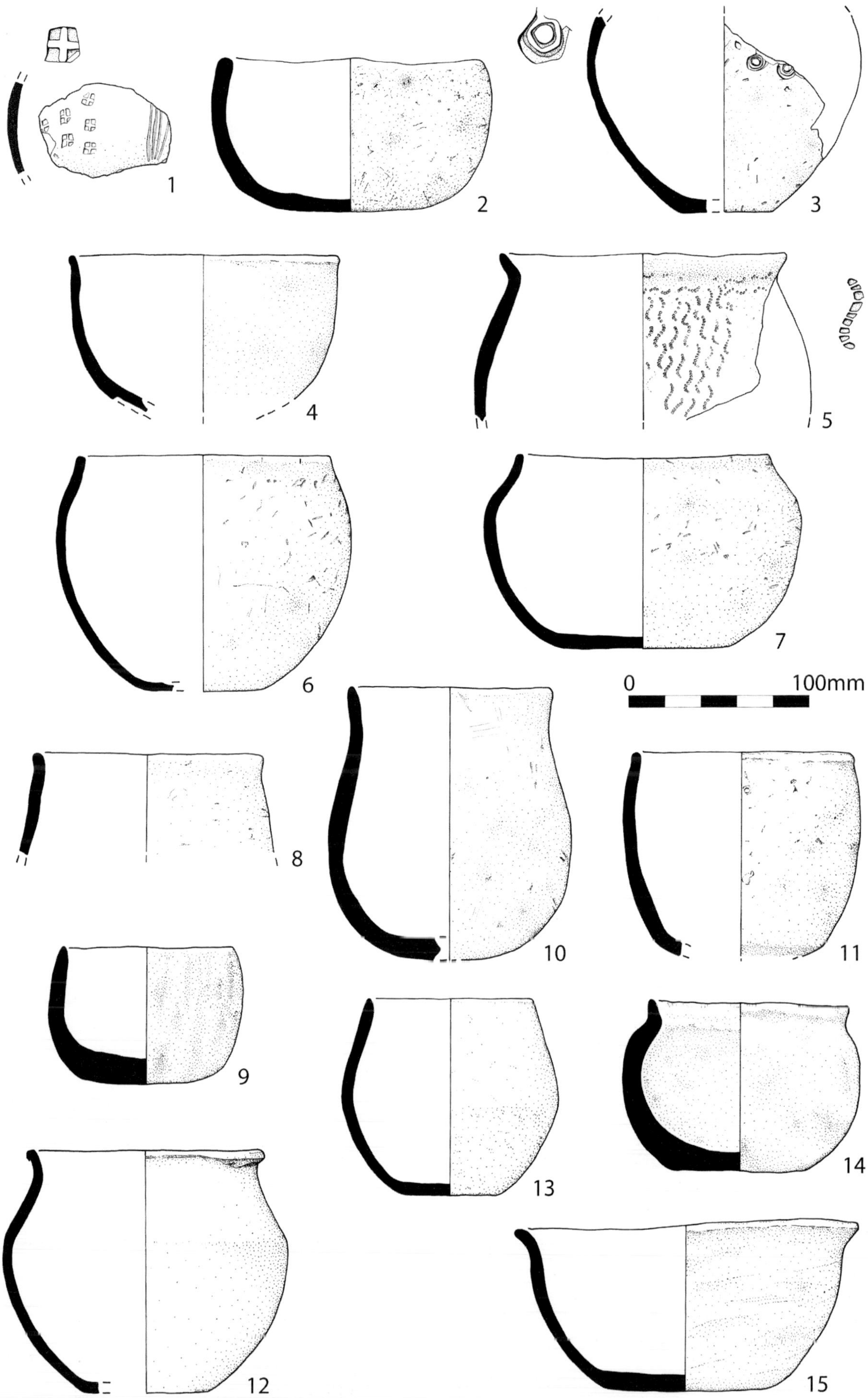

Figure 7.19 Early Anglo-Saxon pottery from Flixton I and II (scale 1:3, stamps shown at 1:1)

12. 'Round-bellied' or sub-biconical granite-tempered bowl (ESCF) with upright beaded rim, burnished. Orange/black externally, black internally. Rim D.130mm, 23% complete. (22/5 in grave inventory)

13. Sand-tempered (ESMS) baggy jar with slight shoulder, vertical rim and flat-angled base, burnished, worn on both surfaces. Reddish brown. Rim D.90mm, 28% complete. (39/3 in grave inventory)

14. Granite-tempered offset-shouldered bowl (ESCF, some flint and chalk), everted rim and flat-angled base, near complete but rim broken, sooted, worn internally. Light brown externally and black inside. Rim D.110mm, 75% complete. (46/1 in grave inventory)

15. Fine sandy curved bowl (ESFS), sooted, worn internally, burnt food residue. Brown-black. Rim D.190mm, 70% complete. (47/1 in grave inventory)

Chapter 8. The Human Remains

by Sue Anderson

I. Flixton I

One small fragment of unburnt bone (008:*0060*) was recovered from the inhumation Grave A. Although in very poor condition, it appeared to be a petrous temporal fragment, possibly juvenile. The bone was collected from the area of the skull so this would certainly fit anatomically. Two further unburnt fragments of bone from the south-east quadrant were an animal tooth (008:*0035*) and a possible bird bone (008:*0052*), both in very poor condition. In conclusion, the inhumation had barely survived, but the remaining fragment suggested that the individual may have been a juvenile.

II. Flixton II

Introduction

Human remains from thirty-three of the sixty-two excavated graves were available for analysis. As two of the graves were double burials, the bones represented a total of thirty-five individuals; no disarticulated bone was found. A full list is provided in Table 8.1.

Methodology

Measurements were taken using the methods described by Brothwell (1981), together with a few from Bass (1971) and Krogman (1978). The maximum mesio-distal and bucco-lingual dimensions of teeth were also recorded. Non-metric dental traits were recorded based on ASU dental plaques (Turner *et al.* 1991). Sexing and ageing techniques follow Brothwell (1981) and the Workshop of European Anthropologists (WEA 1980), with the exception of adult tooth wear scoring which follows Bouts and Pot (1989).

Condition

An assessment of condition of the bone was made for each skeleton, although it is recognised that this is fairly subjective. The assessment of condition took into account the preservation of the bone, not the completeness or otherwise of the skeleton. Eight skeletons were considered to be in 'poor' condition, the rest were 'very poor'. Generally there was a high degree of surface erosion in this assemblage, many bones consisting of flaky fragments of the outer layers which had been separated from the thicker cortical bone and had often either disappeared or were the only part to survive. All skeletons were fragmented and the majority consisted of fragments of tooth enamel and pieces of skull only. Slightly better preservation was seen in the skeletons from the southern section of the site (FLN 062) and this may be related to their burial within the fill of the ring ditch, possibly a slightly less acidic soil than the undisturbed subsoil in which the individuals in the northern part of the main plot (FLN 053) were buried.

Demographic analysis

A summary list of skeletons with age and sex is included in Table 8.1. Details of methods used for ageing and sexing individuals are recorded in the grave inventory.

Two children below the age of 16 years were present in this assemblage, and there was a sub-adult who was probably aged 16–18 years. The proportion of juveniles to adults based on the skeletal remains is 8.6%. This is a relatively low frequency and may be attributable to the generally poor condition of juvenile (and adult) bones in this group. If the grave size is taken into consideration – bearing in mind that this can only provide a very rough guide as graves were often too large or too small for their occupants in this period – fifteen graves were probably those of children, one was a sub-adult, four were uncertain and forty-three were adult. As one of the last, Grave 22, is known to have contained a child as well as an adult, there is a possibility that other children were interred with adults and would be missing from the data as a result. However, based on this crude estimate there were probably at least seventeen children in the excavated areas, perhaps as many as twenty if the uncertain graves represent older juveniles or sub-adults. This would increase the proportion of children to around 30%. The expected proportion of children would be around one third of the group so this is within the normal range, but interpretation is limited by the incomplete excavation of this cemetery.

One child was aged *c*.5 years and the other was *c*.11–12. The fact that there are no infants in the assemblage is almost certainly related to preservation of bone at this site. Based on other groups, approximately 5–10% of all child burials might be expected to be below the age of two years in the Early Anglo-Saxon period. However, in many contemporary groups, the highest death rates are in the 2–5 year or 6–11 year ranges.

Twenty-eight individuals were classified as adult and were probably over the age of eighteen years at death. Of these, ten were thought to be male (including three ?male), four were female (three ?female) and fourteen were unsexable. The skeletal evidence for sex was compared with the gender ascribed by the artefacts (see Chapters 10–11) and, where both types of evidence were available (ten individuals), the results proved to be the same in all but two cases. These were skeletons 053:*0440* from Grave 17 and 062:*1861* from Grave 59, both identified as male from the bones but female from the grave goods. For 053:*0440* the male sex was suggested due to the robusticity of the occipital crest: the position of the skull, at the side of the grave, indicated that the head was not related to the female accessories (see Chapter 10). Skeleton 062:*1861* was recorded as ?male because the mastoid process was large, but the occipital crest of this individual was not pronounced and, given the extremely poor preservation of the skeletal material, it is preferable to rely on the grave good gender in this case. The burial in Grave 61A, skeleton 062:*1875*, has also been tentatively identified as male for reasons described in Chapter 11.

Grave	Skeleton	Sex	Gender*	Age	Condition	Observations
Graves in rectangular plot						
1	053:*0348*	?	M	Y-MA	V poor	
2	053:*0317*	?	M?	Young	V poor	
3	053:*0850*	?	F	Unaged	V poor	
7	053:*0319*	M?	?	Y-MA	V poor	
9	053:*0361*	?	F	Unaged	V poor	
11	053:*0362*	?	F	Adult	V poor	Possible torn ligaments
13	053:*0394*	?	F	Y-MA	V poor	Large carious lesion lower M1
14	053:*0431*	M	M	MA?	V poor	
15	053:*0432*	M	M	MA	V poor	Maxillary sinusitis, possible abscess M1, OP C1-2
17	053:*0440*	M	F	Adult	V poor	Lambdoid wormian bones?
20	053:*0465*	F?	F	Young	Poor	No degeneration of vertebrae
22A	053:*0507*	?	?	Young?	V poor	
22B	053:*0508*	?	?	*c.*11-12	V poor	
23	053:*0527*	?	M	Y-MA	V poor	Carious lesions lower M1-2
26	053:*0573*	?	F	Young	V poor	
27B	053:*0580*	?	M	Unaged	V poor	
28	053:*0577*	M	M	Y-MA	Poor	Carious lesion upper M1. No cribra left orbit.
30	053:*0599*	F?	F	Young	Poor	Triple hypoglossal canal right
32	053:*0617*	M	?	MA?	V poor	Carious lesion upper M2, possible abscess lower M3?
33	053:*0634*	?	F	Young	V poor	
34	053:*0662*	F?	F	Young	Poor	Possible cut in occipital
36	053:*0665*	F	F	Young	V poor	Enamel pearl of premolar
37	053:*0724*	?	M	Adult?	V poor	
41	053:*0732*	M	M	Adult	V poor	Lambdoid wormian bones?
42	053:*0735*	?	F	*c.*5	V poor	
43	053:*0740*	M?	M	Adult	Poor	
51	062:*1870*	?	F	Young	V poor	
Graves associated with ring-ditch/mound						
52	062:*0995*	?	M	Unaged	V poor	
55	062:*1832*	?	M	Young	Poor	Carious lesion upper M1
56	062:*1843*	M	M	Y-MA	Poor	No cribra right orbit
57	062:*1852*	?	?	(Y-)MA?	V poor	
58	062:*1857*	?	?	Adult	V poor	
59	062:*1861*	M?	F	MA-Old	Poor	Slight OP basi-occipital, caries and abscess upper PM2 and caries upper M1, no cribra left orbit.
61A	062:*1875*	?	?	MA	V poor	
61B	062:*1876*	?	?	*c.*16-18?	V poor	

* gender derived from grave goods

Table 8.1 Flixton II, summary of graves with skeletons. Y=young; MA=middle-aged

Ten unsexed adults had gender-specific grave goods, adding a further five males and five females, and one of the children had female-gender artefacts. Four individuals could not be aged from their skeletal remains, but grave good gender suggested that these were two males and two females: the sizes of their graves suggested that at least three were adults. The graves which did not contain bone added a further two adult males, eight adult females and one juvenile female. Nineteen individuals had no clear sex or gender evidence, although dental measurements provided tentative sexing for five of these (one male, four female; see below). The total for adults, based on sex and gender (but giving preference to grave goods for the single discrepancy), was eighteen males and twenty-one females (Tables 8.2–8.3). There was also one male sub-adult and three female children, and a female of uncertain age. The total male:female ratio is therefore 1:1.4, which is not statistically significant.

Table 8.2 summarises the age and sex/gender interpretation for all graves. Categories of age rather than actual age ranges are employed because estimation of adult age at death is difficult with currently available techniques. The data should be taken to represent *biological* rather than chronological age at death. The grave good gender and grave size estimates of age greatly increase the proportions of female and juvenile individuals represented (Table 8.3). This shows that the acidic soil affected the lighter and less robust skeletons of children and women to a much greater extent than those of males. It is likely that older adults are also missing as a result of poor preservation and the apparent high proportion of younger adults may therefore be misleading. The available evidence suggests that fewer than a quarter of the aged adults in this group had reached middle age or older at the time of their death. However at the similarly poorly preserved cemetery of Coddenham,

Age	*Male*	*Female*	*Unsexed*	*Total*
Child (<18)	1	3	12	16
Young adult	2	8		10
Young/Mature	5	2		7
Middle-aged	3	1		4
Mature/Old		1		1
Adult	8	8	7	23
Uncertain		1	5	6
Total	**19**	**24**	**24**	**67**

Table 8.2 Summary of age and sex/gender for all excavated graves

the proportion of middle-aged and older adults was closer to 40% (Anderson forthcoming c), so it may be that the population at Flixton had a lower life expectancy than the later, and richer, group further south.

Metrical and morphological analysis

Preservation was so poor that it was not possible to record any cranial or post-cranial measurements from these remains. Cranial and post-cranial non-metric traits were not scored systematically, although they were noted when present. All recorded measurements and systematically scored non-metric traits relate to the teeth and are discussed below in the section on dental analysis. Analysis of the dental non-metric record did not provide any clear evidence of family relationships, although the overall similarity in morphology of the third molars of 062:*1861* in Grave 59 and 062:*1832* in Grave 55 did suggest that the two might have a genetic relationship. Although both buried in the ring-ditch area of the site, they were not close together.

Non-metric traits which were noted as present consisted of an unusual triple hypoglossal canal in young female 053:*0599* (Grave 30), and possible lambdoid wormian bones in 053:*0440* (Grave 17A) and 053:*0732* (Grave 41).

Dental analysis

Twenty-seven individuals had complete or partial dentitions. Of these, twenty-four were adults, one was a sub-adult and two were children. The twenty-four adults consisted of eight males, four females and twelve unsexed adults of various ages at death, but the group was too small for separation into sex or age categories.

If complete dentitions from all twenty-five adult and sub-adult individuals had been present, there would have been a total of 800 observable positions. However, 556 teeth/positions were missing, leaving 244 observable positions, 121 of which consisted of the enamel part of the tooth only, the roots and alveolar bone having been dissolved. This means that there were 123 positions which could be assessed for abscesses or ante-mortem tooth loss. Ante-mortem loss was recorded in one position; the ante-mortem tooth loss frequency for this group is therefore 0.8%. One abscess was recorded, which gives a frequency of 0.8%. Post-mortem loss from assessable alveoli totalled fifteen. Two teeth in this group were unerupted, the lower right third molar of the youngest individual (062:*1876*, Grave 61B, *c*.16–18 years), whose upper third molars were partially erupted, and the upper right third molar of unsexed young adult 053:*0507* (Grave 22A). A total of 224 teeth were present. Eight carious lesions in the surviving teeth gave a frequency of 3.6% for this dental pathology. The frequencies of dental disease are relatively low in this group, but this is likely to be a result of poor preservation. Although alveolar bone survived in several skeletons, it was generally in very poor condition and difficult to assess for dental pathology.

The origin of carious lesions was recorded where possible. A large interstitial lesion was present in the lower left first molar of 053:*0394* (Grave 13). Interstitial cervical lesions were present in the upper left third molar of 053:*0577* (Grave 28), the upper left second molar of 053:*0617* (Grave 32), the upper left first molar of 062:*1832* (Grave 55), and the upper right first molar of 062:*1861* (Grave 59). Lesions in the lower left first and second molars of 053:*0527* (Grave 23) were occlusal. A very large lesion of unknown origin was present in the upper left second premolar of 062:*1861* (Grave 59), with an open pulp cavity which had resulted in a periodontal abscess. Inflammatory changes were present at the base of alveolus for the lower left ?third molar of 053:*0617* (Grave 32). There may also have been loss of some of the lower teeth ante-mortem, based on the lack of wear of the upper right second molar.

The two juvenile dentitions added a further three deciduous teeth, and three erupted and five unerupted permanent teeth. No caries was present in any of these teeth, reducing the prevalence in erupted permanent teeth to 3.5%.

The poor condition of the teeth generally made recording of calculus and enamel hypoplasia difficult, but both conditions were present. Calculus was particularly heavy on the labial surface of the lower anterior teeth of young female 053:*0665* (Grave 36). Slight enamel hypoplasia had affected the lower canines of 053:*0319* (Grave 7) and 053:*0432* (Grave 15), and the lower molars of 053:*0527* (Grave 23). The presence of this condition suggests that periods of illness or malnutrition had occurred in these individuals. The enamel of several individuals showed signs of having been chipped in life, possibly related to the presence of grit or bone fragments in their food.

Maximum mesio-distal and bucco-lingual measurements of the teeth were recorded for all extant teeth. An attempt was made to apply principal component analysis to the data, but unfortunately the number of individuals for whom both measurements could be taken for any one tooth was no more than fifteen, and often much less. Nevertheless, the results for the twenty-seven individuals included in the plots showed some separation between the sexes. There was some overlap, and males 053:*0431* (Grave 14), 053:*0527* (Grave 23) and 053:*0740* (Grave 43) appeared to be in the female range, but it is likely that unsexed individual 062:*1876* (Grave 61B) was male, and 053:*0507* (Grave 22A), 053:*0508* (Grave 22B), 062:*1852* (Grave 57) may all be female. Unsexed individual 062:*1875* (Grave 61A) also appeared to be female, although some slight burial evidence suggests male (Chapter 11).

Epigenetic traits of the teeth were recorded systematically following the ASU Dental Non Metric Recording System (Turner *et al.* 1991). Unfortunately, as for tooth measurements, there was a high degree of missing data. Recording of this type has only been attempted on one other group studied by the author, so

Grave	*Grave fill*	*Skeleton*	*Sex*	*Gender*	*Teeth sex*	*Age*	*Grave size*
Graves in rectangular plot							
1	053:*0304*	053:*0348*	?	M		Y-MA	adult
2	053:*0306*	053:*0317*	?	M		Young	adult
3	053:*0308*	053:*0850*	?	F		Unaged	?
4	053:*0310*			F			adult
5	053:*0312*			F			adult
6	053:*0314*			M			adult
7	053:*0321*	053:*0319*	M?	?		Y-MA	adult
8	053:*0345*			F			child
9	053:*0350*	053:*0361*	?	F		Unaged	truncated
10	053:*0356*			?			adult
11	053:*0359*	053:*0362*	?	F		Adult	adult
12	053:*0389*			F?			adult
13	053:*0391*	053:*0394*	?	F		Y-MA	adult
14	053:*0396*	053:*0431*	M	?		MA?	adult
15	053:*0398*	053:*0432*	M	M		MA	adult
16	053:*0435*			F?			child
17A 1st	053:*0439*	053:*0440*	M			Adult	adult
17B 2nd				F			adult
18	053:*0442*			?			child?
19	053:*0462*			?			child
20A							adult
20B	053:*0464*	053:*0465*	F?	F		Young	adult
21	053:*0468*			F			adult
22A	053:*0502*	053:*0507*	?	?	F?	Young?	adult
22B	053:*0502*	053:*0508*	?	?	F?	*c.*11-12	adult
23	053:*0505*	053:*0527*	?	M		Y-MA	adult
24	053:*0529*			?			?
25	053:*0531*			?			adult
26	053:*0534*	053:*0573*	?	F		Young	adult
27A 1st	053:*0554*			F			adult
27B 2nd		053:*0580*	?	M		Unaged	adult
28	053:*0576*	053:*0577*	M	M		Y-MA	adult
29	053:*0596*			?			child
30	053:*0598*	053:*0599*	F?	F		Young	adult
31	053:*0613*			F			adult
32	053:*0616*	053:*0617*	M	?		MA?	adult
33	053:*0619*	053:*0634*	?	F		Young	adult
34	053:*0655*	053:*0662*	F?	F		Young	adult
35	053:*0657*			?			adult
36	053:*0664*	053:*0665*	F	F		Young	adult
37	053:*0717*	053:*0724*	?	M		Adult?	adult
38	053:*0720*			?			child
39	053:*0726*			F			adult
40	053:*0728*			F			adult
41	053:*0730*	053:*0732*	M	M		Adult	adult
42	053:*0734*	053:*0735*	?	F		*c.*5	child
43	053:*0738*	053:*0740*	M?	M		Adult	adult
44	053:*0743*			?			child?
45	053:*0748*			?			adult
46	062:*0894*			?			child
47	062:*0898*			?			child
48	062:*0902*			?			child
49	062:*0904*			?			child
50	062:*1547*			?			child
51	062:*1866*	062:*1870*	?	F		Young	adult
Graves associated with ring-ditch/mound							
52	062:*0994*	062:*0995*	?	M		Unaged	adult
53	062:*0998*			M			adult

54	062:*1825*			?			adult
55	062:*1829*	062:*1832*	?	M		Young	adult
56	062:*1841*	062:*1843*	M	M		Y-MA	adult
57	062:*1845*	062:*1852*	?	?	F?	(Y-)MA?	adult
58	062:*1856*	062:*1857*	?	?		Adult	adult
59	062:*1860*	062:*1861*	M?	F		MA-Old	?
60	062:*1863*			?			adult
61A	062:*1873*	062:*1875*	?	?	F?	MA	adult
61B	062:*1873*	062:*1876*	?	?	M	*c.*16-18?	adult
62	062:*1888*			?			child

Table 8.3 Summary of burials at Flixton II. Y=young; MA=middle-aged

only one directly comparable data set was available, that of Coddenham. A study of non-metric traits of teeth from Middle Saxon Brandon and Roman Icklingham has been undertaken (Lloyd-Jones 1997) and this was also compared. Based on nine traits using the mean measure of divergence (MMD), Brandon and Icklingham were found to be statistically significantly different from Coddenham, although they showed no significant differences between each other. Flixton was not significantly different from any of these groups, and so it was tested against two of Lloyd-Jones' groups with the greatest geographical distance, Lechlade and Lankhills (Winchester). Neither of these was significantly different from Flixton either, and it may be that there is too little data from Flixton for reliable comparison. A wider range of traits (sixty-eight in total) was compared between Flixton and Coddenham, and again there was no significant difference. It is hoped that further data from the cemeteries at Eriswell may be available for comparison in the future.

Pathology

Very little evidence for pathological lesions had survived. Middle-aged male 053:*0432* (Grave 15) had maxillary sinusitis, probably caused by an abscess of the first molar. Degenerative changes, consisting of osteophytosis of the first and second cervical vertebrae and the basi-occipital, were present in two individuals, middle-aged male 053:*0432* (Grave 15) and middle-aged/old female 062:*1861* (Grave 59) respectively. Three individuals could be assessed for cribra orbitalia, a lesion of the eye socket which is thought to be associated with iron deficiency anaemia, but none was affected. Bony exostoses were present on an unidentified bone fragment of adult female 053:*0362* (Grave 11) and may have been caused by torn ligaments. A possible unhealed cut on the occipital of young female 053:*0662* (Grave 34) may have been the cause of her death, but the bone was in very poor condition and the diagnosis is uncertain.

Summary and discussion, Flixton II

The preservation of bone in this assemblage was extremely poor and reconstruction of the population buried in the excavated area has been severely limited as a result. However, demographic information has been compiled taking into account biological and artefactual information (Table 8.3). The excavated graves are assumed to have contained a minimum of sixty-seven individuals. These consisted of nineteen males, twenty-four females (including children), and twenty-four individuals for whom sex/gender was indeterminate. All but the very youngest and very oldest members of society were represented by the group, although it is possible that these were amongst those burials which produced no bone. Certainly the group of small graves at the south-east corner of the main component of the Flixton II cemetery in FLN 062 could have contained the remains of infants. The adult age ranges are skewed to the youngest group, but this is again likely to be due to poor preservation of the generally thinner, osteoporotic bones which would be expected in the older age group.

No definite evidence for family relationships within the cemetery was found, and a comparison with other sites in the county suggested that Flixton did not differ significantly in tooth morphology. Even though this would be expected for contemporary groups in a limited geographical area, the small size of the dataset for Flixton may mean that the results are unreliable. Very few pathological conditions could be identified, either amongst the teeth or the bones. Those which were found were all common types and, with the exception of the possible unhealed wound, would not have impinged much on the individuals' daily life.

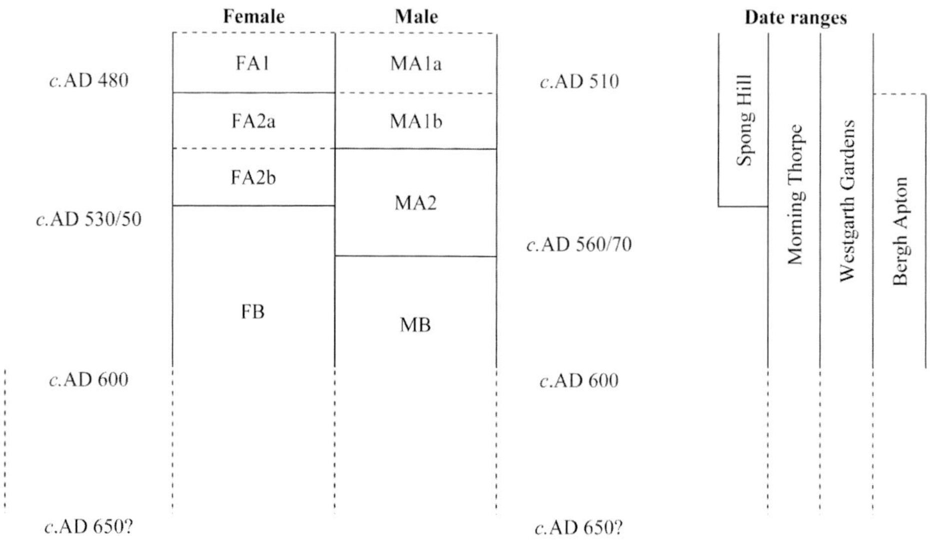

Figure 9.1 East Anglian (EAC) Framework

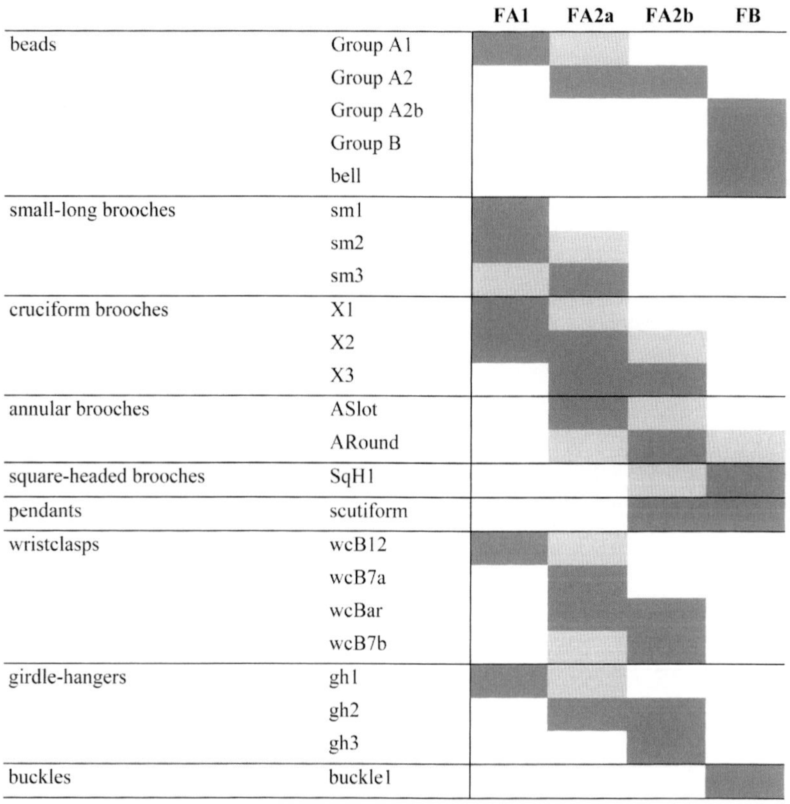

Figure 9.2 Female chronology based on dress accessories and beads

Chapter 9. The Chronology of the Flixton Cemeteries

by Birte Brugmann

I. Introduction

None of the excavated graves at Flixton is coin-dated; bone preservation is poor, and there are only a few inter-cutting graves that indicate burial sequences. Dates for the Flixton material therefore have to be based mostly on external dates for grave-good associations. The grave inventory gives detailed information on the stratigraphic relationships of Graves 5, 6, 7, 9, 33 and 36: Grave 6 cut into the end of Grave 9, Grave 7 cut Grave 5, and Grave 33 disturbed a corner of Grave 36. As described in Chapter 6, in Grave 27 the interment of a later male burial (B) disturbed an earlier female burial (A). In Graves 20, 22 and 61, two bodies were buried side by side, probably, but not necessarily, at the same time.

II. The East Anglian (EAC) framework

Figs 9.1–9.2

The most recent and detailed regional framework on which a site chronology for 5th- and 6th-century material from Flixton can be based was developed for the inhumation graves excavated at Spong Hill, Morning Thorpe, Bergh Apton and Bury St Edmunds Westgarth Gardens (Fig. 9.1; Penn and Brugmann 2007, fig. 5.20). The relative chronological phases of this framework are defined by grave-good associations. The definitions of the three main Phases FA1, FA2 and FB of the 'female' chronology are based on dress accessories and incorporate the results of an analysis of a national sample of Anglo-Saxon glass beads (Fig. 9.2; Brugmann 2004; Penn and Brugmann 2007, fig. 5.9). The definitions of the three main Phases MA1, MA2 and MB of the 'male' chronology are based on weapon combinations (Høilund Nielsen in Penn and Brugmann 2007) and backed up by the preliminary results of an analysis of a national sample of weapon graves carried out by Karen Høilund Nielsen and John Hines. The EAC framework will have to be re-assessed in the light of the final results from this study (Bayliss *et al.* forthcoming).

The absolute dates assigned to the relative chronological phases are derived from Continental frameworks (Penn and Brugmann 2007, 42–75). These dates are unconventionally early, which can make it difficult to correlate the framework with conventional date ranges for types of objects such as knives, or the claw beaker in Grave A at Flixton I. In exceptional cases, the EAC framework can date objects earlier by as much as half a century.

Thirty-eight out of the sixty-three graves excavated at Flixton (I and II) can be dated to one of the East Anglian phases on the basis of grave-good types identified by the small-finds analyses in Chapter 7. Some of the weapon types found at Flixton, however, are not covered by EAC and Karen Høilund Nielsen has kindly commented upon them.

III. Male grave-good assemblages

Grave 1 The shield boss Type COV, dated to Phase MA2, is associated with spearheads of Types Angular Medium 1 and Angular Medium 2b, also dated to Phase MA2.

Grave 15 The shield boss Type COS suggests a date for the grave in Phase MA2.

Grave 23 The spearhead Type Concave Long 1b suggests a date for the grave in Phase MA1.

Grave 27B The shield boss Type SOS dated to Phase MB is associated with a spearhead Type Angular Medium 1.

Grave 28 The spearhead Type Concave Medium 1b suggests a date for the grave in Phase MA1.

Grave 37 The spearhead 37/6 of Type Angular Medium 2b, dated to Phase MA2, was found together with a shield boss Type COV, dated to Phase MA2, to the left of the remains of a skull, the only skeletal remains in the grave. Spearhead 37/1 of Type Concave Long 1a, dated to Phase MA2, was found to the right of the skull, with enough space between them to allow for a possible second body. Whether for one or two individuals, the grave falls in Phase MA2.

Grave 41 The spearhead Type Parallel Long 1 suggests a date for the grave in Phase MB.

Grave 43 In the EAC analysis, the spearhead Type Angular Medium 1 falls in Phase MA2. The EAC study, however, included relatively few late weapon graves, and the national sample analysed by Høilund Nielsen suggests that the type was still in use in Phase MB (K. Høilund Nielsen, pers. comm.).

Grave 52 The shield boss Type SOS is dated to Phase MB and is associated with a spearhead Type Angular Long 1, which does not occur in the EAC study. Høilund Nielsen's national sample suggests it was in use in Phases MA2 and MB (K. Høilund Nielsen, pers. comm.). This suggests a date for the grave in Phase MB

Grave 53 As Grave 52.

Grave 55 The spearhead Type Lanceolate Long 1 could not be firmly dated in the EAC study; Høilund Nielsen's national sample suggests a date in Phases MA2/MB (K. Høilund Nielsen, pers. comm.).

Grave 56 In the EAC analysis, the spearhead Type Parallel Long 2 falls in Phase MB. In Høilund Nielsen's national sample the type is dated to a relative chronological phase with a provisional absolute date range of c.640/50–660/70 AD.

IV. Female grave-good assemblages

Note that in the chronological framework for East Anglia, annular brooches as a class are dated to Phases FA2 and FB.

Grave A The small-long brooches Type *sm2* suggest a date for the grave in Phases FA1/2a. The type of claw beaker associated with these brooches is conventionally dated to the first half of the 6th century; the claw beaker itself is dated relatively late within this span by Broadley (Chapter 7). This may indicate a date for the grave in Phase FA2a rather than FA1.

Grave 3 The association of beads of group A1, dated to FA1/FA2a, with sleeve-clasps of Type wcBar, dated to Phase FA2, indicates a date for the grave in Phase FA2.

Grave 4 The cruciform brooches of Type X1 suggest a date for the grave in Phase FA1 or FA2a. The brooches seem to have been old when buried, which suggests a date in Phase FA2a rather than earlier.

Grave 5 The beads of Group B indicate a date for the grave in Phase FB.

Grave 8 The association of annular brooches with beads of Group A2 places the grave in Phase FA2.

Grave 9 The association of annular brooches with beads of Group B1 suggests a date for the grave in Phase FB.

Grave 11 The association of two annular brooches (one is Type ARound, mainly dated to Phase FA2b), with sleeve clasps (one is Type wcBar dated to Phase FA2), suggests a date for the grave in Phase FA2.

Grave 13 The annular brooch indicates a date in Phase FA2 or FB.

Grave 16 Sleeve-clasps were worn in Phase FA; the single piece in this grave may, however, be intrusive.

Grave 17 The association of sleeve-clasps with an annular brooch suggests a date for the grave in Phase FA2.

Grave 20A/B The association of annular brooches Type ARound, mainly in use in Phase FA2b, with beads of Group A2 place the grave in Phase FA2.

Grave 21 The annular brooches suggest that the grave does not predate Phase FA2.

Grave 26 The association of annular brooches Type ARound mainly in use in Phase FA2b with beads of Group A suggests a date for the grave in Phase FA2.

Grave 27A The small-long brooches of Types sm2 and sm3 dated to Phases FA1/2a associated with beads of Group A suggest a date for the grave in Phases FA1/2a.

Grave 30 The association of annular brooches with sleeve-clasps Type B7b and beads of Group A2 suggests a date for the grave in Phase FA2.

Grave 31 The association of annular brooches with beads of Group A suggests a date for the grave in Phase FA2.

Grave 33 The beads of Group B suggest a date for the grave in Phase FB.

Grave 34 Annular brooches Type ARound were mainly used in Phase FA2b, but cannot date the grave more closely than to Phases FA2/B.

Grave 36 As Grave 34.

Grave 39 The beads of Group B2 suggest a date for the grave in Phase FB.

Grave 40 As Grave 39.

Grave 42 The beads of Group A2 suggest a date for the grave in Phase FA2.

Grave 59 The beads of Group B2 suggest a date for the grave in Phase FB.

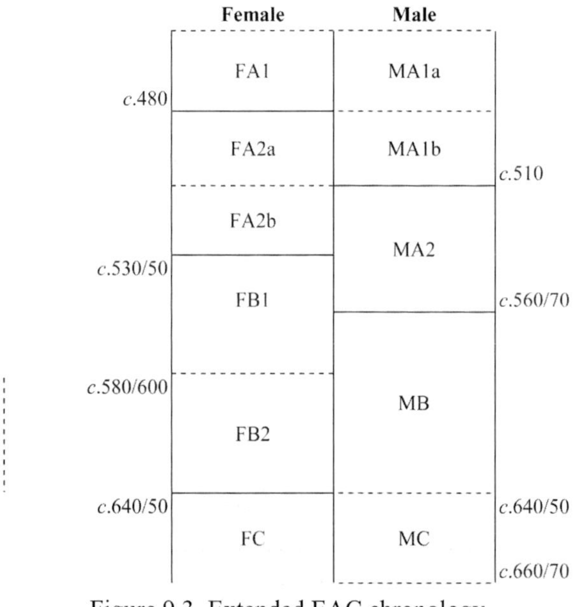

Figure 9.3 Extended EAC chronology

Grave 51 The association of annular brooches, which include Type ARound, with beads of Group A2b suggest a date for the grave in Phase FB.

Grave 61A The buckle Type buckle1 suggests a date for the grave in Phase FB. This date range is supported by the type of fire-steel found with the individual B in this grave (see Riddler, Fire-steel, in Chapter 7).

V. The East Anglian framework extended

Figs 9.3–9.4

The East Anglian Chronology (EAC) framework had to remain vague about the end of Phases MB and FB (Fig. 9.1) because there was enough evidence to suggest that at least Morning Thorpe and Westgarth Gardens were still in use in the 7th century, but not enough to define a detailed phasing based on grave-good associations. At Flixton, there is no evidence for female dress accessories of the so-called 'Final Phase' or Bead Phase C (Brugmann 2004) which would indicate that burial continued beyond the mid-7th century, but the spearhead type in Grave 56 suggests that the cemetery was still in use at the time (see above). This asks for a more detailed phasing of the second half of the 6th century and of the 7th century than the EAC chronology can provide.

A sub-division of Phase FB can be achieved by integrating (a) some aspects of the chronological framework for Anglo-Saxon female costumes developed by Walton Rogers (2007 and this volume, Chapter 10) and (b) the chronological sequence of bead groups B1 and B2 (Brugmann 2004). The late 6th century (AD *c*.580–600) forms a transitional period in which beads of both groups B1 and B2 were in use and in which paired peplos brooches disappear, but single brooches remain (Walton Rogers 2007, 184–9). Beads of Group B1 ran out of fashion in the late 6th century, between AD 580 and 600 (Brugmann 2004, table 3). Phase FB2 ends with the introduction of the 'Final Phase' bead types of Group C around AD 640/50 (Fig. 9.3). The 'Migration Period peplos' costume defined by Walton Rogers (2007, 144–54), ended while beads of Group B1 were in use and the fashion change is thought to have taken place between AD 560 and 580 (Walton Rogers 2007, 180, 184). On this basis, Phase FB can be subdivided into sub-phases FB1 and FB2: Phase FB1 covers the 'Migration Period peplos' in combination with beads of group B1, and Phase FB2 post-dates this dress fashion and is defined by beads of Group B2. According to this definition, the following graves can be more closely dated:

Grave 9 The beads of Group B1 and the pair of annular brooches suggest a date for the grave in Phase FB1.

Grave 13 The single annular brooch implies a date for the grave no later than Phase FB.

Grave 21 The pair of annular brooches at the shoulder suggests a date for the grave no later than Phase FB1.

Grave 34 The pair of annular brooches of Type ARound at the shoulders indicate a date of the grave in Phase FA2/B1.

Grave 36 As Grave 34.

Grave 39 The beads of Group B2 suggest a date of the grave in Phase FB2.

Grave 40 As Grave 39. The type of spindle whorl in this grave supports the late date (see Walton Rogers, Spindle whorl, Chapter 7).

Grave 59 As Grave 39

Grave 51 The beads of Group A2b worn with a 'Migration Period peplos' held by annular brooches Type ARound suggests a date for the grave in Phase FB1.

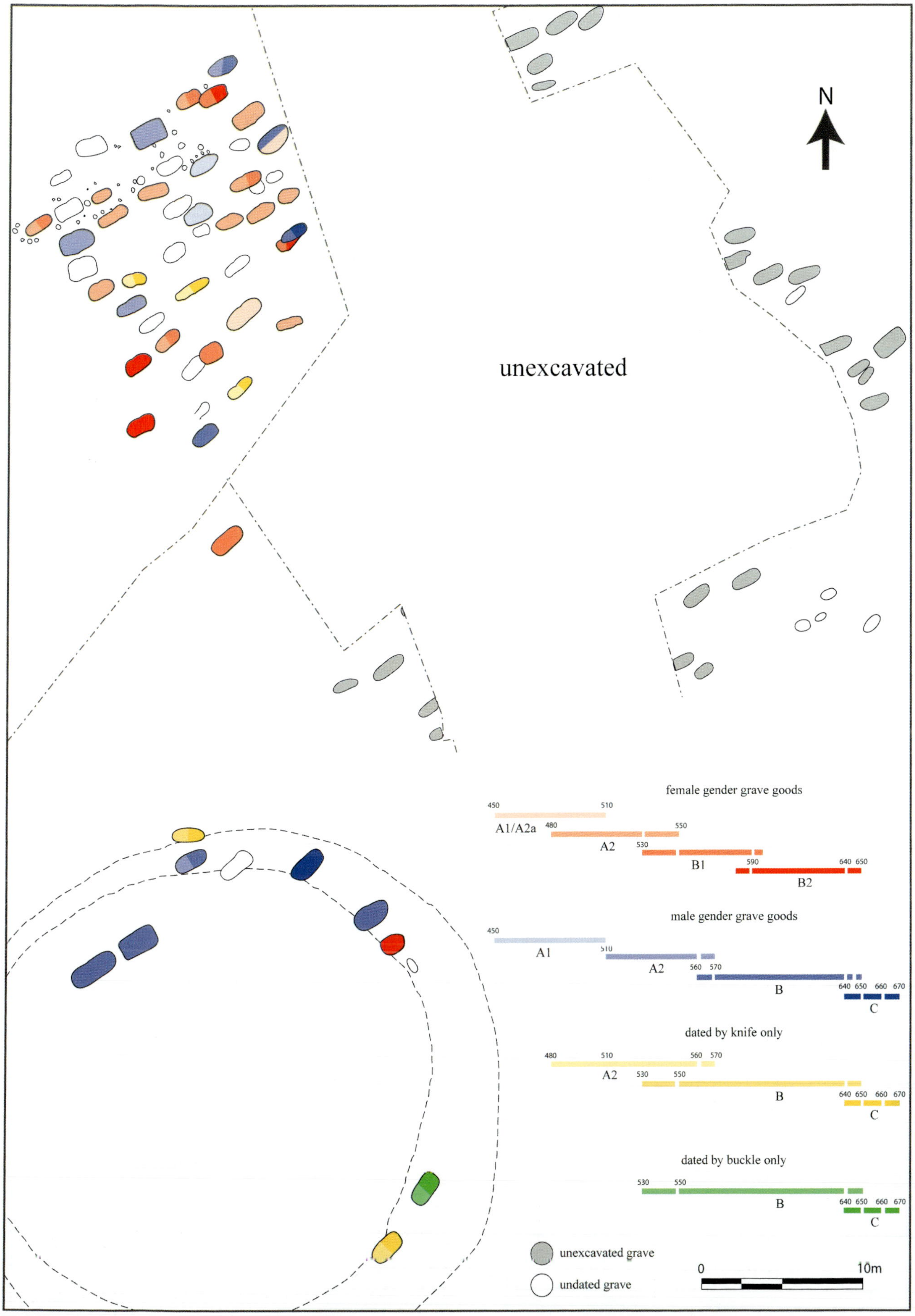

Figure 9.4 Flixton II (FLN 053 and FLN 062): distribution of dated graves

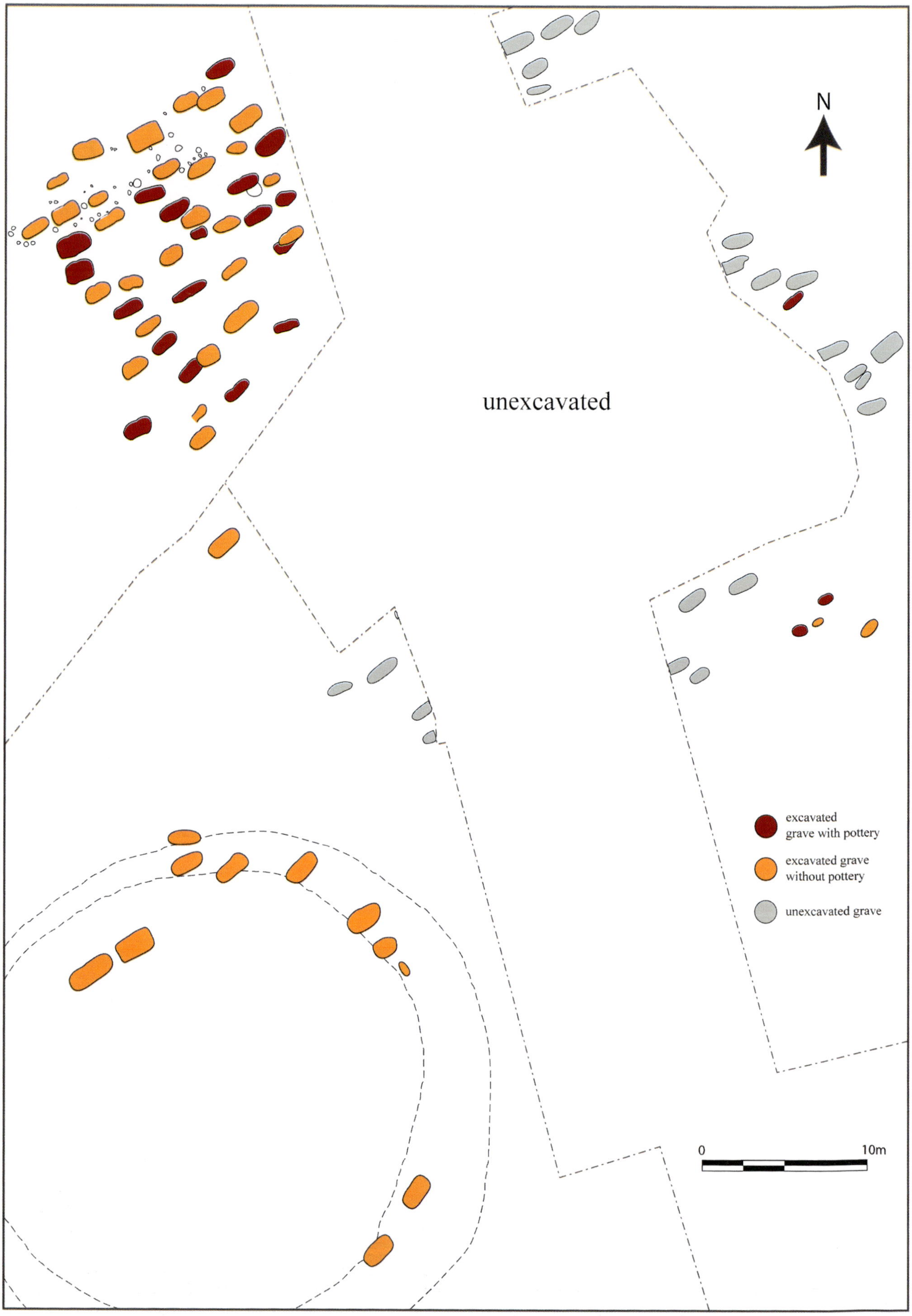

Figure 9.5 Flixton II (FLN 053 and FLN 062): distribution of graves with pottery

Dating evidence for the iron lunulate neck-ring (lunula) from Grave 22 has been discussed by Walton Rogers (Chapter 7.III), who argues for a date-range centred on the first half of the 6th century. The only neck-ring dated by association in the EAC analysis was found in Bergh Apton G50 and was placed in Phase MA2 (Penn and Brugmann 2007, 31). The grave is therefore tentatively dated to Phases FA2/MA2.

For an extension of the chronological framework for male graves, the provisional phasing of the national sample of weapon graves analysed by Karen Høilund Nielsen is used, which provisionally places the spearhead from Grave 56 in a phase dated in absolute terms to AD *c*.640/50–660/70 and here named Phase MC for convenience. Phase MB cannot be subdivided but is thus given a more definitive end date, AD 640/50. An overview of the extended chronological framework is given in Figure 9.3.

The distribution of the dated graves (Fig. 9.4) suggests that the first graves were dug in FLN 053 around AD 500 and that the burial plot was in use throughout the 6th century and possibly still in the first half of the 7th century. It seems possible that confining boundaries of the main Flixton II burial ground (see Chapter 6) led to an extension towards the prehistoric ring ditch to the south (FLN 062) in the second half of the 6th century; the new area was in use at least until the mid 7th century.

There was relatively little re-use of burial space at Flixton, and in only one such case does this narrow down the date range of a grave: Grave 7 was dug into Grave 5, dated to Phase FB, which suggests a date for Grave 7 in the male equivalent of Phase FB/C. Grave 27B dated to Phase MB seems to have been dug into or through Grave 27A, dated to Phases FA1/2a. Evidence from other cemeteries suggests that such an act was not necessarily an accidental disturbance, but more likely to have been a deliberate aspect of early Anglo-Saxon burial practice (see Penn and Brugmann 2007, 87). The same may be true of Grave 33 dated to Phase FB, which disturbed a corner of Grave 36, dated to Phase FA2/B1.

VI. Knives, buckles and pottery

Fig. 9.5

In some of the Flixton graves, knives are the only type of grave good that can be relatively closely dated (see Riddler, Knives, Chapter 7.VI). Unfortunately this does not include knife Type Drinkall A, which is the most common type found at Flixton. Type Drinkall B is conventionally dated to the 6th and early 7th centuries and was found in six graves, four of them dated by associated grave goods to Phases FA2–B1 and MA2–B (Grave 22, 37, 41, 51). This suggests a similar date range for Graves 12 and 18. Type Drinkall D in Grave 2 is conventionally dated to the 6th and 7th centuries. Graves 53 and 55 with knives of this type are dated by associated weapons to phases MB and MA2/B respectively. This may indicate a date for Grave 2 in Phases MA2/B. Type Drinkall E is conventionally dated to the late 6th and 7th centuries, which suggests a date for Graves 54 and 60 in Phases FB/C or MB/C.

The only datable object in Grave 58 is a small iron buckle and buckle plate with a vertical row of rivets, 58/1. This is a type of buckle conventionally dated to the late 6th and 7th centuries (see Walton Rogers, Buckles, Chapter 7.II) and for which the national sample of weapon graves analysed by Høilund Nielsen suggests a date range in Phases MB/C (K. Høilund Nielsen, pers. comm.) (Fig. 9.4). In Grave 53 such a type is associated with weapons dated to Phase MB.

The types of ceramic vessels found in the Flixton graves are not closely datable, although organic-tempered wares in Graves 2, 6, 8, 11, 16, 27B and 30 are probably dated to the 6th and 7th centuries and the granitic pottery of Graves 1, 15 and 21 may be limited to the 6th century (see Anderson, Pottery, Chapter 7.VIII). The EAC analysis indicates that the deposition of pottery in graves was less common after Phase FA2/MA2 (Penn and Brugmann 2007, 68–70). The distribution of graves with pottery (Fig. 9.5) suggests that this was also the case at Flixton. Two graves in the northern part of the main plot dated to Phase FB contained ceramic vessels (Grave 5 and 39) but none of the graves associated with the barrow included pottery as grave goods.

VII. Burial practice

Figs 9.6–9.8

Analysis of the inhumation graves at Spong Hill, Morning Thorpe, Bergh Apton and Westgarth Gardens demonstrated overall changes in burial practice which suggested that the combination of a ceramic vessel and a small knife in a large grave is likely to date earlier than the combination of an iron buckle and a large knife in a small grave (Penn and Brugmann 2007, 70). This tendency, however, does not seem to apply to Flixton in all its aspects because there is no evidence for an overall decrease of grave lengths over time, possibly because the graves dated late include a relatively large number of weapon graves. Most of the graves dug into the prehistoric barrow and ring ditch (FLN 062) are not only long (*c*.2–3m) but also relatively deep on Flixton standards (*c*.0.3–0.7m; Figs 9.6 and 9.7). The FLN 053 graves to the south are mostly shallower, but include a scatter of graves as long as those of FLN 062.

The absence of graves with a remaining depth of more than 0.4m in the northern central part of FLN 053 may indicate the presence of a shallow mound or rise in Anglo-Saxon times which may have attracted the earliest graves in this area. The presence of both shallow and deep graves in the south of FLN 053 and on the fringes of the excavated area, however, suggests that there was also a chronological aspect to grave depths at Flixton, as the relatively deep graves are also mostly the late ones: Graves 9 and 39–41 are dated to Phases FB and MB. This matter is discussed further in Chapters 10–11.

Soil stains at the bottom of many of the shallow graves in the northern part of the main plot indicate the presence coffins or biers which in the EAC study were found mostly in graves dated to Phases FA and MA (Penn and Brugmann 2007, 83–4). The concentration of possible evidence for such features in the early part of the burial plot (Fig. 9.8) and their absence in the graves to the south suggests that this pattern also applies to Flixton. As in the EAC analysis, such features are not directly related to the shape of the grave pit (Fig. 9.8, based on the descriptions in the grave inventory), and rectangular or sub-rectangular grave pits as such are not datable (see Penn and Brugmann 2007, 84).

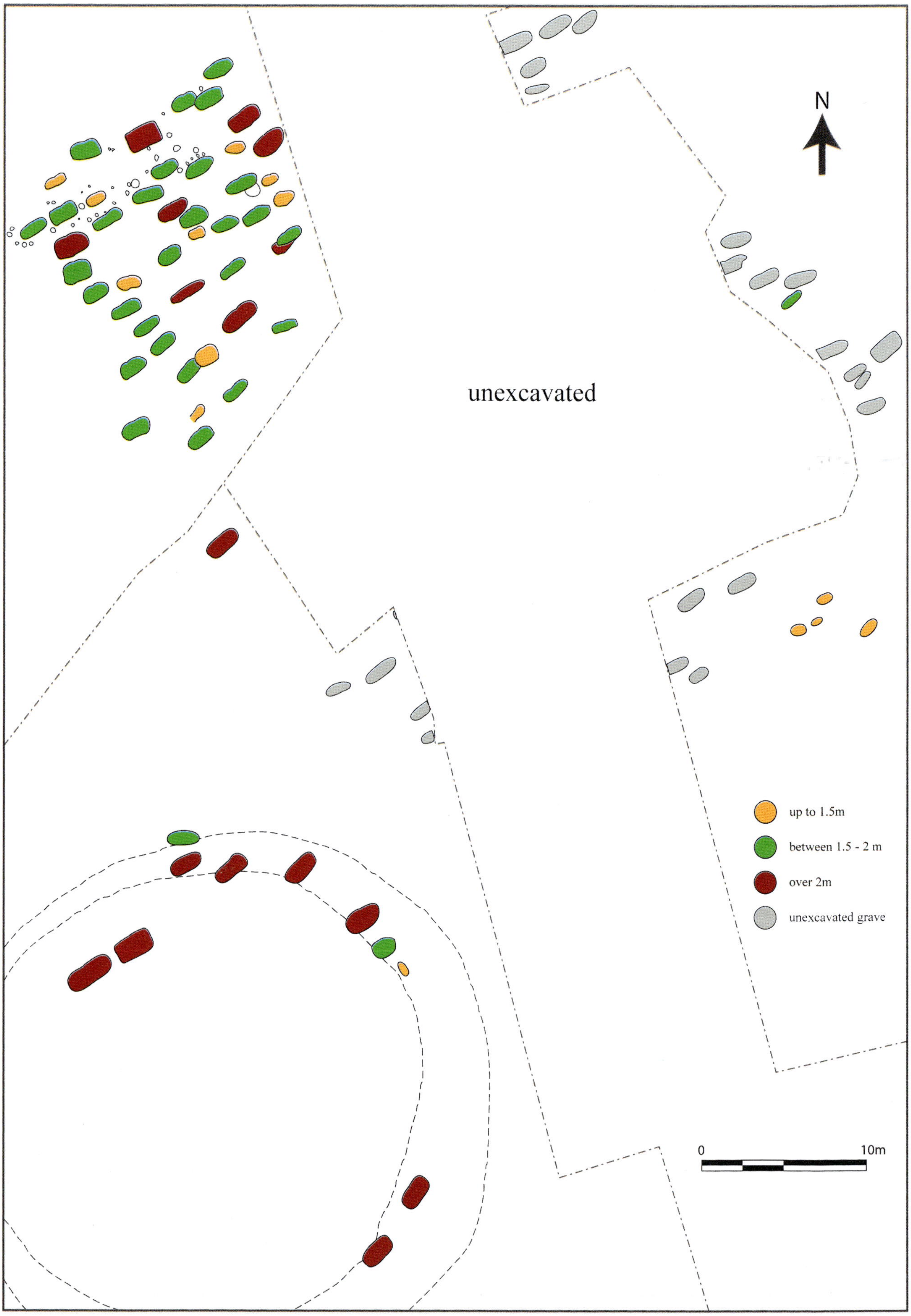

Figure 9.6 Flixton II (FLN 053 and FLN 062): grave lengths

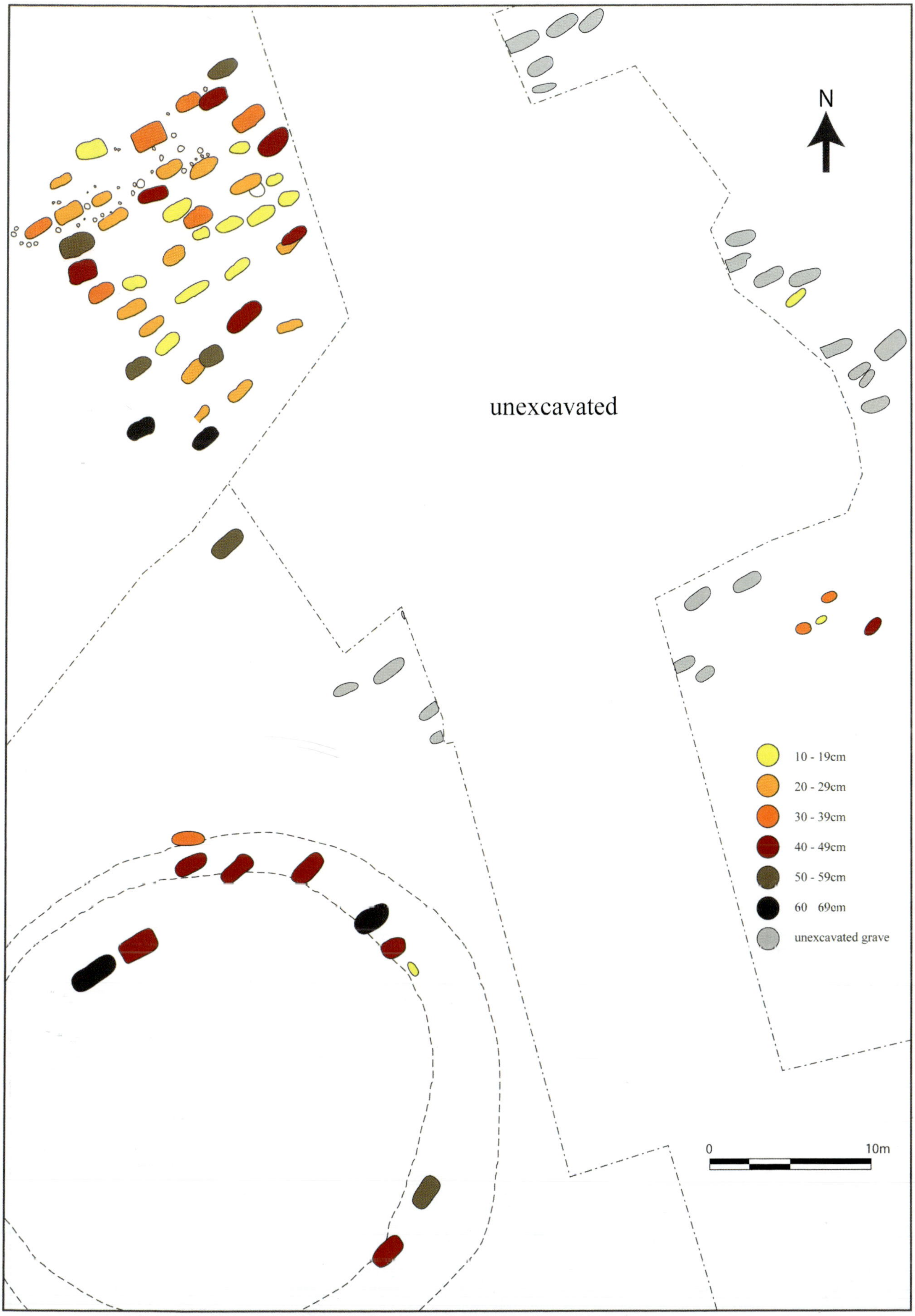

Figure 9.7 Flixton II (FLN 053 and FLN 062): grave depths

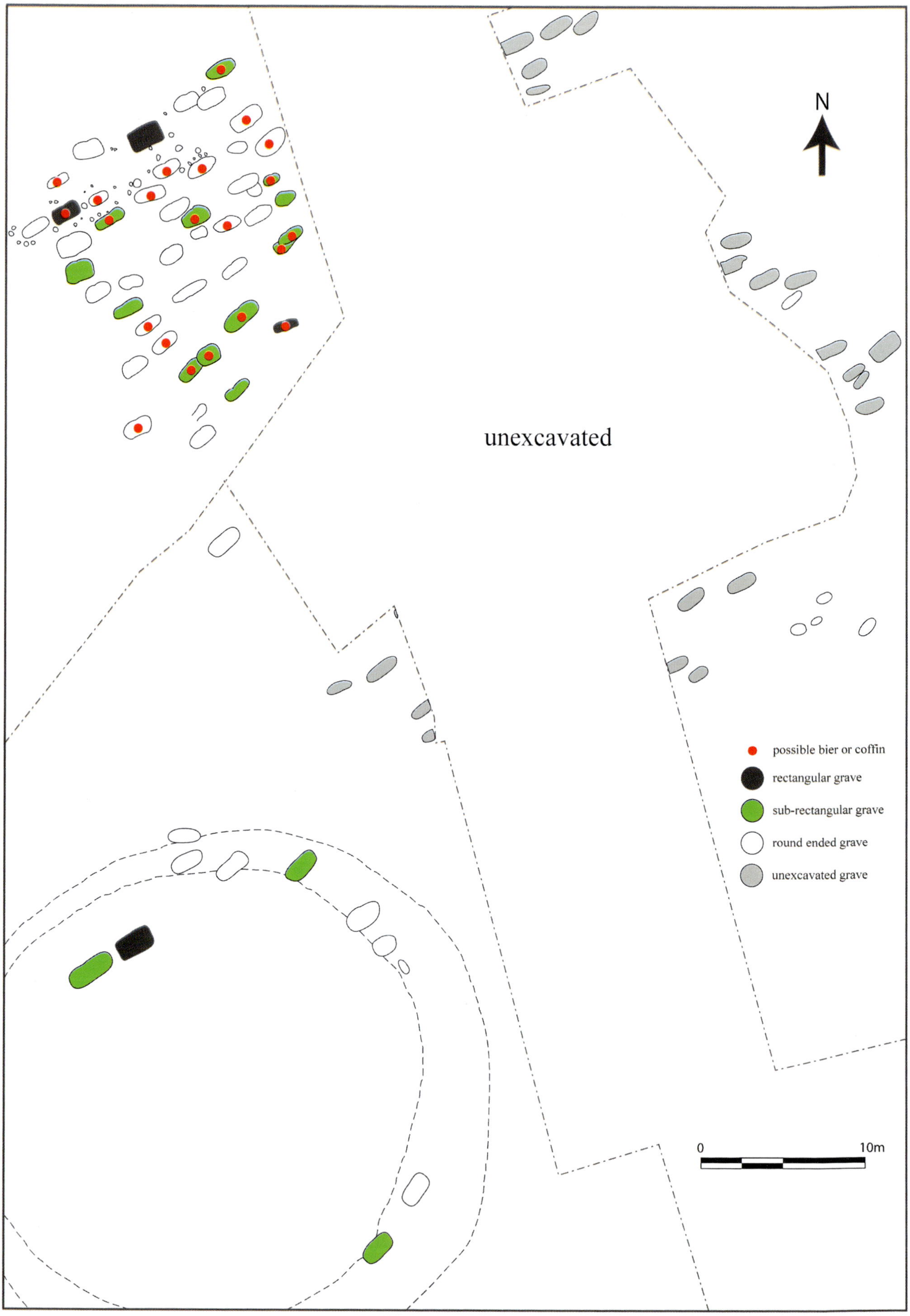

Figure 9.8 Flixton II (FLN 053 and FLN 062): grave shape and presence of coffin/bier

	Grave	Phase	Grave	Phase
Flixton I	A	FA2a?		
Flixton II	1	MA2	32	-
	2	MA2/B	33	FB
	3	FA2a	34	FA2b/B1
	4	FA1/2a	35	-
	5	FB	36	FA2/B1
	6	MA2/B	37	MA2
	7	MA2/B	38	-
	8	FA2	39	FB2
	9	FB1	40	FB2
	10	-	41	MB
	11	FA2	42	FA2
	12	FA2/B	43	MA2/B
	13	FA2/B1	44	-
	14	M-	45	-
	15	MA2	46	-
	16	-	47	-
	17	FA2	48	-
	18	A2/B	49	-
	19	-	50	-
	20A+B	FA2/B1, MA2/B	51	FB1
	21	FA2/B1	52	MB
	22A+B	FA2/MA2	53	MB
	23	MA1	54	B/C
	24	-	55	MA2/B
	25	-	56	MC
	26	FA2	57	-
	27A	FA1/2a	58	MB/C
	27B	MB	59	FB2
	28	MA1	60	B/C
	29	-	61A+B	FB
	30	FA2	62	-
	31	FA2		

Table 9.1 The phases of the graves at Flixton I and II

It would not seem safe to date any of the Flixton graves firmly on the absence or presence of knives, buckles, pots or coffins/biers alone, and the date ranges considered for some of the following graves are therefore only tentative: Grave 6 with a remaining depth of 0.22m and a spear socket, an incomplete vessel and the possible remains of a bier may date in Phase MA. Grave 14 combines one of the largest knives from the site with a buckle type conventionally dated to the 6th century (see Walton Rogers, Buckles, Chapter 7.II) and probable evidence for a bier or container, which may date the grave in Phase MA2 or possibly later; the same may apply to Grave 32 with a slightly shorter knife in a slightly deeper grave, also associated with an iron buckle and possible evidence for a bier. Grave 57 is likely to date no earlier than Phase FB or MB because it was dug into the ring ditch with other late graves.

In the north of the main plot, post-holes were excavated which probably relate to a number of shallow graves in this area (Graves 28, 30, 32, 34–7, 42; for details see Table 6.1, Chapter 6). None of these graves is dated later than Phases MA2 and FB1. There is no evidence for Anglo-Saxon ring ditches at Flixton, although this is not an unusual feature in early East Anglian cemeteries (Penn and Brugmann 2007, 84).

Forty-five out of the sixty-three graves excavated at Flixton (I and II) can be dated according to the phases shown in Fig. 9.4 and Table 9.1.

Chapter 10. Reconstructing the Flixton Women

by Penelope Walton Rogers

I. Introduction

In the early phases of the Anglo-Saxon period, individual communities appear to have been broadly equal to each other in terms of status, but within each community there was considerable social differentiation (Scull 1993, 72–3). National and regional studies of the cemeteries have shown, for example, that gender was strongly indicated in both clothing and accessories; that there were significant age thresholds for both men and women; that there were different ranks and social roles; and that the expression of these matters altered with time (Arnold 1980; Härke 1997; Stoodley 1999a; Penn and Brugmann 2007; Walton Rogers 2007). The cemeteries have been interpreted, on this and other evidence, as the place where individual households – by which is meant a nuclear family with dependants, including servants or slaves – would return to their own plots to bury their dead over successive generations.

At Flixton it was difficult to identify household plots because of the limited areas excavated, but the graves marked by post-holes in the northern part of Flixton II are likely to represent the focus of one such group and it is probable that Flixton I represents another. The differences between male and female and between young and old are easier to see, and the following chapters will therefore consider women, men and children separately, with an additional section on the gender-less domestic items that furnish the grave. The aim will be to reconstruct the appearance of the individuals and their accessories, as they would have been at the time of burial, and to use this material as a base from which to discuss the social make-up of the Flixton community, and how it changed with time.

II. The Flixton women

Twenty-one adults and four children (including Flixton I Grave A) have been identified as female, using the combined evidence of biological sex and gender-signifying accessories (Chapter 8). The number of young females is probably under-represented in these figures, as there were seventeen children where the sex could not be identified, but it will be argued in the next chapter that most of the adult burials without any obvious gender-indicators were male, and very few adult women are likely to have been overlooked.

III. Burial practice

Women tended to have smaller graves than men, which probably reflects their smaller average stature. They followed the trend seen among the men, of larger graves in later phases, although the increase was more marked in the male graves (Table 10.1). In Stoodley's national sample, the increase in length was only clear for men (Stoodley 1999a, 67–8), and, on analysis, it would appear that the Flixton burial sizes for both sexes are below the national average in the early phases, and only rise to meet the standard in Phases FB/MB. In the Norfolk cemeteries, the opposite is true, as some large early graves lift the figures above the national average in Phases FA1 and FA2 (Penn and Brugmann 2007, 76–7). This is the first indication that the excavated section of Flixton II, which in many respects resembles the Norfolk cemeteries, followed a different trajectory in terms of status.

One woman at Flixton was almost certainly buried in a coffin, two had a coffin or bier and seven a bier (or hide or rug); four had grave markers indicated by post-holes (Table 6.1). Where the posture of the body could be identified, it was mostly supine with legs extended, but in Grave 51 (Phase FB1) the woman was turned to the left with legs flexed, in Grave 36 (Phase FA2/B1) she was almost certainly prone, and in Grave 17 (Phase FA2) she appears to have been on her side with head to the east. This last was the grave in which there was a man's skull to one side of the body and it was argued in Chapter 6 that the Norfolk practice of occasionally reversing a female burial is likely to indicate something irregular in the woman's life.

IV. Women's costume

Introduction

How the dead were dressed for burial can be reconstructed from the position of the metal garment fasteners on the body and the arrangement of the textiles in relation to those fasteners. Before the evidence from Flixton is

Phase	*No. of graves*	*Average length (m)*	*Average width (m)*	*Average area (m^2)*	*Depth (m)*
Female					
FA2	8	1.60	0.68	1.27	0.19
FA2/B1	4	1.79	0.76	1.36	0.26
FB	7	1.81	1.07	1.98	0.49
Male					
MA1	2	1.82	0.79	1.44	0.29
MA2 and MA2/B	5	1.94	0.86	1.70	0.39
MB and C	5	2.22	0.98	2.21	0.50

Table 10.1 Size of graves in metres for datable adult burials, arranged by sex/gender and phase (double burials have been omitted)

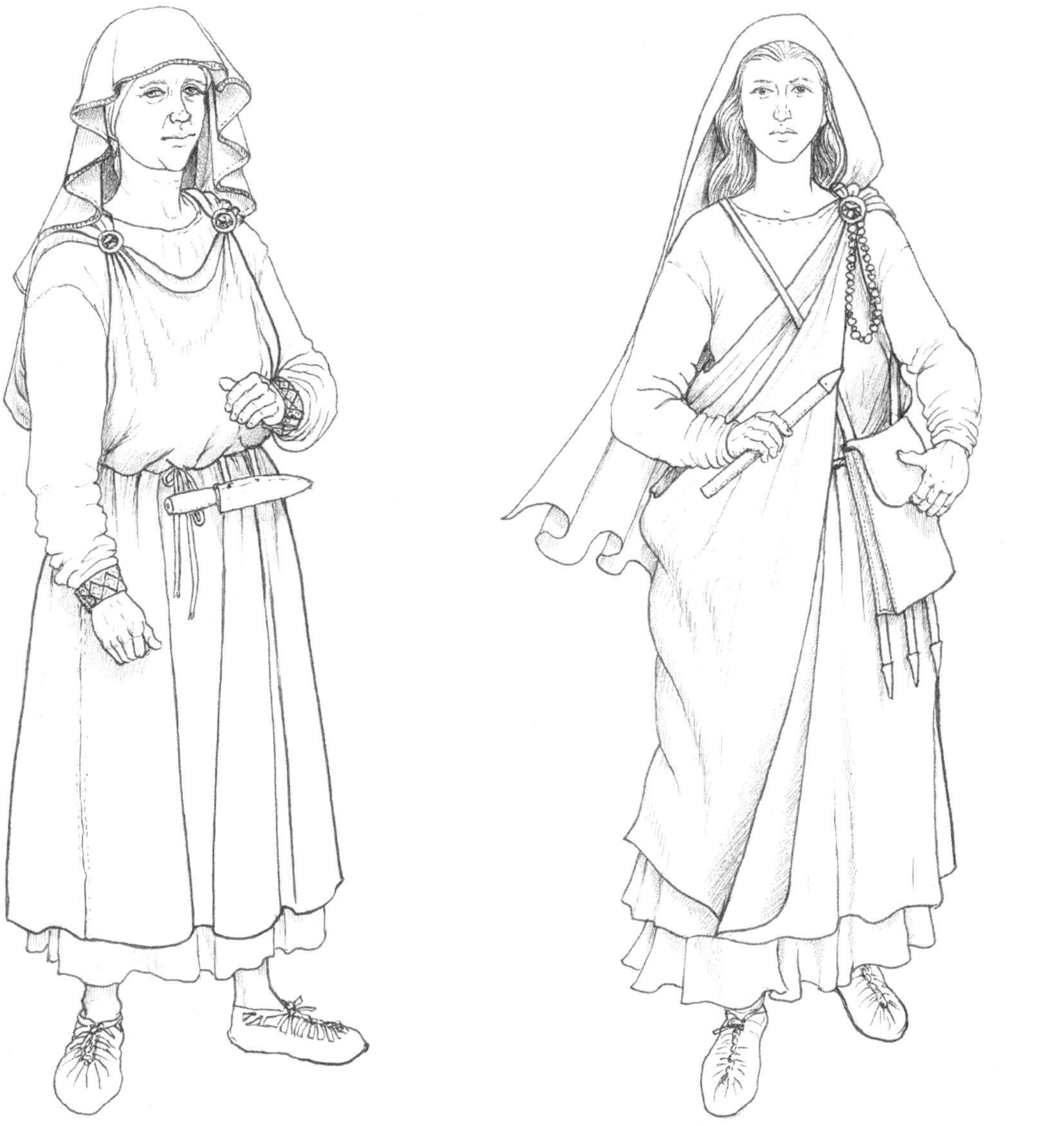

Figure 10.1 Left, the woman from Grave 17 (Phase FA2) in a peplos over a dress with patterned cuffs. Right, the young woman from Grave 9 (Phase FB1) in a single-brooch peplos with a mantle; she has a pouch with a trio of strap ends and carries a staff with an iron ferrule. Anthony Barton, copyright The Anglo-Saxon Laboratory

reviewed, however, some general points that have emerged from a national survey should be made (Walton Rogers 2007). First, it is obvious from the patterns of wear and repair on brooches and textiles that the burial evidence represents clothing worn in life, rather than a funerary costume. Second, the variation in costume details from grave to grave implies that women were not regimented, but were making choices about their clothing – choices that reflected who they were and how they perceived their age-group and their position in society.

Third, within the study of women's costume, there are two overlapping patterns of distribution, of dress fashions on the one hand and of metal garment accessories on the other. Women's costume has proved to have broad national and regional trends and local variations, none of which is exactly congruent with the metal artefact types (Walton Rogers 2007, 139–228). Since women certainly made the clothing and men very probably made the metalwork, these differing patterns have some significance. If this was a 'virilocal' society (see Chapter 14), then women would take their fashions and cloth-making techniques to a new community on marriage, with their own metal garment fasteners, but the metalwork 'know-how' would stay behind. While metal garment accessories are essential for dating the burial and for locating the community where the woman originated, if women are to be made the real focus of the study, the styles of garments that they wore have to be classified first and the identity of the fastener appended to that framework afterwards.

The peplos

Fig. 10.1; Pls 10.1–10.2

In those burials where there is a matching or near-matching pair of brooches towards one end of the grave, the body will almost certainly have been dressed in the 'peplos', which is a tubular garment fastened with a brooch on either shoulder (Fig. 10.1 left; Table 10.2). There are ten examples of paired annular brooches, one pair of small-long brooches (Grave A, possibly a juvenile) and probably also a pair of cruciform brooches, if the unstratified brooch, II/NG1, has been correctly attributed to Grave 4. It is possible that the two non-matching small-long brooches from Grave 27A were used in the same way, but they were disturbed from their original position when the male burial, 27B, was dug through the grave. A single annular brooch from another burial that may have been disturbed, Grave 13, possibly represents the remains of a further peplos, so that there are at least thirteen, and possibly fifteen, peplos-wearers in all. The earliest of the peplos fasteners are likely to be the cruciform and small-long brooches in Graves A, 4 and 27A of Phase FA1/2a, but most of the paired annular brooches belong to Phase FA2, four are either FA2 or FB1 (Graves 13, 21, 34, and 36) and one pair from Grave 51 belongs to Phase FB1 (Table 10.2).

The fabric of the peplos is represented by the textiles looping over the pins of these brooches. In five cases it is wool 2/2 twill, of medium and medium-fine qualities, from 14 x 12 to 16 x 16 threads per cm, and a single example in a late grave, Grave 51, is linen 2/2 twill, also 14 x 12 per cm. This adds to the evidence from sites such as Castledyke, north Lincolnshire, that linen replaced wool in the manufacture of the peplos shortly before the garment disappeared from use (Walton Rogers 1998, 276). The top of the peplos often has a strengthening border along its edge, and in four burials from Phase FA2 this was a plain tablet-woven band (Graves 11, 20A, 30 and 31), but in two, one from Phase FB1 (Grave 51) and the other either FA2 or FB1 (Grave 21), the border was a warp-faced band which may have been an integral part of the cloth. In Grave 20B, an unusually broad tablet-woven band, over 30mm wide, was recorded. In Grave 26 and probably also Grave 36, the annular brooches clasp folds of the fabric and it is possible that in this instance the garment had the fold-down bib which is seen in some of

Grave	*Phase*	*Age (grave size)*	*Shoulder brooches*	*Central fastener*	*Sleeve clasps*	*Beads*	*Other*
4 (disturbed)	FA1/A2a	(adult)	m pair				ring, collar, buckle x 2, knife
27A (disturbed)	FA1/A2a	(adult)	non-m pair			10	knife, bucket pendants
A (Flixton I)	FA2a	juvenile	m pair				claw beaker, ceramic bowl
3	FA2a	(?adult)		complete pin	two pairs	20	ring, knife, buckle, ear scoop, ceramic bowl, unidentified object
8	FA2	(child)	single			5	ceramic bowl
11	FA2	adult	non-m pair	pin frag	two pairs		key/latch-lifter, knife, pouch x 2, ring, wooden vessel, ceramic jar and bowl
17	FA2	(adult)	m pair		two pairs		knife
20A	FA2	?				4	
20A or 20B							latch-lifter, pouch
20B	FA2	young adult	m pair	pin frag		10	buckle, bucket pendants
26	FA2	young adult	non-m pair			14	knife, latch-lifter, ring, buckle
30	FA2	young adult	m pair		one pair	6	ceramic sherds
31	FA2	(adult)	m pair			14	latch-lifter, knife, buckle
42	FA2	child, *c.*5yrs				1	two metal tubes at neck
34	FA2b/B1	young adult	non-m pair				ring
36	FA2/B1	young adult	m pair				knife, buckle
13	FA2/B1	young-mid adult	single				ceramic vessel
21	FA2/B1	(adult)	m pair			1	ring, ceramic jar
12	FA2/B	(adult)		pin frag			knife, ceramic vessel
51	FB1	young adult	non-m pair			40	knife, key, latch-lifter, buckle, pouch, ring
9	FB1	(truncated)	single			23	knife, girdle group, buckle
39	FB2	(adult)				10	knot-ring and ceramic jar
40	FB2	(adult)				14	spindle-and-whorl
59	FB2	mid-age/old (poss male)				12	buckle, knife, pouch
33	FB	young adult or sub-adult				7	knife, ceramic sherds
5	FB	(adult)				9	ceramic jar

Key: m = matching, frag = fragment

Table 10.2 Burials identified as female from sex of human remains and/or gender of artefacts, arranged by phase. Age has been derived from the bones and teeth, but a bracketed identification as an adult or child is based on the size of the grave

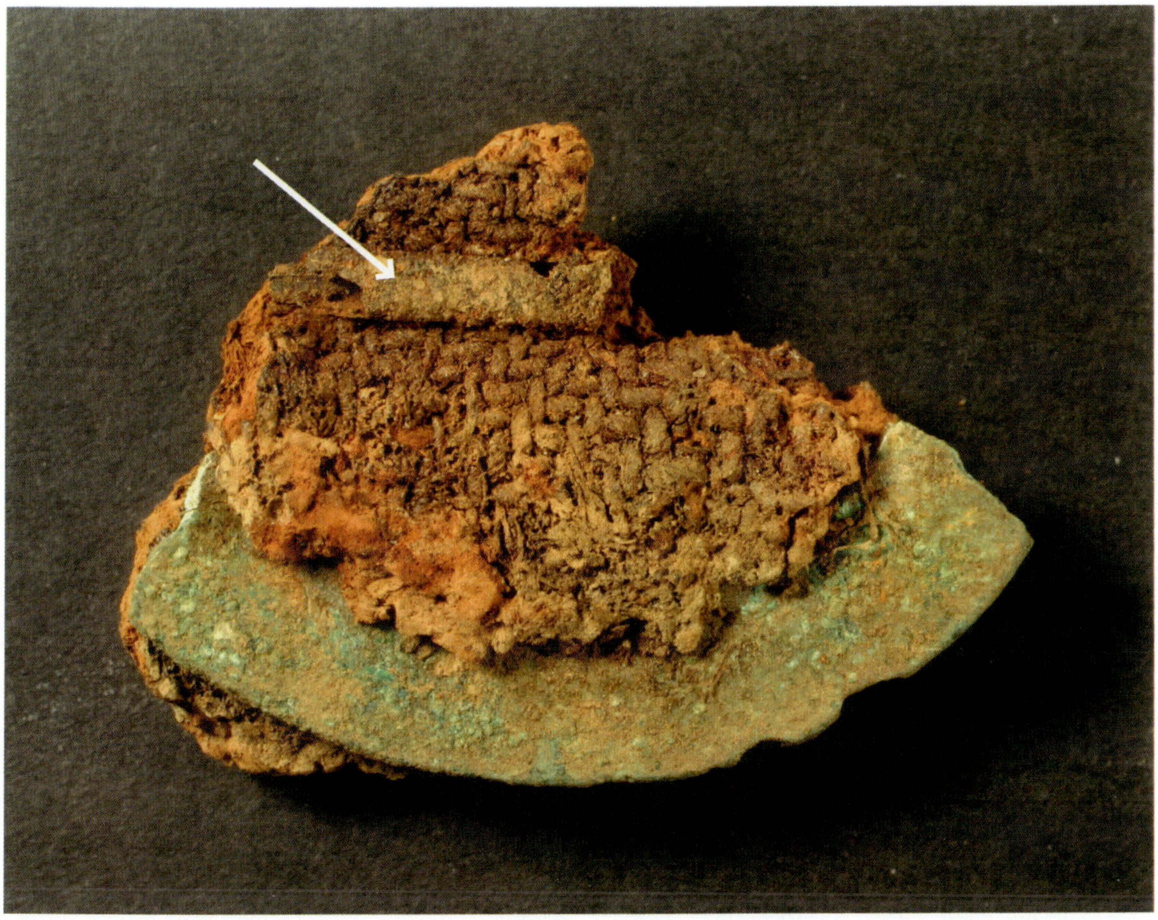

Plate 10.1 Wool twill in flat layers clasped by an annular brooch 34/2 from Grave 34. The arrow points to the iron pin. Photo Vanessa Fell, English Heritage

the peploi from Classical Greece, Viking Age Finland and perhaps also Iron Age Denmark (Walton Rogers 2007, 148–51). More unusually, in Grave 34 the brooch clasps flat layers of the fabric, which may indicate that the garment edges have been overlapped (Pl. 10.1). As well as the textiles on the shoulder brooches, on the front of sleeve clasp 17/3 there is a blue-black wool twill, 12 x 12 per cm, with a seam that is approximately vertical in relation to the body (Pl. 10.2): this may be the fabric of the peplos, preserved where the woman's wrist lay against the gown. It represents the first evidence that the peplos could have a closed side seam (Walton Rogers 2007, 152).

The dress

The peplos was a loose over-garment, usually worn on top of a closer-fitting, long-sleeved dress (Walton Rogers 2007, 154–6). A flat layer of fine wool textile pierced by the annular brooch in Grave 36 probably represents the dress fabric, since the peplos in this grave was made from a heavier material. Peplos brooches are not usually pinned to the inner dress, but it is possible that in this case the people who prepared the body for burial accidentally caught up some of the dress fabric while fastening the peplos. The pairs of metal sleeve clasps found in five graves represent cuff-fasteners on the dress sleeves, and remains of a pair of intricately patterned sleeve cuffs were recorded in Grave 17 (Fig. 10.1 left). Tablet-woven cuffs were also noted in Grave 3, where they were associated with a dress of linen 2/2 twill, 14–16 x 14–16 per cm, a fabric which appeared on a buckle and on the knife at the left waist, as well as on the sleeve clasps. Unusually, there were no peplos brooches in this grave, although there was clearly an outer garment of some sort, represented by a coarser 2/2 twill, 10–12 x 12 per cm, on the buckle and ring at the waist. This costume can be reconstructed as a long-sleeved linen dress under an outer garment of wool twill.

Belts

Buckles were found in nine female burials, only six in a position that suggested they had fastened a belt around the waist, but knotted girdles would probably be worn in the other graves (Walton Rogers 2007, 219–20). Knives, recorded in thirteen female graves, were mostly just below the level of the belt, pointing downwards, which suggests that they were suspended by the mouth end of the sheath, although Ian Riddler has observed that 'where knives occurred together with keys or latch-lifters they were set lower in the grave, aligned with the upper legs'. Only one knife, in Grave 17, lay crossways below the expected area of the waist (Fig. 10.1).

Veils, shawls and cloaks

Lightweight fabrics on the front of the peplos brooches represent the lower part of a veil, draped over the head and shoulders (Walton Rogers 2007, 157–67). There are examples from five graves, in Grave 4 a fine tabby, 16–18 x 12 per cm; in Grave 9 a fine linen tabby, 16–20 x 14 per cm; in Grave 17 a fine textile woven in tabby or 2/1 twill; in Grave 20B a linen tabby, 12 x 10 per cm, a net-like fabric made from fine yarns; and in Grave 26 a fine linen textile of uncertain weave. In Grave 20B the front edges of

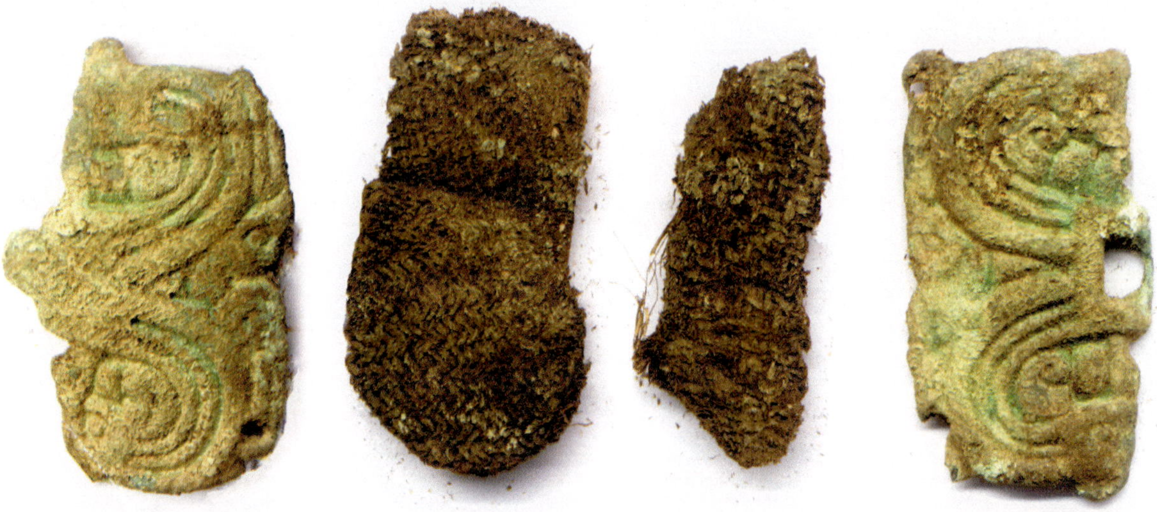

Plate 10.2 Sleeve clasps from Grave 17, 17/3, with organic layer lifted and turned over. There is a double layer of textile and a seam which runs crossways on the left-hand fragment (originally vertical on the body). The textile is a wool twill, dyed blue-black, and was probably part of the peplos. Image: The Anglo-Saxon Laboratory

the veil are represented by two patterned linen tablet-woven borders, approximately 10mm wide, which run vertically over the peplos brooches, and one of these can be picked up again in the complex of metalwork on the chest: this demonstrates that the veil in this instance reached to the mid chest at least. A vertical ribbed border was also present on the veil in Grave 9. The linen tabby veil is well attested in cemeteries of all the Anglo-Saxon regions. The front opening is not often preserved, but the Flixton borders can be compared with a patterned tablet-woven border, 9mm wide, on a fine red veil at West Heslerton G123 (Walton Rogers 1999, I, 156–7), where it ran across the woman's temple; a braided edge on a linen veil from Cleatham G24, Lincs (Coatsworth *et al.* 1996, 7, fig. 1); and gold-brocaded veil borders from women's graves in Kent (Crowfoot and Chadwick Hawkes 1967; Walton Rogers 2007, 96–7, 158). These are consistently narrow, in contrast with the wider cuff and peplos tablet bands.

There were no examples in the Flixton graves of prestige cloak-fasteners, such as florid cruciform or great square-headed brooches, but there were long pins on the chest in Graves 3 and 11 and above the shoulder in Grave 20B. The pin from Grave 11 clearly pierces several folds of poorly preserved textile, which is probably the same as the loose fragment of wool 2/2 twill, 14 x 12 per cm, which was found next to the pin, and on the front of the buckle at the waist and the front of a sleeve clasp just below the waist. It has been argued elsewhere that long pins on the upper chest were sometimes used to fasten the linen veil and sometimes a shawl or mantle draped over the head (Walton Rogers 2007, 159–61). A credible interpretation for Grave 11 therefore would be that the wool textile represents a twill shawl that covered the head, reached to the waist and was fastened on the chest by the pin. A felted fabric in Grave 20B, on the front of a brooch at the shoulder, probably also represents a cloak.

Non-standard costumes

There are three burials which do not fit the standard pattern and incorporate a single annular brooch in the region of the neck or shoulder, Grave 8, Phase FA2, Grave 13, Phase FA2/B1, and Grave 9, Phase FB1, although, as described above, Grave 13 may have been a disturbed grave. A single annular brooch on the shoulder is a fashion sometimes associated with young women, especially teenage girls, and it is thought to represent either a peplos fastened on one shoulder, or a mantle worn directly over the inner dress (Walton Rogers 2007, 152–4). Grave 8 was small enough for a young girl, but the fabric the brooch clasped was a heavy cloak-like material, possibly made from goat hair. It is therefore unclear whether this was a single-brooch peplos or an example of a girl not yet wearing an adult peplos, but buried in a cloak. In Grave 9 the annular brooch clasped several folds of two different fabrics, one a plain twill and the other soft-finished. The soft-finished was the outermost fabric and, since soft-finished textiles were mostly used for cloaks and mantles, it is possible that this represents the old Roman rectangular *pallium* fastened on the shoulder by the peplos brooch (Fig. 10.1 right). The same fashion has been recorded at West Heslerton G78 and G141, North Yorkshire, Scorton G19, North Yorkshire, and Great Chesterford G37, Essex (Walton Rogers 2007, 153–5), although in those instances there was a second brooch on the opposite shoulder, fastening the inner peplos.

Bead strings

Anglo-Saxon peplos-wearing women often wore beads in a row between the brooches, the ends of the string being anchored around the brooch pins. At Flixton, however, only the fourteen beads between the iron annular brooches in Grave 31 could have been worn this way. More commonly they have been suspended in a loop or vertical string from one of the peplos brooches, ten beads (possibly with the three bucket pendants) on the left shoulder in Grave 20B, fourteen beads on the right shoulder in Grave 26, six beads on the right shoulder in

Grave 30 and as a loop from the single annular brooches in Grave 8 (five beads) and probably Grave 9 (twenty-three) (Fig. 10.1 right). These loops would hang vertically in life, but in the burial they have often fallen to one side, which probably explains the single loop of beads and bucket pendants at right angles to the grave side in the disturbed burial Grave 27A. It is tempting to relate these to the late Roman habit of suspending strings of beads from head-dresses and brooches (Stout 2001) and to regard them as another example of Romano-British survival. A single string hanging from a peplos brooch has also been found at Wasperton, G114, Warwickshire (Carver *et al.* 2009, 259), and at Scorton G79 and G104 (Walton Rogers forthcoming b.), which are both cemeteries with a significant Romano-British component. As yet, however, no examples have been identified in the Norfolk cemeteries.

The greatest number of beads comes from Grave 51, where forty were arranged in two rows, beginning above the two annular brooches on the shoulders and dipping down through them. It is probable that there was a cord around the back of the neck which split into two, to carry the two strings at the front: the veil would cover up the back and sides and the beads would be positioned where they were most on show. This necklace has the greatest amount of amber recorded at Flixton and comes from Phase FB1.

Costume in the late burials

The burials reviewed so far represent all the graves with metal garment fasteners or decorative accessories from Phase FA2 and the early part of Phase FB. There remain a further six burials from late graves, after the peplos brooches and metal sleeve clasps had ceased to be worn, where the only costume accessories are a short pin or beads. This represents a substantial shift in fashion. From evidence collected elsewhere, it is possible to reconstruct the costume of this period as a full-length linen chemise with long sleeves, worn under a full-length sleeved wool tunic (or possibly full-length coat); a long veil reaching to the hip; a short string of beads worn around the neck; and perhaps also a lightweight shawl fastened with a short pin (Walton Rogers 2007, 180–9). The only textile preserved in the late graves at Flixton is a piece of medium-weight twill on the knife in Grave 12. There was one, short (incomplete) pin, in Grave 12, and short strings of Group B beads were found in the region of the neck in Graves 5 (nine beads), 33 (seven beads), 39 (ten beads, with a wire ring), 40 (fourteen beads) and 59 (twelve beads).

Summary and interpretation

Most of the women buried in Phase FA2 wore a peplos over a long-sleeved dress. The exceptions are the woman in Grave 3 who was buried in some form of overgarment without peplos brooches and the two bodies with single annular brooches, Graves 8 and 9, one of which was probably a child. Linen head veils are well represented amongst the adults in this group and there is also evidence for a shawl, a soft-finished cloak and a mantle fastened on the shoulder by a peplos brooch. Beads were often hung as a loop from a single brooch, which may be Romano-British, or a discrete Flixton fashion. Some peplos-wearing continued into Phase FB, but during this period the fashion fell away and was replaced by simpler clothing, which required fewer accessories.

The paired brooches with adults and one possible juvenile (Grave A at Flixton I) conforms with the evidence of the national survey, that the Germanic peplos was mostly, although not exclusively, worn by women and girls between ages that approximate to menarche and menopause, up until the 560/580 watershed (Walton Rogers 2007, 178–9, 242). The head veil on the other hand became an increasingly prominent garment during the period in question, changing from shoulder length in Phase FA1, to hip-length or longer by Phase FB/C. There is no evidence for the wearing of the veil before the late teens, and the pin-fastened shawl (which by Phase C cannot be distinguished from the long veil) seems to have been adopted at the same age. It has been argued that the veil (as seen in Graves 4, 9, 17, 20B and 26) and the pinned shawl (Graves 3, 11, 12 and 20B), might be indicative of married status (Walton Rogers 2007, 242–4). If they are, the disappearance of the peplos and the arrival of an engulfing marital veil is very telling. At a national level, this change in costume presaged a period when women outside the royal dynasties seem to have lost ground in relation to men (Walton Rogers 2007, 240–1) and it is possible to read into this kind of evidence a shift in emphasis, from women as individuals to women as wives.

V. Cultural affiliation

Fig. 10.2

Karen Høilund Nielsen has produced a contour map, based on statistical analysis, which illustrates the geographical distribution of the main costume accessory groups of Early Anglo-Saxon England (Høilund Nielsen 1997, 88–9). If her 1.0 contours are taken as marking out the edges of the core 'Anglian' (annular and cruciform brooches and sleeve clasps) and core 'Saxon' (disc and saucer brooches) groups, then Flixton lies inside the 'Anglian' group (Fig. 10.2). This confirms the evidence of the Flixton metalwork, which finds most parallels in the cemeteries to the north. In the rest of Suffolk and in Cambridgeshire, 'Anglian' accessories still predominate, but other brooch types occur, and in Essex 'Saxon' artefacts are equally common.

Flixton also shares with the Norfolk cemeteries evidence for the survival of Romano-British textile techniques (Fig. 10.2). As the map shows, there is a second group at Mucking, Essex, but this is limited to the two Mucking cemeteries, and, although there are 510 records of textiles from seventeen sites in the rest of Suffolk and Essex, there are only three examples of Romano-British techniques, at Snape G5, Ipswich Boss Hall G97 and Bury St Edmunds Westgarth Gardens G13 (database online, ADS 2007). The major cluster in Norfolk therefore seems to be a single discrete group, to which Flixton can now be added. Whatever the cause of this pattern – the survival of the Romano-British population, the intermarriage of immigrant men with local women, or the subjugation of Romano-British women with weaving skills – by the second half of the 5th century, the classic Anglo-Saxon costume had become established as standard wear, although the old textile techniques were still being used in its production in the 6th century.

In his study of the Barrington cemeteries, John Hines (Malim and Hines 1998, 313–7) identified four standard sets of costume accessories, Groups A, B, C and D (see also Høilund Nielsen 1997, 87). Group A, a 'Saxon' set,

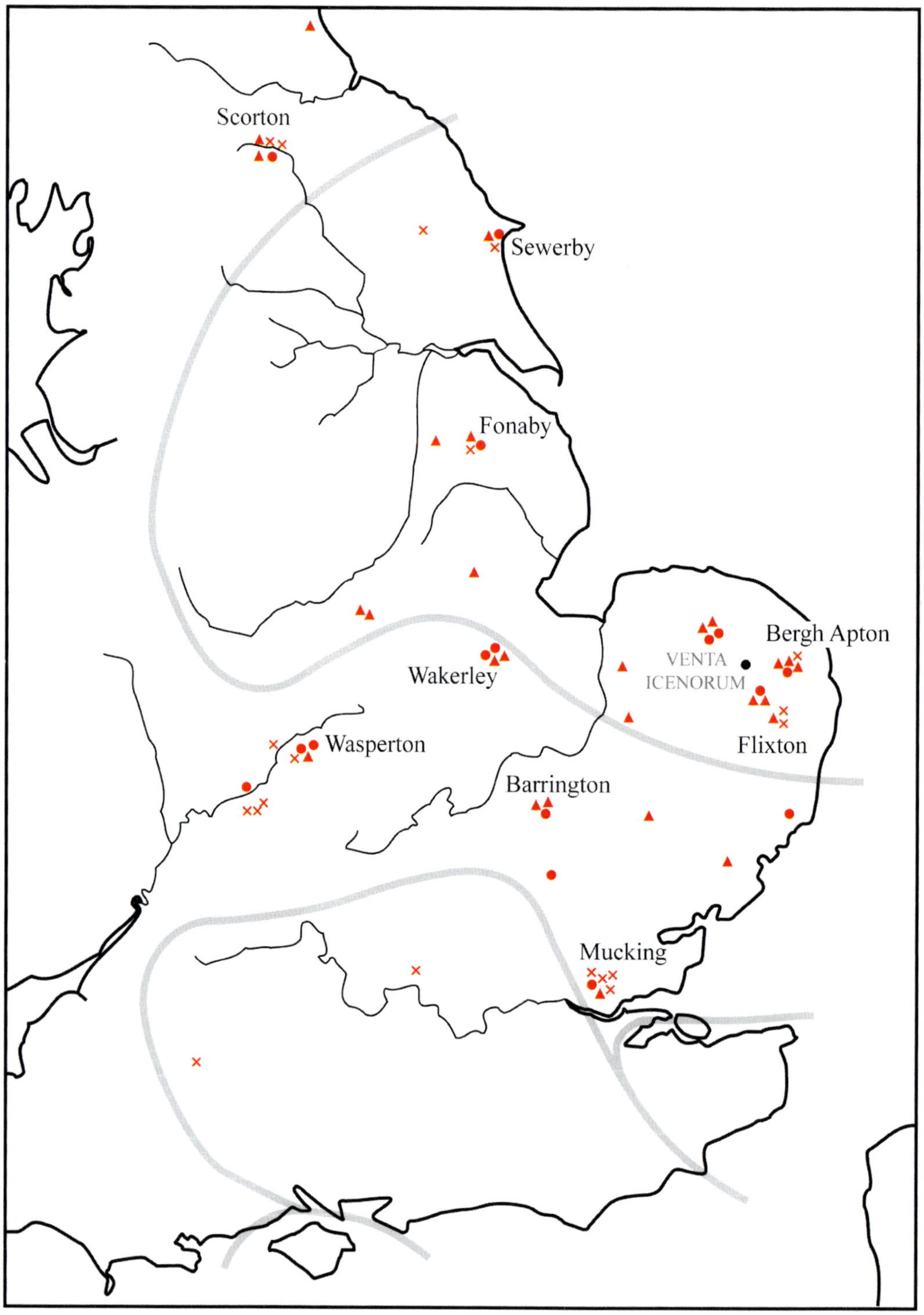

Figure 10.2 The distribution of Romano-British textile techniques. Triangle = 2/1 twill; circle = tubular selvedge; x = soft-finished. The grey lines represent the 1.0 contours in Karen Høilund Nielsen's trend surface map of Anglo-Saxon metalwork (Høilund Nielsen 1997, 88–9). The Anglo Saxon Laboratory

and Group C, a predominantly Cambridgeshire combination, are absent from Flixton. There is one burial, Grave 4, which can be ascribed to Group B, the 'classic Anglian' set, based on its B2 cruciform brooches, although it lacks any of the usual supplementary artefacts, such as the long copper-alloy pin and B17 sleeve clasps. Most of the Flixton adult women's burials can be placed in Group D, because of their annular brooches, supported by *B7b* sleeve clasps in Grave 30 and a long iron pin in Graves 11 and 20. The trefoil-headed brooches in Grave A (Flixton I) and 27A are also considered part of the Group D repertoire, although in 27A the trefoil-headed brooch was combined with a brooch with hooked lappets of Cambridgeshire type. Even without Grave 27A, fourteen of the Flixton women's burials can be attributed to Group D. Group D is regarded as typical of late Anglian graves, although in its earliest phase it overlaps with the other groups and at Flixton there are Group D graves in Phases FA2a to FB1 (*c.*480–*c.*560/80). A subtle change takes place somewhere in the middle of the 6th century. In the EAC study, sleeve clasps were shown to disappear towards the end of phase FA2, while paired annular peplos brooches remained in use in Phase FB1 (Penn and Brugmann 2007, 58, 99), and the same is true at Flixton

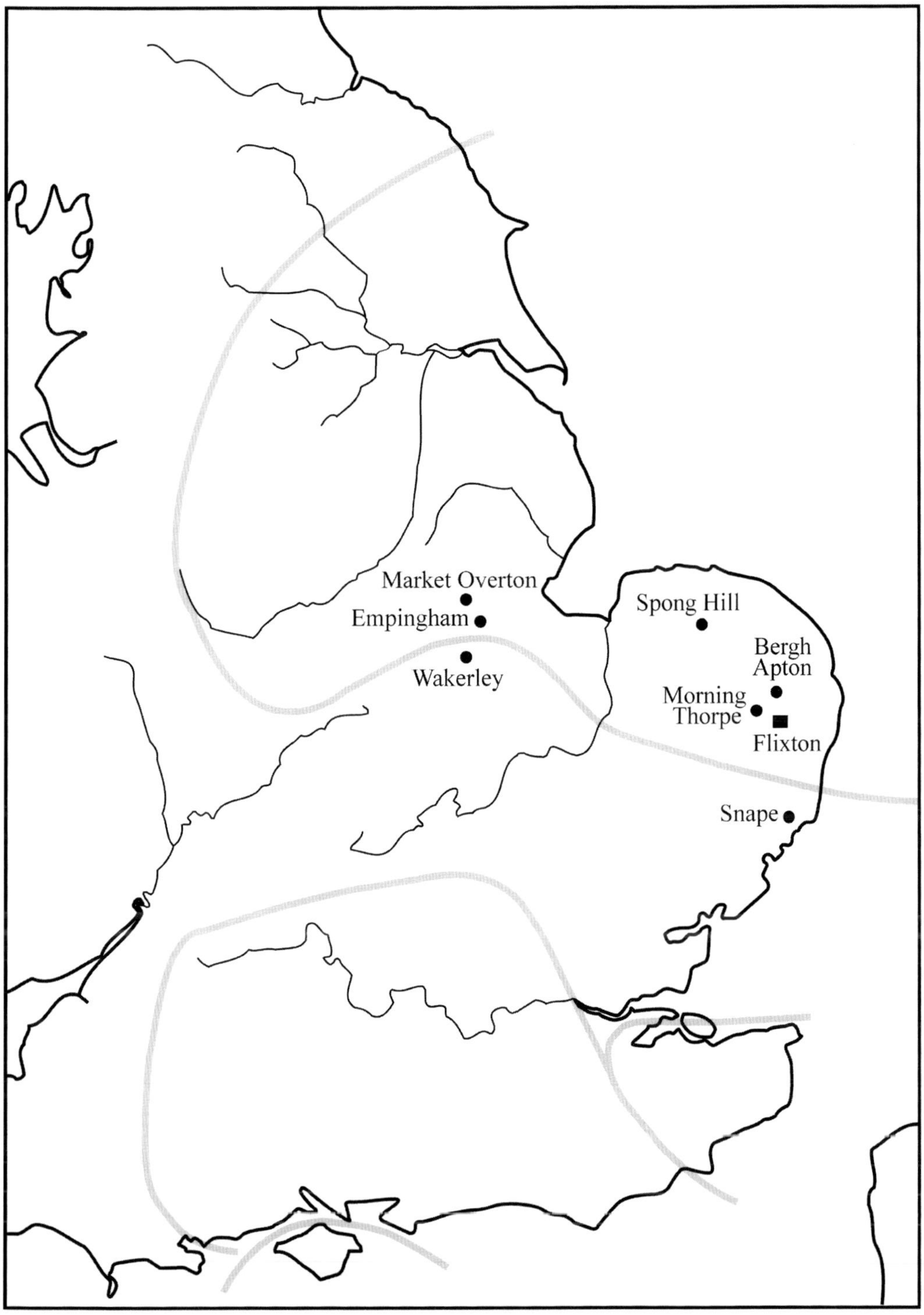

Figure 10.3 The sites in the vicinity of Empingham in relation to Flixton and the Norfolk sites. The Anglo-Saxon Laboratory

(Table 10.2). This may mark a change in the styling of the sleeves, although a decline in the availability of copper alloy is likely to have been the cause (Penn and Brugmann 2007, 91).

There remains the conundrum of Grave 3, the burial with no peplos brooches, which has the long copper-alloy pin and toilet accessory of Group B, combined with B13b clasps of Group C (discussed further below). Apart from this, only six relatively late graves, Graves 5 (Phase FB), 12 (FA2/B), 33 (FB), 39 (FB2), 40 (FB) and 59 (FB2), fall outside the Hines costume-accessory groups. They come from a period when regional variation is less in evidence (Walton Rogers 2007, 184–7).

VI. Evidence for exogamy

Fig. 10.3

Although most of the Flixton women's accessories are typical of East Anglia, or more precisely Norfolk, diffused through the graves are some artefacts which bear comparison with cemeteries much further away, on the Gwash and Welland river system, and especially Empingham II, Rutland (Fig. 10.3). They are the spangle-headed pin with faceted head in Grave 3; the buckle with cut-down back-plate in Grave 26; the segmented annular brooches in Grave 21; the annular brooches with the

	Morning Thorpe *365 graves*	*Bergh Apton* *63 graves*	*Spong Hill* *57 graves*	*Flixton II* *62 graves*
Great square-headed and florid cruciform brooches	*G16*, G214, G288, *G353*, G359, G371	G7, G18	*G2*, *G18*, G24, G57	-
Cruciform brooches of Type D and other 'third fasteners'	*G30*, G80, *G90*, *G91*, G96, G129, G133, G153, G160, G208, G209, G253, G358, G370, G396, G397	G6	*G22*, G38, G39, G45, G58	-
Cast sleeve clasps with Style I ornament	G153, *G353*, G360	-	-	G17
40 or more beads	G16, G30, *G90*, G108G, G108N/O, G253, G309, G322, G337, G342, *G353*, G358P–V, G360, G362, G393, G400, G407	G7, G18, G29, G34, G35, G65	*G5*, *G22*, G24, *G26*, G38, G39	G51

Table 10.3 Valuable female-gender costume accessories from three Norfolk cemeteries, compared with those from Flixton II. Grave numbers in italics indicate burials of Phase FA1

pin-through-lap construction in Graves 34 and 51; and the trio of strap-ends with a stamped line of circles in Grave 9. The lunulate neck-ring in a child's grave, Grave 22, can possibly be added to the list, and the sleeve clasps broadly attributed to the East Midlands from Grave 17 might also belong with the group. Individually, each of these could be dismissed: several of the objects belong to small type groups and a few new finds from East Anglia would change the emphasis of the distribution plot, while the technical features could be a coincidental local development. Together, however, they are not so easy to ignore.

The burials with Empingham-style objects occur in Phases FA2a to FB1 and the material is spread through several female graves. There are no individual female burials which have a full suite of Midlands-style objects, such as openwork disc brooches or square-headed small-long brooches, and there are no comparable artefacts in the male graves (although male-gender objects are less easy to attribute to a specific region). A scenario which might fit the evidence would be one where, early in the community's life, a high-status woman from the Empingham region came to Flixton, perhaps with her maidservants, and while living there she distributed some of her property to her adopted family, some of whom kept the objects for a generation, before they were buried. This is not entirely far-fetched, since among the Germanic peoples diplomatic marriage alliances were not uncommon (Fell 1984, 37, 74; Straume 1995), and gift-giving was one of the social roles of a high-born woman (Fell 1984, 35–6). If such a woman existed, she must have been buried in one of the unexcavated graves, perhaps at Flixton I, but the woman in the coffin in Grave 3 (Phase FA2a) might conceivably represent one of her entourage (see below).

VII. Wealth of the community

Women's accessories are often regarded as indicators of a community's wealth (Ravn 2003, 135), although this is a difficult matter to quantify. When the excavated part of the Flixton cemetery is analysed by the system of counting the number of artefact types in each grave (NAT scores), with the modification for male-gender artefacts introduced by Penn and Brugmann (2007, 89–90), the results at first seem comparable with the Norfolk cemeteries. The average for Flixton I and II is 2.7, which is similar to the 2.8 of Morning Thorpe (*ibid.*). These two cemeteries both include a low-scoring late component, and their averages are therefore below those of Bergh Apton, 3.6, and Spong Hill, 3.7. When compared phase by phase, the Flixton male and female graves rise and fall in parallel with the other cemeteries, and, in common with most large Anglo-Saxon cemeteries, the greatest numbers of artefacts and artefact types are recorded for Phase FA2 (Penn and Brugmann 2007, 90–1).

When the most valuable accessories are counted, however, a different picture emerges. In Table 10.3, those female-gender artefacts that are likely to have had some extra value attached to them have been listed by grave and site. They include the ornate great square-headed and florid cruciform brooches which were used as cloak fasteners; other large brooches worn centrally in addition to a pair of peplos brooches (classified as 'third fasteners'); and bead strings with forty or more beads. Cast sleeve clasps with Style I ornament have been included in the table because of their presence at Flixton, although, as an East Midlands–Cambridgeshire artefact type, they are comparatively rare in East Anglia. The Norfolk graves in the table include nine dated to Phase FA1, but otherwise their date-range is comparable with that of Flixton. This different method of quantifying wealth puts Flixton II well below the Norfolk group in Phase FA2. The sleeve clasps from Grave 17 represent a single exception, although they are very worn and repaired. The number of repaired items and objects used in their broken state, although not without parallels in Norfolk (*e.g.* Hills *et al.* 1984, 6–7), is particularly noticeable in this group.

In Phase FB only one female burial, a poorly furnished example, Grave 33, appears in the northern group, and the emphasis shifts to the central and southern half of the main cemetery. In the southern group, Grave 51 is particularly well furnished within the context of its phase (FB1), with forty beads, a pouch, latch-lifter, key, buckled belt, ring and peplos brooches. There were only four Norfolk graves from Phases FB where there were forty or more beads and none of these had more than fifty: Bergh Apton G18, Morning Thorpe G322, G342 and G400. The artefact evidence for Flixton therefore matches the grave sizes, which put the excavated burials below the national and regional average in the early phases, but equal to other sites in Phase FB.

VIII. Individual women and their place in the cemeteries

Fig. 10.4

The evidence has revealed a number of adult women, modestly dressed in a peplos, long-sleeved dress and head-veil or shawl, without any valuable cloak-fastening brooches or long strings of beads (Tables 10.2 and 10.3). Seven had head veils or pins on the chest, which it has been argued represent married status. The iron keys and latch-lifters in Graves 11, 20A, 26, 31, 51 (of which 11, 20A and 26 are included in the married group) may also indicate a woman with some form of economic control over the household (Meaney 1981, 178–81; Fell 1984, 59–60). In Stoodley's survey (1999a, 111), objects such as these were less common in the over-forty age group, and Graves 26 and 51 were indeed the burials of young adults, although the bone was too poorly preserved to allow age to be identified in the others.

When ranked by the number of accessories, the graves with the highest NAT scores are Graves 3 (FA2a), Grave 11 (FA2) and Grave 51 (FB1). In Grave 3, the woman had been buried in a coffin, which adds to the impression of status. She had no peplos brooches on the shoulders, although the textile evidence indicated that she had been dressed in an inner and outer gown (Table 10.5). On her chest she wore the Wakerley-style pin and her B13b sleeve clasps would be more at home in costume accessories Group C, in the Edix Hill study regarded as a Cambridgeshire group. At her hip was the mysterious object with a copper-alloy hooped handle. The age of this woman could not be established from the bones, but since the peplos was mostly worn in the child-bearing years, it is possible that she was elderly (Walton Rogers 2007, 178–9, 242). If that is the case, in her youth she could have been one of the earliest members of the Flixton community.

The position of this grave towards the middle of the main plot suggests a different cluster from the burials in the northernmost area (Fig. 10.4) Since none of the women in the centre of the northern group can lay claim to any great status and none stands out as a founder grave, it is possible that the largest grave of the middle group, the disturbed burial Grave 4, Phase FA1/2a, should be seen as the founder grave of a female group, and equivalent to the two early male burials at the centre of the northern graves, Grave 23 and 28, and that both clusters relate to the same household. The graves arranged around Grave 4 are almost all female (Graves 3 (FA2a), 9 (FB), 5 (FB), 13 (FA2/B1), 39 (FB2), 40 (FB2), 12 (FA2/B)), genderless without artefacts (Grave 10), or probable males without weaponry (Graves 6, 7 and 14 (no phase)). Only on the south-west corner of this group are there two males with spears, one possibly young, to judge from his flexed posture, Grave 2 (MA2/B), and the other a young adult Grave 41 (MB). If it is correct to see this group as the female core of the main household, then the woman in well furnished Grave 11 becomes an outlier between the two groups, and Grave 51, perhaps an outlier to the south. It is possible, therefore, that the whole of the north-west quadrant of Flixton II represents one household with two cores, one male and the other female, both with children and mixed-sex retinues.

One of the graves in the female group, Grave 40 (Phase FB2), was buried with a short string of beads and a spindle-and-whorl. Most women of this period would be spinners (Walton Rogers 2007, 9–10, 46), but perhaps this one had some special skill in the craft, or it may have been her favourite pastime. Spinning skills would be passed down the female line and this person, buried with a Romano-British whorl, at a site where Romano-British textile crafts have survived, may have traced her ancestry back to a native British woman.

The single female burial at Flixton I was placed at the foot of a barrow in a relatively large grave, with a prestigious glass claw beaker and a hemispherical ceramic bowl, in Phase FA2a. Her costume is represented by only a pair of small-long peplos brooches, but she was probably a juvenile and it can be suggested that she was a young girl from an important family who had not yet reached the age of acquiring more significant garment fasteners. The pierced Roman coins, I/NG5-6, found nearby imply the presence of at least one other female burial, and the ceramics and the metal buckle, I/NG4, confirm a 6th-century date. This burial plot is therefore contemporary with the early phases of Flixton II.

IX. 'Cunning women'

The women of this period would have had different, overlapping social roles and it can be argued that some of the women in the Flixton cemetery carried out the function of a shaman or 'cunning woman'. Audrey Meaney has pointed out that artefacts such as keys and girdle-hangers, may have acquired a symbolic form, but their original purpose was essentially practical (Meaney 1981, 247). This contrasts with other objects which, from her study of their burial position and associated items, and research of written sources, she concluded had a magical or amuletic use (Meaney 1981, 24–7). A hypothesis can now be presented, that strap-end trios, such as those from Graves 9 and 20, belong with Meaney's 'amulet bags' and that, like bucket pendants, they are an archaeological marker for a 'cunning woman' or wise woman (Meaney 1981, 249–62).

Strap-end trios

As Table 10.4 shows, strap-end trios have been found in the burials of women aged up to 35 years who were moderately well dressed, but who lacked the prestıge cloak brooches that would indicate the upper rank of society. These women were often buried with amuletic or talismanic objects, including bucket pendants, scutiform pendant(s), a walnut amulet in a metal frame and an antler ring imitating the female amulets of Roman Britain and Gaul (Greep 1994; Walton Rogers 2007, 26). The small metal collar in Empingham G40 also resembles the mounts seen on animal claw and tooth pendants, such as the beaver-tooth pendant from West Heslerton G113 (Haughton and Powlesland 1999, I, 115–6). The Roman finger ring and strange zoomorphic mount, incorporated into a necklace in Morning Thorpe G384 (Green *et al.* 1987, I, 149–50, II, 342), would fall into the category of amuletic objects (Meaney 1981, 222–7) and the position of the ring at the neck can be compared with the plain cast rings and metal discs encountered at the neck in other graves with amulets (such as West Heslerton G113 and G167). The women with strap-end trios also seem to be linked by burial practice: in the nine graves where layout was clear, they lay on their sides (right or left) with legs

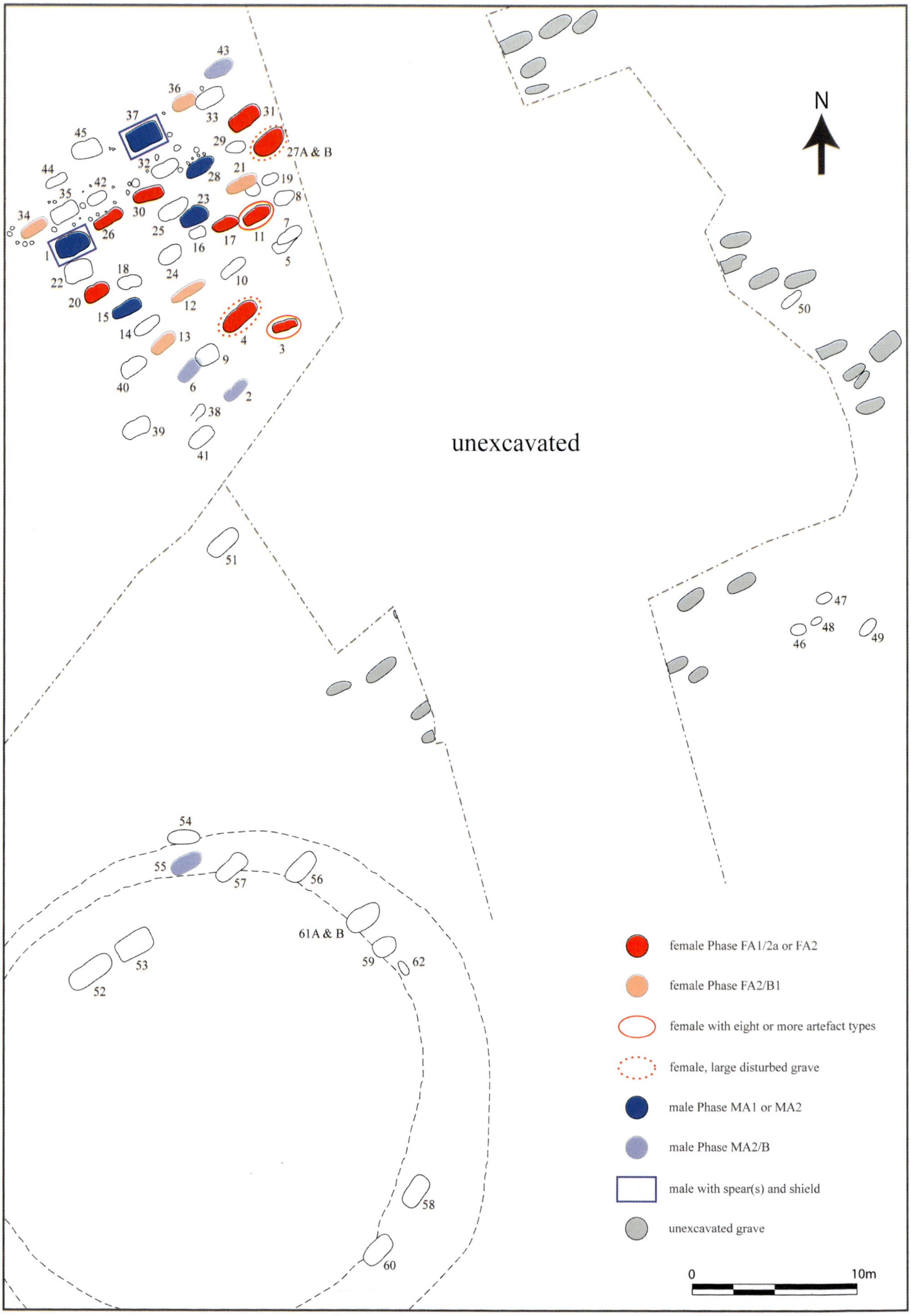

Figure 10.4 The distribution of female and male burials at Flixton II in phases FA2–FB1 and MA1–MA2/B

Site	*Grave*	*Age*	*Peplos brooches*	*Sleeve clasps*	*Third fastener*	*Beads*	*Pendants and amulets*	*Other artefacts (not including ceramics)*	*Position in burial*
West Heslerton, N.Yorks	G132 (2BA768)	15–20 yrs	pair annular			x56	walnut amulet & iron disc pendant	latch-lifter, cu/a ring, cu/a vessel rim, buckle	left thigh
	G139	25–35 yrs	pair annular			x23	scutiform pendant	latch-lifter, girdle-hanger, ivory bag ring	left thigh
	G152	Adult	pair annular	B13a and B20, B7b		x1	bucket pendants x7	latch-lifter, girdle-hanger, ivory bag ring	by knees
	G167	Adult	pair annular		pin type VIII	x123 (A2)	bucket pendants x12	latch-lifter, ivory bag ring, cu/a ring, buckle, knife	right waist
Norton-on-Tees, Cleveland	G35	25–35 yrs	pair annular	B18c	pin fragment	x12	bucket pendants x9	latch-lifter, iron ring, pouch fitting, buckle, knife	by thigh
Morning Thorpe, Norfolk	G253	Young adult	pair annular	B7b, B12	cruciform D	x45 (A2)		key/latch-lifter, girdle-hanger, buckle	left waist
Bergh Apton, Norfolk	G29	?	pair annular			x58 (A2)		latch-lifter, girdle-hanger, cu/a rings, buckles, plate buckle, fire-steel	by ?thigh
	G34	?	pair annular		pin type VIII	x186 (A2)	bucket pendants x9	latch-lifter, buckle, fragment glass vessel, iron chain, knife	by ?knees
	G42	?	pair annular	?B7b	pin type VIII	x38		latch-lifter, iron rod with cu/a handle, wooden vessel	by ?feet
Empingham II, Rutland	G40	25–35 yrs	pair annular	B13b		x44		latch-lifter, girdle-hanger, cu/a collar, ivory bag ring, iron ring, wire ring, lace-tag, buckle, non-matching strap end	left waist
	G98B	?	pair annular	B7b		x27 (A2)	antler ring	girdle-hanger, keys, ivory bag ring, iron rings, two buckles, plate buckle, metal pouch fittings, knife	?
Edix Hill, Cambs	G19B	35 yrs	pair openwork	B7b & B13		x74	bucket pendant x1, silvered disc pendant	iron & cu/a rings, buckles	?

Compiled from data in Haughton and Powlesland 1999, II, Empingham, Edix Hill, Bergh Apton, Morning Thorpe, Norton refs and Brugmann 2004, table 11, West Heslerton G132, 139, 152, 167, N.Yorks, Norton-on-Tees G35, Cleveland, Morning Thorpe G253, Norfolk, Bergh Apton G29, G34, G42, Norfolk, Empingham G40, G98B, Rutland, (Haughton and Powlesland 1999, II, 223–95, Sherlock and Welch 1992, 143–7, Green *et al.* 1987, II, 282–3, Green and Rogerson 1978, 24–32, 66–9, 73–4, Timby 1996, 107–8, 122–3, 187–8, 225).

Table 10.4 Burials with trios of strap-ends and their associated artefacts

flexed, except for West Heslerton G132 where the woman was prone, but still with legs bent backwards.

The position of the strap-end trios, often with clusters of other objects at the waist, hip or thigh, suggests that they relate to a bag or pouch. Ivory bag rings and the rectangular plate buckles regarded as the fasteners for flat purses (Marzinzik 2003, 45, 413–4, Type II.17) have been found with them, but, since strap-end trios are unlikely to form a fastener on the type of bag that has a ring mouth, it is probable that the strap-ends (and plate buckles) represent a secondary pouch. In the grave of a 'cunning woman' at Bidford-on-Avon two pouches were present, one on the chest, seemingly fastened by drawstrings with aglets (tubular tags) and the other at the hip (Dickinson 1993, 45, 50). At Flixton, the strap-end trio, 9/3, in Grave 9, lay immediately below a metal pouch fitting, 9/6, riveted to a piece of animal skin at the left waist. In this grave there was only evidence for one pouch, but in Grave 20, body B, there were two complexes, a pouch fitting, 20B/4, a buckle, 20B/5, and single strap-end, 20B/6, on the chest and a strap-end trio, 20B/3, below an iron latch-lifter and ring at the thigh (if the body had flexed legs: otherwise, they belong with body A). In both graves there was a buckle with the plate turned back and tongue pointing out, which suggests that the strap, unlike a belt worn round the waist, was not under tension when it was buried. In a third grave, Grave 51, there was a pair of strap-ends below a complex that included fine animal skin, a buckle, cast copper-alloy ring, key and latch-lifter, and it can be argued that this is a pouch from which the third strap-end has been lost. The exact appearance of these pouches is unknown, although a flat purse with fold-down flap has been suggested (Walton Rogers 2007, 223–4), or a bag with a drawstring mouth (Crowfoot *et al.* 2005, fig. 1), or it is possible that the strap-ends were decorative and comparable with the row of vertical tags sometimes seen on Merovingian belts (Marzinzik 2003, 310).

Bucket pendants

Bucket pendants have a long history in Europe and it is generally accepted that they had some ideological significance (Meaney 1981, 166–8; Hines 1984, 13–342; Dickinson 1993, 51–2). They have been recorded in only twenty or so Anglo-Saxon graves (Dickinson 1993, 51), so that their appearance in five of the thirteen burials with strap-end trios must be regarded as significant (Table 10.4). At Flixton there were three bucket pendants in the same grave as a strap-end trio, Grave 20, but the burial with seven bucket pendants, Grave 27A, had been disturbed by a second, male, burial, so that the full range of costume accessories has probably been lost. In Grave 27A the pendants seem to have been stitched to leather or skin by means of a cord or thong and there are other burials where they were mounted on a leather bib or pouch (Dickinson 1993, 51). Bucket pendants often contain white material (those from Grave 20B had been stuffed with flax fibre), although its significance is unknown. It has been suggested that bucket pendants symbolised the female role of dispensing ale, or the ritual use of alcohol, or that they were containers for charms (Dickinson 1993, 52). At any rate, they seem to indicate that the wearer had the special knowledge associated with 'cunning women' (Dickinson 1993, 53).

Ferrules

There are further indications of the significance of these burials. In the Bidford grave, at the woman's left hip, there was a hollow antler cone with two perforations which would have allowed it to be pinned to a shaft (Dickinson 1993, 48, 52). Although unique at the time, it can now be compared with the iron ferrule mounted on an ash shaft, 9/1, at the waist or hip of the woman in Grave 9. When ferrules were mounted on spear shafts, it was so that the spear could be fixed in the ground. That being the case, it may be relevant that an 8th-century Continental manuscript states that to 'fix coloured rods in the earth by digging' in order to expel demons was a pagan practice (Meaney 1981, 12). Some metal rings, such as those in Graves 26 and 51 may also have had a use in pagan medicine (Meaney 1981, 12–13, 174).

Amber

According to written sources, amber was believed to have protective and curative properties (Meaney 1981, 70–1, 245). The wearing of amber beads was widespread and it is unlikely that in themselves they indicate any particular social role, but, even so, it is significant that most of the graves with strap-end trios have substantial numbers of amber beads at the neck and that the two graves with the greatest number of amber beads at Flixton are two of the graves already reviewed in this section, Graves 9 (thirteen amber beads) and 51 (thirty-three amber beads).

Interpretation

None of the burials at Flixton had the number of amuletic objects seen in the Bidford grave, and yet certain graves contained accessories that are likely to have been associated with the role of cunning woman. These are Grave 20B (Phase FA2), where there was a pouch with a strap-end trio, a second pouch on the chest and two, or possibly three, bucket pendants; Grave 9 (Phase FB1) with a strap-end trio, a ferrule on an ash staff and thirteen amber beads (Fig. 10.1 Right); and Grave 51 (Phase FB1) with a strap-end pair at the hip, a pouch on the chest, a cast metal ring and thirty-three amber beads. The disturbed grave with bucket pendants, 27A (Phase FA1/A2a), may represent an early member of the group.

The Germanic 'cunning woman' was someone who practised a mixture of beneficent magic, prophecy and healing (Meaney 1981, 253–62; Fell 1984, 31–4; Griffiths 2006, 109–14). Her stock-in-trade would include herbs and ointments which would leave little archaeological evidence (Meaney 1981, 255), as well as the more robust amulets. Special pouches or 'medicine bundles' containing herbs, roots and small objects with magical significance are one of the universal accessories of the shaman (Griffiths 2006, 112–4; Aldhouse-Green and Aldhouse-Green 2005, 34–5). Helen Geake has suggested that women of this kind may also have been the organisers of the funeral, and comparable with the 'angel of death' and her daughters recorded by Ibn Fadlan in the 10th century (Geake 2003, 264–5). The role of 'cunning woman' may well have been hereditary (Meaney 1981, 262), although it need not have been full-time nor would it exclude other social roles. The Flixton burials would allow for approximately one 'cunning woman' per generation, stretching from the foundation of the cemetery to the later 6th century.

Body and burial	*Layout*	*Fibre*	*Weave*	*Count/Spin*	*Position of Textile*	*Interpretation*
Grave 3 Unsexed adult bone poor Coffin stain Phase FA2a	Head probably resting against end of coffin. Beads, toilet accessory 3/6 and crossways pin 3/5 in region of neck: beads in two groups, 11 glass left (3/11) and 9 glass and amber right (3/12). Sleeve clasps 3/8-9 in region of lower chest. Sleeve clasps 3/8–9 in region of lower chest. Knife 3/1, buckle 3/2, ring 3/4 and handle/finial 3/3 in region of left waist. Pot 3/10 to left of ?head	flax/hemp	2/2 twill	14-16/Z x 14-16/Z	On front of buckle 3/2 at left waist; on knife 3/1 nearby and in fold on ring 3/4 next to knife.	There are at least two, possibly three textiles of similar quality, woven in 2/2 twill. The finest twill is likely to be the fabric of a long-sleeved dress with tablet-woven cuffs. The wool twill is probably the fabric of an outer garment. The complex of objects at the left waist includes a suspension ring tied to the knife (or a textile enclosing the knife), by means of a stitched tablet-woven band. From the orientation of the buckle tongue, it is unlikely that the buckle was attached to a strap.
		not ident.	2/2 twill	16/Z x 16/Z	On back and front of sleeve clasp 3/8, with tablet weave.	
		not ident.	tablet, 3 cords SSS	?/Z2S x ?	In association with finer twill and sleeve clasp 3/8	
		wool (SEM)	2/2 twill	14/Z x 14/Z	Flat against ring 3/4, and on front of buckle 3/2.	
		not ident.	tablet, twill- and repp-effect ZSZSZS	12-16 cords/Z x ?	Two lengths of tablet-woven band bind ring 3/4 to crossways object, probably knife 3/1.	
		not ident.	Z2S	D. 1.0-1.25mm	Stitching on tablet band on 3/4	
Grave 4 No bone Possible organic container	Face-down brooch 4/2 and a matching brooch II/NG1, unstratified, suggest grave was disturbed. Buckle 4/7 was next to cruciform brooch 4/2 and near to knife 4/1 Finger ring 4/5 middle of grave.	wool	2/2 twill	8/Z x 8/Z	On front of small buckle 4/7	The coarser wool twill is of blanket quality. The fine tabby on the front of the brooch is likely to represent a head veil extending over a brooch on the shoulder.
		wool	2/2 twill	10/Z x 9/Z	On one face of buckle fragment 4/4	
		not ident.	tabby	16-18/Z x 12/?Z	On front of cruciform brooch 4/2	
		flax/hemp	cords	cabled Z-S-Z	On cruciform brooch 4/2, binding pin support to brooch	
		probably flax	cords or textile	?	On back of cruciform brooch 4/8 at pin hinge	
Grave 8 No bone. Size, 1.35m long, suggests juvenile Phase FA2	Annular brooch 8/1 with 5 amber and glass beads 8/4 towards one end of grave, in middle. Ceramic bowl 8/3 at side of grave.	?goat hair	twill, ?2/2	12/Z x 10/Z	On back of brooch 8/1, curling on to front, probably pinned by it.	This person may have been wearing a goat-hair cloak fastened by the annular brooch. The linen tabby seems poor quality for a veil and may have been a grave cover.
		low-grade flax	tabby	10/Z x 10/Z	On front of brooch 8/1	
Grave 9 Teeth only. Probably a flexed adult (from arrangement of artefacts) Phase FB1	Annular brooch 9/5 and 23 amber and glass beads 9/7 close to teeth, in region of neck and shoulder. If body flexed, there was a ferrule 9/1, knife 9/2 and pouch fitting 9/6 at the left waist and a trio of strap-ends 9/3 in the region of the thighs. A small buckle 9/4 in the region of the front waist, had a plate folded back on the loop.	wool	2/2 twill	12/Z x 10/S	Pinned by annular brooch 9/5.	Two garments pinned by the single annular brooch at the neck/shoulder: probably a wool twill peplos and a soft-finished (napped) mantle. The front edge of a head-veil of linen tabby runs over the front of the brooch. It possibly reaches to the waist. The function of the fine linen 2/1 twill with the strap-ends and pouch fitting is unknown.
		wool (SEM)	?	?	Soft-finished textile pinned by annular brooch 9/5.	
		flax/hemp, prob.flax	tabby	16-20/Z x 14/Z	On front of annular brooch 9/5, curling on to back. Probably also on outer face of pouch fitting 9/6.	
		flax/hemp, prob.flax	tabby repp	20/Z x 10/Z	On front of annular brooch 9/5. Probably border on plain tabby.	
		flax/hemp	2/1 twill	16-18/Z x 14-16/Z	In association with pouch fitting 9/6, and on strap-ends 9/3.	

Grave 11 Adult (jaw and teeth) Probably extended (from arrangement of artefacts) Phase FA2	Pair of annular brooches 11/5 and 11/9 in region of shoulders. Pin 11/11 on diagonal between brooches. Iron buckle 11/12 in region of waist. Sleeve clasps 11/4 below waist. Sleeve clasp 11/1 i-iii lower down grave, probably displaced. Finger ring 11/6 on chest. Knife 11/3 and latch-lifter 11/2 i-ii outside left thigh. Ceramic pot 11/14 above head and wooden cup by cheek.	not ident.	2/2 twill	16/Z x 16/?	On front and back of annular brooch 11/9 and in flat layer on long pin 11/11.	A peplos with a wool tablet-woven border fastened by the annular brooches on the shoulder. The main fabric of this garment may be the finer twill (16 x 16). The long pin fastens folds of an outer garment, possibly the medium-weight twill (12 x 12) found with the pin, and on the front of the sleeve clasps and buckle: a cloak/shawl reaching from shoulder to hip. The coarsest twill at edge of grave probably a blanket grave-lining.
		wool	tablet, ZSZS	?	Tablet band on front of annular brooch 11/5 and probably pierced by pin.	
		flax/hemp	?stitching	Z2S, D.0.4mm	Paired threads on 11/5, probably stitching.	
		kempy wool	2/2 twill	12-14/Z x 12/Z	On front of sleeve clasp 11/4, on front of buckle 11/12, and in folds in association with long pin 11/11	
		not ident.	2/2 twill	10/Z x 9/Z	On end of key/latch-lifter 11/2	
		not ident.	tabby	Z x Z	In association with clasp 11/4.	
		flax	?	?	Probably same as tabby, under 2/2 twill on front of clasp 11/4	
		not ident.	?	?	In folds pierced by pin.11/11.	
Grave 12 No bones. Grave size adult. Phase FA2/B	Cu/a pin 12/1 in region of chest. Knife 12/2 in region of waist. Whole pot 12/3 below waist.	not ident.	twill, ?2/2	14/? x 14/?	On spine of knife 12/2	
Grave 13 Young–middle aged Phase FA2/B1	Annular brooch 13/1 and remains of two pots 13/2 to left of shoulder and centre of grave, possibly disturbed.	wool	?	?	On front of annular brooch 13/1	
		flax/hemp	?	?	On front of annular brooch 13/1	
Grave 14 Male, ?middle-aged no phase	Buckle 14/2 in region of right waist. Knife 14/2 central and vertical.	not ident.	2/2 twill	9/Z x 8/Z	On knife 14/2, outside sheath.	The coarse quality of the twill suggests a blanket or cloak.
Grave 15 Male, middle aged	Shield and its fittings, 15/1, 15/3-8, placed over head. Buckle 15/2 probably from shield strap. Knife 15/9 i in region of waist.	not ident.	?	fine	On shield grip extension 15/5; leather on opposite face.	
		leather	strap	13-15mm wide	Binding shield grip 15/1 ii.	

Grave 17 Adult male skull at side of grave No bones with metalwork Phase FA2	Probably one body with female accessories (B); and separate male skull from an earlier burial (A). Two fragmentary annular brooches, 17/4 i–iii, in region of neck. Two sets of sleeve clasps in region of waist, 17/2–3. Knife 17/1 by thigh.	not ident.	tabby or 2/1 twill	?/Z x ?/Z (fine)	On front of annular brooch 17/4 in folds along pin, and detached.	Probably a peplos fastened by the pair of annular brooches, worn on top of a long-sleeved dress with patterned tablet-woven cuffs. The blue-black wool twill may be from a fold of the peplos which has fallen on to the wrist: the seam would run approximately vertically down the body. The folds of fine textile on the front of the annular brooch are typical of the head veil where it touches the shoulder brooches. Sedge/grasses on top of the burial.
		wool dyed blue-black	2/2 twill	12/Z x 12/Z	Dyed with woad and tannins on white wool. On front of sleeve clasps 17/2 and 17/3. Seam on front of 17/3.	
		wool and flax/hemp in warp, wool only in weft	tablet, 4-hole, patterned	16 warp cords/Z2S x ground and brocading weft, both 14-16/Z2S	On back of sleeve clasps 17/2 and 17/3 and lapping on to front of 17/2. Cuffs 28mm wide with corded borders twisted [selvedge] SZSZ?? on one side and SSZSZS [?selvedge] on other. Patterned zone includes colour effects introduced by linen yarn, areas of twill-effect weave and brocading.	
		wool	Z2S	sewing thread	Stitches on tablet weave and passing through attachment holes of clasps 17/2 and 17/3	
Grave 20 Artefacts and stains suggest two bodies, A and B. Phase A2	A. Beads 20A/11 probably mark the neck/shoulder region.	**Body A or B** 2/2 twill	not ident.	14/Z x 12/Z	On ring 20/2 and strap-ends 20/3	**Body A or B** Garment of medium-weight twill.
	B. Pair of annular brooches 20B/7 and 20B/10 , at the shoulders, a pin 20B/9 vertical beside the head. Beads 20B/12 by left shoulder. Complex of buckle and fittings 20B/4-6 in region of chest.	**Body B** 2/2 twill	wool	11–12/Z x 9–10/Z	On buckle plate of 20B/5, strap end 20B/6 and cu/a fitting 20B/4 i, in region of chest. Weaving gore on 20B/5.	**Body B** The peplos fastened by the annular brooches on the shoulders has tablet-woven borders at least 30mm wide. A long linen tabby veil, with vertical borders of patterned 2-hole tablet weaving, runs over annular brooches on shoulders and over buckle on chest. A cloak of wool twill, probably soft-finished, worn on top of other garments.
Bones of B: young adult ?female	A or B. Ring 20/2, latch-lifter 20/1and strap-ends 20/3 the waist/hip.	tablet, 2-hole, ZSZS patterned	not ident.	12 cords/Z2S x 8–10 weft/?	On front of annular brooches 20B/7 and 20B/10 at shoulders, where vertical; and, detached, with buckle 20B/5 on chest.	
		tablet, 4-hole, ZSZS	flax/hemp and ?wool	8 cords/Z2S x ?	Pierced by pins of both annular brooches 20B/7 and 20B/10; probably two bands on 20B/7.	
		tabby	flax/hemp	12/Z x 10/?	On front of annular brooch 20B/7 and in vertical folds on front of annular brooch 20B/10.	
		2/2 twill	not ident.	12/Z x 12/Z	Felted in places, outermost fabric on front of annular brooch 20/10. Possibly same as wool twill on front of buckle.	

Grave 21 No bones Phase FA2/B1	Pair of segmented annular brooches, 21/2–3, in region of shoulders. A single amber bead 21/6 between the brooches. Iron rings 21/1 and 21/4 in region of knee and thigh respectively.	wool, non-pigmented wool, non-pigmented	2/2 twill warp-faced band or border	16/Z x 16/Z Z x Z	On back of brooch 21/3. Folded edge pierced by pin of brooch 21/2. Either a woven border or an attached band along the edge of the 2/2 twill. On 21/2 the border at the hinge end has been folded down. On 21/3 the border at the pin-tip end has not been folded.	Peplos of fine wool twill with plain warp-faced upper border. At the front the border has been folded down, but not at the back.
Grave 22 A. Young Adult B. Child, 11-12 years Phase FA2	Body A. No artefacts. Body B. Lunula 22B/1 in region of neck, knife 22B/2 at waist.	not ident. not ident.	? ?	Z x ?, coarse Z x ?, fine	On lunula 22B/1 at neck. On lunula 22B/1 at neck.	Body A: no evidence. Body B: two different garments, one fine, one coarse.
Grave 23 Young-middle aged Phase MA1	Buckle 23/3 with knife 23/2 in region of waist. Spear 23/1 on left.	not ident.	tabby	14/Z x 14/Z	In horizontal folds on front of buckle 23/3	Tabby represents an outer garment, possibly a tunic over belted trousers. It is too fine for a cloak.
Grave 26 Young adult Probably supine Phase FA2	Pair of annular brooches 26/1-2 in region of neck/shoulders. Buckle 26/4, knife 26/7, latch-lifter 26/6 and wire suspension ring 26/5 in region of hip. 14 beads 26/9 to right of annular brooch 26/2.	wool not ident. flax/hemp	2/2 twill ? ?	14/Z x 12-14/Z 12/Z x 12/Z ?/Z x ?/Z, fine	Two folded edges clasped by both annular brooches, 26/1-2 On knife 26/7 in region of hip In vertical fold on front of annular brooch 26/2 at right neck.	Peplos of wool twill with folded upper edges clasped by annular brooches on the shoulders. Fine linen head veil reaching on to shoulders. Beads suspended in loop from right-hand brooch.
Grave 27 Burial A: disturbed, no bones Phase FA1/2a Burial B: bones poor. Grave size = ?adult Phase MB	Burial A: A pair of displaced small-long brooches, 27A/2-3, a knife 27/1, bucket pendants 27/4 and 11 glass and amber beads 27/5. Burial B: Shield 27/7 on upper chest with buckle 27/9, spear 27/6 left head, knife 27/8 at waist.	flax/hemp flax/hemp	2/2 twill ?	14-16/Z x 12-14/Z ?	On front of head and bow of small-long brooch 27A/3 of Burial A.	Burial A: probably a peplos fastened by small-long brooches and a string of beads and pendants on chest. A shawl or veil of linen twill. Burial B: no costume evidence.
Grave 30 Young ?female Position of sleeve clasps suggest body probably turned to left side. Phase FA2	Pair of small annular brooches 30/3-4 on shoulders. Sleeve clasps 30/1-2 in region of left chest and waist. 6 glass beads 30/7 on right side of right brooch.	not ident.	tablet	?	Tablet weave looped over pin of annular brooch 30/3	Peplos with a tablet-woven border fastened by pair of small annular brooches. Over sleeved dress. Beads to right of neck, either as necklace or placed separately in grave.
Grave 31 No bone. Size suggests adult extended Coffin or bier Phase FA2	Pair of iron annular brooches 31/1-2 in region of shoulders, associated with a pin 31/3 from a third brooch and 14 amber and glass beads 31/8 strung between brooches. Buckle 31/7 at centre waist. Knife 31/4, ring 31/5 and latch-lifter 31/6 at left hip.	not ident. not ident. not ident.	tablet tabby repp tabby	Z2S x Z2S 12/Z x 8/Z 16/Z x 16/Z	On back of brooch 31/2, across pin. On one face of latch-lifter and ring 31/5-6 On front of small buckle 31/7	Peplos with tablet-woven upper border. Tabby repp may represent a cummerbund (see text). Function of fine tabby on front of buckle at upper waist unclear: perhaps a long veil.

Grave 32 Middle aged male Extended. Grave marker no phase	Knife and buckle 32/1-2 to left of body.	goat hair or coarse wool	twill, possibly pile weave	*c*.9 x 9 per cm	On back of buckle at left waist. Coarse textile with a thick lock of fibre anchored in the weave suggests a pile weave. Pile faces towards buckle.	It is possible that a buckled belt and knife were placed at the side of the body, and the body was resting on a piled rug.
Grave 34 No bone. Grave size = adult Phase FA2b/B1	Pair of annular brooches 34/1-2, slewed to side of neck.	wool	2/2 twill	14/Z x 12/Z	On back of both annular brooches, 34/1-2, on 34/2 a flat layer pierced twice by brooch pin.	Peplos of wool twill. A cloak or cover of slightly finer wool twill.
	Small suspension ring 34/3 centre chest.	wool	2/2 twill	14/Z x 14/Z	On front of brooch 34/2 in loose folds and on ring 34/3 centre chest. Seems to be different from other twill	
Grave 36 Young adult female Phase FA2/B1	Body prone. Pair of annular brooches 36/1-2, face down at shoulders. Buckle 36/4 at centre waist.	?wool	2/2 twill	14/Z x 12/Z	Two folds, one at either end of the pin of brooch 36/2, both pierced by pin. Also on front buckle 36/4 at waist	Peplos of ?wool twill, which may have been worn over another, belted, garment. The finer textile pinned on the right shoulder may be part of the inner dress accidentally caught when fastening the peplos.
	Knife 36/3 at left hip if body face down.	?wool	?	?/Z x ?/Z, fine	Pinned by annular brooch 36/1 at right shoulder. Finer than other textile.	
Grave 37 Skull fragments only Possibly a chamber grave Phase MA2	Spear ferrule 37/7 relates to spearhead 37/6.	not ident.	twill	7/Z x 7/Z	Curled around tip of spear ferrule 37/7 towards foot of grave.	Textile on ferrule is of blanket quality (or perhaps a wrapper).
	Shield with knife 37/11 to right of body. Buckle 37/8 with shield fittings 37/2-5 and 37/10.	wool	2/2 twill	10/Z x 9/Z	On shield grip 37/10, side facing downwards. To right of body.	The textile on the shield grip may be from a grave lining. The buckle with the shield fittings probably represented a carrying strap.
Grave 41 ?Young adult male Phase MB	Spear 41/1 on left side. Knives 41/2-3 region of left waist.	not ident.	?	Z x ?, medium	On and with knives 41/2-3	
Grave 43 Adult ?male Phase MA2/B	Spear 43/1 on left side. Buckle 43/2 left waist.	?wool	?	Z x Z, medium	On back of buckle 43/2 at right waist, and on one head of clench nail/rivet 43/3	
Grave 51 Young adult Phase FB1	Pair annular brooches at shoulders, 51/1–2.	flax/hemp	2/2 twill	14/Z x 12/Z	Pinned by both annular brooches, 51/1-2	Peplos of linen twill pinned by pair of annular brooches. Strengthened upper border.
	Double string of 40 beads around neck 51/10. Buckle 51/3 at waist. Girdle group 51/5-9 at lower thigh and knee.	flax/hemp	2/2 twill	20-24/Z x 12-14/Z	On both annular brooches, looping round pin: almost certainly the border on other linen twill	Wool garment may be a cloak or shawl.
		?wool	2/2 twill	12/Z x 10/Z	On front of annular brooch 51/1. Possibly also on latch-lifter 51/6 at knee.	

Grave 52 Little bone Grave size = adult Phase MB	Spearhead 52/1 probably to right of head. Shield 52/2-3, 5 over waist area. Knife 52/4 at left waist.	wool not ident. not ident. ?hemp	coverlet weave tabby 2/2 twill tabby repp	8/Z+S x 7/Z+S 8/? x 8/? 8-10/ Z x 8-10/S 10/Z x 16/Z	On socket of spearhead 52/1 On upper face of shield boss rim 52/2 Touching shield grip 52/3 but not binding it. On knife blade 52/4 at waist	Coverlet lining grave. Coarse tabby on shield boss is probably a blanket. ZS twill is probably tunic or cloak. Tabby repp may be cummerbund.
Grave 56 Young-mid aged male Phase MC	Spearhead 56/1 to left of head and shoulder. Knife 56/2 at left waist. Buckle 56/3 under head.	not ident.	twill, ?2/2	10/Z x 8/Z	On socket of spearhead 56/1	
Grave 57 Young-mid aged adult no phase	Buckle 57/1 in region of waist	not ident.	?	Z x S, medium	On buckle 57/1 at waist.	
Grave 61 Two bodies A. middle-aged ?female B. 16–18 year old male Phase FB	A. Knife 61A/2 and buckle 61A/1 at waist B. Knife 61B/4 and buckle 61B/3 at waist and fire-steel 61B/5 on right upper waist.	not ident. ?wool	?tabby ?2/2 twill	? 12/Z x 10/?	On knife 61A/2, body A. On front of buckle 61B/3, body B.	

TEXTILES
Fibres were mostly identified with a transmitted-light (optical) microscope fitted with a polarising analyser
[SEM] indicates that the identification has been by scanning electron microscopy (micrographs prepared by Vanessa Fell, English Heritage).
'Counts' are the numbers of threads per cm
Z and S indicate the lie of the fibres in a yarn, when the yarn is held vertically: Z = / and S = \
Z2S indicates a two-ply yarn or cord, twisted in the S direction from two Z-spun yarns
For weaves see Fig. 7.11

COSTUME
The clothing has been described as if the person were alive and standing upright.
'Left' and 'right' indicate the body's left and right.
'Above' and 'below', mean worn higher or lower on the body.
'Inside' and 'outside' mean as worn, 'inside' being closer to the body.
The terms for living body parts – head, neck, breast, arm, waist, hip – replace strict osteological terms, except where they cause ambiguity

Table 10.5 Textiles and their use in costume in the Anglo-Saxon cemetery at Flixton II, Suffolk

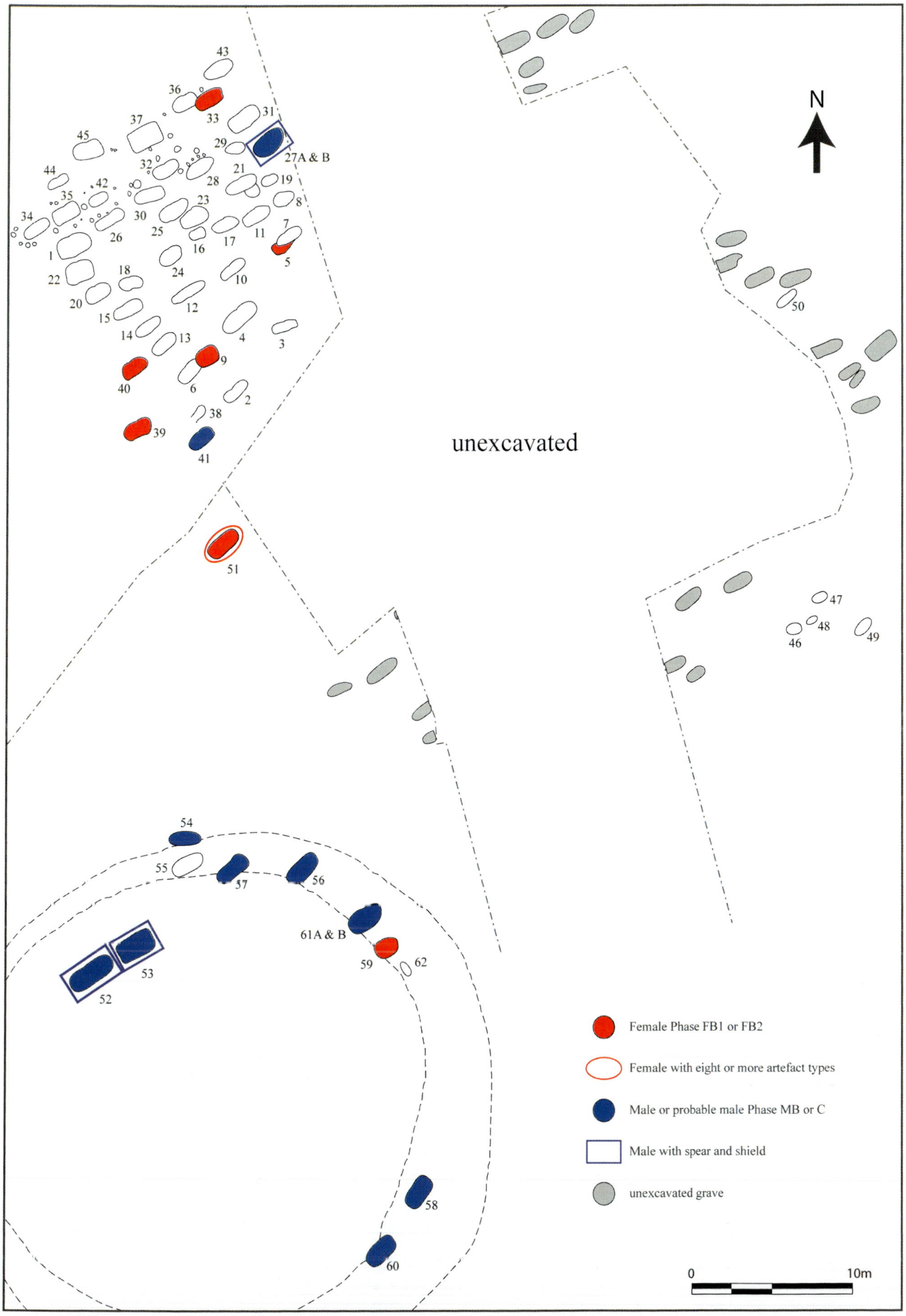

Figure 11.1 The distribution of female and male burials at Flixton II in phases MA2/B–MC and FB1–FB2

Chapter 11. Reconstructing the Flixton Men

by Ian Riddler and Penelope Walton Rogers

I. Introduction

The Early Anglo-Saxon male is best addressed through his weaponry and other aspects of the burial ritual, rather than his costume, for which the evidence is limited. Weapons do not necessarily signify that a man had warrior status, but their types and sizes have proved to form meaningful patterns in relation to age at death and wealth scores, and it is therefore inferred that, whether they were symbolic or functional, weapons are indicators of a man's rank and social role (Härke 1992a, 150–6; 1997, 143–6).

II. The Flixton men

Eighteen adults and one teenager (Grave 61B) have been identified as male through a combination of biological sex and gender-indicating artefacts (Chapter 8). If the male skull at the side of the female-gender occupant of Grave 17 is removed, the number of male adults is reduced to seventeen. A further five adults buried with a knife and/or buckle can probably be added to the list, for the following reasons. Of the eight adult bodies with only a knife and/or a buckle, two were certainly male by sex and one was probably so (Table 11.1). The five datable graves in this group are from late phases, MB and MB/C, and all the examples without identifiable sex come from graves that fall within the size range for males in later phases, with lengths of 1.92 m to 2.27 m (Table 10.1). In Stoodley's survey, knives and buckles were weak male indicators overall, but they became more closely associated with men in the later 6th and 7th centuries (Stoodley 1999a, 30–1, 34, 35, 39, 41), and in the context of the 7th- to early 8th-century cemetery at Harford Farm, Norfolk, bodies with a knife and buckle were interpreted as 'unweaponed' males (Penn 2000, 55–6). Strong correlations of knife-and-buckle graves with males have come also from the Kent cemeteries of Saltwood and Dover Buckland (Riddler forthcoming). The evidence therefore points to the knife/buckle graves at Flixton being male and to most of them being late (only one undated knife-and-buckle burial, Grave 32, male from the osteology, lies in the early part of the cemetery). The following survey is therefore based on revised figures of twenty-two adult males and one male teenager (Table 11.1).

Grave	*Phase*	*Male Sex*	*Age (grave size)*	*Spear*	*Shield*	*Knife*	*Buckle*
23	MA1		young-mid	♦		♦	♦
28	MA1	♦	young-mid	♦		♦	
1	MA2		young-mid	♦♦	♦	♦	
15	MA2	♦	middle		♦	♦	♦
37	MA2		(adult)	♦♦	♦	♦	♦
2	MA2/B		young adult	♦		♦	
6	MA2/B		(small adult)	♦			
7	MA2/B	◊	young-mid	(♦)			♦
43	MA2/B	◊	adult	♦			♦
55	MA2/B		young adult	♦		♦	♦
27B	MB		(adult)	♦	♦	♦	♦
41	MB	♦	?young adult	♦		♦♦	
52	MB		(adult)	♦	♦	♦	
53	MB		adult	♦	♦	♦	♦
61A	FB/MB	(F?)	middle-aged			♦	♦
61B	MB	♦	16-18 years			♦	♦
58	MB/C		adult				♦
54	B/C		(adult)			♦	♦
60	B/C		(adult)			♦	
56	MC	♦	young-mid	♦		♦	♦
14	-	♦	middle-aged			♦	♦
32	-	♦	middle-aged			♦	♦
57	-		young-mid?				♦

♦ = male sex ◊ = possible male; (♦) possible spear shaft

Table 11.1 Male burials at Flixton II

III. Burial practice

Fig. 11.1

The men were buried in, on average, larger, deeper graves than the women, and the disparity between the two grew with time (Table 10.1). This pattern of increasing differentiation between the sexes is a national one and corroborates other evidence for a shift in the balance of power between men and women in the late 6th and 7th centuries (Stoodley 1999a, 72, 104, 118, 141; Walton Rogers 2007, 240–1). There were few differences in terms of grave construction and marking, but this was probably because most of the noteworthy features appeared in early phases. One man was buried in a small chamber grave (Grave 37 in Phase MA2), five were on biers or mats (Graves 23 and 28 in MA1, Grave 27B in MB, and Graves 6 and 14 undated) and three were in graves with associated post-holes (Grave 28 in MA1, Grave 37 in MA2 and Grave 32 undated), which is roughly comparable with the range of practice seen in the women's burials. The predominant posture for men was supine and extended, as it was for the women, but there was an occasional exception, such as the young adult in Grave 2, who had been placed on his right side with legs slightly flexed.

In the early phases, men's graves were intermingled with those of women and children, probably in a household plot (Fig. 10.4). By phases MB and C, however, men were ranged on and around the barrow to the south. Of the eleven graves there, eight held males and one was a double burial including at least one male, Grave 61 (Fig. 11.1; Table 11.1). The remaining two were a female-gender burial, Grave 59 (although tentatively identified as male from the osteology), and one small grave with no skeleton or grave goods, assumed to represent a child (Grave 62). Only two late male graves have been recorded in the main part of the cemetery, one a young adult in a relatively small grave (Grave 41 Phase MB) and the other inserted into the grave of a female (27B Phase MB). Women, in contrast, continued to be buried in the main plot in Phase FB, on the outskirts of the earlier group.

A similar trend has been observed in Wessex, where there are two types of 7th-century burial ground, one made up of mixed sexes arranged in rows and the other of predominantly male graves focused on a barrow (Stoodley 1999b). The nearest parallel in East Anglia is the cemetery at Harford Farm, which was arranged in two plots, one a compact, relatively orderly, mixed-sex group and the other an irregular cluster on and around a ring barrow and dominated by knife-and-buckle burials (with a single female-gender grave) (Penn 2000, fig. 5, 43–5, 68–9). This trend for groups of males to become dissociated from the family cemeteries is thought to coincide with the breakdown of earlier social systems, as the power of the kin group gave way to a male elite (Stoodley 1999b, 104–5). The new elite would still have blood ties, however, and there is some evidence in the morphology of the teeth that the bodies in Graves 55 and 59 were related (Chapter 8).

IV. Burial with weaponry

Figs 11.2–11.4

Weaponry was recovered from 15 of the 23 graves identified as male (Table 11.1). Only spears and shields are represented, and there are no examples of the arrows sometimes found in children's graves, or of the swords, seaxes and axes that indicate especially high status (Härke 1992a, 156–9; 1997, 145) (Fig. 11.2). The weaponed burials occur in Phases MA1, MA2 and MB. Heinrich Härke has argued that those buried with weapons in the 5th and 6th centuries were men who were claiming the status of Germanic descent, but that in the 7th century weapons became limited to a smaller group and lost their ethnic affiliation (Härke 1992a, 155, 164). Phase MB straddles the latter part of the 6th century and the first half of the 7th, but it is likely that the relatively few weaponed burials in Phases MB and MB/C reflect this change in emphasis.

There was a single spear in twelve graves and two spears in two, Graves 1 and 37 (Chapter 7). They were found in all phases of the site, from MA1 to C (Table 11.1), but the two-spear burials were both from Phase MA2, which is the period when the deposition of weapons reached a peak in East Anglia and nationally (Penn and Brugmann 2007, 90–6). The spearheads are mostly of

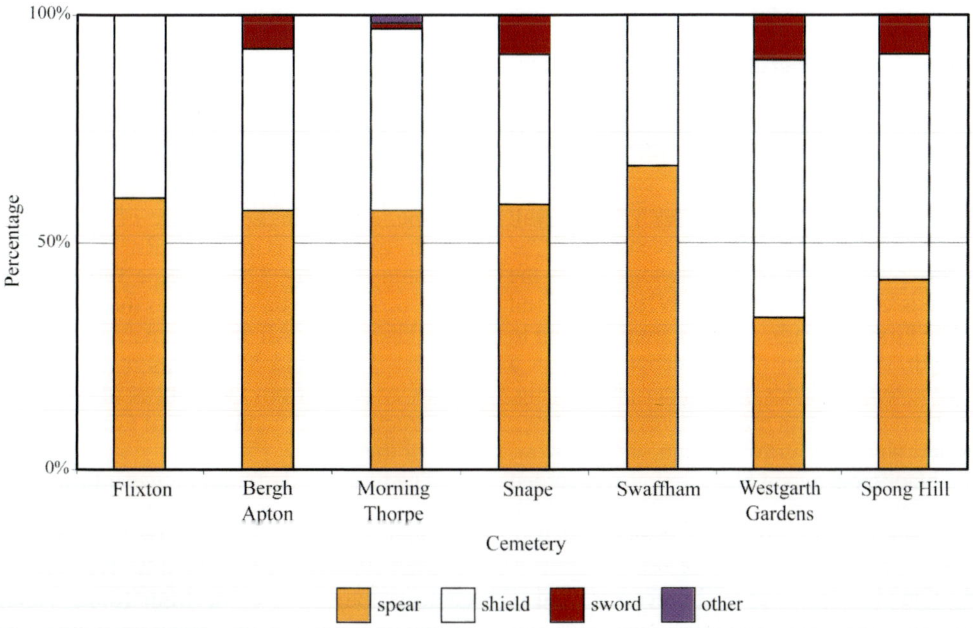

Figure 11.2 Weapon combinations in seven East Anglian cemeteries

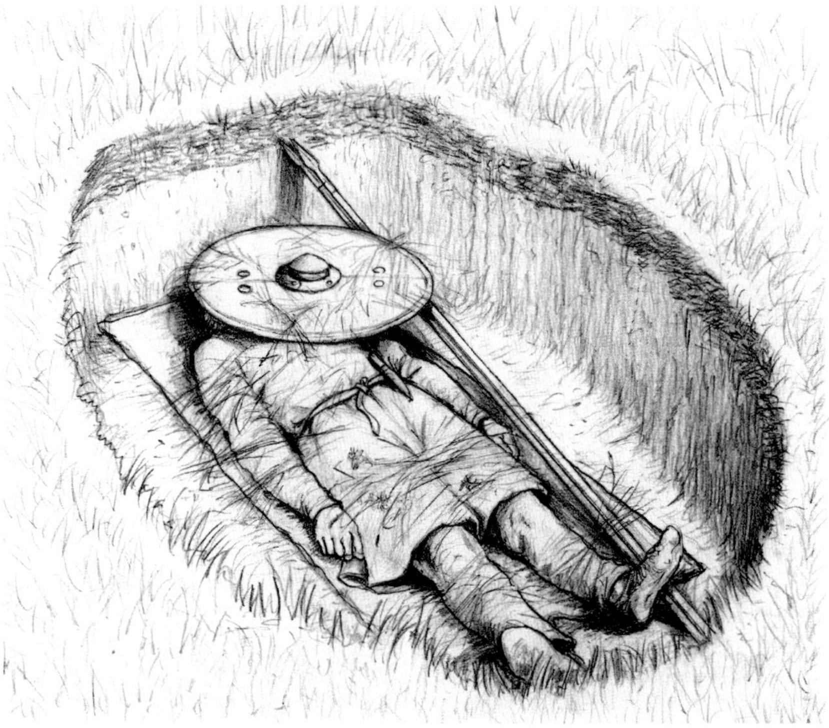

Figure 11.3 Reconstruction of Grave 1, Phase MA2. Anthony Barton, copyright The Anglo-Saxon Laboratory

Swanton's Types E1, E2, E3, H1 and H3, which are commonly found in East Anglia, but two graves had types more often seen in Kent, Type C2, of which there are two examples from Grave 1(Phase MA2) and Type D3 from Grave 55 (Phase MA2/B) (Table 7.6). They were mainly hafted with ash, but there were also examples of hazel, alder and willow/poplar (Table 7.7), and the use of mature timber suggested that some at least had been intended for throwing. One of the spears from Grave 37 had an iron ferrule at the butt end, but the spearhead lay beneath a shield and the orientation of the ferrule suggested that the spear shaft had been broken. Two spearheads (Graves 2 and 6) had lost their blades and this reflects the fact that they were generally found at a high level in the grave, and often towards its outer edge. In a number of cases they were angled so that the tip was higher than the socket and, in one grave (Grave 23), the spearhead reached beyond the edge of the grave. These can be interpreted as long spears placed on the slant in the grave (Fig. 11.3). In life, they must have reached well above the head, although it is impossible to calculate the exact length from the burial evidence.

Härke has noted a correlation between the overall length of a spear and the age of the deceased, but he records that this relationship is less obvious when the spearhead alone is considered (Härke 1992b, 187–8 and abbn 37–8). The Flixton spearheads vary from 204mm to 515mm in length. A diagram of their lengths shows a tendency towards longer blades in the later phases (Fig. 7.17), as was also the case with men's knives (see below). All four of the late weaponed graves on or near the barrow, produced long blades, but a long blade was also recorded in the chamber grave, Grave 37, Phase MA2, which suggests that length was connected with status as well as date.

The shields found in six graves can be reconstructed as the typical circular form with iron boss, hand-grip and studs, fitted on to wooden boards of ash and willow/poplar in Phase MA2 and lime/maple and alder in Phase MB (see Shields, Chapter 7). The minimum diameter, estimated from the distance between the centre of the boss and the outer studs or mounts is consistently 400mm (Fell and Watson 2007, 8), which is inside the average size of 600mm noted by Härke (in Dickinson and Härke 1993, 45). The boards were covered with thin leather on the front and thicker leather on the back. There were decorative mounts on the front of four shields and silver-plating on the flange rivets of one (Grave 15). At least one shield had a carrying strap and Jacqui Watson has suggested that it was attached to the rim with a buckle on one side, and that it might be looped around the hand-grip when it was placed in the burial (Fig. 11.4).

The presence of a small number of spearheads and shields of types seen more commonly in Kent than East Anglia suggests that there may have been links between males in the two areas. Type C2 and D3 spearheads have been found elsewhere in East Anglia, if only in small numbers. There are single examples of type C2 spearheads from cemeteries at Barrington A, Bergh Apton and Snape, as many as five examples from Morning Thorpe, and a single example of a D3 spearhead from Bergh Apton G41 (Green and Rogerson 1978, 31, fig. 87; Swanton 1973, fig. 22). The type 3b(ii) shield from Grave 37 also represents a form seen more commonly in Kent than elsewhere. All three graves with Kentish objects (Graves 1, 37 and 55) represent relatively high status males, to judge from the number of artefacts, grave size, construction, and, in the case of Grave 55, position at the foot of the barrow.

The likelihood of links between East Anglia and Kent has been established for some time, and was outlined by Plunkett in the context of the Hadleigh Road cemetery at Ipswich (Plunkett 1994, 35–45). The initial impetus for contacts may have come from Kent, which retained a virtual monopoly on the exchange of goods with northern France during the 6th century (Evison 1979; Huggett

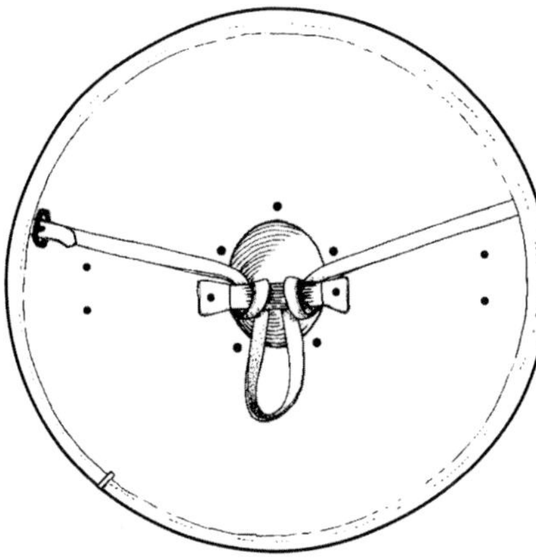

Figure 11.4 A reconstruction of how the leather carrying strap might have been attached to the shield from Grave 15 and how it might have been looped around through the hand-grip when it was placed in the grave.
Jacqui Watson, English Heritage

1988). Over time, however, contacts may have extended in both directions. The recent discovery of ceramics of 6th- to 7th-century date of East Anglian provenance at Springhead in Kent has been linked to a route through the Ipswich area and the Deben estuary (L. Mepham, pers. comm.). Even before the foundation of Ipswich as a settlement, that area may have performed an important role as a gateway into the heart of East Anglia. The evidence from Flixton suggests that these goods were only reaching the senior males in the community.

V. Position of weapons in graves

The spearheads all pointed towards the head of the grave and they were mostly on the left side of the body. In Grave 37, one spear was on the left and the seemingly broken spear with a ferrule was on the right. The only clear examples of spears on the right are the two large burials placed in a prominent position on the barrow in Phase MB, Graves 52 and 53. At a national level, spearheads are found more often on the right of the deceased than the left, although the ratio in East Anglia is roughly 1:1 (Härke 1992b, 126). In some cemeteries the earlier graves have spearheads on the right of the body and the later graves have them on the left (Härke 1992b, 126); but at Flixton the reverse appears to be the case. The high proportion of graves with spearheads on the left has parallels at Bergh Apton, Little Eriswell and Westgarth Gardens (Härke 1988, 13), and at Morning Thorpe, where 62% of the graves had spearheads on that side of the body. It can be argued, therefore, that the local preference – seen at Bergh Apton, Flixton and Morning Thorpe – was to place spearheads on the left side of the body.

Stephanie Spain comments on the shields as follows: 'None of the shield burials was well-furnished and in five burials the only other weapon was the spear. The sixth burial, Grave 15, had no offensive weapon, a custom found nationally but most popular in the Anglian region (Dickinson and Härke 1993, 67–8). Three shields were positioned over the face and shoulders of the deceased (Graves 1, 15 and 53), one over the chest (Grave 27B) and one over the waist (Grave 52). The shield in Grave 37 was clearly deposited vertically, leant against the side of the grave. The preference for upper body positions is mirrored at other cemeteries in the region (Holywell Row, Little Eriswell, Snape, Spong Hill, Swaffham and Westgarth Gardens). The face position, in particular, is well represented and particularly popular at Holywell Row. Burials with shields in this position do not cluster chronologically or spatially at Flixton. Graves 52 and 53 are adjacent, aligned and similarly sized, forming a pair well away from neighbouring graves. The shield fittings confirm that these burials are closely linked and contemporary (Phase MB), yet the shields are placed in different positions within these graves (Grave 52 at the waist and Grave 53 over the face). The presence or positioning of other grave-goods does not suggest any practical reason for this.'

VI. Knives

Fig. 11.5

Although not specifically a male artefact, knives can be considered here because they confirm the changes in status for males in the later phases of the site. Knives were found with eighteen males, including one teenager, thirteen females and three children, which represents just over 50% of the graves. This figure conforms with the overall total of knives found in Early Anglo-Saxon cemeteries, of around 45% to 50% (Härke 1989, 144) or 55% (Stoodley 1999a, 30). Two bodies appear to have had two knives, one being the child in the double burial Grave 22 in Phase A2, and the other a single burial Grave 41 in Phase MB. This last may also represent someone relatively young, as the body appeared to be lying on one side and flexed, a feature more common in males under the age of fifteen (Härke 1997, 128).

Very few of the knives are incomplete and it is likely that they were all originally placed in graves as complete objects. They vary in length from 81mm to 202mm, which is a fairly constrained size range: there are no large knives or seaxes, and none of the knives could be described as a weapon. Rather, they can be viewed as domestic, utilitarian objects, used in daily life. At least twenty-seven had horn handles, in one instance secured by a rivet through the tang, and the handle of the large broad-bladed knife from Grave 37 may have been either repaired or ornamented (see Knives, Chapter 7.VI). Four knives from male burials, Graves 23 (Phase MA1), 37 (MA2), 41 (MB) and 14 (undated) had sheaths.

The size of knife blades can sometimes be correlated with age groups (Härke 1989; Sasse 2001, 98; Riddler and Trevarthen forthcoming), but the poor survival of skeletal remains at Flixton means that correlations have had to be restricted to the twenty-five graves for which the sex/gender could be identified and complete measurements recorded (Fig. 11.5). No particular blade type is specific to either gender, but the men's knives had, on average, marginally longer blades than the women's (male 87.9mm, female 84.3mm). On the other hand, the longest knife in the cemetery was found in the grave of one of the supposed 'cunning women', Grave 51 in Phase FB1: it had a narrow blade, 122mm long, which is just below the longest blade from a female grave seen by Härke, of 128mm (Härke 1989, 146; but *cf.* Härke 1997, 133, where the figure is given as 126mm). As the bar graph shows, blades from male graves lengthened with time but the women's blades did not (Fig. 11.5). The male seax appears at other sites during the later phase (Härke 1989; Stoodley

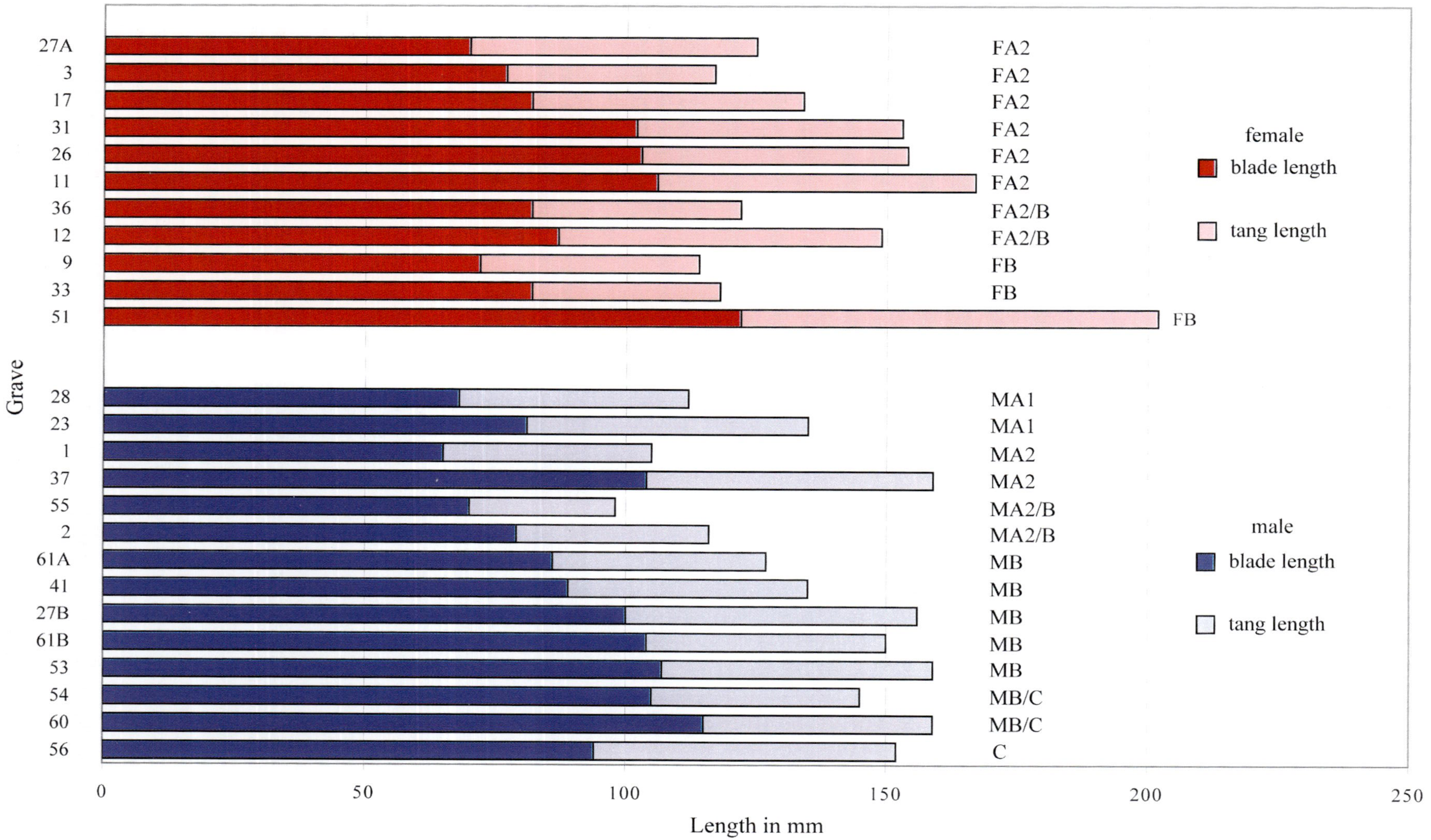

Figure 11.5 Knife lengths arranged by gender and phase

1999a, 35) and the increased size of ordinary knives for men may be a response to this. It can also be compared with the lengthening of spearheads, although, once again, the chamber grave, Grave 37, provides an early example of a long blade.

The extent to which the knives had been used before they were buried can be assessed, if only in very broad terms. It can be difficult to determine the wear patterns on knives, particularly when they do not survive well and most of the metal has corroded away. The clearest indication is provided by the cutting edge, which is thinned and reduced in size through sharpening, particularly in the area close to the choil and tang. Twenty-nine knives could be examined for this characteristic and six of them were heavily worn, whilst a further eight showed slight wear; no wear was visible on the remaining fifteen knives. This provides the possibility that around half of the knives were placed in the grave without having seen extensive use, although this does not necessarily mean that they were completely new.

VII. Other accessories in male graves

Finds other than the spear, shield, knife and buckle are rare in male graves, but in two graves of phase MB there were items associated with the knife, a fire-steel in Grave 61 and an iron implement in Grave 60. The ceramic vessels buried with males in Graves 2 (Phase MA2/B), 43 (MA2/B), 27B (MB) and 6 (undated), will be discussed separately with the ceramics in the graves of women and children.

The fire-steel in Grave 61 (61/5) was in a vertical position in the area of the torso, and may have been suspended on a cord placed through one of its curled terminals, or it could have been attached to a pouch (Geake 1997, 80). Brown has reviewed the function of these objects, suggesting that they primarily served as fire-steels, which could be used on their own or as part of a tinder pouch (Brown 1977). No flint was present in the Flixton grave, but in East Anglian cemeteries fire-steels are often associated with a knife, as at Spong Hill G30, Morning Thorpe G65, G184, G381 and G416, Shudy Camps G57, Snape G31 and Holywell Row G85, and the steel and knife could have been used together to strike a spark (Penn and Brugmann 2007, 34). On the Continent and in England in the 5th and early 6th century, fire-steels are mostly found with men, although they also occur in female graves in later phases (Stoodley 1999a, 35).

The function of the iron tool from Grave 60 (60/2) is unknown, although it bears a resemblance to the mysterious 'spatulate tools' or 'tanged implements' also found with knives in late graves (see Chapter 7). They occur with both sexes (Drinkall and Foreman 1998, 283–4).

VIII. Costume in male burials

The only metal garment fasteners recovered from male graves were buckles, and three of these, Graves 15, 27B and 37, were probably on the shield strap (Fig. 11.4). One buckle came from under the man's head in Grave 56, its function unknown. Eight, however, were recovered from the waist, where they must represent a belt, and in every case where organic remains were preserved, the belt was of skin or leather. In most cases, the buckle was horizontal and the knife lay vertically next to it, usually point-down, as if it had been tucked into the belt. In the earlier graves the buckle was in a central position, but in the later burials, Graves 53, 55, and 58, it was on the left. In one undated burial, Grave 32, the buckle was also on the left but in contact with a tentatively identified pile weave, possibly a rug under the body (Table 10.5). In this grave, the knife was immediately above the buckle and the layout can be compared with that of a 7th-century burial at Harford Farm G44, Norfolk, where the belt and knife were placed alongside the body (Penn 2000, 40). It is possible that this represents the re-appearance of a Roman burial practice, where accessories were placed beside the body, next to where they would have been worn in life (Walton Rogers 2007, 246).

The conventional costume of the Anglo-Saxon male, from the 5th to the 10th century, was a knee-length tunic over close-fitting trousers. Since both tunic and trousers could be belted, it is not always clear which garment is represented by textiles in association with buckles. Textiles at the waist included a medium-weight tabby, 14/Z x 14/Z per cm on the front of the buckle in Grave 23 (Phase MA1), where it appeared in horizontal folds; poorly preserved remains on the front of the buckle in Grave 7 (undated), for which no technical details could be recorded; and a medium-weight fabric, possibly of wool on the back of the buckle in Grave 43 (MA2/B) (Table 10.5). A tabby repp, probably of hemp, which was recorded at the waist in association with a knife in Grave 52 (MB), may represent some form of cummerbund or *fascia ventralis* for carrying small personal effects (Walton Rogers 2007, 220). Apart from these few items, however, most of the textiles in the male graves are likely to represent blankets and covers and will be discussed in Chapter 13.

IX. Metalworking skills

Although there has been no full review of the evidence for this period, it seems likely that the manufacture of metalwork was primarily in the hands of men (Hinton 2000, 111–2). This raises the question of how many of the metal artefacts in the graves could have been made by the men in the settlement at Flixton.

Copper-alloy metalwork from Early Anglo-Saxon graves can be divided into three main categories, which probably reflect different classes of metalworker. First, there are the fine cast objects with Style I ornament and gilding, such as great square-headed brooches, which are likely to have been made by travelling specialist smiths (Hines 1997, 221–2). Next, there are the cast objects such as cruciform brooches, which form recognisable type groups, each with a distribution pattern with a central focus. It can be suggested that these were made in small stationary workshops, exchanged in a regional network, and taken further afield by women marrying outside their clan. The third group includes artefacts, such as annular brooches, made by a range of simple techniques, which form amorphous groups that are difficult to arrange into a type-series. These are more likely to have been made at the individual settlements by people with basic metalworking skills.

The objects found at Flixton that fall into the first two categories will have been brought in from outside the area.

The Class C clasps, 16/2–3, for example, probably belong in the first category and almost certainly originated in the Midlands. The small-long brooches represent the second category and are also predominantly Midlands types, as were the cast segmented annular brooches and the spangle-headed pin. The pair of B2 brooches, 4/2 and II/NG1, are not necessarily foreign to the area, but the repair to the large gash on the headplate of II/NG1 is significant. It would have been relatively easy for anyone with skills in casting to make a mould from the undamaged brooch and to cast a new brooch, and yet it appears to have been repaired with a soldered plate. The remaining artefacts are made from sheet metal, and include features, such as the beaked profile in the annular brooches, which imply a discrete local manufacture. Those which appear to mimic external fashions, such as the annular brooch 8/1, have been inexpertly made. If the pin-through-lap annular brooches represent Midlands technology, they could have been copied locally without any great technical expertise.

On the evidence of the copper alloy metalwork from the excavated graves, there is little to indicate that there was anyone with advanced metalworking skills at Flixton. It is less easy to review the ironwork in the same way, but Janet Lang has noted in her study of the metallurgy of the spears that 'the quality of construction was not particularly good' (Chapter 7.VII). It is too early to comment on the significance of this, given the lack of comparable studies from other cemeteries, although a contrast can be drawn with the higher quality of contemporary spearhead manufacture seen in Kent, at both Dover Buckland and Saltwood. Evidence for the smelting of iron at Thorpe St Andrew, on the outskirts of Norwich, goes back to the 7th century but it is difficult, as yet, to relate this evidence (which consists entirely of metallurgical residues) directly to object manufacture, or even to identify the potential market for this activity (Bishop and Proctor 2011, 79–104). Skilled metalworking was essential to the development of centres of trade and places of power (Hjärthner-Holdar *et al.* 2002) and all evidence, even the negative evidence collected here, needs to be recorded for future reference.

X. Male status

The number of artefact types in male graves is comparable with those in the Norfolk sites, and they peak in Phase MA2 and decline afterwards, as they do elsewhere (Penn and Brugmann 2007, 90–6). Only the grave sizes of the early phases, which are below the national average (Stoodley 1999a, 67–8) and well below the average for Spong Hill and Morning Thorpe (Penn and Brugmann 2007, 77), add to the evidence from the women's graves that the Flixton burials in the early phases follow the standard pattern, but at a reduced level. It would appear that the signalling of male status through weapons was maintained even when the household was relatively poor.

The grave that is the most likely to contain a head of household is Grave 37 in Phase MA2 (Fig. 10.4). This is the chamber grave, containing a long-bladed spear on the man's left, and, on his right, a cluster of objects that includes a shield with a Kentish boss type, a broken spear with a butt ferrule, and a long-bladed knife. This is closely followed by another burial in Phase MA2, Grave 1, which has a large and particularly deep grave pit (0.56m), two Kentish or Kentish-like spears on the body's left side, a shield and a knife. They are both in the northern end of the cemetery and close to the centre of this group are two male graves of phase MA1, which may represent early members of the same family group. They were furnished with spears and knives, both were buried on biers or mats and one, Grave 28, had a grave marker represented by a row of post-holes. In the middle of the same area, there is an undated male grave, 32, buried with just a knife and buckle. Households would have had their own internal ranking and the weaponless burial may represent a servant or slave. Grave 43 appears to be a burial of a man with just a spear and a buckle added on at the edge of the main group in phase MA2 or MB, and, as already described, two further burials, which presumably represent the descendants of the same family, were added in Phase MB (Graves 27B and 41). Because the cemetery has been only partially excavated, it is not clear whether other male graves immediately to the south of the main group represent outlying burials of the same household, or a separate family plot.

In Phase MB–C the emphasis shifts to the barrow to the south, where there are two prominent burials with weapons, Graves 52 and 53 (Fig. 11.1). They have particularly large graves, probably situated higher on the mound than the others, and they have shields and long-bladed spears. Below them at the foot of the barrow lie a further four males (or probable males) including one or more young adults, Graves 54–57. They, too, were buried in large graves and two have long-bladed spears, although none has a shield. One of these men, Grave 55, may have a genetic link to one of the group buried further round on the east side of the mound, Grave 59. The members of this third group have no weapons but include a child, Grave 62, an adult of uncertain sex, Grave 61A, buried with a teenage male, 61B, and an elderly person interpreted as female from the beads and the small size of the grave (length 1.62m), Grave 59. Still further round the mound are two more burials, Graves 58 and 60, adult males to judge from the size of the grave, but with few accessories, and no weapons.

It would be easy to produce a simple ranking for the males of this group based on their weaponry, but this might not tell the full story. The two men with shields and spears lie, unlike the others, with spears on the right, and their shields have matching fittings that suggest an origin outside the area. As already stated, this was a period when weapons were buried with fewer men than previously (Härke 1997, 129, 146; Stoodley 1999a, 72), but there is evidence from mainland Europe at an earlier date that a male leader might be buried without weapons while his retinue was armed (Ravn 2003, 27). A hypothesis can therefore be put forward, that the late burials on the southern barrow represent a family supported by a male retinue. The retinue included a probable kinsman and two men of warrior status, possibly from outside the region, who in burial commanded especial respect.

Chapter 12. Graves with no Gender Indicators and Burials of Children

by Penelope Walton Rogers

I. Introduction

Most of the graves where no gender could be ascribed were shorter than 1.5 m and it has been assumed that they represent the burials of children. There remain five, however, Graves 10, 24, 25, 35 and 45, where the grave cuts were adult size, 1.62 to 2.20m long, but no artefacts were present other than the base of a ceramic vessel in Grave 25 (Table 12.1). A sixth can be added, an adult (A) without artefacts, buried facing a child (B) in Grave 22. It might have been suggested that these were the burials of slaves, were it not for the fact that one of them, Grave 35, was in a coffin, and the grave probably had a superstructure, represented by post-holes, which suggests a certain degree of status.

In Stoodley's survey, wealth was mostly associated with gender-signalling accessories such as weapons or garment fasteners, except in his phase group 1, AD 425–525 (Stoodley 1999a, 94–7). Grave 35 lay at the corner of the northern plot, in an end-to-end row between two other graves with post-holes, one a simply dressed woman, Grave 34 (Phase FA2/B1), and the other a young child, Grave 42 (Phase FA2); it was flanked by an adult male with weapons, Grave 1 (Phase MA2), and another child, Grave 44 (undated) (Fig. 10.4). A date in Phase MA2 or FA2 therefore seems credible and it is possible that this coffined burial represents the early centre of a small family group, perhaps one wing of the main household.

The remaining adult-size graves with no accessories have no significant grave features and are distributed throughout the northern plot. It is possible that they represent further early graves, or the 'servile or semi-servile' element that has been postulated for communities of this period (Scull 1993, 73).

II. Children's burials

Three burials, Graves A (Flixton I), 22B and 42, were recognized as children's from the evidence of teeth and bones, but the remaining thirteen have been identified from the small size of the grave cut (Table 12.1). There was evidence for a coffin or bier in two graves, post-holes in a third and the status of burial next to a mound was claimed by two, one early (Flixton I Grave A), and the other probably late (Grave 62). In Graves 18 and 22B the bodies had been laid on their sides, in Grave 22 the child facing the adult in the same grave. In Grave A the girl was

	Phase	*Age*	*Grave length (m)*	*Burial details*	*Artefacts*
Flixton I					
Grave A	FA2a?	Juvenile	1.90m	Supine extended; grave next to mound	Pair of small-long brooches, glass claw beaker, hemispherical ceramic bowl
Flixton II Rectangular plot					
Grave 8	FA2		1.35m	-	Single annular brooch, 5 beads, metal fitting, small globular ceramic bowl
Grave 16	-		1.05m	-	Part of sleeve clasp, ceramic baggy jar
Grave 18	A2/B		1.48m	On left side	Fragment of fire-steel, knife
Grave 19	-		1.02m	Coffin or bier/hide/rug	-
Grave 22B	A2	11–12 yrs	[1.80m]	On right side; with adult 22A	Lunula, knife, fragment of knife, glass sherd, round-bellied ceramic bowl
Grave 29	-		1.25m	-	-
Grave 38	-		0.80m	-	-
Grave 42	FA2	*c*.5 yrs	1.30m	Post-holes	1 bead and 2 metal tubes
Grave 44	-	-	1.40m	Bier (or hide or rug)	Knife
Grave 46	-	-	0.95m	-	Ceramic bowl
Grave 47	-	-	1.00m	-	Ceramic bowl
Grave 48	-	-	0.70m	-	-
Grave 49	-	-	1.30m	-	-
Grave 50	-	-	1.50m	-	Incomplete ceramic vessel
Flixton II associated with ring-ditch/mound					
Grave 62	-	-	1.00m	Cutting ring-ditch	-

Table 12.1 Graves of children and probable children at Flixton I and II

probably extended and supine, but the posture of the other children was not clear. Children were therefore given the same range of burial treatment as the adults.

As is often the case, artefacts were rare in the children's graves. There were ceramic vessels in Graves 16, 46, 47, 47 and 48, and it has been suggested that the frequent appearance of pots and dishes in children's graves reflects the parents' need symbolically to feed their offspring (Lee 2007, 85). Two children were buried with trinkets, a broken fire-steel in Grave 18 and one half of a sleeve clasp in Grave 16, while two of the older children (as indicated by the grave size) had knives, Graves 18 and 44. As far as costume accessories are concerned, a child of about five years old in Grave 42 was buried with a necklace of a single glass bead and two tubes, the girl in one of the larger graves, Grave 8, had accessories approaching those of an adult, the probable juvenile in Grave A had peplos brooches (already discussed in Chapter 10), and the 11–12 year old in Grave 22B wore an iron lunulate neck-ring. This last may be an indicator of the child's status. The review of graves with neck-rings (Chapter 7.III) has shown that, at a time when children were usually buried with few artefacts, the lunula-wearers often had good quality, sometimes adult, accessories. This was a period when the children of important families could be fostered into other households (Fell 1984, 81–2), and the significance of children buried with extensive accessories, especially those with metal neck-rings, has yet to be explored.

The poor preservation of skeletons at Flixton made it impossible to sub-divide the children by age, but there is nothing in the grave sizes to contradict the evidence collected elsewhere, that children under the age of three are rarely found (and perhaps were rarely buried) in cemeteries (Crawford 1993, 84–5; Lucy 1994, 26–7). They might be buried with artefacts by the age of three, but 10–12 years was the main threshold at which they acquired gender-signalling accessories (Härke 1997, 126–30). The cluster of four small undated graves in the south-east quadrant of Flixton II, however, is significant, as children were integrated with the adults in the northern part of the cemetery. The datable adult graves in the southerly section are all late and it is possible that this grouping of children is related to the same change in social structure that caused the predominantly male group to appear on or next to the barrow (Chapter 11). The decline in importance of kinship and family links at this time is likely to have affected the status and treatment of children (Härke 1997, 126), and it is clear that once churchyard burials had been established, very young children were often buried in separate groups (Crawford 1993, 88–9).

Chapter 13. Furnishing the Grave

by Penelope Walton Rogers

I. Introduction

The remaining objects in the Flixton graves represent domestic furnishings and utensils which the funeral party will have brought with them from the settlement. They include bed covers, a variety of pottery vessels, a wooden cup and a glass claw beaker. The glassware and ceramics are examples of vessels which can be found as sherds in settlement excavations, and the combination of evidence from occupation sites and cemeteries helps identify their pattern of use and their significance within the burial ritual. Organic materials, on the other hand, rarely survive in the free-draining soils of Anglo-Saxon settlements, and the textile covers and the wooden cup, preserved here by their association with corroding metalwork, are representatives of what was probably a much broader range of soft furnishings and wooden containers in use in a typical Anglo-Saxon settlement. Finds of this kind place the people buried at Flixton within the everyday, domestic context of their lives.

II. Coverlets, blankets and rugs

The monk Goscelin described how, when secretary to Bishop Herman in 1058, he had to furnish his poor lodgings with curtains, hangings and rugs for the benches (Barlow 1962, 93). Bed-clothes, seat-covers and wall-hangings also appear in the wills of women of the 10th and 11th centuries (Owen 1979; Fell 1984, 44) and there is every reason to suppose that similar fabrics were used to make comfortable the Anglo-Saxon halls of the 5th and 6th centuries. Traces of blankets and bedding have been found in several Early Anglo-Saxon graves, most notably at Snape, where staining marked out their full extent and small areas of textile preserved within the stained layer proved to be the remains, two or three layers thick, of coverlets and blankets (Snape G36, G37, G43: Filmer-Sankey and Pestell 2001). Elsewhere, remains of checked wool blankets, bed linen, feather pillows, mattresses and cushions have been recorded (Walton Rogers 2007, 73–86, 224–7).

In the Flixton graves, a thick wool twill, 8/Z x 8/Z per cm, under the body in Grave 4, is likely to represent a blanket, and there are similar remains curling around the end of the spear ferrule from Grave 37, where the butt end of the spear met the floor of the grave. Remains probably representing blankets or cloaks placed over the grave include a 2/2 twill 9/Z x 8/Z on the knife in Grave 14, another 10/Z x 9/Z on the ring and latch-lifter at the edge of the grave in Grave 11, and a tabby weave 8/? x 8/? on the rim of the shield boss in Grave 52. To these may be added the patterned coverlet weave to the right of the head, also in Grave 52, and a tentatively identified pile weave beside the body in Grave 32.

The plain wool blankets are likely to represent the work of women living in the local settlements, since they are simply a variation of the finer clothing fabrics they were producing on the warp-weighted loom. The coverlet weave, however, is only the second example of a textile type thought to be a variation on the Byzantine or Syrian coverlets imported into Britain (see Specialist textiles, Chapter 7.IV). It is possible that they are copies woven on the same loom as the 2/1 twills found in the Norfolk cemeteries, but if so they would require specialist skills and a considerable investment of time. If they really are East Anglian products, they would very probably be produced in some form of protected or supported workshop. Both the originals and the copies are reversible fabrics with strong geometric patterns, the back face being a negative of the front. They can be grouped with other heavy, patterned textiles which have been classified as coverlets, based on the nature of the fabrics and their position in the grave. The pile weave, if such it is, belongs in the same general category and possibly represents another import into Britain (see Specialist textiles, Chapter 7.IV). Textiles of this nature would form a suitable subject for gift-giving, either as an exchange between noble houses or as payment for services rendered. By the 7th century they were concentrated in men's graves and it is clear that patterned fabrics, hangings and piled rugs had become associated with rank (Walton Rogers 2007, 238–41). Grave 32 is undated, but Grave 52 represents one of the two males buried with spear and shield in a significant position on the southern barrow (Chapter 11).

III. Pottery vessels

by Sue Anderson

Most vessels at this site showed evidence for use in the form of sooting or burnt food residue, and the degree of wear on many suggests that this was probably not just a one-off use as part of the burial ceremony. The vessels within the cemetery were all relatively small. This is not necessarily reflected in the rim diameter measurements, as these are not proportional to the size of the vessel in the Saxon period. Sizes at the settlement varied from 50mm to 200mm, with the majority falling between 120-160mm. As the vessels from the Flixton settlement were more fragmented, it was not possible to be certain of their overall size, but the impression was that they ranged from small to relatively large. Those in the cemetery were generally of a similar size to each other, and may be of a more 'personal' nature, perhaps even the individual's preferred food vessel in life.

A study of the distribution of pottery vessels by gender and age showed that pottery occurred in sixteen adult and six juvenile graves. However in two adult and one juvenile graves these consisted of body sherds only and in these cases the pottery may be residual rather than an intentional inclusion. If these are discounted, there were vessels from six adult male, six adult female and two juvenile female graves, the remainder being unsexed. The spread is therefore not significantly different between the sexes.

The position of the more complete vessels in each grave was recorded on the grave plans. Eight were found close to the head, seven close to the waist or hips and four close to the feet. There was no gender difference apparent for the head and waist, but all three of the sexable graves containing pots by the feet were female. The sample is small, however, and unlikely to be significant. Analysis of soil samples taken from the pots provided no clue as to what, if anything, they contained on deposition. However the fact that all had clearly been used as cooking vessels does suggest that they would have contained some form of food, or perhaps that they were intended to be used for food in the afterlife. Remains of pots in the grave fill have been discussed in relation to the funeral feast (Feasting the dead, Chapter 6.X).

IV. The wooden cup

by Penelope Walton Rogers
Fig. 13.1

The maplewood vessel found in the region of the neck in a female-gender burial, Grave 11, is probably a drinking cup (see Wooden vessel, Chapter 7.VIII) and because it was made from burr wood (a burr is an abnormal outgrowth, in which the grain becomes contorted), it would have had an attractive speckled and whorled appearance (Fig. 13.1). Burr-wood cups were still in use in the Late Anglo-Saxon period and they are probably indicated by the phrase 'two cups decorated with dots' (OE *twa treowanan gesplottode cuppan*) in the 10th-century will of Wynflæd (Morris 2000, 2182, 2186). This cup would have been a valuable object (Morris 2000, 2182), although perhaps not as prestigious as the bottles and cups from Sutton Hoo and Taplow, with their ornamental metal fittings (Bruce-Mitford 1983, 3/1, 347–73).

Wooden vessels were probably more common in burials than we realise – Carole Morris estimates that two in every three inhumations may have had one – but detecting and identifying them depends on the presence of metal fittings and repairs, or the survival of circular dark soil stains (Morris 1994, 30–2). There is little comparative material from the early settlements, where conditions are even less suitable for the preservation of wood, but if the vessels found in 9th- to 11th-century urban sites are taken as a guide, there will have been a wide range of shapes and sizes in everyday domestic use (Morris 2000, 2165–98). In the cemeteries, on the other hand, a bowl of 240mm diameter in Spong Hill G34 is unusual (Morris 1994, 31), and most vessels are small cups and gourd-shaped bottles, with a rim diameter of 45mm to 105mm (Morris 2000, 2182; Bruce-Mitford 1983, 3/1, 347–73). These smaller vessels have been found in the burials of men and women equally, and by the head, perhaps intentionally close to the mouth, is one of the most common positions (Morris 1994, 32). As was suggested for the ceramic vessels, it is possible that they represent personal property, while the larger vessels from the settlements were communal or household items.

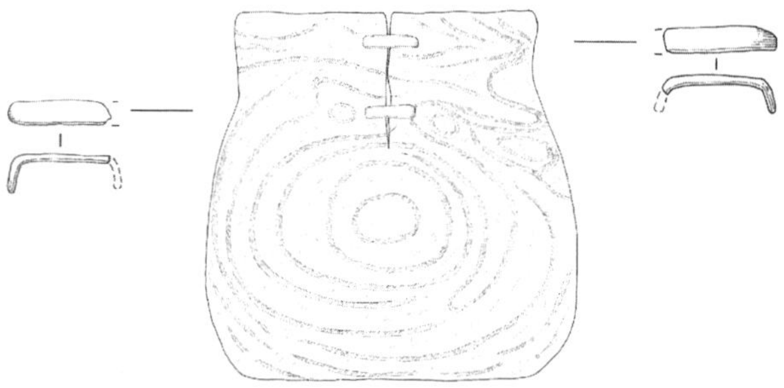

Figure 13.1 A reconstruction of the burr-wood vessel from Grave 11 (scale; staples at 1:1). Note how the staples could have been used to repair a crack in the vessel rim. For the rim mounts and alternative shapes for the rim, see Figure 7.18. Jacqui Watson, English Heritage

V. The claw beaker

by Rose Broadley

Occurrence and use

In addition to the body of evidence from cemetery sites, fragments of claw beakers and other types of Anglo-Saxon glass vessels are increasingly being discovered in settlement contexts (for example, West Stow and Brandon in Suffolk, and Hamwic and York nationally). Settlement contexts are always frustratingly lacking in large fragments, let alone substantially complete vessels, but the glass evidence from these sites does provide an indication that the same types of vessel that were placed in graves were in daily use at the same time.

However, fragments from 6th-century settlement sites are rare, and it is often difficult to interpret how the glass was used from the archaeological contexts in which the few known examples have been found. One interesting and local case is the fragment of a Type 3c claw beaker found in Hut 50 at West Stow – here there is a clear association with one of the largest buildings in a settlement that mainly consisted of *Grubenhäuser*. It is difficult to say whether that particular building was used for community gatherings and feasts, but wider archaeological evidence suggests that the feast hall was certainly the social context in which such beautiful glass vessels were used. For example, four glass claw beakers were found alongside two extremely rare silver-rimmed drinking horns in the late 6th-century burial at Taplow, Buckinghamshire, and the same combination of glass and silver is also seen elsewhere in the richest graves, such as Sutton Hoo and Prittlewell. This association between silver-mounted vessels that unquestionably had a formal and high-profile function and high-quality glass vessels is a clear indication that glass vessels performed a similar function in society.

Claw beakers were definitely drinking vessels, despite that fact that drinking from replicas reveals that they are quite difficult to use in this way – liquid tends to splash out of the claws when the glass is raised to drain it. The wealthy probably drank *beor* (a drink thought to have been made from fermented fruit), mead and wine from glass and other expensive and rare vessels during ceremonial feasting and drinking in a great hall. Surviving contemporary literature clearly reveals that the Anglo-Saxon feast hall was at the heart of early English society, and that drinking was a major part of the festivities that took place there. Marjorie A. Brown cites the poem *The Wanderer*, in which the writer 'remembers his happiness in terms of the hall and its generous lord' (Brown 1998, 2):

Where has gone the place of the banquets? Where are the pleasures of the hall? Alas, the gleaming chalice; alas, the armoured warrior; alas, the majesty of the prince! (lines 92–95a)

The literature clearly illustrates that most of the ritual associated with feasting involved drinking, not eating; that it was the duty of rulers to provide drink to their followers; and that shared consumption of drink sealed bonds and reinforced the social hierarchy within the community. It is difficult to find specific references to glass vessels in heroic literature due to the poetic conventions used and the complexity of translation (the reference above to a 'gleaming chalice' is typically non-specific), and a similar problem applies to illustrations in Anglo-Saxon documents: there is often no indication of the material that a depicted vessel is made of. We may infer, however, that glass vessels would have been used alongside silver and silver-mounted vessels and perhaps imported pottery in a position of prominence in the feast-hall setting.

The significance of the object in the grave

Relatively recent work on cremation burials at Spong Hill in Norfolk, Mucking in Essex and Loveden in Lincolnshire suggests that burial with a glass vessel may not have been as rare in East Anglia as inhumation burials alone have previously suggested (Evison 2000, 48), but this find is still a distinct indicator of the high status of the person with which is was buried. The red marbling and decoration in particular are characteristics of a very rare and high-quality product, as illustrated by the fact that the closest parallels are the globular beaker from the ship burial in Mound 2 at Sutton Hoo and the claw beakers from the boat cemetery at Valsgärde, Sweden.

There is no question that it was an Anglo-Saxon tradition to place complete glass vessels in inhumation graves (Evison 2000, 48), so this vessel would not have been broken in antiquity – in this case the glass was probably crushed by the settlement of the soil around it over a long period of time. A fragment of skull survived, and its position tells us that the glass vessel was originally placed near the head of the burial. Whether this is significant or not is open to question – no comprehensive survey of where glass vessels were usually placed in inhumation burials has been completed, perhaps because it is unclear what inferences could be drawn from the results. It seems sufficient to observe that in most cases the glass vessels were placed at the head or sometimes at the foot of the body, where they would have been clearly visible during the burial rite. During the rite, the placing of the glass vessel in the grave would have been a pivotal moment – if one assumes that the two brooches found in the grave were part of the dress of the body, the glass vessel and the pottery bowl would have been the only items placed in the grave separately from the body itself. The glass vessel would also have been a visual focal point, with its bright red and green colour gleaming in the light, almost as described in *Beowulf*: 'And they buried torques in the barrow, and jewels' (*trans* Heaney 1999, 78 line 3163).

The small-long brooches show that this claw beaker was buried with a female body. This is unremarkable as glass vessels were buried fairly evenly with men and women with a slight bias towards women, although no precise data has been gathered for East Anglia. In Kent the ratio is similar to that for pottery vessels: approximately 60% buried with women and 40% with men (Richardson 2005, I, 162). More unusually, the osteoarchaeological evidence suggests that the grave belonged to a juvenile. Few glass vessels have been found with juveniles, particularly in East Anglia, although the picture in this region may be skewed by the greater difficulty in identification of melted glass as vessel glass in cremation cemeteries. One similar case may be Grave 148 at Morning Thorpe in Norfolk, in which a double burial surrounded by five post-holes contained a male and a female, both juvenile. Amongst the grave goods was a 5th- or early 6th-century glass cone beaker with opaque white marvered festooned trails (Evison 2000, 61–2), which had been placed inside a pot, although the position of the vessels implies that they were associated with the male occupant (Green *et al.* 1987, 76–7). Kentish examples are more numerous – *e.g.* Chatham Lines, Grave IV (excavated 1779); Mill Hill II, Deal, Graves 32 and 33 (ex. 1986); Buckland, Dover, Graves 20 (ex. 1951–3), 254, and 326, 347, 422, and 432 (ex. 1994); Kingston Down Grave 205 (ex. 1771); and Barfriston, Grave 28 (ex. 1772–3) (Richardson 2005, II, 138, 147, 162, 182, 187–9, 195–6, 247 and 346), but even in Kent juveniles are significantly under-represented amongst burials containing glass vessels: 25.5% of burials with glass vessels were 0–18 year olds, whereas that group represented 31.9% of the total sample (Richardson 2005, I, 162). Furthermore, half of the examples above are from the Buckland cemetery in Dover, which is extraordinary in the number of burials and the level of wealth represented by the grave goods.

It has been argued that this is likely to have been a girl at an age between the adoption of the peplos and the acquisition of adult accoutrements (see Chapter 10). It is surprising that such a fine glass vessel was buried with a teenage girl, but perhaps she was already the leading woman in her wealthy father's household at the time of her death and thus the honour was appropriate, or perhaps the glass vessel was intended to represent the role she would have had if she had lived as consort to an important man in the community after her marriage. In richer graves, glass vessels helped to create an image of the deceased person as a generous host or hostess – a leader or consort who welded alliances while softening important visitors with games, drink and music. The mourners at this funeral may have wanted to honour and enhance the political and social standing of the girl's family with these associations and the siting of the burial next to a prehistoric feature in the landscape may also have been part of the construction of a powerful past and present identity both for the deceased individual and the collective.

VI. Conclusion

It has been argued by others that artefacts in graves represent a conscious attempt to signal gender and status (Stoodley 1999a), possibly as a tableau for the kinsfolk at the funeral to observe (Carver 1998, 116–27; Geake 2003, 260). While there can be little doubt that the funerals of princes had such a purpose, as they still do today, it is less easy to see the evidence for this in more ordinary graves, where much was hidden from view by over-garments and blankets. There is little correspondence between the clothing and accessories in Anglo-Saxon graves and those of the 18th and 19th centuries, when garments and coffin upholstery were made specifically for the viewing of the body (Litten 1991). On the other hand, they bear a close resemblance to the property bequeathed in Late Anglo-Saxon wills. In these, weaponry, and vestments associated with a particular office, appear to have been the concern of men, while clothes, necklaces, brooches and items such as a 'spinning box' are more frequently among the bequests of women, while cups of different types and materials appear in the wills of both sexes (Whitelock 1930). An alternative view of the burial evidence would be that the garments and their accessories are those worn in life (Walton Rogers 2007, 245–7) and that small ceramic dishes, wooden cups, and hand tools such as a spindle-and-whorl, represent the dead's personal property. Large vessels and craft equipment such as looms, which are more likely to have been communal property, did not enter the grave. This is not to dispute the fact that many objects, such as weapons, had a social significance, but to place greater emphasis on the idea of ownership. At a time when people lived in relatively large households, the distinction between what belonged to the family and what belonged to an individual may have been carried through into the burial.

Chapter 14. The Flixton Cemeteries in Context

I. The early landscape

When the Early Anglo-Saxon settlers arrived in the region at the end of the 5th century, the landscape had been continually developing under varying degrees of human influence for in excess of four and a half millennia, throughout the Neolithic, Bronze Age, Iron Age and Roman periods. The incoming settlers would have been confronted with a landscape that, while almost certainly suffering decline in formal management during the final years of the Roman period and earlier 5th century, would still have included a palimpsest of features generated during these earlier periods. At Flixton, the situation was no different. The influx of people, albeit possibly limited in numbers, would have found a landscape that, while not necessarily occupied to the same degree as it had been previously, would still have borne the scars of earlier activity. It was this environment then that would have influenced their own choice of location and into which they ultimately would become established.

In East Anglia, the sites where Early Anglo-Saxon activity has been recorded are essentially riverine. In comparison, the pattern of Roman settlement was far more extensive with the heavy soils of the clay plateau also cultivated, although, again, concentrated areas of occupation and activity followed the more accommodating soils of the river valleys. There is considerable debate regarding the character of the native British population encountered by the 5th-century immigrants, but what is certain for the Waveney Valley is that sites with evidence for activity beyond AD 360 are few and far between, although they do continue to occupy the same general area as in the earlier Roman period. The nearest site to Flixton on the southern, Suffolk, side of the River Waveney which has produced Late Roman evidence is 2.5km to the south east, at South Elmham St Margaret, where there is Oxford Ware pottery.

It is also clear that the indigenous population immediately prior to the arrival of the Early Anglo-Saxon settlers is, effectively, archaeologically invisible. This lack of archaeological evidence could be due to a reduction of the number of people in the landscape, combined with their impoverishment following the localised, if not uniform, breakdown of organised society and its associated infrastructure at the end of the Roman period. This impoverishment would have led to a lack of the durable material wealth that could survive into the archaeological record. Whichever of these factors was the most dominant, the environment encountered by the settlers would not have been entirely hostile and where opposition was encountered it was not likely to have been a significant or continuing problem.

II. Settlement of the Waveney Valley

Fig. 14.1

The distribution of Early Anglo-Saxon cemeteries and settlements in East Anglia shows a population concentrated in three main zones (Scull 1992; West 1998, 268–70). The first is focused on the east-flowing rivers in Norfolk and includes sites such as Morning Thorpe, Spong Hill and Bergh Apton. The second forms a curving band around the fen edge in western Norfolk, north-west Suffolk and Cambridgeshire: the sites on the Suffolk rivers draining westwards into the fens belong to this group. The third is in south-east Suffolk in the area of the Rivers Alde, Deben and Gipping-Orwell, where Sutton Hoo is the most prominent site. Flixton lies immediately to the south of the east-central Norfolk group and many of the burials in cemetery II show an affinity, in terms of material culture, with that area. The early settlers, however, did not necessarily arrive from the north.

The Anglo-Saxon settlement of Suffolk is believed to have begun with Germanic mercenaries or colonists who established themselves at the heads of the Orwell and Deben estuaries and made their way via the Gipping corridor to the valleys of the Lark and the Black Bourn in the north-west (West 1998, 291; 1999, 44). From here there would be easy routes into the Waveney and its major tributary the Dove, and there was clearly an Anglo-Saxon presence of some sort in the upper Waveney and Dove valleys by the mid 5th century (Fig. 14.1). There is a supporting-arm brooch dated to the first half of the 5th century at Eye (HER: EYE 003), near the confluence of the Dove with the Waveney (PAS: SF-10133), and early cruciform brooches of Mortimer Type A, from west to east, at Thornham Magna (HER: TMM 007), Mendham (HER: MDM 105), Flixton I (see Chapter 7), South Elmham St Margaret (West 1998, 95, 244) and Pewter Hill, Kirby Cane (Penn and Ashley 2003, 310–11). In both river valleys there are also small-long brooches of EAC types *sm1* and *sm2*, which belong mostly to the 5th century (see Chapter 7.II). These finds are least common, however, in the middle and lower stretches of the valley, and the settlement close to the coast at Bloodmoor Hill, Carlton Colville, does not appear to have been founded until the 6th century (Lucy *et al.* 2009). The greatest concentration of 5th-century evidence occurs to the west of Flixton.

The sites in the upper Waveney and the Dove clearly had some form of contact with the Cambridgeshire and fen-edge settlements in the 5th and early 6th centuries. Small-long brooches with a square head, or the squared-up version of the cross-shaped head (the 'cross potent' and 'cross pattée' types), which occur more commonly in the Midlands, north-west Suffolk and Cambridgeshire (Leeds 1945, 14–26), have been found upriver from Flixton, at Eye (PAS: SF-10047, 10161, 10187–8, 10820, 10823), Yaxley (PAS: SF-28C002, 27E973) and Palgrave (PAS: SF-9DE194, A1CCF2, 183153); and there is a Midlands-style openwork brooch from Oakley (West 1998, 86, 236). The pattern continues at Flixton, where there is a small-long brooch with hooked lappets of Cambridgeshire type in one of the earliest burials, Grave 27A (Phase FA1/2a). The post-holes for grave markers, which begin with Grave 28 in Phase MA1, also have their nearest parallels in

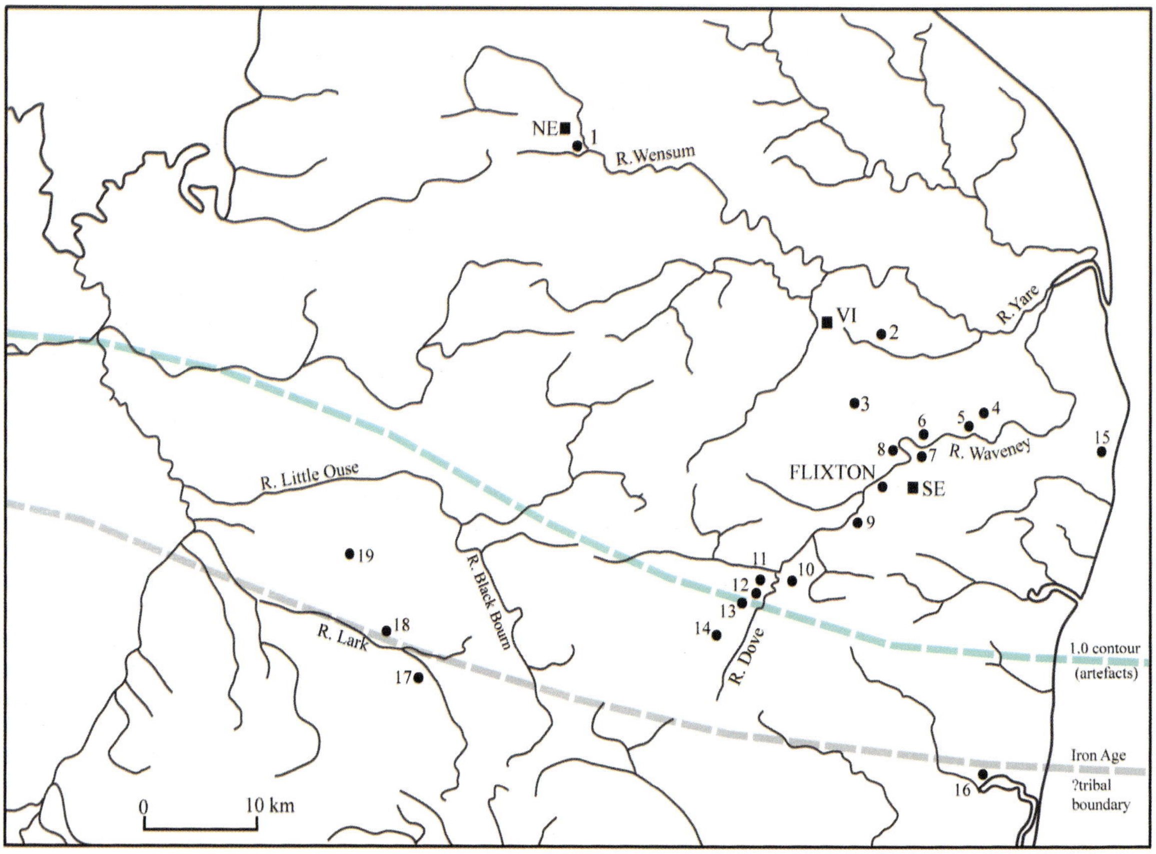

●
1. Spong Hill
2. Bergh Apton
3. Morning Thorpe
4. Stockton
5. Kirby Cane
6. Broome
7. Bungay
8. Earsham
9. Mendham
10. Hoxne
11. Oakley
12. Eye
13. Yaxley
14. Thornham Magna
15. Carlton Colville (Bloodmoor Hill)
16. Snape
17. Bury St Edmunds
18. West Stow
19. Eriswell

■
NE North Elmham

SE South Elmham

VI Venta Icenorum

Figure 14.1 Early Anglo-Saxon sites in Norfolk and north Suffolk and the probable Iceni territorial boundary (after Dymond and Martin 1999, 41). The 1.0 contour line marks the point at which the 'Anglian' artefacts in the northern zone become increasingly diluted by other types (after Høilund Nielsen 1997, figs 22–3). The Anglo-Saxon Laboratory

Cambridgeshire (Chapter 6). That the settlers came along the river valley from the west, therefore, seems a likely proposition.

The Flixton settlement and cemeteries are on the west side of a cluster of sites that includes, on the Norfolk side of the river, a settlement at Broome (Yarmouth Road, 36289), cremations at Earsham, inhumations at Broome, Stockton and Kirby Cane; and on the Suffolk side, cremations and inhumations at Bungay (Clough and Green 1973; West 1998, 13–14; Penn and Ashley 2003). They are separated by about 18km from the sites at the Dove-Waveney confluence, and, downriver, the next significant sites are 15–20km away at Aldeby, Norfolk (34099), and Bloodmoor Hill, Suffolk (Lucy *et al.* 2009). If the settlers arrived in Flixton from the west, once established they would have found themselves in closer proximity to the Norfolk group: Morning Thorpe and Bergh Apton are only 9 km and 14 km away as the crow flies.

The Norfolk cemeteries are grouped around the former capital of the *civitas* of the Iceni, Venta Icenorum, at Caistor-St-Edmund (Caistor-by-Norwich). The Anglo-Saxon settlement of East Anglia is deemed to have been a slow occupation by small groups of people, and there is evidence that the communities around Venta Icenorum retained some of the administrative importance of the former capital well into the 6th century (Myres and Green 1973, 12–14; Scull 1992, 8–14). The boundary between Norfolk and Suffolk now runs along the Waveney, but the southern edge of Iceni territory, and the Roman *civitas* that followed it, originally lay further to the south (Fig. 14.1; Mattingly and Jones 1990, fig. 5.11; Dymond and Martin 1999, 41). The contour line outlining the core northern area of 'Anglian' artefacts runs parallel to the Iceni boundary (Fig. 14.1). The Anglo-Saxon period saw the occupied areas shrinking back into the river systems, so that boundaries may have become more nebulous, but it is likely that the Flixton area of the Waveney Valley was still perceived at the end of the 5th century as part of a territory ruled from the north.

III. Settling at Flixton

The first arrivals at Flixton would have been confronted with a series of monumental earthworks standing in what is likely to have become a somewhat overgrown setting (Chapter 16). Vestiges of the Roman agricultural landscape, including an extensive rectilinear field system, may still have been present: dating evidence suggests that the field ditches had become redundant during the earlier Roman period, but the boundaries could have been maintained as hedges until considerably later. Certainly, the circular mounds of Early Bronze Age barrows would have been visible, and probably also the linear mound of the earlier Neolithic long barrow in the bottom of the shallow valley.

It was probably the earthworks that attracted the settlers to this particular spot and they worked the layout of the monuments into their use of the site. The large barrow on the low ridge parallel to the river became the western end of the settlement, and the two new burial grounds were placed so that, from the settlement, they both had a visual relationship with a smaller barrow. The two burial grounds have proved to be quite different in character. Flixton I was probably a small plot, positioned on the lower slope of a barrow, and it included the grave with the high-status glass claw beaker. Flixton II, on the other hand, was contained within a rectangular plot and included a group of people whose level of wealth was below that of contemporary populations (Chapter 10) and whose life expectancy (with the caveats described in Chapter 8) was also low. The people buried there were not slaves, since the men had spears, and they display the typical social structure of an Early Anglo-Saxon household, yet there must have been some social distinction between them and the group buried at Flixton I. This is highly unusual for the early 6th century, when communities and households are regarded as having been broadly equal to each other in status (Scull 1993, 73; Härke 1997, 146–7).

There do not appear to be any other examples of this enclosed layout from the early phase of settlement in East Anglia. There is a parallel, however, at Dover Buckland, Kent, where approximately twenty-five graves were placed in a tight rectangle measuring 15 x 10m (Plot A, Evison 1987, 14, 19, 136, 142–5, 175). The excavator suggested that this represented an enclosure allocated to the immigrants by the British, at a time when they were struggling to gain a toe-hold in the country (Evison 1987, 143). It was argued that when the burial plot was begun in the final quarter of the 5th century, Dover was distant from the main area of Germanic settlement, and that graves only began to appear outside the first plot, in the early-to-mid 6th century, as the incomers either became integrated, or gained the upper hand (Evison 1987, 143).

This theory could be applied to Flixton. If the area was still perceived as part of the old Iceni territory controlled from central Norfolk, then the enclosed burial plot at Flixton II could represent an allocation of land to new settlers from outside the region. If the presence of a claw beaker combined with burial on a mound is regarded as an indicator of status, then perhaps the people at Flixton I were in a position to oversee the new arrivals. No distinction can be made between native and immigrant in this case, however. There was already a Germanic presence at Venta Icenorum by the 5th century, and the immigrants most probably aligned themselves with the government of the old territory (Myres and Green 1973, 8–14; Scull 1992, 14); and if the new arrivals at Flixton were Germanic in origin, they are likely to have been second- or third-generation immigrants. Regardless of their ethnic background, it can be hypothesised that the main population at Flixton II was made up of newcomers from the west, who had settled inside a territory which took its authority from the north.

An alternative explanation, that the enclosed plot represents a local British population, acculturated to the Anglo-Saxon way of life, who came under the control of a small dominant group, is less easy to maintain. There is no evidence for such a population at Flixton in the late 4th or 5th century and artefacts such as the Cambridgeshire brooch in an early burial, Grave 27A (Phase FA1/2a), would be difficult to explain in these terms. The absence of Romano-British textile techniques and Norfolk-type beads in the earliest graves, attributed to Phases MA1 (Graves 23 and 28), FA1/2a (Graves 4 and 27A) and FA2a (Grave 3), is also compatible with the theory that the first settlers came from outside the region.

IV. Date-range and population size

The earliest burials at Fixton II are Graves 4, 23, 27A and 28, from Phases MA1 and FA1/FA2a (*c*.450–510), and Grave 3 from Phase FA2a (*c*.480–510), while the single grave at Flixton I probably also belongs in Phase FA2a (Chapter 9). In theory, it is possible that the graves in the unexcavated areas were earlier still, but 5th-century evidence from the settlement is sparse, and a foundation for both cemetery and settlement at, or shortly before, AD 500 seems plausible. There is no evidence in the metal-detected finds that Flixton I continued later than Phase FA2, but the main plot at Flixton II was still being used in Phases MB (*c*.560/570–640/50) and FB2 (*c*.590–640/50), when Graves 27B, 39, 40 and 41 were inserted. By Phase FB/MB burials were also being placed on the ring barrow to the south and the latest burials in this area are Graves 56 from Phase C (AD *c*.640/50 to *c*.660/70), and perhaps also Graves 54 and 58 from Phase MB or C. The cemetery had probably gone out of use by the mid 7th century.

When complete cemeteries are excavated and the ages of the skeletons recorded, the size of the population burying their dead can be estimated by multiplying the total number of bodies by the mean age at death and then dividing the result by the number of years that the cemetery was in use (Boddington 1987, 184). For Flixton this can be only a very rough approximation, but it seems worth the exercise, despite the problems inherent in such calculations (Boddington 1987, 185–93). If Flixton II was in use for 130–160 years, the total number buried is assumed to be 210 (the excavator estimated 200 for the rectangular plot) and the mean age at death is set at 20 years (following Scull 2009a), then the population burying at Flixton II would be between twenty-six and thirty-two at any one time. If the number of individuals in a household is regarded as nine to twelve (Härke 1997, 140) or ten to fifteen (Penn and Brugmann 2007, 94), this would indicate two or three contemporary households, and Flixton I would probably add a further household in the earliest phase. However inexact these figures, they are not incompatible with the six 'halls' from a similar date-span excavated in the settlement. They represent a medium-sized community for the period, substantially smaller than Mucking, but only slightly smaller than West Stow (Härke 1997, 140).

V. Cultural connections

Regardless of where they originated, during Phase FA2 the Flixton community became firmly established as part of the Norfolk group. The artefacts, burial practice and Romano-British textile techniques all find parallels in the major Norfolk cemeteries. At the same time, any contacts with the settlements upriver were probably diminishing. The annular brooches so common at Flixton and on the north side of the river are comparatively rare among the Suffolk sites at the Dove-Waveney confluence, even though the artefacts (florid cruciform brooches from Eye, Yaxley and Hoxne, silver bell bead(s) from Hoxne and a gilded square-headed brooch from Mendham) suggest that occupation in this area continued well into the 6th century (PAS: SF-4B6E83, SF-323565; SF-1E0527, SF-1A1C04; HER: Mendham, TM2728 8090 and TM2750 8069; EYE 060, SF-27978; YAX 016, SF-30912; West 1998, 44–5, 166). Although Flixton is on the south side of the river, the Roman road, Stone Street, crossed the Waveney at Bungay (Clough and Green 1973; Dymond and Martin 1999, 43) and by this route Flixton would be only an afternoon's walk from Morning Thorpe.

The evidence in the Norfolk cemeteries for Romano-British textile techniques, now used in Germanic costume styles, indicate that some practical aspects of women's lives had survived in that area (Walton Rogers 2007, 230–32). The presence of these same textile techniques at Flixton is particularly significant, because cloth production will have been in the hands of women (Walton Rogers 2007, 41–7). The four examples from three female graves, Graves 17 (Phase FA2), 20 (Phase FA2) and 9 (Phase FB1) suggest some form of contact with those women of the Norfolk communities who had retained Romano-British skills, and the woman buried with spinning equipment derived from a Romano-British tradition, Grave 40, (Phase FB) implies that they were integrated into the Flixton settlement.

VI. Households and the position of women

It has been argued in Chapters 10 and 11 that the forty-five or so graves in the north-west quadrant of Flixton II represent the members of one household buried over several generations, from around AD 500 to the early 7th century. They include an irregular string of graves with superstructures (represented by post-holes), ranged along the northern side of the cemetery, and the hearth pit outside the north-west corner probably represents the site of their funeral feasts. Men, women and children are mingled together, as is to be expected of an Anglo-Saxon household (Härke 1997, 137–41; Stoodley 1999a, 126, 131). At this time, a household is likely to have been made up of a nuclear family and their dependants, including slaves or servants, but if sons married and stayed at home, its make-up would have become increasingly complex. Some of the clusters of mixed graves may represent one of these smaller family units within the main household.

Although men and women were essentially integrated in the early phases, when the senior males, represented by burial with spear and shield, and the women with the greatest numbers of artefacts were plotted, a gender division emerged (Fig. 10.4). It is difficult to make confident statements when the eastern end of the household plot is probably missing, but the evidence as it stands suggests separate zones for prominent males and prominent females. The kinship system of the 5th and 6th centuries has been described as 'patrilineal', based on later documentary sources (Scull 1993, 73), but bilateral with a weak patrilateral bias has also been proposed (Härke 1997, 137). In other cemeteries men and women of equivalent rank have been recorded in approximately equal numbers through the different phases (Evison 1987, 146–50; Welch 1992, 81–2), which suggests a degree of equality in life, and this is matched by the evidence from Flixton II in Phase FA2–FB1. If it is correct to see four of the women in this plot as hereditary 'cunning women', they may have boosted the status of the female side of the family.

Most authors agree that societies of this period were 'patrilocal' or 'virilocal' (Scull 1993, 73; Härke 1997, 137; Hines 2002, 91–4), which signifies that the woman would move to the man's household on marriage. For many women that would mean marriage into some nearby settlement and this would provide a route by which women's costume styles and accessories could transfer from one place to another. The Flixton 'beaked' annular brooches of Phase FA2 could have reached Morning Thorpe and Bergh Apton by this means (Chapter 7.II), and the Romano-British textile techniques and Norfolk-type beads could have arrived in Flixton with women marrying into the settlement. The excavations have also produced evidence for a more far-reaching marriage alliance.

The arguments for a connection with the cemeteries of the Gwash–Welland river system and, especially Empingham, have been set out in Chapter 10. The evidence has been recorded in at least six female-gender graves in Phases FA2 to FB1 (*c*.480/520–560/80) and it is limited to the Flixton cemetery: no comparable evidence could be found in the Norfolk sites or anywhere else in East Anglia. If it is accepted as genuine, then one explanation could be that a woman from the Empingham area, perhaps the daughter of a prominent family with her female retinue, joined the Flixton community in a political or diplomatic marriage.

The reasons for such an alliance are not immediately clear. The Wakerley–Empingham–Market Overton area was densely settled in the 6th century (Timby 1996, 1–3, 97), and iron ore in the Wakerley area was extracted and smelted in the Iron Age and Roman period, although it has yet to be shown that this activity continued into the post-Roman period (Adams and Jackson 1988, 78): iron ore might have been a valuable resource for an East Anglian community. At the same time, it is a curious feature of the Empingham II cemetery that there were a number of women particularly well-provided with accessories, alongside men with especially low mortality rates (Stoodley 1999a, 120). The position of such women in 6th-century England has yet to be fully explored

If this high-status Empingham woman did exist, it is to be expected that she was buried at Flixton I, in view of the poor status of the excavated Flixton II household in Phase FA2, or, less probably, in the unexcavated section of Flixton II. In Phase FB1 the women of Flixton II seem to have improved their lot and reached parity with the rest of the Norfolk region in terms of grave size and wealth, but this was only to find that at a national level the structure of society was changing, and not in a way that was favourable to women.

VII. The later 6th and 7th century

The later 6th and 7th centuries (Phases FB2, MB and C) saw substantial changes at Flixton. Some graves were added on the outskirts of the original plot and one man accompanied by spear and shield, Grave 27B, was inserted into the grave of a woman buried in Phase FA1/2a, 27A, at the same time as a new group emerged on and around the barrow to the south. It has been argued that the new burial plot represents a family with a male retinue, some of whom were warriors (Chapter 11). The similarities between two of the graves, Graves 52 and 53, their non-local shield mounts, the positioning of the spear on the right instead of the left, and their separation from the rest of the group, have been used to argue that they came from outside the area. Perhaps one may speculate that these two men were part of a warrior band, who would give loyalty and military service to a chieftain or warlord in return for gifts and patronage (Ravn 2003, 8–12). The patterned coverlet in Grave 52 represents exactly the type of object that would have been used in this form of gift-exchange (Chapter 13). Significantly, its closest parallel lies at Snape, in the south-east of the county and, as the power of the old Iceni territory declined, it is probable that the people living in the Waveney Valley were looking towards the Sandlings area of Suffolk for leadership.

Flixton may have been gaining in importance because of its position. As the Wuffings took control of East Anglia, a settlement that lay on a west–east route, close to a Roman road that crossed the river and led into the heart of the former Iceni territory, probably had some strategic significance. There is some evidence that this area was still regarded as part of a northern zone in the 7th century. The northern of the two East Anglian bishoprics was almost certainly established at South Elmham, on the south side of the Waveney at this time (Scarfe 2002, 88–9; Dymond and Martin 1999, 46) and it was probably not until the 9th century that the northern seat moved into present-day Norfolk, at North Elmham (Dymond and Martin 1999, 22).

At the same time, the move to the barrow runs parallel with broader changes in society. One theory for this period is that the internal ranking within the early communities led, through peer competition and competitive exclusion, to temporary chiefdoms, and that these in turn gave rise to the establishment of a more permanent regional structure under a dynastic ruler (Scull 1993, 72–7; 1999, 19–22). The later stages of this development correspond with the raising of barrows in the south-east of the country, first at Snape and then at Sutton Hoo (Carver 1998, 107–36; Filmer-Sankey and Pestell 2001, 194–6; Carver 2005, 497). In this light, burial on the prehistoric barrow at Flixton can be seen as part of the increasing social differentiation of the late 6th and 7th centuries. As at Sutton Hoo, the women present among the male elite are few and, at a national level, most women seem to be slipping down the social scale (Chapter 10).

VIII. The end of Flixton II

Burial on the barrow had ceased by the middle of the 7th century, the final burial there being that of an adult male, Grave 56, in Phase C (*c*.640/50–660/70), at a time when the excavated evidence suggests that the settlement was already deserted. If the burials on the barrow represent an elite group, then perhaps they failed to win the next round of the competition, as described in Scull's model. On the other hand, the Flixton hamlet may simply have moved. As society changed during the course of the 7th century, so did the pattern of settlement, from a network of broadly equal sites to a more hierarchical arrangement. Royal residences and centres of administration became differentiated from centres for craft and trade, and rural settlements became concerned with food production to serve the others (Härke 1997, 146–8; Scull 2002, 308–12; Reynolds 2003, 130–1; Newman 2005, 483; Carver 2005, 498). In the Waveney Valley these developments probably coincided with a change in religion. Christianity was introduced into the area at a relatively early date, due to the activity of Bishop Felix (d. 647), who helped to establish the Church of Rome in East Anglia (Plunkett 2005, 101–2), ahead of the mission from the Church of Iona in AD 653. There is evidence that he received Flixton (which possibly derives its name from his), along with South Elmham, as an endowment from the Wuffings (Scarfe 2002, 94). At this time, ecclesiastical sites were establishing their own settlement hierarchy (Härke 1997, 147) and some consequent re-organisation of lands may have caused the Flixton community to move, perhaps to the present-day village.

IX. Conclusion

The two Anglo-Saxon burial grounds at Flixton have been only partially excavated, and yet the general character of the site has been successfully recorded and the findings pave the way for further investigation of the settlement. Although in many ways the cemeteries have proved to be typical of the Early Anglo-Saxon period, there are aspects of the site which are particularly significant, if not unique. The settlement of Anglo-Saxon England was immensely complex and locally variable (Higham 2007) and it is these inconsistencies between sites that are the most significant (Hines 2002). If we are ever to piece together the history of this period, each site has to be allowed to tell its own story, and Flixton's story has been one of a community on the outskirts of a major territory, evolving and restructuring to meet changing circumstances, before finally disappearing back into the landscape of barrows in which it had first appeared.

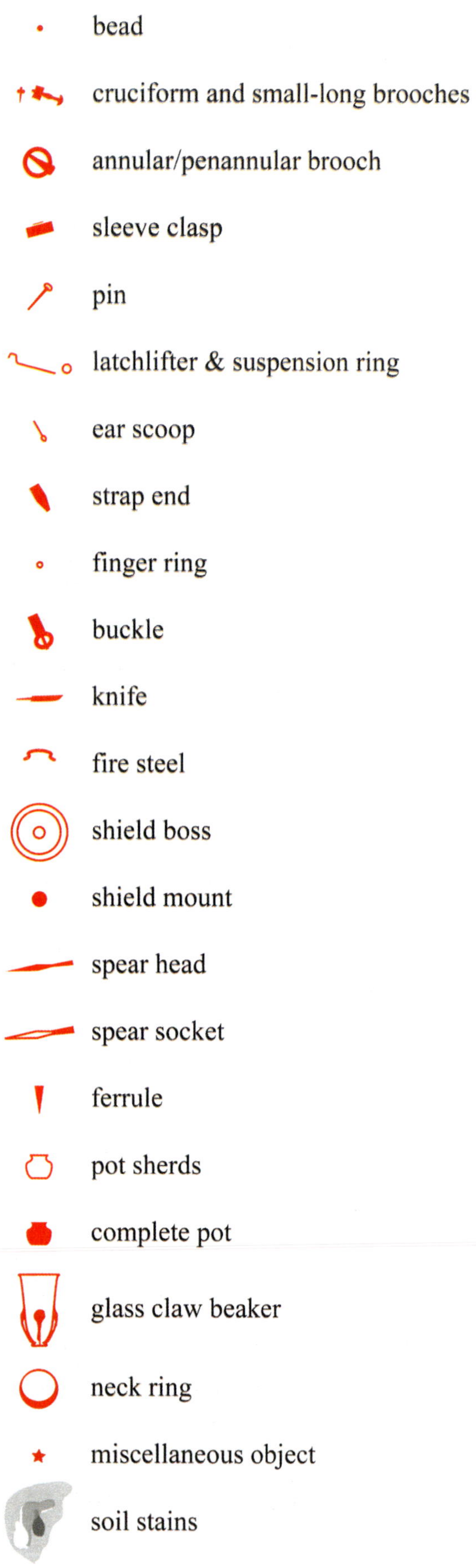

Figure 15.1 Key to grave plans

Chapter 15. Inventory of Graves

I. Introduction

The inventory has been compiled by the following:

Sue Anderson	ceramics and human bone
Stuart Boulter	description of grave
Rose Broadley	glass beaker
Birte Brugmann	glass and amber beads
David Earle Robinson	plant remains from Graves 2 and 55
Vanessa Fell	X-ray fluorescence of metalwork (see also Table 15.1 at end), horn and skin products on knives and scanning electron microscopy
Allan R. Hall	plant remains from Grave 17
Janet Lang	metallography of spearheads
Jude Plouviez	Roman coins
Ian Riddler	knives, spearheads and other ironwork
Stephanie Spain	shields
Penelope Walton Rogers	brooches, pins, clasps, buckles, metal beads, textiles, skin/leather straps, optical microscopy of fibres and dye analysis
Jacqui Watson	mineral-preserved wood

Numbers in bold are the numbers used in the text, on the grave plans and on the illustrated finds within the inventory. The numbers following individual artefact entries represent the site code and then the original small-find number in italics. In the object descriptions, where appropriate, D. = diameter, Ht. = height, Th. = thickness, L. = length, W. = width. The grave inventory is followed by a key to the bead terminology and a table of the results of the X-ray fluorescence analysis (Table 15.1). Figure 15.1 presents a key to the artefact symbols used on the grave plans.

II. Flixton I (FLN 008)

Grave A (008:*0113*)
Figs 15.2–15.3; Pls 7.17–7.18
Dimensions: 1.9m x 0.7m
Orientation: 239°
Container for body: None recognised
Finds gender: Female
Age and Sex: Possible juvenile, indeterminate sex
Body position: Supine, extended, head to west.
Description: An essentially sub-rectangular cut with a small irregularity on its southern side which may represent the collapse caused by an 'unknown foot' that is described on the context sheet. The grave was located on the southern side, and cut the inner edge, of ring-ditch 008:*0100* and survived to a depth of 0.15m. A record of the grave fill was not made, but was almost certainly a mixture of sand and gravel reflecting the surrounding natural subsoil and fill of the ring-ditch into which it had been cut.

Only a very small proportion of the skeleton had survived, one bone fragment (skull) along with a small area of staining that may have been related to the location of the body. However, the grave shape and finds distribution suggests that the body had been supine and extended while the bone fragment is consistent with the head lying to the west. No evidence was recorded of a container for the body.

Two small-long brooches (A/1 and A/2), one of which was fragmentary, were found lying together central to the grave and towards its western end. A complete, but fragmented glass claw beaker (A/3) lay in the south-east corner with its top facing the western end of the grave. The approximate position of a ceramic bowl (A/4) places it overlapping the western end of the grave adjacent to the claw beaker.

A/1 Fragments of a copper-alloy **small-long brooch** with trefoil head and lengthways facets on the foot stem: foot terminal missing. Single-lug pin support and pin catch both broken. Type: EAC *sm2*. Fragments 28 x 28mm and 24 x 8mm; reconstructed L.65mm. 008:*0056*.

A/2 Copper-alloy **small-long brooch** with trefoil head and sub-triangular foot. Single-lug pin support and iron corrosion representing absent pin; pin catch broken. Stamped decoration on head and foot terminal, made with hollow triangle punch. Type: EAC *sm2*. L.65mm, W.29mm. 008:*0057*.

A/3 Fragments of a complete glass **claw beaker**. Pale translucent green glass marbled with very dark red glass. Rounded rim. Two rows of four claws, featuring thick indented vertical trails and offset to form a zigzag. Very fine dark red trailing both above and below the claws. Concave foot at base, with pontil mark on underside. Type: Evison 3c. Ht.167mm; rim D.*c.*98mm; foot D.37mm. 008:*0058*.

A/4 Near-complete hemispherical **bowl** with flat base and plain rim, coarse granitic inclusions, patchy brown/black. Inner surface worn to expose grits, external surface smoothed and sooted. Rim D.*c.*60mm, 25% complete (see also Fig. 7.19.2). 008:*0008*.

Flixton I, artefacts not from graves (NG)
Fig. 15.3

I/NG1 Body sherds of ?sub-biconical or globular **vessel**, medium sandy with occasional coarse quartz inclusions, light brown externally and blackened internally. Decorated with square cross stamps: Briscoe Type C3ai (see also Fig. 7.19.1). 008:*0006*.

I/NG2 Fragment of iron **buckle** with remains of oval loop and complete tongue. Thin layer of skin/leather pierced by tongue. Type: possibly Marzinzik I.11a. W.34mm x 25mm. 008:*0007*.

I/NG3 Fragment of a small copper-alloy **cruciform brooch**, including head, top knob and incomplete wings and bow. It has reflexed wings and a full-round knob cast with the brooch. Single lug pin support and remains of iron pin spring. 22 x 13mm. 008:*0061*.

I/NG4 Cast copper-alloy **buckle** loop with inset axis and depression in tongue rest; front is flat, back is concave. Type: see Chapter 7.II. 008:*0062*.

I/NG5 Fragment of **Roman coin** with two circular perforations close to rim. Coin identified as a worn bronze *nummus*, with damaged margins, probably Crispus, AD 318–24. Obverse —]L[—]IS[——]NOB C; reverse [Caesarum] NOSTROR[um, wreath, VOT / X. Mint illegible. Coin D.19mm, perforations D.2mm. 008:*0065*.

I/NG6 Fragment of **Roman coin** with circular perforation close to rim. Coin identified as an extremely corroded bronze *nummus*, probably AD 348–60. Obverse illegible; reverse probably 'Fel Temp Reparatio', Fallen Horseman type. Coin D.15mm, perforation D.2mm. 008:*0066*.

III. Flixton II: rectangular plot (FLN 053 and FLN 062)

Grave 1 (053:*0303*)
Figs 15.2 and 15.4
Dimensions: 2.1m x 1.3m
Orientation: 244°
Container for body: None recognised
Finds gender: Male

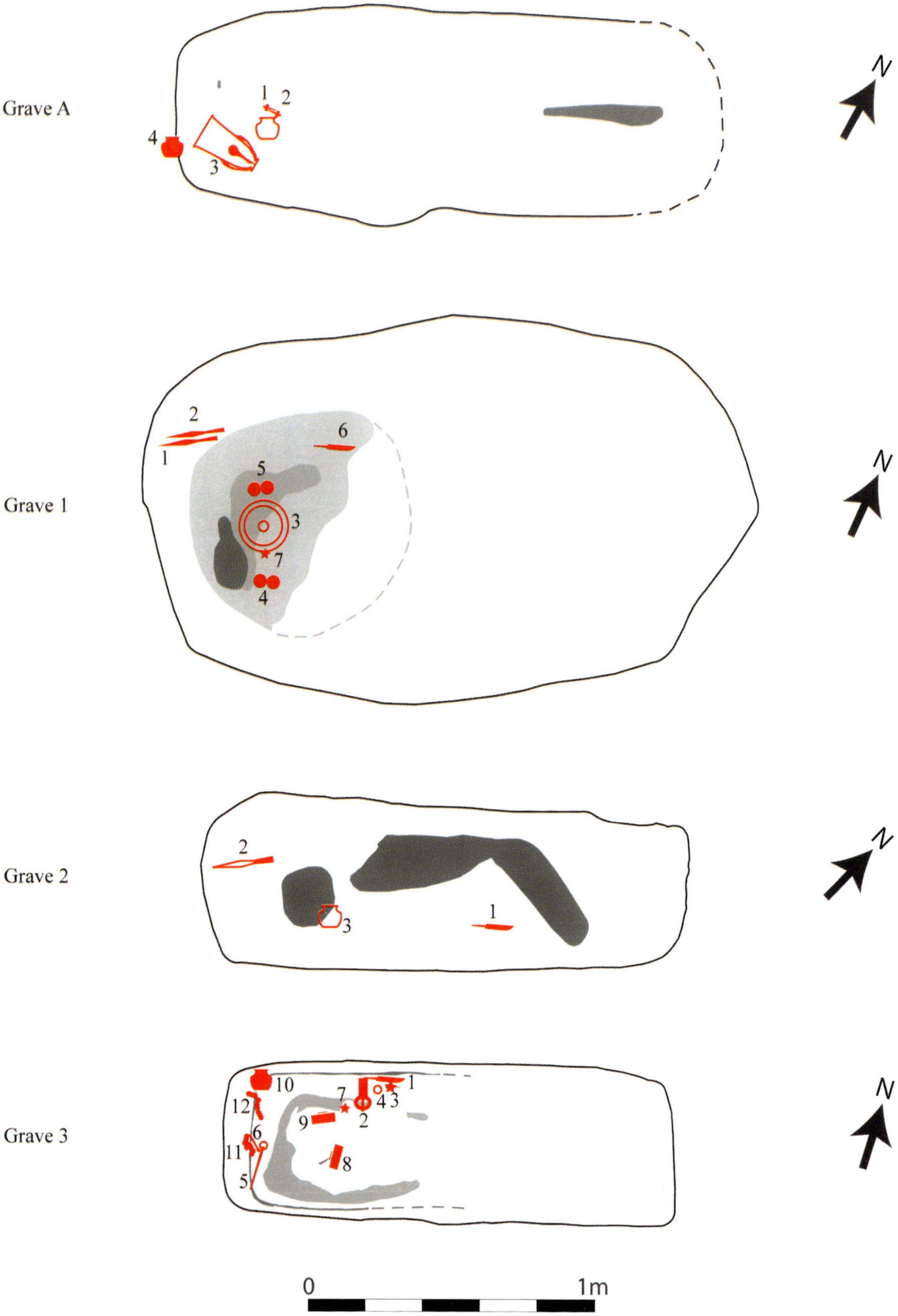

Figure 15.2 Plans of Flixton I Grave A and Flixton II Graves 1–3 (scale 1:20)

Age and Sex: Young to middle-aged, indeterminate sex
Skeletal remains: Very poor, flaky. Fragments of left parietal, temporal and mandible (17 teeth survive), and pieces of proximal humerus and shaft (preserved by shield boss). Tooth wear moderate.
Body position: Indeterminate, head to west
Associated features: None recognised

Description: A well-rounded almost oval cut. Detailed plan shows an irregularity on the south-east corner that was not present on photograph. The fill (053:*0304*) comprised relatively homogenous light brown silty sand with gravel inclusions. The grave survived to a maximum depth of 0.56m with near vertical sides to the north and west with a shallower

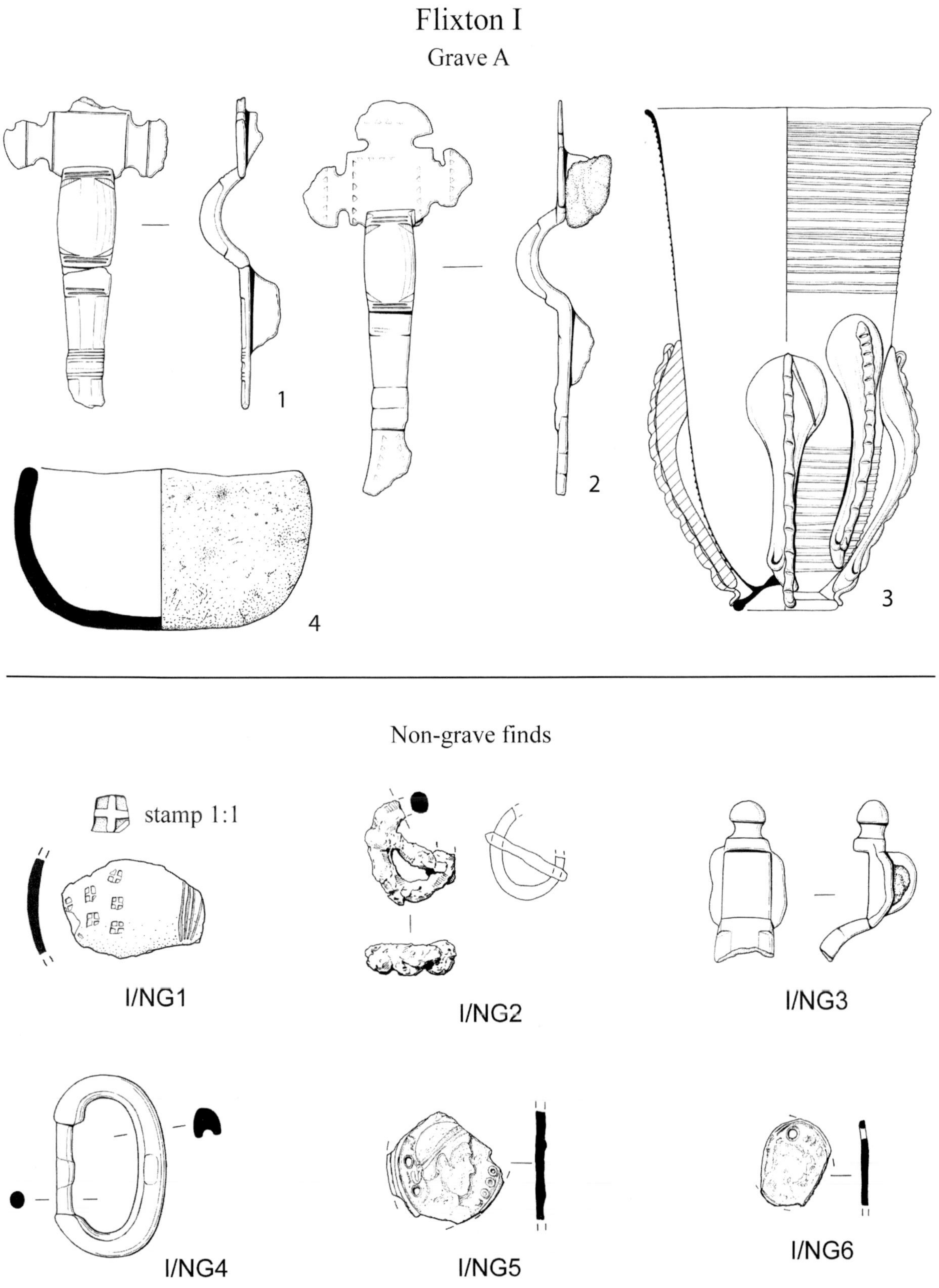

Figure 15.3 Grave goods; Flixton I Grave A (scales: 1 and 2 at 1:1; 3 at 1:2; 4 at 1:3) and unstratified (NG) cemetery finds from Flixton I (scales: 1 at 1:3; pottery stamp at 1:1; 2 at 1:2; 3–6 at 1:1)

slope to the south and east. The base of the grave was level along its long axis but exhibited a more rounded profile across its width.

Skeletal remains (053:*0348*) were limited to fragments of skull, teeth and other small pieces preserved by the shield boss (1/3 i). There was no direct evidence for a container for the body although a surface cleaning undertaken prior to excavation did reveal a faint but regular rectangular shape in the fill that may have been associated with a coffin or other container. This could have been the result of overburden dropping down into a collapsed container, variable subsidence/compaction at the centre of the grave compared to the edge or, alternatively, tip-lines formed as the grave was backfilled.

Two spearheads (1/1 and 1/2) within the upper fill of the grave were the first finds recovered from the site which alerted the excavation team to the presence of the cemetery. However, the most exceptional thing about this grave was the stain and fittings relating to a shield (1/3 i–ii, 1/4, 1/5 and 1/7), the circular shape of which could clearly be seen, although

Flixton II
Grave 1

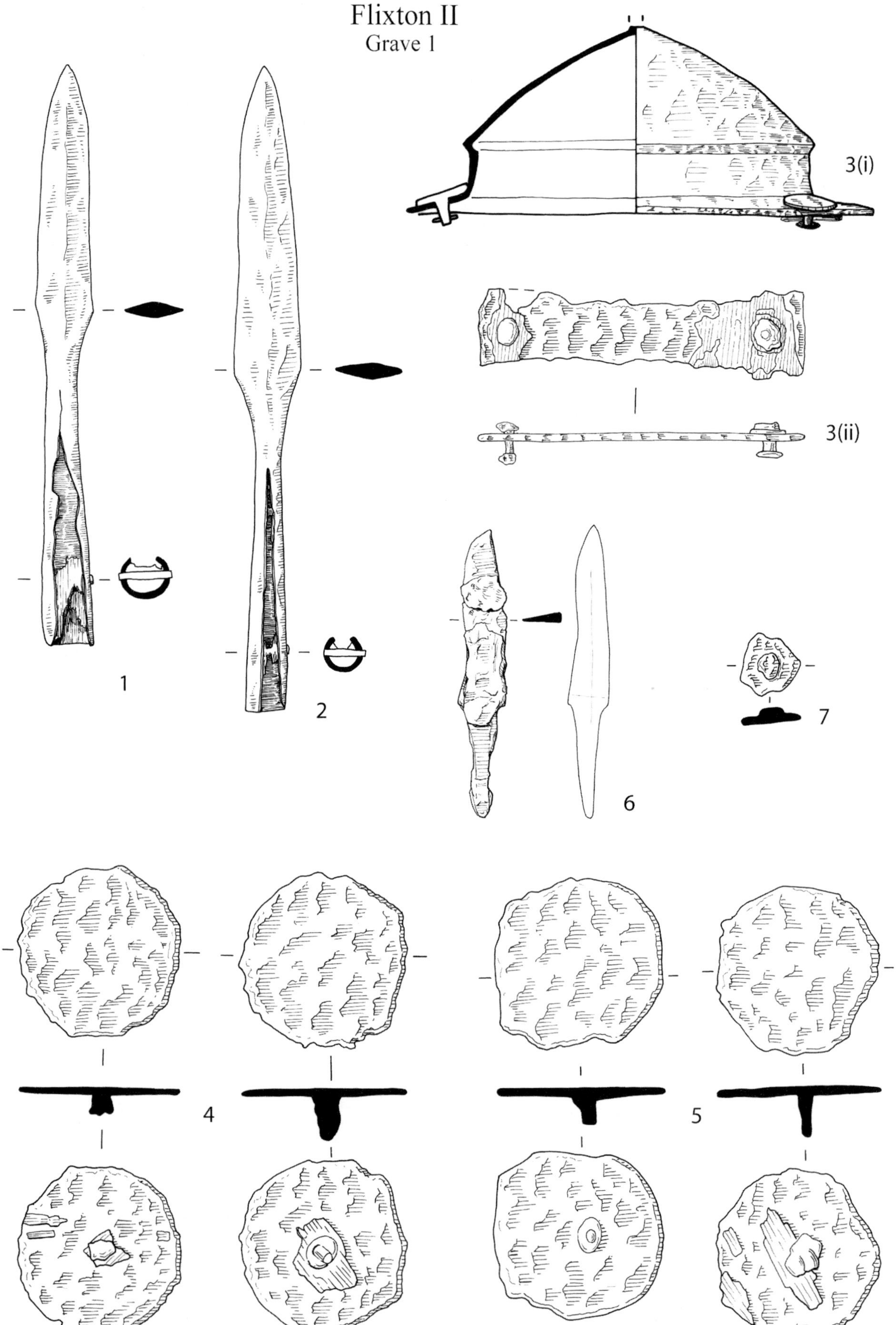

Figure 15.4 Grave goods; Flixton II Grave 1 (scale: 1–7 at 1:2)

not appearing fully on plan or photographs as the eastern side was lost during excavation. An iron knife (1/6) lay within the area of the shield stain on its north-east side, its long axis aligned with that of the grave. Two pot sherds (1/8) were also recovered from the fill.

1/1 Complete iron **spearhead**, broad cleft to socket with abundant wood remains. Lateral nail 22mm above base. Cleft socket occupies most of lower part with short length of solid metal of rectangular section leading to narrow blade, scarcely wider than socket. Blade widens in convex curves with straight tapering sides, curved inwards near apex to tip. Lentoid section. Type: Swanton C2, EAC Angular Medium 1. L.209mm, W.20mm. Mineral-preserved wood in socket: *Alnus* sp. (alder). 053:*0119*.

1/2 Complete iron **spearhead**. Cleft socket extends for practically all of shank, with wood remains over its lower part. Blade widens in concave curves and is well rounded at its widest point, tapering thereafter to rounded tip with slightly concave sides. Lentoid in section. Type: Swanton Type C2; EAC Angular Medium 2b. L.233mm, W.24mm. Mineral-preserved wood in socket: *Fraxinus* sp. (ash), made from mature timber. 053:*0120*.

1/3 (i) Iron **shield boss**. Incomplete, missing apex. Carinated convex cone boss with low wall (Ht.15mm), broad flange (W.25mm) and five flat disc-headed rivets (D.20mm), three with broken copper-alloy washers. Type: Dickinson and Härke 3; Spain 3a; EAC COV. Shield board made from ash (TLS), with leather on the front *c*.2.2mm thick, and back 3.6 – 4.0mm thick. 053:*0148*.
(ii) Iron **shield grip**. Strap grip (W.19mm) expanding towards terminals (W.27mm, 30mm). Fastened at each end by a flat disc-headed rivet (D.15mm) with copper-alloy washer (D.10mm). L.120mm. On opposite face from wood, two layers of organic materials, decayed textile or skin product. 053:*0148*.

1/4 Iron **shield board mounts**. Pair of large disc-shaped mounts. D.60mm. Part of a set of four. 053:*1184*.

1/5 Iron **shield board mounts**. Pair of large disc-shaped mounts. D.60mm. Part of a set of four. Plant stems on the front. 053:*1185*.

1/6 Iron **knife**, complete. Narrow tang, widening evenly to shoulder and choil. Back curved lightly throughout, sinuous cutting edge rising to tip. Faint weld line running approximately halfway through blade and on to tang. Type: Drinkall A. L.105mm, blade W.11mm. Faint traces of horn on one side of tang. Mineral-preserved textile on top. 053:*1186*.

1/7 Iron **shield rivet**. Incomplete, shank missing. Top part of a flat disc-shaped rivet (D.20mm). 053:*1189*.

1/8 Two **sherds** (base and body) of a grass/granite-tempered (ESOM) vessel with sparse red grog/ferrous fragments. Buff/brown externally, dark grey internally (from fill 053:*0304*, not formally located or illustrated). 053:*0304*.

Grave 2 (053:*0305*)
Figs 15.2 and 15.5
Dimensions: 1.7m x 0.6m
Orientation: 229°
Container for body: None recognised
Finds gender: Male
Age and Sex: Young adult, sex indeterminate
Skeletal remains: Very poor. A few fragments of teeth only, some too small to identify. Tooth wear slight.
Body position: On right side facing south, legs slightly flexed, head to west
Associated features: None recognised
Description: A sub-rectangular cut that survived to a maximum depth of 0.22m with a fill (053:*0306*) comprising relatively homogenous dark brown sand with gravel inclusions. In profile, the long sides and eastern end were almost vertical while the western end had a more gentle slope merging into the base.

Skeletal remains (053:*0317*) were limited to teeth, although a significant stain was interpreted as relating to the head, torso and upper legs and it was from these that the flexed attitude of the body was deduced. No evidence for a container for the body was recorded.

A fragment from an iron spear socket (2/2) lay towards the western end of the grave while an iron knife (2/1) lay fairly central to the grave, level with the waist area of the body as indicated by the body stain. Four sherds of pottery (2/3) were found associated with the skull stain.

2/1 Iron **knife**, complete. Narrow tang with rounded end, widening in light curve to rounded shoulder and choil. Back curved throughout, cutting edge sinuous and rising slightly to tip. Faint trace of medial weld line. Type: Drinkall D. L.116mm, blade W.12mm. 053:*0136*.

2/2 Lower part of a cleft iron **spearhead socket**, with abundant wood remains. Noticeably open cleft, tapering towards blade and oval in section rather than circular. L.73mm. Plant matter over socket identified as straw, most probably grass or sedge. Mineral-preserved wood in socket: *Fraxinus* sp. (ash). 053:*0138*.

2/3 Four sherds of a grass-tempered (ESO1) sub-biconical **jar** with flat-angled base, decorated with type A2 ring stamps above the slight carination, smoothed but outer surface spalled, sooted. Grey surfaces, red-brown core. (see also Fig. 7.19.3). 053:*0316*.

Grave 3 (053:*0307*)
Figs 15.2, 15.5 and 15.6; Pl. 7.4a
Dimensions: 1.57m x 0.55m
Orientation: 252°
Container for body: Possible coffin of bier recorded at western end of grave
Finds gender: Female
Age and Sex: Indeterminate age and sex although grave size suggests adult
Skeletal remains: Very poor. A few flakes of unidentified green-stained bone, in association with iron ring 3/4
Body position: Stain and finds suggest supine and extended
Associated features: None recognised
Description: A rectangular cut with only minimal rounding of the corners surviving to a depth of 0.22m at its eastern end, reducing to nothing at its western end. The profiles show relatively steep sides to the south and east with more gently sloping to the north and no survival to the west where it had probably been disrupted during machining. The base of the grave was flat across its width but sloped up by as much as 0.05m from east to west. Fill 053:*0308* comprised relatively homogenous brown sand with gravel inclusions.

Skeletal remains were almost entirely absent with only a few flakes of green stained bone (053:*0850*) found adhering to small find 3/4. However, a soil stain towards the western end of the grave appeared to define the upper arms, shoulders and upper spine of the body which, along with the location of the grave goods and size of grave, suggests that the body was supine and extended. A dark brown soil stain running around the western end of the grave, but lost to the east, certainly represents a container for the body. The regularity of this stain makes it one of the few candidates for a genuine coffin recognised at the site, although it could equally represent a rectangular bier.

This was one of the more richly furnished graves. Fifteen sherds from a ceramic bowl (3/10) were located in the north-west corner of the grave cut in association with the possible coffin stain. Other grave goods at the western end, around the area that would have been occupied by the head and shoulders of the body, included a copper-alloy toilet accessory (3/6), two groups of beads (totalling twenty) and a large copper alloy pin (3/5). A group of three objects, a knife (3/1), a buckle (3/2) and a ring (3/4), all of iron, were located approximately halfway down the north side of the grave on the left side of the body close to the waist. Other finds located within the area of the torso included fragments of sleeve clasps (3/7–9), that would have been attached to garments buried with the body, and a cast copper fitting (3/3).

3/1 Iron **knife**, incomplete and in two pieces, lacking part of blade. Rounded end to tang, widening on one side only, with no visible shoulder or choil. Straight back curving at end to tip, curved cutting edge rising to tip. Blade broken, part of it now missing. Type: Drinkall B. L.117mm, blade W.9mm. Horn remains on tang extend to length of 40mm on one side. Mineral-preserved textile in association. 053:*0145a*.

3/2 Large iron **buckle** with oval loop, enlarged tongue rest, and remains of an iron plate with decorated rivet. Rivet head, 18–19mm diameter, has encircling grooves. Tongue has slipped around ring and points away from the loop. Type: Marzinzik II.20 or II.21. 38 x 27mm; plate largest fragment 24 x 21mm. Two different textiles on ?back. 053:*0145b*.

3/3 Cast copper-alloy **object**, of uncertain function. It has a ring, 25mm diameter, with a rectangular bezel, 13 x 9mm, on one side, and a thick arm with three encircling ridges on the opposite side. The arm is the casing for an iron bar. L.32mm, W.25mm. 053:*0146*.

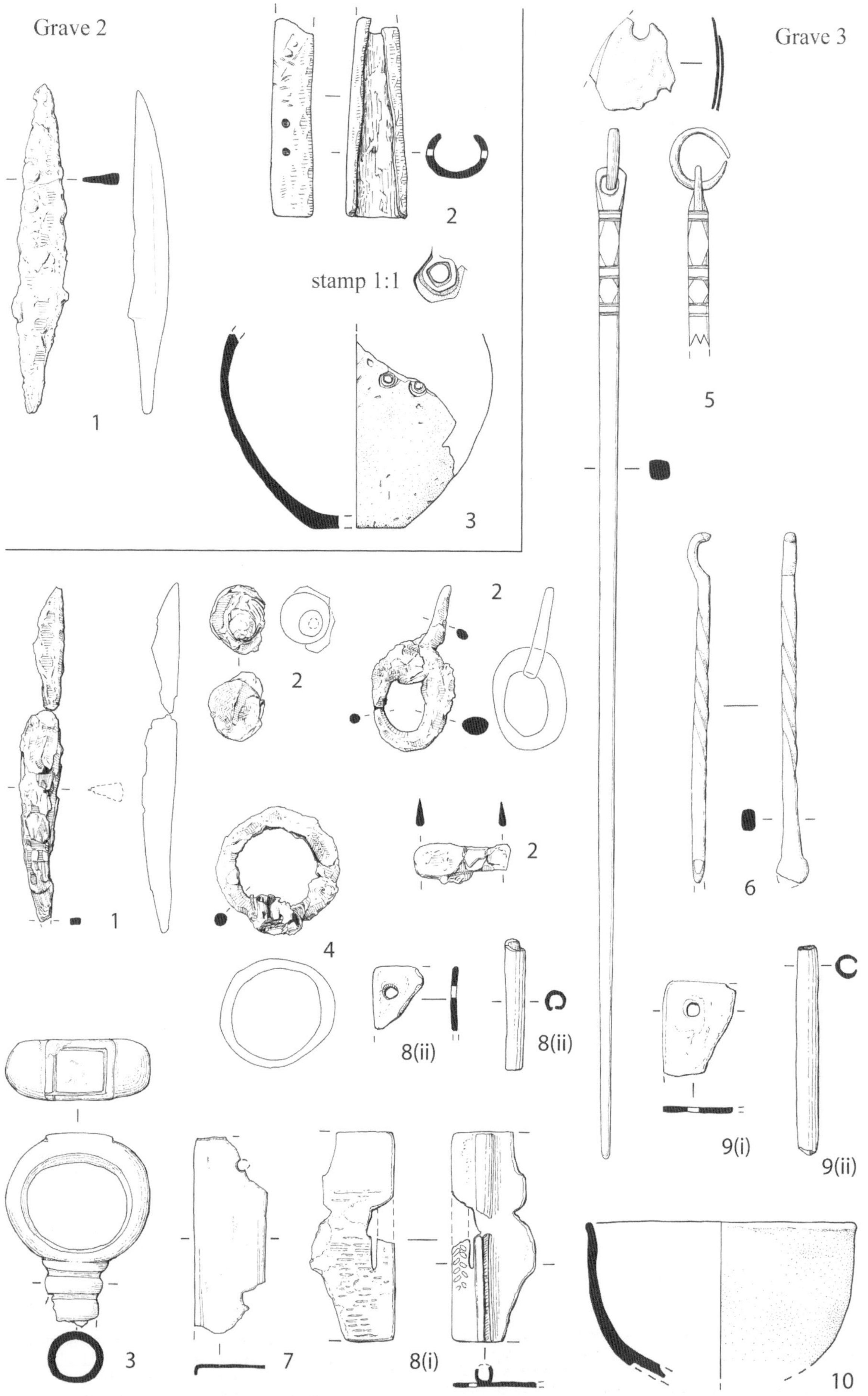

Figure 15.5 Grave goods; Flixton II Grave 2 (scales: 1 and 2 at 1:2; 3 at 1:3; pottery stamp at 1:1) and Flixton II Grave 3 (scales: 1, 2 and 4 at 1:2; 3 and 5–9 at 1:1; 10 at 1:3)

3/4 Iron **ring**, with circular section. D.44mm, ring Th.5mm. Extensive textile remains suggest it was originally tied to a straight object. Bone 053:*0850* found in association. 053:*1150*.

3/5 Long copper-alloy **pin** with ring attachment and detached spangles. Head flattened and perforated (perforation 3mm diameter), to take a pinch ring 11mm diameter, made from 2mm wire. Fragments of flat copper-alloy plates with perforations 3.5mm diameter represent two triangular spangles, reconstructed as 18mm tall x 15mm wide. Beneath head of pin there is a 17mm length of ornament, consisting of two diamond faceted zones bounded by pairs of ridges/grooves. The plain shank is rounded square in section. Type: Ross VIII. L.175mm, D.(shank)3mm, W.(head)6mm. 053:*1153*.

3/6 Near-complete copper-alloy **toilet accessory** with a twisted shank, flat round terminal at one end and broken suspension loop at other. L.62.5mm; W. across terminal 6mm; thickness of shank 3mm. 053:*1155*.

3/7 Fragments of copper-alloy plate, 1mm thick, including a finished edge with two fine incised lines parallel to the edge: possibly from a **sleeve clasp**. Largest 19 x 13mm. 053:*1188*.

3/8 Fragments of a pair of copper-alloy **sleeve clasps**. Type: Hines B13b.
(i) A plain catch-piece with a slot for the catch and a rolled tube. L.37mm, W.>11mm; tube D.4mm. Poorly preserved textile on front and back.
(ii) A corner fragment, 10 x 10mm, with a circular attachment hole 2.5mm diameter, and a fragment of rolled tube, D.3.5mm.
Also fragments of a bone plate <1mm thick, pierced by an iron rivet. 23 x 7mm. 053:*1190*.
Remains of decayed wood in association.

3/9 Fragments of a copper-alloy **sleeve clasp** including (i) piece of flat plate with an attachment hole, 2.5mm diameter, and (ii) rolled tube with five groups of transverse incised lines. Type: Hines B13b. Fragment (i) 16 x 13mm; tube (ii) L.36mm, D.4mm. 053:*1191*.

3/10 Small straight-sided medium sandy **bowl** (ESMS with occasional burnt-out organics) with vertical rim and flat-rounded base, slight spalling and cracking, worn and sooted internally, smoothed externally. Brown with blackened areas inside. Rim D.150mm, 15% complete. (see also Fig. 7.19.4). 053:*0315*.

3/11 Beads 053:*1154*, *1158–1167* (*in situ* plan Fig. 15.6; Pl. 7.4a *1154*, *1165–66*). Brugmann Group A1.
Eleven glass **beads**: Type *Blue:* 1 very short, globular, D.11–15mm (*1164*); 8 short, annular, D.6–10mm (*1154*, *1158–1162*, *1165–66*); 2 fragmented (*1163*, *1167*)

3/12 Beads 053:*1174–1182* (*in situ* plan Fig. 15.6; Pl. 7.4a *1174–5*, *1177–1182*) Brugmann Group A1.
Four amber **beads** (total weight 7.9g; worn): 1 short, irregular, D.26mm (*1179*); 2 short, irregular, D.16–21mm (*1178*, *1181*); 1 medium, rounded, D.11–15mm (*1180*)
Five glass **beads**: Type *Blue:* 2 short, asymmetrical globular, D.11–15mm (*1174–5*).
Type *Traffic Light:* 1 medium, globular; D.11–15mm (*1177*).
Type *Polychrome1:* 1 medium, globular; D.11–15mm (*1182*).
Type *Polychrome5:* 1 globular, fragmented (*1176*).

Grave 4 (053:*0309*)
Figs 15.7 and 15.8
Dimensions: 2.6m x 0.98m
Orientation: 228°
Container for body: Indeterminate grey sandy stain
Finds gender: Female
Age and Sex: Indeterminate age and sex
Skeletal remains: None
Body position: Indeterminate, but size of grave suggests extended. Two grave fills and disturbance of artefacts suggest female burial followed by a second burial.
Associated features: None recognised
Description: A large sub-rectangular cut with well-rounded ends surviving to a depth of 0.4m. The profiles show near vertical edges at both ends with more gently sloping concave edges along the sides with a relatively flat bottom. Two fills (collectively 053:*0310*) were recognised after surface cleaning, a central dark brown sand with gravel inclusions and an outer fill of orange sand that was similar to the natural subsoil at that juncture.

There was no skeletal material surviving or staining that may have represented the vestiges of a body, although the grave goods indicate that the head was likely to have been to the west. A dark grey sand stain forming the junction between the inner and outer fills on the southern side of the grave may have been evidence for a container for the body.

A copper-alloy cruciform brooch (4/2) was found close to the long axis of the grave just to the west of centre. The upside down position of this object may indicate disturbance. Another incomplete brooch (II/NG1) and further fragments (II/NG2 and II/NG3) were unstratified, but their similarities with 4/2 have been considered as evidence to suggest that they originated in Grave 4 and were subsequently displaced. An iron knife was located approximately one third of the way down the north side of the grave, as measured from its western end (4/1). Other finds included a group of four, an iron collar (4/3), a fragment from an iron buckle (4/4), a fragment of copper-alloy sheet (4/6) and a small iron buckle (4/7), found in close association with brooch 4/2. Fragments from a possible lead finger ring (4/5) were recorded in a central position in the western half of the grave.

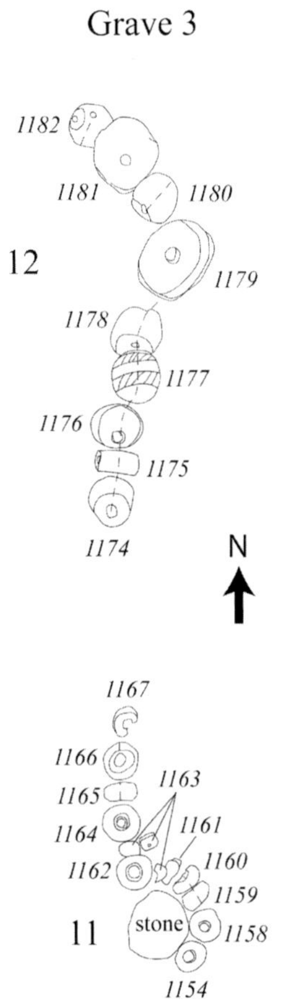

Figure 15.6 Flixton II Grave 3, *in situ* plan of bead groups 11 and 12. All contexts numbers are site 053 (scale 1:2)

4/1 Iron **knife**, fragmentary, lacking end of tang. Tang widens to distinct shoulder and rounded choil. Back straight and then angled down lightly to rounded tip, cutting edge shows little wear, straight and then curving to tip. Abundant horn remains on both sides of tang. Slightly curved vertical handle line defined by horn at shoulder. Type: Drinkall C. Blade W.16mm. Skin product on both sides of blade, up to 4mm thick. Imprint of textile on one face. 053:*0139*.

4/2 Copper-alloy **cruciform brooch** with no lappets, slightly flared wings and heart-shaped nose. The top knob has been cast with the brooch, but the side knobs, presumably separately cast, are missing. The animal head has square eyes and is separated from the bow by two broad flat ridges. Ornament is punched ring-and-dot, of which there are five in the centre of the head, two parallel rows of four on the bow and two on the nose. The pin support is a single lug cast with the brooch and has remains of a transverse iron bar on one side; the pin catch is cast with the brooch and turned to the left (viewed from back with foot pointing down); and the pin is absent. Type: Mortimer B2; EAC *Xform1*. L.103mm, W. (across head) 39mm. Bow L.22.5mm x W.16mm x Ht.11mm. Foot L.48mm x W. (across nose) 19mm. Textile on front, and cords around and over pin support, top knob and transverse bar. 053:*0141*.

4/3 Iron **collar**. D.27mm, Ht.13mm, Th.10mm. Textile on one face. 053:*0142*.

4/4 Fragment of iron object, possibly a **buckle** loop. 32 x 19mm. L.>19mm, W.32mm. Textile on back, front and inside loop. 053:*0143*.

4/5 Fragments of a lead (XRF) **ring** with circular section, possibly finger ring. D.25–26mm; band D.3–4mm. 053:*0144*.

4/6 Corner fragment of copper-alloy **sheet**. Th.<1mm, with a circular perforation, 4mm diameter. 11 x 9mm. Not illustrated. 053:*1151*.

4/7 Small iron **buckle** with oval loop and no plate. Tongue points diagonally upwards. Type: Marzinzik I.11a-i. 20 x 18mm. 053:*1152*.

Unstratified (context 053:0001) but probably from Grave 4
Fig. 15.7

II/NG1 Copper-alloy **cruciform brooch**, matching 4/2, except for punched ring-and-dot ornament, which comprises two parallel rows of six along the bow, and, on the foot, pairs of shallow transverse grooves that seem to meet in the centre. Decoration is shallow and worn. One wing has been damaged in antiquity and an angular piece is missing. The remains of a tin-based metal coating on the wing and the headplate (XRF) suggest that the brooch has had a soldered repair. The pin is recently broken and remains of the tip are present in the catch. L.104mm, W.39mm. Bow L.22.5mm x W.15.5mm x Ht.11mm high. Foot L.49mm x W. (across nose) 19mm. Poorly preserved textile or cordage on the back. 053:*1157*.

II/NG2 Cast copper-alloy **knob** from a **cruciform brooch**, probably 4/2. Plain with semi-circular section; transverse slot to fit edge of brooch and axial iron rod inside. 13mm x 10.5mm. 053:*0137*.

II/NG3 Cast copper-alloy **knob** from a **cruciform brooch**, same as 053:*0137*. 13mm x 10mm.

Grave 5 (053:*0311*)
Figs 15.8–15.9; Pl. 7.4a
Dimensions: *c*.2.1m x 1.8m
Orientation: 227°
Container for body: Stain covering western end of grave base may represent a coffin or bier
Finds gender: Female
Age and Sex: Indeterminate age and sex although grave size suggests adult
Skeletal remains: None.
Body position: Indeterminate although grave goods suggest head to west
Associated features: Cut by Grave 7
Description: A sub-rectangular cut with slight tapering towards the west and moderately rounded ends. The eastern end of Grave 5 appears to coincide with that of cutting Grave 7. Within the 0.25m deep cut, the excavated fill (053:*0312*) comprised relatively homogenous brown silty sand with inclusions of gravel.

Skeletal remains were completely absent although a rectangular (0.3m x 0.15m) area of darker stain was recorded within the more extensive stain on the base of the grave towards its western end. Given the location of grave goods, this could represent the position of the skull although other organic objects or materials could be responsible.

Potsherd 5/1 appears on plan to be in cutting Grave 7, but was considered during excavation to have been in Grave 5 and subsequently disturbed by the later grave cut. However, this was by no means certain. Other grave goods comprised a group of nine beads (collectively 5/2a–i) located towards the western end of the grave in an area that would have been close to the neck and shoulders of the body.

5/1 Rim and body of a fine sandy globular **jar** (ESFS with occasional quartz conglomerates) with everted rim, burnt food residue inside, smoothed/burnished externally, with Briscoe's type H2ai segmented-S stamps. Red-brown to black externally, black internally. Rim D.160mm, 15% complete.(see also Fig. 7.19.5). 053:*0318*.

5/2 Beads 053:*0147a–i* (Pl. 7.4a *0147a–e* and *i*). Brugmann Group B.
Five amber **beads** (total weight 2.2g; worn): 1 long, faceted, D.6–10mm (*0147f*); 1 medium, faceted, D.11–15mm (*0147i*); 3 medium, faceted, D.6–10mm (*0147e*, *g–h*).
Four glass **beads**: Type *Cylindrical, Round:* 2 medium, cylindrical, red, D.6–10mm (*0147a–b*); 2 medium, cylindrical, blue, D.6–10mm (*0147c–d*).

Grave 6 (053:*0313*)
Figs 15.8–15.9
Dimensions: 1.7m x 0.8m
Orientation: 223°
Container for body: Extensive area of staining at eastern end and some towards west, possible bier
Finds gender: Male
Age and Sex: Indeterminate age and sex; grave size suggests adult
Skeletal remains: None
Body position: Indeterminate
Associated features: ?Cuts Grave 9
Description: An essentially sub-rectangular cut with a more rounded western end and gently curving sides. During excavation it was thought that Grave 6 cut Grave 9. However, this was based on limited stratigraphic information with the two features only overlapping by 0.1m with very little differentiation in their fills and on that basis this relationship must be considered to be tenuous. Within the 0.22m deep cut, the fill (053:*0314*) comprised relatively homogenous brown sand with gravel inclusions.

No skeletal remains were recorded and no element of the basal stain within the grave was obviously associated with a body. With no evidence for a container other than the basal stain, its interpretation as a possible bier was considered more favourably than the bottom of a coffin.
Nine pot sherds (6/2), all from the same vessel, were recorded towards the south-west corner of the grave with a fragmentary iron spear socket (6/1) in the north-west corner, all at a high level in the fill. Given that the pot sherds were relatively widely spaced and that the spear socket was incomplete, it seems reasonable to suggest that there had been some post-depositional damage.

6/1 Fragmentary cleft iron **spearhead socket**, circular in section. Lateral nail 17mm above socket base. L.61mm. Mineral-preserved wood in socket: *Fraxinus* sp. (ash) made from mature timber. 053:*1183*.

6/2 Baggy/globular grass-tempered (ESO1) **jar** with short vertical/inturned rim and rounded base, burnt food residue inside, sooted, slight burnishing. Grey/brown externally, black internally. Rim D.160mm, 10% complete (see also Fig. 7.19.6). 053:*0351*.

Grave 7 (053:*0320*)
Figs 15.8–15.9
Dimensions: 1.52m x 0.6m
Orientation: 242°
Container for body: Extensive stain on base of grave, possible bier
Finds gender: Uncertain
Age and Sex: Young–middle aged ?male
Skeletal remains: Very poor, skull flaky. Fragments of left side of cranial vault, face and mandible, 14 teeth. Tooth wear moderate. Zygoma robust.
Body position: Extended, supine, head to west
Associated features: Cuts Grave 5
Description: Exhibited a sub-rectangular cut, although narrowing towards the west with moderately rounded ends. The grave was 0.44m deep with a flat bottom and near vertical edges and a fill (053:*0321*) comprising relatively homogenous brown silty sand with gravel.

Skeletal remains (053:*0319*) were limited to sections of the skull with the extensive stain over the base of the feature interpreted as part of a container for the body, possibly a bier. A second stain at a higher level running for 0.7m down the southern edge of the grave was of indeterminate origin, possibly part of a coffin or even the shaft of a spear. While no spear-head was recovered from this grave, it could have been disturbed during soil-stripping. Indeed, a fragment (053:NG/7) of possible spearhead was recovered from the upcast bund adjacent to the cemetery area, along with a number of other objects that must have originally been deposited as grave goods.

An iron buckle (7/1) was found within the extensive basal stain towards the western end of the grave in the area that, judging from the position of the skull, would have been occupied by torso of the body.

7/1 Iron **buckle** with oval-to-D-shape loop and no plate. Type: Marzinzik I.10d-i. 25 x 20mm. Traces of textile on front of tongue. 053:*1168*.

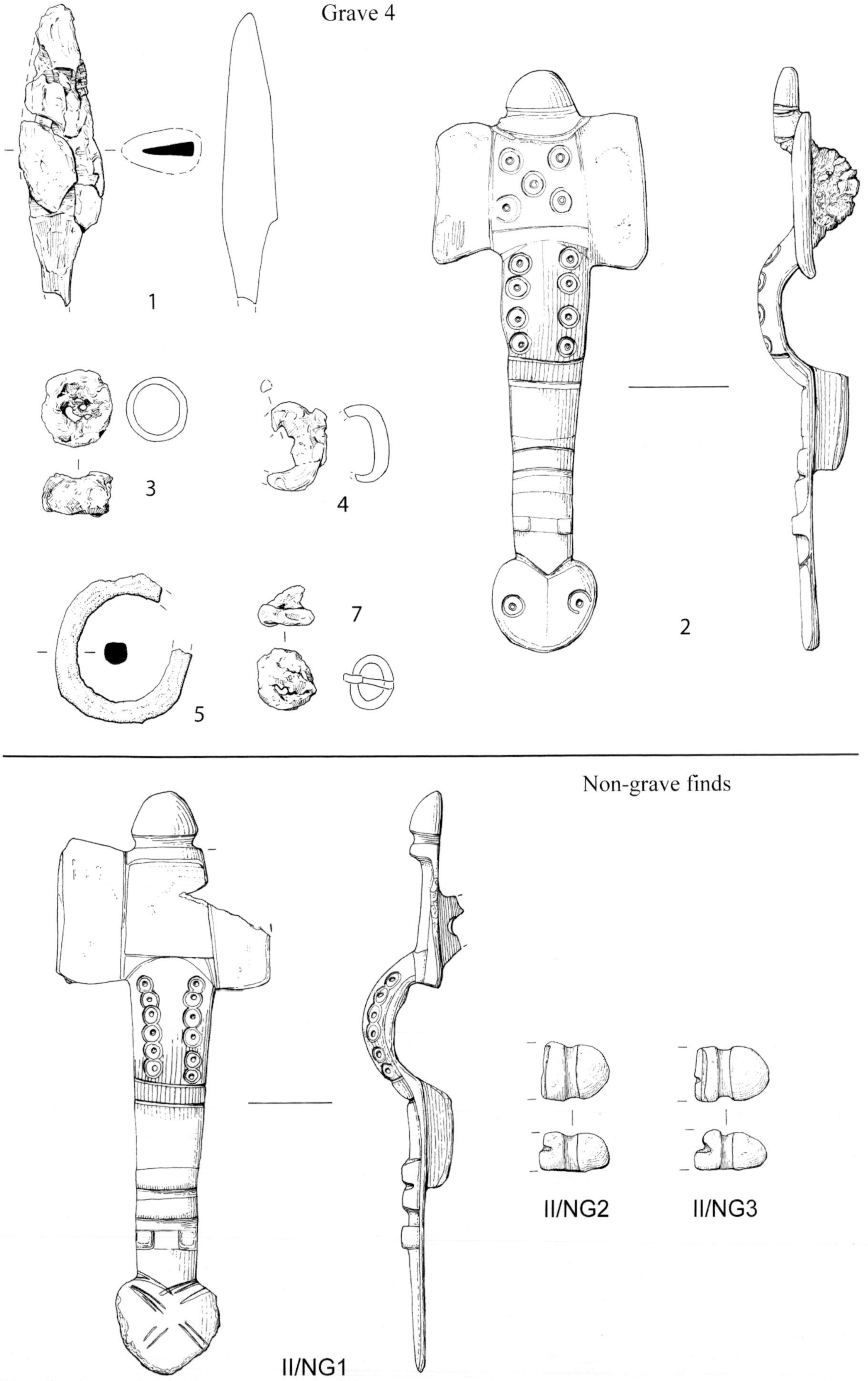

Figure 15.7 Grave goods; Flixton II Grave 4 (scales: 1, 3, 4 and 7 at 1:2; 2 at 1:1) and unstratified (NG) cemetery finds likely to be from Grave 4 (scale: 1:1)

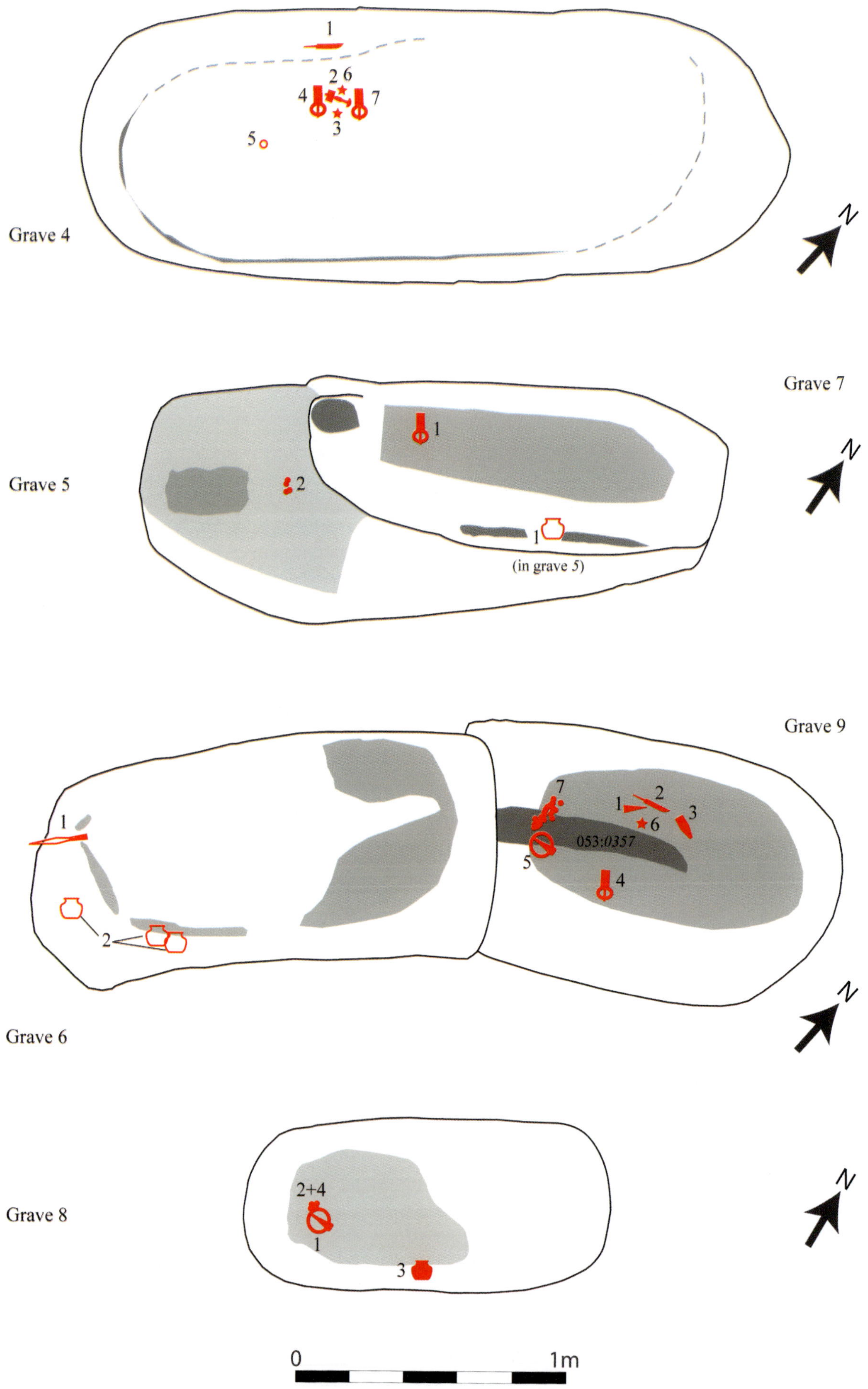

Figure 15.8 Plans of Flixton II Graves 4–9 (scale 1:20)

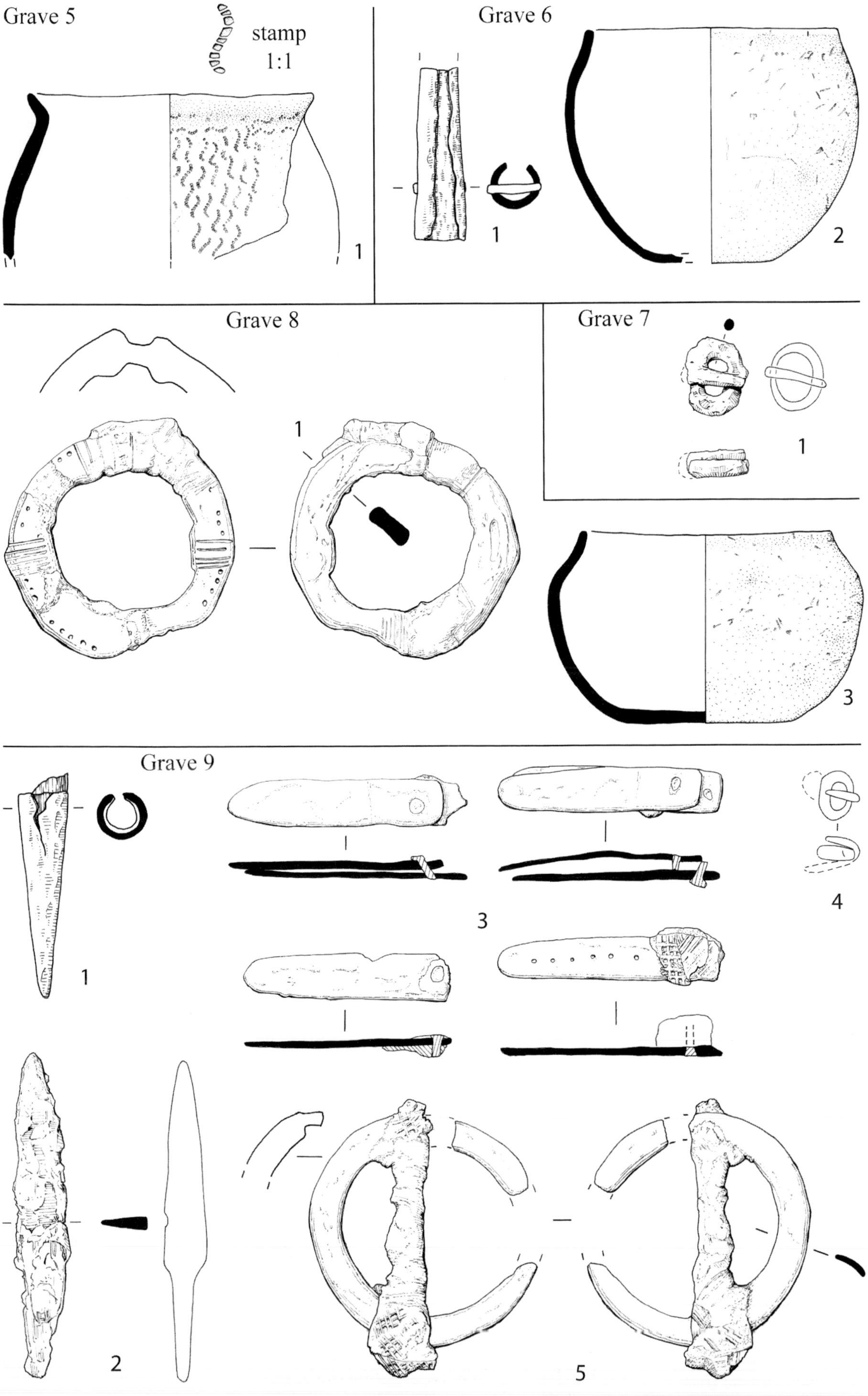

Figure 15.9 Grave goods; Flixton II Grave 5 (scales: 1 at 1:3; pottery stamp at 1:1), Flixton II Grave 6 (scales: 1 at 1:2; 2 at 1:3), Flixton II Grave 7 (scale: 1 at 1:2), Flixton II Grave 8 (scales: 1 at 1:1; 3 at 1:3) and Flixton II Grave 9 (scales: 1, 2 and 4 at 1:2; 3 and 5 at 1:1)

Grave 8 (053:*0344*)
Figs 15.8–15.9, Pl. 7.4a
Dimensions: 1.35m x 0.6m
Orientation: 239°
Container for body: None recognised
Finds gender: Female
Age and Sex: Indeterminate age and sex although grave size may indicate a child
Skeletal remains: None
Body position: Indeterminate, but grave goods suggest head to west
Associated features: None recognised
Description: A sub-rectangular cut with well-rounded ends (shown as almost oval on the smaller scale site plan) only surviving to a depth of 0.18m with a fill (053:*0345*) comprising homogenous brown silty sand with gravel inclusions.

No skeletal remains were recorded and an amorphous stain located towards the western end of the grave was insufficiently defined to interpret it as either a body stain or vestiges of a container.

A group of seven pot sherds (8/3) was found central to the southern edge of the grave while a small group of finds comprising an annular brooch (8/1), an associated copper-alloy disc (8/2) and five beads (8/4) were recorded central to the western end of the grave. This area would have been occupied by the neck and shoulders of the body, providing the head to the west interpretation was correct.

8/1 Copper-alloy **annular brooch** with a thick flat ring and four zones expanded widthways, so that the inner edge is stepped in places. Ornament consists of two transverse grooves on either side of the pin emplacement; two groups of four grooves in the expanded zones at 90° and 270°; and a row of punched dots around the outer edge between the transverse grooves. Bar pin emplacement 4.5mm long x 3.5mm wide. Iron pin has an irregular section, 2mm wide. D.41mm; ring 6.5–7mm wide x 3.5mm thick. Well preserved textiles on front and back of brooch. 053:*1169*.

8/2 Copper-alloy fragment, part of a **perforated disc**. D.9mm (+), inner D.2.5.mm, Th.3.0mm. Not illustrated. 053:*1430*.

8/3 Small globular offset-shouldered grass-tempered (ESO1) **bowl** with vertical rim and flat-rounded base, sooted. Oxidised orange-brown externally, dark grey internally. Rim D.150mm, 11%. (see also Fig. 7.19.7). 053:*0347*.

8/4 Beads 053:*1170–3*, *1429* (Pl. 7.4a *1170–3*). Brugmann Group A2.
One amber **bead** (weight 0.3g; worn): 1 very short, irregular, D.11–15mm (*1170*).
Four glass **beads**: Type *Constricted Cylindrical:* 1 very long, cylindrical, D.3–5mm (*1173*).
Type *Constricted Cylindrical variant:* 1 very long, cylindrical; wound, perforated sides constricted, D.3–5mm (*1172*)
Type *Polychrome4:* 1 medium, cylindrical-globular; translucent green wide crossing trails on a white body, D.6–10mm (*1429*)
Other bead: blue-green globular: 1 medium, globular, D.6–10mm (*1171*).

Grave 9 (053:*0349*)
Figs 15.8–15.10, Pl. 7.4a
Dimensions: 1.3m x 0.9m
Orientation: 239°
Container for body: Possible bier
Finds gender: Female
Age and Sex: Indeterminate age and sex
Skeletal remains: Very poor. Tiny fragments of tooth enamel only, not identifiable.
Body position: Indeterminate, finds indicate head to west, must be crouched if adult
Associated features: Cut by Grave 6
Description: An essentially sub-rectangular cut with a rounded end to east, squared to west. Exhibited a steep sided profile, almost vertical to the east, with a relatively flat bottom and survived to a depth of 0.55m. The fill (053:*0350*) comprised relatively homogenous brown silty sand with gravel inclusions.

Skeletal remains (053:*0361*) were limited to tiny fragments of tooth enamel. Two discrete stains were recorded: a dark grey/brown sandy stain 053:*0357*, which had the appearance of a plank of wood, was 0.1m wide and 0.75m long and dipped steeply into the grave from west to east, and an oval-shaped basal stain of dark brown silty sand, possibly representing a bier.

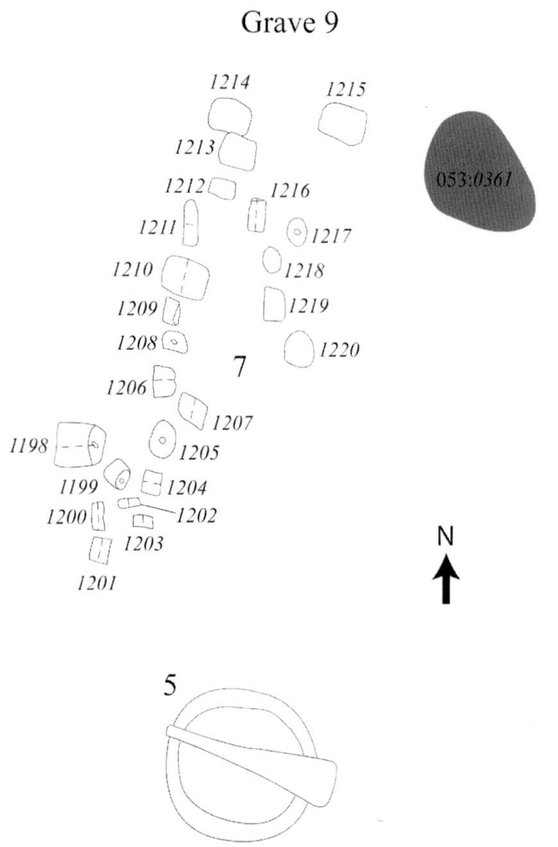

Figure 15.10 Flixton II Grave 9, *in situ* plan of annular brooch 5 and bead group 7. All contexts numbers are site FLN 053 (scale 1:2)

A relatively well-furnished grave with all finds recorded within the confines of the basal stain. Four finds were grouped just to the north of centre of the basal stain, an iron ferrule (9/1), an iron knife (9/2), a stack of three copper-alloy strap-ends (9/3) and a copper-alloy plate (9/6), the latter probably a pouch fitting. The position of this group of objects approximately halfway down the grave suggests they were attached at the waist of the body. A small iron buckle (9/4) was found close to the southern edge of the basal stain. A further group of objects, an annular brooch (9/5) and twenty-three beads (9/7), were positioned towards the western end of the basal stain in an area that would have been close to the head and shoulders of a body lain out with its head to the west.

9/1 Complete iron **ferrule**, conical in shape, tapering to pointed tip. Circular in section. Wood remains at apex, exterior accreted in sand throughout. Slight mineral-preserved wood remains visible in the socket: *Fraxinus* sp. (ash) made from mature timber. L.73mm. 053:*1192*.

9/2 Iron **knife**, complete with rounded end to tang, widening to rounded shoulder and choil. Back curves lightly throughout to blunt tip. Cutting edge shows slight wear, rising to tip. Horn remains particularly abundant on one side of tang, leading to near-vertical handle line. Type: Drinkall A. L.114mm, blade W.15mm. Traces of skin product on both sides of blade. Mineral-preserved textile in association. 053:*1193*.

9/3 Three two-plate copper-alloy **strap-ends**, arranged in a vertical stack. Each pair of plates has a tapering rounded tip, a line of punched dots along the outer face of both plates and an iron rivet, 2.5mm diameter, holding the two plates together at the square end. L. (each strap-end) 39mm, W.8mm. 053:*1194*.
Between each pair of plates, reaching to a line 13mm from the square end, is the remains of a leather/skin strap, pierced by the rivet. A fold of textile is preserved in the corrosion products of the rivet of the topmost strap-end.

9/4 Small iron **buckle** with small iron plate folded back on itself. Type: probably Marzinzik II.22a. Loop W.18 x 13mm. 053:*1195*.

9/5 Fragments of a ?complete copper-alloy **annular brooch** with a flat ring sloping outwards and downwards. Broken at bar-type pin emplacement. Iron pin. Traces of transverse grooves on front. D.39mm; ring W.4.5–5.5mm. Extensive textile remains on front and back. 053:*1221*.

9/6 Fragments of copper-alloy **plate**, probably a **pouch fitting**. The best preserved fragment includes a flat piece of plate attached by a ?cu/a rivet to a curved piece resembling the rim of a jug. On the inner face of the flat section is a layer of animal skin, attached by the same rivet. Largest fragment, 14 x 8mm. Textile on outer face. Not illustrated. 053:*1223*.

9/7 Beads 053:*1198–1220* (see 1:2 *in situ* plan Fig. 15.10; Pl. 7.4a *1198–9*, *1201–3*, *1205*, *1209–1210*, *1218–9*). Brugmann Group B1.
Thirteen amber **beads** (total weight 7.5g; slight signs of wear): 2 long, faceted, D.11–15mm (*1209*, *1211*); 1 very long, faceted, D.3–5mm (*1216*); 6 medium, faceted, D.11–15mm (*1206–7*, *1213–5*, *1220*); 3 medium, faceted, D.6–10mm (*1200*, *1203*, *1218*); 1 medium, rounded, D.6–10mm (*1204*).
Ten glass **beads**: Type *Blue*? 2 highly fragmented (*1208*, *1212*).
Type *Traffic Light:* 1 medium, globular (asymmetrical), D.6–10mm (*1201*).
Type *Melon:* 1 medium, 9 ribs, yellow, D.11–15mm (*1198*).
Type *Cylindrical, Pentagonal:* 1 long, cylindrical, pentagonal cross section, yellow; larger end of perforation has a square cross-section, D.6–10mm (*1219*).
Type *Dot34:* 1 medium, globular, D.16–21mm (*1210*).
Type *Polychrome6:* 2 medium, globular, D.6–10mm (*1199*, *1205*).
Other beads: red globular: 2 short, globular, D.6–10mm (*1202*, *1217*).

Grave 10 (053:*0355*)
Fig. 15.11
Dimensions: 1.78m x 0.58m
Orientation: 227°
Container for body: None recognised
Finds gender: No grave goods
Age and Sex: Indeterminate age and sex, size of grave suggests adult
Skeletal remains: None
Body position: Indeterminate, grave size suggests extended while possible skull stain suggests head to west
Associated features: None recognised
Description: A parallel-sided cut with a rounded end to the west, a more pointed eastern end, with a flat bottom and a depth of only 0.14m, although increasing to 0.18m in a small area at the western end conforming to the possible stain left by the head. The fill (053:*0356*) comprised relatively homogenous brown silty sand with gravel inclusions.

Skeletal material was totally absent and the only indication of a body was a circular stain towards the western end of the grave that may have represented the location of the skull.
No grave goods were recorded in this grave.

Grave 11 (053:*0358*)
Figs 15.11–15.13
Dimensions: 1.94m x 0.6m
Orientation: 240°
Container for body: None recognised
Finds gender: Female
Age and Sex: Adult of indeterminate sex
Skeletal remains: Very poor. One tooth and a few fragments of unidentified bone. Third molar erupted. One fragment has possible exostoses suggesting a torn ligamentous attachment.
Body position: Grave shape and finds suggest extended and supine
Associated features: None recognised
Description: A parallel-sided cut with rounded ends. North and east sides were gently sloping while those to the south and east were almost vertical. With a maximum depth of 0.18m, its even base sloped up gently from east to west. The excavated fill (053:*0359*) comprised relatively homogenous brown silty sand with gravel inclusions.

Skeletal remains (053:*0362*) were fragmentary but concentrated in the area adjacent to the main group of grave goods that also coincided with a distinct soil stain.

A complete pot had clearly been placed central to the grave towards its western end (11/14) and had since suffered some post-depositional damage. Six sherds (11/13 i–ii) relating to two other vessels were recovered, including one that may have come from the same vessel (6/2) as sherds recorded in Grave 6. These were probably re-deposited. Three fragments of sleeve clasp (11/1 i–iii) were found close to the southern edge of the grave towards its eastern end, probably not in their original position. An iron key or latch-lifter (11/2 i), iron ring (11/2 ii) and knife (11/3) lay close to the northern edge of the grave approximately two-thirds of the way down from its western end and may have been attached in the waist area of the body. Another sleeve clasp (11/4 i) and part of a second similar clasp (11/4 ii) were recorded just to the west of and more centrally placed in the grave than the 11/2–3 objects, and could also have been in its original position on the body. A small iron buckle (11/12) was found lying close to sleeve clasps 11/4 i–ii. In addition, there was a group of objects clustered together in the area immediately east of the skull fragments (053:*0362*) in a position relating to the neck and shoulders of the body. These included an annular brooch (11/5), fragments of a cast copper-alloy finger ring (11/6), two copper-alloy staples (11/7 and 11/8), fragments of another annular brooch (11/9), a rolled copper-alloy tube (11/10) and a large iron pin (11/11).

11/1 Three fragments of copper-alloy plate, 1mm thick. (i) Fragment of the hook-piece of a **sleeve clasp**; 18 x 10mm. (ii) a fragment with serrated edge; 10 x 8mm; (iii) fragment, 7mm x 8mm. Not illustrated. 053:*1196*.

11/2 (i) Iron **key** or **latch-lifter** with three inward bends at the working end, and a loop, 18mm diameter, curled on the same axis, at the suspension end. Shank has square section, 8 x 7mm. L.145mm; bent sections approximately, 20mm, 35mm and 15mm. Remains of textile.
(ii) Fragments of an iron **ring** in association with 11/2 i and 11/3. Near-circular section. D.52mm, Thickness of ring 5–6mm. 053:*1197a*.

11/3 Iron **knife**, complete, with rounded end to narrow tang, which widens evenly to rounded shoulder and choil. Back lightly curved throughout, leading to blunt tip. Cutting edge slightly worn, rising to tip. Faint trace of straight, vertical handle line at shoulder. Type: Drinkall A. L.167mm, blade W.20mm. Traces of mineralised organic remains on blade, possibly from a sheath. 053:*1197b*.

11/4 (i) Near-complete catch-piece from a pair of copper-alloy **sleeve clasps**. A separately cast flat rib has fine transverse and thick diagonal grooves and there is a double row of fine punched ellipses, parallel to the rear edge. The catch is a plain slot, 8mm long. Two attachment holes are broken. Type: Hines B13a. W.34mm, L.15mm. Textile remains on front.
(ii) Fragments from a second **clasp**, including a separately cast flat rib similar to (i) although the transverse grooves are much coarser. 34 x 5 x 1.5mm. 053:*1222*.

11/5 Fragments of a complete copper-alloy **annular brooch** with a flat ring of irregular width. Five groups of cast transverse grooves on upper face. Bar pin emplacement, 4mm long x 3mm thick. Iron pin, circular section, 2.5mm diameter. Poorly preserved textiles on and around pin and pin emplacement. Imprint of large fungus in corrosion on back. D.47mm; ring W.7–8mm. 053:*1224*.

11/6 Fragments of a cast copper-alloy **finger ring**, with a D-shaped section. D.25mm; band 2.5mm wide x 3.0mm deep. Black organic remains on inner surface may be human tissue. 053:*1225*.

11/7 Fragment of a rectangular-section copper-alloy **staple**. L.13mm, arm 4mm; W.3mm. 053:*1226*.

11/8 Almost complete rectangular-section copper-alloy **staple**. L.14mm, arm 4mm; W.3mm. Embedded in mineral-preserved wood, 15 x 4mm. 053:*1227*.

11/9 Fragment of a copper-alloy **annular brooch** of the flat ring type, with perforation for pin emplacement, 3mm diameter, and remains of iron pin. The ring widens at the perforation. L.22mm; ring width 7mm at perforation. Poorly preserved textile. 053:*1228*.

11/10 Fragment of wood, pierced by a **rolled tube** of copper-alloy sheet, 2mm diameter, with remains of a flat plate on one end. 20 x 9 x 4mm. 053:*1229*.

11/11 Iron **pin** with head incomplete, probably a flattened shape. Shank has rounded section. L.127mm; broken head W.10mm. Shank pierces folds of mineral-preserved textile. 053:*1230*.

11/12 Iron **buckle** with narrow oval loop and no plate. Type: Marzinzik I.11a-i. 28 x 19mm. Thin layer of skin/leather pierced by tongue. Remains of textile on front. 053:*1231*.

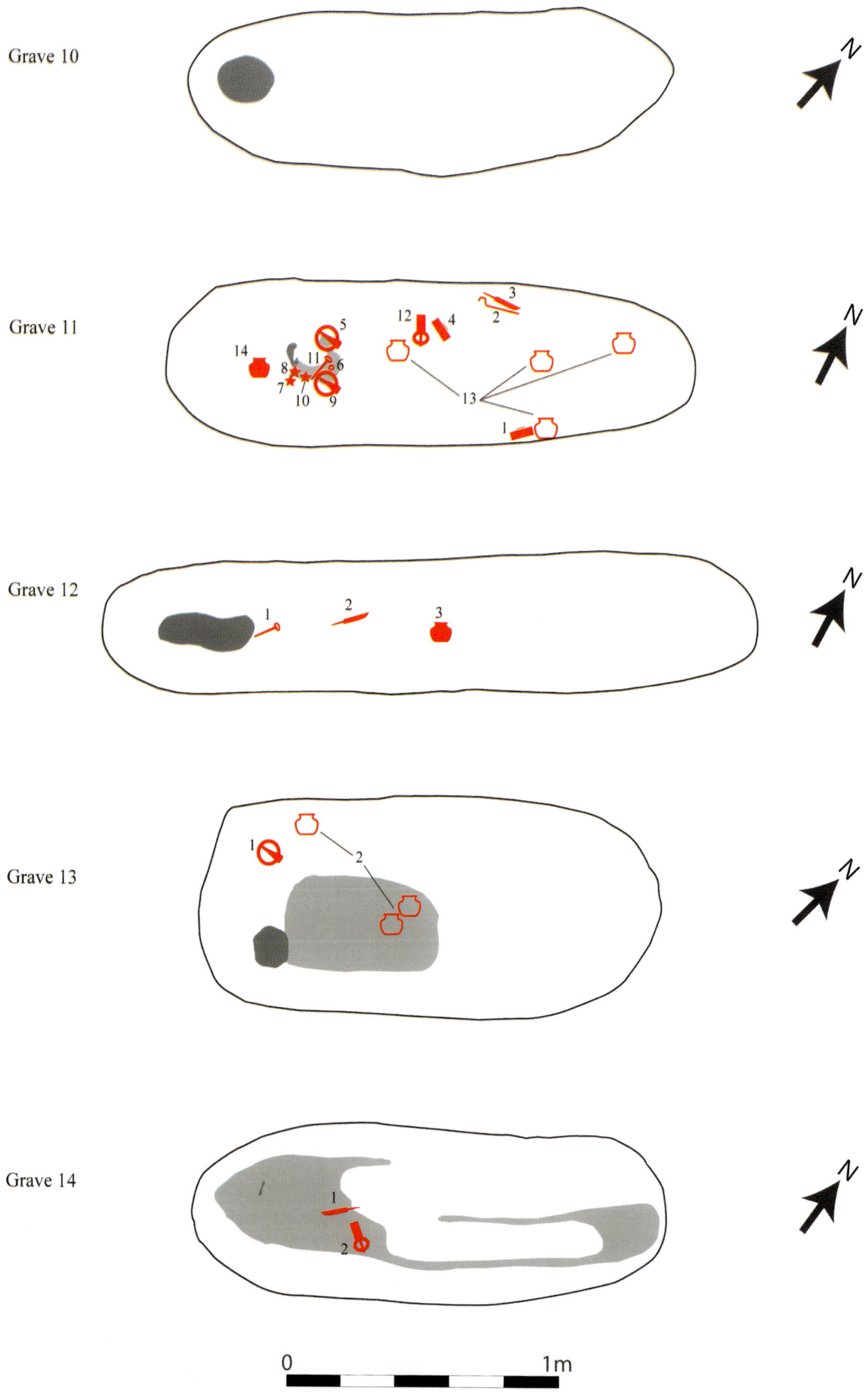

Figure 15.11 Plans of Flixton II Graves 10–14 (scale 1:20)

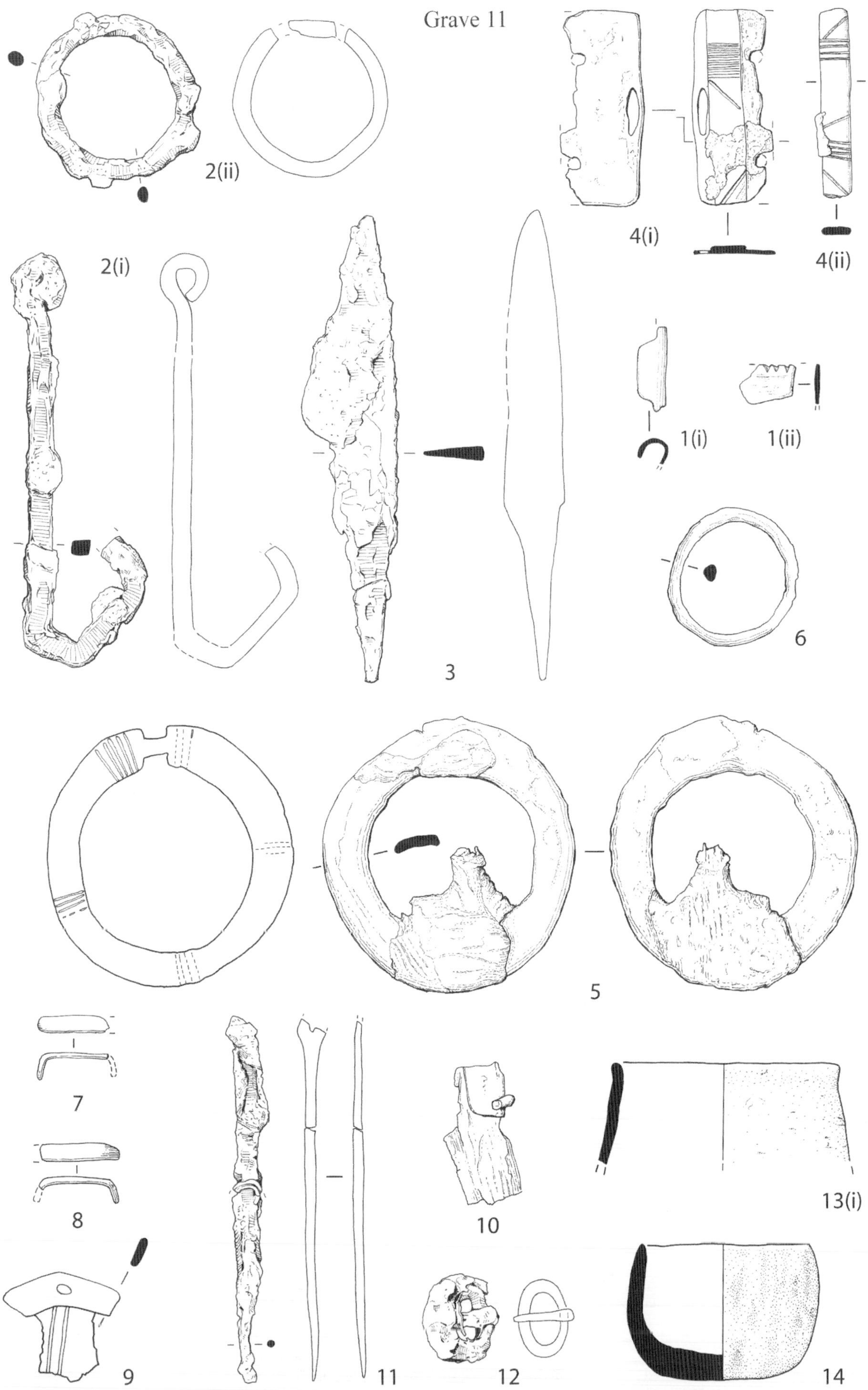

Figure 15.12 Flixton II Grave 11 (scales: 1 and 4–10 at 1:1; 2, 3, 11 and 12 at 1:2; 13(i) and 14 at 1:3)

Grave 11

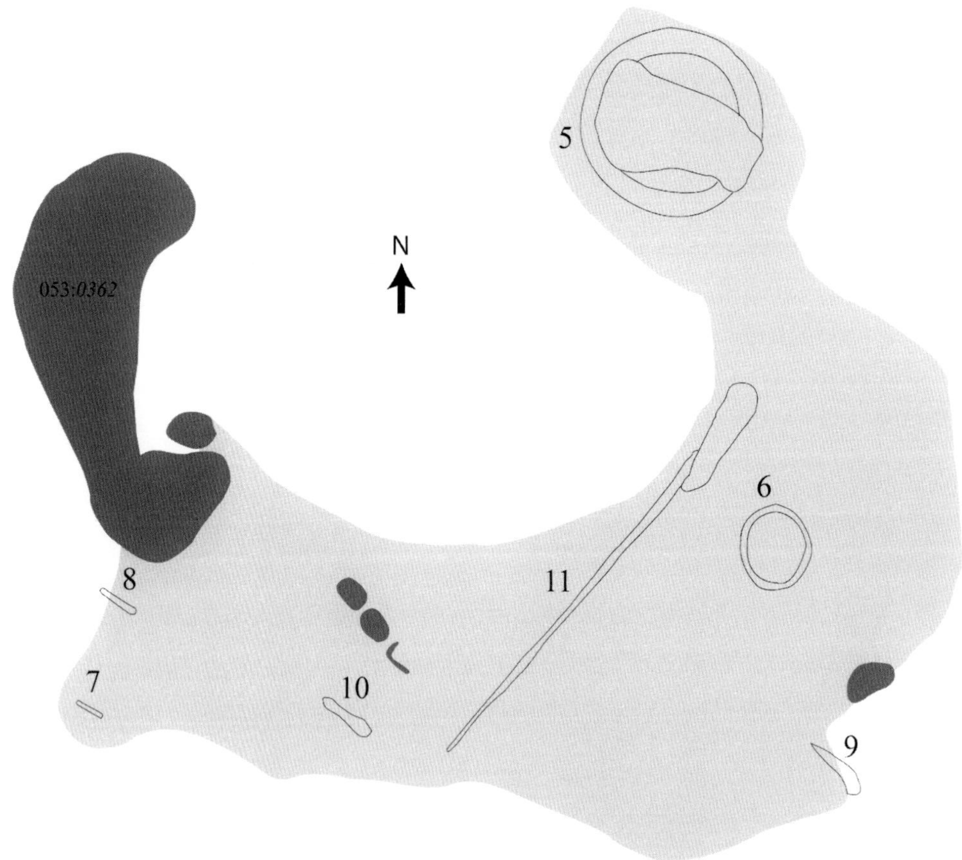

Figure 15.13 Flixton II Grave 11, *in situ* plan of grave goods 5–11. All contexts numbers are site 053 (scale 1:2)

11/13 (i) ?Biconical grass-tempered (ESO1) **jar** with short vertical rim, smoothed. Grey. Rim D.120mm, 8% complete. Possibly redeposited. (retained under grave fill number) (see also Fig. 7.19.8)..
(ii) One body **sherd** (ESO1), abraded, sooted, smoothed. Grey/brown externally, black internally. Possibly the same vessel as 6/2 in Grave 6 (retained under grave fill number). Not illustrated. 053:*0359*.

11/14 Inturned-rim globular grass-tempered **bowl** (ESO2, large voids probably from seeds) with thick rounded base, sooted, smoothed externally. Dark grey/brown. Rim D.120mm, 45% complete (base 100%). (see also Fig. 7.19.9). 053:*0360*.

Grave 12 (053:*0388*)
Figs 15.11 and 15.14
Dimensions: 2.4m x 0.48m
Orientation: 239°
Container for body: None recognised
Finds gender: Possibly female
Age and Sex: Grave size suggests adult of indeterminate sex
Skeletal remains: None
Body position: Indeterminate, grave size suggests extended while possible skull stain and orientation of knife grave good suggests head to west
Associated features: None recognised
Description: A long thin parallel-sided cut with rounded ends that survived only to a depth of 0.1m with a gently dished base. The fill (053:*0389*) comprised relatively homogenous brown silty sand with gravel, although a slightly darker, dirtier band was recorded on its north side towards the eastern end.

No skeletal material was recorded, but an amorphous dark stain towards the western end may have been the location of the skull.

A fragment of a copper-alloy pin (12/1) was located central to the grave towards the western end close to where the neck or shoulders would be if the body had been laid out head to the west. An iron knife (12/2) was also found lying central to the grave and may have been attached at the waist area of the body. A cluster of forty pot sherds (12/3) recorded central to the grave to the east of the knife were in poor condition and while probably originally representing a single whole pot, had suffered a fair degree of post-depositional damage and deterioration.

12/1 Fragment of copper-alloy **pin**, including lower shank but not tip. Near-circular section. L.49mm, D.3.5mm. 053:*1232*.

12/2 Iron **knife**, complete with tang widening evenly from rounded end to shoulder and choil. Back lightly curved throughout to sharp tip. Cutting edge sinuous and rising to tip. Faint trace of medial weld line. Type: Drinkall B. L.149mm, blade width 14mm. Traces of horn on one side of tang. Skin product, 3mm thick, in places on both sides of blade. Textile near tip. 053:*1234*.

12/3 Body sherds in poor condition, grass/granitic-tempered (ESOM) **vessel**, smoothed. Red-brown externally, dark grey internally. Not illustrated. 053:*0393*.

Grave 13 (053:*0390*)
Figs 15.11 and 15.14
Dimensions: 1.7m x 0.8m
Orientation: 227°
Container for body: Possible bier
Finds gender: Female
Age and Sex: Young-middle aged, indeterminate sex
Skeletal remains: Very poor. Tooth fragments (10 teeth) and small amount of left temporal and mandibular bone only. Tooth wear slight to moderate, large carious lesion in lower left first molar.
Body position: Indeterminate, skull stain indicates head to west
Associated features: None recognised
Description: Parallel-sided cut with a rounded east end, somewhat more squared to the west. The fill (053:*0391*) within the shallow, 0.12m deep,

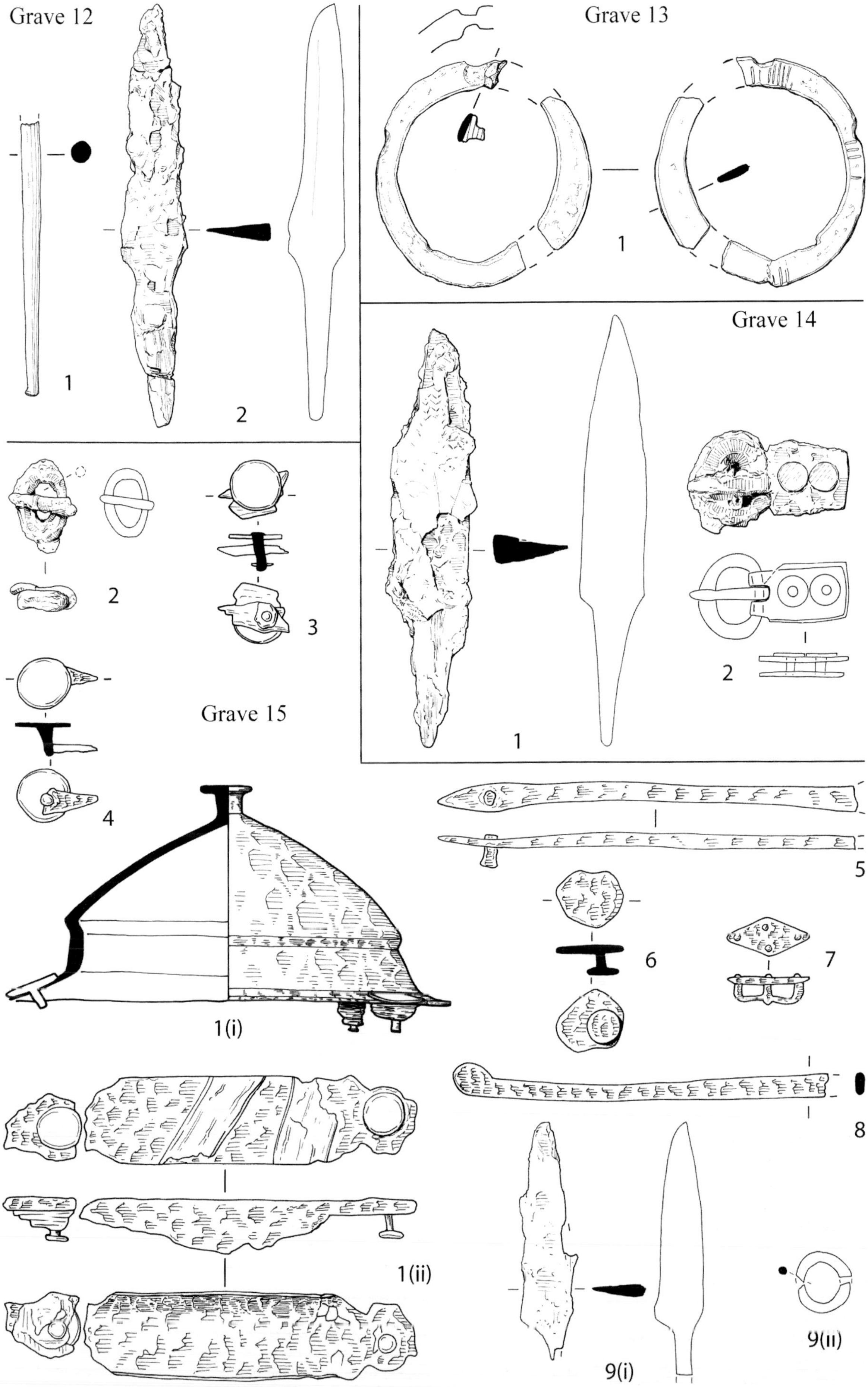

Figure 15.14 Flixton II Grave 12 (scales: 1 at 1:1; 2 at 1:2), Flixton II Grave 13 (scale: 1 at 1:1) Flixton II Grave 14 (scale: 1 and 2 at 1:2) and Flixton II Grave 15 (scale: 1–9 at 1:2)

cut comprised homogenous brown silty sand with gravel inclusions. Profiles revealed steeply sloping sides to the south, east and west, with a more gently sloping edge to the north.

Skeletal material (053:*0394*) was limited to a few fragments of skull associated with a circular stain towards the western end of the grave. Given the location of the skull, an adjacent area of staining measuring 0.55 by 0.35m may represent the torso of the body or part of a container such as a bier.

Fragments of an annular brooch were found towards the north-west corner of the grave, somewhat divorced from the skull (053:*0394*) and so possibly not in its original position. Two sherds each from two separate vessels (13/2 i–ii) were recovered from the grave fill, three central to the grave associated with the most extensive basal stain and another sherd close to the annular brooch. It is unclear whether these represented deliberate deposition as grave goods or accidental inclusion.

13/1 Fragments from an incomplete copper-alloy **annular brooch** with a flat ring of irregular width. Groups of cast transverse grooves on the upper face. Poorly formed bar-type pin emplacement, 3 x 3mm. Iron pin represented by corrosion at emplacement. D.38–40mm; ring width 4–6mm. Remains of textile over pin emplacement. 053:*1233*.

13/2 (i) Base and body sherd of sandy **vessel** (ESMS with occasional burnt-out organics and coarse quartz), sooted, smoothed/burnished externally, worn internally. Dark grey/buff. Not illustrated.
(ii) Two body **sherds** of a grass/granitic-tempered vessel (ESOM), grass-wiped. Red-brown externally, dark grey-black internally. Not illustrated. 053:*0392*.

Grave 14 (053:*0395*)
Figs 15.11 and 15.14
Dimensions: 1.7m x 0.65m
Orientation: 233°
Container for body: Extensive stain on base of grave, probably a combination of body stain and container such as a bier
Finds gender: Uncertain
Age and Sex: ?Middle aged, male
Skeletal remains: Very poor, flaky. Left temporal and mandible fragments, nine teeth. Tooth wear moderate. Large mastoid process suggests male.
Body position: Extended, grave goods suggest supine, head to west
Associated features: None recognised
Description: A parallel-sided round ended cut surviving to a maximum depth of 0.2m with a flat base and moderately sloping sides. The fill (053:*0396*) comprised homogenous brown silty sand with gravel inclusions.

Skeletal material (053:*0431*) was limited a few fragments of skull. Where present, the relatively extensive staining in the base of the grave followed the shape of its edge and on that basis is not likely to represent a coffin. Linear components towards the eastern end may represent the location of the legs.

Grave goods were limited to an iron knife (14/1), positioned on the central long axis of the grave approximately 0.6m from its western end in an area that would have been occupied by the torso of the body, and an iron buckle (14/2) immediately to the south-east.

14/1 Iron **knife**, complete. Rounded end to narrow tang, which widens evenly to shoulder and choil. Back curves lightly throughout to rounded tip. Cutting edge sinuous, rising to tip. Lightly curved vertical handle line at shoulder. Horn remains on end of tang on both sides. Type: Drinkall A. L.149mm, blade W.21mm. Skin product 1mm thick on both sides of blade and traces of grain pattern near tip suggests calf. Above this, textile. 053:*1235*.

14/2 Iron **buckle** with D-shaped loop, enlarged tongue-rest and rectangular iron plate. The two rivets fixing the plate have silver disc-shaped heads (XRF), 11mm diameter; rivet shanks are *c*.3.5mm diameter. Type: Marzinzik II.20. Loop 31 x 26mm; plate W.26mm, L.30mm. Remains of a leather strap, 3–4mm thick, are preserved between the front and back part of the plates and part of the grain layer is present on the back of the tongue. 053:*1236*.

Grave 15 (053:*0397*)
Figs 15.14–15.15
Dimensions: 1.9m x 0.7m
Orientation: 242°
Container for body: None recognised
Finds gender: Male
Age and Sex: Middle aged, male
Skeletal remains: Very poor, flaky and fragile. Left temporal, maxilla, right mandible, 17 teeth, atlas and axis. Some degeneration, tooth wear moderate to heavy. Large vertebrae, robust mandible. Enamel hypoplasia of lower right canine. Slight pitting left maxillary sinus. Osteophyte C1–2 facet for odontoid process.
Body position: Probably supine and extended with head to the west
Associated features: None recognised
Description: Essentially a sub-rectangular cut with moderately rounded ends and tapering slightly towards the east. The profiles of the 0.2m deep cut reveal a relatively level base along its long axis with steep steeply sloping edges at each end, but shallower sloping sides that carried and maintained a continuous curve across the bottom of the grave. The fill (053:*0398*) comprised homogenous brown silty sand with gravel inclusions.

Skeletal material (053:*0432*) was only preserved in the area immediately beneath the shield boss. A dark sandy stain surrounding the shield boss is likely to represent the body of the shield itself, while an amorphous curving area of discolouration to the sand in the base of the grave may relate to the position of the body.

The majority of the grave goods were associated with a shield that had been placed over the head of the body at the western end of the grave and comprised a shield boss and shield grip (15/1 i and 15/1 ii respectively), two iron shield grip extensions (15/5 and 15/8), four shield rivets and mounts (15/3–4 and 15/6–7) and an iron buckle (15/2). An iron knife and associated iron ring (15/9 i–ii) was found on the central long axis of the grave approximately 1.05m from its western end and may have been attached at the waist of the body. Eight pot sherds (15/10) were recovered from the grave fill. These were in poor condition.

15/1 (i) Iron **shield boss**. Carinated convex cone boss with large disc apex (D.18mm), broad flange (W.20mm), tall wall (Ht.25mm) and plated flat disc-headed rivets (D.18mm), one with complete shank (L.10mm) and washer (D.8mm). Type: Dickinson and Härke 3; EAC COS. D.160mm, Ht.85mm.
(ii) Iron **shield grip**. Incomplete. Flanged central section from a long grip (L 80mm) with a circular plate housing a copper-alloy flat disc-headed rivet (D 16mm) at each end, one with a washer (D 8mm). L 152mm. See also 15/5 and 15/8. Strap of leather/skin, 13–15mm wide, wrapped around grip. 053:*1237*.

15/2 Iron **buckle** with narrow oval loop and no plate. Type: Marzinzik I.11a–i. 28 x 18mm. 053:*1238*.

15/3 Copper-alloy **shield rivet**. Flat disc-headed rivet with copper-alloy washer. D.18mm. 053:*1239*.

15/4 Copper-alloy **shield rivet**. Flat disc-headed rivet. D.18mm. 053:*1240*.

15/5 Iron **shield grip extension**. Narrow extension (L.120mm, W.10mm) from a long grip with lozenge-shaped terminal (L.35mm) housing a rivet shank. L.155mm. See also 15/1 ii and 15/8. Traces of fine textile on one face and skin product on the other. 053:*1241*.

15/6 Iron **shield rivet or mount**. Incomplete. Disc-shaped rivet or mount (D.20mm approx.) with washer (D.12mm). 053:*1242*.

15/7 Iron **shield mount**. Lozenge-shaped mount with four tiny knob-headed rivets. Very probably a repair patch. L.32mm, W.15mm. 053:*1243*.

15/8 Iron **shield grip extension**. Narrow extension (L.120mm, W.12mm) from a long grip with disc-shaped terminal (D.14mm). L.135mm. See also 15/1 ii and 15/5. 053:*1244*.

15/9 (i) Iron **knife**, fragmentary, lacking end of tang, which has parallel sides, widening over upper part to shoulder and choil. Back straight and then angled down to rounded tip, cutting edge worn and sinuous, rising to tip. Clear medial weld line. Type: Drinkall C. L.89mm, blade W.14mm.
(ii) Fragment of iron **ring** in association with knife. Th.5mm, original D.*c*.25mm. 053:*1246*.

15/10 Body sherds in poor condition, grass/granitic-tempered (ESOM) **vessel**, smoothed. Buff-brown externally, dark grey internally. Not illustrated. 053:*0433*.

Grave 16 (053:*0434*)
Figs 15.15–15.16
Dimensions: 1.05m x 0.5m
Orientation: 253°
Container for body: None recognised
Finds gender: ?Female
Age and Sex: Child from size of grave, indeterminate sex
Skeletal remains: None

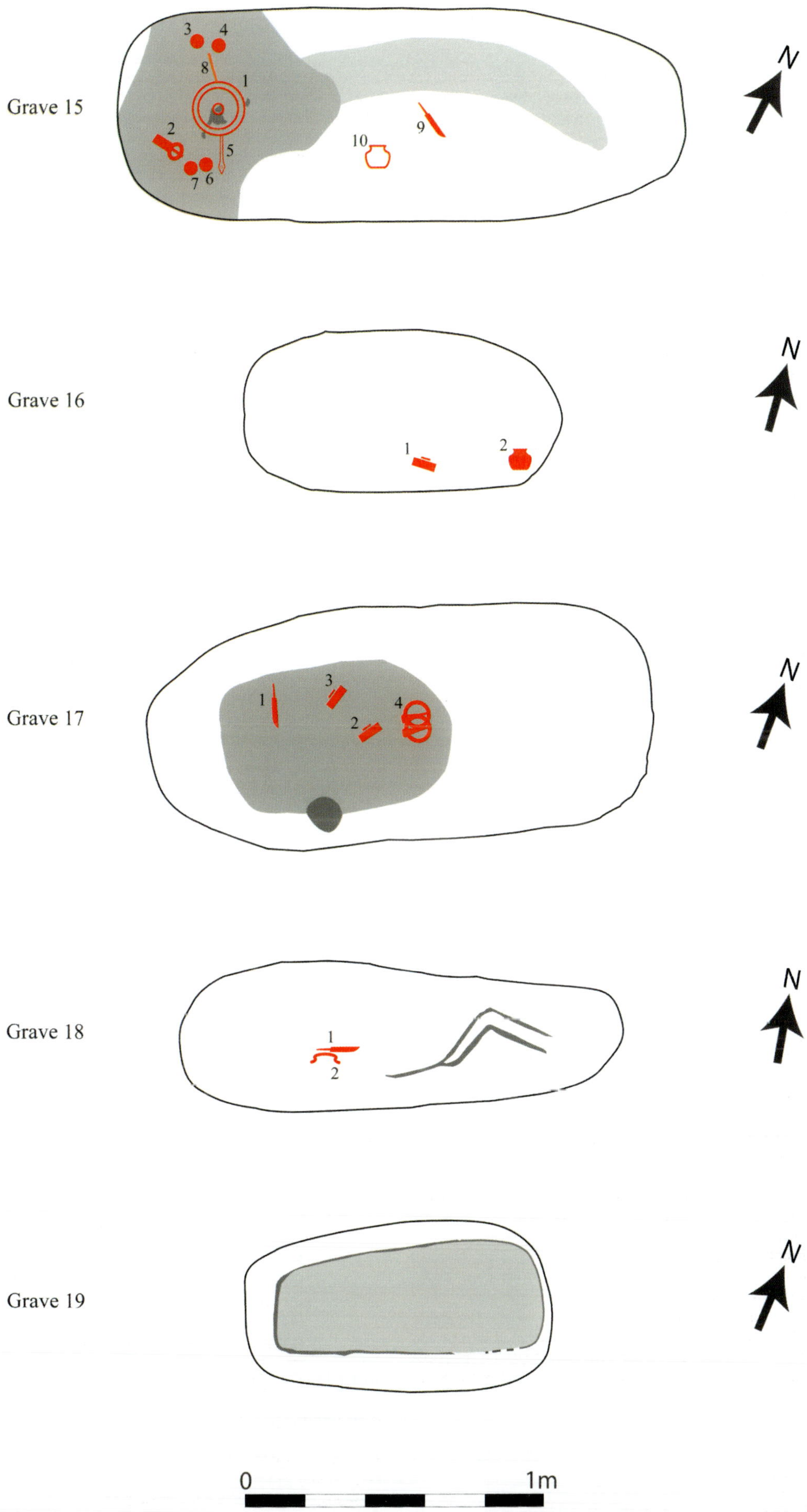

Figure 15.15 Plans of Flixton II Graves 15–19 (scale 1:20)

Body position: Indeterminate
Associated features: None recognised
Description: Parallel-sided cut with a rounded end to east, more squared to west with a surviving depth of 0.1m and a shallow dished profile. The fill (053:*0435*) comprised relatively homogenous brown sand with gravel inclusions.

No skeletal material was recorded and there were no soil stains that could indicate the presence of a container for the body or the location/attitude of the body itself.

Sixty-five sherds were recovered from a pottery vessel (16/2) placed in the south-east corner of the grave. The pot was incomplete and in poor condition, probably the result of post-depositional damage and deterioration. A near complete catch-piece from a pair of sleeve clasps (16/1) was found close to the southern edge of the grave just to the east of centre.

16/1 A near-complete catch-piece from a pair of copper-alloy **sleeve clasps**. Plain, rectangular; no indication of lost ornament; two intact attachment holes, 2.5mm diameter. Type: Hines B7. W.38mm, L.17mm. 053:*1247*.

16/2 Very fragmented grass-tempered (ESO1 with occasional chalk) baggy **jar** with vertical rim and rounded base, smoothed. Orange-brown externally, grey internally. Rim D.110mm, 6% complete. (see also Fig. 7.19.10). 053:*0436*.

Grave 17 (053:*0438*)
Figs 15.15–15.16
Dimensions: 1.7m x 0.76m
Orientation: 69°
Container for body: Indeterminate stain in base of grave
Finds gender: Female
Age and Sex: Adult, male (skull)
Skeletal remains: Very poor. Fragments of occipital and left parietal. Robust occipital crest.
Body position: Female with head to east, male skull at side
Associated features: None recognised
Description: A parallel-sided cut with rounded ends surviving to a depth of only 0.1m with a vertical edge to the west and more gently sloping sides to the north, south and east. The fill (053:*0439*) comprised relatively homogenous brown sand with gravel inclusions.

Skeletal material (053:*0440*) was limited to fragments of skull located central to the southern edge of an oval-shaped stain which itself was located towards the western end of the grave. The position of the skull in the grave is unusual and was not consistent with the distribution of the grave goods if they were directly related. In addition, the skull was identified as male, while the grave goods were clearly female gender. The oval-shaped stain of dark brown sand, measuring 0.75m by 0.5m, could represent a container for the body or have been generated by the body itself.

All of the grave goods were within the area of the basal stain. An iron knife (17/1) was found towards the north-west corner of the basal stain, with its long axis across the grave, with two pairs of sleeve clasps (17/2–3) close by two the east. Fragments of two annular brooches (17/4 i–iii) were recorded central to the grave towards the eastern end of the stain, close to 17/2. The position of the finds is suggestive of a body buried in a crouched attitude with its head to the east, although this would have left an unusually large distance between the head and the eastern end of the grave. It is possible that the female burial is a secondary burial in an earlier male grave.

17/1 Iron **knife**, complete, with rounded end to tang, widening evenly to stepped shoulder and rounded choil. Tang pierced by circular perforation, *c.*25mm from end. Back slopes in straight line towards tip, curving over last section. Pronounced diagonal line rises from choil along lower part of blade. Faint vertical handle line at shoulder. Type: Drinkall A. L.134mm, blade W.14mm. Skin product on blade. 053:*1248*.

17/2 A non-matching pair (i and ii) of cast copper-alloy **sleeve clasps** with curving profile, Style I animal ornament and gilding on the catch plate only (XRF). Both parts: Type Hines C1. There are textile remains and sedge/grasses (see Chapter 7.IV) on the front of both plates; and remains of the textile cuff on the back of one.
(i) The hook-piece has one thick and three thin ridges forming the everted coils of the epsilon; a simple animal head on the end of both coils and the centre of the coil is open. A pair of animals face each other along the rear edge. Five extra perforations have been drilled. The remains of the hook are represented by a thin plate, attached, probably with a tin-lead solder (XRF), to a tab cast with the clasp. No attachment lugs visible. W. (across cuff) 45mm x L.24mm.
(ii) The catch-piece belongs to the same set as 17/3. It has one thick and two thin ridges forming the epsilon and the animal head at the end of the coils is segmented with a curled snout. A pair of animals face each other along the rear edge. One of the attachment lugs appears to have been broken in antiquity, the other more recently. The catch itself has been cast with the plate. W.34mm x L.20mm. 053:*1249*.

17/3 A matching pair (i and ii) of cast copper-alloy **sleeve clasps** with curving profile, Style I animal ornament and gilding on both plates (XRF). Type: Hines C1. There are textile remains and grasses on the front and remains of the textile cuff on the back. The cast ornament is as described for 17/2 ii catch-piece, with minor differences in the animals along the back edge (see Chapter 7.II).
(i) The hook-piece has a triangular hooked plate attached with a tin solder (XRF) to a tab cast with the clasp. The two attachment loops at the corners of the back edge are intact. W. (across cuff) 35mm x L.24mm.
(ii) The catch-piece has one broken attachment loop. W.35mm x L.20mm. 053:*1250*.

17/4 (i–ii) Fragments of a copper-alloy **annular brooch**, with flat section of variable width, 5–7mm. A row of punched solid circles, 0.8mm diameter, runs along both the outer and the inner edge. Remains of a bar pin emplacement. Approximately half of the brooch is present, but it may be reconstructed as *c.*38mm diameter. A further fragment (iii; not illustrated) with a bar pin emplacement indicates that there was a **second annular brooch** of the same type. Textile remains detached and on pin. 053:*1251*.

Grave 18 (053:*0441*)
Figs 15.15–15.16
Dimensions: 1.48m x 0.5m
Orientation: 262°
Container for body: None recognised
Finds gender: Uncertain
Age and Sex: ?Child, indeterminate sex
Skeletal remains: None
Body position: Flexed, lying on left side, head to west
Associated features: None recognised
Description: A round ended cut with sides tapering towards the east and surviving to a depth of only 0.1m. The profiles reveal shallow sloping edges with those at the sides maintaining a continuous curve across the base. The fill (053:*0442*) comprised relatively homogenous brown sand with gravel, although some stratification was recorded with a thin band of stone-free grey/brown sand running around the western end of the grave and widening out along its northern side.

No skeletal remains were recovered, but the position of the legs and lower spine defined by a dark sandy stain on the base of the grave. There was no evidence of a container for the body.

Two associated iron finds, a knife (18/1) and an incomplete fire-steel (18/2) were located central to the grave with their long axis conforming to that of the burial. The position of these finds within the grave suggests that they would have been attached at the lower torso of the body, but possibly above the waist.

18/1 Iron **knife**, complete with narrow and relatively short tang, which has rounded end. Tang widens to rounded shoulder and choil. Both back and cutting edge taper evenly to rounded tip. Handle line at shoulder, straight but slightly off vertical. Possible trace of faint medial weld line. Traces of horn remains on one side of tang. Type: Drinkall B. L.113mm, blade W.12mm. Mineralised skin product on blade and textile on top near tip. 053:*1252a*.

18/2 Incomplete iron **fire-steel** with straight shank of rectangular section, 8 x 4mm, and rounded hook terminal. Fractured at approximate mid point. L.70mm. 053:*1252b*.

Grave 19 (053:*0461*)
Fig. 15.15
Dimensions: 1.02m x 0.55m
Orientation: 246°
Container for body: Regular sub-rectangular stain, possible coffin or bier
Finds gender: Uncertain, no grave goods
Age and Sex: ?Child based on grave size, indeterminate sex
Skeletal remains: None
Body position: Indeterminate

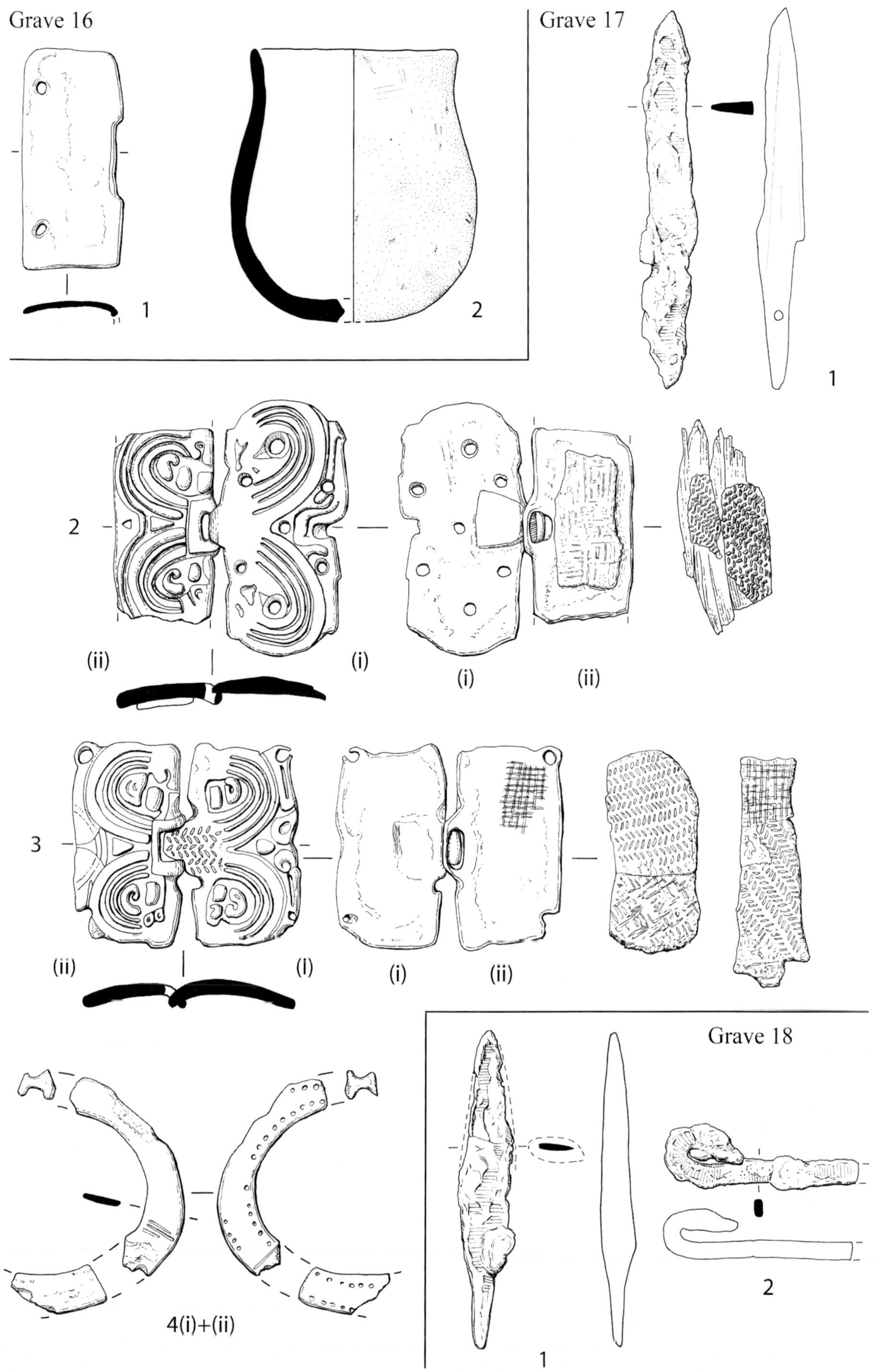

Figure 15.16 Grave goods; Flixton II Grave 16 (scales: 1 at 1:1; 2 at 1:3), Flixton II Grave 17 (scales: 1 at 1:2; 2–4 at 1:1) and Flixton II Grave 18 (scales: 1 and 2 at 1:2)

Associated features: None recognised
Description: A sub-rectangular cut with moderately rounded corners, a slight taper to the west and surviving to a depth of 0.14m. The profiles have relatively steep sides with an almost flat base. Fill (053:*0462*) comprised relatively homogenous brown sand with gravel inclusions.

No skeletal remains were recorded. A regular shaped rectilinear soil stain (053:*0466*) measuring 0.89m by 0.36m and forming a shallow trough approximately 0.07m deep has been interpreted as a wooden coffin or bier, although other organic materials cannot be entirely dismissed.

No grave goods.

Grave 20 (053:*0463*)
Figs 15.17–15.19; Pl. 7.4a
Dimensions: 1.68m x 0.86m
Orientation: 242°
Container for body: None recognised
Finds gender: Female
Age and Sex: Two bodies, (A) of indeterminate age and sex on south side of grave and (B) a young adult ?female to the north.
Skeletal remains: (A) None; (B) Poor, but vertebrae and ribs with copper staining are well preserved. Right zygoma, petrous temporal and fragment of mandible, six teeth, C5–T1 vertebrae, rib fragments. No degeneration of surviving vertebrae, tooth wear slight. Small teeth.
Body position: The grave goods with body (A) indicate head to west. Skeleton and grave goods of the northernmost (B) indicate supine, head to west, legs could be flexed.
Associated features: None recognised
Description: A parallel-sided cut with a rounded end to the east, squarer to the west and surviving to a depth of 0.32m. The profiles reveal vertical edges and a flat bottom. The fill (053:*0464*) comprised relatively homogenous brown sand with gravel inclusions.

The positions of the grave goods provide evidence suggesting that this was a double burial. However, the skeletal remains (053:*0465*) were limited to fragments from the skull and upper body from the northernmost of the two individuals (B). An amorphous dark sand stain running eastwards away from the skull also relates to the position of the northern body (B), while a circular stain close to the south-west corner was attributed to the second, southernmost of the two bodies (A).

Grave goods, which from their location may have been at the thigh of Body B or perhaps the waist of Body A, comprised an iron latch-lifter (20/1), an iron suspension ring (20/2) and fragments of two copper-alloy strap-ends with the imprint of a third (20/3). A group of four beads (20A/11:*1261–1264*) were closely associated with the circular stain in the south-west corner of the grave in a position conforming to neck and shoulders of the southernmost body. Grave goods certainly associated with the northernmost body (B) were all located towards the north-west corner of the grave in an area that would have been occupied by the neck and shoulders. The finds comprised a composite object of iron and copper alloy (20B/4 i–iii), an iron buckle (20B/5), fragments from a strap-end (20B/6), a pair of copper-alloy annular brooches (20B/7 and 20B/10), the latter with three associated copper-alloy bucket beads (20B/8) and a fragment from an iron pin (20B/9). In addition, a group of ten beads (20B/12: *1265–70(a+b), 1271–3*) were recorded.

Body A or B

20/1 Iron **latch-lifter** with a working end which has one outward bend followed by two inwards bends, and a suspension end with a loop, 11mm diameter, curled on the same axis. Shank is rectangular section, 10 x 5mm. L.170mm; bent sections 23mm, 30mm, 23mm. Poorly preserved textile remains on surface but no details could be recorded. 053:*1253*.

20/2 Iron suspension **ring**, with oval section. D.35mm, Th.5mm. Traces of textile on surface. 053:*1254*.

20/3 Fragments of two copper-alloy two-plate **strap-ends**, back-to-back, with imprint of a third strap-end. Tapering, but tips missing; undecorated. Circular rivet hole on each plate, 2mm diameter. L. (largest fragment) 30mm; W.6.5mm tapering to 5mm. Detached textile remains. Largest fragment only illustrated. 053:*1255*.

Body B

20B/4 (i) A copper-alloy **fitting** made from sheet metal 16mm wide, folded over an iron rod or wire 5mm diameter, and riveted to a second copper-alloy sheet also 16mm wide. The ?iron rivet is 3mm diameter. 19 x 16mm. Two further fragments (ii) of copper-alloy sheet with iron rivets were also found, one illustrated. Possibly an elaborate (or repaired) buckle.
(iii) Triangular fragment of iron plate, 40 x 30mm. Not illustrated. 053:*1256*.

20B/5 Iron **buckle** (i) with D-shaped loop and detached rectangular iron plate (ii) (only one half of plate recovered). The plate is slightly tapering (23mm to 21mm wide) and has remains of a copper-alloy rivet at the broader end (iii). The buckle tongue has been pulled upwards and sideways. Marzinzik II.19a. Loop 36 x 26mm; plate W.23 x L.42mm. Traces of leather/skin on one face of plate. Remains of a distorted textile on the other face. 053:*1257*.

20B/6 Fragments of a copper-alloy two-plate **strap-end**, undecorated, with rounded rectangular end. The plates are 1mm thick; the attachment end is missing. W.9mm, L. (largest fragment) 25mm. On inner face of one fragment, 9 x 7mm of leather/skin, 1.5–2.0mm thick. Textile remains on outer face of one fragment. 053:*1258*.

20B/7 Copper-alloy oval **annular brooch** with flat band of irregular width and thickness. Pierced circular pin emplacement, 3mm diameter; band widens at perforation. Iron pin with circular section, 2mm diameter. Groups of shallow badly formed transverse grooves, possibly six groups in all. 53 x 45mm; band W.7–10mm x Th.1.0–2.5mm. Extensive textile remains. 053:*1259a*.

20B/8 Copper-alloy **bucket pendant**, complete apart from part of strap; and fragments of one, or possibly two, more. Made from sheet metal: a disc-shaped base, a curled strip with butted edges for sides, and a strip for the carrying strap. Fibre stuffing inside bucket is raw, fully processed flax, *Linum usitatissimum* L. D.9mm, Ht.7.5mm. 053:*1259b*.

20B/9 Fragment of iron **pin** shank, head end broken in antiquity. Round cross-section. L.92mm, D.5mm. 053:*1260*.

20B/10 Copper-alloy oval **annular brooch**, pair to 20B/7. 54 x 50mm; band 8–11mm wide x 1.5–2.0mm thick. Extensive textile remains. 053:*1274*

Body A

20A/11 Beads 053:*1261–4* (see *in situ* 1:2 plan Fig. 15.19a; Pl. 7.4a *1261, 1264*). Brugmann Group A2.
Two amber **beads**: medium faceted (*1262–3*)
Two glass **beads**: Type *Norfolk Short?:* 1 short, globular (irregular); smaller end of perforation has square cross-section, D.6–10mm (*1264*).
Other bead: white globular: 1 short, globular (irregular), D.6–10mm (*1261*).

Body B

20B/12 Beads 053:*1265–1270a–b, 1271–3* (see *in situ* 1:2 plan Fig. 15.19b; Pl. 7.4a *1265–7, 1269, 1270a, 1271–3*). Brugmann Group A2.
Four amber **beads** (total weight 1.7g; worn): 1 medium, wedge-shaped, D.11–15mm (*1270a*); 2 medium, faceted, D.6–10mm (*1269, 1272*); 1 medium, rounded, D.6–10mm (*1271*).
Six glass **beads**: Type *Constricted, Cylindrical:* 2 very long, cylindrical, D.3–5mm (*1266, 1268*); 1 cylindrical; fragment stuck in the perforation of an amber bead, D.3–5mm (*1270b*).
Type *Cloak:* 2 medium, cylindrical/globular (asymmetrical), D.6–10mm (*1265, 1267*).
Type *BlueGreen Spiral:* 1 very short, globular, D.16–21mm (*1273*).

Grave 21 (053:*0467*)
Figs 15.17 and 15.20; Pl. 7.4a
Dimensions: 1.87m x 0.8m
Orientation: 244°
Container for body: None recognised
Finds gender: Female
Age and Sex: Grave size suggests adult, indeterminate sex
Skeletal remains: None
Body position: Location of grave goods suggests supine, head to west
Associated features: Pit 053:*0499*
Description: Parallel-sided cut with rounded ends and surviving for a maximum depth of 0.24m at its eastern end, but reducing to 0.16m at its western end. Flat-bottomed profile with near vertical sides and a fill (053:*0468*) comprising relatively homogenous brown sand with gravel inclusions and exhibiting a stonier band around the ends and continuing along its southern side. A shallow circular feature (053:*0499*) cut by the

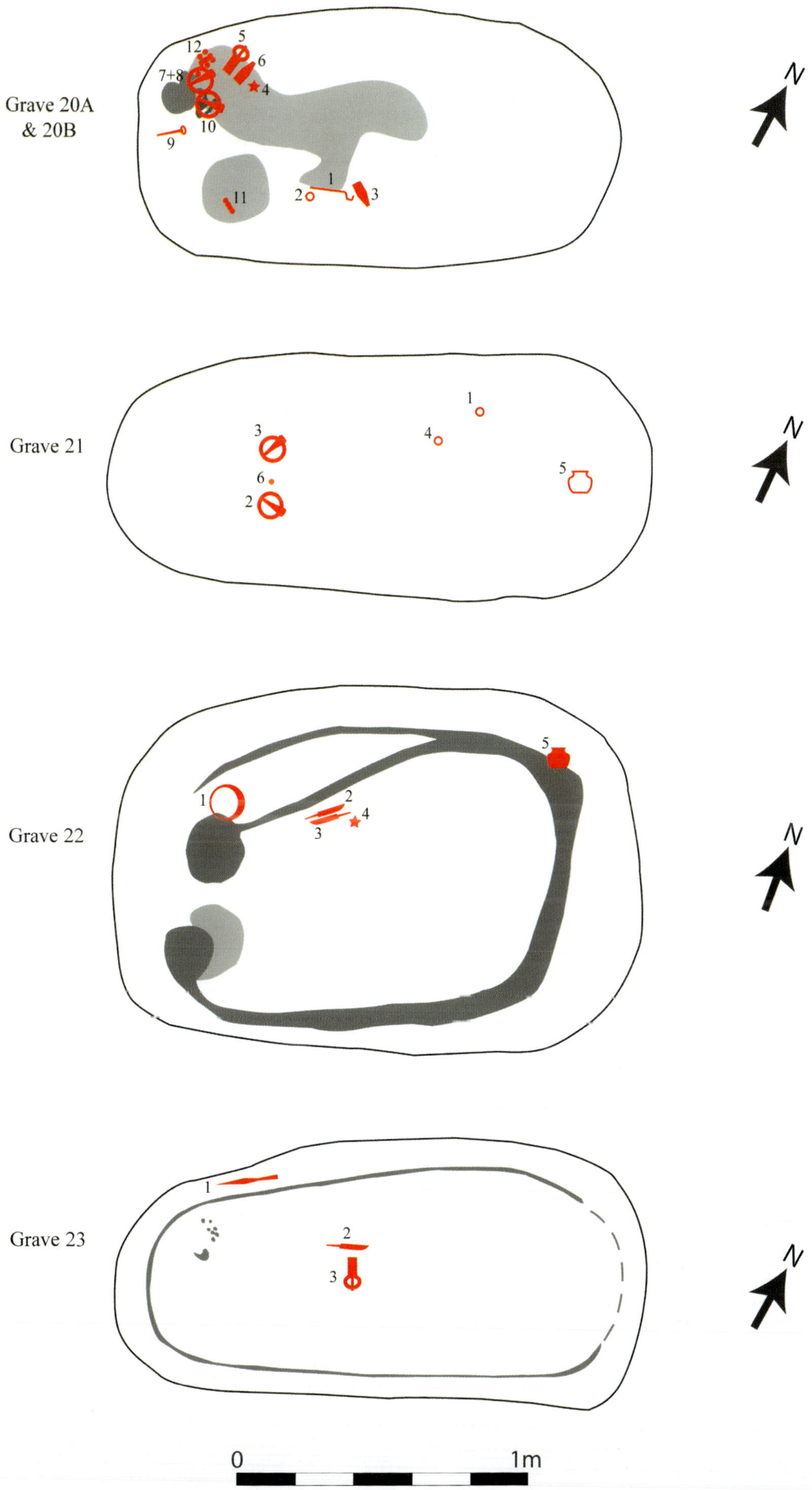

Figure 15.17 Plans of Flixton II Graves 20–23 (scale 1:20)

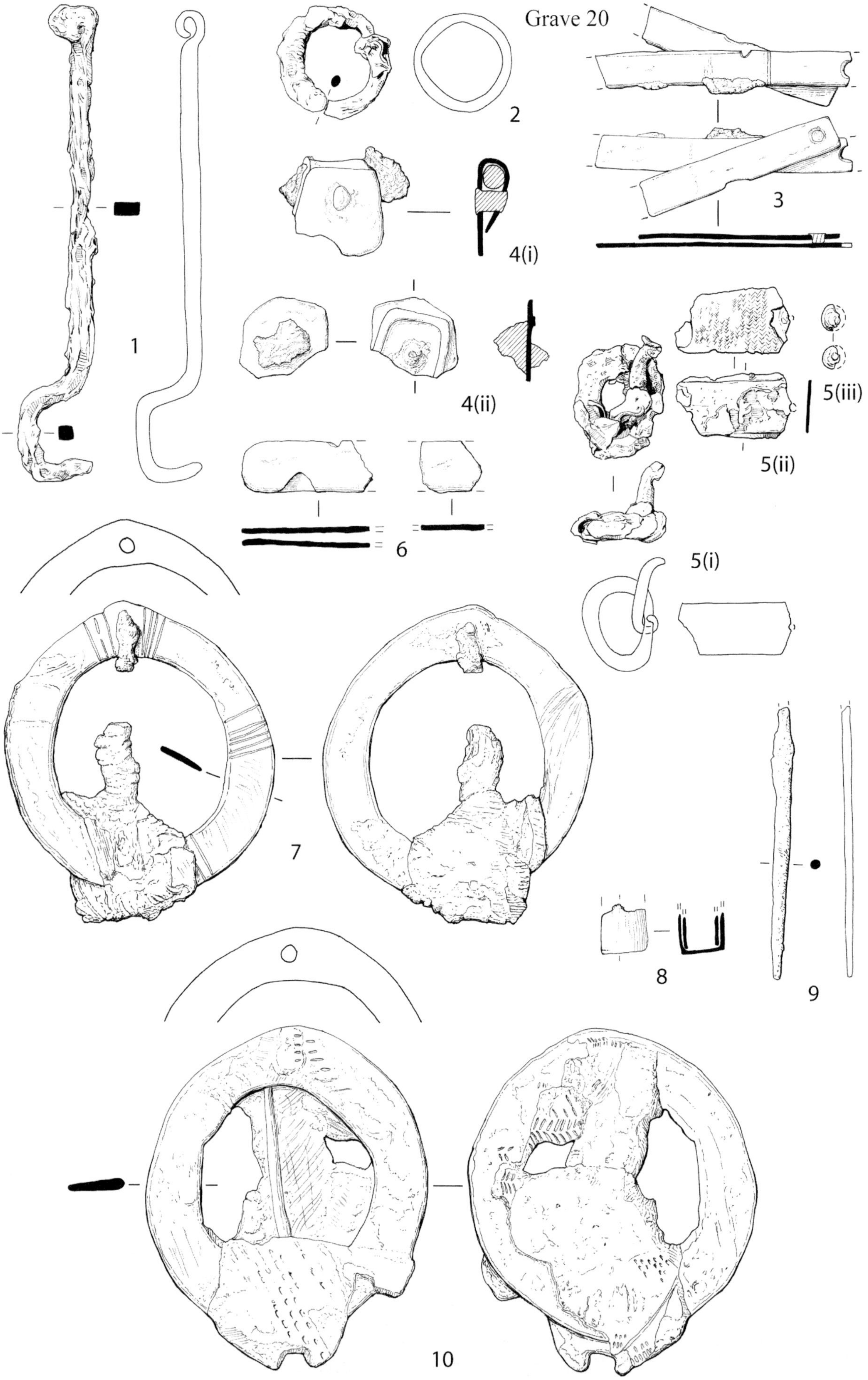

Figure 15.18 Grave goods; Flixton II Grave 20 (scales: 1, 2, 5 and 9 at 1:2; 3, 4, 6, 7 and 10 at 1:1)

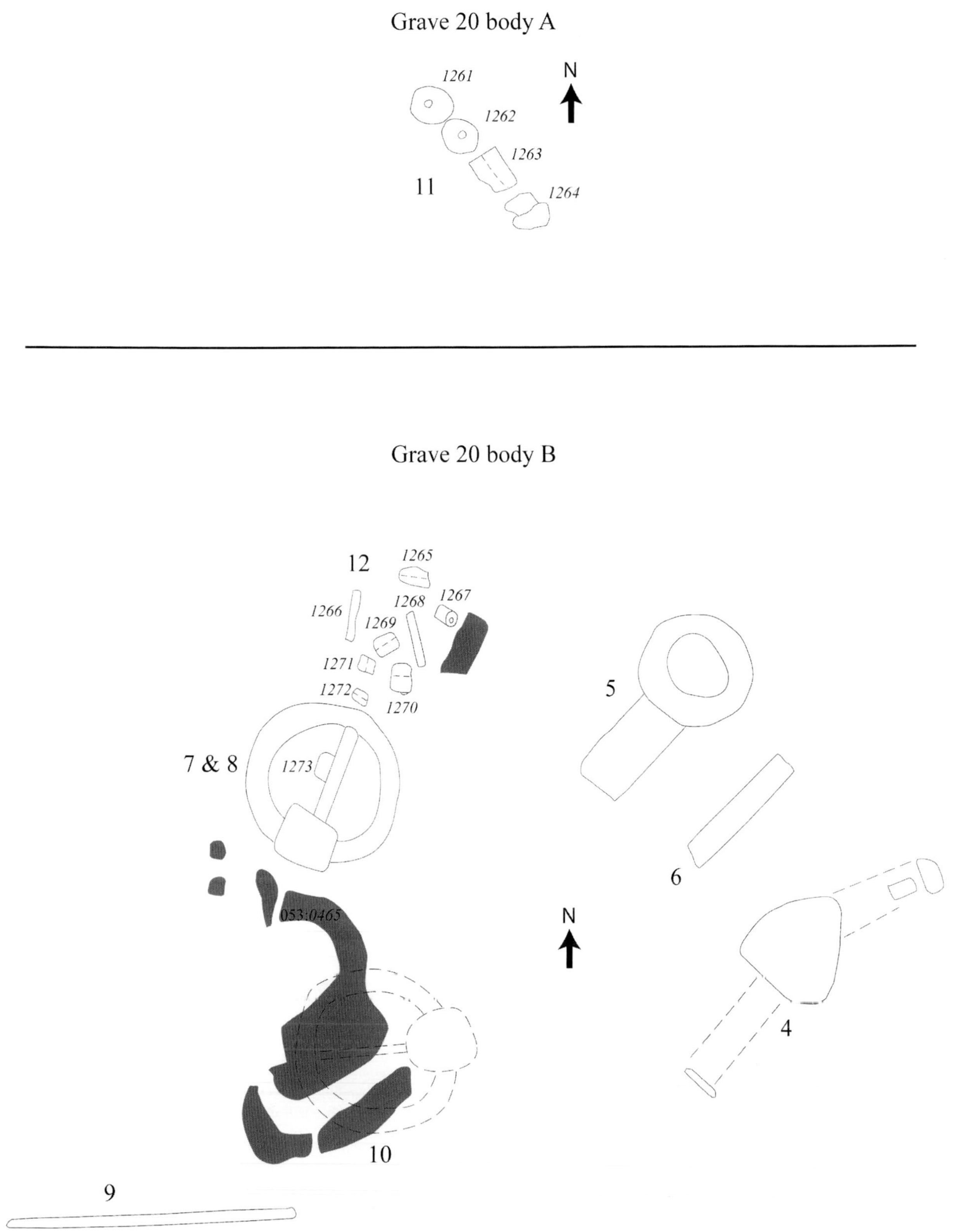

Figure 15.19 Flixton II Grave 20, *in situ* plan of bead group 11 (body A) and grave goods 4–10 with bead group 12 (body B). All contexts numbers are site FLN 053 (scale 1:2)

southern edge of the grave was treated as if it were itself another grave (shown unnumbered on Fig. 6.1). However, the homogenous brown silty sand fill (053:*0500*) suggests that this was a pit and possibly natural in origin.

No skeletal remains were recovered and no soil stains were present that may have represented a container for the body or the body itself.

Two large pot sherds (21/5) were located central to the eastern end of the grave and may have represented the deposition of a whole vessel that had subsequently been damaged. An iron suspension ring (21/4) and another, smaller, iron ring (21/1) were recorded in the eastern half of the grave towards its northern side with the former in a position that would suggest it was attached near the waist of the body. Other finds comprised two annular brooches (21/2 and 21/3) with an associated bead (21/6;*1278*) all forming a group in what would almost certainly have been the neck and shoulder area of the body.

21/1 Small iron **ring**. D.25mm, Th.4.5mm. 053:*1275*.

21/2 Cast copper-alloy **annular brooch** with flat segmented ring: sections formed from eleven transverse grooves. Constricted pin emplacement. Iron pin *c*.3mm wide. D.42mm; band W.6.5mm x Th.3mm. Extensive textile remains. 053:*1276*.

21/3 Cast copper-alloy **annular brooch**, pair to 21/2. Pin absent. D.41mm; ring W.6mm x Th.2.5mm. Textile on front and back. 053:*1277*.

21/4 Iron suspension **ring** with elliptical ring section. D.38mm, ring section 5–6 x 3–4mm. Traces of textile on outer face. 053:*1279*.

21/5 Baggy **jar**, grass/granitic-tempered (ESOM but organics sparse), very small vertical rim with signs of wear or deliberate rubbing, sooted, burnt food residue internally. Buff-brown externally, black internally. Rim D.120mm, 6% complete. (see also Fig. 7.19.11). 053:*0469*.

21/6 Beads 053:*1278* (Pl. 7.4a *1278*).
One amber **bead** (weight 2.6g; worn): short, irregular, D.16–21mm (*1278*).

Grave 22 (053:*0501*)
Figs 15.17 and 15.20
Dimensions: 1.8m x 1.2m
Orientation: 250°
Container for body: None recognised
Finds gender: (A) No grave goods, (B) Uncertain
Age and Sex: (A) (skel 053:*0507*) young adult, indeterminate sex; (B) (skel 053:*0508*) child, aged 11–12 years, indeterminate sex.
Skeletal remains: (A) Very poor. A few fragments of cranial vault and four incomplete teeth. Tooth wear slight. (B) Very poor. Five permanent and one deciduous molars only.
Body position: Uncertain, but heads to west, (A) possibly on left side facing north, (B) on right side facing south
Associated features: None recognised
Description: A sub-rectangular cut with moderately rounded corners and surviving for a depth of 0.46m with vertical sides and a flat base. The fill (053:*0502*) comprised homogenous brown silty sand and gravel.

Skeletal remains were limited to fragments of skull and teeth, although the associated stains and locations of the bone fragments clearly identified this as a double grave with two individuals (skeletons 053:*0507* and *0508*) facing each other. There was no obvious evidence for a container and the linear stains associated with the skulls have been interpreted as relating to the location of the bodies themselves.

All of the included grave goods appear to have been associated with the northernmost of the two bodies (B). A pottery vessel (22B/5), surviving as twenty-one sherds, had been place in the north-east corner of the grave, while an iron lunula or neck-ring (22B/1) was found close to the skull and was probably *in situ*. An iron knife (22B/2), another knife blade fragment (22B/3) and a sherd of glass (22B/4) were found closely associated, approximately halfway down the grave on its northern and were probably attached to the body in the waist area.

22B/1 Fragments of an iron **lunula**, or neck-ring, with plain flat front area and thin (rounded rectangular section) arms. Fastened by a simple hook through a hole in the flattened and expanded end of one arm. D.*c*.120mm; front section 11 x 2mm; side arms 5 x 3mm. Remains of two different textiles. 053:*1280*.

22B/2 Iron **knife**, complete with short, narrow tang widening markedly to rounded choil and shoulder. Back slopes in straight line towards tip, curving over last part. Cutting edge straight, rising throughout diagonally towards tip. Horn remains spread over tang on both sides, vertical handle line lightly curved. Type: Drinkall A. L.81mm, blade W.14mm. Traces of skin product on both sides of blade. 053:*1282a*.

22B/3 Heavily corroded blade fragment, probably from a **knife**. Back curves lightly towards tip, cutting edge straight and rising to tip. Back portion of blade and tang missing. Type: Drinkall B. L.78mm, blade W.14mm. Skin product up to 5mm thick on both sides of blade. 053:*1282b*.

22B/4 Single pale-green **glass sherd**, with a defined rounded edge. Slightly curved, and possibly from the rim of a bowl. W.29mm at is widest point. 053:*1282c*.

22B/5 'Round-bellied' or sub-biconical granite-tempered **bowl** (ESCF) with upright, slightly flaring, beaded rim, burnished. Orange/black externally, black internally. Rim D.130mm, 23% complete. (see also Fig. 7.19.12). 053:*0503*.

Grave 23 (053:*0504*)
Figs 15.17 and 15.21
Dimensions: 1.83m x 0.88m
Orientation: 239°
Container for body: Extensive stain on base of grave, possible bier
Finds gender: Male
Age and Sex: Young-middle aged, indeterminate sex
Skeletal remains: Very poor. Six teeth only, two carious. Tooth wear slight-moderate.
Body position: Uncertain, but probably supine and extended
Associated features: None recognised
Description: Essentially a sub-rectangular cut with a rounded west end, a squarer east end, the whole slightly tapering towards the west with a surviving depth of 0.34m. The profiles reveal steep, near vertical edges at the ends with gentler slopes along the sides that were maintained across the base of the grave as a continuous curve. The fill (053:*0505*) comprised relatively homogenous brown silty sand and gravel.

Skeletal remains (053:*0527*) were limited to a few teeth. Any additional body stain was obscured by the extensive brown sandy stain (053:*0506*) that covered the whole base of the grave, forming a shallow trough that followed the contours and shape of the feature. On that basis it was considered that this was not a coffin, more likely representing a wooden bier or some other organic material on which the body had been lain.

An iron spearhead (23/1) was recorded against the northern side of the grave towards the western end with its blade pointed to the west. Other grave goods were limited to an iron knife (23/2) and associated iron buckle (23/3). The knife was centrally positioned in the grave and was probably attached at the waist of the body.

23/1 Complete iron **spearhead** with short, wide cleft socket extending over practically all of shank. Blade widens from shank in convex curves with widest point just above junction. Tapers with straight sides to rounded tip. Lentoid in section and quite flat. Abundant mineral-preserved wood remains in socket: *Fraxinus* sp. (ash) made from mature timber. Type: Swanton E2; EAC Concave Long 1b. L.307mm, W.32mm. 053:*1281*.

23/2 Iron **knife,** complete, with long, narrow tang, rounded end, widening gradually to distinct shoulder and choil. Straight back curving over front part to rounded tip, slightly sinuous cutting edge rising to tip. Clear vertical handle line at shoulder. Medial weld line visible in part, mainly at front of blade. Type: Drinkall A. L.135mm, blade W.13mm. Remains of seam in skin-product sheath (2mm thick) running along spine: three stitch holes in a 5mm length. 053:*1283a*.

23/3 Iron **buckle** with oval loop and no plate. Type: Marzinzik I.11a-i. 22mm x 15mm. Remains of leather/skin strap, 14 x 10mm, on back at hinge. Folds of textile on front.. 053:*1283b*.

Grave 24 (053:*0528*)
Fig. 15.22
Dimensions: 1.62m x 0.9m
Orientation: 234°
Container for body: None recognised
Finds gender: No grave goods
Age and Sex: Indeterminate age and sex
Skeletal remains: None
Body position: Indeterminate
Associated features: None recognised
Description: A parallel-sided cut with rounded ends, which survived to a depth of 0.26m. North, south and western edges were vertical while that to the east was less severe. The fill (053:*0529*) comprised relatively homogenous brown silty sand with gravel inclusions.

No skeletal material or body stain was recorded and there was no evidence surviving of a container for the body or the presence of grave goods.

No grave goods.

Grave 25 (053:*0530*)
Fig. 15.22
Dimensions: 2.2m x 0.75m
Orientation: 239°
Container for body: None recognised
Finds gender: Uncertain
Age and Sex: Grave size suggests adult, indeterminate sex
Body position: Indeterminate
Associated features: None recognised
Description: Essentially a sub-rectangular cut with a rounded western end, squarer to the east and surviving to a depth of 0.15m. The profiles exhibit vertical sides with a flat bottom. The fill (053:*0531*) comprised relatively homogenous brown silty sand with gravel inclusions.

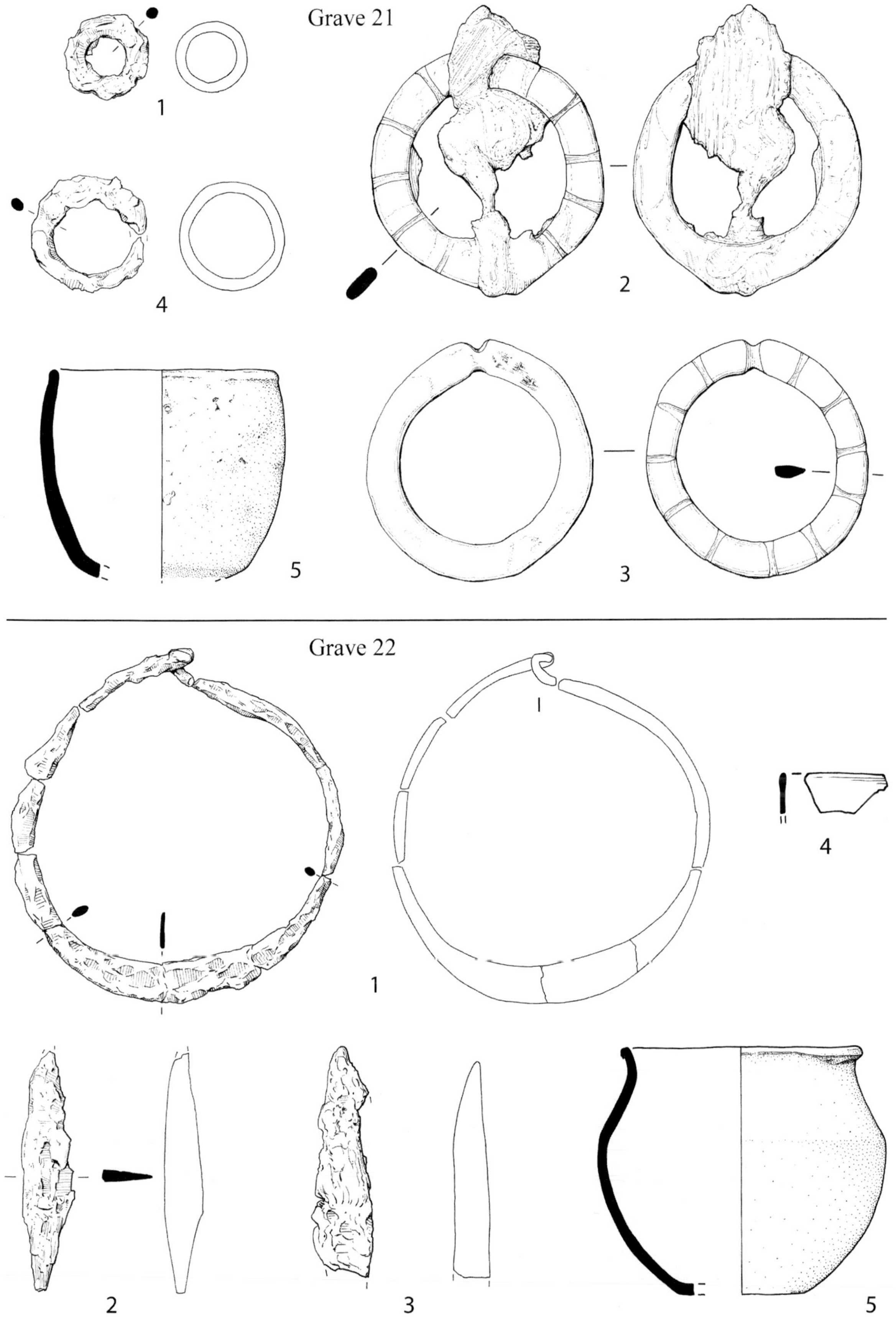

Figure 15.20 Grave goods; Flixton II Grave 21 (scales: 1 and 4 at 1:2; 2 and 3 at 1:1; 5 at 1:3) and Flixton II Grave 22 (scales: 1–4 at 1:2; 5 at 1:3)

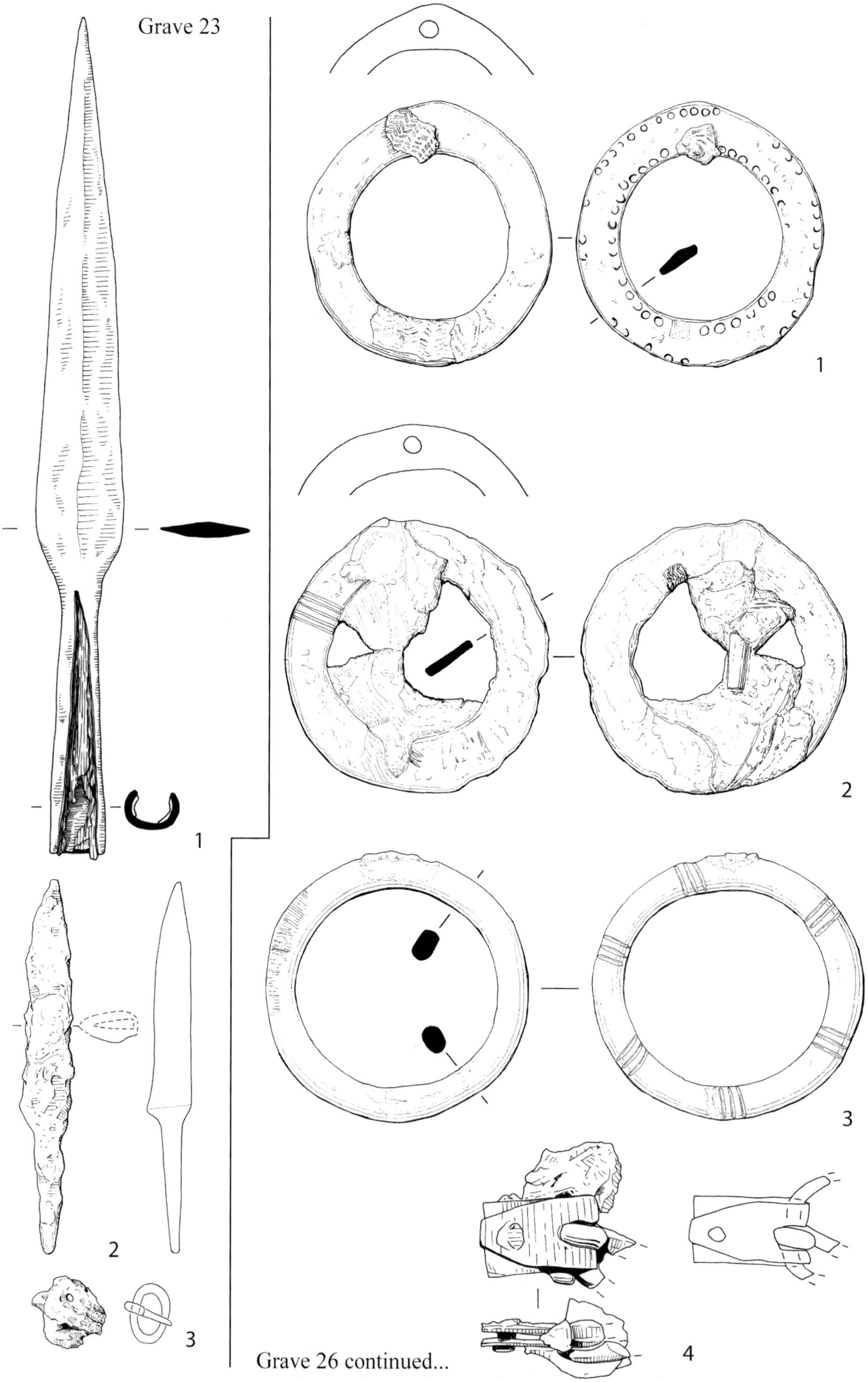

Figure 15.21 Grave goods; Flixton II Grave 23 (scale: 1–3 at 1:2) and Flixton II Grave 26 (scale: 1–4 at 1:1)

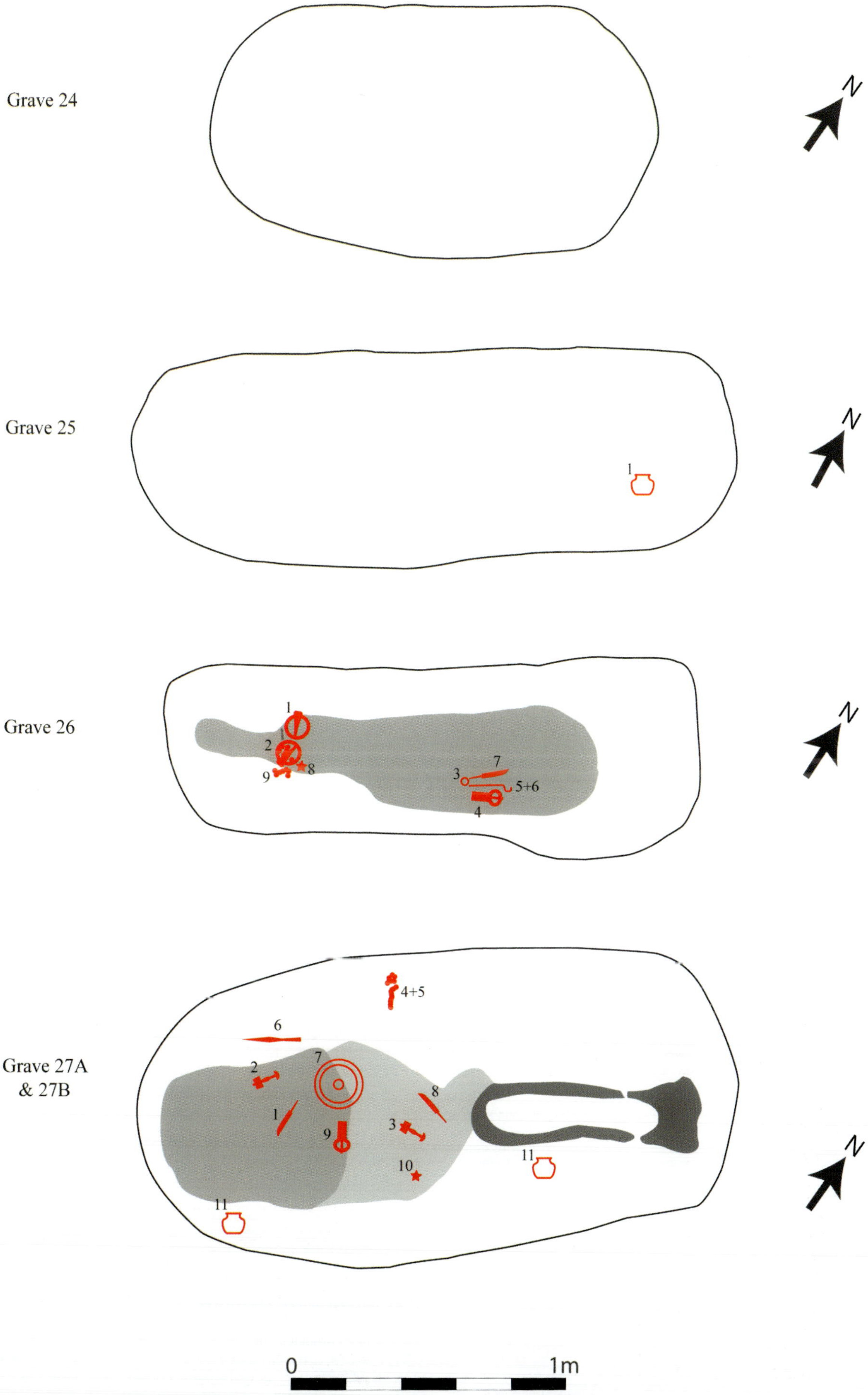

Figure 15.22 Plans of Flixton II Graves 24–27 (scale 1:20)

No skeletal remains or soil stains were recorded.

A single sherd of pot (25/1) was recovered from the fill towards the eastern end of the grave. It was unclear whether this represented accidental inclusion, the deliberate deposition of a single sherd or the vestiges of a whole vessel that had suffered from post-depositional damage. The final option seems the most unlikely as even substantial disturbance would have left identifiable traces in the form of small pot fragments.

25/1 Thick rounded **base** fragment, grass-tempered (ESO1), smoothed. Orange/brown externally, dark grey internally. Not illustrated. 053:*0532*.

Grave 26 (053:*0533*)
Figs 15.22–15.24; Pl. 7.4a
Dimensions: 1.95m x 0.6m
Orientation: 237°
Container for body: Extensive stain on base of grave, possible bier
Finds gender: Female
Age and Sex: Young adult, indeterminate sex
Skeletal remains: Very poor, copper staining. Nine teeth only. Tooth wear slight.
Body position: Grave size and grave goods suggest supine, extended with head to west
Associated features: None positively attributed to 053:*0533*, small post-holes to north are more likely to be associated with Grave 42.
Description: Sub-rectangular cut with rounded corners and a somewhat bulbous eastern end, surviving to a depth of 0.26m. Exhibited relatively steep edges throughout and a flat bottom. The fill (053:*0534*) comprised relatively homogenous brown silty sand with gravel inclusions.

Skeletal remains (053:*0573*) were limited to teeth. An extensive stain on the base of the grave could be have been related to the position of the body. However, its shape was also suggestive of a container into which the body had been placed, possibly a bier.

The grave goods formed two distinct groups, both located within the extensive basal stain. A western group, in the area that would have coincided with the neck and shoulders of the body, comprised two annular brooches (26/1 and 26/2), a fragment of copper alloy plate (26/8) and fourteen beads (26/9:*1293–1306*). The second group, located approximately two-thirds of the way down the grave and probably attached close to the waist, comprised a copper alloy ring (26/3), an iron buckle (26/4), a copper-alloy sliding-knot ring (26/5), an iron latch-lifter (26/6) and an incomplete iron knife (26/7).

26/1 Copper-alloy **annular brooch** with an almost flat ring of elliptical section and regular width. Pierced circular pin emplacement, 3.5mm diameter; outer edge of ring widens at emplacement. Remains of iron pin in perforation. Punched small rings around inner and outer edge and transverse grooves on ring where pin tip would be: ornament very worn. D.46mm; band W.8mm. Well-preserved textile on back. 053:*1284*.

26/2 Copper-alloy **annular brooch** with a flat, thick ring of irregular width. Pierced circular pin emplacement, 2.5mm diameter. Iron pin, 2.5mm diameter. Cast transverse grooves to one side of perforation and on opposite side of ring. D.50mm; band 9–11mm x 2.3mm thick. Textile remains pierced by pin. 053:*1285*.

26/3 Copper-alloy **ring** with circular-section band. Six groups of three transverse grooves arranged around band. Some parts are flattened from wear. D.49mm; ring D.5.5mm. Mineral-preserved fibres and textile. 053:*1286*.

26/4 **Buckle** with round iron loop, iron tongue and copper-alloy plate. The plate is rectangular on one side and tapered on the other, and has been fixed with a single rivet with domed heads (on both sides), 4mm diameter. Marzinzik II.19b. 22 x 22mm; plate W.14mm x L.20mm. 053:*1287a*.

26/5 Copper-alloy wire **sliding-knot ring**, bent out of shape, made from circular-section wire, 2mm diameter. D.*c*.20mm. 053:*1287b*.

26/6 Iron **latch-lifter** with an incomplete working end, and a broken suspension end incorporating an outward curled loop and remains of an iron ring. Rectangular section, 7 x 4mm, thickening to 9 x 5mm towards the suspension end. L.190mm. 053:*1287c*.

26/7 Iron **knife**, incomplete with lightly rounded end to tang, widening to shoulder and rounded choil. Abundant horn surviving on both sides with vertical handle line at shoulder. Straight back, curving slightly over last quarter towards tip, which is missing. Sinuous cutting edge rising towards tip,

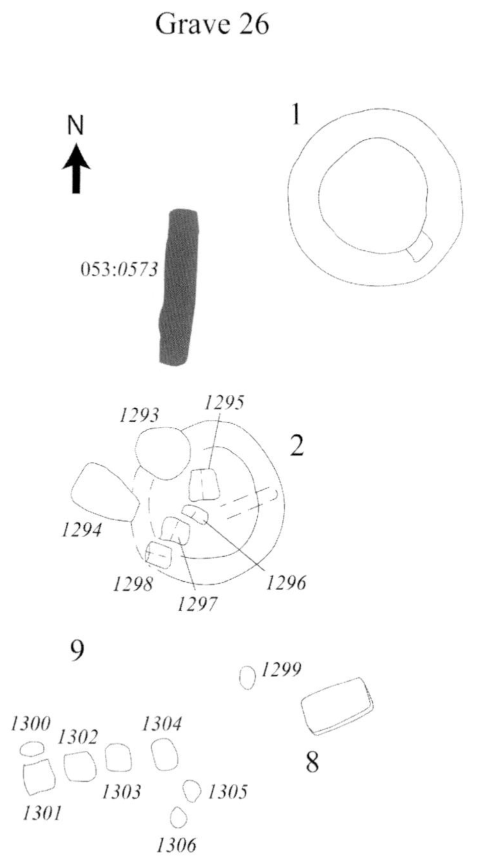

Figure 15.23 Flixton II Grave 26, *in situ* plan of grave goods 1, 2, 8 and bead group 9. All contexts numbers are site FLN 053 (scale 1:2)

seemingly broken in antiquity. Upper quarter of blade has distinct metallurgy, different from remainder. Type: Drinkall B or C. Estimated original length 154mm, blade W.18mm. Skin product 2mm thick on one side of blade under textile on one face. Traces of plant material above. 053:*1288*.

26/8 Fragment of copper-alloy **plate**, 1.5mm thick. 19 x 12mm. 053:*1292*.

26/9 Beads 053:*1293–1306* (see *in situ* 1:2 plan Fig. 15.23; Pl. 7.4a *1293–4*, *1296–8*, *1300*, *1305–6*). Brugmann Group A. Ten amber **beads** (total weight 5.3g; slight signs of wear): 1 short, chip lost, D.16–21mm (*1293*); 1 short, irregular, D.16–21mm (*1294*); 2 medium, faceted, D.11–15mm (*1295*, *1302*); 1 medium, faceted, D.6–10mm (*1298*); 5 medium, rounded, D.6–10mm (*1297*, *1299*, *1301*, *1303–4*).
Four glass **beads**: Type *Norfolk short variant*?: 1 short, globular (irregular), D.6–10mm (*1300*).
Other beads: white globular: 1 short, globular; D.6–10mm (*1296*); yellow: 1 short, cylindrical, D.6–10mm (*1306*); 1 short, globular, D.6–10mm (*1305*).

Grave 27 (053:*0553*)
Figs 15.22, 15.24–15.25; Pl. 7.4b
Dimensions: 2.2m x 1.1m
Orientation: 230°
Container for body: Extensive stain on base of grave, possible bier
Finds gender: Two sets of grave goods, one female (A) and one male (B)
Age and Sex: Only one body recognised (B), indeterminate age, grave size suggests adult, indeterminate sex
Skeletal remains: (A) None. (B) Very, very poor. A few tiny scraps of unidentified bone.
Body position: Supine, head to west
Associated features: None recognised
Description: Rounded, almost oval cut surviving to a depth of 0.46m. Steep, near-vertical sides were recorded throughout with a flat bottom. The fill (053:*0554*) comprised relatively homogenous brown silty sand with gravel inclusions.

Skeletal remains (053:*0580*) were limited to a few tiny fragments preserved close to the shield boss (27B/7). However, an extensive stain

Grave 26 ...continued

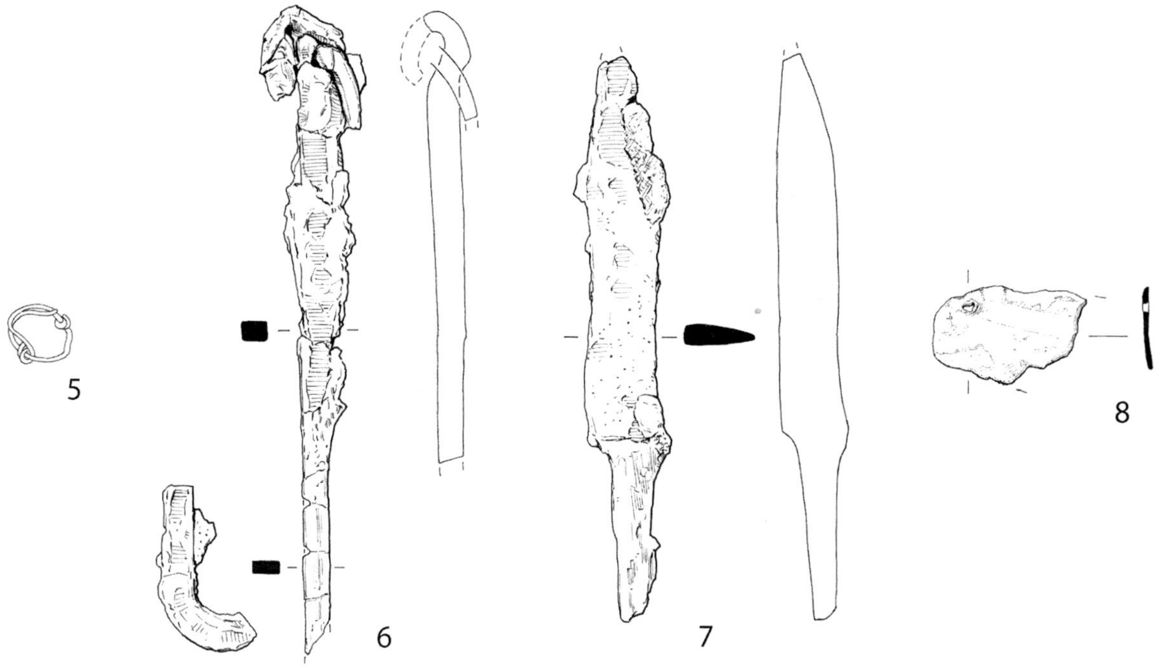

Grave 27A

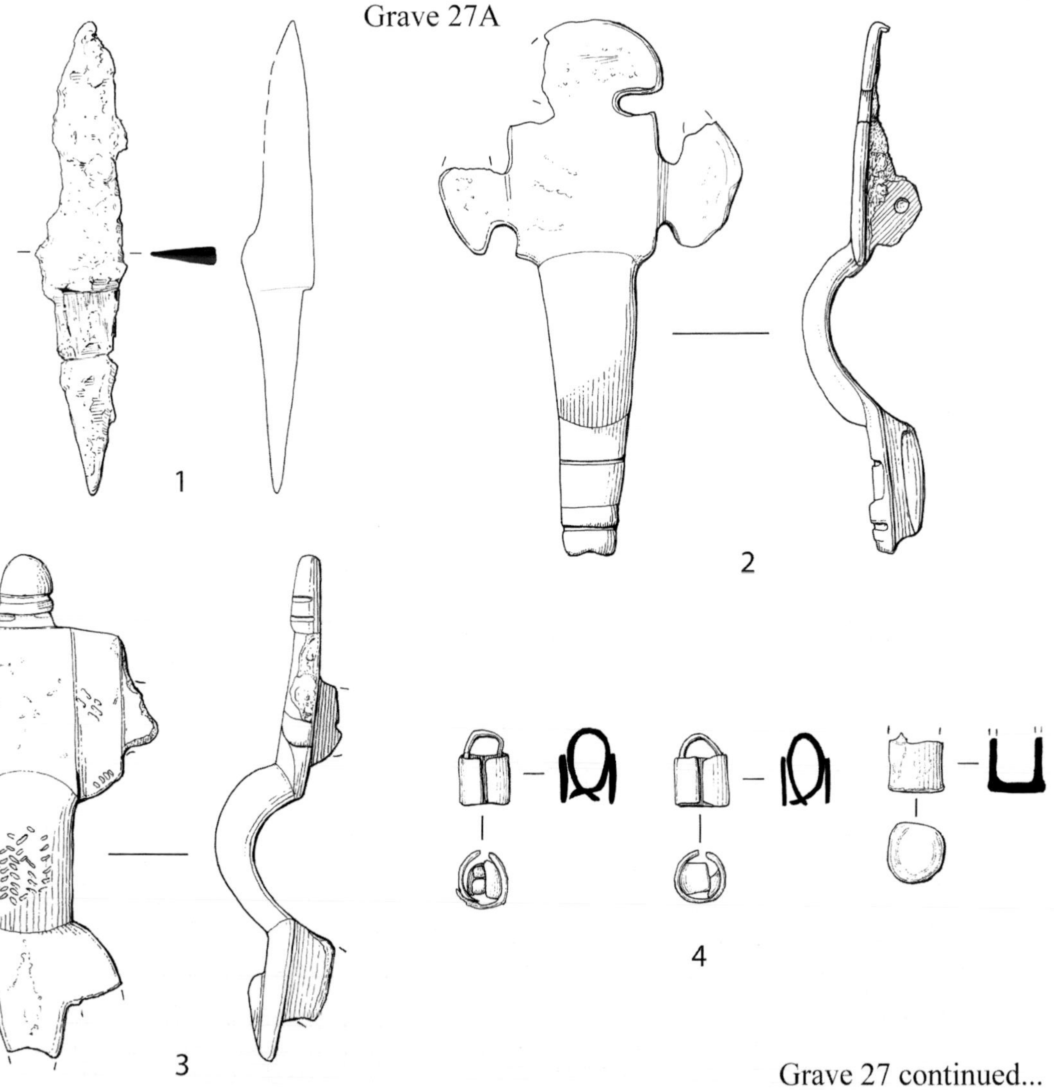

Grave 27 continued...

Figure 15.24 Grave goods; Flixton II Grave 26 (scales: 5–7 at 1:2; 8 at 1:1) and Flixton II Grave 27 body A (scales: 1 at 1:2; 2–4 at 1:1)

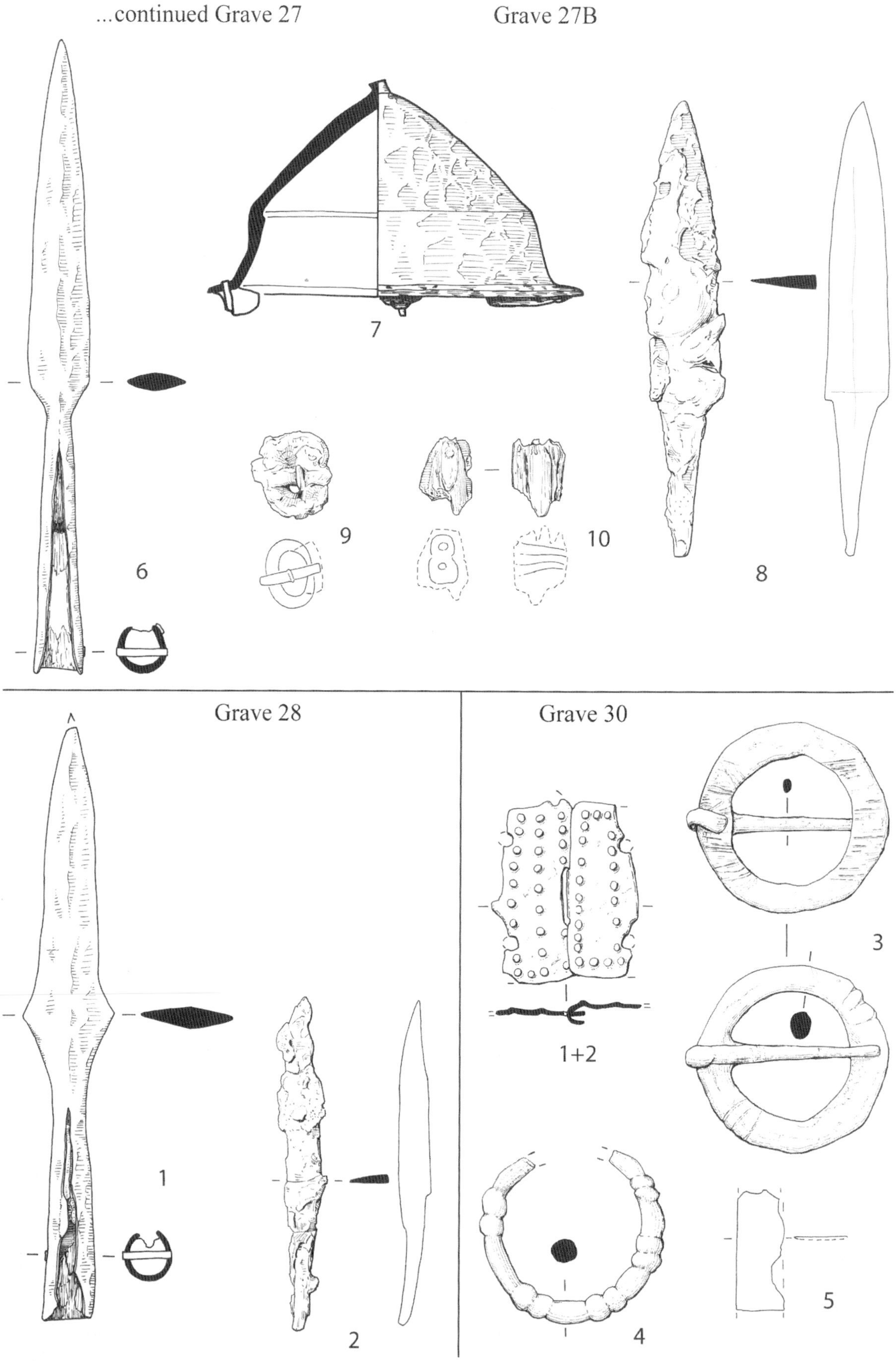

Figure 15.25 Grave goods; Flixton II Grave 27 body B (scale: 6–10 at 1:2), Flixton II Grave 28 (scale: 1 and 2 at 1:2) and Flixton II Grave 30 (scales: 1–4 at 1:1; 5 at 1:2)

on the base of the grave included clear impressions of legs, a right arm and a pelvis with a more amorphous area towards the west possibly indicative of the torso or a container such as bier.

While apparently associated with one cut, the finds evidence suggests that the grave relates to two individuals; one with female gender grave goods and one with male gender grave goods. Two brooches (27A/2 and 27A/3) and an iron knife (27A/1) were encountered at high level and appeared to have been disturbed and not in the position that they would have been worn. A group of seven copper-alloy bucket beads (collectively 27A/4) and ten other beads (27A/5) were located close to the northern edge of the grave just to the west of centre and are consistent with their being associated with the partially disturbed burial with female grave goods. In contrast, the shield boss (27B/7), a spearhead (27B/6), a second knife (27B/8) and an iron buckle (27B/9) were entirely in keeping with a position that relates them directly to the recorded body stain in the base of the grave. In addition, a fragment from a socketed object (27B/10), recorded towards the southern side of basal stain approximately halfway up the grave, was also attributed to body B. It does then seem likely that an initial burial, with female gender grave goods, was at least partially disturbed by a subsequent burial with male gender grave goods. Given that stratigraphic relationships between graves in the cemetery are rare, it seems reasonable to suggest that such a total disturbance of an earlier burial was deliberate. In addition to these grave goods, seven pottery sherds (27/11) were recorded with all but one located in the eastern end of the grave towards its southern edge. While two vessels may have been represented, sherd 053:*0574*, in the western end of the grave, was from the same pot as the majority of 27/11 and can be considered as evidence for post-depositional disturbance. Whether the pot was in the initial burial, later disturbed by the second interment, or broken as a result of later disruption is unclear.

Body A

27A/1 Complete iron **knife**. Tang widens markedly from narrow end to stepped shoulder and rounded choil. Back curves lightly throughout to blunt tip, sinuous cutting edge rises to tip. Horn remains present on one side of tang with distinct vertical handle line at shoulder. Less obvious on other side. Medial weld line extending into tang. Type: Drinkall A. L.125mm, blade W.13mm. On blade traces of mineralised organic material, possibly skin product, and textile near tip. 053:*1289*.

27A/2 Copper-alloy **small-long brooch** with trefoil head. Foot missing, broken in antiquity. The pin support is a single lug, cast with the brooch; the pin catch is also cast and turned to the left; the remains of an iron pin are present at the pin support. Type: EAC *sm2*. L.70mm, W.41mm across head. Bow L.22.5mm, W.12mm, Ht.12.5mm. 053:*1290*.

27A/3 Incomplete copper-alloy **small-long brooch** with cruciform head and downward-pointing lappets. All three knobs are cast with brooch. Foot incomplete and side knobs broken (recent breaks, due to corrosion). The pin support is a single lug, cast with the brooch, but now broken; the pin catch is also cast and turned to the left; the pin is absent. The metal has a grey core, caused by decay of leaded bronze (XRF). L.65mm, W.34mm (across head). Type: EAC *sm3*. Bow L.21mm, W.13mm, Ht.11mm. Textile remains on the front of the brooch. 053:*1291*.

27A/4 Six complete copper-alloy **bucket pendants** and fragments of at least one more. Made from sheet metal, with disc-shaped bases (sometimes absent), curled sides with a butted join and narrow strip handles with ends braced against the inner face of the walls. No material inside, but decayed leather/skin in association and remains of cord or thong running across underside of handle. D.8mm, Ht.wall 7mm, handle strip 3.5mm wide. 053:*1315*.

27A/5 Beads 053:*1307–1314*, *1319–1321* (see *in situ* 1:2 plan Fig. 15.26; Pl. 7.4b *1307*, *1310–2*). Brugmann Group A.
Seven amber **beads** (total weight 0.4g; slight signs of wear): 1 medium, faceted, D.6–10mm (*1311*); 6 medium, faceted, D.3–5mm (*1308–9*, *1310*, *1313–4*, *1319*).
Four glass **beads**: Type *Constricted, Segmented:* 3 medium, globular, D.3–5mm (*1312*, *1320–1*).
Type *Polychrome3:* 1 medium, globular, D.11–15mm (*1307*).

Body B

27B/6 Complete iron **spearhead** with cleft socket encompassing most of shank, short length of solid iron above. Narrow blade with widest part just above junction with shank, tapering

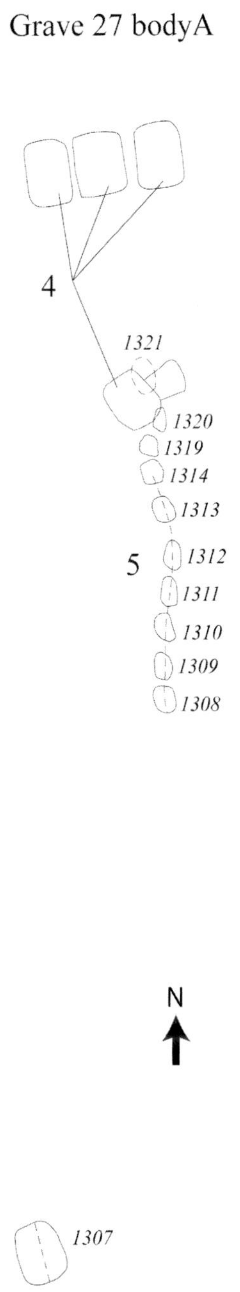

Figure 15.26 Flixton II Grave 27 body A, *in situ* plan of bucket pendant group 4 and bead group 5. All contexts numbers are site FLN 053 (scale 1:2)

with straight sides to pointed tip. Lentoid to lozengiform in section. Heavily accreted in sand. Type: Swanton E2; EAC Angular Medium 1. L.213mm, W.23mm. Mineral-preserved wood in socket: possibly *Fraxinus* sp. (ash) and made from mature timber. 053:*1316*.

27B/7 Iron **shield boss**, incomplete. Small boss with fairly straight cone, slightly sloping wall (Ht.20mm), narrow flange (W.12mm) and small disc-headed apex (D.7mm approx.). Type: Dickinson and Härke 6; EAC SOS. D.130mm, Ht.75mm. 053:*1322*.

27B/8 Iron **knife**, complete. Bent and distorted tang widens evenly to distinct shoulder and stepped choil. Noticeable handle line at shoulder. Back straight and curving lightly to tip, cutting edge slightly worn but straight and rising to tip. Clear and obvious weld line along middle of blade. Type: Drinkall A. L.156mm, blade W.19mm. Traces of horn on tang. Extensive skin-product sheath survives on both sides of blade, wraps over the blade back and is joined at the cutting edge. 053:*1323*.

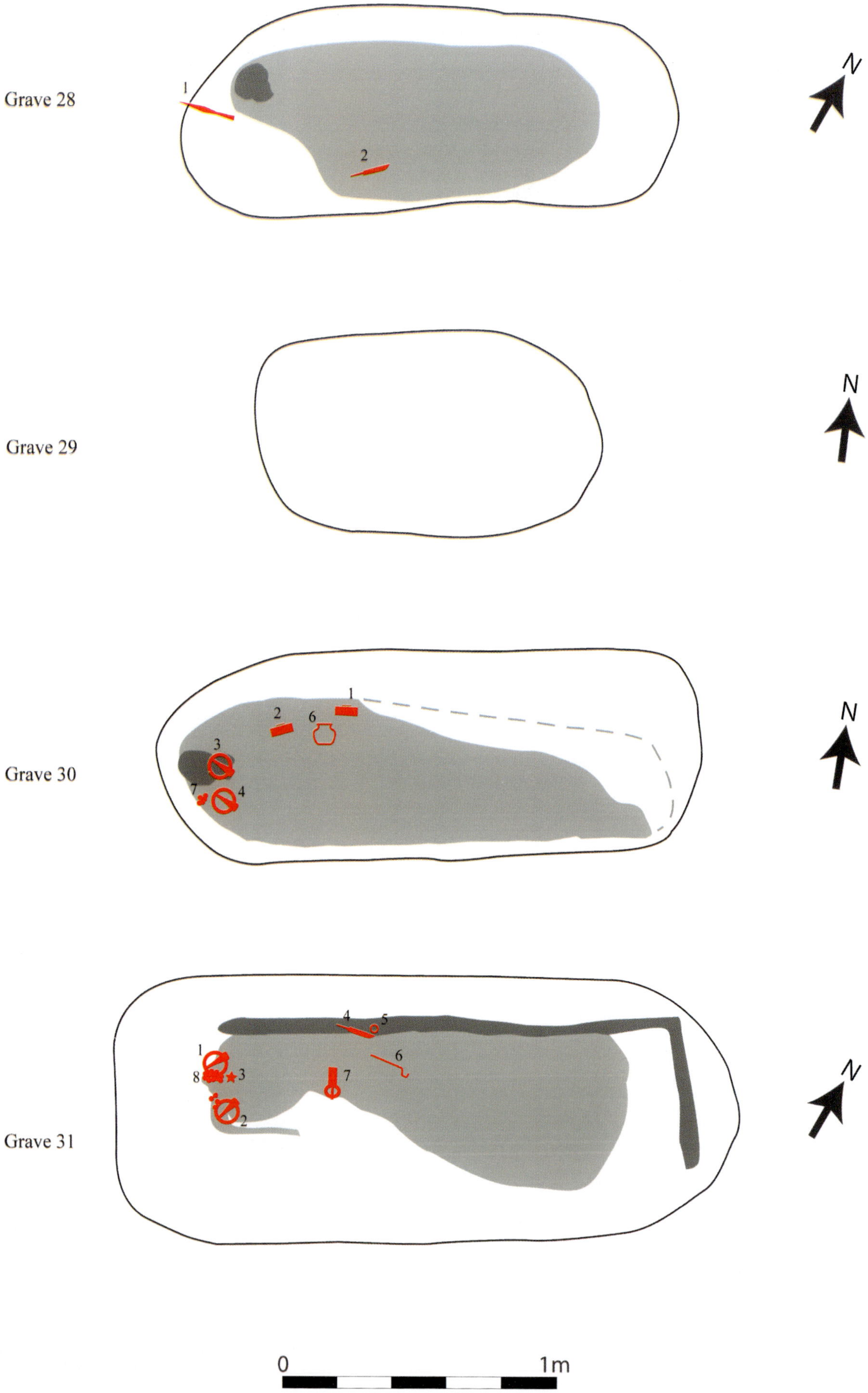

Figure 15.27 Plans of Flixton II Graves 28–31 (scale 1:20)

27B/9 Iron **buckle** with D-shaped loop, iron tongue and no belt plate. The tongue pierces a layer of leather or skin and further remains of strap by axis. Type: Marzinzik I.10a-i. W.30mm x 23mm. Textile remains on back and side of buckle. 053:*1324*.

27B/10 Fragment of a **socketed iron object**, enclosing mineral-preserved ?horn. L.27mm, W.19mm, Ht.17mm. 053:*1325*.

27B/11 (i) Base and body sherds of globular **vessel** with rounded base, grass-tempered (ESO1), smoothed, sooted, burnt food residue internally. Buff-brown externally, black internally. 100% base. Contexts 053:*0574* and 053:*0578*. Not illustrated.
(ii) Three abraded granite-tempered **sherds**, probably one vessel. Grey-brown externally, grey internally. Contexts 053:*0578* and 053:*0579*. Not illustrated. 053:*0574*, *0578* and *0579*.

Grave 28 (053:*0575*)
Figs 15.25 and 15.27
Dimensions: 1.8m x 0.7m
Orientation: 236°
Container for body: Extensive stain on base of grave, possible bier
Finds gender: Male
Age and Sex: Young–middle aged, male
Skeletal remains: Poor, powdery and fragile. Fragments of left side of skull: frontal, maxilla, parietal, temporal, mandible, 15 teeth.
Body position: Supine, head to west
Associated features: Series of five post-holes parallel and external to northern edge of grave
Description: A parallel-sided, round-ended cut surviving to a depth of 0.24m. Profiles reveal steeply sloping edges on the sides and west end, shallower sloping edge to the east. The fill (053:*0576*) comprised relatively homogenous brown silty sand with gravel inclusions.

Skeletal remains (053:*0577*) were limited to fragments of skull and teeth. An extensive stain that covered the majority of the grave base had no well-defined components that could relate directly to a body and it seems more likely that it represented the vestiges of a container, possibly a bier.

An iron spearhead (28/1) was recorded central to the western end of the grave with its point outside of the excavated grave edge and may have been pushed into the side due to it being too long to fit comfortably. One other grave good, an iron knife (28/2) was located almost central to the grave towards its southern side within the extensive basal stain. The location of this object is consistent with it being attached at the waist area of the body.

A series of five circular post-holes (053:*0581*, *0600*, *0602*, *0604* and *0606*) formed a gently curving arc immediately north of the grave cut, with a sixth post-hole (053:*0608*) further north again, but possibly unrelated (all shown unnumbered on Fig. 6.1) While it could be argued that the post-hole at the western end of the arc (053:*0600*) and 053:*0608* are associated with Grave 32 rather than Grave 28 or, in the case of 053:*0608*, not related to the graves at all, the position of these features does suggest that the posts they would have contained functioned as grave markers. Alternatively, they may have been structural, possibly as revetting or curbing around a mound or platform. The post-holes were all small, between 0.2m and 0.3m in diameter with depths also ranging between 0.2m and 0.3m and fills comprising homogenous brown silty sand.

28/1 Complete iron **spearhead**, cleft socket extending for practically all of shank with lateral nail 20mm above base. Blade widens in concave curves to its widest point just above junction with shank, tapering thereafter with curved edges before tapering to rounded point. Lentoid in section. Type: Swanton H1, EAC Concave Medium 1b. L.204mm, W.35mm. Abundant mineral-preserved wood in socket: *Fraxinus* sp. (ash) made from mature timber. 053:*1317*.

28/2 Iron **knife**, complete with narrow tang widening gradually to stepped shoulder and rounded choil. Back curves towards tip, rising over last part, tip thin and sharp. Sinuous cutting edge rises to tip. Type: Drinkall F. L.112mm, blade W.9mm. Traces of horn on tang edges and along part of one side. 053:*1318*.

Grave 29 (053:*0595*)
Fig. 15.27
Dimensions: 1.25m x 0.7m
Orientation: 260°
Container for body: None recognised
Finds gender: No grave goods
Age and Sex: Grave size suggests child, indeterminate sex
Skeletal remains: None
Body position: Indeterminate
Associated features: None recognised
Description: An oval cut with very gently sloping sides and a relatively flat bottom, only surviving to a depth of 0.1m. The fill (053:*0596*) comprised homogenous brown silty sand with gravel inclusions.

No skeletal remains or soil stains were recorded.

No grave goods.

Grave 30 (053:*0597*)
Figs 15.25, 15.27–15.28; Pl. 7.4b
Dimensions: 1.97m x 0.7m
Orientation: 256°
Container for body: Extensive brown stain over base of secondary cut, possible bier
Finds gender: Female
Age and Sex: Young adult ?female
Skeletal remains: Poor, thoracic preservation due to copper staining. Fragments of left side and base of skull, 6 teeth, C1–2, left clavicle, arches of upper thoracic vertebrae. Tooth wear slight. Mandible rounded, occipital crests small, vertebral arches small.
Body position: Supine, head to west
Associated features: Three post-holes north of grave, association tenuous
Description: A parallel-sided cut with a rounded west end and square east end. Exhibits a secondary deeper cut along the southern side of the grave measuring 1.8m by 0.5m in which the body and associated grave goods had been placed. The profiles reveal that the wider cut was 0.12m deep increasing to 0.4m in the secondary cut, the latter exhibiting steeply angled sides with the former shallower sloping except on its southern side where it coincided with the secondary cut. The fill (053:*0598*) comprised relatively homogenous brown silty sand with gravel inclusions.

Skeletal remains (053:*0599*) were limited to fragments of skull, clavicle and vertebrae. An extensive stain covering the whole of the base of the secondary cut could have been associated with a container for the body, possibly a bier. Other than the secondary cut, there was no other evidence that might suggest that there were two superimposed burials.

Four sherds of pot (30/6) were recorded approximately central to the western half of the grave. While almost certainly representing a deliberate deposition, it is unclear whether it had originally been placed in the grave as a complete vessel and subsequently suffered post-depositional damage, or had been introduced as already broken sherds representing only part of the whole pot. A pair of sleeve clasps (30/1 and 30/2) were located towards the northern side in the western half of the grave and two annular brooches (30/3 and 30/4) were found in association with six beads (30/7) in the neck and shoulder region of the body. These objects were all considered to have been in their original positions, probably attached to garments worn by the body.

Three circular post-holes (053:*0673*, *0675* and *0684*) were recorded to the north of the western end of the grave (all shown unnumbered on Fig. 6.1). However, with the absence of similar features around the remainder of the grave it seems difficult positively to associate them to the burial. Both 053:*0673* and 053:*0675* were *c*.0.2m in diameter with depths of 0.3m and 0.2m respectively while 053:*0684* was 0.4m in diameter with a depth of 0.4m. The fills of all three features comprised brown silty sand with gravel (053:*0684*) and charcoal.

30/1–2 A pair of almost complete copper-alloy **sleeve clasps**. The rectangular pieces both have two rows of repoussé dots and remains of two attachment holes, 2.5mm diameter, close to the rear edge. The catch is a plain slot 11mm long. Type: Hines B7; EAC *B7b*. L.31mm, W.catch-piece 15mm, W.hook-piece 13mm. Black organic material in association appears to be human tissue. 30/1 is 053:*1326* and 30/2 is 053:*1327*.

30/3 Small copper-alloy **annular brooch** with near-circular ring section and two areas of cast beading on opposite sides of the ring. The copper-alloy pin has an oval section, 2mm diameter mid shank, and the end is looped over the ring without an emplacement. D.32mm; ring W.5mm. Poorly preserved textile remains. 053:*1359*.

30/4 Small copper-alloy **annular brooch**, incomplete, with near-circular ring section and cast bead-and-reel ornament. The iron pin, now fragmentary, has a circular section, 2mm diameter, and was originally looped over the ring, without an emplacement. D.32mm; ring W.4mm. 053:*1360*.

30/5 A thin **fragment** of corroded iron, possibly the remains of a knife blade. 44 x 17mm. Not on grave plan. 053:*0127*.

Grave 30

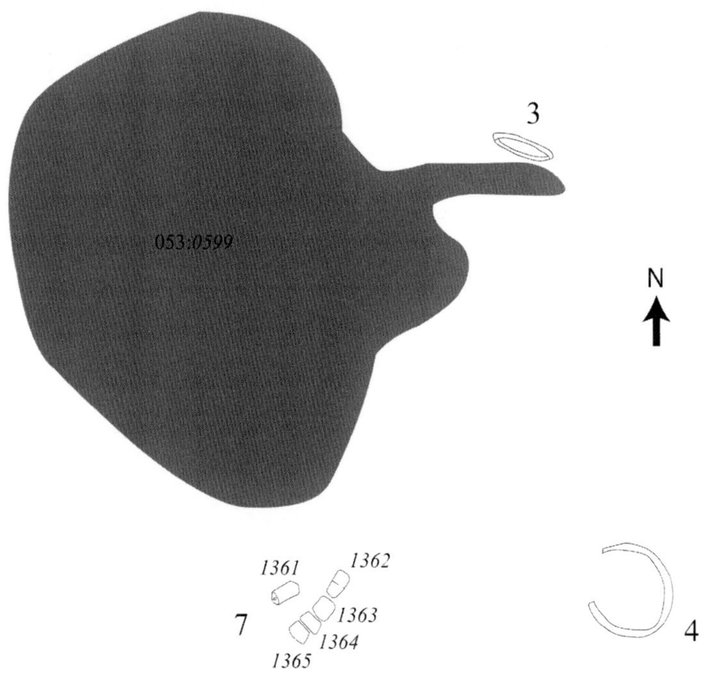

Figure 15.28 Flixton II Grave 30, *in situ* plan of grave goods 3, 4 and bead group 7. All contexts numbers are site FLN 053 (scale 1:2)

30/6 Four **sherds** of a thick-walled grass-tempered vessel. Grey/brown. Not illustrated. 053:*0611*.

30/7 Beads 053:*1361–5*, *1374* (see *in situ* 1:2 plan Fig. 15.28; Pl. 7.4b *1361–3*, *1365*, *1374*), Brugmann Group A2.
Six glass **beads**: Type *Norfolk Melon:* 1 long, 4 ribs, D.6–10mm (*1361*); 1 medium, 4 ribs, D.6–10mm (*1374*).
Other beads: yellow large: 4 short, globular (asymmetrical), D.6–10mm (*1362–5*).

Grave 31 (053:*0612*)
Figs 15.27, 15.29–15.30; Pl. 7.4a
Dimensions: 2.26m x 0.9m
Orientation: 236°
Container for body: Straight edged stain, possibly coffin or bier
Finds gender: Female
Age and Sex: Grave size suggests adult, indeterminate sex
Body position: Indeterminate, grave size suggests extended, grave goods indicate head to west
Associated features: None recognised
Description: A parallel-sided cut with squared western end, rounded to the east and surviving for a depth of 0.3m. Exhibited a relatively steep sided profile and contained a fill (053:*0613*) comprising relatively homogenous brown silty sand with gravel inclusions.

Skeletal remains were completely absent, but elements of a brown sandy stain (053:*0614*) on the base of the grave possibly relate to the body. In addition, the stain had a clearly defined straight edge running down the north side of the grave before turning at 90° across the grave and has been interpreted as relating to either a coffin or another type of container for the body such as a bier.

A well-furnished grave with a complex group of grave goods located towards the centre of the western end of the grave in an area that would have been occupied by the neck and shoulders of the body. This group comprised iron annular brooches (31/1 and 31/2), an iron brooch pin (31/3) and fourteen beads (31/8). A second group of finds was recorded approximately halfway up the grave close to its northern edge, comprising an iron knife (31/4) and an iron suspension ring (31/5) and there was an iron latch-lifter (31/6) further towards the middle of the grave. These finds were probably attached close to the waist area of the body. In addition, a small iron buckle with long plate (31/7) was found in the area between the other two groups of finds that would have been occupied by the torso of the body.

31/1 Iron **annular brooch** with rounded ring section; pin tip missing. D.37mm; ring W.4.5mm. Poorly preserved textile on front. 053:*1352*.

31/2 Iron **annular brooch** with rounded ring section and long iron pin. D.36mm; ring W.5.5mm; pin L.45mm. Poorly preserved textile. 053:*1353*.

31/3 Iron **brooch pin**, probably from a copper-alloy annular brooch, with rounded section and an intact looped end. L.42mm, D.2.5mm. 053:*1354*.

31/4 Iron **knife**, complete with rounded end to narrow tang. Widens evenly to shoulder and choil. Abundant horn remains on both sides of tang, extending to shoulder with sinuous vertical handle line. Straight back curving gradually to rounded point, straight cutting edge. Medial weld line along blade, extending into tang. Type: Drinkall A. L.153mm, blade W.14mm. Some skin product on both sides. 053:*1355*.

31/5 Iron suspension **ring** with, attached by looped end, the broken end of a key or latch-lifter with a square-section shank. Ring D.21mm, Th.4mm. Shank L.28mm, section 10 x 8mm. Poorly preserved textile remains. 053:*1356*.

31/6 Fragment of iron **latch-lifter or pot hook**, probably related to 31/5. The working end has three inward bends, the shank is square section, 9 x 8mm, and the suspension end is missing. L.100mm; bent lengths 45mm, 35mm, 15mm. Poorly preserved textile remains. 053:*1357*.

31/7 Small iron **buckle** with oval-to-circular loop, and long tapering iron plate, incomplete at rear edge. The plate is fastened with an iron rivet, 5mm diameter. Type: Marzinzik II.16. Loop 21 x 18mm; plate W.18mm, L.>55mm. Textile remains on front. 053:*1358*.

31/8 **Beads** 053:*1328–1340*, *1351* (see in situ 1:2 plan Fig. 15.30; Pl. 7.4b *1328*, *1330–1*, *1333*, *1335–8*, *1351*), Brugmann Group A.
Nine amber **beads** (total weight 13.1g; worn): 1 short, irregular, D.33mm (*1351*); 1 short, irregular, D.6–10mm (*1336*); 3 medium, faceted, D.11–15mm (*1331–2*, *1334*); 1 medium, faceted, D.7mm (*1329*), 3 medium rounded, D.6–10mm (*1328*, *1339*, *1340*).
Five glass **beads**:Type *Norfolk Short* variant?*:* 1 medium, globular, D.6–10mm (*1330*).
Type *Polyhchrome7:* 2 short, globular, D.11–15mm (*1333*, *1335*).

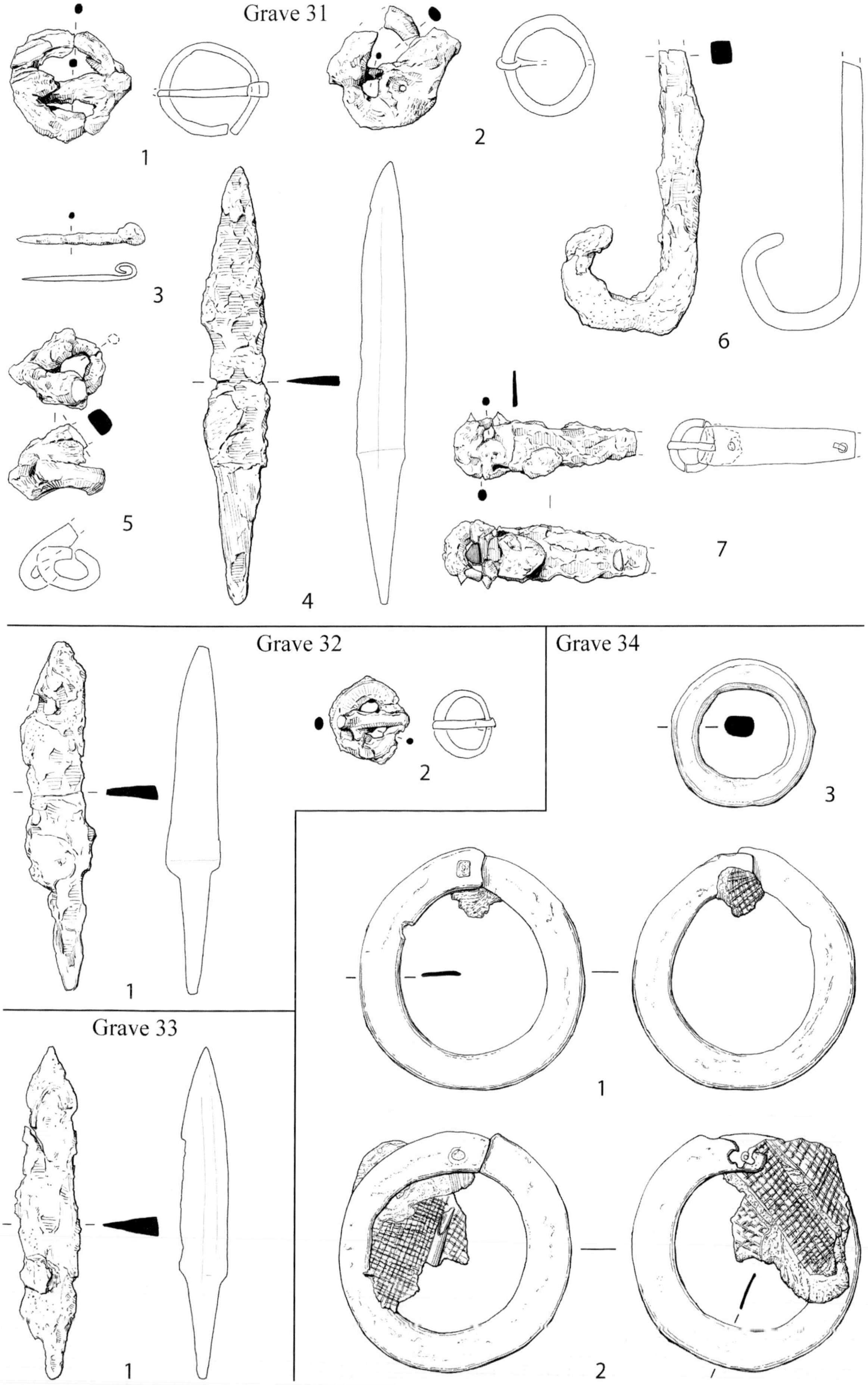

Figure 15.29 Grave goods; Flixton II Grave 31 (scale: 1–7 at 1:2), Flixton II Grave 32 (scale: 1 and 2 at 1:2), Flixton II Grave 33 (scale: 1 at 1:2) and Flixton II Grave 34 (scale: 1–3 at 1:1)

Other beads: white globular: 2 short, globular, D.6–10mm (*1337*, *1338*).

Grave 32 (053:*0615*)
Figs 15.29 and 15.31
Dimensions: 1.75m x 0.7m
Orientation: 244°
Container for body: Extensive oval-shaped stain on base of grave, possible bier
Finds gender: Uncertain
Age and Sex: Middle aged male
Skeletal remains: Very poor. Fragments of left temporal, occipital and mandible, five molars. Tooth wear moderate. Large occipital crest and mastoid process. Carious upper left second molar, periodontal disease of left mandible.
Body position: Extended, probably supine, head to west
Associated features: Four post-holes close to the grave cut were possibly related
Description: A parallel-sided irregular-ended cut with a flat bottom and moderately sloping sides, survived to a depth of 0.26m. The fill (053:*0616*) comprised relatively homogenous brown silty sand with gravel inclusions.

Skeletal remains (053:*0617*) were limited to a few fragments of skull and teeth. An extensive oval shaped stain in the base of the grave was considered to represent a container for the corpse rather than vestiges of the body itself, with its oval shape favouring a bier rather than a coffin.

An iron knife (32/1) was found associated with an iron buckle (32/2) within the basal stain central to the northern edge of the grave. These items may have been on the body at the waist, or to the side of the body.

Three circular post-holes (053:*0622*, *0624* and *0626*) recorded in an arc to the north of the grave could be associated with it as markers or part of an above-ground structure (all shown unnumbered on Fig. 6.1). Also, post-hole 053:*0600*, already described with Grave 28, may actually relate to Grave 32. These features varied between 0.2m and 0.4m in diameter with depths of between 0.15m and 0.34m and fills comprising homogenous brown silty sand with occasional gravel inclusions.

32/1 Iron **knife**, complete with rounded end to tang. Widens to rounded shoulder and choil. Straight back curves over front section to rounded tip. Cutting edge shows little wear, straight and rising to tip. Vertical handle line slightly in front of shoulder. Slight traces of horn on one side of tang. Type: Drinkall A/C. L.124mm, blade W.16mm. Traces of skin product on both sides of blade. 053:*1342*.

32/2 Iron **buckle** with D-shaped loop, no plate, enlarged tongue-rest and tongue which is wider towards tip. Marzinzik I.10b-i. 28 x 22mm. Textile on back. 053:*1343*.

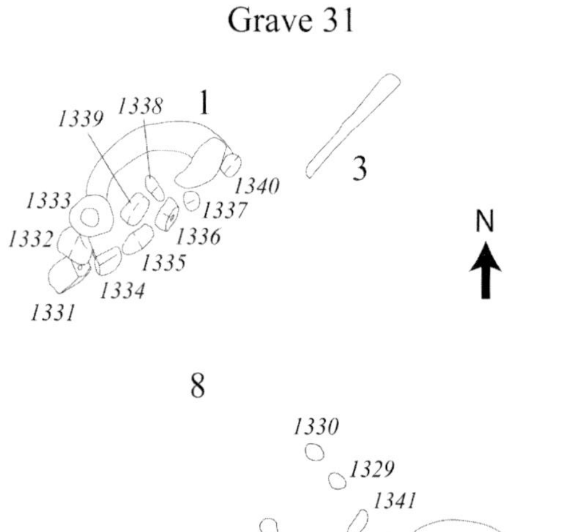

Figure 15.30 Flixton II Grave 31, *in situ* plan of grave goods 1–3 and bead group 8. All contexts numbers are site 053 (scale 1:2)

Grave 33 (053:*0618*)
Figs 15.29 and 15.31; Pl. 7.4b
Dimensions: 1.93m x 0.85m
Orientation: 240°
Container for body: None recognised
Finds gender: Female
Age and Sex: Young adult or sub-adult, indeterminate sex
Skeletal remains: Very poor, fragile. Three teeth only. Third molars unerupted?
Body position: Grave shape and grave goods suggest extended, supine, head to west
Associated features: Cuts Grave 36. A post-hole immediately to the north was more likely to be associated with the adjacent Grave 36.
Description: A parallel-sided cut with a rounded east end, squarer to the west and surviving to a depth 0.44m with steep, near vertical sided edges and a flat bottom. The fill (053:*0619*) comprised relatively homogenous brown silty sand with gravel inclusions.

Skeletal remains (053:*0634*) were limited to a few fragments of skull and teeth. A dark grey/black sand stain in the base of the grave almost certainly marked the general position of the body.

An iron knife (33/1) was found within the basal stain close to and central to the northern edge of the grave and was probably attached at or near the waist of the body. In addition, a group of seven beads (33/2) were recovered from the area towards the western end of the grave that would have been occupied by the neck and shoulders of the body. A single sherd of pottery (33/3) was found in grave fill 053:*0619*. It was unclear whether it had been deliberately included or had been introduced accidentally.

33/1 Iron **knife**, complete with rounded end to tang. Widens evenly to shoulder and choil. Straight back curving to tip, straight cutting edge rising to tip. Medial weld line extending to tang. Possible vertical handle line just in front of shoulder. Type: Drinkall A. L.118mm, blade W.16mm. Traces of skin product 2mm thick and plant material intermittently on at least one side of the blade. 053:*1344*.

33/2 Beads 053:*1345–1350*, *1366* (Pl. 7.4b *1345*, *1347–1350*, *1366*). Brugmann Group B.
Two amber **beads** (total weight 0.8g; worn): 1 medium, faceted, D.11–15mm (*1348*); 1 medium, rounded, D.6–10mm (*1366*).
Five glass **beads**: Type *Cylindrical, Round:* 1 short, cylindrical; white, D.6–10mm (*1349*).
Type *Koch20 RedYellow:* 1 medium, globular, D.6–10mm (*1350*).
Other beads: yellow small: 3 medium, globular, D.3–5mm (*1345–7*).

33/3 One grass-tempered body **sherd**, soot internally. Buff externally, black internally. From fill 053:*0619*. Not illustrated or on grave plan. 053:*0619*.

Grave 34 (053:*0654*)
Figs 15.29 and 15.31
Dimensions: 1.85m x 0.65m
Orientation: 238°
Container for body: None recognised
Finds gender: Female
Age and Sex: Young adult ?female
Skeletal remains: Poor. Fragments of right parietal, temporals and basi-occipital, four teeth. Tooth wear slight. Small mastoid process.
Body position: Grave size and grave goods position suggests extended, supine, head to west
Associated features: Six post-holes, five to the west and one south-east of the grave, may be associated with Grave 34
Description: A parallel-sided, round ended cut with a maximum depth of 0.3m. The profiles reveal a variable, but generally steeply sloping side and a level base along its long axis, but gently curving across its width. The fill (053:*0655*) comprised relatively homogenous brown silty sand with gravel inclusions.

Skeletal remains (053:*0662*) were limited to a few fragments of skull and teeth. A dark brown sandy soil stain surrounding the area with the skull and associated grave goods may have related to the body or represented the vestiges of the container into which it had been placed.

Two annular brooches (34/1 and 34/2) were found towards the western end of the grave within the basal stain close to the remains of the skull (053:*0662*). A copper-alloy suspension ring (34/3) was located in the area immediately to the east of skull.

Five post-holes (053:*0638*, *0640*, *0642*, *0644* and *0646*) formed an arc around the western end of the grave, with another (053:*0636*) immediately to the south-east of the grave, the latter just as likely to be associated with adjacent Grave 35 as Grave 34 (all shown unnumbered

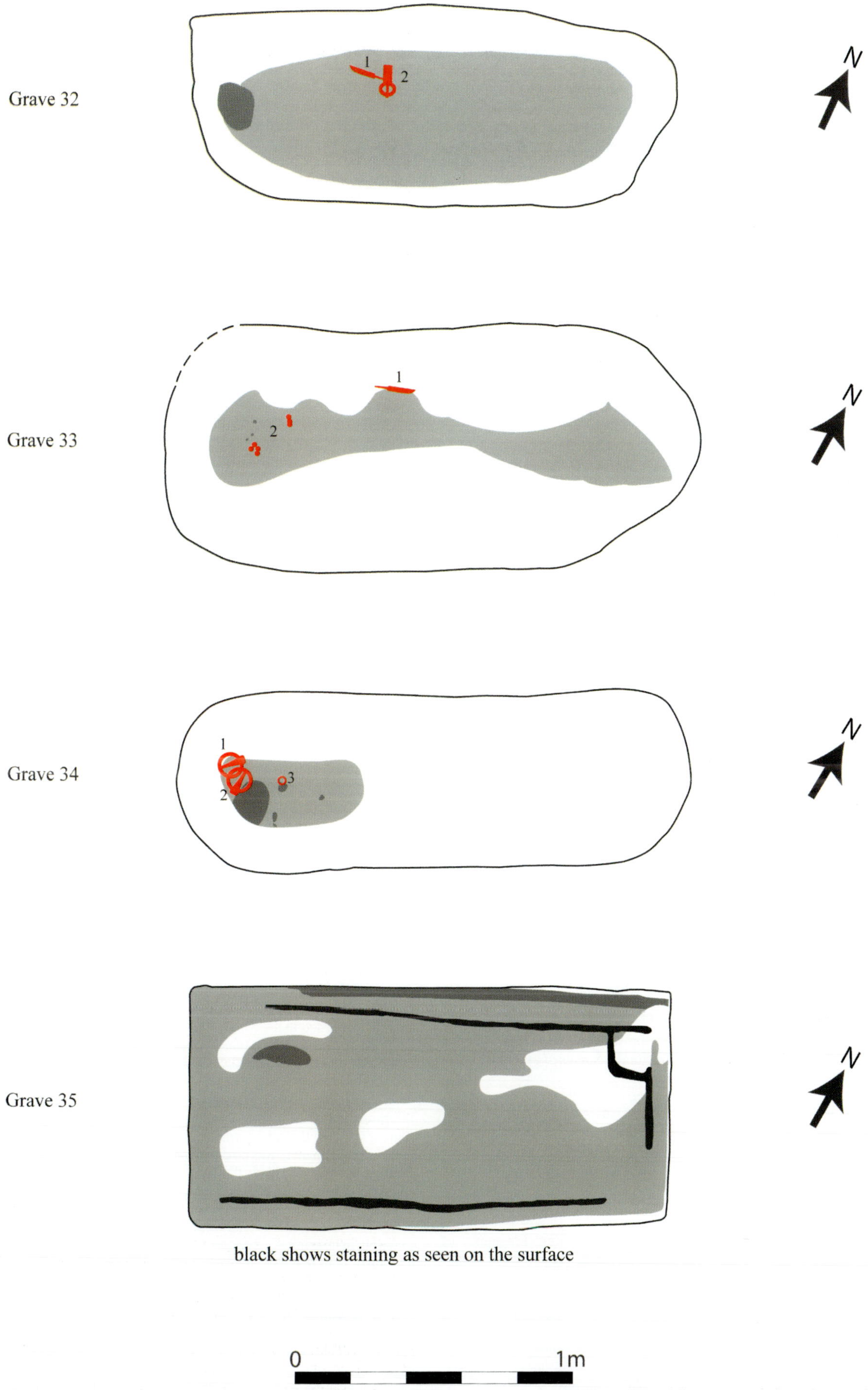

Figure 15.31 Plans of Flixton II Graves 32–35 (scale 1:20)

on Fig. 6.1). The circular post-holes ranged from 0.15m to 0.4m in diameter with a maximum depth of 0.25m and fills comprising homogenous brown silty sand with occasional gravel inclusions. These features could have been related to grave markers or performed structurally as curbing or revetting of a soil mound.

34/1 Fragments of a complete copper-alloy **annular brooch** with flat ring; undecorated. Open ends of ring overlapped and pierced by circular pin emplacement, 3mm diameter. Iron pin represented by corrosion products only. D.40mm; band W.6–7mm. Textile remains on ?back. 053:*1367*.

34/2 Fragments of a complete copper-alloy **annular brooch** with flat ring; undecorated. Open ends of ring overlapped and pierced by pin emplacement which is made up of three overlapping circular perforations. Iron pin, flattened oval section, 2.5mm x 1.5mm. Irregularities in metal suggest a poor casting. D.44mm; band W.7–8mm. Extensive textile remains, some pierced by pin. 053:*1368*.

34/3 Small cast copper-alloy **ring**. D.22mm, Th.5mm, Ht.3mm. Textile remains on one face. 053:*1369*

Grave 35 (053:*0656*)
Fig. 15.31
Dimensions: 1.7m x 0.83m
Orientation: 240°
Container for body: Dark brown/black stain indicative of a coffin or in this instance, more likely a chamber
Finds gender: No grave goods
Age and Sex: Grave size suggests adult, indeterminate sex
Skeletal remains: None
Body position: Indeterminate, possible skull stain suggests head to west
Associated features: Six post-holes could be associated, but their juxtaposition to other adjacent graves makes positive attribution difficult.
Description: A regular rectangular cut surviving to a depth 0.22m with relatively steeply sloping sides throughout. The excavated fill (053:*0657*) comprised homogenous brown silty sand with gravel inclusions.

Skeletal remains were completely absent, but undulating stains on the base of the grave could have been associated with the body. Linear stains recorded during surface cleaning were considered to be clear evidence for the presence of a coffin or chamber. Given that a stain covered the entire base of the grave, right up to its junction with the sides and ends, then it seems reasonable to favour a chamber rather than a coffin. The position of stains seen at a higher level, where they occurred between 0.05 and 0.15m from the sides and eastern end of the grave cut, were probably the result of post-depositional collapse within the chamber.

No grave goods.

Six circular post-holes could be tentatively associated with grave 053:*0656* (all shown unnumbered on Fig. 6.1). Post-hole 053:*0636* to the south-west has already been described with adjacent Grave 053:*0654*. Of the remaining five, two (053:*0652* and *0686*) lay to the north, two more (053:*0650* and *0688*) were to the south and the fifth (053:*0692*) immediately to the east. Those to the north and south were all small, measuring less than 0.2m in diameter with depths not exceeding 0.2m. Post-hole 053:*0692* was larger, 0.3m in diameter with a depth of 0.22m. All fills comprised homogenous grey/brown silty sand. Their function was unclear, but grave markers or structural elements of a mound or curb seems most likely.

Grave 36 (053:*0663*)
Figs 15.32–15.33
Dimensions: 1.75m x 0.8m
Orientation: 242°
Container for body: None recognised
Finds gender: Female
Age and Sex: Young adult female
Skeletal remains: Very poor, fragile, copper staining. Fragments of frontal, right maxilla and mandible, 21 teeth. Tooth wear slight. Mandible and glabella gracile
Body position: Extended, prone, head to west
Associated features: Cut by adjacent Grave 33. Two post-holes external to grave on its long axis.
Description: A parallel-sided round ended cut surviving to a depth of 0.38m with steep, near vertical edges. The fill (053:*0664*) comprised homogenous brown silty sand with gravel inclusions.

While skeletal remains (053:*0665*) were limited to fragments of skull and teeth, the legs and pelvic area were clearly defined as a brown sandy stain.

Two copper-alloy annular brooches (36/1 and 36/2) were located towards the western end of the grave close to the skull fragments in the area that would have been occupied by the head and shoulders of the body. The fact that both brooches were upside down suggests that the body had been buried in a prone position. An iron knife (36/3) was found towards the southern side of the grave in association with the clear body stain and was attached at the left side of the waist. Similarly, an iron buckle (36/4), recorded central to the body stain, would also have been attached close to the waist.

Stratigraphically, Grave 36 was recorded as being cut by the north-west corner of adjacent Grave 33. Two post-holes (053:*0671* to the north east and *0682* to the south-west) could be associated with this grave, both located within 0.6m of the grave edge, one at each end close to its long axis (both shown unnumbered on Fig. 6.1). With the absence of other features to the north and south of the grave, it seems likely that these accommodated grave markers rather than performing a structural function.

36/1 Copper-alloy oval **annular brooch** with flat ring of irregular width; undecorated. Bar pin emplacement, L.3mm x W.2.5mm. Iron pin. 43 x 38mm; ring W.5.5–7mm. Poorly preserved textile pierced by pin. 053:*1370*.

36/2 Copper-alloy oval **annular brooch** with flat-elliptical ring, undecorated. Bar pin emplacement, 2.5 x 2.5mm. Iron pin W.3mm. D.41–43mm; ring W.6–7mm. Textile remains pierced by pin. Decayed bone adhering to back. 053:*1371*.

36/3 Iron **knife**, complete with rounded end to short and broad tang. Widens to angled shoulder and rounded choil. Back curves throughout to lightly rounded tip. Cutting edge straight, rising to tip. Slightly angled handle line in front of shoulder. Type: Drinkall A. L.122mm, blade W.11mm. Slight traces of horn towards end of tang on one side. Traces of skin product on both sides of the blade and may also have covered most of the handle. 053:*1372*.

36/4 Iron **buckle** with D-shaped loop and no plate. Type: Marzinzik I.10a-i. 27 x 23mm. Traces of a leather strap, less than 2mm thick on back of loop and tongue. Textile remains on front. 053:*1373*.

Grave 37 (053:*0716*)
Figs 15.32–15.34
Dimensions: 2.10m x 1.25m
Orientation: 244°
Container for body: None recognised
Finds gender: Male
Age and Sex: Probably adult (confirmed by grave size), indeterminate sex
Skeletal remains: Very poor. Fragments of occipital, left temporal and two lower molars. Tooth wear not heavy.
Body position: Probably extended, supine, head to west
Associated features: Two post-holes were close to the grave and could be related
Description: A regular rectangular cut surviving to a depth of 0.32m with steep, near vertical sides. The fill (053:*0717*) comprised homogenous brown silty, very stony sand.

Skeletal remains (053:*0724*) were limited to fragments of skull. Staining recorded in the base of the grave did not obviously represent a body or a container for a body. A circular stain on the south side was tentatively interpreted as the vestiges of the organic component of the shield. However, the associated shield boss (37/2) lay immediately to the west and unless post-depositional movement had occurred, then this interpretation is difficult to sustain. The overall large dimensions and regular shape of the cut are what would be expected of a chamber grave and even though there was no direct evidence for the presence of a timber lining it is considered likely that one would originally have been present.

Two iron spearheads were recorded, the first (37/1), lying parallel to the long axis of the grave in its north-west corner with its point to the west. The second (37/6) was similarly parallel to the long axis of the grave but in its south-west corner with its point to the west and lay behind a group of finds that indicated that the shield had been placed on top of it. An iron ferrule (37/7), found towards the south-east corner of the grave, almost certainly belonged with this second spear. The shield boss (37/2) was accompanied by other shield fittings; four shield board mounts (37/3–5 and 37/9), an iron shield grip (37/10) and an iron buckle (37/8). One additional item, an iron knife (37/11) was found underneath the shield boss.

Two circular post-holes (053:*0630* and *0745*), the former to the south-east of the grave and the latter immediately to the south, may be associated (both shown unnumbered on Fig. 6.1). Both were small, less than 0.2m in diameter with depths of approximately 0.15m and fills

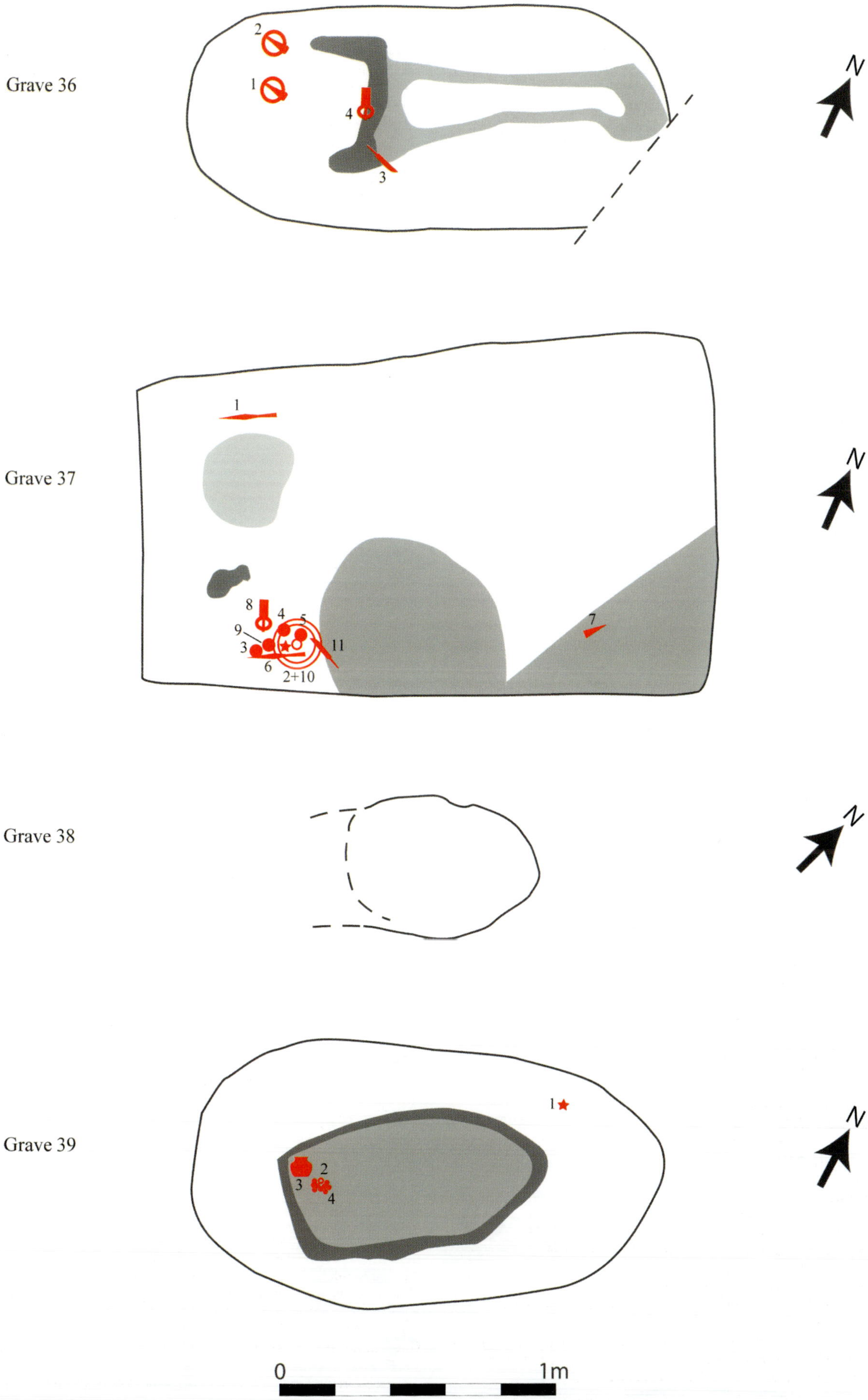

Figure 15.32 Plans of Flixton II Graves 36–39 (scale 1:20)

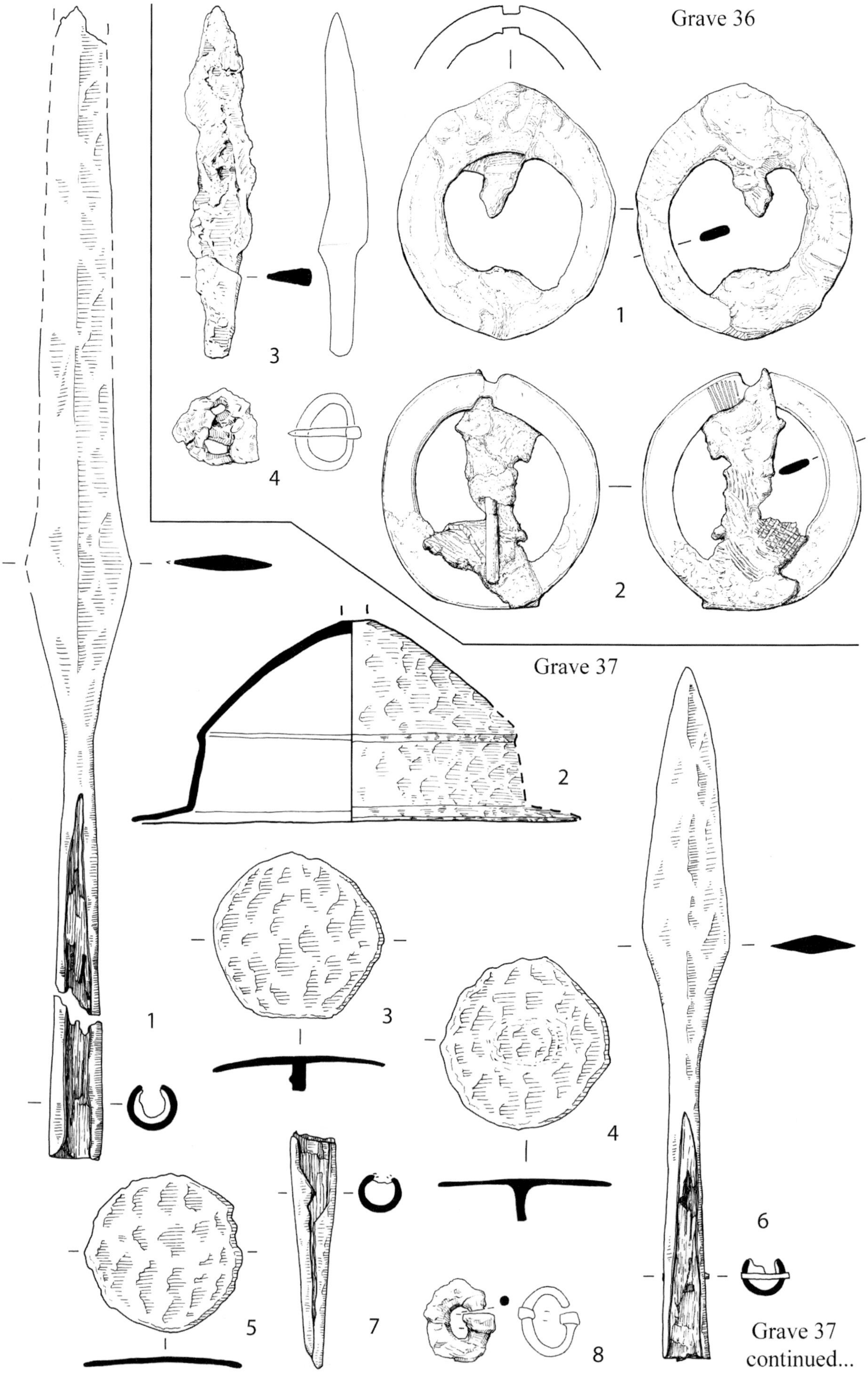

Figure 15.33 Grave goods; Flixton II Grave 36 (scales: 1 and 2 at 1:1; 3 and 4 at 1:2) and Flixton II Grave 37 (scale: 1–8 at 1:2)

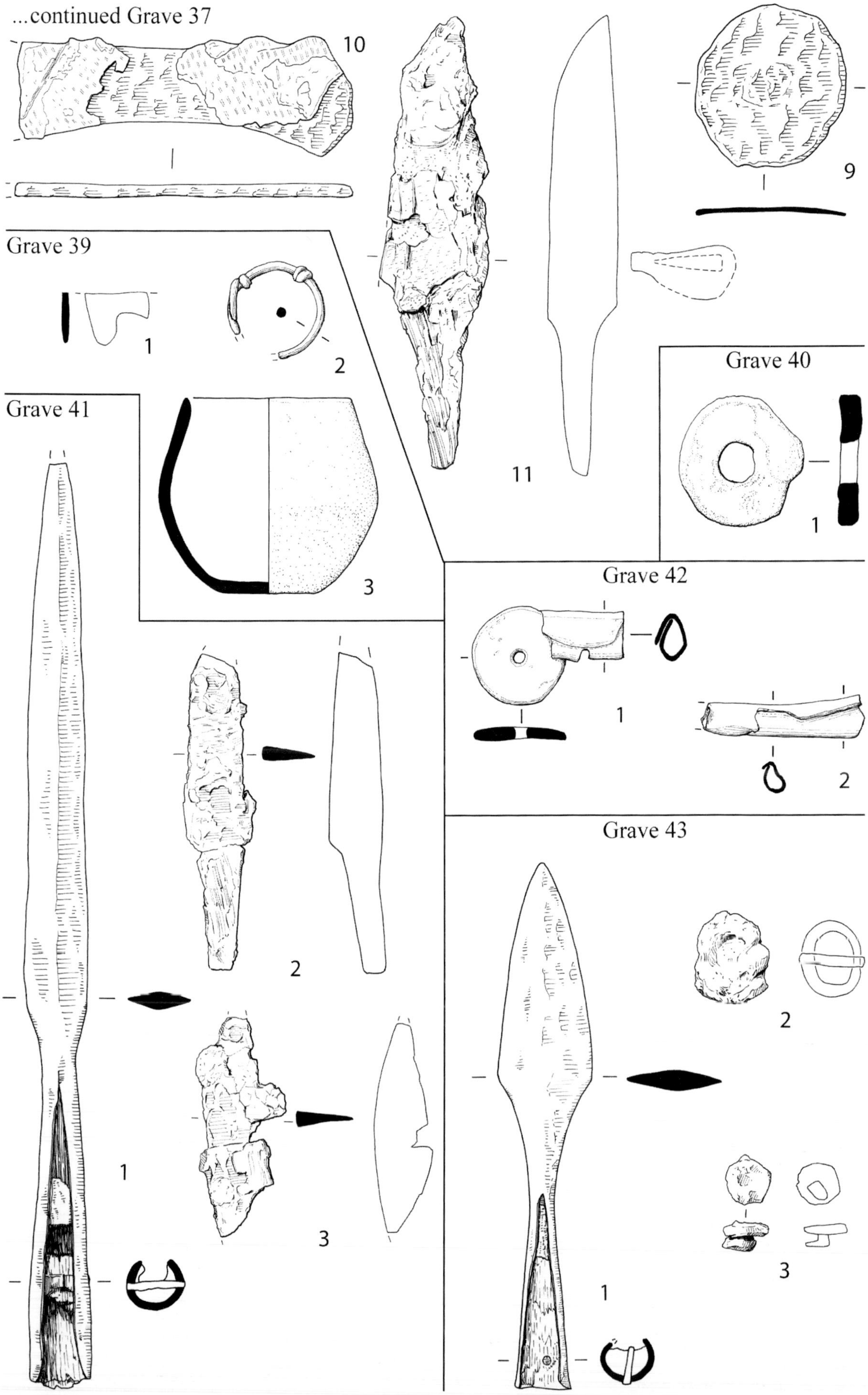

Figure 15.34 Grave goods; Flixton II Grave 37 (scale: 9–11 at 1:2), Flixton II Grave 39 (scales: 1 at 1:2; 2 at 1:1; 3 at 1:3), Flixton II Grave 40 (scale: 1 at 1:1), Flixton II Grave 41 (scale: 1–3 at 1:2), Flixton II Grave 42 (scale: 1 and 2 at 1:1) and Flixton II Grave 43 (scale: 1–3 at 1:2)

comprising homogenous brown silty sand. The lack of any formal arrangement or symmetry to these features makes them hard to interpret.

37/1 Complete iron **spearhead**, cleft socket encompassing most of shank with short length of solid iron below blade. Widens with convex curve on one side and concave curve on other, providing asymmetric shape. Widest point at lower part of the blade, narrowing with curved edges and straightening before tapering to tip. Lentoid in section across lower part of blade. Type: Swanton H3, EAC Concave Long 1a. L.425mm, W.42mm. Mineral-preserved wood in socket: *Fraxinus* sp. (ash) made from mature timber. 053:*1375*.

37/2 Iron **shield boss**. Incomplete, apex and flange missing. Uncarinated boss with tall, straight wall (Ht.30mm), shallow convex cone and two flat disc-headed rivets (D.20mm, L. of shank 8mm, 10mm). Type: Dickinson and Härke 3; Spain 3b(ii); EAC COV. D.160mm approx., Ht.75mm. 053:*1376*.

37/3 Iron **shield board mount**. Complete. Large disc-shaped mount. D.60mm. One of a pair. 053:*1377*.

37/4 Iron **shield board mount**. Incomplete, broken shank. Large disc-shaped mount. D.60mm. One of a pair. 053:*1378*.

37/5 Iron **shield board mount**. Incomplete, broken shank. Large disc-shaped mount. D.55mm. One of a pair. 053:*1379*.

37/6 Complete iron **spearhead** with cleft socket extending along most of shank and short length of solid metal of rectangular section above. Iron ring set laterally across lower part of socket. Blade widens in long convex curves with angular widest point at lower part. Narrows with curved edges, tapering in light curves to rounded tip. Lentoid section. Type: Swanton H2, EAC Angular Medium 2b. L.250mm, W.26mm. Accreted in sand throughout. Mineral-preserved wood in socket: *Fraxinus* sp. (ash). 053:*1380*.

37/7 Complete iron **ferrule**, conical in shape and of circular section, tapering evenly to rounded tip. L.91mm. Mineral-preserved wood enclosed by ferrule: *Fraxinus* sp. (ash). Textile curling around tip. 053:*1381*.

37/8 Iron **buckle** with incomplete loop, oval to D-shaped, and no plate. Type: Marzinzik I.10d-i. 27 x 20mm. Remains of leather/skin strap, <1.5mm thick, on axis beside tongue. 053:*1382*.

37/9 Iron **shield board mount**. Incomplete, broken shank. Large disc-shaped mount. D.55mm. One of a pair. 053:*1383*.

37/10 Iron **shield grip**. Incomplete, one terminal missing. Strap grip (W.27mm) expanding towards terminals (W.44mm). Survives in two joining fragments. L.115mm. On outer face of grip, textile covered by skin/leather. 053:*1386*.

37/11 Iron **knife**, complete. Broad tang with rounded end widens to shoulder and choil, rising more for shoulder. Straight back throughout, lightly convex but not curving to tip. Cutting edge straight, rising up to tip. Noticeably broad blade. Type: Drinkall B. L.159mm, blade W.26mm. Abundant remains of horn on tang, which, on one side has the grain orientated diagonally, suggesting a possible repair to the handle. On one side of the blade there are extensive remains of a skin product up to 2mm thick, with a grain pattern. A fibre in a single follicle has been identified as cattle hair, probably calf, from its diameter of 40–50 microns and a cuticular scale pattern which is irregular mosaic with smooth near-to-close margins. 053:*1387*.

Grave 38 (053:*0719*)
Fig. 15.32
Dimensions: 0.8m x 0.5m (possibly truncated to the south-west)
Orientation: 223°
Container for body: None recognised
Finds gender: No grave goods
Age and Sex: Grave size suggests child, indeterminate sex
Skeletal remains: None
Body position: Indeterminate
Associated features: None recognised
Description: An oval-shaped cut with gently sloping sides and an irregular base, surviving to a maximum depth of 0.24m. The fill (053:*0720*) comprised homogenous brown silty, stony sand.

No skeletal remains or soil stains were recorded. The general orientation and shape of this feature prompted its excavation as a grave. However, after the removal of the fill, that interpretation became less certain due to its irregular edges and base. The feature, in its excavated form, certainly would not accommodate an adult body, although there

Grave 39

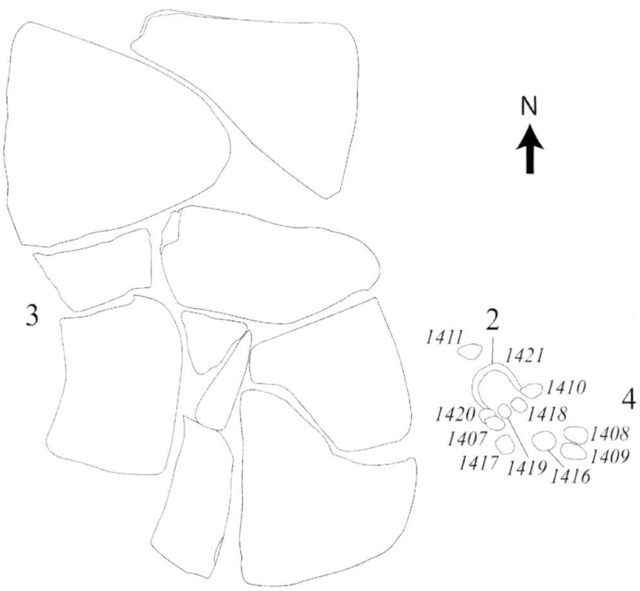

Figure 15.35 Flixton II Grave 39, *in situ* plan of grave goods 2, 3 and bead group 4. All contexts numbers are site FLN 053 (scale 1:2)

was a suggestion that the western end had been truncated. While entered in the records as a grave, this interpretation should be viewed with some caution.

No grave goods.

Grave 39 (053:*0725*)
Figs 15.32, 15.34–15.35; Pl. 7.4b
Dimensions: 1.7m x 0.95m
Orientation: 244°
Container for body: Trough-like stain in base of grave, possible bier or body stain
Finds gender: Female
Age and Sex: Grave size suggests adult, indeterminate sex
Body position: Indeterminate, head to west
Associated features: None recognised
Description: A near oval-shaped cut with steeply sloping sides, a flattish base sloping slightly down to the north and surviving to a depth of 0.64m. The fill 053:*0726* generally comprised homogenous brown silty, stony sand that became lighter in colour and more consolidated where it overlay basal stain 053:*0736*.

No skeletal remains were recorded. A brown roughly oval-shaped sandy trough-like stain (053:*0736*), measuring 1m by 0.5m lay central to the base of grave. The origin of this was uncertain. Given the location of the grave goods, it is clear that the stain defined an area coinciding with the torso of the body. Alternatively, if representing a container, either a coffin or a bier, the body would need to be that of a child or tightly crouched sub-adult. On balance then, it seems more likely that the body rather than the container into which it had been placed generated stain 053:*0736*.

With the exception of iron fragment 39/1, the grave goods were formed a discrete group at the western end of the basal stain. Fifty-eight sherds from a single pot (39/3) were recorded lying adjacent to ten beads (39/4) and a sliding-knot ring (39/2). While no identifiable body stain was present, it is likely that the beads lay in the general area occupied by the neck and shoulders of the body.

39/1 Iron **fragment**, possibly part of a buckle plate. 25 x 18mm. 053:*1384*.

39/2 Fragments of a copper-alloy wire **sliding-knot ring**. Wire circular section, 2mm diameter. D. reconstructed as 18mm. 053:*1421*.

39/3 Sand-tempered (ESMS) baggy **jar** with slight shoulder, vertical rim and flat-angled base, burnished, worn on both surfaces. Reddish brown. Rim D.90mm, 28% complete. (see also Fig. 7.19.13). 053:*0739*.

39/4 Beads 053:*1407–1411, 1416–1420* (see *in situ* 1:2 plan Fig. 15.35; Pl. 7.4b *1407–1411, 1416, 1418–9*). Brugmann Group B2.
One amber **bead** (weight 0.3g; worn): medium, rounded, D.6–10mm (*1409*).
Nine glass **beads**: Type *Cylindrical, Round:* 2 medium, cylindrical, yellow, D.6–10mm (*1407, 1419*); 1 medium, cylindrical, red, D. 6–10mm (*1410*); 1 medium, cylindrical, blue, D. 6–10mm (*1411*).
Type *Koch34 RedWhite:* 2 short, globular; body snapped off another bead segment, D.6–10mm (*1417–8*); 1 medium, globular, body snapped off another bead segment, D.6–10mm (*1420*); 1 short, cylindrical, body snapped off another bead segment, D.6–10mm (*1416*).
Type *Koch34 WhiteBlue:* 1 short, cylindrical, D. 6–10mm (*1408*).

Grave 40 (053:*0727*)
Figs 15.34, 15.36–15.37; Pl. 7.4b
Dimensions: 1.7m x 0.86m
Orientation: 239°
Container for body: None recognised
Finds gender: Female
Age and Sex: Grave size suggests adult, indeterminate sex
Skeletal remains: None
Body position: Indeterminate, head to west
Associated features: Cuts amorphous area of natural subsoil
Description: A parallel-sided, round-ended cut with steeply sloping sides and surviving to a depth of 0.54m. The fill (053:*0728*) comprised homogenous brown silty, stony sand.

No skeletal remains or stains were recorded in this grave.

A lead spindle whorl (40/1) was located towards the centre of the western end of the grave with a group of fourteen beads (40/2) approximately 0.25m further to the east. While no identifiable body stain was present, it seems likely that the beads lay in the general area occupied by the neck and shoulders of the body.

40/1 Lead disc-shaped **spindle whorl**, cast with former for spindle hole. Walton Rogers B1. Mineral-preserved wood represents remains of spindle, with grain running down spindle hole. D.23mm, Th.5mm; spindle hole D.8mm. The wood remains were not well enough preserved to allow identification of the species. 053:*1385*.

40/2 Beads 053:*1389–1401, 1403* (see 1:2 plan Fig. 15.36; Pl. 7.4b *1389–1390, 1393, 1396–8, 1403*). Brugmann Group B2.
Nine amber **beads** (total weight 4.3g; worn): 3 medium, faceted, D.11–15mm (*1392, 1396, 1401*); 6 medium, faceted, D.6–10mm (*1391, 1394–5, 1397, 1399, 1401*)
Five glass **beads**: Type *Cylindrical, Round:* 1 medium, cylindrical; yellow; D.6–10mm (*1398*).
Type *Cylindrical, Pentagonal-related:* 1 long, cylindrical, slightly pentagonal cross-section; white; D.6–10mm (*1390*).
Type *Koch20 RedWhite:* 1 medium, globular; D.6–10mm (*1403*).
Type *Koch34 RedWhite:* 1 short, globular; D.6–10mm (*1393*).
Type *Polychrome2:* 1 short, globular; D.11–15mm (*1389*).

Grave 41 (053:*0729*)
Figs 15.34 and 15.37
Dimensions: 1.75m x 0.9m
Orientation: 233°
Container for body: None recognised
Finds gender: Male
Age and Sex: Adult, male
Skeletal remains: Very poor. Fragments of left parietal and occipital. Cranial sutures open, possibly young? Large occipital crest.
Body position: Extended, supine, head to west
Associated features: None recognised
Description: An essentially oval, but somewhat irregular cut with steeply sloping sides to the east, west and north, locally gentler to the south, exhibiting a relatively flat bottom and surviving to a depth of 0.65m. The fill (053:*0730*) comprised homogenous brown silty, stony sand.

Skeletal remains (053:*0732*) were limited to fragments of skull. A linear brown sandy stain (053:*0731*) at the eastern end of the grave clearly represented the legs of the body.

An iron spearhead (41/1), was found lying parallel to the long axis of the grave in its north-west corner with its point to the west. Two iron knives (41/2 and 41/3) were recorded approximately halfway down the grave in an area that would suggest that the knives were attached to the body at or near the waist.

Grave 40

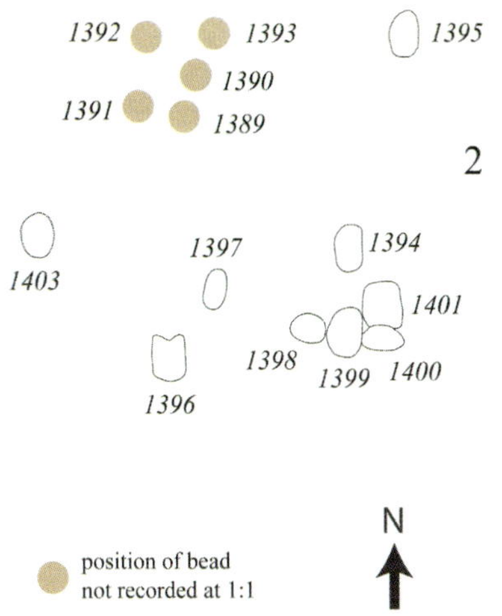

Figure 15.36 Flixton II Grave 40, *in situ* bead group 2. All contexts numbers are site FLN 053 (scale 1:2)

41/1 Complete iron **spearhead** with wide cleft socket encompassing practically all of shank, short length of solid iron stem above. Lateral nail in socket, 35mm above base, set at slight angle. Blade long and narrow, widening in convex curves with widest point over lower part. Tapers evenly with straight sides to rounded tip. Lentoid in section. Type: Swanton E2, EAC Parallel Long 1. L.341mm, W.25mm. Abundant mineral-preserved wood in socket: *Fraxinus* sp. (ash) made from mature timber. 053:*1388*.

41/2 Iron **knife**, complete. Broad tang with flat end widening gradually to shoulder and choil. Straight cutting edge and back, both tapering towards tip, which is missing. Abundant horn remains on one side of tang, with vertical handle line of horn on opposite side. Type: Drinkall B. L.135mm, blade W.17mm. 053:*1406a*.

41/3 Fragment of middle part of iron **knife**. Part of the tang survives, widening to indistinct shoulder. Traces of vertical handle line at shoulder. Surviving section of blade has straight and parallel back and cutting edge. Type unclear. 78 x 20mm. Bulky mineralised skin product on the blade, at least 5mm thick, representing the remains of a sheath that was joined at the cutting edge, where there are six stitch holes visible in 7mm. 053:*1406b*.

Grave 42 (053:*0733*)
Figs 15.34 and 15.37; Pl. 7.4b
Dimensions: 1.3m x 0.6m
Orientation: 246°
Container for body: Extensive stain at eastern end of grave, possible bier
Finds gender: Female
Age and Sex: Child, aged about five, indeterminate sex
Skeletal remains: Very poor. Tooth fragments only (one deciduous, three permanent unerupted).
Body position: indeterminate, head to west
Associated features: A series of ten post-holes surrounding grave
Description: A parallel-sided, round-ended cut with steep, near vertical sides, a flattish bottom that dished up slightly towards its margins and survived to a depth of 0.2m. The fill (053:*0734*) comprised homogenous grey/brown silty sand with gravel inclusions.

Skeletal remains (053:*0735*) were limited to fragments of teeth. An extensive grey sandy stain recorded towards at the eastern end of the grave followed the shape of the grave edge, and given the location of the teeth fragments would have encompassed the whole body. While not positively identifiable as the vestiges of a bier, this would seem the most reasonable of the possibilities. The size of this grave was clearly greater than the minimum that would have been required to accommodate a child of the size and age indicated by the position and character of the skeletal remains.

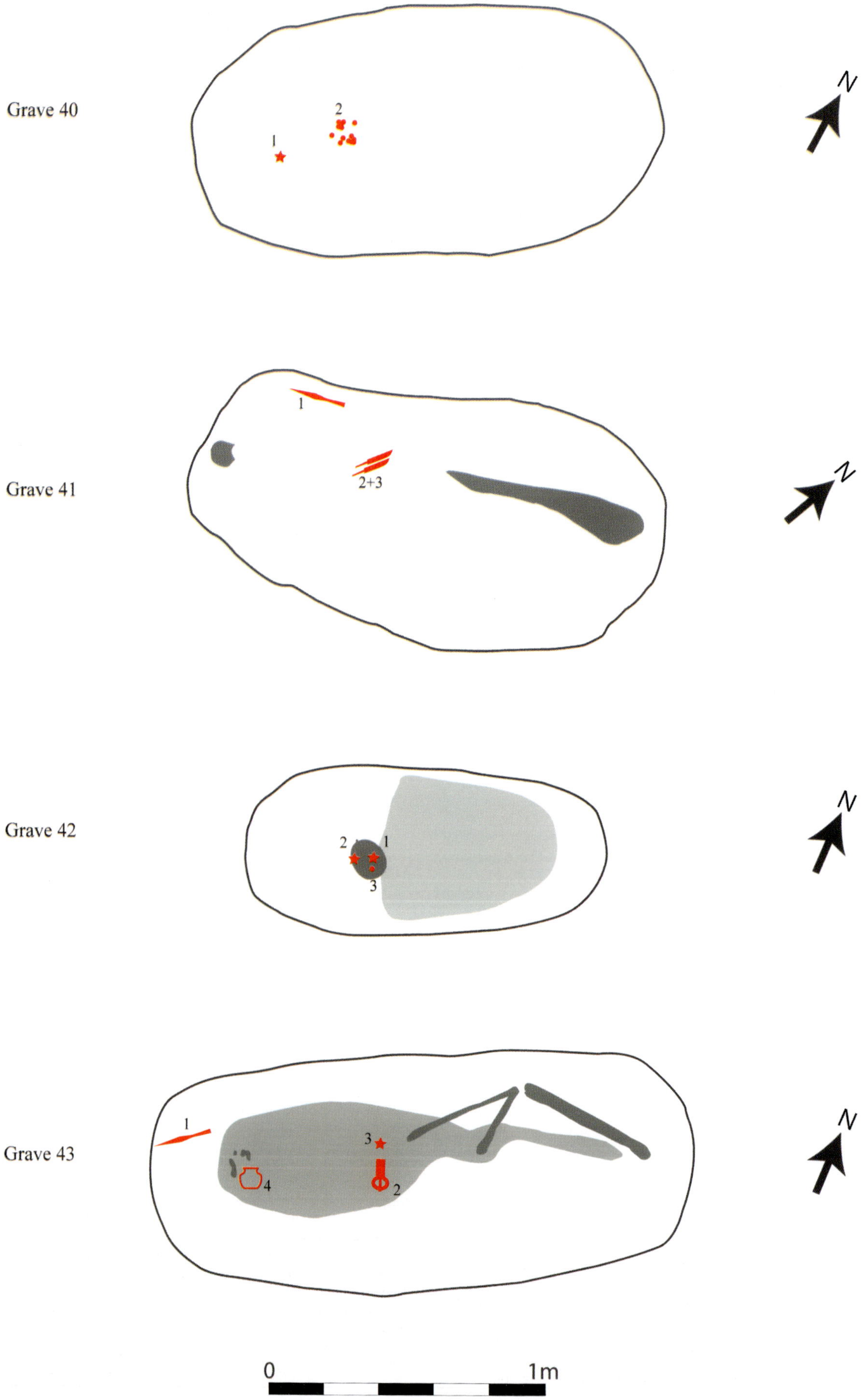

Figure 15.37 Plans of Flixton II Graves 40–43 (scale 1:20)

Grave goods were limited to two rolled tubes of copper alloy sheet (42/1 and 42/2) and a single bead (42/3), all recorded close to the central long axis of the grave just into its western half. The juxtaposition of the surviving teeth (053:*0735*) immediately to the east suggests that the finds lay in the general area occupied by the neck and shoulders of the body.

While it was not always easy positively to associate individual post-holes with graves, a series of ten of these features formed an equidistantly spaced sub-rectangular arrangement around Grave 42 and were recorded with a degree of certainty (all shown unnumbered on Fig. 6.1). The formally arranged circular post-holes included a line of four (053:*0702*, *0704*, *0706* and *0710*) to the north of the grave, another line of four (053:*0690*, *0694*, *0696* and *0698*) to the south, and single post-holes at each end (053:*0692* and *0700*). With the exception of post-hole 053:*0692*, which has previously been described with Grave 35, and post-hole 053:*0690*, they were all small, with diameters of approximately 0.2m and depths ranging from 0.06m to 0.3m. Post-hole 053:*0690* was 0.3m in diameter with a depth of 0.4m. The fills generally comprised homogenous grey/brown silty sand with occasional gravel and pebble inclusions. Assuming that the majority of these features were genuinely related to Grave 42, they represent the best evidence for an above ground structure associated directly with a grave in the Flixton cemeteries, probably a curbed or revetted mound.

42/1 Small tube of copper-alloy sheet with copper-alloy disc with central perforation attached. Tube L.15 x 7mm; disc D.16mm; perforation D.2mm. 053:*1402*.

42/2 Small tube of copper-alloy sheet, sides pinched in. D.5.5mm, L.28mm. 053:*1404*.

42/3 Beads 053:*1405* (Pl. 7.4b *1405*). Brugmann Group A2. One glass **bead**: Type *Norfolk Melon*: 1 medium, 4 ribs, D.6–10mm (*1405*).

Grave 43 (053:*0737*)
Figs 15.34 and 15.37
Dimensions: 1.97m x 0.85m
Orientation: 242°
Container for body: None obvious, extensive staining on base of grave probably related to body but may represent bier
Finds gender: Male
Age and Sex: Adult, ?male
Skeletal remains: Poor, flaky. Fragments of left temporal and parietal, two molars. M3 erupted. Mastoid process appears large, but is incomplete.
Body position: Legs flexed to north, head to west
Associated features: None recognised
Description: A sub-rectangular cut with a somewhat bowed south side and moderately rounded ends. The profiles exhibit near vertical sides to the south and east, steeply sloping to the north and west with a surviving depth of 0.52m. The fill (053:*0738*) comprised homogenous grey/brown silty sand with gravel inclusions.

Skeletal remains (053:*0740*) were limited to fragments of skull and teeth. Extensive staining in the base of the grave clearly reflected the position of the body with the legs well-defined and a large amorphous area representing the torso and skull. However, it was unclear whether this stain also represented the vestiges of a container such as a bier.

An iron spearhead (43/1) was found lying parallel to the long axis of the grave in its north-west corner with its point to the west. An iron buckle (43/2) and a possibly associated stud/rivet (43/3) were located approximately central to the grave within the body stain in an area that suggests that the item was attached at or near the waist of the body. A group of seven pot sherds (43/4) were recorded towards the western end of the grave in close association with the skull fragments and teeth (053:*0740*). While it seems likely, given the prominent location in the grave, that the pottery represents deliberate deposition, it is unclear whether this occurred as a few sherds, or as a complete vessel that subsequently suffered post-depositional damage.

43/1 Complete iron **spearhead** with wide cleft socket, lateral nail extending out of cleft rather than across it, set just above base. Short length of stem above socket, blade widening in concave curves, widest point over lower section, tapering with curved, convex sides to tip. Noticeably wide blade. Lentoid in section. Type: Swanton E1, EAC Angular Medium 1. L.188mm, W.35mm. Abundant mineral-preserved wood in socket: *Salix* sp. (willow) or *Populus* sp. (poplar). 053.*1412*.

43/2 Iron **buckle** with oval-to-D-shape loop and no plate. Type: Marzinzik I.10d-i. 31 x 23mm. Poorly preserved textile on back. 053:*1413*.

43/3 Iron **stud/rivet**, one head larger than the other: probably the rivet from the strap on which buckle 43/2 was mounted. D.17mm, Ht.10mm. 053:*1414*.

43/4 Grass-tempered body **sherds**, sooted, worn internally. Black external surface, red-black inside. Not illustrated. 053:*0744*.

Grave 44 (053:*0742*)
Figs 15.38 and 15.40
Dimensions: 1.4m x 0.5m
Orientation: 244°
Container for body: Extensive stain on base of grave, possible bier
Finds gender: Indeterminate
Age and Sex: Grave size suggests child, indeterminate sex
Skeletal remains: None
Body position: Head to west
Associated features: None recognised
Description: A parallel-sided cut with a rounded west end, more squared to the east with an angled south-east corner. The profiles reveal relatively shallow sloping edges, a level base along its long axis, but gently dished across its width. Surviving to a depth of 0.2m with the excavated fill (053:*0743*) comprising homogenous grey/brown silty sand with gravel inclusions.

No skeletal remains were recorded. An extensive stain on the north side and eastern end of the grave may represent the general position of the body or the vestiges of a container, possibly a bier, into which the corpse had been placed.

An iron knife (44/1) was found centrally placed with its long axis parallel to that of the grave within the basal stain in an area that would suggest it was attached to the body in an area close to the waist.

44/1 Iron **knife**, fragmentary, lacking most of tang. Back curves lightly throughout to rounded tip, cutting edge slightly sinuous and rising to tip. Faint trace of possible handle line at shoulder. Type: Drinkall A. L.86mm, blade W.14mm. Traces of horn on one side of tang. Some skin product on both sides of blade and over the back and cutting edge. 053:*1415*.

Grave 45 (053:*0747*)
Fig. 15.38
Dimensions: 1.8m x 0.96m
Orientation: 253°
Container for body: None recognised
Finds gender: No grave goods
Age and Sex: Grave size suggests adult, indeterminate sex
Body position: Indeterminate
Associated features: None recognised
Description: A sub-rectangular cut with moderately rounded corners, surviving to a depth of 0.14m with near vertical sides to the east, north and west, but more gently sloping to the south. The fill (053:*0748*) comprised relatively homogenous grey/brown silty sand with gravel inclusions and some recent biogenic disturbance.

No skeletal remains or soil stains were recorded that would indicate the position of the body or presence of a container into which it had been placed.

No grave goods.

Grave 46 (062:*0893*)
Figs 15.38 and 15.40
Dimensions: 0.95m x 0.6m
Orientation: 253°
Container for body: None recognised
Finds gender: Indeterminate
Age and Sex: Size of grave suggests child, indeterminate sex
Skeletal remains: None
Body position: Indeterminate
Associated features: None recognised
Description: An oval-shaped cut with steep, almost vertical sides and a flattish bottom, surviving to a depth of 0.34m. The fill (062:*0894*) comprised mid grey/brown silty sand.

No skeletal remains or soil stains were recorded that would indicate the position of the body or the presence of a container into which it had been placed.

A whole pot (46/1) had been placed in the grave just to the east of centre.

46/1 Granite tempered offset shouldered **bowl** (ESCF, some flint and chalk), slightly everted rim and flat-angled base, near complete but rim broken, sooted, worn internally. Light brown externally and black inside. Rim D.110mm, 75% complete. (see also Fig. 7.19.14). 062:*0893*.

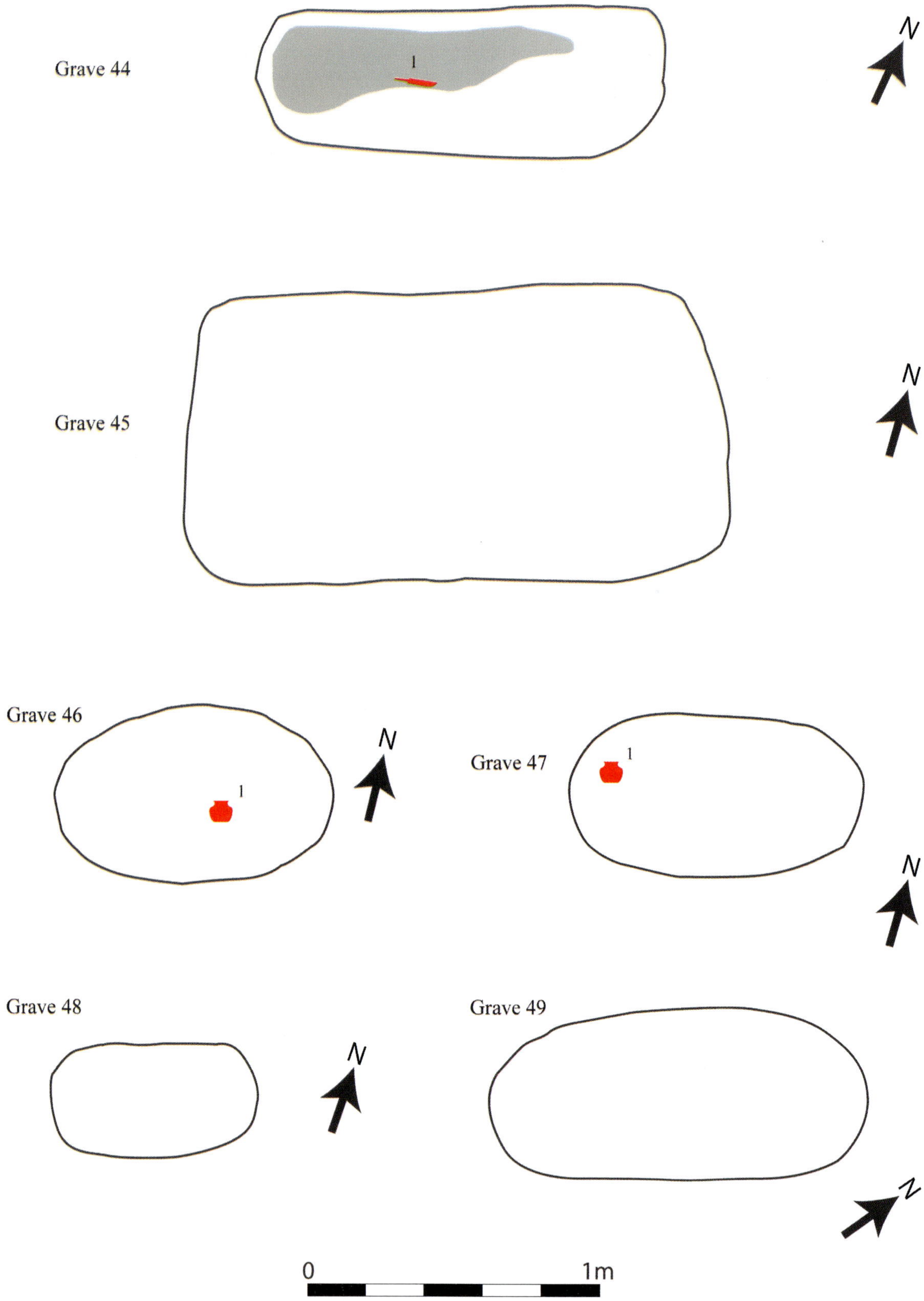

Figure 15.38 Plans of Flixton II Graves 44–49 (scale 1:20)

Grave 47 (062:*0897*)
Figs 15.38 and 15.40
Dimensions: 1.0m x 0.54m
Orientation: 250°
Container for body: None recognised
Finds gender: Indeterminate
Age and Sex: Grave size suggests child, indeterminate sex
Skeletal remains: None
Body position: Indeterminate
Associated features: None recognised
Description: A parallel if slightly bow-sided cut with rounded ends and surviving to a depth of 0.34m. The profiles reveal relatively gently sloping sides to the north, south and west with a steeper edge to the east. The fill (062:*0898*) comprised homogenous grey/brown silty sand with occasional stones.

No skeletal remains or soil stains were recorded that would indicate the position of the body or presence of a container into which it had been placed.

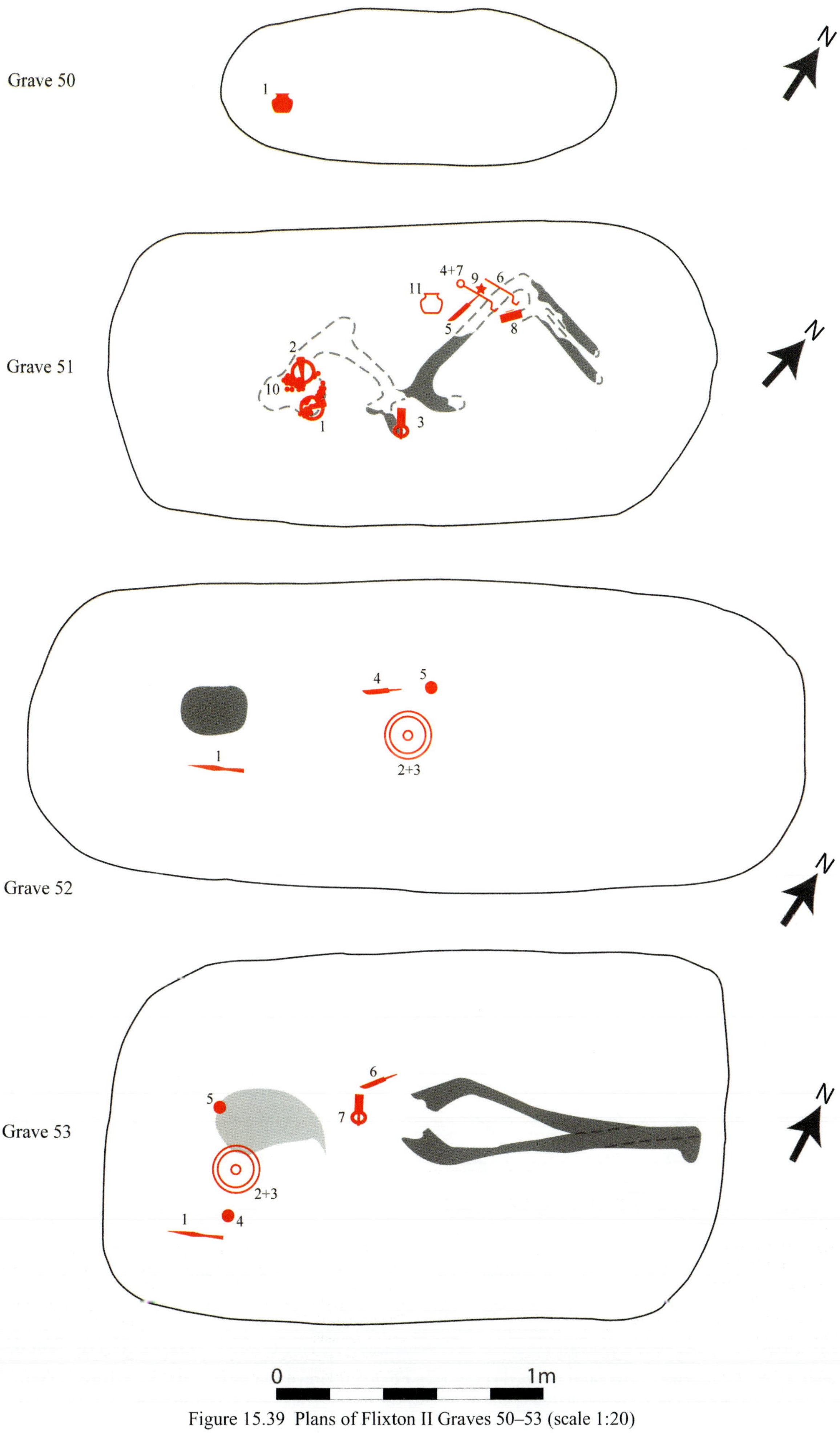

Figure 15.39 Plans of Flixton II Graves 50–53 (scale 1:20)

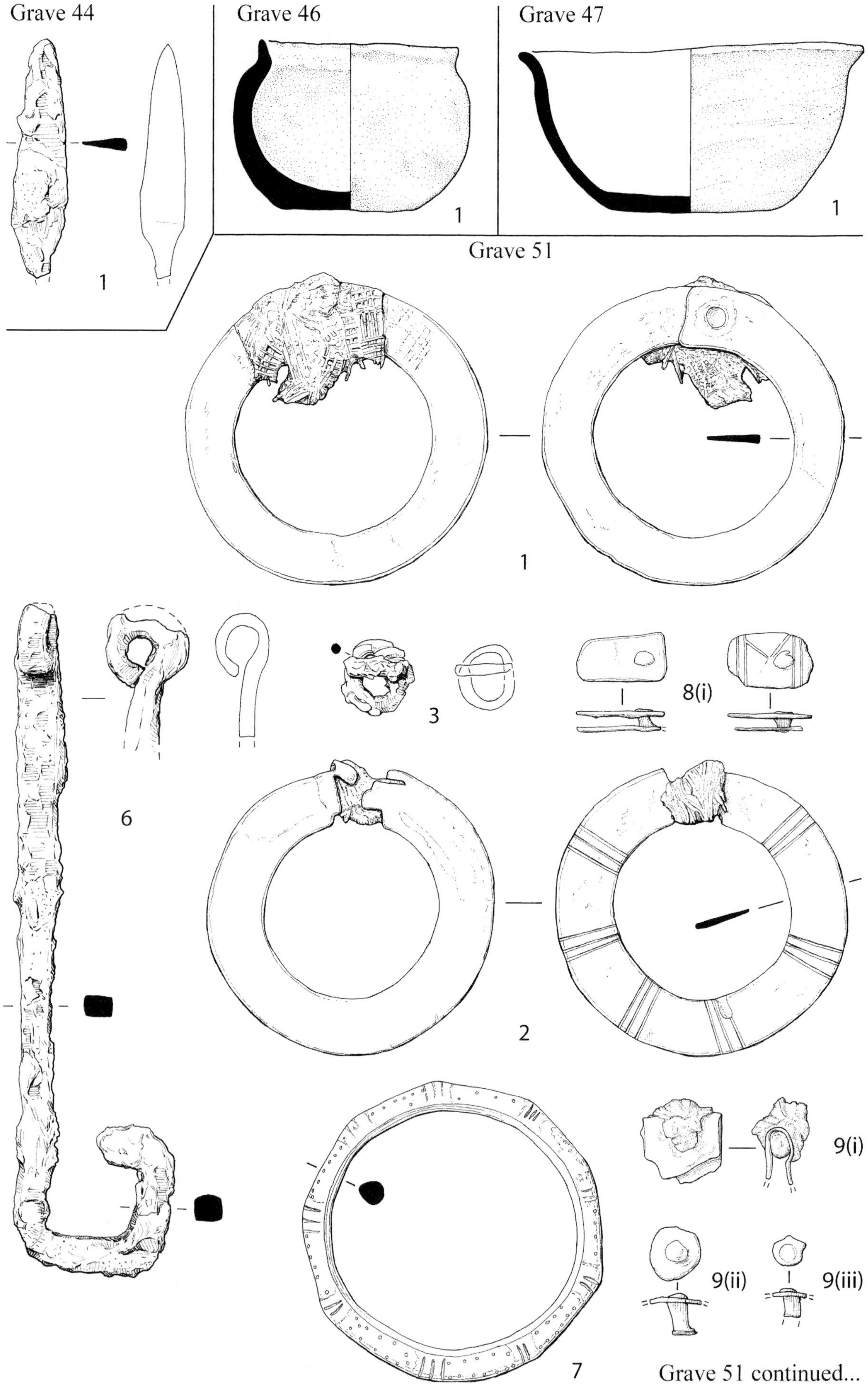

Figure 15.40 Grave goods; Flixton II Grave 44 (1 at 1:2), Flixton II Grave 46 (scale: 1 at 1:3), Flixton II Grave 47 (scale: 1 at 1:3) and Flixton II Grave 51 (scales: 1, 2, 7, 8 and 9 at 1:1; 3 and 6 at 1:2)

A whole pot (47/1) had been placed at the western end of the grave, but exhibited some post-depositional damage. A single sherd from a second vessel was also recovered.

47/1 Fine sandy curved **bowl** (ESFS), sooted, worn internally, burnt food residue. Brown-black. Rim D.190mm, 70% complete. (see also Fig. 7.19.15). 062:*0899*.
Also, an abraded fine sandy sherd (from fill 062:*0898*, not formally located or illustrated).

Grave 48 (062:*0901*)
Fig. 15.38
Dimensions: 0.7m x 0.38m
Orientation: 243°
Container for body: None recognised
Finds gender: No grave goods
Age and Sex: Grave size suggests child, indeterminate sex
Skeletal remains: None
Body position: Indeterminate
Associated features: None recognised
Description: A parallel-sided cut with moderately rounded ends, relatively gently sloping sides and surviving to a depth of 0.16m. The fill (062:*0902*) comprised mid grey/brown silty sand with occasional stones.

No skeletal remains or soil stains were recorded that would indicate the position of the body or presence of a container into which it had been placed.

Two abraded sherds of possible Early Anglo-Saxon pot were recovered from the grave fill (48/1).

48/1 Two abraded fine sandy **sherds** (from fill 062:*0902*, not formally located or illustrated). 062:*0902*.

Grave 49 (062:*0903*)
Fig. 15.38
Dimensions: 1.3m x 0.56m
Orientation: 224°
Container for body: None recognised
Finds gender: No grave goods
Age and Sex: Grave size suggests child, indeterminate sex
Skeletal remains: None
Body position: Indeterminate
Associated features: None recognised
Description: A parallel-sided cut with rounded ends, relatively gently sloping sides and surviving to a depth of 0.45m. The fill (062:*0904*) comprised mid grey/brown silty sand with occasional stones.

No skeletal remains or soil stains were recorded that would indicate the position of the body or the presence of a container into which it had been placed.

No grave goods.

Grave 50 (062:*1546*)
Fig. 15.39
Dimensions: 1.5m x 0.56m
Orientation: 239°
Container for body: None recognised
Finds gender: Indeterminate
Age and Sex: Indeterminate age and sex, grave size possibly suggests child
Skeletal remains: None
Body position: Indeterminate
Associated features: None recognised
Description: A near parallel-sided cut with rounded ends with an uneven base and shallow sloping sides and surviving to a maximum depth of 0.16m. The excavated fill (062:*1547*) comprised dark grey/brown stony, silty sand, mottled with orange sand.

No skeletal remains or soil stains were recorded that would indicate the position of the body or the presence of a container into which it had been placed.

The base and sides of a pottery vessel (50/1) were recorded at the western end of the grave. Almost certainly deposited complete, the pot was exposed during machining and while this did cause some damage, ploughing had already taken its toll.

50/1 Base and body sherds of grass/granitic-tempered **vessel** with rounded base. Not illustrated. 062:*1552*.

Grave 51 (062:*1865*)
Figs 15.39–15.42; Pl. 7.4b
Dimensions: 2.3m x 1.10m
Orientation: 227°
Container for body: None recognised
Finds gender: Female
Age and Sex: Young adult, indeterminate sex
Skeletal remains: Very poor. Fragments of left mandible, left clavicle and seven teeth. Tooth wear slight.
Body position: Flexed, almost crouched, body lying on left side, head to west
Associated features: None recognised
Description: A parallel-sided cut with a rounded east end, squarer to the west, surviving to a depth of 0.5m and exhibiting a flat bottom with near vertical sides, to the north, south and east, less steeply sloping to the west. The fill (062:*1866*) comprised grey/brown silty sand mixed with orange stony sand.

Skeletal remains (062:*1870*) were limited to fragments of skull, teeth and left clavicle, but a brown sandy stain clearly defined the position of the legs with a less distinct area of staining in the vicinity of the torso and head. No stains were present that could positively be associated with a container for the body.

One of the more richly-furnished graves with two principal groups of grave goods. In the area coinciding with the neck and shoulders of the body two annular brooches (51/1–2) were found with forty accompanying beads (51/10). The second group was recorded in the eastern half of the grave towards its northern edge, overlying the body stain in the area conforming to its upper legs. These included an iron slide key (51/4), an iron knife (51/5), a key/latch-lifter (51/6), a copper alloy purse ring (51/7), two copper alloy strap-ends (collectively 51/8) and a composite object (51/9). Given the character of these finds, it is likely that they were suspended from the waist of the body. In addition, an iron buckle (51/3) was recorded centrally in the grave and would have been attached at or near the waist of the body. Three sherds of prehistoric (earlier Iron Age) pottery (51/11) were found close to the eastern group of finds and may have been deliberately placed.

51/1 Copper-alloy **annular brooch** with flat ring, undecorated. Open ends of ring overlapped and pierced by circular pin emplacement, 3mm diameter. Iron pin, 3.5mm wide. D.55mm; ring W.9–10mm. Extensive textile remains on front and back of brooch. 062:*1347*.

51/2 Copper-alloy **annular brooch** with flat ring. Bar pin emplacement, 8.5mm long x 5.5mm wide. Remains of iron pin present at pin hinge. Ornament consists of five unevenly spaced groups of three transverse grooves. D.53mm, ring W.9.5–10.5mm. Textile remains on brooch and detached. 062:*1348*.

51/3 Fragments of an iron **buckle** with near-circular loop and no plate. Type: Marzinzik I.12a-i. 24 x 23mm. 062:*1349*.

51/4 Iron slide **key** with broken working end, originally forked and the ends turned back 43mm. Suspension end has a loop, 22mm diameter, curled on the opposite axis from the hooks. Shank square section, 9 x 9mm. A curved fragment of copper-alloy sheet, 13 x 7mm, is corroded to the shank. L.200mm. 062:*1350*.

51/5 Iron **knife**, complete with rounded end to narrow tang. Widens to rounded choil and no real shoulder. Back of blade straight throughout, descending just slightly to rounded tip. Cutting edge sinuous, rising to tip. Vertical handle line just in front of shoulder. Type: Drinkall B. L.202mm, blade W.17mm. Abundant horn remains on one side of tang, present but less visible on other side. Traces of skin product on both sides of blade. 062:*1351*.

51/6 Large iron **latch-lifter or pot hook** with three inward bends at the working end and suspension end with a loop, 24mm diameter, curled on the opposite axis. Shank has square section, 9 x 9mm; widening at the loop to 15 x 6mm. L.235mm, bent sections, 46mm, 46mm, 26mm. Traces of poorly preserved textile on one face. 062:*1352*.

51/7 Cast copper-alloy **purse ring** with triangular section. The two outer surfaces are ornamented with nine zones of two parallel punched dots separated by expanded areas with transverse lines. D.55mm; W.ring 5mm. 062:*1353*.

51/8 (i) Two short copper-alloy **strap-ends**, both made from two rounded-rectangular plates held together by a single copper-alloy rivet. One strap-end is decorated on one plate with paired incised lines forming a diagonal cross flanked by transverse lines. Both 16 x 9mm.
(ii) A thin fragment of **skin/leather**, 18 x 12mm and a second, smaller, piece which clearly originates in the riveted area between the plates of one of the strap-end. Not illustrated. 062:*1359*.

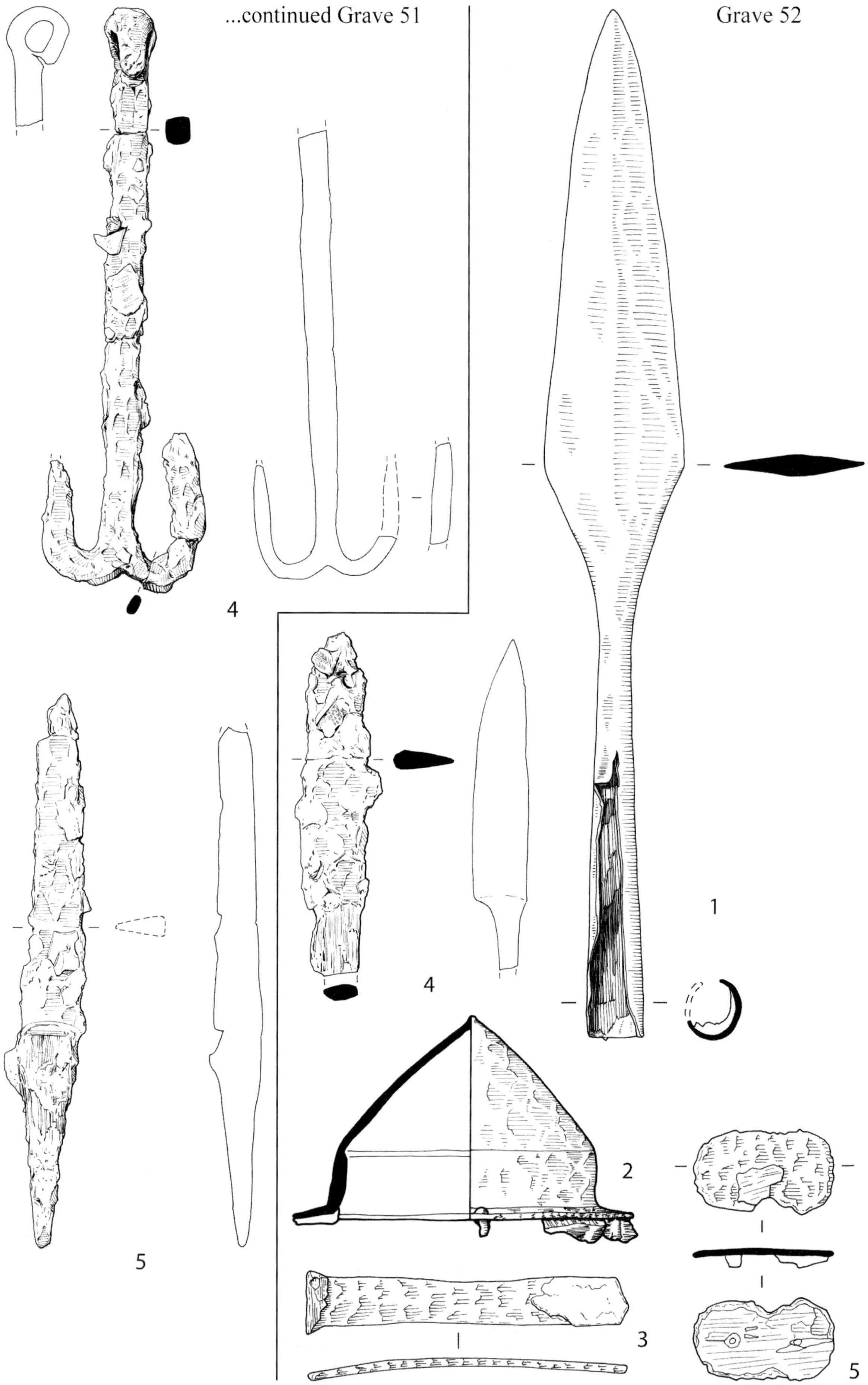

Figure 15.41 Flixton II Grave 51 (scale: 4 and 5 at 1:2) and Flixton II Grave 52 (scale: 1–5 at 1:2)

51/9 (i) Fragment of a copper-alloy **buckle** plate, with remains of iron loop and iron tongue. Marzinzik II. W.15mm x L.>12mm.

(ii) Copper-alloy **rivet/nail** with separately made circular head, 10mm diameter, slotted on to shank 3.5mm thick. L.7mm.

(iii) Copper-alloy rivet, as (ii). L.4mm.

(iv) Fragment of **skin/leather**, >1mm thick. 17 x 8mm. Not illustrated. 062:*1360*.

51/10 Beads 062:*1317–1346, 1354–8, 1361–5* (see *in situ* 1:2 plan Fig. 15.42; Pl. 7.4b *1317, 1321, 1329, 1338, 1343–4, 1355, 1357–8, 1361–2, 1365*). Brugmann Group A2b.

Thirty-three amber **beads** (total weight 45.9g; worn): 1 medium, faceted, D.30mm (*1317*); 5 medium, faceted, D.16–21mm (*1319, 1326, 1327, 1338, 1341*); 15 medium, faceted, D.11–15mm (*1318, 1320, 1322–5, 1328, 1331, 1333, 1339–1340, 1344–5, 1363–4*); 1 medium, faceted, D.6–10mm (*1343*); 7 medium, rounded, D.11–15mm (*1330, 1332, 1334–7, 1361*); 3 medium, rounded, D.6–10mm (*1329, 1342, 1356*); 1 short, rounded, D.16–21mm (*1365*).

Seven glass **beads**: Type *Melon:* 2 short, 8 ribs, yellow, D.11–15mm (*1321, 1362*).

Other beads: yellow large: 1 short, globular, D.6–10mm (*1357*); red globular: 4 short, globular, D.6–10mm (*1346, 1354–5, 1358*).

51/11 Three adjoining body **sherds**, quartz and grog tempered, undecorated. Earlier Iron Age. Not illustrated. 062:*1871*.

IV. Flixton II, graves associated with the ring-ditch/mound (FLN 062)

Grave 52 (062:*0993*)
Figs 15.39 and 15.41
Dimensions: 2.92m x 1.05m
Orientation: 237°
Container for body: None recognised
Finds gender: Male
Age and Sex: Grave size suggests adult, indeterminate sex
Skeletal remains: Very poor. Very tiny fragments of bone, recorded as an arm on site.
Body position: Indeterminate, head to west
Associated features: Internal to ring-ditch FLN 010
Description: A large sub-rectangular cut with rounded corners, steeply sloping sides, flat-bottomed and surviving to a depth of 0.6m. The excavated fill (062:*0994*) comprised mid grey/brown slightly silty sand with occasional stones and charcoal flecks.

Skeletal remains (062:*0995*) were limited to a few tiny fragments of bone. A rectangular, 0.25m by 0.17m, area of staining (062:*0996*), recorded on the base of the grave cut towards its western end, was interpreted as the vestiges of the skull. There was no evidence of a container for the body.

An iron spearhead (52/1) was found lying parallel to the long axis of the grave immediately to the south of the possible skull stain (062:*0996*) towards the western end of the grave. In the centre of the grave a shield boss (52/2) was recorded along with a shield grip (52/3), a shield board mount (52/5) and an iron knife (52/4), the latter probably attached at or near the waist of the body.

52/1 Near-complete iron **spearhead**, broken across socket, part of cleft missing. Cleft extends along most of shank with short length of solid metal stem of rectangular section beyond. Blade widens in concave curves, widest part over lower section. Tapers with straight edges to rounded tip. Lentoid in section. Abundant wood remains in socket. Accreted in sand with straw on one side across blade edge and socket. Type: Swanton E3, EAC Angular Long 1. L.370mm, W.52mm. Mineral-preserved wood in socket: *Corylus* sp. (hazel) made from mature timber. On the tip of the blade is a fragment of wood, *Fraxinus* sp. (ash) with a tangential surface. Textile, detached and on socket. 062:*1268*.

52/2 Iron **shield boss**. Incomplete, missing apex. Small uncarinated boss with only slightly convex cone, straight wall (Ht.20mm) and narrow flange (W.12mm). Type: Dickinson and Härke 6; EAC SOS. D.120mm, Ht.75mm. Textile on rim. 062:*1269a*.

52/3 Iron **shield grip**. Incomplete, one end and both terminals missing. Narrow strap grip (W.13mm) expanding towards terminals (W.15mm, 21mm). L.120mm. Textile on grip but not binding it. 062:*1269b*.

Grave 51

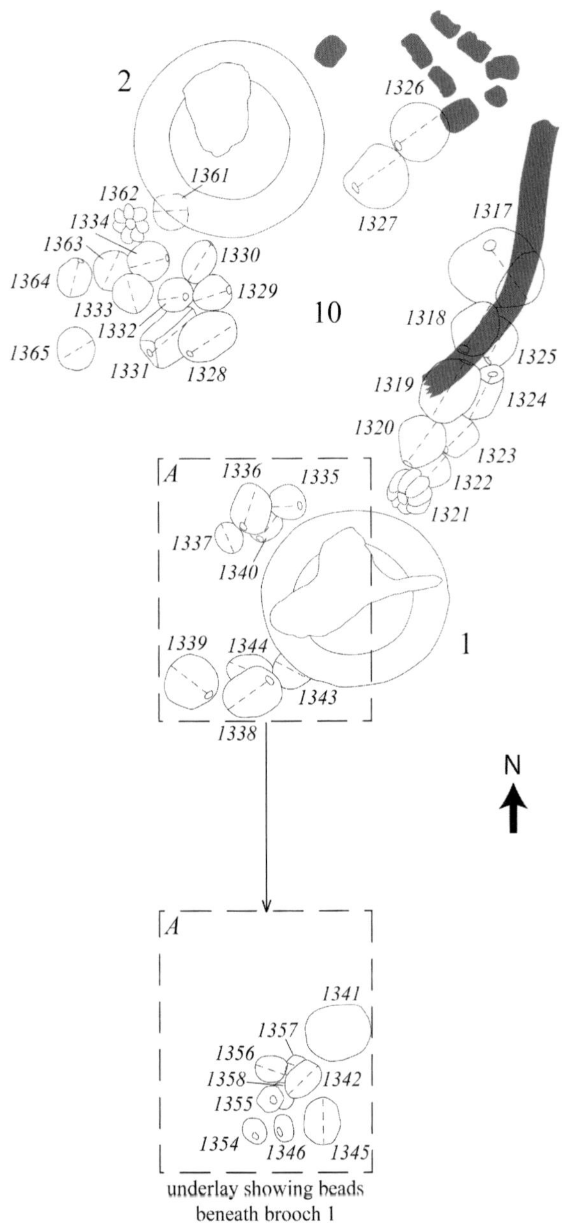

Figure 15.42 Flixton II Grave 51, *in situ* plan of grave goods 1, 2, and bead group 10. All contexts numbers are site FLN 062 (scale 1:2)

52/4 Iron **knife**, fragmentary, lacking end of tang. Widens in curve to shoulder, with less pronounced widening to choil. Slightly curved handle line at shoulder. Back straight then curving to rounded tip. Cutting edge is straight, rising to tip. Type: Drinkall A. L.124mm, blade W.20mm. Abundant horn remains on both sides of tang. Abundant remains of skin product on both sides of the blade, 1.5mm thick and joined at blade edge. Textile on top on one face. 062:*1270*.

52/5 Iron **shield board mount**. Double-rivet style mount formed from a pair of conjoined flat disc-headed rivets (D.25mm approx.). L.50mm. 062:*1271*.

Grave 53 (062:*0997*)
Figs 15.39 and 15.43
Dimensions: 2.3m x 1.35m
Orientation: 241°
Container for body: None recognised

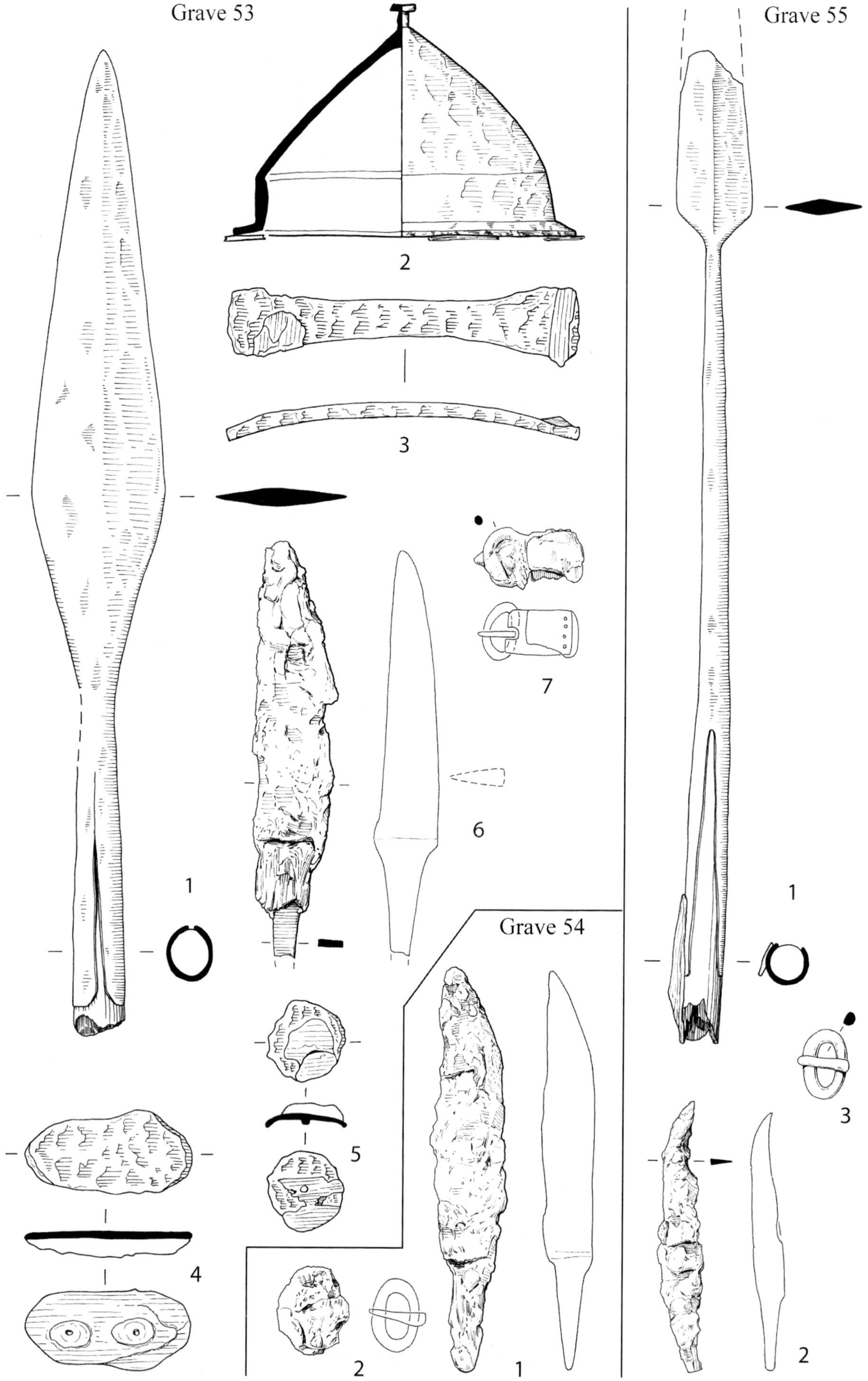

Figure 15.43 Grave goods; Flixton II Grave 53 (scale: 1–7 at 1:2), Flixton II Grave 54 (scale: 1 and 2 at 1:2) and Flixton II Grave 55 (scale: 1–3 at 1:2)

Finds gender: Male
Age and Sex: Grave size suggests adult, indeterminate sex.
Body position: Extended, supine, legs crossed at ankles, head to west
Associated features: Internal to ring-ditch FLN 010
Description: A large, wide sub-rectangular cut with rounded corners, steeply sloping sides, flat-bottomed and surviving to a depth of 0.47m. The excavated fill comprised a mixture of orange/yellow stony sand and brown silty sand with some biogenic disturbance, probably roots, towards its base.

Skeletal remains were totally absent, but a clear indication of the position of the legs was provided by a brown sandy stain (062:*0999*) central to the eastern end of the grave. A more amorphous soil stain (062:*1827*) immediately north of shield boss and grip (062:*1275*) was considered to represent vestiges of the organic component, wood and leather, of the shield itself.

An iron spearhead (53/1) was found lying parallel to the long axis of the grave towards its south-west corner. Immediately to the north was a shield boss (53/2) with associated fittings comprising a shield grip (53/3), an iron shield board mount (53/4) and an iron shield rivet or mount (53/5). An iron knife (53/6) was recorded halfway along the grave, just to the north of centre and, similarly to an iron buckle (53/7), was probably attached at or near the waist of the body.

53/1 Complete iron **spearhead** with cleft socket occupying most of shank. Short length of stem of rectangular section. Blade widens in convex curves, widest point over lower section, tapering in straight lines to rounded tip. Lentoid in section. Type: Swanton E2, EAC Angular Long 1. L.347mm, W.50mm. Mineral-preserved wood in socket: *Fraxinus* sp. (ash) made from mature timber. 062:*1274*.

53/2 Iron **shield boss**. Incomplete. Small uncarinated boss with convex cone, straight wall (Ht.17mm), narrow flange (W.12mm) and small disc-headed apex (D.10mm) positioned slightly off-centre giving a 'lopsided' appearance. Type: Dickinson and Härke 6; EAC closest to SOS. D.120mm, Ht.85mm. 062:*1275a*.

53/3 Iron **shield grip**. Strap grip (W.15mm) expanding towards terminals (W.25mm, 30mm). L.110mm. 062:*1275b*.

53/4 Iron **shield board mount**. Incomplete. Double-rivet style mount formed from a pair of conjoined flat disc-headed rivets (D.24mm). L.60mm. 062:*1276*.

53/5 Iron **shield rivet or mount**. Incomplete. Hollow convex disc-shaped mount or rivet. D.25mm. 062:*1277*.

53/6 Iron **knife**, complete. Tang widens to distinct shoulder and choil with vertical handle line at shoulder. Abundant horn remains on both sides of tang. Back lightly angled downwards, curving to tip. Cutting edge is straight and slightly sinuous, leading to rounded tip. Type: Drinkall D. L.159mm, blade W.24mm. Some skin product on both sides of the blade. 062:*1278*.

53/7 Iron **buckle** with oval loop and rectangular iron plate fixed with a row of four tin rivets (XRF), 1.5mm diameter, along the rear edge. Type: Marzinzik II.24a. Loop 21 x 17mm; plate W. *c*.7mm x *c*.20mm long. Poorly preserved remains of leather/skin between plates. 062:*1279*.

Grave 54 (062:*1824*)
Figs 15.43–15.44
Dimensions: 1.92m x 0.82m
Orientation: 267°
Container for body: None recognised
Finds gender: Indeterminate
Age and Sex: Indeterminate age and sex
Skeletal remains: None
Body position: Indeterminate, grave good suggest head to west
Associated features: Cuts outer edge of ring-ditch FLN 010
Description: An essentially parallel-sided cut with a rounded west end and a squarer end to the east. Surviving to a depth of 0.3m at its eastern end, its western end had been truncated, almost to its base, by a modern farm track. Where intact, the sides sloped relatively steeply. The fill (062:*1825*) comprised grey/brown silty sand mixed with orange silty sand with frequent stones. As the grave cut the backfill of ring-ditch FLN 010, it is logical to assume that the fill of the grave was at least in part derived from that of the earlier feature.

No skeletal remains were recorded. A circular stain (062:*1826*), measuring approximately 0.25m in diameter, was located centrally on the base of the grave in association with the grave goods. While not having any diagnostic attributes, the location of this stain in an area that was likely to have been occupied by the body would suggest that it was this and the juxtaposition of the grave goods that provided a locally favourable environment for preservation.

An iron knife (54/1) and an iron buckle (54/2) were found just to the west of centre in the grave in an area that would suggest they were attached at or near the waist of the body.

54/1 Iron **knife**, complete with rounded end to tang. Widens evenly to stepped choil and shoulder. Clear vertical handle line at shoulder, with abundant horn remains on both sides, following shape of tang. Straight edge to back of blade, angled down over last third to rounded tip. Cutting edge straight with no trace of wear. Clear medial weld line along blade. Type: Drinkall E. L.145mm, blade W.20mm. Some skin product on both sides of blade and textile on top, on one face. 062:*1272*.

54/2 Iron **buckle** with oval loop and no plate. Type: Marzinzik I.11a-i. 27 x 19mm. 062:*1273*.

Grave 55 (062:*1828*)
Figs 15.43–15.44
Dimensions: 2.05m x 0.85m
Orientation: 244°
Container for body: None recognised
Finds gender: Male
Age and Sex: Young adult, indeterminate sex
Skeletal remains: Poor. Fragments of left temporal, mandible, acetabulum, R. tibia shaft, talus and calcaneus. Tooth wear slight.
Body position: Extended, supine, head to west
Associated features: Entirely cut into ring-ditch FLN 010
Description: A parallel-sided, round ended cut surviving to a depth of 0.45m with a flat bottom. The cut exhibited steeply sloping sides on its north side and eastern end, reducing towards the base. Gentler sloping sides were present to the south and west with that at the western end describing a continuous curve down and merging with the base. Cut entirely into the upper fill of ring-ditch FLN 010, the excavated fill (062:*1829*) of the grave was derived from that of the earlier feature and comprised mixed brown silty sand and yellow sand with some gravel inclusions. Residual finds included five sherds of prehistoric pottery, a single sherd of Roman pottery and a number of struck flints.

Skeletal remains (062:*1832*) included fragments of skull and both legs. No stains relating to the rest of the body or a container were found to be present.

An iron spearhead (55/1) was found lying parallel to the long axis of the grave in its north-west corner. An iron knife (55/2) and a iron buckle (55/3) were recorded just into the western half of the grave, the latter central and the former towards the north side, both in an area suggesting they were attached at or near the waist of the body.

55/1 Complete iron **spearhead** with long cleft socket leading to solid shank of circular section. Small leaf-shaped blade of lentoid section widens in convex curves and tapers with curved sides to rounded tip. Type: Swanton D3; EAC Lanceolate Long 1. L.365mm, W.29mm. Plant material on socket identified as straw, most probably grass or sedge. Mineral-preserved wood in socket: probably *Fraxinus* sp. (ash) made from mature timber. A section of wood on the exterior of the socket: from its shape and grain alignment, part of the hafting. 062:*1284*.

55/2 Iron **knife**, complete. Narrow tang widens to shoulder and choil. Back curved throughout, whilst the cutting edge is straight but tip is curved down, drooping below level of cutting edge, if only by small amount. Vertical handle line just in front of shoulder. Type: Drinkall D. L.98mm, blade W.10mm. Abundant horn remains on tang. Traces of skin product. 062:*1285*.

55/3 Iron **buckle** with oval loop, enlarged tongue rest and no plate. Type: Marzinzik I.11b. 26 x 17mm. 062:*1286*.

Grave 56 (062:*1842*)
Figs 15.44–15.45
Dimensions: 2.2m x 0.8m
Orientation: 225°
Container for body: None recognised
Finds gender: Male
Age and Sex: Young-middle aged, male
Skeletal remains: Poor. Fragments of base of skull, maxilla and mandible, both hip joints, right tibia shaft. Tooth wear slight-moderate. Large mastoid process and occipital crest.
Body position: Extended, supine, head to west
Associated features: Almost entirely cut into ring-ditch FLN 010

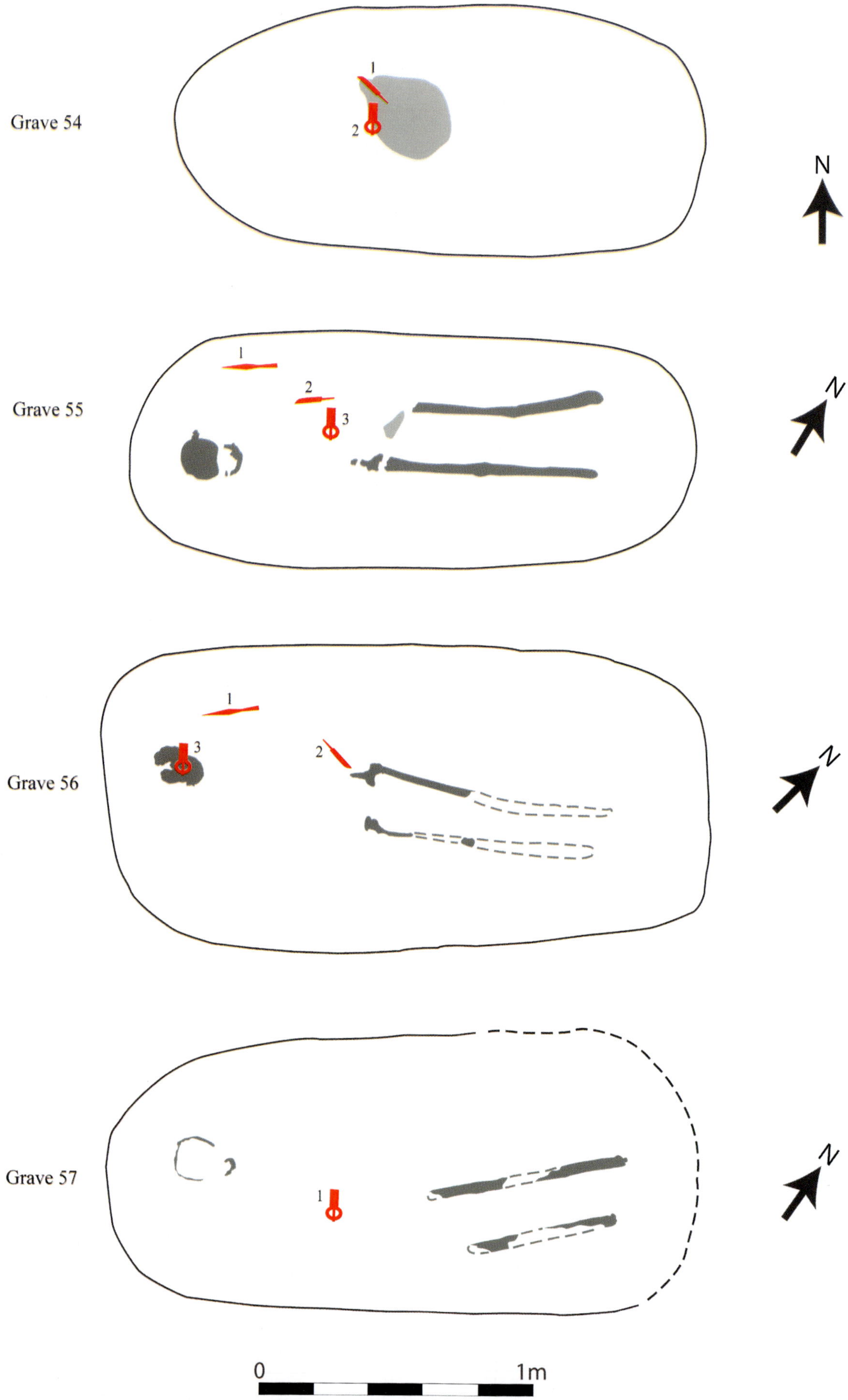

Figure 15.44 Plans of Flixton II Graves 54–57 (scale 1:20)

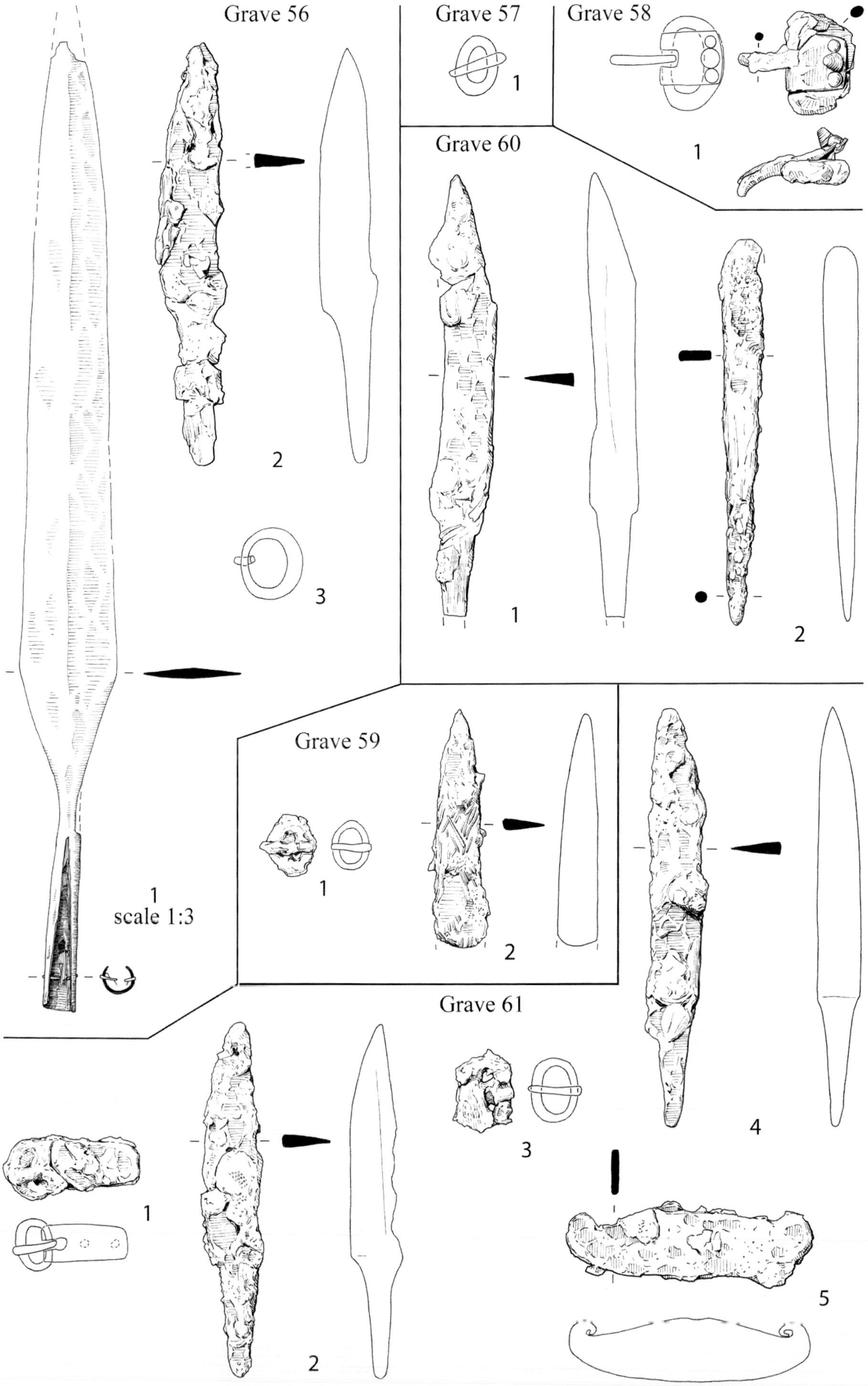

Figure 15.45 Grave goods; Flixton II Grave 56 (scales: 1 at 1:3; 2 and 3 at 1:2), Flixton II Grave 57 (scale: 1 at 1:2), Flixton II Grave 58 (scale: 1 at 1:2), Flixton II Grave 59 (scale: 1 and 2 at 1:2), Flixton II Grave 60 (scale: 1 and 2 at 1:2) and Flixton II Grave 61 (scale: 1–5 at 1:2)

Description: A large sub-rectangular cut with rounded corners and surviving to a depth of 0.48m. The profiles exhibited a steep, almost vertical eastern end, more gently sloping to the west. The sides were moderately steep, maintaining a curve that continued down onto the relatively flat base. Cut almost entirely into the upper fill of ring-ditch FLN 010, the fill of the grave (062:*1841*) was derived from that of the earlier feature and comprised relatively homogenous brown silty sand with some gravel inclusions. Residual finds included fragments of Roman brick/tile, fired clay and a number of struck flints.

Skeletal remains (062:*1843*) included parts of the skull and legs, with the rest of the legs defined by brown sandy stains. No stains relating to the rest of the body or a container were found to be present.

An iron spearhead (56/1) was found lying parallel to the long axis of the grave in its north-west corner while an iron buckle (56/3) was recorded beneath the skull (062:*1843*). In addition, an iron knife (56/2) had been approximately centrally placed in the grave and had been almost certainly attached at or near the waist of the body.

56/1 Complete iron **spearhead** with short cleft socket and small length of solid stem of oval section. Lateral nail set 17mm above base. Sword-like blade widens in short concave curves, widest part over lower section. Straight sides taper gradually to tip, curved over upper part. Lentoid in section. Type: Swanton E3; EAC Parallel Long 2. L.515mm, W.52mm. Mineral-preserved wood in socket: *Fraxinus* sp. (ash). Textile on socket. 062:*1288*.

56/2 Iron **knife**, complete with rounded end to broad tang. Widens to shoulder and choil in curves. Back straight and angled down over last quarter to tip, which is sharp. Cutting edge slightly sinuous but generally straight, rising to tip. Slight traces of horn at one end of tang on one side. Vertical handle line in front of shoulder. Type: Drinkall C. L.152mm, blade W.20mm. Possible skin product on one side. On the blade back and orientated longitudinally plant remains, probably wood, 35mm long. 062:*1289*.

56/3 Iron **buckle** with D-shaped loop, enlarged tongue rest and no plate. Type: Marzinzik I.10b–i. 26 x 22mm. 062:*1301*.

Grave 57 (062:*1844*)
Figs 15.44–15.45
Dimensions: 2.15m x 1.0m
Orientation: 232°
Container for body: None recognised
Finds gender: Indeterminate
Age and Sex: Young–middle aged adult, indeterminate sex
Skeletal remains: Very poor. Distal left tibia and calcaneus, and seven tooth fragments. Tooth wear moderate.
Body position: Extended, supine, head to west
Associated features: Cuts inner edge of ring-ditch FLN 010
Description: A parallel-sided round-ended cut surviving to a depth of 0.48m with steeply sloping north side, south side and eastern end, with a shallower sloping edge at its western end. The bottom sloped relatively steeply from west to east, falling by almost 0.2m along its length. As a result of the grave cutting ring-ditch FLN 010, the homogenous brown silty sand with gravel fill (062:*1845*) was at least partially derived from the upper fill of the earlier feature. Residual finds included two sherds of prehistoric pottery, four sherds of Roman pottery, a fragment of Roman tile and a few struck flints.

Skeletal remains (062:*1852*) were limited to fragments of skull and lower leg, the latter continuing as a brown sandy stain. No other soil stains relating to the rest of the body or a container were found to be present.

An iron buckle (57/1) was found just to the south-west of centre in the grave in an area that suggests the item was attached at or near the waist of the body.

57/1 Small iron **buckle** with oval loop and no plate. Type: Marzinzik I.11a–i. 22 x 16mm. Textile on one side. 062:*1295*.

Grave 58 (062:*1855*)
Figs 15.45–15.46
Dimensions: 2.02m x 0.97m
Orientation: 215°
Container for body: None recognised
Finds gender: Indeterminate
Age and Sex: Adult, indeterminate sex
Skeletal remains: Very poor. Fragments of skull base and atlas.
Body position: Supine, extended, left leg slightly flexed and crossed over right leg, head to west
Associated features: Entirely cut into ring-ditch FLN 010
Description: A parallel-sided cut with rounded end to the south-west, squared to the north-east and surviving to a depth of 0.57m with steeply sloping sides with curving at their junction the flat bottom. The fill (062:*1856*), which was almost entirely derived from the upper fill of ring-ditch FLN 010, comprised a heterogeneous mix of brown/grey silty sand and stony orange sand.

Skeletal remains (062:*1857*) were limited to fragments of skull, but an extensive brown sand stain clearly defined the position and attitude of the entire body. No stains were present that would indicate a container for the body.

An iron buckle (58/1) was found just to the north-west of centre in the grave in an area that suggests the item was attached at or near the left side of the waist of the body.

58/1 Iron **buckle** with D-shaped loop and rectangular iron plate, the plate folded back over the loop and the tongue pointing outward. There are three copper-alloy rivets with ornamental heads along the rear edge of the plate, the outer ones dome-headed, 4 and 5mm diameter x 2mm high, and the central one formed from concentric rings, which give it a stepped profile, 6mm diameter x 6mm high. Type: Marzinzik II.24a. Loop 35 x 23mm; plate W.22 x L.23mm. Remains of leather/skin between front and back of plate. 062:*1296*.

Grave 59 (062:*1859*)
Fig. 15.45–15.46; Pl. 7.4b
Dimensions: 1.62m x 1.08m
Orientation: 251°
Container for body: None recognised
Finds gender: Female
Age and Sex: Middle aged to old, ?male
Skeletal remains: Poor. Fragments of skull base, frontal, maxilla and mandible, 18 teeth, tibia shafts. Some degeneration, tooth wear advanced. Mastoid process large but occipital crest not pronounced. Caries of two teeth, one with abscess; one lower molar lost ante-mortem.
Body position: Extended, supine, head to west
Associated features: Almost entirely cut into ring-ditch FLN 010
Description: A squat essentially parallel-sided cut with moderately rounded ends and a maximum depth of 0.48m. The base of the grave sloped markedly along its long axis, falling by 0.2m from west to east and by a similar amount from north to south across its width. Whether this reflects a genuine eccentricity in the original excavation or post-depositional subsidence in the underlying ditch is unclear. Derived substantially from the fill of the earlier ditch, the fill of the grave (062:*1860*) comprised relatively homogenous brown silty, stony sand. A single piece of Roman tile was recovered as a residual find.

Skeletal remains (062:*1861*) were limited to fragments of skull and lower leg. No other soil stains relating to the rest of the body or a container were found to be present.

Part of an iron knife (59/2), a small iron buckle (59/1) and thin iron rod or pin (59/3 i), the latter in association with mineralised organic remains (59/3 ii), were recorded in the western half of the grave, both in an area that would have been occupied by the upper torso of the body, the knife on the right side and the buckle to the left. A group of twelve beads (59/4) were found beneath the jaw and were almost certainly worn at the neck.

59/1 Small iron **buckle** with D-shaped loop and no plate. Type: Marzinzik I.10a-i. 19 x 15mm. 062:*1302*.

59/2 Fragment of iron **knife** blade only. Back curves lightly throughout and descends to rounded tip. Cutting edge slightly sinuous, rising to tip. Type: Drinkall A. L.84mm, blade W.15mm. Non-orientated plant debris. 062:*1303*.

59/3 (i) Fragments of thin iron **rod** or **pin**. Total L.*c*.38mm, D.2mm. Not illustrated.
(ii) Mineralised organic remains, probably a piece of **leather**, 2mm thick, folded in two. 24 x 20mm. Not illustrated. 062:*1304a–b*.

59/4 Beads 062:*1305–1316* (Pl. 7.4b *1305, 1307–1310, 1312–5*). Brugmann Group B2.
One amber **bead** (weight 2.1 g; worn): functional part of a carefully shaped ?globular bead with two perforations, D.16–21mm (*1305*).
Eleven glass **beads**: Type *Cylindrical, Round:* 1 short, cylindrical, white, D.6–10mm (*1308*).
Type *Koch34 RedWhite:* 5 medium, globular, body snapped off another bead segment, D.6–10mm (*1306, 1309, 1311, 1315–6*); 1 medium, cylindrical, body snapped off another bead segment, D.6–10mm (*1310*).
Type *Koch34 RedWhite variant:* 1 medium, globular, white spiral on red body, D.6–10mm (*1307*).

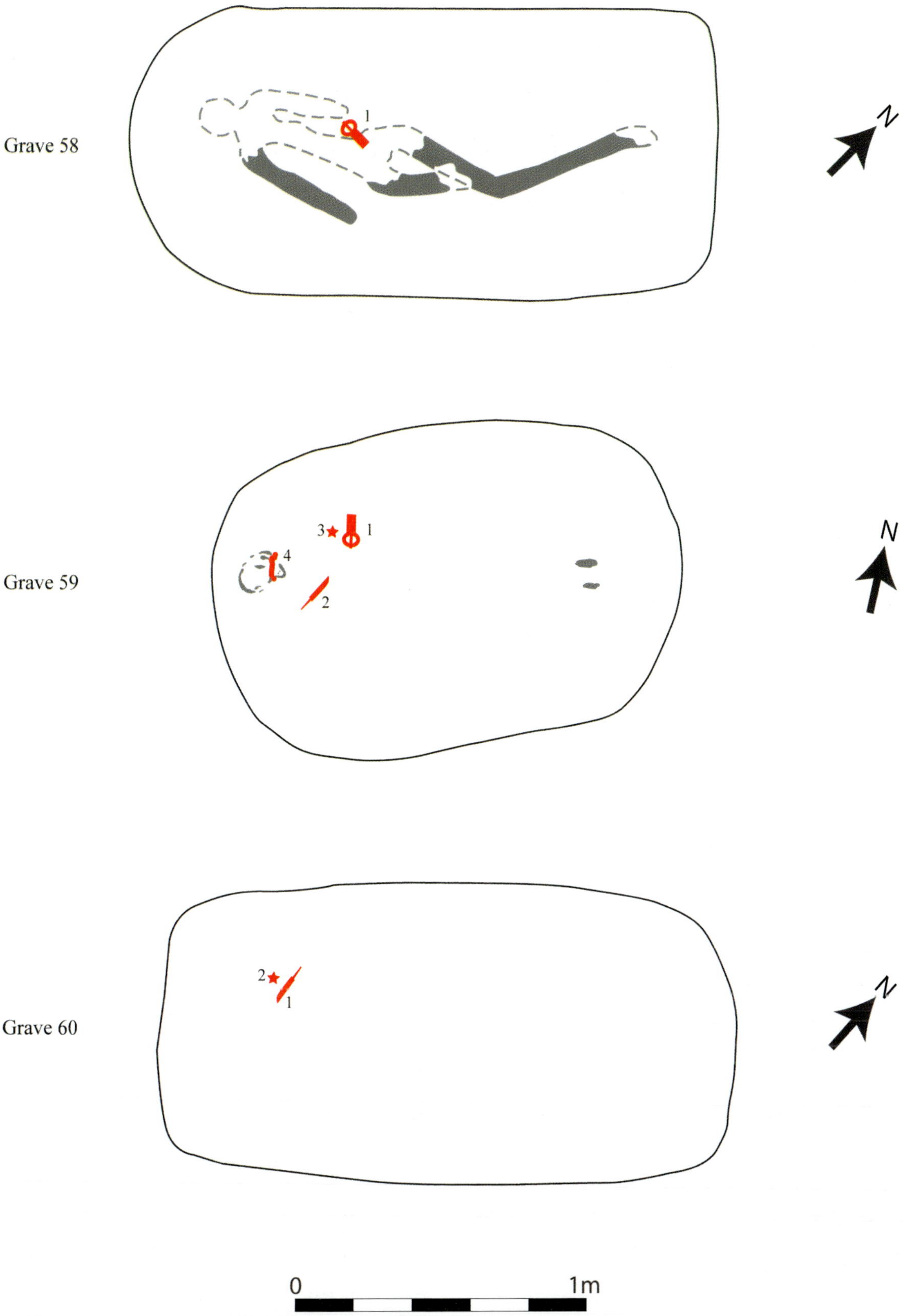

Figure 15.46 Plans of Flixton II Graves 58–60 (scale 1:20)

Type *Koch34 RedYellow-related:* 1 medium, globular, body snapped off another bead segment, trail not marvered in, D.6–10mm (*1313*).

Type *Koch34 WhiteBlue:* 1 short, globular, D.6–10mm (*1314*).
Other beads: yellow: 1 short, globular, D.6–10mm (*1312*).

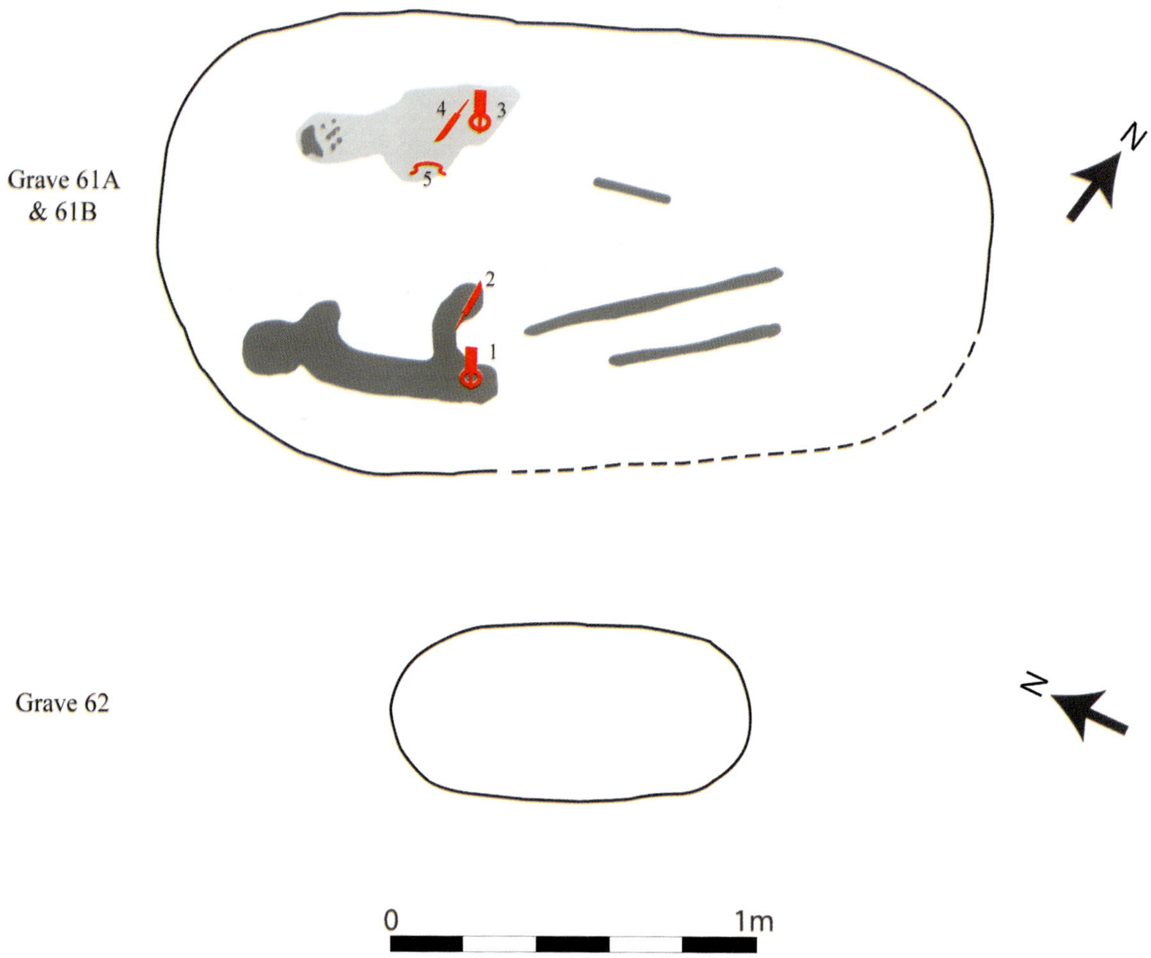

Figure 15.47 Plans of Flixton II Graves 61 and 62 (scale 1:20)

Grave 60 (062:*1862*)
Figs 15.45–15.46
Dimensions: 2.0m x 1.0m
Orientation: 225°
Container for body: None recognised
Finds gender: Indeterminate
Age and Sex: Size of grave suggests adult, indeterminate sex
Skeletal remains: None
Body position: Indeterminate
Associated features: Almost entirely cut into ring-ditch FLN 010
Description: A sub-rectangular cut with moderately rounded corners surviving to a depth of 0.45m with a flat bottom. The fill (062:*1863*), which would almost entirely have been derived from the underlying ring-ditch, comprised grey/brown silty, stony sand. Three struck flints were recovered as residual finds.

No skeletal remains, body stain or vestiges of a container were recorded.

An iron knife (60/1) was recorded towards north-west corner of the grave in close association with an iron tool (60/2). With no evidence for the position of the body, it is unclear at which point they would have been attached.

60/1 Iron **knife**, complete with short tang widening to distinct shoulder and choil. Back straight and angled down to tip over last third. Cutting edge straight with no trace of wear, rises just slightly at end to tip. Clear medial weld line. Horn remains on one side of tang, faint trace of possible handle line at shoulder. Type: Drinkall E. L.159mm, blade W.18mm. 062:*1297*.

60/2 Iron spatulate **tool**. Flat section, 4.5mm thick, tapering to a blunt point at one end and rounded at the other. L.135mm, W.15mm. 062:*1298*.

Grave 61 (062:*1872*)
Figs 15.45 and 15.47
Dimensions: 2.27m x 1.22m
Orientation: 238°
Container for body: None recognised
Finds gender: Indeterminate for both bodies
Age and Sex: Two bodies, (A) to the south (062:*1875*) middle aged, sex undetermined; and (B) to the north (062:*1876*) a *c*.16–18 year old, possibly male (from teeth)
Skeletal remains: (A) Very poor. Fragments of petrous temporals, occipital and C1–2, four molars. Tooth wear moderate-heavy. (B) Very poor. Fragments of occipital and nine teeth.
Body position: Both supine, heads to west
Associated features: Almost entirely cut into ring-ditch FLN 010
Description: A parallel-sided cut with rounded ends, surviving to a depth of 0.65m with steeply sloping sides and a bottom which sloped down from west to east, falling approximately 0.1m over its length. The fill (062:*1873*), which would almost entirely have been derived from the earlier ring-ditch, comprised grey/brown silty sand, locally stony. Residual finds included three sherds of prehistoric pottery, three sherds of Roman pottery and two struck flints.

Skeletal remains were limited to fragments of skull and teeth for both of the bodies (062:*1875* and *1876*) in this double burial. In addition, brown sandy body stains associated with the torso and legs were recorded for both bodies, those of 062:*1875* more extensive than 062:*1876*.

Grave goods associated with the southernmost body were limited to an iron buckle (61A/1) and an iron knife (61A/2); both in locations indicating that they were attached at or near the waist, the knife on the left side with the buckle more centrally placed. The finds attributed to the northernmost body were all recorded in the area of the torso and comprised an iron buckle (61B/3), an iron knife (61B/4) and an iron fire-steel (61B/5).

Body A

61A/1 Iron **buckle** with oval frame and rectangular iron plate; no rivets visible. Marzinzik II.19a. Loop 19 x 14mm; plates W.14mm x 27mm. Laminating layers of leather/skin between front and back of plate. 062:*1300*.

61A/2 Iron **knife**, complete. Tang has rounded end and widens to distinct shoulder and choil. Back straight and angled over last third to tip. Cutting edge ragged near choil and straight thereafter, rising to rounded tip. Clear weld line for cutting edge. Possible trace of handle line just beyond shoulder. Type: Drinkall C/A. L.127mm, blade W.17mm. Traces of horn on one side of tang. Thin skin product on both sides of blade and textile on top. 062:*1366*.

Body B

61B/3 Iron **buckle** with oval loop, enlarged tongue rest and no plate. 23 x 18mm. Textile remains on front. Type: Marzinzik I.11b. 062:*1367*.

61B/4 Iron **knife**, complete. Narrow tang with rounded end, widening to distinct shoulder and choil. Vertical handle line at shoulder. Back straight and curves to tip, cutting edge straight and parallel with back, rising to tip. Type: Drinkall A. L.150mm, blade W.18mm. Traces of horn on one side of tang. 062:*1368*.

61B/5 Complete iron **fire-steel**, lower edge lightly curved throughout, rising at both ends to curled terminals, one of which is perforated. Upper edge rounded and curved. L.89mm, W.14mm. 062:*1369*.

Grave 62 (062:*1887*)
Fig. 15.47
Dimensions: 1.00m x 0.47m
Orientation: 320°
Container for body: None recognised
Finds gender: No grave goods
Age and Sex: Grave size suggests child
Skeletal remains: None
Body position: Indeterminate
Associated features: Entirely cut into ring-ditch FLN 010
Description: A parallel-sided cut with rounded ends, surviving to a depth of 0.14m with gently sloping sides and a flat bottom. The fill (062:*1888*), which would have entirely been derived from the earlier ring-ditch feature, comprised brown silty sand. This feature was identified during surface cleaning as minor variation in fill and the edges were not well-defined. Given that the feature was orientated substantially differently to the other graves and there were no grave goods, skeletal remains or body stains, then its interpretation as a burial must be considered doubtful.

Flixton II: objects from FLN 053, not from graves (NG)
Fig. 15.48

II/NG/1-3 appear in the inventory with Grave 4, above.

II/NG4 Curved fragment of cast copper-alloy **object**, possibly a Roman bow brooch. 11 x 7mm. 053:*0124*.

II/NG5 Fragment of cast copper-alloy **brooch** with remains of a single-lug pin attachment. 18 x 13 x 2mm.. 053:*0126*.

II/NG6 Iron **shield boss**. Incomplete. Heavily carinated boss with straight cone, low wall (Ht.15mm), broad flange (W.25mm) with flat disc-headed rivets (D.20mm approx.) and large disc-headed apex (D.32mm). Type: Dickinson and Härke 1; EAC closest to SOC2. D.150mm, Ht.75mm. 053:*0132*.

II/NG7 Bent iron **strip**, fragmented and heavily corroded. L.100mm, W.12mm. 053:*0135*.

II/NG8 Incomplete pair of copper-alloy **sleeve clasps**. Plain, probably Hines B7 but rear edge missing on both halves. Catch is a plain slot, 16mm long; hook extension 13–14mm across. W.39mm, L. catch-piece 15mm, L. hook-piece 9mm. 053:*0149*.

II/NG9 Small iron **buckle** with near circular loop and no plate. Type: Marzinzik I.12a-i. 19 x 18–19mm. 053:*1245*.

II/NG10 Fragment of iron **spearhead** including upper part of cleft socket and small part of blade. Socket tapers to short length of solid stem of rectangular section with rounded edges. Blade widens from stem in convex curves, lentoid in section. Slight traces of wood in socket. L.60mm, W.27mm. 053:*1423*.

II/NG11 Iron **buckle** with D-shaped loop and rectangular plate. Type: Marzinzik II.19a. Loop *c*.30 x 23mm; plate 30 x 26mm. Textile on front and back. 053:*1436*.

V. Key to bead entries in catalogue
by Birte Brugmann

Descriptions are based on visual examination of the beads in November 2006. The unedited descriptions of the individual beads, which are more detailed than in the published catalogue, are held in the project archive in printed form.

Measurements
The maximum diameter of the beads is given in 5mm ranges. For size ranges of individual glass bead types see Table 7.3. The proportion of the beads indicates their length:

very short	1:4
short	1:2
medium	1:1
long	1.5:1
very long	2:1

Shapes

Glass beads
The outline of the longitudinal section of most of the Flixton beads is rounded or square. A rounded section is described as globular or annular depending on the proportion of the bead and the size of the perforation. Short or very short beads with a perforation that measures *c*.half the diameter of the cross section of the bead or more are described as annular; all other beads with a rounded longitudinal section are described as globular, including those that may described as barrel-shaped due to a large perforation or flattened perforated sides. Such 'barrel-shaped' beads medium in proportion are described as 'globular, perforated sides marvered flat'. Beads with a square or sub-square longitudinal section are described as cylindricals. Their cross sections are described only if it they are not round but ribbed or square.

Amber beads
See section on Glass and amber beads in Chapter 7.

Segments
Glass beads are made of one segment if not described otherwise.

Perforations
Perforations have a round or slightly oval cross-section if not described as square. Abrasions on amber beads that have changed cross sections are not described. For the diameter of perforations of glass beads in relation to bead sizes see 'shapes'. 'Sharp edges to perforation' refers to a technical detail that may in the future help to distinguish between earlier and later wound monochrome beads on a statistical basis.

Colours
The colour descriptions are based on visual examination in daylight and differentiate between white, yellow, green, blue, red (brown/'terracotta' /brick-red) for opaque beads and brown (including 'pink') for translucent beads, 'light' used for the colour variations in so-called 'gold-in-glass' beads and translucent 'white' beads, and 'dark' for any beads that appear black in daylight. For the difficulties that would be attached to a more detailed description see Brugmann (2004, 24).

Bead types
The glass bead types referred to in the catalogue in italics are described in detail in Table 7.3. For brevity, the catalogue omits attributes of glass beads if these are defined as part of the type description given in Table 7.3.

Glass bead making techniques
See the type descriptions in Table 7.3.

Opacity and translucency
See the type descriptions in Table 7.3.

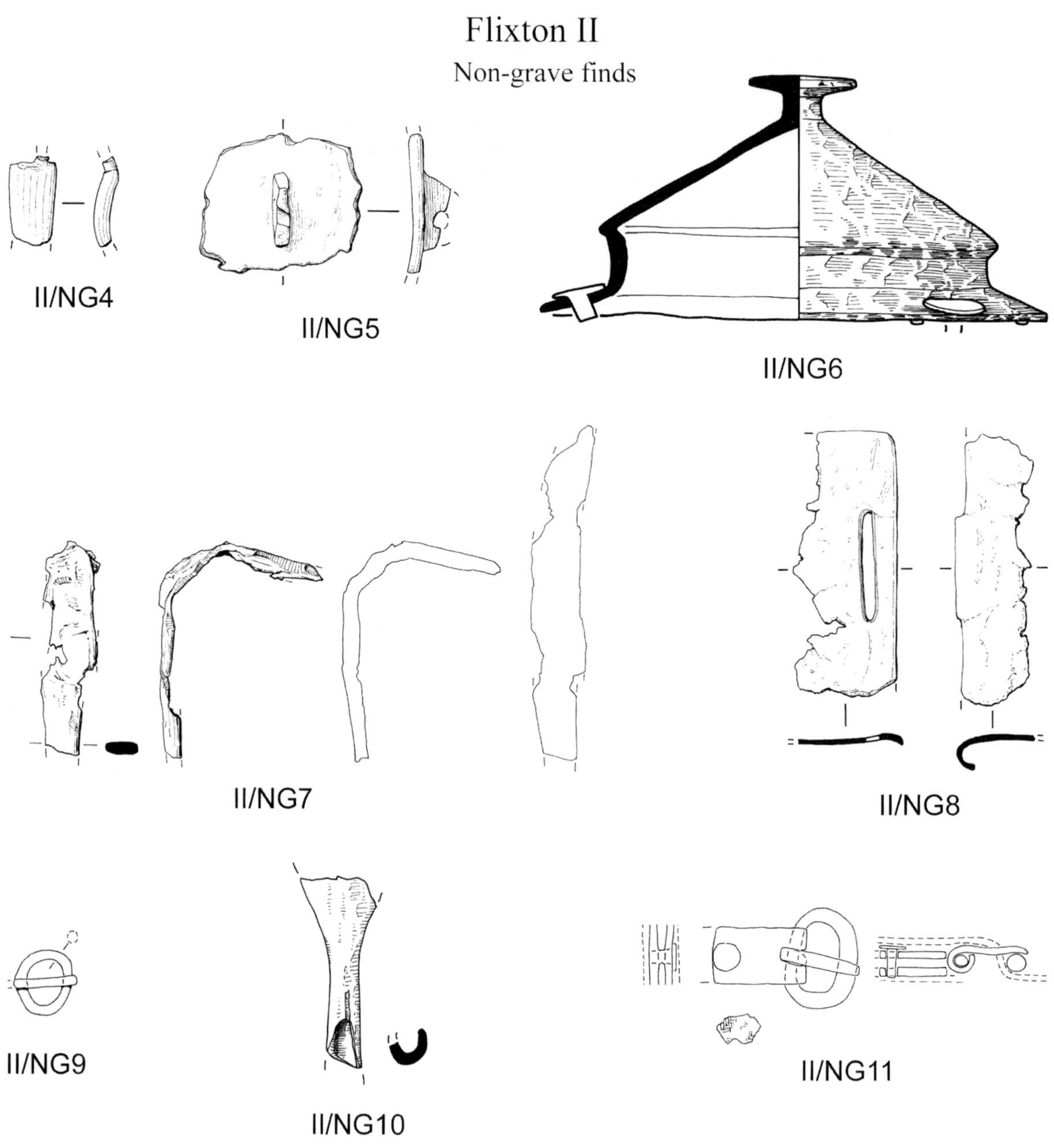

Figure 15.48 Unstratified (NG) cemetery finds from Flixton II (scales: 1, 2 and 5 at 1:1; 3, 4 and 6–8 at 1:2)

Weight

The beads were weighed by Vanessa Fell (Fell and Watson 2007, Appendix 1). Weights were determined on the same balance and corrected to *c.*0.1g.

VI. X-ray fluorescence analysis

by Vanessa Fell

The composition of selected metal finds was determined by X-ray fluorescence analysis, which is a surface analytical technique (Table 15.1). Because of corrosion effects, the results are qualitative only, but they serve to indicate the presence of applied metals, such as solder and coatings. Analyses were made on a small area of each item, 0.3mm diameter, under vacuum at 40kV, 220μA in an Eagle II X-ray fluorescent spectrometer with a lithium-drifted silicon detector.

Object No.	*Area analysed*	*Result*	*Interpretation*
4/5 Ring	Fractured metal edge	Pb	Almost pure lead
II/NG1 Brooch	White metal on the wings near to a probable repair on copper alloy brooch	Cu Sn (Pb)	The area bearing the white metal on the front of the wings was shown to comprise copper and tin, although the tin did not show as strongly as suspected. Nevertheless, there was more tin here than on the reverse of the brooch and on the top of the bow.
14/2 Buckle	White metal rivet heads	Ag (Cu S Au)	The rivet heads were made of silver containing small amounts of copper and a trace of gold. Sulphur was also determined, which will come from the black tarnish.
15/1 Shield boss	Rivet 1 head	Ag	The top layer of the rivet head was silver, which was attached to a copper or bronze base.
	Rivet 2 head	Ag	As rivet head 1
	Rivet 3 head	Ag	As rivet head 1
	Rivet 4 head, detached	Cu Sn (Pb)	The rivet head was bronze containing some lead. The appearance suggests that the rivet head once had another layer attached, like rivet 1.
	Rivet 5, detached	Cu Sn (Pb)	The rivet head was bronze containing some lead. The appearance suggests that the rivet head once had another layer attached, like rivet 1. The washer did not reveal any tin, suggesting that plain copper was used.
	Rivet 15/3 head	Cu Zn (Sn Pb)	A low-zinc brass with small amounts of tin and lead.
	Rivet 15/3 washer	Cu	The washer was copper with insignificant amounts of tin.
	Rivet 15/4 head	Cu Sn (Pb)	A low-tin bronze with some lead.
17/2 Sleeve clasp	Hook piece, rear, edge	Cu Sn (Pb Zn)	Bronze with a trace of lead and zinc
	Hook piece, front	Cu Sn (Pb Zn)	Part of the rear surface
	Hook piece, possible edge of solder	Cu Sn Pb	There was much more tin and lead here compared with the base metal, suggesting that the hook was attached with a tin-lead solder.
	Catch piece	Cu Au Sn Pb	Gilding on a leaded bronze. No mercury was detected in the gilding. No gilding was determined on the rear.
	Catch piece, rear	Cu Sn Pb (Zn)	Leaded bronze
27A/3 Brooch	Broken pin catch	Cu Sn Pb (Fe)	The pinkish-grey corroded metal visible at the modern break was a leaded bronze, which showed no evidence of the suspected silver alloy. Similarly, a dark area on the front of the brooch was a leaded bronze
51/1 Brooch	Yellow metal on the front	Cu (Zn Pb)	The alloy is a low-zinc brass with traces of lead. No gold was detected.
53/4 Decorative shield mount	Countersunk area in the wood around a broken rivet stem	Fe Sn Ca	Low levels of tin and calcium. The tin may be from a corroded bronze rivet head that has re-deposited some tin around the rivet stem.
	Rivet stem	Fe (Cu Pb)	The iron stem had traces of copper and lead, which may have derived from a corroded bronze rivet head
53/7 Buckle	Two fractured rivets from an iron buckle	Sn (Fe Cu Pb)	Both rivets revealed tin with very small amounts of lead and copper. The rivets seem to be made of a tin alloy with low levels of lead and copper, although the composition may have altered through corrosion in the acid soil.

Brackets indicate minor and trace peaks

Table 15.1 X-ray fluorescence analysis

Part IV

Flixton, the Bigger Picture

Chapter 16. The Excavations at Flixton and their Wider Context

by Stuart Boulter

I. Introduction

Fig. 16.1

The following sections provide a brief description of the significant archaeological deposits relating to the periods of activity recorded in the phases of the quarry opened up after those covered in this volume, and other known contemporary sites in the Waveney Valley (Fig. 16.1). The inclusion of this chapter was based on the need to provide some context for the archaeology detailed in Parts II–III and at least make more widely available a summary of the material that will be included in greater detail in later Flixton volumes. The overall phasing and dating framework is summarised in Table 2.1.

II. Prehistoric

Flixton chronology, Period I.a. Palaeolithic (*c.*10,000+ BP)

The earliest evidence for human activity recorded in the quarry is represented by a series of flint artefacts recovered from the quarry gravels themselves. These were all unstratified with the exception of one hand-axe recovered as a residual find in the upcast spoil from the excavation of an Early Anglo-Saxon sunken featured building (SFB). No analytical work has yet been carried out on these implements, but clearly there are differences in their morphological characteristics and degree of post-depositional damage. This would fit well with the geological evidence which suggests that the succession of sediments seen at Flixton includes both pre-anglian and anglian deposits, the former only seen in the deepest parts of the quarry (J. Rose, pers. comm.). The earliest of the hand-axes are probably pre-anglian and suffered re-working before their secondary deposition in anglian deposits. However, the presence of a classic Levallois flake, from an industry so far unknown from sediments earlier than OIS 8 (oxygen isotope stage 8) (*c.*250,000 BP) (D. Schreve, pers. comm.), at least provides a *terminus post quem* for some of the Flixton sediments.

Flixton chronology, Period I.b. Mesolithic (*c.*8000–4000 BC)

Evidence for Mesolithic activity was sparse and limited to a few unstratified worked flints.

Flixton chronology, Period I.c. Early Neolithic (*c.*4000–3200 BC)

Most Early Neolithic features comprised small clusters of pits along with more isolated examples. There were two exceptions, both monumental structures: a ring-ditch and a long barrow (Fig. 16.1a). At this stage, dating has been provided by the artefactual evidence (primarily ceramics and worked flint), although further analysis will include radiocarbon and thermoluminescence dating.

In the FLN 062 area, at a distance of some 120m south of the Early Anglo-Saxon cemetery, a 7.5m-diameter ring-ditch was recorded. No associated features were found to be present and its dating was based solely on ceramic evidence. The fill of the ditch included significant numbers of similarly coloured flint cobbles throughout, many exhibiting frost shattering. While cobbles such as these were available from the local geology, they had clearly been collected together for a specific purpose, possibly forming a mound or cairn-like structure within the area enclosed by the ditch. Erosion by natural processes could have resulted in their deposition into the ditch, or it may have been deliberately dismantled.

The second monumental structure was a long barrow in the area excavated as FLN 069 and located in the base of the shallow south-west to north-east facing valley. This feature almost certainly survived as an upstanding earthwork in the landscape for some considerable time and may have directly influenced the position of later monuments such as the FLN 013 timber circle, the Early Bronze Age round barrows and even the Late Iron Age/Early Roman timber circle. While not obviously having any direct influence on the location of the Early Anglo-Saxon cemeteries and settlement, it would probably have still been visible and may have been looked upon as a 'special place' in the landscape. At the time of writing, no analysis has as yet been undertaken on the associated finds or the potentially complicated progressive construction and closure phases of the monument. In overall plan, however, the monument took the form of a relatively straight-sided, apsidal-ended, continuously-ditched enclosure some 40m long and 15m wide. A central *c.*11m long, *c.*1.3m wide trough-like feature was located at the eastern end of the monument, lying on its long axis. Immediately to the east, a line of large post-holes flanked what must have represented the entrance to the trough-like chamber and formed a north-east facing façade-like structure. A pit located central to its eastern end was filled primarily with flint cobbles, a number of which also formed alignments along the adjacent edges of the trough with a large pile also forming a blockage across its full width approximately 2m to the west of the pit. In addition, lines of post-holes were recorded parallel with and internal to the surrounding ditch on the sides of the monument and turning at right-angles across the apsidal west end. Post-holes immediately west of the internal trough suggested there was further compartmentalisation within the structure. A large pit was recorded in the narrow strip between the southern side of the ditch and its internal post-holes and was clearly inserted to respect the monument or *vice versa*. Significant finds from this pit included a large shale

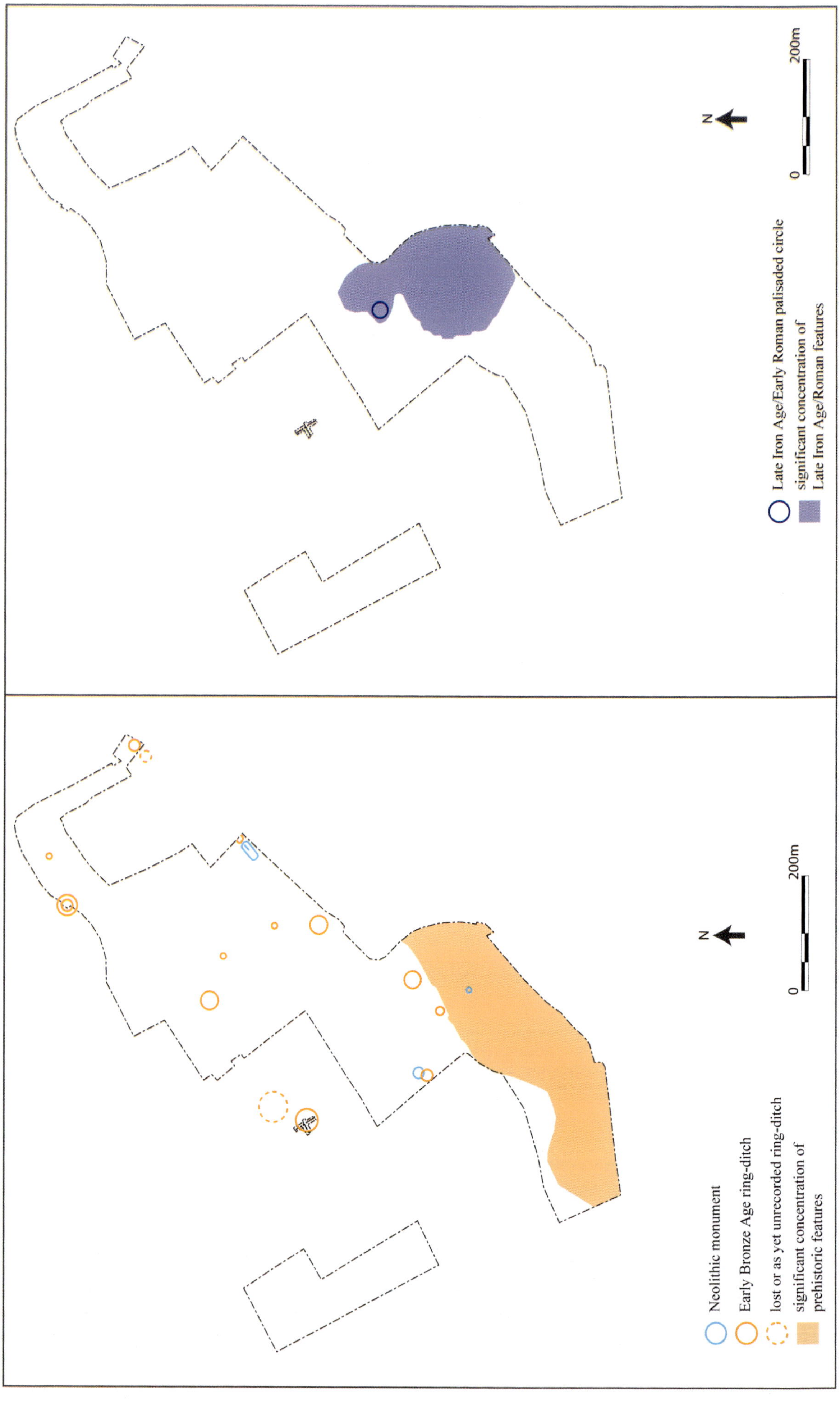
Late Iron Age/Early Roman palisaded circle
significant concentration of Late Iron Age/Roman features
N
0
200m
Neolithic monument
Early Bronze Age ring-ditch
lost or as yet unrecorded ring-ditch
significant concentration of prehistoric features
N
0
200m

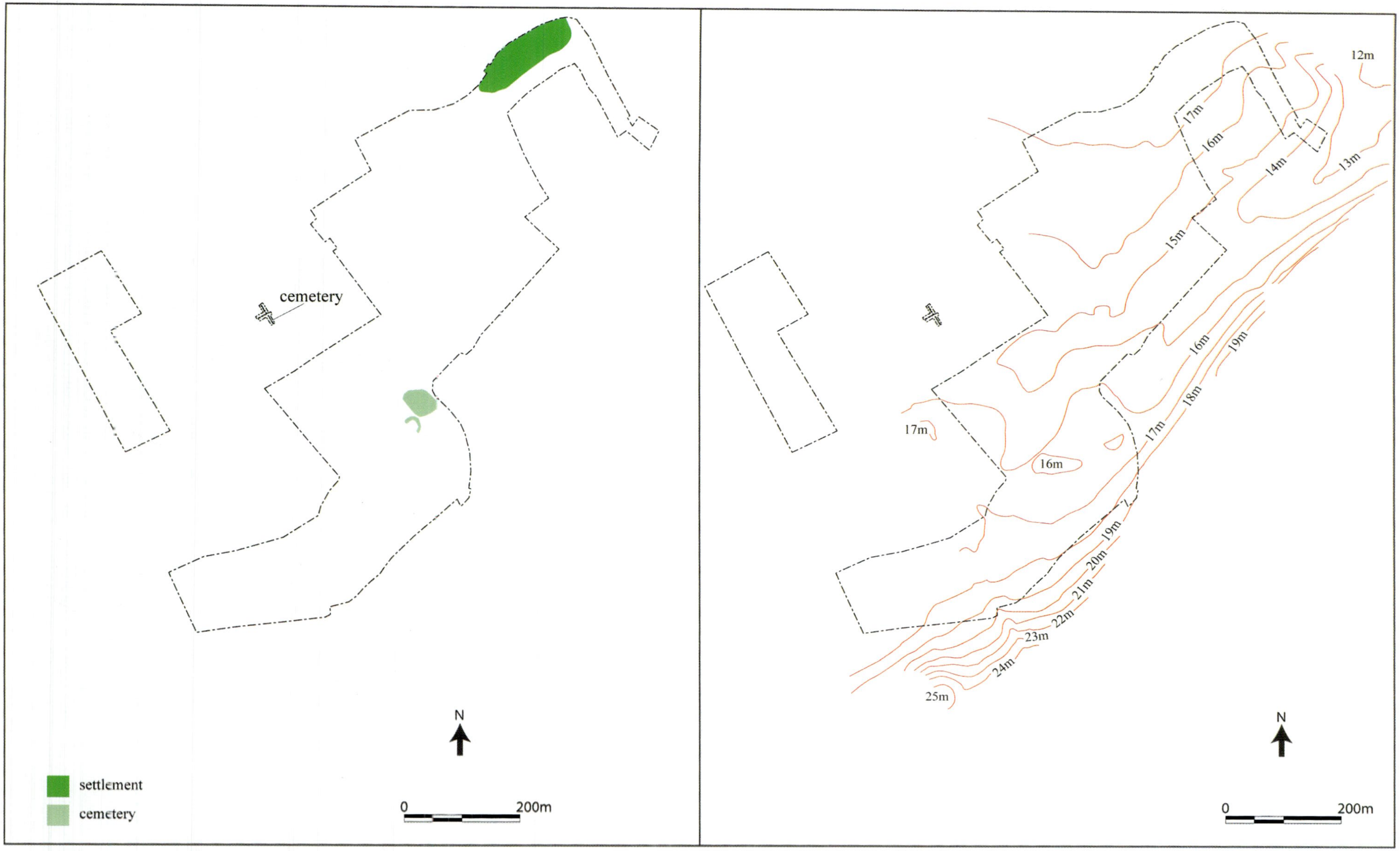

Figure 16.1 Flixton Park Quarry, significant archaeology and contour survey. (a) Prehistoric archaeology (b) Late Iron Age and Roman archaeology (c) Early Anglo-Saxon archaeology (cemetery and settlement) (d) Contour survey

bead and a whole Mildenhall Ware bowl, the latter placed in its upper fill.

The Flixton long barrow is not an isolated monument with at least one, if not two, similar features known from the northern side of the Waveney at Broome Heath some 6km to the north-east. One of these, MNF 10597, survives as a standing earthwork and forms part of a Scheduled Ancient Monument (SAM 152). It is also likely that there are other ploughed out examples which, like that at Flixton, have not been identified on aerial photographs. The impression is then, that major undertakings in monument construction were occurring on a widespread, albeit dispersed, scale within the Waveney Valley during the earlier Neolithic period and the landscape, which may only have been occupied on a transient, seasonal basis, was beginning to develop aspects of its later monumental character. It is unknown what combination of factors provided the impetus for these first excursions into monument building although, at Flixton, the presence of the shallow valley/depression clearly played its part. The long barrow was located in the bottom of this landscape feature with its long axis conforming to the orientation of the valley. The monument would have been highly visible to observers from all directions, but particularly to those standing on the boulder clay plateau to the south (Fig. 16.1a and d). Evidence for other activity of this date in the areas around the monuments was extremely limited with a few pits producing diagnostic artefactual evidence and a number of residual worked flints in later features. However, results of the micromorphological analysis of a pre-long barrow palaeosol (French 2008) suggests that major soil changes occurred prior to its construction, almost certainly the result of human activity relating to the process of deliberate deforestation.

Flixton chronology, Periods I.d. Late Neolithic (*c*.3200–2400 BC) and I.e. Early Bronze Age (*c*.2400–1500 BC)

Late Neolithic and Early Bronze Age deposits have been recorded throughout the Flixton excavations, effectively limited to significant monumental structures (the timber circle in FLN 013 and ring-ditches) or dispersed groups of pits. Other than these larger monuments, structural evidence was not positively identified, but shallow lain deposits are not likely to have survived damage by recent agricultural processes. This does mean that the character of the processes that generated the pits is hard to assess. However, given the length of time involved, the number of features is actually quite small and is indicative of a relatively low level of activity, possibly on a transient or seasonal basis.

HER entries for the Waveney Valley include widely distributed evidence for later Neolithic and Early Bronze Age activity and there is no reason to believe that the levels recorded at Flixton Park are anything other than representative.

Unfortunately, structures such as the FLN 013 timber circle are all but invisible unless uncovered during formal soil-stripping. While the FLN 013 ring-ditch had previously been identified on aerial photographs, and was subsequently confirmed by geophysical survey, the earlier structure had not shown up at all. It is possible that the extreme rarity of this type of monument in the archaeological record, certainly in the East Anglian region, is at least in part due to the difficulty in recognising them other than within formally excavated areas. Having said that, they are certainly not represented in the same order as the generally later round barrows, as other examples would have been identified at sites such as Flixton. While the difficulties with recognition and the interpretation of the function of these monuments remain, it is hard to predict at what frequency they are likely to have occurred in the landscape. However, while taking these problems into consideration, this class of monument does appear to be extremely rare and this alone suggests that their function was specialised.

Within the quarry itself, the monument occupies a shallow north-east facing spur at the head of the shallow valley/depression occupied by the Early Neolithic long barrow (Fig. 16.1a and d). When the long axis of the barrow is projected to the south-west it runs directly through the post-hole circle. The long barrow would have been clearly visible from the position chosen for the post-hole circle and it is difficult to see how this site could have been selected without this in mind. However, this may not have been the only factor, as the overall aspect of the site located on the shallow spur overlooked from the clay plateau to the south, would have offered the monument a fair degree of prominence in the landscape.

On balance, the most attractive interpretation remains a limited access scenario, with the monument performing at least one specialised function which, although the evidence in this case is scant, could be astronomically related or funerary in nature. However, while the primary function of the monument is likely to have been associated with a specialised activity occurring on a periodic or, at least, punctuated basis, these could still sit comfortably alongside its ability to provide a more general focus in the landscape for less specific and more mundane activities not requiring direct access to its interior. In this way, the catchment area for one of these monuments would probably depend on the territorial range of the occupying group or loosely linked groups of people that still considered themselves to be part of a single wider community.

Ring-ditches representing the ploughed-out remains of round barrows have regularly been encountered during soil-stripping at the two Flixton quarries, the majority of which were not previously known from aerial photographs. Thirteen have now been excavated at Flixton, with at least one other lost without record and another known from aerial photographs to be located in a future phase of the quarry. The ring-ditches form a dispersed group along the gravel terrace and generally do not appear to have been preferentially sited with relation to the shallow valley/depression which may have influenced the location of the earlier, Neolithic, monuments (Fig. 16.1a and b). All of the ring-ditches, however, would have been visible from vantage points along the edge of the clay plateau to the south. On typological grounds it is considered likely that most, if not all, of these features were Early Bronze Age in date. However, with the exception of FLN 013 detailed in this volume and two other ring-ditches with primary deposits including datable ceramics (Table 16.1), there was a lack of direct dating evidence. One exception, a small example in FLN 062 (16.1a), already discussed above, was associated with Early Neolithic pottery and this may be considered the exception rather than the rule. These features were all thought to represent funerary

Site Code (and context)	Overall diameter	Width	Depth	General description	Associated burials and features
FLN 008	40m?	4.7m	1.69m	Ditch only seen in limited trenches and edge of quarry. Presumed to be a continuous circle. Accompanying mound may partially have been constructed in association with later windmill	Dispersed pottery sherds from a collared urn and some calcined bone fragments suggest that at least one urned cremation had been present
FLN 012	20m?	?	?	Ploughed out. Continuous circle seen on aerial photographs, as yet unexcavated. Immediately adjacent to FLN 011/086	
FLN 013	20m	2.0–3.3 m	1.0m	Ploughed out. Continuous circle, cut Late Neolithic timber circle	One unurned cremation burial approximately central to enclosed area
FLN 045	60m?	?	?	Ploughed out. Continuous circle seen on aerial photographs, lost to quarrying without record	
FLN 055/059	12m	1.0m	0.9m	Ploughed out. Continuous circle	Large 'grave-shaped' central pit. Unurned cremation at base, possibly two secondary burials at higher level associated with organic staining
FLN 061 (*0202*)	30m	4.0m	1.5m	Ploughed out. Continuous circle, Associated ground discolouration revealed the location of an external bank and internal berm.	Large 'grave-shaped' central pit. Evidence for a bier or coffin with a Beaker deposited as a grave-good. No skeletal remains surviving
FLN 061 (*0218*)	38 and 28m	2.0 and 5.0m	0.7 and 0.5m	Ploughed out. Double continuous circle	None recognised
FLN 061 (*1494*)	11m	1.0m	0.3m	Ploughed out. Penannular with opening to the north-east	A shallow rectangular pit was located relatively centrally to the enclosed area. No staining or skeletal remains, but location and size suggest a crouched inhumation
FLN 010/062	35m	5.6m	1.4m	Ploughed out. Upper fill contained significant quantities of Roman material. Feature later became the focus of Early Anglo Saxon burials	None recognised
FLN 062	7.5m	1.0m	0.4m	Ploughed out. Fill included large quantity of frost-shattered flint cobbles. Ceramic evidence of Early Neolithic date	None recognised
FLN 064	8m	1.4m	0.5m	Ploughed out. Continuous circle	A shallow rectangular pit was located centrally to the enclosed area. No staining or skeletal remains, but location and size suggest a crouched inhumation. Possible unurned cremation external to and 2m south-west of ditch
FLN 069 (*0036*)	11m	1.5m		Ploughed out. Continuous circle	Small square enclosure defined by gullies, open to south-east. Pit within enclosure contained two biconical urns. A third urn was found in another pit to the south of the enclosed area. A minimum of three and maximum seven individuals were represented. Finds included a fragment of copper alloy wire and faience beads
FLN 069 (*0100*)	35m	1.55m		Ploughed out. Continuous circle constructed from a series of straighter segments	'Grave-shaped' pit towards central area, no staining or skeletal remains, but location and size suggest a inhumation burial
FLN 069 (*0245*)	1.2m	0.7m	0.3m	Ploughed out. Only half within excavated area immediately east of Long Barrow. Opposed butt-ends forming entrance to south-west, somewhat irregular shaped	None positively attributed. Pit full of cobbles towards centre of enclosed area
FLN 011/086	19m	1.2m	0.7m	Ploughed out. Continuous circle constructed from a series of straighter segments.	None recognised

Table 16.1 Details of the Flixton ring-ditches

monuments, although human remains were not always encountered, and while all exhibited the commonality of a defining circular ditch, their overall dimensions and character varied considerably (Table 16.1). These marked differences could have occurred due to burial practices changing over time, but other factors such as different origins/ethnicity and status of those buried must also be considered. The latter was highlighted by the presence of an assemblage of finds, including 'Wessex-type' biconical urns and faience beads, that are rare finds in East Anglia. In addition to the funerary related monuments, a single isolated inhumation burial (identified as such without the presence of skeletal material) was recorded in a vertical sided oval-shaped grave with a bier or coffin and a Beaker pot deposited as a grave good.

The most commonly recorded features of Late Neolithic and Early Bronze Age date at Flixton were pits, mostly less than 1m in diameter and with depths not usually exceeding 0.5m, although occasional exceptions did occur. While not forming any well-defined concentrations, there were loose groupings of features. Interestingly, while the currency of Grooved Ware pottery is believed to overlap considerably with Beaker pottery, at Flixton the two wares were both present, but were mutually exclusive. It is unclear whether here this does represent a chronological difference or a deliberate separation of contemporary material. It may be significant that within the loose groups of features, Grooved Ware pits were sometimes found in close association with Beaker pits. The general impression given by the finds assemblages recovered from these pits is consistent with that found for sites FLN 013 and FLN 053 (see Chapter 3). It has been argued that examples of the three depositional scenarios recognised by Garrow (2006) for East Anglian Sites ('general', 'selective' and 'arranged') were represented, although the latter is more difficult to prove. The types of activity represented are difficult to characterise as structural evidence is absent. While the FLN 013 post-hole circle formed a focus for a group of pits that were thought to be broadly contemporary, these features were similar in character to those recorded in the wider area of the quarry. The activities represented by these features certainly did not suggest periods of prolonged occupation, and the impression given is one of an open landscape becoming progressively dotted with monumental structures, particularly during the Early Bronze Age, and being utilised on a transient, possibly seasonal basis. The unusual character recognised in some of the finds assemblages could be the result of closure deposits buried at the end of each episodic occupation.

Flixton chronology, Period I.f.–I.h. Late Bronze Age to Late Iron Age (*c*.1000–100BC)

There was clear evidence to suggest that activity at Flixton continued during the later Bronze Age and Iron Age, although given the length of time covered by these periods, the intensity of occupation appears to have been relatively low and dispersed.

The most significant deposits, a series of predominantly four- and six-posted structures, were hard to date precisely, although by their association with more securely dated contexts it is suggested that the majority at least can be attributed to the later Bronze Age and earlier Iron Age. Many of these structures were clearly arranged in such a way that they defined two straight edges and a right-angled corner of a feature-free area, it was on that basis they were considered to be broadly contemporary. While there was no evidence with which to deduce the function of these structures, they were similar to those often interpreted elsewhere as post-holes for posts supporting elevated granaries. Until the most recent phases of excavation, when a series of circular post-built structures were recorded, there was no evidence for any round-houses to accompany the four- and six-posted structures.

III. Late Iron Age/Roman

The concentrated area of activity relating to this period has been highlighted in Figure 16.1b. However, it is likely that when adjacent areas are opened up it will be found that a number of as yet undated field boundary ditches are contemporary, extending this area of influence, albeit peripheral to the main area of settlement.

During the later Iron Age there is evidence for the formal organisation of the landscape, with a rectilinear ditch system developing on the southern side of the shallow valley/depression in the terrace gravels, immediately north of their junction with the rising clay soils to the south. The Late Iron Age/Early Roman deposits in FLN 053, those detailed in this volume, lay to the north of the ditched fields/enclosures, beyond the limit of what appears to have been the formally managed land.

In addition to the palisaded circle, one other enigmatic structure was recorded some 140m to the south-west, still outside the confines of the ditched fields/enclosures, but sharing a similar alignment. Rectangular in plan, measuring 14m from north-east to south-west and 11m from north-west to south-east, the building/structure was defined by eighteen external post-holes (six down each side and five across the ends) with a further three rows of six forming three internal aisles, a total of thirty-six. There was no obvious evidence indicating the location of an entrance. While there was no reason to suggest that more than one phase of construction was represented, the arrangement of post-holes does suggest that two discrete elements were present. However, the problem with a single-phase structure is the close proximity of the post-holes with little room to move between. Very few artefacts were recovered from the post-holes; the external fills were sterile, with the finds exclusively recovered from the post-pipes. The ceramic evidence suggested an early to mid 1st century date which, similarly to the FLN 053 features, could not be positively assigned pre- or post-Conquest status.

No close parallels for this structure have been identified and the possible interpretations range from it representing an almost industrial-scale granary raised on a raft of posts, or a shrine. There was no direct artefactual evidence for the latter, other than the presence of two gold coins (both 'Irstead' type quarter staters) and two silver coins, all attributable to the Iceni (P. de Jersey, pers. comm.), recovered in the immediate or close vicinity, which perhaps suggests an elevated status or unusual character for the site. While there was no environmental evidence to support the granary theory, this interpretation does seem to be the most attractive and there are examples from the continent, *e.g.* the 2nd–3rd-century phase of a site at Flögeln-Eekhöltjen in Germany (Welch 1992, fig. 17), where granary structures supported on up to sixteen posts have been recorded, although here they are closely associated with significant numbers of domestic buildings. While the Flixton structure is on an even larger scale, with double the number of posts, and predating the Flögeln-Eekhöltjen examples, these represented an established tradition and the similarities are compelling.

Another unusual feature was a multiple burial that had been cut into the middle of an early to middle 1st-century pit. Three adults (two women and a man) and one teenager of indeterminate sex appeared to have been unceremoniously dumped in a single grave cut (Anderson 2006b). Analysis suggested that there were indicators for family relationships between some or all of the individuals. Furthermore, the male had been decapitated peri-mortem, and one of the females had suffered cuts to the head suggesting that they may have suffered a violent end. All of the skeletons exhibited evidence of physical stress during life and the three adults were all short, possibly due to poor nutrition. A radiocarbon determination (SUERC-1190; 1985±35 BP) undertaken on a fragment of fibula gave a calibrated date of 60BC–AD120 at 95% confidence. Combining this with the artefactual evidence from the grave, and the pit that it cut, places the burial towards the middle to upper limit of this date range. Given that the site lay within the territory of the Iceni, the possibility that there was a connection with the Boudiccan revolt and the subsequent reprisals that took place has to be postulated, although the evidence for other disruption at that time has not been identified at Flixton.

In the wider area of the Flixton quarry site, Roman activity continued on into the 4th century, with the latest coin recovered dating to 353AD, although the number of features was much reduced. While this could simply have been due to the contraction of the settlement core or a lateral shift in its location, there is evidence for some form of widespread disruption in east Suffolk at that time, as previously noted in excavation at sites such as Hacheston (Blagg *et al.* 2004, 199) and from metal-detecting assemblages. Towards the southern end of the Roman feature concentration, a layer of subsoil was encountered between the overlying topsoil and natural sand/gravels representing a contemporary, *in situ* buried soil. This artefact-rich layer produced a mixture of domestic and semi-industrial material and the majority of the Roman coinage so far recovered at Flixton. Associated structures included two conventional aisled buildings, one with a south-facing porch, and two updraft pottery kilns. The latter were different in detail, but from the included ceramic finds were both probably in use, at the earliest, from the end of the 1st century, possibly continuing in use throughout the 2nd century and becoming redundant, at the latest, in the first few years of the 3rd century. A similar kiln was previously excavated in the adjacent Homersfield Quarry during the 1950s (Smedley and Owles 1959, 168–84).

The overall impression given by the formally excavated Late Iron Age and Roman archaeology at Flixton, and from other known sites and contemporary finds-spots in adjacent areas of the Waveney Valley, is of dispersed activity throughout, probably associated with a series of relatively closely spaced farms/homesteads or small farming communities. However, within that landscape, there are also the enigmatic structures, such as the palisaded circle and multi-aisled building, which may perform a more specialised function, possibly on behalf of the wider community. It has also become clear that evidence for activity dating later than the middle of the 4th century AD is extremely rare in the Waveney Valley. If we are to believe that the earlier Roman levels of population continued beyond that time, then they must have been severely impoverished as they have continued to remain archaeologically invisible despite the relatively large-scale excavations that have now been undertaken.

IV. Early Anglo-Saxon

The local and regional context of the Early Anglo-Saxon cemeteries at Flixton has been discussed in depth in Chapter 14 and need not be repeated. However, the contemporary settlement evidence excavated in Flixton Park Quarry is worthy of mention here. An extensive area of Early Anglo-Saxon occupation was identified in 2001 and excavated in 2002. The settlement occupied a shallow north-east to south-west orientated ridge overlooking the water meadows of the River Waveney to the north and the shallow parallel valley/depression within the river terrace gravels to the south (Fig. 16.1c and d). While continuing on beyond the northern edge of the quarry, the western, southern and eastern extents of the settlement area were recorded. Buildings and their associated features were found to cover an area of 350m by 80m, although the concentration of structures was greatest towards the north-west end of this area. It is, however, by no means certain how many of the buildings were present at any one time and the whole of this area may not have been occupied contemporaneously. The artefactual evidence was relatively limited, but suggested that the occupation could have begun in the late 5th, spanning the 6th and continuing into the very early 7th century. While this coincides broadly with the currency of the excavated portions of the Flixton cemeteries, there was no direct evidence proving that the occupants of the settlement were those subsequently buried in Flixton I and Flixton II. Both cemeteries were located in excess of 500m away from the settlement, the former to the south-west and the latter to the south. One point in favour of there being a direct link between at least the main Flixton cemetery and the settlement is their topographic relationship: both occupying prominent positions on opposite sides of the shallow valley/depression with each being highly visible from the other (Fig. 16.1c and d).

Twenty-four buildings were recorded. Six of these were of the general type described at sites such as West Stow as 'halls' (West 1985, 112). There were twelve SFBs (sunken featured buildings) and six miscellaneous structures. The 'halls' were rectangular in shape, characterised by their closely spaced post-holes and weak- cornered construction indicating that the weight of the roof was supported by the sides of the structure. One of the 'halls' was large, measuring 13m by 6m, and appears to be larger than any previously excavated examples in the region. Evidence for internal partitions was sometimes present as were secondary external post-settings providing additional buttressing to the supporting long walls. Entrances were usually in the long wall, although this was not consistently the case.

The SFBs varied in both size and character with the range of types consistent with those seen at contemporary sites excavated in the region. Of the twelve examples excavated, two did not have any associated post-holes, one had seven or eight post-holes and nine had two post-holes. The majority of the artefactual evidence was recovered from these features.

Six of the structures were termed miscellaneous as they did not fit the pattern of the other two identified building types. Five of these comprised discrete groups of post-holes defining a roughly rectangular area, but the exact layout of these structures could not be ascertained in detail. The sixth, however, was a curious hybrid of the two main building types with a shallow pit, a large post-hole at each end and four more along each side in shallow slots.

In addition to the buildings, the southern end of what was probably a rectangular ditched enclosure was recorded, measuring 60m at its ends and in excess of 60m on its sides. A large external ditch was mirrored by a lesser internal ditch, both with opposed butt-ends in the middle of the southern end forming an entrance to the interior. The centre of the enclosure was marked by a small square enclosure (9m by 9m) surrounded by a continuous ditch. Within the area confined by the ditch was a large circular pit with a 1m-square setting in its base with a continuous row of flint cobbles around its edge.

Artefactual evidence was scarce, but did suggest an Early Anglo-Saxon date. However, the dominant alignment of the Early Anglo-Saxon buildings was contrary to that of the enclosure and its chronological relationship with the settlement remains unclear. Proposed future work may help in this respect as it will include a radiocarbon determination on the articulated remains of a horse found in the external ditch.

One interpretation of this complex of features has been provided by John Blair (pers. comm.), who has worked extensively on Anglo-Saxon shrines and sanctuaries and their development from earlier prototypes (Blair 1995), and is in no doubt that this is what is represented at Flixton.

We have, then, at Flixton both settlement evidence and cemeteries which, on balance, were likely to have been directly related. The artefacts from the settlement are consistent with those deposited as grave goods in the cemetery, both chronologically and economically: they are generally not spectacular and appear to represent what must be considered to be an average population with regard to status and wealth at that time. It is unclear then, whether the unusually large 'hall' and the possible broadly contemporary shrine have any significance regarding the character and associations of the population. It has been suggested by Norman Scarfe (Scarfe 2002, 90–95) that, contrary to the accepted derivation of the name Flixton (farm of Flick), the first element actually relates to Bishop Felix. He further surmises that a group of parishes, today comprising the Elmhams, Homersfield and Flixton, were part of a royal estate of the Wuffings that formed part of their original endowment to Felix in the first half of the 7th century. If this were the case, then the settlement at Flixton which, from the cemetery evidence at least, appears to have continued from the end of the 5th century to the middle of the 7th century, was occupied continuously throughout the period during which the ruling power emerged in East Anglia. Tom Plunkett states that the late 550s mark a distinct horizon in the formation of English powers (Plunkett 2005, 55) and, if Scarfe is to be believed, the development of Flixton and its adjacent parishes into a royal estate, probably during the second half of the 6th century, would have had marked implications for the local population. Future interpretation of the Flixton site, with its unusually large 'hall' and the possible shrine or sanctuary, will need to take into account the influence that would have been asserted by a close royal connection.

V. Medieval and later

No securely dated medieval deposits have been identified at Flixton, although some of the undated ditch features may actually belong in this period. Artefactual evidence is limited to a few metal detector finds. Of these, the majority were recovered from close to the line of the former Flixton to Homersfield road which, until the late 1800s, ran through the middle of Flixton Park before being diverted to its present position to the north: the others were found in association with the medieval/early post-medieval windmill remains in FLN 008. While the flanking ditches and metalled surface of this road recorded in the excavations probably relate to its later phases, it almost certainly follows the line of its medieval predecessor.

The post-medieval archaeology could be divided into three main categories. Firstly there are residual landscape features, mainly field boundaries that became redundant during the landscaping of the parklands around Flixton Hall. Secondly, there are features directly associated with Flixton Hall and its surrounding parklands, which include boundary ditches, dew-pond, wells, drains, a barn, tree-plantings and a ditched folly structure. Thirdly, modern features associated with more recent farming activities and World War I training trenches are present.

Bibliography

Adams, B. and Jackson, D., 1989 'The Anglo-Saxon Cemetery at Wakerley, Northamptonshire; Excavations by Mr D. Jackson', *Northamptonshire Archaeol.* 22, 69–183

ADS, 2007 http://ads.ahds.ac.uk/catalogue/archive/clothing_eh_2007

Alarcaõ, A.M. and da Ponte, S., 1982 'O tempereiro e a antiquidade do tear horizontal de padais', *Conimbriga* 21, 163–8

Aldhouse-Green, M. and Aldhouse-Green, S., 2005 *The Quest for the Shamen: Shape-Shifters, Sorcerers and Spirit-Healers of Ancient Europe*, (London, Thames and Hudson)

Alkemade, M., 1997 'Elite lifestyle and the transformation of the Roman world in Northern Gaul' with catalogue entries by Peddermors, A. and Pol, A., in Webster, L. and Brown, M., *The Transformation of the Roman World, AD 400–900*, 180–93 (London, British Museum)

Anderson, S., 2000 'Roman and post-Roman pottery', in Fern C., *Sutton Hoo Visitor Centre, Tranmer House, Bromeswell, Suffolk, Site BML 018*, SCCAS Report No. 2007/116 (assessment report)

Anderson, S., 2003 'Post-Roman pottery' in Caruth, J. and Anderson, S., *RAF Lakenheath, Anglo-Saxon Cemeteries ERL104, ERL046 and ERL114. A Report on the Archaeological Excavations 1997–2002*, SCCAS Report No. 2003/78 (assessment report)

Anderson, S., 2006a 'Post-Roman Pottery', in Boulter, S.P., *Assessment 2: An assessment of the Archaeology Recorded in New Phases 5, 6, 7 (a and b), 9, 11 and 12 of Flixton Park Quarry (FLN 056, FLN 057, FLN 058, FLN 061, FLN 062, FLN 063 and FLN 064)* (SCCAS Report No. 2006/54)

Anderson, S., 2006b 'Human skeletal remains', in Boulter, S.P., *Assessment 2: An assessment of the Archaeology Recorded in New Phases 5, 6, 7 (a and b), 9, 11 and 12 of Flixton Park Quarry (FLN 056, FLN 057, FLN 058, FLN 061, FLN 062, FLN 063 and FLN 064)* (SCCAS Report No. 2006/54)

Anderson, S., 2009 'Non-textile-related fired clay and daub', in Lucy, S., Tipper, J. and Dickens, A., *The Anglo-Saxon Settlement and Cemetery at Bloodmoor Hill, Carlton Colville, Suffolk*, E. Anglian Archaeol. 131, 246–9

Anderson, S., forthcoming a 'Fired clay', in Tester. A., Anderson, S., Carr. R.D. and Riddler, I., *A High Status Middle Saxon Settlement on the Fen Edge: Staunch Meadow, Brandon, Suffolk*, E. Anglian Archaeol.

Anderson, S., forthcoming b 'The Early Saxon Pottery', in Walton Rogers, P., forthcoming, *Tyttel's* halh, *the Early Anglo-Saxon site at Tittleshall, Norfolk: Bacton to King's Lynn Gas Pipeline Vol. 2*, E. Anglian Archaeol.

Anderson, S., forthcoming c 'Human skeletal remains', in Penn, K., *The Shrubland Hall Anglo-Saxon Cemetery, Coddenham, Suffolk*, E. Anglian Archaeol.

Annable, F.K. and Eagles, B.N., 2010 *The Anglo-Saxon Cemetery at Blacknall Field, Pewsey, Wiltshire*, Wiltshire Archaeological and Natural History Society Monograph No. 4 (Devizes)

Appleyard, H. M., 1978 *Guide to the Identification of Animal Fibres* (Leeds, WIRA)

Archibald, M., Brown, M. and Webster, L., 1997 'Heirs of Rome: the shaping of Britain AD 400–900', in Webster, L. and Brown, M., *The Transformation of the Roman World, AD 400–900*, 208–48 (London, British Museum)

Arnold, C., 1980 'Wealth and social structure: a matter of life and death', in Rahtz, P., Dickinson, T. and Watts, L. (eds), *Anglo-Saxon Cemeteries in 1979*, Brit. Archaeol. Rep. 82, 81–142 (Oxford)

Arwidsson, G., 1932 'Some glass vessels from the boat cemetery at Valsgärde', *Acta Archaeologica* III: 251–66

Ashwin, T. and Bates, S., 2000 *Norwich Southern Bypass Part I: Excavations at Bixley, Caistor St Edmund, Trowse*, E. Anglian Archaeol. 91

Avent, R. and Howlett, T., 1980 'Excavations in Roman Long Melford 1970–1977', *Proc. Suffolk Inst. Archaeol. Hist.* 34, 229–49

Baldwin Brown, G., 1915 *The Arts in Early England* (London, Dutton)

Ball, D. F., 1964 'Loss-on-ignition as an estimate of organic matter and organic carbon in non-calcareous soils', *J. Soil Science* 15, 84–92

Bamford, H., 1982 *Beaker Domestic Sites in the Fen Edge and East Anglia*, E. Anglian Archaeol. 16

Barlow, F. (ed. and trans.), 1962 *The Life of King Edward (Vita Ædwardi Regis)* (London, Nelson)

Bass, W., 1971 *Human Osteology* (Missouri Archaeol. Soc.)

Bates, S., 2004 'Worked Flint', in Boulter, S. P., *Assessment 2: An assessment of the Archaeology Recorded in New Phases 5, 6, 7 (a and b), 9, 11 and 12 of Flixton Park Quarry (FLN 056, FLN 057, FLN 058, FLN 061, FLN 062, FLN 063 and FLN 064)* (SCCAS Report No. 2006/54)

Bayley, J., Dungworth, D. and Paynter, S., 2001 *Archaeometallurgy*, Centre for Archaeol. Guidelines (London, English Heritage)

Bayliss, A., Høilund Nielsen, K., Hines, J., McCormac, G. and Scull, C., forthcoming *Anglo-Saxon Graves and Grave-Goods of the sixth and seventh Centuries: a Chronological Framework*, (Leeds, Society for Medieval Archaeololgy)

Bender Jørgensen, L., 1992 *North European Textiles until AD 1000* (Aarhus, Aarhus University Press)

Bethell, P. and Máté, I., 1989 'The use of phosphate analysis in archaeology: a critique', in Henderson, J. (ed.), *Scientific Analysis in Archaeology*, Oxford University Committee for Archaeology, Monograph 19, 1–29

Bishop, B. and Proctor, J., 2011 *Settlement, Ceremony and Industry on Mousehold Heath. Excavations at Laurel Farm (Phase II), Broadland Business Park, Thorpe St Andrew, Norfolk*, PCA Monogr. 13 (London)

Blagg, T., Plouviez, J. and Tester, A., 2004 *Excavations at a Large Romano-British Settlement at Hacheston, Suffolk, 1973–74*, E. Anglian Archaeol.106

Blair, J., 1995 'Anglo-Saxon Pagan Shrines and their Prototypes', *Anglo-Saxon Stud. Archaeol. Hist.* 8, 1–28

Blakelock, E. and McDonnell, G., 2007 — 'A review of metallographic analyses of early medieval knives', *Historical Metallurgy* 41, 40–56

Boddington, A., 1987 — 'From bones to population: the problem of numbers', in Boddington, A., Garland, N. and Janaway, R.C. (eds), *Death Decay and Reconstruction*, 180–97 (Manchester, Manchester University Press)

Boeles, P.C.J.A., 1951 — *Friesland tot de Elfde Eeuw* ('S-Gravenhage, Nijhoff)

Böhme, H.W., 1974 — *Germanische Grabfunde des 4. bis 5. Jahrhunderts zwischen Unterer Elbe und Loire (Studien zur Chronologie und Bevölkerungsgeschichte)* (Munich, Beck)

Böhner, K., 1958 — *Die Fränkischen Altertümer des Trierer Landes*, Germanische Denkmäler der Völkerwanderungszeit, serie B1 (Berlin)

Boulter, S.P., 1996a — *Flixton Park, Flixton (FLN 013) Assessment Report* (SCCAS Report No. 96/13)

Boulter, S.P., 1996b — *Flixton Park, Flixton (FLN 013), An Assessment of the Archaeological Deposits Identified During Topsoil Stripping of Area 4b* (SCCAS Report No. 96/65)

Boulter, S.P., 1997 — *Flixton Park, Flixton (FLN 053), Preliminary Record of Archaeological Deposits Recorded during Soil Stripping in Area 5* (SCCAS Report No. 97/46)

Boulter, S.P., 1998 — *RMC Atlas Aggregates Ltd Quarry, Flixton Park, Flixton (FLN 013), Archaeological Excavation and Monitoring Archive Report* (SCCAS Report No. 97/53)

Boulter, S.P., 2004 — *Tarmac Quarry, Flixton, Suffolk, Record of an Archaeological Evaluation* (SCCAS Report No. 2003/107)

Boulter, S.P., 2005 — *Handford Road, Ipswich (IPS 280), Archaeological Assessment Report (Volume 1: Text)* (SCCAS Report No. 2004/87)

Boulter, S.P., 2006a — *A Reassessment of, and Updated Project Design for the Archaeological Deposits Excavated at Flixton Park Quarry Under the Site Codes FLN 013 and FLN 053; Also Includes FLN 008 and part of FLN 062* (SCCAS Report No. 2006/12)

Boulter, S.P., 2006b — *Assessment 2: An assessment of the Archaeology Recorded in New Phases 5, 6, 7 (a and b), 9, 11 and 12 of Flixton Park Quarry (FLN 056, FLN 057, FLN 058, FLN 061, FLN 062, FLN 063 and FLN 064)* (SCCAS Report No. 2006/54)

Boulter, S.P. and Anderson, S., 2000 — *Flixton Park Quarry, Flixton, An Assessment of the Archaeology Recorded in the Areas Excavated as FLN 013 and FLN 053* (Version 1) (SCCAS Report No. 2000/21)

Bouts, W. and Pot, Tj., 1989 — 'Computerized recording and analysis of excavated human dental remains' in Roberts, C. A., Lee, F. and Bintliff, J. (eds), *Burial Archaeology: current research, methods and developments*, Brit. Archaeol. Rep. British Ser. 211 (Oxford)

Boyle, A., Dodd, A., Miles, D. and Mudd, A., 1995 — *Two Oxfordshire Anglo-Saxon Cemeteries: Berinsfield and Didcot*, Thames Valley Landscapes Monogr. 8 (Oxford, Oxford Archaeological Unit)

Boyle, A., Jennings, D., Miles, D. and Palmer, S., 1998 — *The Anglo-Saxon Cemetery at Butler's Field, Lechlade, Gloucestershire. Volume 1: Prehistoric and Roman activity and Anglo-Saxon Grave Catalogue*, Thames Valley Landscapes Monogr. 10 (Oxford, Oxford Archaeological Unit)

Bradley, R., 1998 — *The Significance of Monuments* (London, Routledge)

Bradley, R., 2000a — *An Archaeology of Natural Places* (London, Routledge)

Bradley, R., 2000b — *The Good Stones: A New Investigation of the Clava Cairns* (Edinburgh, Society of Antiquaries of Scotland)

Brennand, M. and Taylor, M., 2003 — 'The survey and excavation of a Bronze Age timber circle at Holme-next-the Sea, Norfolk, 1998–9', *Proc. Prehist. Soc.* 69, 1–84

Briscoe, D., in archive — *Flixton, Suffolk, FLN 008 (Flixton Quarry) – Archive Site Ref: SUF-283*. Report for the Archive of Anglo-Saxon Pottery Stamps and Suffolk C.C. Archaeological Service

Bronk Ramsey, C., 1995 — 'Radicarbon calibration and analysis of stratigraphy', *Radiocarbon* 36, 425–30

Bronk Ramsey, C., 1998 — 'Probability and dating', *Radiocarbon* 40, 461–74

Bronk Ramsey, C., 2001 — 'Development of the radiocarbon dating program', *Radiocarbon* 43, 355–63

Brothwell, D., 1981 — *Digging up Bones* (London, British Museum of Natural History/Oxford University Press)

Brown, D., 1977 — 'Firesteels and pursemounts again', *Bonner Jahrbucher*, 177, 451–77

Brown, M.A., 1998 — 'The Feast Hall in Anglo-Saxon Society', in Carlin, M. and Rosenthal, J.T. (eds), *Food and Eating in Medieval Europe*, 1–13 (London and Rio Grande, Ohio, The Hambledon Press)

Bruce-Mitford, R. L. S., 1978 — *The Sutton Hoo Ship Burial, 2: Arms, Armour and Regalia* (London, British Museum)

Bruce-Mitford, R., 1983 — *The Sutton Hoo Ship Burial, 3: Silver, Hanging Bowls, Drinking Vessels, Containers, Musical Instruments, Textiles, Minor Objects* (London, British Museum)

Brugmann, B., 2004 — *Glass Beads from Early Anglo-Saxon Graves* (Oxford, Oxbow)

Brugmann, B., 2010 — 'Beads', in Annable, F.K. and Eagles, B.N., *The Anglo-Saxon Cemetery at Blacknall Field, Pewsey, Wiltshire*, Wiltshire Archaeological and Natural History Society Monograph No. 4, 42–50 (Devizes)

Brugmann, B., forthcoming a — 'Beads', in Walton Rogers, P., forthcoming, *Tyttel's* halh, *the Early Anglo-Saxon site at Tittleshall, Norfolk: Bacton to King's Lynn Gas Pipeline Vol. 2*, E. Anglian Archaeol.

Brugmann, B., forthcoming b — 'Beads', in Parfitt, K. and Anderson, T., *The Anglo-Saxon Cemetery at Dover Buckland, Kent. The 1994 Excavations*, Canterbury Archaeol. Trust Monogr., new series (Canterbury)

Bulleid, A. and Gray, H. St George, 1911 — *The Glastonbury Lake Village. A Full Description of the Excavations and the relics discovered, 1892–1907* (The Glastonbury Antiquarian Society)

Butler, C., 2005 — *Prehistoric Flintwork* (Stroud, Tempus)

Cameron, E., 2000 — *Sheaths and Scabbards in England AD 400–1100*, Brit. Archaeol. Rep. Brit. Ser. 301 (Oxford)

Carver, M.O.H., 1998 — *Sutton Hoo: Burial Ground of Kings?* (London, British Museum)

Carver, M.O.H., 2005 — *Sutton Hoo: A Seventh-Century Princely Burial Ground and its Context* (London, British Museum)

Carver, M., Hills, C. and Scheschkewitz, J., 2009 — *Wasperton: A Roman, British and Anglo-Saxon Community in Central England*, Anglo-Saxon Studies 11 (Woodbridge, Boydell)

Catling, D. and Grayson, J., 1982 — *Identification of Vegetable Fibres* (London, Chapman and Hall)

Chadwick Hawkes, S. and Grainger, G., 2006, — *The Anglo-Saxon Cemetery at Finglesham, Kent*, Oxford University School of Archaeology Monograph 64 (Oxford)

Chadwick Hawkes, S., 2000 — 'The Anglo-Saxon cemetery of Bifrons in the parish of Patrixbourne, East Kent', in *Anglo-Saxon Studies in Archaeology and History*, 11, 1–94

Chamberlain, A., 2003 — 'The significance of the orientation', in Brennand, M. and Taylor, M. 'The survey and excavation of a Bronze Age timber circle at Holme-next-the Sea, Norfolk, 1998–9', *Proc. Prehist. Soc.* 69, 1–84

Chatwin, P.B, 1925 — 'Anglo-Saxon finds at Warwick', *Antiquaries J.* 5, 268–72

Clark, A.J., 1996 — *Seeing beneath the Soil*, 2nd ed. (London, Batsford)

Clark, J.D.G., 1934 — 'Derivative forms of the petit tranchet in Britain', *Archaeol. J.* 91, 34–58

Clarke, D.V., Cowie, T.G. and Foxon, A., 1985 — *Symbols of Power at the Time of Stonehenge* (Edinburgh, HMSO)

Clarke, G., 1979 — *The Roman Cemetery at Lankhills*, Winchester Studies, 3 (Oxford, Clarendon)

Cleal, R., 1984 — 'The Later Neolithic in Eastern England', in Bradley, R. and Gardiner J. (eds), *Neolithic Studies, A Review of Some Current Research*, Brit. Archaeol. Rep. Brit. Ser. 133 (Oxford)

Cleal, R., 1993 — 'Pottery and Fired Clay', in Healy, F., Cleal, R. and Kinnes, I., *Excavations on Redgate Hill, Hunstanton, 1970 and 1971*, E. Anglian Archaeol. 57

Cleal, R., 1999 — 'The What, Where, When and Why of Grooved Ware', in Cleal, R. and MacSween, A. (eds) *Grooved Ware in Britain and Ireland*, Neolithic Studies Group Seminar Papers 3 (Oxford, Oxbow)

Clough, T.H.K. and Green, B., 1973 — 'Gazetteer of Anglo-Saxon cremations and burials in East Anglia', in Myres, J.N.L. and Green, B., *The Anglo-Saxon Cemeteries of Caistor-by-Norwich and Markshall, Norfolk*, 258–63 (London, Soc. Antiq. Lond.)

Coatsworth, E., Fitzgerald, M., Leahy, K. and Owen-Crocker, G., 1996 — 'Anglo-Saxon Textiles from Cleatham, Humberside', *Textile History* 27(1), 5–17

Cockayne, O., 1864–6 — *Leechdoms, Wortcunning and Starcraft of Early England* (London, HMSO)

Cook, A. and Dacre, 1985 — *Excavations at Portway, Andover, 1973–1975*, Oxford Committee for Archaeology Monogr. 4 (Oxford)

Craddock, J., 1979 — 'The Anglo-Saxon cemetery at Saxonbury, Lewes, East Sussex', *Sussex Archaeol. Collect.* 117, 85–102

Craven, J., forthcoming — *New Executive Villas, Center Parcs, Elveden, ELV 067* (SCCAS report)

Crawford, S., 1993 — 'Children, life and the afterlife in Anglo-Saxon England', *Anglo-Saxon Stud. Archaeol. Hist.* 6, 83–91

Crowfoot, E., 1989 — 'The textiles', in Adams, B. and Jackson, D., 'The Anglo-Saxon Cemetery at Wakerley, Northamptonshire; Excavations by Mr D. Jackson', *Northamptonshire Archaeol.* 22, 69–183

Crowfoot, E., 2001 — 'The textiles', in Filmer-Sankey, W. and Pestell, T., *Snape Anglo Saxon Cemetery: Excavations and Surveys 1824–1992*, E. Anglian Archaeol. 95, 207–12

Crowfoot, E. and Chadwick Hawkes, S., 1967 — 'Early Anglo-Saxon gold braids', *Medieval Archaeol.* 2, 42–86, 109–10

Crowfoot, E., 2009 — 'The textiles', in Hirst, S.and Clark, D., *Excavations at Mucking: Volume 3, The Anglo-Saxon Cemeteries*, part i, 428-436 (London, Museum of London Archaeology)

Crowfoot, E., Edwards, G. and Watson, J., 2005 — Organic material associated with metalwork from the early Anglo-Saxon cemetery at Blacknall Field, Pewsey, Wiltshire (Centre for Archaeology Reports, 31/2005)

Crowther, J., 1997 — 'Soil phosphate surveys: critical approaches to sampling, analysis and interpretation', *Archaeol. Prospection* 4, 93–102

D'Amato, R. and Sumner, G., 2005 — *Roman Military Clothing (3). AD 400–640, Men-at-Arms* (Oxford, Osprey)

Darvill, T., 1997 — 'Ever increasing circles: the sacred geographies of Stonehenge and its landscape', in Cunliffe, B. and Renfrew, C., *Science and Stonehenge*, 167–202 (Oxford, British Academy/Oxford University Press)

Davis, S., 1992 — *A Rapid Method for Recording Information about Mammal Bones from Archaeological Sites* (Ancient Monuments Lab. Report 19/92)

Dick, W.A. and Tabatabai, M.A., 1977 — 'An alkaline oxidation method for the determination of total phosphorus in soils', *J. Soil Sci. Soc. America* 41, 511–14

Dickinson, T.M., 1976 — *The Anglo-Saxon Burial Sites of the Upper Thames Region, and their Bearing on the History of Wessex, circa AD 400–700* (unpubl. DPhil thesis, Univ. of Oxford)

Dickinson, T.M., 1982 — 'Fowler's Type G penannular brooches reconsidered', *Medieval Archaeol.* 26, 41–68

Dickinson, T.M., 1993 — 'An Anglo-Saxon 'cunning woman' from Bidford-on-Avon', in Carver, M.O.H. (ed.), *In Search of Cult: in Honour of Philip Rahtz*, 45–54 (Woodbridge, Boydell)

Dickinson, T. and Härke, H., 1993 — *Early Anglo-Saxon Shields*, *Archaeologia* 110 (London, Soc. Antiq. Lond.)

Down, A. and Welch, M.G., 1990 — *Apple Down and the Mardens*, Chichester Excavations 7 (Chichester)

Drinkall, G. and Foreman, M., 1998 — *The Anglo-Saxon Cemetery at Castledyke South, Barton-on-Humber*, Sheffield Excavation Reports 6 (Sheffield)

Dymond, D. and Martin, E., 1999 — *An Historic Atlas of Suffolk*, 3rd ed. (Lavenham, Lavenham Press)

Edlin, H.L., 1949 — *Woodland Crafts in Britain* (London, Batsford)

English Heritage, 1991 — *Management of Archaeological Projects 2* (London, English Heritage)

Evison, V.I., 1979 — *Wheel-Thrown Pottery in Anglo-Saxon Graves* (London, Royal Archaeological Institute)

Evison, V.I., 1982 — 'Anglo-Saxon glass claw beakers', *Archaeologia* 107, 43–76

Evison, V.I., 1987 — *Dover: The Buckland Anglo-Saxon Cemetery*, HBMC Archaeological Report 3 (London)

Evison, V.I., 1988 — 'Some Vendel, Viking and Saxon glass', in Hårdh, B., Larsson, L., Olavsson, D. and Petré, R. (eds), *Trade and Exchange in Prehistory*, Acta Archaeologica Lundensia Series in 8 no. 16, 237–45.

Evison, V.I., 1994a — *An Anglo-Saxon Cemetery at Great Chesterford, Essex*, Counc. Brit. Archaeol. Res. Rep. 91

Evison, V.I., 1994b — 'Anglo-Saxon glass from cremations', in Hills, C., Penn, K. and Rickett, R., *Spong Hill Part V, Catalogue of Cremations (Nos. 2800–3334)*, E. Anglian Archaeol. 67, 23–30.

Evison, V.I., 2000 — 'Glass vessels in England, AD 400–1100', in Price, J. (ed.), *Glass in Britain and Ireland AD 350–1100*, British Museum Occasional Paper No. 127, 47–104 (London)

Evison, V.I. and Hill, P., 1996 — *Two Anglo-Saxon Cemeteries at Beckford, Hereford and Worcester*, Counc. Brit. Archaeol. Res. Rep. 103

Faussett, B., 1856 — *Inventorium Sepulchrale: An Account of Some Antiquities dug up at Gilton, Kingston, Sibertswold, Barfriston, Beakesbourne, Chartham, and Crundale, in the County of Kent, from AD 1757 to AD 1773* (London, privately published)

Fell, C., 1984 — *Women in Anglo-Saxon England* (Oxford, Blackwell)

Fell, V. and Watson, J., 2007 — *Flixton Quarry, Suffolk, Investigative Conservation of the Anglo-Saxon Cemetery material from Sites FLN 053 and FLN 062.* Archaeological Conservation Report, English Heritage, Research Dept. Rpt. Series no. 43/2007

Filmer-Sankey, W., 1992 — 'Snape Anglo-Saxon cemetery: the current state of knowledge', in Carver, M.O.H. (ed.), *The Age of Sutton Hoo: The Seventh Century in North-Western Europe*, 39–52 (Woodbridge, Boydell)

Filmer-Sankey, W. and Pestell, T., 2001 — *Snape Anglo Saxon Cemetery: Excavations and Surveys 1824–1992,* E. Anglian Archaeol. 95

Forbes, R.J., 1964 — *Studies in Ancient Technology* IV (2nd ed.) (Leiden, Brill)

Fowler, E., 1960 — 'The origins and development of the penannular brooch in Europe', *Proc. Prehist. Soc.* 26, 149–77

French, C.A.I., 1991 — 'Excavation of Deeping St Nicholas Barrow Site 28, Lincolnshire', *Antiquity* 65, 580–82

French, C.A.I., 2008 — *Flixton Quarry, Suffolk: Micromorphological analysis of the pre-long barrow palaeosol* (unpubl. assessment report for SCCAS)

Frere, S.S., 1957 — 'Late Roman objects from Charlton, Hampshire', *Antiq. J.* 37, 218–20

Friedenson, V. and Friedenson, S., 1987 — 'Anglo-Saxon pottery: stamps and fabrics', in Green, B., Rogerson, A. and White, S., *The Anglo-Saxon Cemetery at Morning Thorpe, Norfolk. Volume I: Catalogue*, E. Anglian Archaeol. 36, 13–15

Gale, R. and Cutler, D., 2000 — *Plants in Archaeology* (Kew, Royal Botanic Gardens)

Garrow, D., 2006 — *Pits, Settlement and Deposition during the Neolithic and Early Bronze Age in East Anglia*, Brit. Archaeol. Rep. Brit. Ser. 414 (Oxford)

Garwood, P., 1999 — 'Grooved Ware in Southern Britain; Chronology and Interpretation', in Cleal, R. and MacSween, A. (eds), *Grooved Ware in Britain and Ireland*, Neolithic Studies Group Seminar Papers 3 (Oxford, Oxbow)

Geake, H., 1997 — *The Use of Grave Goods in Conversion-Period England, c.600–c.850,* Brit. Archaeol. Rep. Brit. Ser. 261 (Oxford)

Geake, H., 2003 — 'The control of burial practice in Anglo-Saxon England', in Carver, M.O.H. (ed), *The Cross goes North: Processes of Conversion in Northern Europe, AD 300–1300*, 259–69 (York, York Medieval Press)

Geijer, A., 1938 — *Birka III: Die Textilfunde aus den Gräbern* (Uppsala, Almqvist and Wiksells)

Gibson, A., 1998 — *Stonehenge and Timber Circles* (Stroud, Tempus)

Gibson, A., 1999 — 'Grooved Ware and timber circles. Interpretation', in Cleal, R. and MacSween, A. (eds), *Grooved Ware in Britain and Ireland*, Neolithic Studies Group Seminar Papers 3 (Oxford, Oxbow)

Godwin, H., 1956 — *The History of the British Flora* (Cambridge, Cambridge University Press)

Going, C.J., 1987 — *The Mansio and other Sites in the South-eastern Sector of Caesaromagus: the Roman pottery*, Chelmsford Archaeol. Trust Rep. 3.2/Counc. Brit. Archaeol. Res. Rep. 62

Green, B. and Rogerson, A., 1978 — *The Anglo-Saxon Cemetery at Bergh Apton, Norfolk*, E. Anglian Archaeol. 7

Green, B., Rogerson, A. and White, S.G., 1987 — *The Anglo-Saxon Cemetery at Morning Thorpe, Norfolk*, E. Anglian Archaeol. 36

Green, S., 1984 — 'Flint arrowheads: typology and interpretation', *The Newsletter of the Lithic Studies Society* No. 5

Greep, S.J., 1994 — 'Antler roundel pendants from Britain and the North-Western Roman provinces', *Britannia*, 25, 79–97, pls II–IV

Gregory, T., 1992 — *Excavations in Thetford, 1980–1982, Fison Way, Volume One,.* E. Anglian Archaeol. 53

Grierson, S., 1986 — *The Colour Cauldron: The History and Use of Natural Dyes in Scotland* (Perth, Newmiln)

Griffiths, B., 2006 — *Aspects of Anglo-Saxon Magic* (Hockwold-cum-Wilton, Anglo-Saxon Books)

Hamerow, H., 1993 — *Excavations at Mucking Volume 2: The Anglo-Saxon Settlement* (London, English Heritage/ British Museum)

Hansen, E., 1990 — *Tablet Weaving: History, Techniques, Colours, Patterns* (Højbjerg, Hovedland)

Härke, H., 1988 — 'Remarks and Observations on the weapons', in West, S., *The Anglo-Saxon Cemetery at Westgarth Gardens, Bury St Edmunds, Suffolk*, E. Anglian Archaeol. 38, 11–14

Härke, H., 1989 — 'Knives in early Saxon burial: blade length and age at death', *Medieval Archaeol.* 33, 144–8

Härke, H., 1992a *Angelsächsische Waffengräber des 5. bis 7. Jahrhunderts*, Zeitschrift für Archäologie des Mittelalters, Beiheft 6 (Cologne)

Härke, H., 1992b 'Changing symbols in a changing society: the Anglo-Saxon weapon burial rite in the seventh century', in Carver, M.O.H. (ed.), *The Age of Sutton Hoo: The Seventh Century in North-Western Europe*, 149–65 (Woodbridge, Boydell)

Härke, H., 1995 'Weapon Burials and Knives', in Boyle, A., Dodd, A., Miles, D. and Mudd, A., *Berinsfield and Didcot. Two Oxfordshire Anglo-Saxon Cemeteries*, Thames Valley Landscapes Monograph 8, (Oxford) 67–75

Härke, H., 1997 'Early Anglo-Saxon social structure', in Hines, J. (ed), *The Anglo-Saxons from the Migration Period to the Eighth Century: an Ethnographic Perspective*. (Woodbridge, Boydell) 125–70

Hartmann, M., 1981 *Romanen und Alemannen: der Aargau im Frühmittelalter* (Brugg, Vindonissa-Museum)

Haughton, C. and Powlesland, D., 1999 *West Heslerton, The Anglian Cemetery* (2 vols) (West Heslerton, The Landscape Research Centre)

Hawkes, C.F. and Hull, M.R., 1947 *Camulodunum*, Rep. Res. Comm. Soc. Antiq. Lond. No. 14 (London, Soc. Antiq. Lond.)

Hawkes, S.C., 1973 'The dating and social significance of the burials in the Polhill cemetery', in Philp, B., *Excavations in West Kent 1960–1970*, 186–201 (Dover, Kent. Archaeological Rescue Unit)

Healy, F., 1988 *The Anglo-Saxon Cemetery at Spong Hill, North Elmham, Part VI: Occupation during the Seventh to Second Millennia*, E. Anglian Archaeol. 39

Heaney, S. (trans.), 1999 *Beowulf: A New Translation* (London, Faber and Faber)

Heirmann, K., 2006 *Early and Middle Pleistocene sedimentology and Lithostratigraphy at Flixton, northern Suffolk UK* (unpubl. MSc project submission, Royal Holloway, Univ. of London)

Heron, C., 2001 'Geochemical prospecting', in Brothwell, D.R. and Pollard, A.M. (eds), *Handbook of Archaeological Sciences*, 565–73 (Chichester, Wiley)

Higham, N. (ed.), 2007 *Britons in Anglo-Saxon England* (Woodbridge, Boydell)

Hills, C., 1977 *The Anglo-Saxon Cemetery at Spong Hill, North Elmham, Part I: Catalogue of Cremations*, E. Anglian Archaeol. 6

Hills, C. and Penn, K., 1981 *The Anglo-Saxon Cemetery at Spong Hill, North Elmham, Part II: Catalogue of Cremations*, E. Anglian Archaeol. 11

Hills, C., Penn, K. and Rickett, R., 1984 *The Anglo-Saxon Cemetery at Spong Hill, North Elmham, Part III, Catalogue of Inhumations*, E. Anglian Archaeol. 21

Hills, C., Penn, K. and Rickett, R., 1987 *The Anglo-Saxon Cemetery at Spong Hill, North Elmham, Part IV, Catalogue of Cremations*, E. Anglian Archaeol. 34

Hills, C. and Wade-Martins, P., 1976 'The Anglo-Saxon Cemetery at the Paddocks, Swaffham', in *Norfolk*, E. Anglian Archaeol. 2, 1–44

Hines, J., 1984 *The Scandinavian Character of Anglian England in the Pre-Viking Period*, Brit. Archaeol. Rep. Brit. Ser. 124 (Oxford)

Hines, J., 1993 *Clasps – Hektespenner – Agraffen: Anglo-Scandinavian Clasps of Classes A–C of the Third to Sixth Centuries AD* (Stockholm, Almqvist and Wiksell)

Hines, J., 1997 *A New Corpus of Anglo-Saxon Great Square-Headed Brooches*, Rep. Res. Comm. Soc. Antiq. 51 (London, Soc. Antiq. Lond.)

Hines, J., 1999 'The sixth-century transition in Anglian England: an analysis of female graves from Cambridgeshire', in Hines, J., Høilund Nielsen, K., and Siegmund, F. (eds), *The Pace of Change: Studies in Early-Medieval Chronology*, Cardiff Studies in Archaeology, 65–79 (Oxford, Oxbow)

Hines, J., 2002 'Lies, damned lies and the *curriculum vitae*: reflections on statistics and the populations of Early Anglo-Saxon inhumation cemeteries' in Lucy, S. and Reynolds, A., *Burial in Early Medieval England and Wales*, Soc. Medieval Archaeol. Monograph Ser. 17, 88–102 (London)

Hinton, D.A., 2000 *A Smith in Lindsey: The Anglo-Saxon Grave at Tattershall Thorpe, Lincolnshire*, Soc. Medieval. Archaeol. Monograph Ser. 16 (London)

Hirst, S.M., 1985 *An Anglo-Saxon Inhumation Cemetery at Sewerby, East Yorkshire*, York Univ. Archaeol. Publ. 4 (York)

Hjärthner-Holdar, E., Lamm, K. and Magnus, B., 2002 'Metalworking and central places', in Hårdh, B. and Larsson, L. (eds), 'Central Places in the Migration and the Merovingian Periods', *Papers from the 52nd Sachsensymposium*, Lund, August 2001,159–84

Hogarth, A.C., 1973 'Structural features in Anglo-Saxon graves', *Archaeol. J.* 130, 104–19

Høilund Nielsen, K., 1997 'The schism of Anglo-Saxon chronology', in Kjeld, J. and Høilund Nielsen, K. (eds), *Burial and Society: The Chronological and Social Analysis of Archaeological Burial Data*, 71–99 (Aarhus, Aarhus University Press)

Huggett, J.W., 1988 'Imported grave-goods and the Early Anglo-Saxon economy', *Medieval Archaeol.* 32, 63–96

Joffroy, R., 1974 *Le Cimetière de Lavoye (Meuse): Nécropole Mérovingienne* (Paris, Picard)

Johnson, A.E., 1996 *Land at Flixton Park, Waveney District, Suffolk, Topsoil Magnetic Susceptibility, Gradiometer and Woodland Survey* (Oxford Archaeotechnics Limited unpubl. report for RMC (UK) Limited)

Kazanski, M., 2002 *La Necropole Gallo-Romaine et Merovingienne de Breny (Aisne)*, Europe medievale 4 (Montagnac, Monique Mergoil)

Kinnes, I., Gibson, A., Ambers, J., Bowman, S., Leese, M. and Boast, R., 1991 'Radiocarbon dating and British Beakers: the British Museum programme', *Scott. Archaeol. Rev.* 8, 35–78

Koch, U., 2001 *Das Alamannisch-Fränkische Gräberfeld bei Pleidelsheim*, Forschungen und Berichte zur Vor- und Frühgeschichte in Baden-Württemberg 60 (Stuttgart)

Krogman, W., 1978 *The Human Skeleton in Forensic Medicine* (Illinois, C.C. Thomas)

Lane, A. and Campbell, E., 2000 *Dunadd. An Early Dalriadic Capital*, Cardiff Studies in Archaeology (Oxford)

Lang, J., forthcoming, 'Metallographic examination of spearheads from Graves 264, 299, 323 and 393A', in Parfitt, K. and

Anderson, T., *The Anglo-Saxon Cemetery at Dover Buckland, Kent. Excavations 1997*

Lee, C., 2007 *Feasting the Dead: Food and Drink in Anglo-Saxon Burial Rituals*, Anglo-Saxon Studies 9 (Woodbridge, Boydell)

Leeds, E.T. and Pocock, M., 1971 'A survey of the Anglo-Saxon cruciform brooches of florid type', *Medieval Archaeol.* 15, 13–36

Leeds, E.T., 1945 The distribution of the Angles and Saxons archaeologically considered, *Archaeologia,* 91, 1–106

Lethbridge, T.C., 1931 *Recent Excavations in Anglo-Saxon Cemeteries in Cambridgeshire and Suffolk* (Cambridge, Cambridge Antiq. Soc.)

Litten, J., 1991 *The English Way of Death: The Common Funeral since 1450* (London, Hale)

Lloyd-Jones, J., 1997 'Calculating bio-distance using dental morphology', in Anderson, S. and Boyle, K. (eds), *Computing and Statistics in Osteoarchaeology* (Oxford, Oxbow)

Longworth, I., 1971 'The Neolithic Pottery', in Wainwright, G. J.and Longworth, I. H., *Durrington Walls Excavations 1966*, 68 (London, Soc. Antiq. Lond.)

Lucy, S., 1994 'Children in early medieval cemeteries', *Archaeological Review from Cambridge* 13 (2), 21–34

Lucy, S., 2000 *The Anglo-Saxon Way of Death* (Stroud, Sutton)

Lucy, S., Tipper, J. and Dickens, A., 2009 *The Anglo-Saxon Settlement and Cemetery at Bloodmoor Hill, Carlton Colville, Suffolk.* E. Anglian Archaeol. 131

Lyons, A.L., 2000 'The Roman pottery', in Bates, S., 'Excavations at Quidney Farm, Saham Toney, Norfolk 1995', *Britannia* 31, 201–37

MacDonald, P., Manning, W.H. and Riddler, I.D., 2008 'The Small Finds', in Bennett, P., Clark, P., Hicks, A., Rady, J. and Riddler, I., *At the Great Crossroads. Prehistoric, Roman and Medieval Discoveries on the Isle of Thanet 1994–95*, Canterbury Archaeol. Trust Occ. Pap. 4, 190–233 (Canterbury)

MacGregor, A. and Bolick, E., 1993 *Ashmolean Museum, Oxford: A Summary Catalogue of the Anglo-Saxon Collections (Non-Ferrous Metals)* (Oxford)

Malim, T. and Hines, J., 1998 *The Anglo-Saxon Cemetery at Edix Hill (Barrington A), Cambridgeshire*, Counc. Brit. Archaeol. Res. Rep. 112

Manning, W.H., 1985 *Catalogue of the Romano-British Iron Tools, Fittings and Weapons in the British Museum* (London, British Museum)

Martin, E., 1988a *Burgh: The Iron Age and Roman Enclosure*, E. Anglian Archaeol. 40

Martin, E., 1988b 'The Iron Age', in Dymond, D. and Martin, E., *An Historical Atlas of Suffolk* (Lavenham, Lavenham Press)

Martin, E., 1993 *Settlements on Hill-tops: Seven Prehistoric Sites in Suffolk*, E. Anglian Archaeol. 65

Martin, M., 1997 'Wealth and treasure in the west, 4th–7th century', in Webster, L. and Brown, M., *The Transformation of the Roman World, AD 400–900*, 48–66 (London, British Museum)

Marzinzik, S., 2003 *Early Anglo-Saxon Belt Buckles (late 5th to early 8th centuries AD): their Classification and Context*, Brit. Archaeol. Rep. Brit. Ser. 357 (Oxford)

Mattingly, D. and Jones, G.D.B., 1990 *Atlas of Roman Britain* (Oxford, Blackwell)

McKinley, J.I., 2004 'Compiling a skeletal inventory: cremated human bone', in Brickley, M. and McKinley, J.I. (eds), *Guidelines to the Standards for Recording Human Remains*, IFA Paper No. 7

McKinley, J.I., 1994 *The Anglo-Saxon Cemetery at Spong Hill, North Elmham Part VIII: The Cremations*, E. Anglian Archaeol. 69

Meaney, A.L. and Hawkes, S.C., 1970 *The Anglo-Saxon Cemeteries at Winnall, Winchester, Hampshire*, Soc. Medieval Archaeol. Monogr. Ser. 4 (London)

Meaney, A., 1981 *Anglo-Saxon Amulets and Curing Stones*, Brit. Archaeol. Rep. Brit. Ser. 96 (Oxford)

Meaney, A., 1998 'Girdle groups: reconstruction and comparative study', in Malim, T. and Hines, J., *The Anglo-Saxon Cemetery at Edix Hill (Barrington A), Cambridgeshire*, Counc. Brit. Archaeol. Res. Rep. 112, 268–75

Mercer, R., 1981 *Grimes Graves, Norfolk; Excavations 1971–72. Volume 1*, Dept. of the Environment Report 11 (London)

MGC, 1992 *Standards in the Museum Care of Archaeological Collections* (London, Museums and Galleries Commission)

Mitchell, A., 1974 *A Field Guide to the Trees of Britain and Northern Europe* (London, Collins)

Morris, C.A., 1994 'Finds connected with wooden artefacts, woodworking and other tools', in Hills, C., Penn, K. and Rickett, R., *Spong Hill Part V, Catalogue of Cremations*, E. Anglian Archaeol. 67, 30–5

Morris, C.A., 2000 *Wood and Woodworking in Anglo-Scandinavian and Medieval York*, The Archaeology of York 17/13 (York, Counc. Brit. Archaeol./York Archaeol. Trust)

Mortimer, C., 1990 *Some Aspects of Early Medieval Copper-alloy Technology, as illustrated by a study of the Anglian Cruciform Brooch* (unpubl. PhD thesis, Univ. of Oxford)

Mould, Q., 1993 'Structural fittings, iron', in Darling, M.J. and Gurney, D., *Caister-on-Sea. Excavations by Charles Green, 1951–1955*, E. Anglian Archaeol. 60, 103–4

Myres, J.N.L. and Green, B., 1973 *The Anglo-Saxon Cemeteries of Caistor-by-Norwich and Markshall, Norfolk* (London, Soc. Antiq. Lond.)

Myres, J., 1977 *A Corpus of Anglo-Saxon Pottery of the Pagan Period* (Cambridge, Cambridge University Press)

Newman, J., 2005 'Survey in the Deben Valley', in Carver, M.O.H., *Sutton Hoo: A Seventh-Century Princely Burial Ground and its Context*, 477–87 (London, British Museum)

Owen, G.R., 1979 'Wynflæd's wardrobe', *Anglo-Saxon England* 8, 195–222

Panseri, C., Carino, C. and Leoni, M., 1957 'Richerche metallografiche sopra alcune lame Etrusche di acciaio', in Panseri, C. (ed.), *Documenti e contribute per la storia della metallurgia, Quaderno II*, Asociazione Italiana di Metallurgia, Milano, 19–23

Parfitt, K. and Brugmann, B., 1997 *The Anglo-Saxon Cemetery on Mill Hill, Deal, Kent*, Soc. Medieval. Archaeol. Monogr. Ser., 14. (London)

Parker Pearson, M., 1996 'Food, Fertility and Front Doors in the First Millenium BC', in Champion, T.C. and Collis, J.R (eds), *The Iron Age in Britain: Recent Trends* (Sheffield, J.R. Collis Publications)

Parker Pearson, M, Cleal, R., Marshall, P., Needham, S., Pollard, J., Richards, C., Ruggles, C., Sheridan, A., Thomas, J., Tilley, C., Welham, K., Chamberlain, A., Chenery, C., Evans, J., Knusel, C., Linford, N., Martin, L., Montgomery, J., Payne, A. and Richards, M., 2007 'The age of Stonehenge', *Antiquity* 81, 617–39

PCRG, 2010 *The Study of Prehistoric Pottery: General Policies and Guidelines for Analysis and Publication*, Prehistoric Ceramic Res. Group, Occ. Pap. No 1–2. 3rd edn. http://www.pcrg.org.uk/News_pages/PCRG Guidelines 3rd Edition (2010).pdf

Penn, K., 1998 *An Anglo-Saxon Cemetery at Oxborough, West Norfolk*, E. Anglian Archaeol. 5

Penn, K., 2000 *Norwich Southern Bypass, Part II: Anglo-Saxon Cemetery at Harford Farm, Caistor St Edmund*, E. Anglian Archaeol. 92

Penn, K. and Ashley, S., 2003 'Two Early Saxon Cemeteries in south Norfolk', *Norfolk Archaeology* 44, 304–15

Penn, K., and Brugmann, B., 2007 *Aspects of Anglo-Saxon Inhumation Burial: Morning Thorpe, Spong Hill, Bergh Apton and Westgarth Gardens*, E. Anglian Archaeol. 119

Percival, S., 2004 *The Deposition of Grooved Ware pottery at Flixton Park, Suffolk* (unpubl. MA thesis, Univ. of Southampton)

Plunkett, S., 1994 *Guardians of the Gipping. Anglo-Saxon Treasures from Hadleigh Road, Ipswich* (Ipswich, Ipswich Borough Council)

Plunkett, S., 2005 *Suffolk In Anglo–Saxon Times* (Stroud, Tempus)

Pollard, J., 1995 'The Durrington 68 Timber Circle: A Forgotten Late Neolithic Monument', *The Wiltshire Archaeological and Natural History Magazine* 88, 122–5

Pollard, J. and Ruggles, C., 2001 'Shifting Perceptions: Spatial Order, Cosmology, and Patterns of Deposition at Stonehenge', *Cambridge Archaeol. J.* 11(1), 69–90

Pollington, S., 2001 *The English Warrior from Earliest Times till 1066* (Hockwold-cum-Wilton, Anglo Saxon Books)

Pope, R., 2007 'Ritual and the roundhouse: a critique of recent ideas on the use of domestic space in later British prehistory', in Haselgrove, C. and Pope, R. (eds), *The Earlier Iron Age in Britain and the Near Continent* (Oxbow Books)

Porter, V., 1990. *Small Woods and Hedgerows* (London, Pelham Books)

Price, J. and Cottam, S., 1998 *Romano-British Glass Vessels: a Handbook*, CBA Practical Handbook in Archaeology 14

Pryor, F., 1985 'Maxey Timber Circle', *Current Archaeol.* 96, 11–13

Ravn, M., 2003 *Death Ritual and Germanic Social Structure (c.AD 200–600)*, Brit. Archaeol. Rep. Int. Ser. 1164 (Oxford)

Reimer, P.J., Brown, T. and Reimer, R.W., 2004 'IntCal04 Terrestrial radiocarbon age calibration, 026 Cal Kyr BP', *Radiocarbon* 46, 1029–58

Reynolds, A., 2003 'Boundaries and settlements in later sixth to eleventh-century England', *Anglo-Saxon Stud. Archaeol. Hist.* 12, 98–136

Richards, C., 1993 'Contextual analysis of the Grooved Ware at Balfarg', in Barclay, G.J. and. Russell-White, C.J., 'Excavations in the ceremonial complex of the 4th to 2nd millennium BC at Balfarg/Balbirnie, Glenrothes, Fife', *Proc. Soc. Antiq. Scot.* 123, 43–210

Richardson, A., 2005 *The Anglo-Saxon Cemeteries of Kent, vols I and II*, Brit. Archaeol. Rep. Brit. Ser. 391

Riddler, I.D., 2001 *Channel Tunnel (CT 1987–1988). The Small Finds* (unpubl. report for Canterbury Archaeological Trust)

Riddler, I.D. and Walton Rogers, P., 2006 'Early Medieval Small Finds', in Parfitt, K., Corke, B. and Cotter, J., *Townwall Street, Dover. Excavations 1996*, The Archaeology of Canterbury New Series Volume 3, Canterbury, 256–305

Riddler, I.D. and Trevarthen, M., forthcoming *The Prehistoric, Roman and Anglo-Saxon Funerary Landscape at Saltwood Tunnel, Kent*, Channel Tunnel Rail Link Monogr. Ser. (London)

Riddler, I.D., forthcoming 'The Knives', in Parfitt, K. and Anderson, T., *The Anglo-Saxon Cemetery at Dover Buckland, Kent. The 1994 Excavations*, Canterbury Archaeol. Trust Monogr., new series (Canterbury)

Robins, P., 2000, 'Struck flint', in Ashwin, T. and Bates, S., *Norwich Southern Bypass Part I: Excavations at Bixley, Caistor St Edmund, Trowse*, E. Anglian Archaeol. 91

Roes, A., 1958 'The toothed blades from Chalton', *Antiq. J.* 38, 244–5

Ross, S., 1991 *Dress Pins from Anglo-Saxon England: Their Production and Typo-Chronological Development* (unpubl. DPhil thesis, Univ. of Oxford)

Ruggles, C., 1999 *Astronomy in Prehistoric Britain and Ireland* (London, Yale University Press)

Ruggles, C., 2007 'Interpreting solstitial alignments in Late Neolithic Wessex', *Archaeoastronomy: The Journal of Astronomy in Culture* 21, 1–27

Sage, W., 1984 *Das Reihengräberfeld von Altenerding in Oberbayern* (Berlin, Mann)

Samuels, L.E., 1980 *Optical microscopy of carbon steels* (Ohio, American Society for Metals)

Sasse, B., 2001 *Ein frühmittelalterliches Reihengräberfeld bei Eichstetten am Kaiserstuhl*, Forschungen und Berichte zur Vor- und Frühgeschichte in Baden-Württemberg 75 (Stuttgart)

Saville, A., 1981 'The Flint Assemblage', in Mercer, R.J., *Grimes Graves, Norfolk. Excavations 1971–72: Volume II* (London, HMSO)

Scarfe, N., 2002 *The Suffolk Landscape* (London, Phillimore)

Scollar, I., Tabbagh, A., Hesse, A. and Herzog, I., 1990 — *Archaeological Prospecting and Remote Sensing* (Cambridge, Cambridge University Press)

Scull, C.J., 1992 — 'Before Sutton Hoo: structures of power and society in early East Anglia', in Carver, M.O.H. (ed.), *The Age of Sutton Hoo: The Seventh Century in North-Western Europe*, 3–23 (Woodbridge, Boydell)

Scull, C.J., 1993 — 'Archaeology, Early Anglo-Saxon society and the origins of Anglo-Saxon kingdoms', *Anglo-Saxon Stud. Archaeol. Hist.* 6, 65–82

Scull, C.J., 1995 — 'Approaches to material culture and social dynamics of the Migration Period in eastern England', in Bintliff, J. and Hamerow, H. (eds), *Europe between Late Antiquity and the Middle Ages; Recent Archaeological and Historical Research in Western and Southern Europe*, Brit. Arch. Rep. Int. Ser. 617, 71–83 (Oxford)

Scull, C.J., 2002 — 'Ipswich: development and contexts of an urban precursor in the seventh century', in Hårdh, B. and Larsson, L. (eds) 'Central Places in the Migration and the Merovingian Periods', *Papers from the 52nd Sachsensymposium*, Lund, August 2001, 303–16

Scull, C.J., 2009a — 'The Human Burials', in S. Lucy, J. Tipper and A. Dickens, *The Anglo-Saxon Settlement and Cemetery at Bloodmoor Hill, Carlton Colville, Suffolk*, E. Anglian Archaeol. 131, 385–426

Scull, C.J., 2009b — *Early Medieval (late 5th–early 8th centuries AD) Cemeteries at Boss Hall and Buttermarket, Ipswich, Suffolk*, Leeds: Society for Medieval Archaeology Monograph 27

Sherlock, S.J. and Welch, M.G., 1992 — *An Anglo Saxon Cemetery at Norton, Cleveland*, Counc. Brit. Archaeol. Res. Rep. 82

Smedley, N. and Owles, E., 1959 — 'Some Suffolk Kilns: 1, A Romano-British Pottery Kiln at Homersfield', *Proc. Suffolk Inst. Archaeol. Hist.* 28, 168–84

Spain, S., 2000 — *The Shield in Early Anglo-Saxon Kent: A computer-assisted analysis of shield bosses and an investigation into the use of the shield in the burial rite* (unpubl. MA dissertation, Univ. of York)

Stoodley, N., 2002 — 'Multiple burials, multiple meaning? Interpreting the early Anglo-Saxon multiple interment', in Lucy, S. and Reynolds, A. (eds), *Burial in Early Medieval England and Wales*, Soc. Medieval Archaeol. Monogr. Ser. 17 103–21 (London)

Stoodley, N., 1999a — *The Spindle and the Spear: A Critical Enquiry into the Construction and Meaning of Gender in the Early Anglo-Saxon Burial Rite*, Brit. Archaeol. Rep. Brit. Ser. 288 (Oxford)

Stoodley, N., 1999b — 'Burial rites, gender and the creation of kingdoms: the evidence from seventh century England', *Anglo-Saxon Stud. Archaeol. Hist.* 10, 99–108

Stout, A.M., 2001 — 'Jewellery as a symbol of status in the Roman Empire', in Sebesta, J.L. and Bonfante, L., *The World of Roman Costume*, 77–100 (Wisconsin, University of Wisconsin)

Straume, E.M., 1995 — 'On the question of exogamy as a basis for distribution in the Germanic Iron Age', in Gjøstein Resi, H. (ed.), *Produksjon og Samfunn: Beretning fra 2. nordiske jernaldersymposium på Granavolden Gjæstgiveri 7–10 mai 1992* (*Varia* 30), 97–101 (Oslo, Universitetets Oldsaksamling)

Stuiver, M. and Reimer, P.J., 1986 — 'A computer program for radiocarbon age calculation', *Radiocarbon* 28, 1022–30

Swanton, M.J., 1973 — *The Spearheads of the Anglo-Saxon Settlements* (London, Roy. Archaeol. Inst.)

Swanton, M.J., 1974 — *A Corpus of Pagan Anglo-Saxon Spear Types*, Brit. Archaeol. Rep. Brit. Ser. 7 (Oxford)

Swanton, M.J., 1964 — 'An Anglian cemetery at Londesborough in East Yorkshire', *Yorkshire Archaeol. J.* 41, 262–86

Swift, E., 2000 — *The End of the Roman Empire: An Archaeological Investigation* (Stroud, Tempus)

Taylor, P., 1997 — *A Neolithic Lunar Observatory* (unpubl. paper)

Textile Institute, 1975 — *Identification of Textile Materials* (Manchester, The Textile Institute)

Thom, A., 1971 — *Megalithic Lunar Observatories* (Oxford, Oxford University Press)

Thomas, J., 1991 — *Understanding the Neolithic* (London, Routledge)

Thompson, I., 1982 — *Grog-tempered Belgic Pottery of South-Eastern England*, Brit. Archaeol. Rep. Brit. Ser. 108 (Oxford)

Timby, J.R, 1996 — *The Anglo-Saxon Cemetery at Empingham II, Rutland*, Oxbow Monogr. 70

Tipper, J., 2009 — 'Pottery', in Lucy, S., Tipper, J. and Dickens, A., *The Anglo-Saxon Settlement and Cemetery at Bloodmoor Hill, Carlton Colville, Suffolk*, E. Anglian Archaeol. 131, 202–43

Tite, M.S. and Mullins, C., 1971 — 'Enhancement of magnetic susceptibility of soils on archaeological sites', *Archaeometry* 13, 209–19

Turner, C.G. II, Nichol, C.R. and Scott, G.R., 1991 — 'Scoring procedures for key morphological traits of the permanent dentition: the Arizona State University Dental Anthropology System', in Kelley, M.A. and Larsen, C.S. (eds), *Advances in Dental Anthropology*, 13–31 (New York, Wiley-Liss)

Tutin, T.G., Heywood, V.H., Burgess, N.A., Moore, D.M., Valentine, D.H., Walters, S.M. and Webb, D.A. (eds), 1964–80 — *Flora Europaea* (5 vols) (Cambridge)

Tyers, P.A., 1996 — 'Atlas and guide to Roman pottery in Britain', in *Roman Pottery in Britain*, 83–201 (London, Batsford)

Tyler, S., and Major, H., 2005 — *The Early Anglo-Saxon Cemetery and Later Saxon Settlement at Springfield Lyons, Essex*, E. Anglian Archaeol. 111

Urbon, B., 1991 — 'Spanschäftung für Lanzen und Pfeile', *Funderberche aus Bade-Würtenberg*, 16, 127–31

Vyner, B.E., 1988 — 'The Street House Wossit: the excavation of a Late Neolithic and Early Bronze Age palisaded ritual monument at Street House, Loftus, Cleveland', *Proc. Prehist. Soc.* 54, 173–202

Wainwright, G.J., 1979 — *Mount Pleasant, Dorset: excavations 1970–71*, Soc. Antiq. Lond. Res. Rep. 37 (London)

Wainwright, G.J. and Longworth, I.H., 1971 — *Durrington Walls: Excavations 1966 and 1968* (London, Soc. Antiq. Lond.)

Walton Rogers, P., 1997 *Textile Production at 16–22 Coppergate*, The Archaeology of York 17/11, (York, Counc. Brit. Archaeol.)

Walton Rogers, P., 1998 'Textiles and clothing', in Drinkall, G. and Foreman, M, *The Anglo-Saxon Cemetery at Castledyke South, Barton-on-Humber*, Sheffield Excavation Rep. 6, 274–9 (Sheffield, Sheffield Academic Press)

Walton Rogers, P., 1999 'The textiles', in Haughton, C. and Powlesland, D., *West Heslerton, The Anglian Cemetery*, 143–71 (West Heslerton, The Landscape Research Centre)

Walton Rogers, P., 2001a 'Tests for dye in textile samples', in Filmer-Sankey, W., and Pestell, T., *Snape Anglo Saxon Cemetery: Excavations and Surveys 1824–1992*, E. Anglian Archaeol. 95

Walton Rogers, P., 2001b 'The re-appearance of an old Roman loom in medieval England', in Walton Rogers, P., Bender Jørgensen, L. and Rast-Eicher, A. (eds), *The Roman Textile Industry and its Influence: A Birthday Tribute to John Peter Wild*, 158–71 (Oxford, Oxbow)

Walton Rogers, P., 2005 'The textiles from Mounds 5, 7, 14 and 17', in Carver, M. O. H., *Sutton Hoo: A Seventh-Century Princely Burial Ground and its Context*, 262–8 (London, British Museum)

Walton Rogers, P., 2006 'Textiles and clothing', in Williams, P. and Newman, R., *Market Lavington, Wiltshire, an Anglo-Saxon Cemetery and Settlement: Excavations at Grove Farm, 1986–1990*, 111–17 (Salisbury, Wessex Archaeology)

Walton Rogers, P., 2007 *Cloth and Clothing in Early Anglo-Saxon England, AD 450–700* (York, Counc. Brit. Archaeol.)

Walton Rogers, P., forthcoming a 'Costume and textiles', in Parfitt, K. and Anderson, T., *The Anglo-Saxon Cemetery at Dover Buckland, Kent. The 1994 Excavations*, Canterbury Archaeol. Trust Monogr., new series (Canterbury)

Walton Rogers, P., forthcoming b 'Costume and textiles', in Speed, G. and Powlesland, D., *Excavations at Hollow Banks Quarry, Scorton, N. Yorks*

Walton, P. and Taylor, G.W., 1991 'The characterisation of dyes in textiles from archaeological excavations', *Chromatography and Analysis*, 17 (June 1991), 5–7

Watson, J, 2003 'Mineral preserved organic material associated with metalwork', in Chadwick Hawkes, S. and Grainger, G., *The Anglo-Saxon Cemetery at Worthy Park, Kingsworthy Near Winchester, Hampshire*, Oxford University School of Archaeol. Monogr. 59, 196–200

Watson, J. and Edwards, G., 1990 'Conservation of material from Anglo-Saxon cemeteries', in Southworth, E. (ed.), *Anglo-Saxon Cemeteries: A Reappraisal* (Proceedings of a conference held at Liverpool Museum in 1986), 97–106 (Stroud, Alan Sutton)

Watson, J., 1984, 'Appendix 1: Organic material associated with metal objects', in Hills, C., Penn, K and Rickett, R., *The Anglo-Saxon Cemetery at Spong Hill, North Elmham, Part III, Catalogue of Inhumations*, E. Anglian Archaeol. 21, 157–9

Watson, J., 1995 'Wood usage in Anglo-Saxon shields', *Anglo-Saxon Stud. Archaeol. Hist.* 7, 35–48

Watson, J., 2001 'Organic material associated with metalwork from the Anglo-Saxon cemetery at Boss Hall, Ipswich', *Centre for Archaeology Report Series*, 88/2001

Watson, J., 2002 'Organic material associated with metalwork from the Anglo-Saxon cemetery at Edix Hill, Barrington, Cambridgeshire', *Centre for Archaeology Report Series*, 88/2002

WEA, 1980 'Recommendations for age and sex diagnoses of skeletons', *J. Human Evolution* 9, 517–49

Welch, M., 1992 *Anglo-Saxon England* (London, Batsford/English Heritage)

Welch, M., 1983 *Early Anglo-Saxon Sussex*, Brit. Archaeol. Rep. 112 (Oxford)

Werner, J., 1988 'Danèeny and Brangstrup. Untersuchungen zur Èernjachov-Kultur zwischen Sereth und Dnestr und zu den "Reichstumszentren" auf Fünen', *Bonner Jahrbücher* 188, 241–86

Werner, J., 1991 Eiserne Wollkämme der jüngeren Kaiserzeit aus dem freien Germanien, *Germania* 69, 608–11

West, S.E., 1985 *West Stow, The Anglo Saxon Village*, E. Anglian Archaeol. 24

West, S.E., 1988 *The Anglo-Saxon Cemetery at Westgarth Gardens, Bury St Edmunds, Suffolk*, E. Anglian Archaeol. 38

West, S.E., 1990 *West Stow, The Prehistoric and Romano British Occupation*, E. Anglian Archaeol. 40

West, S.E., 1998 *A Corpus of Anglo-Saxon Material from Suffolk*, E. Anglian. Archaeol. 84

Whitelock, D. (ed. and trans.), 1930 *Anglo-Saxon Wills* (Cambridge, Cambridge University Press)

Wiexzorek, A., Périn, P., von Welck, K. and Menghin, W. (eds), 1997 *Die Franken: Altagskultur im Frankenreich* (Mainz, von Zabern)

Wild, J.P., 1970 *Textile Manufacture in the Northern Roman Provinces* (Cambridge, Cambridge University Press)

Wild, J.P., 1984–5 'A socketed toothed terminal from the Saalburg vicus', *Saalburg Jahrbuch* 40–1, 28–9

Williams, D. and Vince, A., 1997 'The characterization and interpretation of Early to Middle Saxon granitic tempered pottery in England', *Medieval Archaeol.* 41, 214–20

Williams, H., 1997 'Ancient landscape and the dead: the reuse of Prehistoric and Roman monuments as Early Anglo-Saxon burial sites', *Medieval Archaeol.* 41, 1–32

Wilson, P.R., Cardwell, P., Cramp, R.J., Evands, J., Taylor-Wilson, R.H, Thompson, A. and Wacher, J.S., 1996 'Early Anglian Catterick and *Catraeth*', *Medieval Archaeol.* 40, 1–61

WYAS, 1997 *Flixton Park, Waveney, Suffolk, Archaeological Field Walking and Geophysical Survey* (Archaeological Services, WYAS unpubl. report for RMC (UK) Limited)

Index

Illustrations are indicated by page numbers in *italics* or by *illus* where figures are scattered throughout the text. Places are in Suffolk unless indicated otherwise.

East Anglian Archaeology

is a serial publication sponsored by ALGAO EE and English Heritage. It is the main vehicle for publishing final reports on archaeological excavations and surveys in the region. For information about titles in the series, visit **www.eaareports.org.uk**. Reports can be obtained from:

Oxbow Books, 10 Hythe Bridge Street, Oxford OX1 2EW

or directly from the organisation publishing a particular volume.

Reports available so far:

No.1,	1975	Suffolk: various papers
No.2,	1976	Norfolk: various papers
No.3,	1977	Suffolk: various papers
No.4,	1976	Norfolk: Late Saxon town of Thetford
No.5,	1977	Norfolk: various papers on Roman sites
No.6,	1977	Norfolk: Spong Hill Anglo-Saxon cemetery, Part I
No.7,	1978	Norfolk: Bergh Apton Anglo-Saxon cemetery
No.8,	1978	Norfolk: various papers
No.9,	1980	Norfolk: North Elmham Park
No.10,	1980	Norfolk: village sites in Launditch Hundred
No.11,	1981	Norfolk: Spong Hill, Part II: Catalogue of Cremations
No.12,	1981	The barrows of East Anglia
No.13,	1981	Norwich: Eighteen centuries of pottery from Norwich
No.14,	1982	Norfolk: various papers
No.15,	1982	Norwich: Excavations in Norwich 1971–1978; Part I
No.16,	1982	Norfolk: Beaker domestic sites in the Fen-edge and East Anglia
No.17,	1983	Norfolk: Waterfront excavations and Thetford-type Ware production, Norwich
No.18,	1983	Norfolk: The archaeology of Witton
No.19,	1983	Norfolk: Two post-medieval earthenware pottery groups from Fulmodeston
No.20,	1983	Norfolk: Burgh Castle: excavation by Charles Green, 1958–61
No.21,	1984	Norfolk: Spong Hill, Part III: Catalogue of Inhumations
No.22,	1984	Norfolk: Excavations in Thetford, 1948–59 and 1973–80
No.23,	1985	Norfolk: Excavations at Brancaster 1974 and 1977
No.24,	1985	Suffolk: West Stow, the Anglo-Saxon village
No.25,	1985	Essex: Excavations by Mr H.P.Cooper on the Roman site at Hill Farm, Gestingthorpe, Essex
No.26,	1985	Norwich: Excavations in Norwich 1971–78; Part II
No.27,	1985	Cambridgeshire: The Fenland Project No.1: Archaeology and Environment in the Lower Welland Valley
No.28,	1985	Norfolk: Excavations within the north-east bailey of Norwich Castle, 1978
No.29,	1986	Norfolk: Barrow excavations in Norfolk, 1950–82
No.30,	1986	Norfolk: Excavations at Thornham, Warham, Wighton and Caistor St Edmund, Norfolk
No.31,	1986	Norfolk: Settlement, religion and industry on the Fen-edge; three Romano-British sites in Norfolk
No.32,	1987	Norfolk: Three Norman Churches in Norfolk
No.33,	1987	Essex: Excavation of a Cropmark Enclosure Complex at Woodham Walter, Essex, 1976 and An Assessment of Excavated Enclosures in Essex
No.34,	1987	Norfolk: Spong Hill, Part IV: Catalogue of Cremations
No.35,	1987	Cambridgeshire: The Fenland Project No.2: Fenland Landscapes and Settlement, Peterborough–March
No.36,	1987	Norfolk: The Anglo-Saxon Cemetery at Morningthorpe
No.37,	1987	Norfolk: Excavations at St Martin-at-Palace Plain, Norwich, 1981
No.38,	1987	Suffolk: The Anglo-Saxon Cemetery at Westgarth Gardens, Bury St Edmunds
No.39,	1988	Norfolk: Spong Hill, Part VI: Occupation during the 7th–2nd millennia BC
No.40,	1988	Suffolk: Burgh: The Iron Age and Roman Enclosure
No.41,	1988	Essex: Excavations at Great Dunmow, Essex: a Romano-British small town in the Trinovantian Civitas
No.42,	1988	Essex: Archaeology and Environment in South Essex, Rescue Archaeology along the Gray's By-pass 1979–80
No.43,	1988	Essex: Excavation at the North Ring, Mucking, Essex: A Late Bronze Age Enclosure
No.44,	1988	Norfolk: Six Deserted Villages in Norfolk
No.45,	1988	Norfolk: The Fenland Project No. 3: Marshland and the Nar Valley, Norfolk
No.46,	1989	Norfolk: The Deserted Medieval Village of Thuxton
No.47,	1989	Suffolk: West Stow: Early Anglo-Saxon Animal Husbandry
No.48,	1989	Suffolk: West Stow, Suffolk: The Prehistoric and Romano-British Occupations
No.49,	1990	Norfolk: The Evolution of Settlement in Three Parishes in South-East Norfolk
No.50,	1993	Proceedings of the Flatlands and Wetlands Conference
No.51,	1991	Norfolk: The Ruined and Disused Churches of Norfolk
No.52,	1991	Norfolk: The Fenland Project No. 4, The Wissey Embayment and Fen Causeway
No.53,	1992	Norfolk: Excavations in Thetford, 1980–82, Fison Way
No.54,	1992	Norfolk: The Iron Age Forts of Norfolk
No.55,	1992	Lincolnshire: The Fenland Project No.5: Lincolnshire Survey, The South-West Fens
No.56,	1992	Cambridgeshire: The Fenland Project No.6: The South-Western Cambridgeshire Fens
No.57,	1993	Norfolk and Lincolnshire: Excavations at Redgate Hill Hunstanton; and Tattershall Thorpe
No.58,	1993	Norwich: Households: The Medieval and Post-Medieval Finds from Norwich Survey Excavations 1971–1978
No.59,	1993	Fenland: The South-West Fen Dyke Survey Project 1982–86
No.60,	1993	Norfolk: Caister-on-Sea: Excavations by Charles Green, 1951–55
No.61,	1993	Fenland: The Fenland Project No.7: Excavations in Peterborough and the Lower Welland Valley 1960–1969
No.62,	1993	Norfolk: Excavations in Thetford by B.K. Davison, between 1964 and 1970
No.63,	1993	Norfolk: Illington: A Study of a Breckland Parish and its Anglo-Saxon Cemetery
No.64,	1994	Norfolk: The Late Saxon and Medieval Pottery Industry of Grimston: Excavations 1962–92
No.65,	1993	Suffolk: Settlements on Hill-tops: Seven Prehistoric Sites in Suffolk
No.66,	1993	Lincolnshire: The Fenland Project No.8: Lincolnshire Survey, the Northern Fen-Edge
No.67,	1994	Norfolk: Spong Hill, Part V: Catalogue of Cremations
No.68,	1994	Norfolk: Excavations at Fishergate, Norwich 1985
No.69,	1994	Norfolk: Spong Hill, Part VIII: The Cremations
No.70,	1994	Fenland: The Fenland Project No.9: Flandrian Environmental Change in Fenland
No.71,	1995	Essex: The Archaeology of the Essex Coast Vol.I: The Hullbridge Survey Project
No.72,	1995	Norfolk: Excavations at Redcastle Furze, Thetford, 1988–9
No.73,	1995	Norfolk: Spong Hill, Part VII: Iron Age, Roman and Early Saxon Settlement
No.74,	1995	Norfolk: A Late Neolithic, Saxon and Medieval Site at Middle Harling
No.75,	1995	Essex: North Shoebury: Settlement and Economy in South-east Essex 1500–AD1500
No.76,	1996	Nene Valley: Orton Hall Farm: A Roman and Early Anglo-Saxon Farmstead
No.77,	1996	Norfolk: Barrow Excavations in Norfolk, 1984–88
No.78,	1996	Norfolk:The Fenland Project No.11: The Wissey Embayment: Evidence for pre-Iron Age Occupation
No.79,	1996	Cambridgeshire: The Fenland Project No.10: Cambridgeshire Survey, the Isle of Ely and Wisbech
No.80,	1997	Norfolk: Barton Bendish and Caldecote: fieldwork in south-west Norfolk
No.81,	1997	Norfolk: Castle Rising Castle
No.82,	1998	Essex: Archaeology and the Landscape in the Lower Blackwater Valley
No.83,	1998	Essex: Excavations south of Chignall Roman Villa 1977–81
No.84,	1998	Suffolk: A Corpus of Anglo-Saxon Material
No.85,	1998	Suffolk: Towards a Landscape History of Walsham le Willows
No.86,	1998	Essex: Excavations at the Orsett 'Cock' Enclosure
No.87,	1999	Norfolk: Excavations in Thetford, North of the River, 1989–90
No.88,	1999	Essex: Excavations at Ivy Chimneys, Witham 1978–83
No.89,	1999	Lincolnshire: Salterns: Excavations at Helpringham, Holbeach St Johns and Bicker Haven
No.90,	1999	Essex:The Archaeology of Ardleigh, Excavations 1955–80
No.91,	2000	Norfolk: Excavations on the Norwich Southern Bypass, 1989–91 Part I Bixley, Caistor St Edmund, Trowse
No.92,	2000	Norfolk: Excavations on the Norwich Southern Bypass, 1989–91 Part II Harford Farm Anglo-Saxon Cemetery
No.93,	2001	Norfolk: Excavations on the Snettisham Bypass, 1989
No.94,	2001	Lincolnshire: Excavations at Billingborough, 1975–8
No.95,	2001	Suffolk: Snape Anglo-Saxon Cemetery: Excavations and Surveys
No.96,	2001	Norfolk: Two Medieval Churches in Norfolk
No.97,	2001	Cambridgeshire: Monument 97, Orton Longueville
No.98,	2002	Essex: Excavations at Little Oakley, 1951–78
No.99,	2002	Norfolk: Excavations at Melford Meadows, Brettenham, 1994
No.100,	2002	Norwich: Excavations in Norwich 1971–78, Part III
No.101,	2002	Norfolk: Medieval Armorial Horse Furniture in Norfolk